Biology Now!

Tommy Murtagh

Gill & Macmillan

Gill & Macmillan Ltd
Hume Avenue
Park West
Dublin 12
with associated companies throughout the world
www.gillmacmillan.ie

© 2002 Tommy Murtagh
0 7171 3198 X
Index compiled by Jann Kelly
Print origination by Compuscript Ltd., Shannon
Colour reproduction by Ultragraphics, Dublin

The paper used in this book is made from the wood
pulp of managed forests.
For every tree felled, at least one tree is planted,
thereby renewing natural resources.

A catalogue record is available for this book from the
British Library.

1 3 5 4 2

My-etest

Test yourself on our FREE website www.my-etest.com!
Check out how well you score!
Just register once, keep your email as your password,
and come back to test yourself regularly.
Packed full of extra questions,
my-etest.com lets you revise
— at your own pace
— when you want
— where you want.

Author's Acknowledgments

Many thanks to Deirdre Greenan, Mairéad O'Keeffe and Hubert Mahony at Gill & Macmillan. Their patience and encouragement made such a difference to me. Never was my experience less than positive. I don't know how they do everything so well.

Thanks to Ruadháin Bonham for his timely contribution and to his mum, Caitríona, for her infectious enthusiasm. Thanks too to Cynthia Kelleher for the use of her garden and for her half of the non-identical twins. Thanks to Michael Dunne, Mairéad McNamara and Anne Hanley of Maryfield College for their support and encouragement. They have always been inspiring teachers and the best colleagues I could wish for.

I'd like to record special thanks to my mother, Maureen Murtagh, and fond memories at this time of my father, Michael Murtagh, who did it all before me.

Very special thanks to my wonderful children: Orla, Claire, David and Ronan. Their constant interruptions paced all of my work nicely for me. Honestly kids, you'll get more attention from now on.

This book is dedicated to my wife, Ann, who makes everything I do worthwhile. Her support was, as usual, brilliant.

Acknowledgments

For permission to reproduce photographs used in the book grateful acknowledgment is made to the following:

Biofotos; Frank Lane Picture Agency: Angel Natural Visions; Hulton Archive; Mary Evan Picture Library; Natural History Photographic Agency; Oxford Scientific Films; Sally Richard Greenhill; Science Photo Library; theartarchive.

Contents

A red dotted line down the side of text indicates material for higher level only.
Numbers in square brackets refer to Department of Education and Science syllabus.

Chapter 1

Introduction and the Scientific Method

IN THIS CHAPTER: [110]

Main issues

Definition and extent of biology.
The scientific method.
Rules of experimentation.

Background

None necessary.

Applications

The advantages in studying biology.
Obtaining useful results from good experiments.

Learning objectives

After your study of this chapter, you should be able to:

- define the word '*biology*';
- describe the extent of biology;
- explain a *hypothesis*;
- present the strengths and weaknesses of the scientific method;
- criticise and improve poor investigations;
- design an experiment.

DEFINITION OF 'BIOLOGY' [111]

Biology is the study of life ('*bios—ology*' means '*life—study*').

Fig. 1.1. Plant and animal interaction.

Biologists study the living world and the problems that relate to it. Biology is a subject that covers a vast number of topics and involves just about every other branch of natural science, including physics, chemistry, mathematics, geology and geography.

In the past, biology was simply subdivided into *botany* (a study of plants), *zoology* (a study of animals) and then, later, *microbiology* (a study of micro-organisms). Nowadays, given the size of the subject and the diversity of life, modern biology tends to specialise in many different areas as shown on the chart on page 4.

THE SCIENTIFIC METHOD [112]

Biology is an enormous subject and it needs good methods of study. Biologists are looking for solutions to the problems of the living world and they use study methods and processes to lead to worthwhile discoveries. Not all of the study methods used in the past to try and 'advance' scientific knowledge were good ones. For example, Aristotle (384–322 BC) was the founder of biology and contributed enormously to

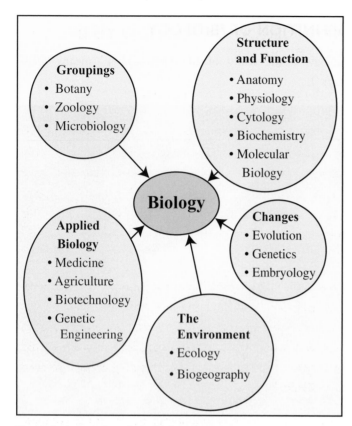

Fig. 1.2. Areas of study in biology.

many aspects of the subject. His techniques of study, however, were sometimes flawed. He 'believed' in spontaneous generation rather than testing for it, and he also declared that males and females had different numbers of teeth. He preferred to construct arguments and philosophies to support his case rather than any experimental proof.

Nowadays, scientists use the process of the 'scientific method' based on observations and experiments. Their aim is to use it to explain the existence, development and functions of all aspects of the natural world.

The main features of the method are as follows:

- observations and measurements are made;
- a *hypothesis* is developed (a working assumption or 'an educated guess');
- experiments are designed to test the hypothesis;
- the experimental data is collected and recorded;
- the data is interpreted;
- conclusions are drawn;
- the hypothesis is modified in light of the results;
- any consistency of results leads to a *theory* or *principle*;

- theories and principles are communicated to others;
- the theories and principles now add to the 'bank of knowledge' and can be used for more observations and hypotheses.

For example:

Observation: mustard seeds only germinate when water is present.

Hypothesis: water is necessary for seed germination.

Experiment design: 50 similar seeds divided into two groups: one group given water, the other kept dry. Both groups kept in otherwise identical conditions.

Results: only the seeds with water germinated.

More experiments: different seeds are tested.

Outcome: the hypothesis is supported.

Finally: the hypothesis becomes a theory: water *is* necessary for germination.

It is important to understand that the theory is never *proved* in the way a mathematical result might be, i.e. that other alternatives are impossible. The theory is only adopted as true until a better theory replaces it. Therefore, it should be stated that water is necessary for germination — as far as we know at present!

The strengths of the scientific method

- It is completely unprejudiced.
- The results obtained are repeatable and any sceptic ('non-believer') can reproduce them.
- All its theories are falsifiable, i.e. it is *possible* that they can be disproved.*
- Present theories are not expected to explain future experiments.
- It does not make moral judgements

---

* The theory that there is a Loch Ness monster that hides when humans approach is *unfalsifiable* and therefore a flawed one. The theory that there is *no* monster is better: it is *falsifiable* — if a monster is found, the theory will be proved false and happily discarded. You could apply the same reasoning to the 'theories' of UFOs, aliens on the moon and abominable snowmen.

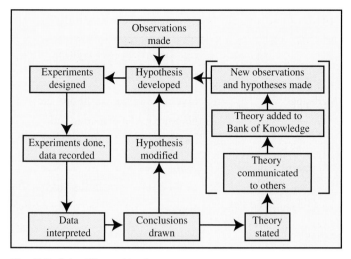

Fig. 1.3. Scientific method.

- Good scientists are not 'blinkered' and are happy to be proved wrong.
- Results are always communicated to others regardless of how they turn out.
- Others will always judge the value of any contribution.

Scientific theories are always *tentative* — they are the best that are available given the current data. Any present-day explanation is liable to be replaced by a new one in the future.

The weaknesses of the scientific method

- It is limited by the extent of our current knowledge.
- It is limited by our ability to interpret results.
- It applies to a natural world that is under constant change.
- It often relies on accidental discoveries and chance.
- Its ethics may be contentious — some aspects of experimentation may be unacceptable.
- Historically, some scientists have tended to cling to disproved hypotheses or to dismiss experimental results that they did not expect.

EXPERIMENTATION (OR HOW TO DESIGN AN EXPERIMENT) [113]

Variables, constants and controls

A *variable* is any condition that changes during an experiment. In experiment design, it is important to remember that many variables can affect the outcome. Generally one variable, the subject of the experiment, is allowed to change during the experiment and all others are held constant. This avoids confusion and will prevent criticism of an 'unfair' experiment.

In the case of the germination investigation described above, water availability can be varied in the experiment but light, temperature and oxygen should be kept at a constant level. Likewise experimental equipment including glassware should not change and seed samples should be big enough to even out individual differences.

It is also important to have a *control* experiment to compare the outcome to. In the germination example, a sample of seeds without water is *the experiment* and a similar sample *with* water is the *control* (a 'normal' situation for comparison).

All experiments, including the ones within this course, should be conducted with the following points in mind:

Every experiment should have:

- careful planning and design;
- a safe procedure;
- a control experiment for comparison;
- a large sample size;
- generally only one or two factors varied at any one time;
- all other factors held constant;
- reproducible results clearly presented.

AREAS OF STUDY IN BIOLOGY

Major groupings of organisms

Botany	The study of plants, e.g. nettles, mosses, oak trees.
Zoology	The study of animals, e.g. cats, slugs, jellyfish and humans.
Bacteriology	The study of bacteria, e.g. those that are used to make yoghurt or those that cause food poisoning.
Virology	The study of viruses, e.g. those causing measles, chicken pox and AIDS.
Mycology	The study of fungi, e.g. mushrooms, yeast, bread mould, ringworm.

Areas of structure and function

Anatomy	The structures within living organisms, e.g. the chambers and valves of the human heart.
Physiology	The activities within an organism, e.g. how plants turn to the light or how muscles contract.
Cytology	The study of cells and cell structures, e.g. how food and oxygen enter cells.
Biochemistry	The chemical reactions within organisms, e.g. how energy is extracted from food.
Molecular biology	The molecules within cells, e.g. studying proteins, carbohydrates or DNA.

Areas of applied biology

Biotechnology	Using biology in industry to make a saleable product,

e.g. the processes of brewing or cheese making.

Medicine	Investigating human health and illness, e.g. the diagnosis and treatment of heart disease.
Veterinary medicine	Animal health and welfare, e.g. treating infections in cats and dogs.
Agriculture	More efficient maintenance of livestock, crops and forests, e.g. pest control to protect cereals.
Genetic engineering	Introducing new genes into cells, e.g. manufacturing human insulin for diabetics.

Areas of interaction with the environment

Ecology	The study of life in its natural environment, e.g. the relationships between predators and prey.
Biogeography	The study of where organisms are found and why they are found there, e.g. kangaroos are found only in Australia.

Areas involving change

Evolution	Charting population changes over time, e.g. the appearance and disappearance of dinosaurs.
Genetics	Studying the mechanism of inheritance, e.g. how dark-haired parents might have a fair-haired child.
Embryology	The development of embryos, e.g. how chickens grow within eggs.

SUMMARY

- Biology is the study of life.
- Modern biology specialises in many different areas.
- The *scientific method* is used to study biology.
- A *hypothesis* is a working assumption or an 'educated guess'.
- A *theory* is a hypothesis confirmed by experiment.
- The scientific method has many strengths and some weaknesses.
- A *variable* is any condition that changes during an experiment.
- Many variables can affect the outcome of any experiment.
- Normally only *one variable* is *changed* during an experiment.
- All other conditions must be held constant.
- A *control* experiment is necessary for comparison.

KEY WORDS

Biology	The study of life.
Scientific method	A process of investigation based on observations and experiments.
Hypothesis	A working assumption or 'educated guess'.
Theory	An hypothesis confirmed by experiment.
Variable	Any condition that can change during an experiment.
Control	A 'normal' situation used in experiments for comparison.

QUESTIONS

1. How should you test Aristotle's theory that men have more teeth than women?
2. What is the difference between an hypothesis and a theory?
3. Design an experiment to test the hypothesis that exercise increases the heart rate.
4. Design experiments to determine whether:
   a. snails can respond to music;
   b. a watched pot never boils;
   c. people can tell the difference between margarine and butter;
   d. flies always take off backwards.
5. Criticise the following investigation and suggest improvements:
   a. *I saw someone on TV bending a spoon just by using his mental energy.*
   b. *I couldn't understand how he did it but it could be that mental energy was involved.*
   c. *I've heard other stories about mental energy that are definitely true.*
   d. *Tests have shown that mental energy exists and it is a very attractive idea to me.*
   e. *I now firmly believe in mental energy, as scientists don't know everything.*
6. A student observes that the slugs in their garden only eat certain parts of the dahlia plants. Suggest *two* hypotheses that might explain this and design an experiment to test either of them.

OPTIONAL ACTIVITIES

Consider and discuss any of the following statements:

- The Earth is flat.
- Tobacco company research has shown that the dangers of smoking are greatly exaggerated.
- Scientists don't test 'alternative science' claims, as it is a waste of their time.
- Scientists don't want to be proved wrong.

Now test yourself at
www.my-etest.com

Chapter 2
The Characteristics of Life

IN THIS CHAPTER: [120]

Main issues

The needs of living organisms.
How organisms respond to these needs.
A definition of life.

Background

The diversity of biology.

Learning objectives

After your study of this chapter, you should be able to:

- distinguish between living organisms and non-living matter;
- summarise the main characteristics of living organisms;
- understand the terms *metabolism* and *continuity*;
- explain the *five* responses of organisms to their needs;
- consider an investigation of the life proesses of a living organism;
- recognise that a completely acceptable definition of life is difficult to find.

A SEARCH FOR A DEFINITION OF 'LIFE' [121]

Fig. 2.1. Iris and buttercup.

Fig. 2.2. Rabbits greeting each other.

As biology is the study of life and living things (or *living organisms*), it is important for a biologist to have a clear idea as to what *living* means. Many people associate *life* with all sorts of things: plants, animals, bacteria, fire, running water, cars, etc. It can be difficult to describe exactly what *life* is.

The common features and behaviours of living organisms are:

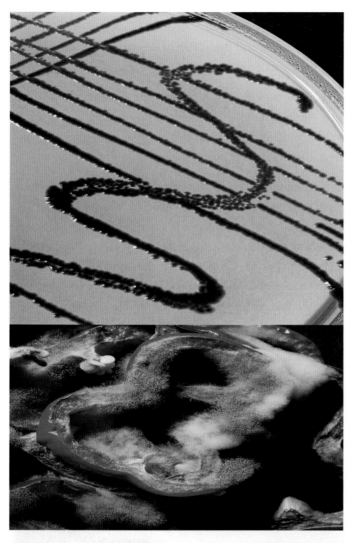

Fig. 2.3. *Salmonella* bacteria on nutrient agar. Fungi on a red pepper.

Movement	Animals tend to move more than plants, as they need to find their food.
Reproduction	This is an organism's ability to make copies of itself to take its place after its own death.
Sensitivity	The ability to respond to external events.
Growth	Using food to increase in size and complexity.
Respiration	This is the controlled release of energy from food. It is a chemical event that happens in all living cells at all times (not to be confused with *breathing* which is only found in *some* living organisms).
Excretion	Getting rid of the wastes produced by the organism's chemical reactions.
Nutrition	The need for nutrients to supply energy and matter.

(*Use the acronym MRS GREN or make up your own to remember the list.*)

Fig. 2.4. Humans responding.

All living organisms carry out large numbers of chemical reactions — collectively known as their *metabolism*. These chemical reactions of life can be divided into two groups:

Anabolism	Where small chemicals are joined to form larger ones (e.g. forming muscle protein from amino acids or making food by photosynthesis);
Catabolism	Where large chemicals are broken into smaller ones (e.g. the breakdown of food during digestion or respiration).

Metabolism is the total of the chemical processes occurring within a living organism.

Another feature of life is *continuity*. All living organisms do their best to survive in their environment and then reproduce in order that life on Earth may continue. This driving force is always present and life continues regardless of individual deaths. Living organisms are directed by many 'selfish genes' that are programmed for immortality.

A DEFINITION OF 'LIFE'   [122]

There is no satisfactory definition for what constitutes 'life'. Life involves an interaction of processes towards the twin needs of metabolism and continuity. These are *functional needs* — they are processes that have to be *done*. In simple terms, organisms want to survive and reproduce and they are programmed to do what is best towards these ends.

CHARACTERISTICS OF 'LIFE'   [123]

There are five fundamental *responses* that organisms will show in order to stay 'alive'. These are:

- organisation;
- nutrition;
- excretion;
- reproduction;
- behaviour.

Organisation

All living organisms are made from cells.

Some organisms are *unicellular*: they consist of only one single cell (e.g. bacteria) and carry out all of their life processes within that one cell.

Most organisms are *multicellular*: they consist of many cells joined together and use different cells to carry out their different life processes.

Cells have the effect of *organising* the structures and chemicals within themselves. A random mixing of chemicals would result in chaos within the organism and would not serve the need to stay alive.

Cells themselves are further organised into tissues and organs, which are grouped into complete systems. In humans, for example, similar *muscle cells* are grouped to make *muscle tissue* and this tissue is used to form the biceps *muscle* of the upper arm. All of the muscles in the human body form the *muscle system* and this, together with other systems, helps to form the complete human organism. This structural 'layering' makes the complete human highly organised and better able to conduct his or her metabolism. Any disruption in organisation would create a huge difficulty for human metabolism and continuity.

Organisation does not stop with the complete organism: individuals are further grouped into populations, which further increases their chances of survival and reproduction.

Organisation is discussed further in chapter 11.

Fig. 2.5. Social organisation in a wasps' nest.

Nutrition

Nutrition is the process of obtaining and using food to provide energy and matter. Nutrition is needed to maintain

Fig. 2.6. Dormouse feeding on hawthorn berries.

everything that an organism does. Animals obtain their food by feeding off other organisms and plants make their own food from simple chemicals and sunlight energy — the process of photosynthesis. The energy within food can always be traced back, through feeding relationships, to its original source, the sun. This flow of energy is discussed in chapter 4.

Excretion

Excretion is the removal of the waste products of metabolism. These products are toxic to the organism and must be removed before they build up into dangerous quantities. Excretion not only removes toxic wastes but also helps the organism to maintain a constant internal environment regardless of conditions on the outside. In humans and higher animals, excretion is done through the highly organised structures of the lungs, the urinary system, the skin and the liver. Plant excretion is through the stomata of their leaves. Excretion is discussed in chapters 21 and 22.

Reproduction

Reproduction is an organism's ability to make copies of itself. These copies can take its place after its own death. Organisms must reproduce for the continuity of life.

There are two types of reproduction — *sexual* and *asexual*.

Sexual reproduction generally involves two parents who make special, reproductive cells called gametes (or sex cells). These gametes join together (fertilisation) and form a zygote. This zygote then develops into a new individual. Sexual reproduction involves a blending of genetic information and creates variety within a population. Sexual reproduction is found in all animals and plants, most fungi and some bacteria.

Fig. 2.7. Breathing and movement.

Fig. 2.8. Chick hatching from its egg.

Asexual (non-sexual) reproduction is when part of a single parent splits from the parent and develops into a new individual. No sex cells are involved and the new individual is genetically identical to its single parent. Examples include the division of bacteria in two.

Reproduction is discussed in chapters 27 and 28.

Behaviour

Living organisms are constantly responding to their changing environment. They behave in a huge variety of ways, which they calculate to have *survival value*. Animals use their muscles and glands to respond to changes detected by their sense organs: eyes, ears, skin, etc. Their behaviour will help them avoid danger and find food. Plants respond to changes in light and temperature by altering their growth.

Behaviour is discussed in chapters 23 and 24.

Fig. 2.9. Caddis fly larva.

No one single response is enough to define life. Life involves an interaction of *all* of the above five responses in order to achieve metabolism and continuity. Everything is done so that the organism can survive, carry out its metabolism and then reproduce.

SUMMARY

- All organisms have a need for metabolism and continuity.
- Organisms have five basic responses to their needs: organisation, nutrition, excretion, behaviour and reproduction.
- A satisfactory definition of 'life' is hard to arrive at and not yet agreed on.

KEY WORDS

Metabolism	The total of the chemical proesses occurring within a living organism.
Anabolism	The joining of small chemicals to form larger chemicals.
Catabolism	The breaking up of large chemicals to form smaller chemicals.
Continuity	All living organisms do their best to survive in their environment and then reproduce in order that life on Earth may continue.
Organisation	A structured plan designed to improve efficiency and increase the chances of survival.
Nutrition	The process of obtaining and using food to provide energy and matter.
Excretion	The removal of the waste products of metabolism.
Reproduction	An organism's ability to make copies of itself.
Behaviour	The constant response of living organisms to their changing environment.

QUESTIONS

1. What are the two functional needs of all organisms?
2. Explain the difference between anabolism and catabolism.

3. State which of the following are examples of anabolism and which are of catabolism:

   a. digestion;
   b. photosynthesis;
   c. respiration;
   d. growth;
   e. manufacture of tears;
   e. muscle contraction.

4. What is meant by the *continuity of life*?
5. Why do organisms need food?
6. What is the main difference between animals and plants?
7. What advantage is it to organisms to be made from cells?
8. What is the difference between a tissue and an organ?
9. Why is reproduction necessary?
10. Why is animal behaviour generally more complicated than plant behaviour?

OPTIONAL ACTIVITIES

■ Discuss whether the following are living or not: a cat; a jellyfish; grass; a computer; a robot; a lighted candle; a car engine; a teddy bear; running water.
■ If possible, select a living organism and investigate its responses to its needs. Suitable choices might be: aquarium fish, small mammals, woodlice, insects, earthworms or any plants. Keep records of all observations under the following headings:

1. name of species;
2. description;
3. maintenance requirements, such as food, living conditions, light, water levels etc.;
4. changes in size, form, colour etc.;
5. behaviour, including method of feeding;
6. comparisons with non-living material.

Present your investigation in a form that communicates well to others.

Now test yourself at www.my-etest.com

Chapter 3
Nutrition

Mandatory activity

#10 Testing for starch, fat, reducing sugar and protein in food.

FUNCTION OF FOOD   [131]

Nutrition, for living organisms, refers to the processes of obtaining energy and matter in order to survive.

Energy and matter are found together in chemicals called *nutrients* and these nutrients can be found in *foods*. Living organisms either try to make their own foods from simple nutrients and an extra energy input, or else locate foods 'ready-made' and ready to eat. All living organisms, without exception, have a requirement for food containing the vital nutrients. Organisms will not be able to grow, move, reproduce or do anything without food. The energy and materials contained within food are needed for metabolism and continuity.

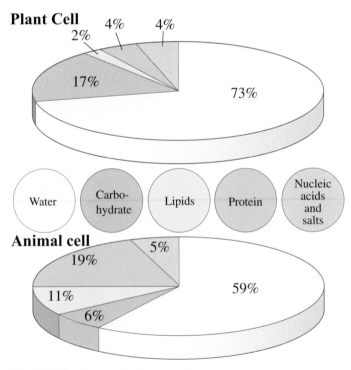

Fig. 3.1. Pie charts of cell contents.

Nutrients are grouped according to whether or not they contain the element carbon (chemical symbol C).

Organic nutrients	Contain *carbon* and originate from other living organisms. Examples include *proteins, fats* and *oils* (*lipids*), *carbohydrates* and *vitamins*.
Inorganic nutrients	Do not contain carbon (except for carbon dioxide). Examples include *dissolved salts* such as *sodium chloride* and *calcium phosphate*, *trace elements* such as *iron, copper* and *zinc, carbon dioxide* (*CO_2*) and *water* (*H_2O*).
Autotrophic nutrition	Is a method of nutrition where foods are made from inorganic nutrients and usually sunlight energy. The formation of organic nutrients always requires an energy input — generally light energy or maybe chemical energy. Plants use light to make their own food by photosynthesis. (Autotrophic means '*self-feeding*'.)
Heterotrophic nutrition	Is a method of nutrition where existing foods are broken down to provide ready-made nutrients. Animals obtain their food by eating existing foods that they locate in their habitat. (Heterotrophic means '*other-feeding*'.)

THE CHEMICAL ELEMENTS PRESENT IN FOOD — BIOELEMENTS [132]

Foods contain many different chemical elements: some in large amounts, many in tiny amounts or *traces*. All these bioelements are originally gathered by plants (from the air, water and soil) and then passed along food chains for all other organisms.

Fig. 3.2. Barn owl feeding.

The six common bioelements in food are carbon, hydrogen, nitrogen, oxygen, phosphorus and sulphur. Also found in food are sodium, magnesium, chlorine, potassium and calcium — all of these present as parts of dissolved salts in water. Iron, copper, zinc and other elements are found in tiny amounts in food. These are termed *trace elements*.

Plants obtain hydrogen and oxygen from soil water and carbon from atmospheric carbon dioxide. All of the other elements in food are initially absorbed by plants in dissolved salts in soil water. The role of plants in nutrition is crucial. By gathering all of these elements and then assembling them through photosynthesis, plants make food and oxygen for themselves and for all other organisms. Food (containing the bioelements) is passed from the plants to all of the other organisms through feeding relationships or *food chains* (see chapter 4).

BIOMOLECULES [133]

Biomolecules are the basic chemical structures found within most organic chemicals. They are found in food and within the bodies of all living organisms.

They contain carbon, hydrogen and oxygen elements (and sometimes nitrogen, phosphorus, sulphur and others) joined together in different ratios to form more complicated molecular units.

Table 3.1. The bioelements of food

Element	Chemical symbol	Initial entry into food chains on land
Hydrogen	H	A component of the soil water absorbed by plants.
Oxygen	O	A component of the soil water absorbed by plants.
Carbon	C	A component of carbon dioxide in air.
Nitrogen	N	
Phosphorus	P	
Sulphur	S	
Sodium	Na	Found by plants in dissolved salts in soil water, common in food.
Magnesium	Mg	
Chlorine	Cl	
Potassium	K	
Calcium	Ca	
Iron	Fe	
Copper	Cu	In dissolved salts in soil water, found as trace elements in food.
Zinc	Zn	
Others		

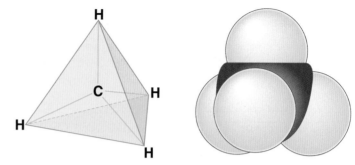

Fig. 3.3. The tetrahedral shape of methane (CH_4).

All biomolecules are constructed around carbon atoms — these atoms form a 'skeleton' for every organic chemical that exists. The carbon atoms may join to form chains, rings or branched structures. Carbon is capable of forming up to four chemical bonds at one time. When it does, it takes on a three-dimensional, tetrahedral shape. This shape is found throughout biomolecules and adds to their own 3-D structure.

BIOMOLECULAR SOURCES AND THE COMPONENTS OF FOOD   [134]

Carbohydrates ('sugars and starches')

Examples include: glucose; sucrose; lactose; ribose; starch; glycogen; cellulose; and chitin.

All carbohydrates contain the elements carbon, hydrogen and oxygen with hydrogen and oxygen always in a ratio of 2:1. Their general formula can be written as $C_x(H_2O)_y$.

For example, the chemical formula of glucose is $C_6(H_2O)_6$ or $C_6H_{12}O_6$. The formula for sucrose is $C_{12}(H_2O)_{11}$ (or $C_{12}H_{22}O_{11}$) and ribose is $C_5(H_2O)_5$.

Carbohydrates are classified as follows:

1. *Monosaccharides* contain single sugar biomolecules with three, four, five or six carbon atoms in each unit and a general formula of $(CH_2O)_n$. Glucose, fructose and ribose are monosaccharides.

All monosaccharides are easily absorbed by cells and give up their energy quickly. They are the smallest carbohydrate units.

2. *Disaccharides* are made from pairs of single sugars biomolecules joined. The joining is termed *condensation* and involves the release of some water from the molecules. Breaking the units apart is termed *hydrolysis* and happens during digestion. Water molecules are added back to the molecules.

Common disaccharides are:

- Sucrose (in sugar beet) — made from glucose and fructose molecules joined.
- Lactose (in milk) — made from glucose and galactose molecules joined.
- Maltose (in malted barley seeds) — made from two glucose molecules joined.

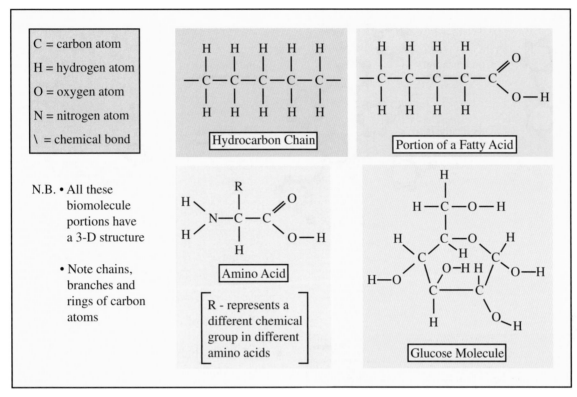

Fig. 3.4. Portions of biomolecules.

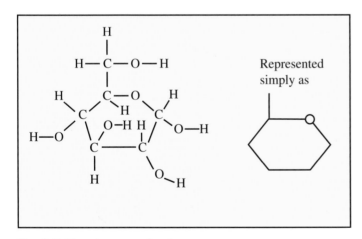

Fig. 3.5. The glucose molecule.

(*Trisaccharides* are made from three sugar units joined, *tetrasaccharides* from four, *pentasaccharides* from five and so on.)

3. *Polysaccharides* are made from long chains of *many* sugar biomolecules joined. The joining is again by condensation. Polysaccharide chains may be *branched*, e.g. glycogen in animal muscle, *cross-linked*, e.g. cellulose in plant cell walls (cross-links give a very strong structure) or *spiral*, e.g. starch in potatoes and rice.

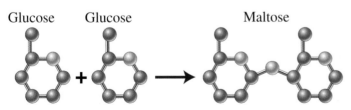

Glucose   Glucose   Maltose

Fig. 3.6. Forming a disaccharide.

| *Condensation* | is the joining of molecules together with the *release of some water*, e.g. photosynthesis. |
| *Hydrolysis* | is the separation of molecules with the *addition of water*, e.g. digestion. |

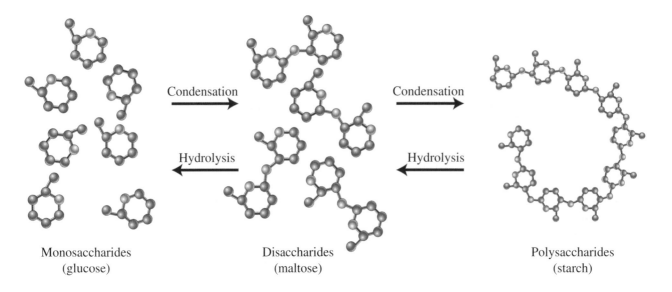

Monosaccharides
(glucose)

Disaccharides
(maltose)

Polysaccharides
(starch)

Fig. 3.7

Table 3.2.

Carbohydrate	Important sources
glucose	grapes, honey
fructose	honey, sweet fruit
sucrose	sweets, cakes, biscuits (contain sugar)
maltose	malted barley seeds — used for beer-making
lactose	milk (but not cheese or yoghurt)
starch	potatoes, flour, pasta, rice (plant sources)
glycogen	meat, liver (animal sources)
cellulose	vegetables, cereals, nuts, fruit (plant cells or fibre)

Carbohydrate-rich foods

The functions of carbohydrates are as follows:

- *Fuels* — carbohydrates have a high energy content and release their energy quickly during respiration. They are primary sources of energy for cell metabolism.
- *Support* — cellulose forms plant cell walls, chitin forms the exoskeleton of arthropods and the cell walls of fungi. Deoxyribose forms the supporting framework of the DNA molecule.

Lipids

Examples of these are: fats; oils; waxes; and phospholipids.

All lipids contain carbon, hydrogen and oxygen atoms but with a different ratio of hydrogen:oxygen atoms.

Most lipids are constructed from *glycerol* molecules and *fatty acid* molecules joined together. A typical fat or oil is made from three fatty acids attached to a glycerol molecule as shown. The joining is again by condensation and some water is released during this process. This smallest fat is called a *triglyceride*.

Fatty acids are a major component of lipids. They contain long chains of carbon atoms and are described as either *saturated* or *unsaturated*. Saturated fatty acids (no double bonds in the carbon chain) are found in animal fats. Animal fats tend to be *solid* at room temperature (e.g. butter, lard).

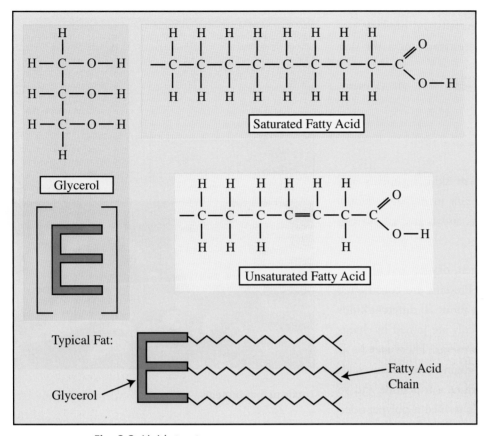

Fig. 3.8. Lipid structure.

Unsaturated fatty acids (with some double bonds in the carbon chain) are found in plant fats. Plant fats tend to be *liquid* at room temperature and are properly called *oils*.

Waxes contain altered forms of fatty acids (called esters). They are used for waterproofing in plants and animals.

Phospholipids differ from fats in that one of the three fatty acid chains is replaced by a phosphate group. They are found in all cell membranes.

All fats are insoluble in water — they are *hydrophobic* ('water-fearing') — but they do dissolve in organic solvents like alcohol, ether or chloroform. Phospholipid molecules are hydrophobic at one end and *hydrophilic* ('water-loving') at the other.

Foods rich in lipids include the following:

– Butter, margarine, lard, suet, egg yolk, cod liver oil, 'meat fat', cheese and milk, which are rich in *animal fats* (*with saturated fatty acids*).

– Sunflower oil, maize oil, nuts and olives, which are rich in *plant oils* (*with unsaturated fatty acids*).

The functions of lipids consist of:

■ *Fuels* — Lipids have twice the energy of carbohydrates and are likewise primary sources of energy for cell metabolism.

■ *Protection* — Waxes form a waterproof covering on all

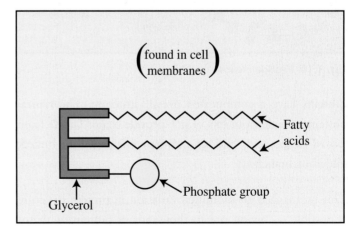

Fig. 3.9. A phospholipid.

leaves and assist plants in life on land. Fats under the skin protect animals and humans from falls and bruising.

- *Insulation* — Fat stored in adipose tissue under the skin is a heat insulator.
- *Structural* — Phospholipids are used to form all cell membranes.

Proteins

Examples of protein are: *collagen* in skin, ligaments and bone; *keratin* in hair and nails; *myosin* in muscle; *albumin* in egg white; the *food stores* in peas and beans; all *enzymes* and *antibodies*.

All proteins contain carbon, hydrogen, oxygen and nitrogen atoms (sulphur is often present). Proteins are constructed from *amino acids* of which there are about 20 different kinds occurring in Nature. The amino acids are joined in chains (condensation again) to form the proteins. There may be as many as 600 amino acids in any chain. Two amino acids joined together form a dipeptide, three a tripeptide and so on. A chain of many amino acids is termed a polypeptide.

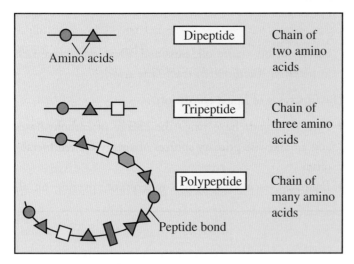

Fig. 3.10. Peptide chains.

Proteins have a complicated overall structure. The typical protein is made from lots of polypeptide chains (made from lots of amino acids joined) and these chains will be linked, folded or branched.

This means that an unlimited variation in protein structure is possible — giving rise to thousands of proteins with totally different properties. The *order of amino acids* in a chain

Table 3.3.

Good sources of protein	
1st class proteins (from animals)	*2nd class proteins (from plants)*
meat	sunflower oil
fish	maize oil
eggs	corn oil
cheese	olive oil
milk	peas, beans, nuts

Foods rich in proteins

can be varied and so too can the *linking and folding* of these chains.

For example, folded chains may produce a soft protein with fluid properties like egg white, whereas linked or branched chains can be tough enough to form the hooves of a horse!

This huge variation is necessary as the typical organism requires thousands of *different* enzymes (which are proteins) in order to maintain itself. The same degree of variation is not needed in lipids or carbohydrates.

(The correct structure in enzymes is extremely important. For example, a single amino acid in the 'wrong' place in an enzyme in the iris of the eye can result in blue eyes rather than brown eyes — or may produce a less trivial change. Virtually all of the enormous amount of information contained in a DNA molecule is concerned with the instructions for joining amino acids in the correct order to produce enzymes. The correct enzymes will then be able to direct and maintain the living organism properly (see chapter 12).

Plants can synthesise their own amino acids from simple chemicals, but the enzymes and other proteins of animals and humans must be assembled from amino acids obtained from the diet. All of these essential amino acids must be available to the animal.

- *Essential amino acids* — There are nine amino acids that are not easily made by animals or humans and *must* be included in the diet. They are always contained in proteins that come from animal sources, e.g. meat or fish (known as 1st. class proteins).
- *Non-essential amino acids* — These are amino acids that can be synthesised from any protein including plant proteins (known as 2nd. class proteins).

Vegetarians, despite their dietary preference, still need all essential amino acids in their diet. They obtain them all by mixing different plant proteins together within their meals. No single plant protein contains all of the essential amino acids together, but a mixture of plant proteins will.

Fig. 3.11. The food pyramid.

The functions of proteins are as follows:

- *Metabolic regulators* — Almost all enzymes are proteins. Every chemical process in biology is directed and regulated by a specific enzyme.
- *Fuels* — Proteins contain as much energy as carbohydrates but generally only release this energy if other fuels are unavailable. Proteins are secondary sources of energy for cell metabolism. They generally only give up their energy in cases of extreme starvation.
- *Structural* — Hair, nails and hooves are made from keratin. Collagen in skin, the tendons of muscles and the ligaments between bones give strength and support.
- *Movement* — Actin and myosin produce movement in muscles.
- *Communication* — Many hormones are formed from protein.
- *Growth and repair* — Amino acids are needed to grow and maintain almost all tissue in living organisms.

Vitamins

These are organic nutrients needed only in tiny amounts but essential to all living organisms. They are synthesised by all plants and are required in the diet of all animals.

They are referred to by letters and numbers e.g. vitamin A, B_2, D, — or by chemical names. Vitamins A, D, E and K are fat-soluble, the B group vitamins and vitamin C are water-soluble.

- **Vitamin C** (ascorbic acid) is a water-soluble vitamin found in citrus fruits and green vegetables. It is needed for the formation of connective tissue in animals and humans. A deficiency of vitamin C leads to the condition of *scurvy* in humans, monkeys, apes and chimpanzees. Most other mammals can make their own vitamin C and are never deficient.

  Symptoms of scurvy:
  Bleeding gums, large bruises just under the skin, bleeding on the surfaces of bones and eventual collapse of internal organs resulting in haemorrhage and death!
  Scurvy was common amongst sailors during the Age of Sail in the 17th and 18th centuries. Sailors were at sea

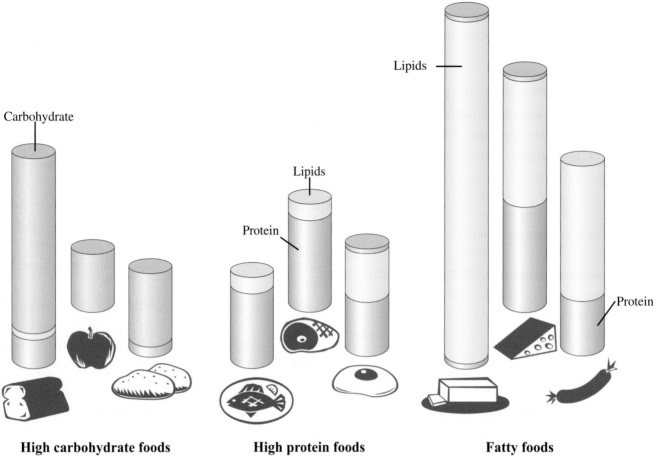

High carbohydrate foods   **High protein foods**   **Fatty foods**

Fig. 3.12. Contents of some foods.

for very long periods of time and soon had little fresh food. English sailors were called *Limeys* as the Royal Navy took limes and lime-juice on board to prevent the disease.

- **Vitamin D** (calciferol) is a fat-soluble vitamin found in fish liver oil, milk, eggs and dairy products. It is needed in the diet for absorbing calcium and phosphorus from food, for hardening bones and for aiding blood clotting. It can be synthesised in the skin on exposure to sunlight.

A deficiency of vitamin D leads to *rickets* in children or *osteomalacia* (sick bones) in adults.

Symptoms of rickets in children:
Swollen abdomen, weakness, diarrhoea, bending of the long bones especially the legs.

Treatment is to replace the missing vitamin by correcting the diet but any delay can result in permanently misshap-

en bones, particularly in the weight-bearing pelvis and legs.

Rickets (once known as *the English Disease*) is now very rare in Ireland.

Mandatory activity #10:
Testing for starch, fat, reducing sugar
and protein in food

Qualitative tests for common nutrients

MATERIALS REQUIRED

Variety of food samples (egg white, egg yolk, castor oil seeds, peas and beans, butter, oil, margarine, apple, baby food, stock cubes, cereals, potato, rice, pasta, bread, table sugar, glucose powder, lemon juice, orange segments etc.).

Table 3.4.

Vitamin	Name	Source	Function	Deficiency disease
A	retinol	liver, dairy products, green vegetables.	Helps vision, growth of mucous membranes	Night blindness, complete blindness in children, dry eyes, dry skin.
B1	thiamine	all food especially white bread, yeast	Respiration	Beriberi, which involves nerve degeneration and tissue wasting.
B2	riboflavin	all foods, yeast.	Respiration	no specific disease
B3	niacin	meat, yeast, coffee.	Respiration and photosynthesis	Pellagra — (diarrhoea, dermatitis and dementia).
C	ascorbic acid	citrus fruits, vegetables	Maintains connective tissue	Scurvy
D	calciferol	milk, eggs, cheese, butter, made in skin with sunlight	Calcium metabolism	Rickets in children, Osteomalacia in adults.
E	tocopherol	plant oils, e.g. sunflower oil.	Helps absorption of some fatty acids.	not known.
K	phylloquinone	dark green vegetables, bacteria in intestine	Blood clotting	Haemorrhage, delayed blood clotting.

Recording chart.

Test tubes.

Dropping pipettes.

Spatula.

Reducing sugar solution (e.g. glucose or fructose).

Benedict's solution *or* Fehling's solution I and II.

Water bath.

Starch solution (starch, salt and water).

Iodine solution.

10% sodium hydroxide solution.

1% copper sulphate solution.

Brown paper.

Heat source.

DCPIP solution.

Microscope.

Slide holders.

- Prepare a chart to show the results of the tests carried out on a range of food samples and controls.
- Carry out a control experiment for each test — carry out each test with water rather than food and compare the results.

- All tests, except for that for lipids, are carried out in test tubes. Test tubes should be no more than one-third full at any time.
- Only the reducing sugar test requires heat.
- Wear safety glasses for all tests. Some of the chemicals used can be hazardous.
- It is only necessary to test small samples of food.
- Clean each test tube as soon as you are finished with it.

1. Protein:

- Add a little sodium hydroxide or potassium hydroxide to a solution of the food.
- Add a drop of copper sulphate solution down the side of the tube.
- Do not heat.
- A blue ring at the surface indicates protein.
- The solution turns purple on shaking.
- Repeat the test with water and compare — the control experiment.

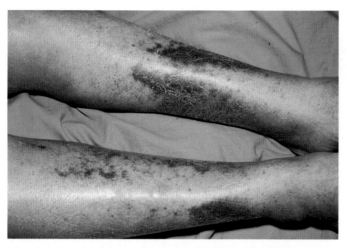

Fig. 3.13. Subcutaneous bleeding over the shins, due to scurvy.

2. Lipid:

- Rub the food onto brown paper and hold up to the light.
- Look for a greasy, translucent (lets the light through) stain.
- Repeat with water and compare.
- Alternatively, grind the food in a mortar and add to water in a test tube.
- Boil gently and look for oil droplets rising to the surface.

3. Starch:

- Add iodine solution to the moist food.
- Look for a colour change from golden to navy or black.
- Repeat the test with water and compare — the control experiment.
- Alternatively, place a thin slice of food sample, e.g. potato on a slide and add iodine to one side.
- Observe the starch grains in the potato cells.

4. Reducing sugar:

- Place about 2 cm of food sample in a test tube and add an equal amount of Benedict's reagent or Fehling's solution I and II.
- Warm the test tube gently — do not boil.
- A brown or brick-red precipitate indicates reducing sugar.
- A green colour indicates relatively little sugar.
- Repeat with water and compare for the control experiment.

- Alternatively, place a thin slice of apple on a microscope slide.
- Add the test reagents and observe.
- Using a slide holder, warm the slide gently on a small flame.
- Add a drop of water if the tissue begins to dry.
- Let the slide cool and re-examine the tissue.
- Look for changes. Are the changes evenly spread through the tissue?

5. Vitamin C (optional test):

- Add 2 cm of DCPIP solution to a test tube.
- Drip the food solution into the tube and observe.
- Look for a change from blue to pink and then colourless.
- Repeat with water and compare for the control experiment.

ENERGY TRANSFER REACTIONS [135]

Thousands of chemical reactions are taking place in all cells at all times — the *cell's metabolism*.

These reactions are regulated by specific enzymes and always involve *energy transfers* from one chemical to another.

In some reactions (*anabolic reactions*), relatively small chemicals are joined to make larger biomolecules and an *input of energy* is required from somewhere to form the new chemical bonds. Energy is transferred from some source (either sunlight or food) to construct the new chemicals. Examples of this include *photosynthesis* in plants where sunlight energy is used to construct carbohydrate from water and carbon dioxide, or *muscle development* in animals where energy from food is used to join dietary amino acids to form new protein.

In other reactions (*catabolic reactions*), large biomolecules are broken down into smaller chemicals with a *release of energy* from the broken chemical bonds. One example of this is during *respiration* where glucose is broken down to produce carbon dioxide, water and energy. The released energy is now available to the cells.

Both photosynthesis and respiration have typical metabolic pathways; they are not single step reactions as their equa-

Table 3.5. Food tests

Tests for the presence of common nutrients in food			
Nutrient	**Materials**	**Method**	**Results**
Protein	Copper sulphate and sodium hydroxide solutions	Add some sodium hydroxide to the moist food. Then gently pour copper sulphate solution down the side of the tube.	A deep violet colour is a positive result (indicates that some protein is present).
Lipid	Brown paper	Rub the food onto the paper, warm gently and hold the paper up to the light.	A greasy, *translucent* stain is positive.
Starch	Iodine solution	Add iodine solution to the food sample.	A navy or black colour is positive for starch.
Glucose	Benedict's solution *or* Fehling's solution I and II	Add to the sample, warm gently.	A brick red colour is positive for glucose or other *reducing sugars*.
Vitamin C (optional)	DCPIP	Add to the moist food	A change from blue to pink or colourless is positive for vitamin C.

tions might suggest but complex sequences of reactions and intermediates directed by cell enzymes.

Energy transfer reactions are discussed in detail in chapter 8.

[136]–[137]

MINERALS

Minerals are inorganic nutrients obtained within *mineral salts*. Their functions are:

1. *To form parts of rigid structures*, e.g. calcium (Ca) in bones and teeth and in plant cell walls.
2. *To form soft body tissues*, e.g. sulphur (S) is used for making proteins in plants and animals.
3. *To function in cellular and body fluids*, e.g. iron (Fe) is needed for the formation of haemoglobin in red blood cells. Magnesium (Mg) is used to make plant chlorophyll. Magnesium, cobalt (Co) and zinc (Zn) are used to switch on or *activate* many enzymes in plants and animals. Phosphorus (P) is used for forming ATP.

(*Mineral salts* are common metal-containing compounds often dissolved in water. They tend to have two-part names such as *sodium chloride* ($NaCl$), *calcium phosphate* ($CaPO_4$), *iron sulphate* ($FeSO_4$) and *magnesium sulphate* ($MgSO_4$). They usually break (*dissociate*) into their component parts when dissolved in water.

They are found in soil water and within almost any food material.)

WATER

Water (H_2O) is an inorganic chemical found in abundance on our planet.

Life originated in water and evolved in its constant presence so it is no surprise that water is essential for all living organisms and continues to hold many different life forms.

All biochemical reactions take place in water and so all organisms require water in their lives. The human body is about 60% water by weight. Individual cells are usually 75% water but can contain up to 90%.

Table 3.6. Summary of the roles of biomolecules

Biomolecules	Structural roles	Metabolic roles
Carbohydrates	Cellulose in cell walls, chitin in arthropod exoskeletons, deoxyribose in DNA	Primary sources of energy, e.g. starch, glycogen and glucose in cells
Lipids	Formation of cell membranes, protection (e.g. surrounding the kidney), insulation (e.g. under the skin)	Primary sources of energy, formation of some hormones
Proteins	Keratin in hair, nails, wool, horns, hooves, connective tissue, myosin in muscles general growth and repair	Secondary sources of energy, enzyme formation, hormone formation
Vitamins	—	Activation of enzymes, tissue development

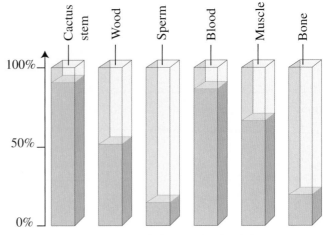

Fig. 3.14. Water content of plant and animal tissue.

The importance of water has a lot to do with its unusual physical and chemical properties:

- *Water is an excellent solvent.* More chemicals dissolve in water than in any other solvent. Chemicals cannot react with each other without coming into contact first. Water brings chemicals into intimate contact by dissolving them and then mixing them.

- *Water can flow.* It can be used to transport dissolved chemicals from one site to another. It is a participant in the movement of materials in and out of cells and it can be used to adjust and control cell shape (discussed in chapters 10 and 17).

- *Water has a high heat capacity.* It takes a relatively large amount of heat energy to raise its temperature. This means that it is slow to heat up and slow to cool down

— it tends to resist changes in temperature and so makes the body of an organism less prone to sudden temperature changes.

(If your body contained 60% *cooking oil* instead of water, a brief period of sunbathing could raise your temperature by about 10°C — with fatal consequences to your enzymes and then to you! Likewise, a cold night would cause your body temperature to fall rapidly. Cooking oil has a much lower specific heat capacity than water — it is quite easy to heat up or cool down and is not suitable as a background liquid within organisms.)

- *Water has a high surface tension.* Its surface behaves like a thin skin that helps to form water droplets, assists the lives of many aquatic insects (who can walk on it!) and aids the transport of water up through the stems of plants.
- *Water is a participant in major chemical reactions.* It is specifically required for photosynthesis and digestion and it is manufactured and released during respiration.

SUMMARY

- All living organisms need nutrients to provide energy and materials for metabolism and continuity.
- Organisms are composed of bioelements. The six most important are: carbon; hydrogen; nitrogen; oxygen; phosphorus; and sulphur.
- Atoms of the bioelements bond in different ratios to form biomolecules.
- The four major types of biomolecule are carbohydrates, lipids, proteins and vitamins.

- Biomolecules can be:

  - joined together (in anabolism);
  - broken apart (in catabolism);
  - used for energy transfer;
  - used as structural units;
  - used to regulate metabolism and continuity.

- Minerals are needed in small but essential amounts by all organisms.
- Water is essential for life.

KEY WORDS

Nutrition	The process of obtaining energy and matter in order to survive.
Nutrients	Chemicals that supply energy and matter to organisms.
Organic nutrients	Contain *carbon*.
Inorganic nutrients	Do not contain carbon.
Autotrophic nutrition	When foods are made from inorganic nutrients and usually sunlight energy.
Heterotrophic nutrition	When existing foods are broken down to provide ready-made nutrients. Animals obtain food by eating.
Trace elements	Elements essential in the diet but only required in tiny amounts.
Biomolecules	The basic chemical structures found within most organic chemicals.
Monosaccharides	Are the simplest sugar biomolecules.
Disaccharides	Are made from pairs of single sugar biomolecules joined.
Polysaccharides	Are made from long chains of *many* sugar biomolecules joined.

Condensation	Is the joining of molecules together with the *release of some water*, e.g. during photosynthesis.
Hydrolysis	Is the separation of molecules with the *addition of water*, e.g. during digestion.
Triglyceride	The smallest lipid unit — made from three fatty acids attached to one glycerol molecule.
Phospholipids	Fat-like substances with one fatty acid replaced by a phosphate molecule.

QUESTIONS

1. Explain the meaning and the significance of the statement: 'We are what we eat'.
2. What are nutrients and why are they important?
3. What is the fundamental difference between plants and animals as regards nutrients?
4. What are biomolecules? Name four kinds of biomolecule found in living cells. State three uses that cells might make of biomolecules.
5. What is the structural difference between a disaccharide and a polysaccharide?
6. Maltose is a disaccharide made from two glucose molecules ($C_6H_{12}O_6$) joined. Why is the formula for maltose $C_{12}H_{22}O_{11}$ and not $C_{12}H_{24}O_{12}$?
7. What is the difference between fats and oils?
8. Draw labelled diagrams of a triglyceride and a phospholipid.
9. Describe both the structural and metabolic roles of proteins.
10. Comment on the fact that proteins can have a much more varied structure than lipids or carbohydrates.
11. Name a water-soluble and a fat-soluble vitamin and for each, state a good source, the function of the vitamin and the consequences of a deficiency.
12. Give three examples of the need for minerals.

13. Describe a laboratory test for each of the following in food and suggest a control for each test:

    a. protein;
    b. lipid;
    c. reducing sugar;
    d. starch.

OPTIONAL ACTIVITIES

- Carry out a survey of eating habits within the school. Design a questionnaire to gather information and present a report to the school on how to provide a balanced diet.
- Compare different juices and drinks for vitamin C content. Count how many drops of each are needed to decolourise the same amount of the same DCPIP solution. Present your results as a bar chart and comment on your findings. Examine the drink labels and comment on the manufacturer's claims.

Now test yourself at
www.my-etest.com

Chapter 4
Ecology

DEFINITION OF ECOLOGY   [141]

Ecology is the study of plants and animals within their natural environment: how they interact with each other and with their surroundings.

Ecology is essential for building up a complete picture of the lives of all living organisms on this planet. In particular, ecology is a vital study if we are to judge the impact of humans on the environment. Despite our relatively late arrival on the planet, we have used our expanded intelligence to assume a very high degree of control on environmental conditions and this has had both beneficial and harmful effects on the natural world (see section [149]).

Fig. 4.1. Humans and the environment.

ESSENTIAL TERMS IN ECOLOGY
[142]–[144]

Ecology	The study of the interaction of living organisms with each other and with their natural environment.	*Population*	A group of organisms of one species, e.g. a crab population. Population members breed within the population and not outside it.
Habitat	The place where an organism lives. An oak tree lives in a woodland, a crab lives at the rocky seashore.	*Community*	The organisms that live in the habitat. A community is a group of populations.

Ecosystem	The habitat and community combined. All ecosystems have living (*biotic*) and non-living (*abiotic*) components with nutrient recycling, an energy input from the sun and an energy flow. Examples of ecosystems include a rocky seashore, a woodland, a bog, a freshwater pond, an old brick wall and a meadow.
Biosphere	The part of the Earth, including its atmosphere, which is inhabited by organisms. The biosphere extends from the bottom of the sea (or the depth of soil on land) to the tops of the highest mountains. It resembles a thin shell around the outside of the surface of the planet. The nature of its biological contents is determined mostly by temperature and by the availability of food and light.
	The biosphere is a true ecosystem as no one part is completely isolated from any other. It is a *global ecosystem*.
Biome	An ecological zone extending over a very large area. Examples include deserts, tropical rainforests, deciduous rainforests, tundra, grasslands and coral reefs.
Producer	An organism that makes its own food by photosynthesis or chemosynthesis. All plants are producers – they make food for themselves and for other organisms using light energy and inorganic nutrients. Plants are *autotrophic* ('self-feeding').
Consumer	An organism that obtains its food from eating other organisms. All animals are consumers — they cannot make their own food and must find, eat and digest 'ready-made' food. Animals are *heterotrophic* ('other-feeding'). Consumers are named according to their diet as follows:
Herbivore	An animal that feeds exclusively on plant material.
Carnivore	An animal that feeds exclusively on other animals.
Omnivore	An animal that feeds on both plants and animals.
Detrivore	An organism that feeds on dead plants and animals and on animal waste.
Decomposers	Microorganisms (fungi and bacteria) that bring about the decay of dead plants and animals. Decomposers are important in that they recycle the inorganic nutrients in dead plant and animal tissue.

ENVIRONMENTAL FACTORS   [145]

These are factors within the ecosystem that affect the *distribution* and *abundance* of plants and animals.

Abiotic factors are *non-living* factors such as temperature, water availability and soil type.

Biotic factors are *living* factors, resulting from the presence and activities of other living organisms.

Abiotic factors

Climatic factors are related to the climate of the ecosystem. Climate influences the lives and distribution of all organisms.

- *Light* — Ragworms hate light and burrow deep into beach sand. Honeysuckle climbs over other plants to obtain more sunlight. Light duration and light intensity changes with the seasons and plants are most active during the long, bright days.
- *Temperature* — Plant seeds germinate in spring as temperatures start to rise.
- *Water availability* — Marine sponges thrive in the high humidity of rock crevices in rock pools. Ferns needs dry air for spore release. Cacti are adapted to retain scarce water.
- *Wind* — Exposed seashores have rough wave action resulting in fewer limpets. Grasses use wind for pollination.

Edaphic factors are related to soil. They are factors such as soil type, soil pH, soil air and moisture. Most ecosystems have soil in them somewhere, e.g. the splash zone of the rocky shore and the mud of ponds.

- *Aeration* — Soil air is needed for root respiration.
- *Drainage* — Willows need a high soil water content.
- *Humus content* — Humus is a black, jelly-like substance formed from decaying organic matter. It improves soil drainage and aeration, and increases soil mineral content.
- *Mineral content* — The correct minerals are essential for healthy plant growth. Orchids and yew require high levels of soil calcium.
- *Soil pH* — This affects the solubility – and so the availability – of minerals. Soil pH itself is influenced by climate, by the nature of the underlying rock and by humus content. Different plants are encouraged by different pHs: heathers prefer acid soils, whereas orchids prefer basic soils. Soil in Ireland can have a pH of between 3.5 and 8.5. Soil pH is easily measured (see section [154]) and adjusted.

Geographic factors are related to the geography of the ecosystem.

- *Aspect* — Mosses and *Pleurococcus* prefer to face north.
- *Slope* — This affects drainage. Willow trees require more soil water than pine trees.
- *Altitude* — Temperatures decrease with altitude and gen-

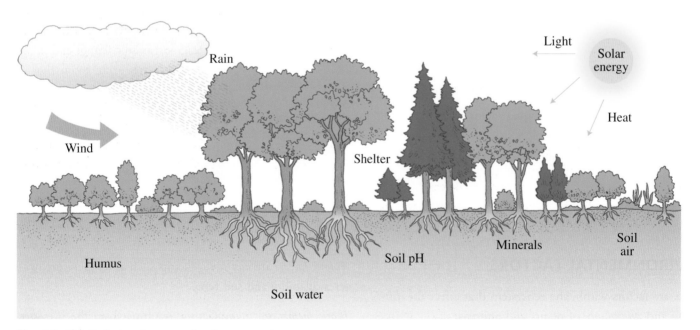

Fig. 4.2. Abiotic factors in a woodland.

erally conditions become more harsh with high winds and thinner soil. As altitude increases, upright plants with large leaves give way to small alpine plants growing in flattened mats or in rock crevices.

- *Shelter* — Rocks, walls and ditches can favour certain organisms. Barnacles and limpets must be attached to rocks to feed.

Chemical factors are related to the chemistry of the ecosystem

- *Oxygen* — 21% of the atmosphere is oxygen, so oxygen is freely available on land. Stagnant ponds can favour the growth of anaerobic bacteria.

- *Salinity* — Freshwater and saltwater fish generally cannot interchange habitats. Green algae in rock pools can withstand the dilution of salt by rainwater.

- *pH* — Small ponds can be slightly alkaline by day due to CO_2 uptake for photosynthesis and then slightly acidic at night due to CO_2 release from plant respiration.

- *Mineral availability* — All are available from seawater at the seashore. Alkaline soils are low in phosphorus.

Biotic factors

These are factors connected with the presence and activities of living organisms in the environment and are best seen in terms of relationships. Examples of relationships include *competition* with others for food, the relationship between *predators* and their *prey*, the effects of *parasites*, and the impact of *humans*.

N.B.

- The division between abiotic and biotic factors is not always clear. Tall grass is a biotic factor for grasshoppers that eat it, but an abiotic factor for mice that shelter within it.

- All factors interact in some way. High altitude brings lower temperatures and more wind. Poor light reduces water losses and increases humidity. Oak trees increase shading, shelter and humidity for organisms near them. Soil pH affects mineral solubility.

- Specific *aquatic* environmental factors include:

  – light penetration in water — poor penetration means that aquatic plants must stay near the water surface.

  – wave action — seashore plants and animals may have to resist the forces of waves and currents.

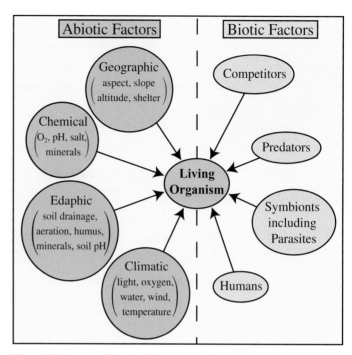

Fig. 4.3. Factors affecting living organisms.

ENERGY FLOW   [146]

Ecosystems cannot function without a constant input of energy. The primary source of energy for all living organisms is the sun. Light energy from the sun is trapped by green plants, converted to chemical energy and stored in food (the process of *photosynthesis*). Plants are producers of food for themselves and for all other organisms on Earth. Animals (herbivores) eat the plants and use the food energy to maintain their own lives. Other animals eat some of these herbivores and so obtain their energy. This feeding relationship establishes *a pathway of energy flow* from one organism to the next.

A *food chain* is the pathway along which *energy* (in food) is transferred in an ecosystem. Each species in the chain obtains its energy by eating the species preceding it. Plants at the beginning of the chain obtain their energy directly from the sun.

A *grazing food chain* is one where the initial plant is living. The following are examples are grazing chains:

grass → grasshoppers → frogs → hawks
honeysuckle → aphids → ladybirds → thrushes
seaweed → winkles → crabs → herring gulls
phytoplankton → zooplankton → copepod → herring

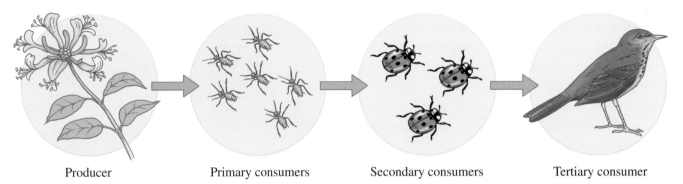

| Producer | Primary consumers | Secondary consumers | Tertiary consumer |

Fig. 4.4. A food (energy) chain.

A *detritus food chain* is one where the chain begins with dead organic matter and animal waste (detritus):

detritus → edible crab → seagull

fallen leaves → earthworms → blackbirds → hawks

The following points should be noted in any food chain:

- Food chains (except detritus food chains) begin with a plant or part of a plant — the producer of food for every chain member.
- The second chain member is always a herbivore or omnivore.
- Other members will be carnivores, omnivores or maybe detrivores and decomposers.
- Arrows in the chain represent *energy flow* and must not point the other way. (Imagine the energy 'flowing' into the mouth of the next consumer.)
- Each step in the chain is termed a *trophic level* or feeding level (plants occupy the first trophic level, herbivores the second and so on).
- The numbers of organisms occupying each level *usually* decrease from left to right. This is for various reasons:
  - food chains lose very large amounts of energy at every step. This also restricts the length of food chains to no more than four or five levels;
  - predators tend to be larger than their prey and so eat multiples of them;
  - small animals reproduce faster than larger ones;
  - animal mobility tends to increase along the chain making successive predations more difficult.

Food Webs

Isolated food chains are unusual in ecology. In practice consumers usually have a choice in what they eat — they are members of *food webs*.

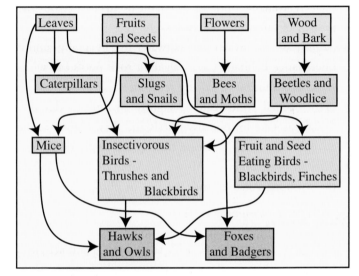

Fig. 4.5. Woodland food web.

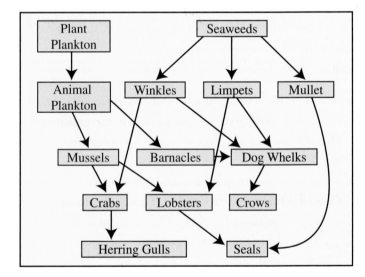

Fig. 4.6. Marine food web.

A food web is a set of interconnected food chains. Food webs give a more complete picture of what is eating what in the ecosystem.

N.B. The trophic level of any animal varies with the food chosen — many animals feed at a range of trophic levels. For example, in the woodland web above, hawks occupy the third trophic level when eating mice and the fourth trophic level when eating thrushes.

ENERGY LOSSES IN FOOD CHAINS

At best, only about 6% of the energy at any trophic level in a food chain will be passed on to the next level. This energy is contained within the eggs and tissues that are food to the next consumer. The other 94% is 'lost' from the chain through movements, excretion, nerve transmission, heat loss after respiration, and death.

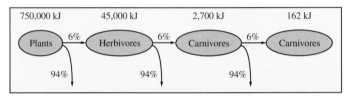

Fig. 4.7. Energy losses in a food chain.

For example, if the plants of the chain contained 750,000 kilojoules of energy, only 45,000 kJ (6%) would be available to the herbivores that come next. Likewise, the next step of the chain would receive only 2,700 kJ (6% of 45,000) and the next step only 162 kJ. This ongoing loss means that food chains can never have many levels and also makes life difficult for organisms situated at the end of the chain.

The food chain is similar to a perforated water pipe — very wasteful and struggling to transport water (or energy) over a large distance. This energy loss, however, does ensure that population numbers do not get too large for the habitat.

PYRAMID OF NUMBERS

As numbers tend to decrease in food chains due to the energy losses, the chain is often represented by a pyramid, with the blocks of the pyramid representing the numbers of organisms occupying each trophic level.

Constructing the pyramid:

1. Count the producers and place them at the bottom of the pyramid.

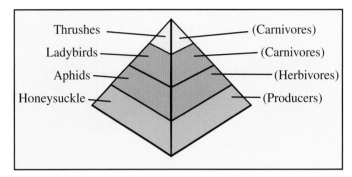

Fig. 4.8. Simple, regular pyramid of numbers.

honeysuckle → aphids → ladybirds → thrushes

2. Count the consumers and place them according to their feeding status (herbivores followed by carnivores, etc.).
3. Complete the pyramid by counting and placing the top carnivores at the apex.

The pyramid shape demonstrates that:

- numbers decrease along the food chain;
- plants, being at the first trophic level, support all the chain members directly or indirectly;
- energy losses are taking place;
- extra trophic levels would be difficult to support.

[H14 I]

The pyramid is really a bar chart representing the numbers found at each step in the food chain. Pyramids should be drawn accurately with the ratio of volumes corresponding to the ratio of numbers measured. In practice though, this accuracy of drawing is too difficult. Usually the diagram is taken as a simple *representation* of the decrease in numbers. The pyramid is used to compare different communities of the ecosystem.

The data needed to construct pyramids are easy to collect, but sometimes unusual shapes are obtained! For example, in the food chain:

oak tree → aphids → ladybirds → thrushes

The pyramid shape is returned as in fig. 4.9.

The pyramid shape is distorted because the producers are physically large but not very numerous.

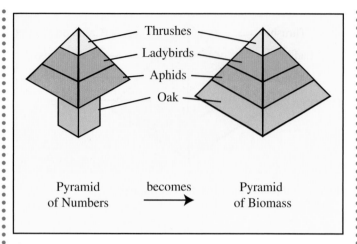

Fig. 4.9. Distorted pyramid shape.

In a food chain containing parasites and microorganisms:

oak tree → aphids → ladybirds → mites → bacteria

part of the pyramid of numbers is inverted.

These unusual shapes point out the one major flaw with these pyramid representations — *organism size* is not taken into account. The pyramid shape is always restored if the organisms are weighed (*biomass*) at each trophic level — something that is not always easy to do! Total population biomass is measured as dry weight in kg/m².

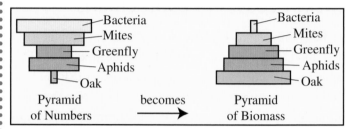

Fig. 4.10. Inverted pyramid restored.

(oak tree → aphids → ladybirds → mites → bacteria)

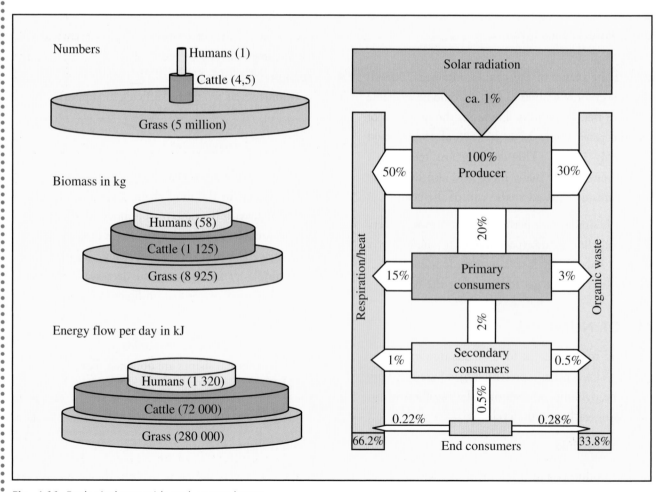

Fig. 4.11. Ecological pyramids and energy losses.

NICHE [147]

The term *niche* describes the position occupied by an organism in its ecosystem — and its relationship with the organisms around it. Niche includes all aspects of these relationships — feeding, mating, shelter, behaviour, etc. Food niche describes feeding relationships only. For example, the food niche of greenfly is to eat honeysuckle and be eaten by ladybirds. *A niche is the functional role of an organism in an ecosystem.* The niche of an organism also includes its abiotic requirements, e.g. its needs regarding moisture, warmth and light.

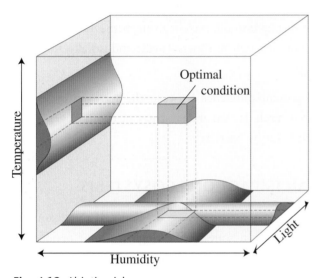

Fig. 4.12. Abiotic niche.

No two species in any balanced ecosystem occupy exactly the same niche. Barnacles and limpets are often found on the same rocks but they are not in competition with each other for food. The barnacle is a filter feeder, eating plankton while the limpet eats seaweed. Mice and voles eat the same food within the woodland but voles feed by day and mice by night. The evolution of niches reduces competition.

NUTRIENT RECYCLING [148]

When plants and animals die, their nutrient content is not wasted. Bacteria and fungi decompose the remains and release the nutrients back into the abiotic environment (into the soil, nearby water and surrounding air). These nutrients are then taken up by other plants and used to make new organic material. This material is passed on down the food chains and is reused by all the chain members. When death

occurs for these members, the nutrients are again returned to the abiotic environment and the cycling of nutrients continues in this circular way. This ensures that there is no real longterm drain on the Earth's nutrients, despite millions of years of plant and animal activity.

All inorganic nutrients are recycled in this way. The diagrams show the recycling of carbon-based and nitrogen-based nutrients.

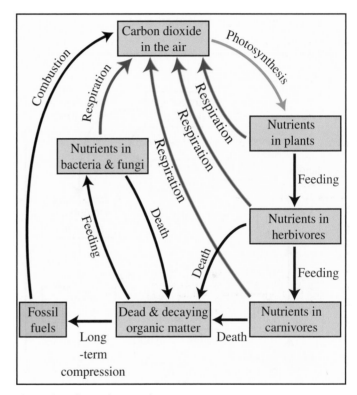

Fig. 4.13. The carbon cycle.

Carbon forms the backbone of all organic nutrients — carbohydrates, lipids, proteins and fats (see chapter 3). Plants obtain their carbon by absorbing carbon dioxide gas from the atmosphere. They use it in the process of photosynthesis to form carbohydrates and then convert these into proteins, lipids and vitamins. These carbon-based nutrients are passed to all other organisms through food chains. Respiration of all organisms, including plants, converts nutrients back into carbon dioxide and returns it to the atmosphere. In certain geological conditions and over long periods of time, dead organic matter becomes fossil fuels such as coal, oil, peat and natural gas. Carbon dioxide is formed and released to the atmosphere when these are burned.

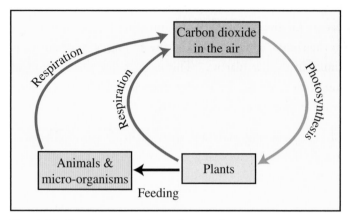

Fig. 4.14. Simple view of the carbon cycle.

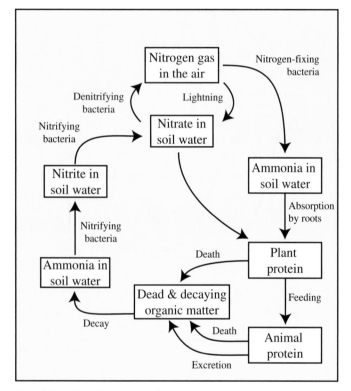

Fig. 4.15. The nitrogen cycle.

Although 78% of the Earth's atmosphere is nitrogen gas, this is not a form of nitrogen that can be utilised directly by plants and animals. Nitrogen gas must first be 'fixed', i.e. converted to a usable form of nitrogen — either ammonia or nitrate.

- *Nitrogen-fixing bacteria* in the soil convert atmospheric nitrogen gas into ammonia. This accounts for about 90% of all nitrogen fixation.
- *Lightning storms* and *fuel burning in car engines* produce nitrates, which are washed by rain into the soil water. This accounts for only 10% of nitrogen fixation.

Both ammonia and nitrates are absorbed by plant roots and converted to plant protein.

Plant proteins are passed along food chains to become animal proteins. When organisms die, their proteins are converted to ammonia by bacterial decomposition. *Nitrifying bacteria* in the soil then convert ammonia into nitrites and then nitrates. These can be absorbed by other plants to continue the cycle. A further group of bacteria — *denitrifying bacteria* — convert soil nitrates into nitrogen gas. This is a considerable loss of nitrogen from the cycle but only happens in conditions of low oxygen (*anaerobic* conditions) due perhaps to flooding or accumulation of sewage. A further input of nitrate into the cycle is through the addition to the soil of nitrogen-rich fertilisers (made industrially from nitrogen gas).

One important difference between the nitrogen cycle and the carbon cycle is that many stages of the nitrogen cycle are carried out by bacteria.

HUMAN IMPACT ON ECOSYSTEMS [149]

Humans are very recent arrivals on Earth. If the history of life was reduced in scale to one single 24-hour period, we would only appear on the planet at 11.59 p.m. and our recorded history would only occupy 1/4 second before midnight.

Before our arrival, many enormous changes had already taken place — including periods of global warming, ice ages and movements of landmasses — but we have had a huge impact in a very short period of time. We are presently in a period of accelerated environmental change — change that is having both beneficial and harmful impacts on the planet Earth. The assessment of these impacts is an ongoing and important debate.

Some Beneficial Human Impacts

1. AGRICULTURE

In the last hundred years, food production has increased faster than the human population. Science and technology have been brought to bear on the methods of agriculture and have increased efficiency. Breeding and genetic engi-

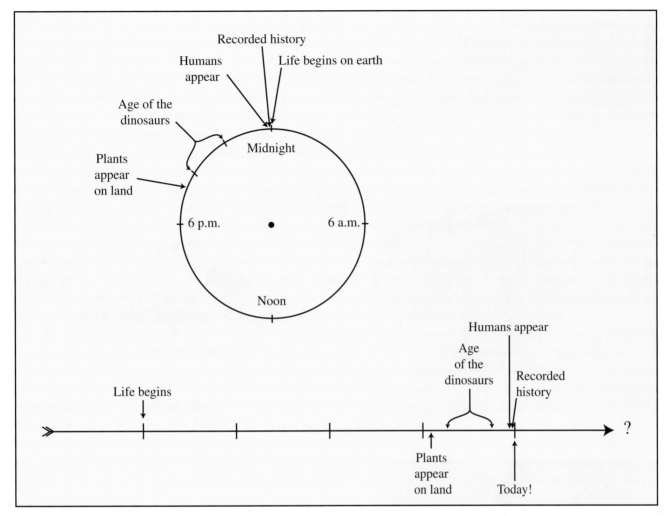

Fig. 4.16. 24-hour clock for life on Earth.

neering produce new species of plants and animals — in particular, new varieties of cereals. Crops are more pest-resistant, drainage is improved, predators are controlled, animals are better fed and housed. Many parts of the world still suffer from appalling famine as a result of war, politics and poor distribution of food, but humans will always be able to produce as much food as the world needs.

2. TRANSPORT AND COMMUNICATION

Humans have evolved the *'global village'*. It is now possible to see and talk to anyone anywhere in the world at any time. It is also possible to travel to any place in the world within a day. Satellites, telephones, the Internet, aeroplanes, radio and television and other media ensure that information on anything is available to anyone. The exchange of scientific information on the Internet alone is considered to have

speeded up recent scientific advance by a factor of ten. Satellite imaging provides information about weather, animal migrations, oil pollution, algal bloom, iceberg movements, land erosion and impending famine.

3. HEALTH AND MEDICINE

Human health is greatly improved in recent years. Advances in food preparation, water quality and sewage systems, together with better education on hygiene and on the importance of diet and exercise, have greatly increased the average human lifespan. Advances in surgery and preventative medicine protect humans from illness, disease and defects. Studies in contraception and reproduction can assist in curbing the human population explosion. All of these advances in turn benefit animal populations.

Fig. 4.17. Cultivation of the land.

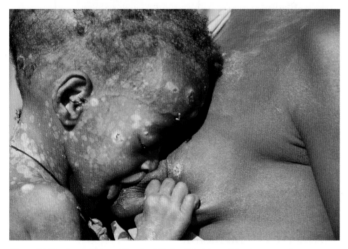

Fig. 4.18. A malnourished child with Kwashiorkor syndrome.

4. CONSERVATION AND RESOURCE MANAGEMENT

Conservation is the wise management of the environment. Humans have a responsibility towards the environment and must always take steps to see that it is protected and maintained. The methods and benefits of conservation are discussed later.

Harmful Impact — Pollution

Pollution is any human addition to the environment that leaves it less able to sustain life. It is the most harmful human impact. Examples include pollution of air, fresh water, the sea, the soil on land, radiation pollution and even light and noise pollution. Chemicals of human origin that harm the environment are termed *pollutants*.

Fig. 4.19. An oiled, immature razorbill.

Note that pollutants are produced from *human* activities. The same chemicals made by natural processes over millions of years are generally absorbed by the environment and are not considered polluting; although they might place stress on certain living organisms in the short term. For example, naturally-made CO_2 from respiration is not a pollutant, but excess CO_2 from burning fossil fuels is. Sulphur dioxide from marshes and volcanoes is not a pollutant, but SO_2 from factory chimneys is.

Some pollutants are chemicals that are normally present in the environment but reach a much higher lever due to human activity, for example, carbon dioxide in the air or nitrates in river water. Other pollutants are chemicals which never exist in the normal environment, such as oil slicks at sea or CFCs in the atmosphere.

Examples of pollution include:

1. CO_2 AND THE 'GREENHOUSE EFFECT' — GLOBAL WARMING

Radiant heat from the sun passes through the atmosphere and warms the Earth. Some of this heat is radiated from the Earth back towards outer space and has to pass through the atmosphere again. Water vapour and carbon dioxide in the atmosphere trap some of this heat and radiate it back towards the Earth. In this way, the atmosphere acts as an 'insulating jacket' around the Earth, sending some of the escaping heat back again.

The world's plants (mainly the forests on land and phytoplankton and algae at sea) act as CO_2 sinks. They absorb CO_2 for photosynthesis and so balance the production of CO_2 by respiration. Over the last two hundred years, CO_2 levels have been rising in the atmosphere due to the burning of fossil fuels such as coal, oil, peat and gas. In the early 1800s, CO_2 levels (measured in air trapped in ice and in old scientific equipment) were about 250 parts per million; by 1957 they had risen to 315 ppm. They currently stand at about 360 ppm. Carbon dioxide in the atmosphere traps reflected heat from the Earth's surface and redirects it back to the Earth. Increased CO_2 levels have caused a slow rise in the Earth's temperature — *global warming.*

Possible consequences of global warming include:

- a rise in sea levels due to melting of the polar icecaps and thermal expansion of the oceans;
- changes in wind and rainfall patterns producing climate changes.

Some scientists, however, are of the opinion that temperature increases in the future will be slight and might even improve conditions for plants.

2. CFCs and ozone damage

Ozone (O_3) is a pale blue gas formed from oxygen gas (O_2). It forms in the upper atmosphere from the action of the sun's ultraviolet radiation on O_2 molecules. Ozone is also formed inside car engines and during electrical discharge from generators, electric trains, lifts or electric storms. Ozone forms a layer in the atmosphere about 30 km up, which filters the ultraviolet radiation of the sun. It absorbs the ultra violet (UV) components that can damage DNA in living tissue but does not absorb the UV responsible for sunburn and sun tanning. Chlorofluorocarbons (CFCs) have been used inside fridges and aerosols over the last 50 years. If CFCs escape, they rise to the ozone layer and re-convert O_3 into O_2. The resulting 'hole' in the ozone layer allows more UV radiation to reach living organisms and increases the rate of genetic mutation. Currently there are large holes over the north and south poles and the ozone layer is much thinner than it used to be. Although further CFC production is now banned, they will remain in the atmosphere for up to 100 years before they break down.

3. Acidic oxides and acid rain

Even the cleanest rain is acidic. CO_2 in the atmosphere dissolves in rainwater to form carbonic acid. This gives rain in unpolluted air a pH of about 5.5. The term *acid rain* refers to *very* acid rain with a pH of 4.5 or less.

The burning of fossil fuels (coal, oil, gas, petrol) releases acidic oxides into the air — particularly sulphur dioxide (SO_2) and nitrogen oxides (NO_x). SO_2 dissolves in rainwater to form sulphurous acid (H_2SO_3) or reacts with chemical particles in the air to form sulphuric acid (H_2SO_4). The resulting rain is highly acidic and can be carried by the wind over huge distances.

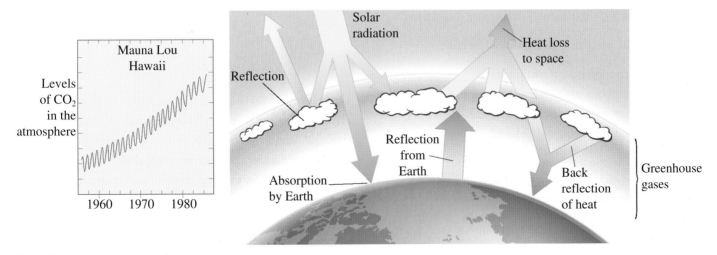

Fig. 4.20. The greenhouse effect.

Effects of acid rain:

- Acid rain reduces soil pH. Phosphorus binds to soil particles and is unavailable to plant roots. Aluminium becomes soluble and poisonous and with potassium, calcium and magnesium is washed (*leached*) from the soil into lakes and water supplies. The soil is impoverished and fish die in the highly mineralised water.
- Acid rain erodes limestone buildings.
- Acid rain causes breathing difficulties in many people as it irritates the delicate linings of the lungs.
- Acid rain inhibits chlorophyll formation and burns the leaves of plants directly.

The acid-rain problem is complicated by the fact that many countries unavoidably 'export' their acid rain over huge distances. This is described as a 'trans-boundary problem'. Norway suffers greatly from acid pollutions originally formed in the English Midlands and in the Ruhr valley of Germany. Ireland can consider itself lucky that the prevailing wind direction tends to be from the Atlantic Ocean rather than from across Europe.

Strategies for dealing with the acid-rain problem include reducing the burning of fossil fuels, using catalysts to treat chimney gases ('scrubbers' are fitted to the insides of chimneys) and exploring the possibilities of alternative, 'clean' energy sources.

Conservation

Conservation is the protection and wise management of the environment. It involves using an understanding of ecological principles to restore the natural balance of ecosystems.

The benefits in practising conservation include:

- existing environments are maintained;
- endangered species are preserved for reproduction;
- the *balance of nature* is maintained;
- pollution and its effects are reduced.

Conservation of the environment by humans is an active process and can be approached in different ways:

1. MAINTAINING EXISTING ENVIRONMENTS

Parklands, natural forests and wildlife refuges need to be

Fig. 4.21. Spruce forest killed by acid rain.

protected. Indiscriminate tree felling and the destruction of environments for building need to be controlled. Ecosystems should be monitored for any changes.

2. SPECIES CONSERVATION

Once lost, species of plants and animals can never be recovered. Besides the fact that living organisms are both attractive and useful, a diversity of life is needed for a proper balance of nature. Legislation is required to prevent illegal importing of organisms and to ensure that unnecessary losses such as hunting do not take place. Wildlife sanctuaries, zoos and botanical gardens all play important roles in species conservation. Education and information exchange can help to change attitudes to species loss.

Fig. 4.22. Endangered species: gorilla, rhino, lemurs, panda.

3. POLLUTION CONTROL

Particularly important areas include CO_2 management, CFC legislation, acid-rain monitoring, waste management and ecological education. In Ireland, much of this is done by the Environment Protection Agency.

Conservation in practice

THE FISHING INDUSTRY

All fish feed directly or indirectly on *plankton* — microscopic plants and animals in the water. There are many freshwater fish in Ireland but almost all commercial fishing is of marine fish.

Fish stocks are not spread evenly throughout the world's oceans; rather they are concentrated in areas where currents and wind bring up minerals from the seabed which are necessary to maintain the plankton. Fish also congregate around areas of natural erosion or human activity — both of which also provide the necessary supply of plankton minerals.

Commercial fishing is done by one of two methods:

- Drift net fishing for surface (pelagic) fish such as mackerel and herring. Nets float near the water surface and the fish are trapped by their gills.
- Trawling for bottom-feeding (demersal) fish such as cod and flatfish. A huge, cone-shaped net is dragged over the seabed.

Dangers to fish stocks

- Pollution of the seawater by nitrates from agriculture, sewage, oil spillages and toxic chemicals. All of these will particularly devastate the plankton numbers and so reduce the numbers of all others in the food chains. Also pollutants tend to concentrate as they proceed through the chains, so the fish at the ends of the chains suffer the highest concentrations (see the explanation of *biological magnification* on page 43).

Fig. 4.23. Fish kill due to pollution.

- Overfishing of fish stocks. Modern fishing methods are extremely efficient, often creating a situation where fish breeding does not take place fast enough to keep pace with the losses.

Conservation methods

- Legislative control over the spread of pollutants, such as oil, nitrates and anti-fouling paint on ship hulls, is rigorously applied.

- Legislation over fishing methods is applied. Many EC rules exist over boat sizes, days at sea, fishing quotas, mesh sizes and net design. These rules are difficult to enforce given the area of sea to be covered and the number of fishery protection vessels available.
- Research into marine lifecycles, fish migration and the effects of pollution is essential and continuing.
- Fish farming is designed to protect and maintain fish species and to increase fish numbers. Large-scale marine fish farming is not yet considered entirely practical or ecologically sound.

THE FORESTRY INDUSTRY

Fig. 4.24. The 'lungs' of the Earth.

Were it not for humans, the Irish countryside would be mostly covered by deciduous forest: ash or elm on basic soils and oak wood on acid soils. As human populations developed their agricultural methods, natural woodlands were destroyed to provide wood for fuel and building, and land for farming, housing and roads. It can be difficult enough to find a natural forest anywhere in Ireland now. Virtually all 'natural' sights (fields, hedges, ditches, pine forests, walls, etc.) are due to human intervention. The practice of felling trees faster than they grow has altered the landscape completely and has created various ecological problems. These problems are important in Ireland but perhaps more important worldwide, particularly in tropical rainforests and in the boreal forests near the North Pole. In these huge areas, the problems are multiplied by the vast scale of deforestation and the vulnerability of the poor communities affected. In Bangladesh many thousands have died due to lowland flood-

ing as a result of deforestation in the mountains hundreds of miles away. Soil erosion produced silting in rivers that eventually burst their banks. The flooding also caused huge crop losses and the spread of disease.

- *Young forests* are important CO_2 'sinks'. They absorb CO_2 from the atmosphere and prevent its build-up. (*Mature* forests tend to only absorb as much CO_2 as they create in respiration.)
- Cutting down of trees brings about soil erosion and the silting of nearby waterways.
- Forests generally absorb and control rainwater. Flooding is more likely in areas that have lost their trees.
- Forest destruction can lead to losses of particular species of plant and animal.

Conservation methods in Ireland

- Tree felling is regulated. Only mature trees are felled, young trees are left undamaged and new trees are planted to replace the losses. The reclaiming of forest land for construction is protected by law.
- Biological diversity is monitored and protected by the Environment Protection Agency.
- Alternative building materials are considered.
- Mixtures of broadleaf (deciduous) and conifer trees are used when replanting to retain a balance of species.
- Public awareness of forest destruction and forest importance is improved by educational programmes, visitors' centres and the promotion of forests as public amenities.

PESTICIDES IN AGRICULTURE

Pesticides are chemical designed to kill living organisms. They have been produced by humans to kills specific pests, such as insects that destroy crops or disease-carrying fleas that infest wild mammals. Categories of pesticide include:

— *herbicides*, designed to kill plants;
— *molluscicides*, to kill slugs and snails;
— *insecticides*, to kill insects;
— *rodenticides*, to kill rats and mice.

Although pesticides have been of great benefit and can increase productivity, there is now recognition that they can

Fig. 4.25. Spraying wheat to control aphids.

also have harmful effects. In 1962, the American ecologist, Rachel Carson, drew attention to the unexpected consequences of pesticide use. In her book, *Silent Spring*, she gave examples of pesticides accumulating at the ends of food chains. *Organochlorides*, such as DDT, had commonly been used for insect control since the late 1940s. These chemicals were very successful in insect control but would linger in rivers and lakes rather than break down. They were absorbed by plankton and so entered the food chains of the ecosystem. DDT accumulated in body fat and, as predators tend to eat many of their prey, reached high concentrations in the top carnivores. Many birds and fish died from the use of this insecticide. The eggs of predatory birds also tended to have very thin eggshells that broke easily.

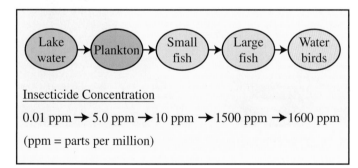

Insecticide Concentration

0.01 ppm → 5.0 ppm → 10 ppm → 1500 ppm → 1600 ppm

(ppm = parts per million)

Fig. 4.26. Food chain concentration of insecticide.

Pesticides also constitute a direct health risks to the humans who have to handle and distribute them.

(*Biological magnification* often occurs when toxins or pollutants enter food chains. Unlike energy, toxins do not leak from the food chain; instead they become concentrated as predators eat multiples of prey. Top carnivores receive such high concentrations of toxins that they die or become sterile.)

Solutions

- Use *biodegradable pesticides*, such as *organophosphates*, which tend to break down with time.
- Use *biological pest control*. Aphids can be controlled by the introduction of ladybirds and hoverflies. Fungi are used to kill specific weeds in cornfields.
- *Selective use* of pesticides. Small doses of one or two pesticides often have a similar effect to large doses of many.

Waste management

Modern urban communities produce vast amounts of rubbish. The average Irish person can produce up to 1/2 tonne of rubbish every year. This rubbish is mostly house dust and dirt (containing human skin cells and hair!), paper, food scraps, metal (soft-drinks cans, tin foil and food containers), glass and plastic. Traditional disposal of this rubbish has been to use landfill sites where everything is buried. Alternatively, the rubbish is burned (*incinerated*).

These waste-disposal methods have problems associated with them:

- the availability of suitable landfill sites;
- the toxic or polluting content of chimney fumes (including CO_2, other acidic oxides and toxic products such as dioxin);
- the formation of methane gas under ground.

Possible solutions:

- Lifestyle changes are essential in order to reduce the amounts of waste. Many people suffer from a 'disposable' mentality. Educational programmes are needed at all age levels to alter attitudes to personal littering and waste.
- Microorganisms may be used soon to degrade the rubbish and may produce useful by-products such as fuel pellets.
- Paper use should be reduced and all paper recycled.
- Biodegradable materials (such as brown paper bags) should be used in place of non-biodegradable plastics (such as supermarket bags). Taxes may have to be placed on the supply of plastic bags in shops.

- Rubbish sorting makes rubbish disposal more efficient. Metals, paper, plastics and glass of different colours should all be sorted by the rubbish producers. Pilot schemes have been run by many county councils and have generally indicated that most householders are willing to cooperate.

- Incineration temperatures must be increased to avoid the production of toxins (e.g. dioxin) from burning plastics. Catalytic scrubbers must be fitted inside chimneys.

Other specific waste problems include:

FISHERIES WASTE

Fish waste from fish landing and cleaning is a major pollutant of marinas and harbours. Accumulated fish waste leads to unpleasant odours, infestations of rats and maggots and low oxygen levels in the harbour water due to decomposition of waste by bacteria. Solutions include establishing recognised fish cleaning areas, rules concerning cleaning and disposal and the implementing of fish composting.

FORESTRY WASTE

Slash debris from tree felling can block waterways and stream channels. This affects the oxygen levels of the water. Solutions include using selective cutting rather than clearing large areas, protecting streams from slash debris and collecting debris for use as a fuel.

AQUACULTURE WASTE

Aquaculture can be defined as the farming of aquatic organisms (e.g. fish, shellfish, crustaceans or aquatic plants) in natural or controlled marine or freshwater environments. As a result of intensive feeding, fish farms can produce large volumes of highly concentrated wastes — mostly consisting of organic debris and high levels of minerals, particularly phosphate. Untreated waste falls as sediment to the bottoms of rivers and seabeds and the quality of these habitats will decrease. Solutions include control of the amount and content of fish food used, proper water treatment, use of closed water systems and careful siting of fish farms with regard to water currents and water depth.

AGRICULTURE WASTE

Sewage disposal is a problem in both urban and agricultural communities. In the past, large volumes of sewage or animal effluent from farms have been released, untreated, into rivers, lakes and the sea. The problems associated with this are:

- Animal and human faeces contain large amounts of biodegradable material. To decompose the organic matter bacteria use up the oxygen in water. The low oxygen levels kill fish and other aquatic life and upset the ecological balance of the water.

- Many bacterial and viral pathogens are found in faeces. These can enter water supplies and cause epidemics of typhoid fever, cholera, polio and other diseases.

- Faeces may contain the eggs of tapeworms and other parasites.

Fig. 4.27. River contaminated with sewage.

Proper sewage treatment in a sewage works is essential for dense, urban communities and intensive farming. Treatment usually involves initial settling to remove non-biodegradable solids, then aeration and treatment with *aerobic bacteria* to degrade the organic material. Sewage treatment removes the threat of pathogens, minimises the release of unpleasant smells and avoids the destruction of natural water environments.

ECOLOGICAL RELATIONSHIPS   [H14II]

The following relationships are significant in the ecosystem as they control population numbers and bring about a '*balance of nature*'.

1. *Competition* — When organisms of the same or different species 'fight' for necessary resources that are in short supply. Plants compete for light, water, minerals and space. Animals compete for food, water, territory and mates.

   - *Contest competition* — An active, physical confrontation between two organisms that results in one obtaining the resource. For example, two dogs may fight over a single bone. One dog may have stronger muscles, better senses and sharper teeth and so be more likely to win.
   - *Scramble competition* — Each organism tries to acquire as much of the resource as possible. For example an ivy plant and a hawthorn tree may compete for available light. The ivy obtains an advantage by using adventitious roots to grip the hawthorn and climb higher.

Competition restricts population sizes — only successful competitors will survive and reproduce. Competition is therefore a driving force behind evolution (see chapter 14). Adaptive techniques such as sharp teeth in carnivores or climbing abilities in ivy are selected in response to the need to survive competition.

2. *Predation* — One organism, the *predator*, kills and eats another organism, the *prey*. Wolves killing deer, spiders eating ladybirds and seagulls eating crabs are all examples. Predators must gain more energy from the prey than they expend in capturing and killing it.

Predation has many positive effects on any ecosystem:

1. Predation stabilises the community.
2. Predators control the number of herbivores and so prevent overgrazing.
3. Predators eliminate the less well-adapted prey.

The predator/prey relationship between wolves and deer in Alaska is examined in the following section. The populations of both wolves and deer are interconnected

Fig. 4.28. Sparrowhawk.

(see page 46). In this relationship, both predators and prey have evolved *adaptive techniques* to improve their chances of survival. The wolves have very keen hearing and eyesight, they have strong muscles and sharp teeth. They use camouflage to conceal themselves and they

Fig. 4.29. Mistletoe.

hunt in organised packs. The deer also have keen hearing and eyesight, they are quick to turn and run and they use both camouflage and disruptive hind markings to evade the wolves.

3. *Parasitism* — One organism, the *parasite*, benefits from another, the *host*, and does harm to it. Examples include lice (*ectoparasites*) within the feathers of seagulls, roundworms (*endoparasites*) within a red squirrel. Parasites do harm to their hosts but are usually careful not to kill them too rapidly!

4. *Mutualism* — Describes two organisms of different species, both of which benefit from a close relationship. A lichen on a wall or seashore rock is composed of an alga and a fungus intertwined. The alga obtains support and a mineral supply from the fungus, the fungus obtains food from the alga.

Fig. 4.30. Lichens from Clara bog.

5. *Commensalism* — Where one organism obtains benefit from another and leaves it completely unaffected — neither harmed nor helped. An example of this is the bacterial population within the intestine of humans and other animals.

Parasitism, mutualism and commensalism are all examples of *symbiosis* ('living together') — where two or-ganisms have a close, specific relationship with each other.

6. *Human interaction* — The impact of humans on ecosystems is obviously enormous and can easily alter the distribution and abundance of organisms. Humans have had both positive and negative effects on ecosystems. Some of these effects have been discussed above.

POPULATION DYNAMICS WITHIN THE PREDATOR–PREY RELATIONSHIP [H14III]

A '*population*' is defined as a group of organisms of the one species. *Population density* is a measurement of the numbers of this species over a stated area.

Population increases are due to increases in the birth rate and immigration and *population decreases* are due to increases in the mortality rate and emigration.

Most population numbers tend to fluctuate in the short term, but find an overall balance in the long term where births and immigrations are equal to deaths and emigrations. Mortality rates tend to be very high in nature, with many organisms dying before they can reproduce. Deaths are due to predation, parasites and lack of food rather than due to old age. A high mortality rate is important to populations — it protects the stock of food and eliminates less well-adapted organisms.

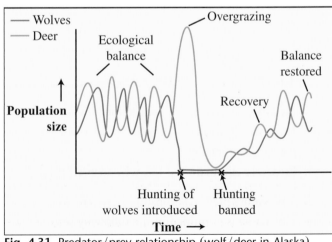

Fig. 4.31. Predator/prey relationship (wolf/deer in Alaska).

N.B.

- When the deer population increased, the wolf population had more food and increased too.
- As the wolf population increased, the number of deer being killed increased bringing about a decline in the deer population.
- When the deer population declined, there was less food for the wolves and they declined too.
- This led to an increase in the deer population.
- This cycle continued over years and had obviously found a natural balance to do with availability of food for both populations.
- When the wolf population was drastically reduced due to hunting, the resulting explosion of the deer population led to *overgrazing* of the vegetation. This produced huge mortality and emigration in the deer population with a collapse of the relationship.
- After the banning of hunting, a balance was slowly re-established in the two populations.

The populations are controlled by *negative feedback*, where a drop in numbers is generally self-correcting. Over a long period of time, the deer evolve structures and behaviours to survive predation better, e.g. better camouflage, quicker reactions and sharper eyesight. The wolves, of course, also evolve better predation techniques to cope with the evolving prey.

The main variables in this relationship are:

- the availability and abundance of plant food for the deer;
- the availability and abundance of food for the wolves;
- the ability of the deer to detect danger and avoid it;
- the ability of the wolves to recognise the prey and stalk it successfully, using camouflage, careful movement, organisation of the pack, etc.;
- the impact of humans when hunting began.

In addition, the following also influenced the population numbers:

- the interaction with other members of the food web;
- the possibility of immigration and emigration for both deer and wolves;
- the birth rates and death rates of both deer and wolves;
- the ability of both populations to adapt and evolve.

HUMAN CONTROL OF THE HUMAN POPULATION CURVE

Most population curves in nature take on a sigmoid (S) shape as follows:

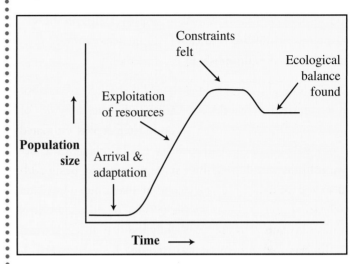

Fig. 4.32. Normal population curve.

1. Organisms arrive and then adapt to their new environment.
2. Growth takes place rapidly due to newly-available food.
3. Growth constraints are felt — predation, overcrowding, available food, etc.
4. Growth settles at a level that the environment can support.

The human population curve, however, has not been susceptible to the normal constraints of nature and looks very different.

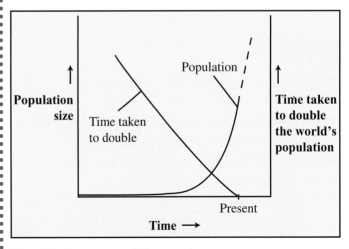

Fig. 4.33. Human population curve.

In nature, growth curves shaped like the human population curve (exponential curves) tend to collapse — due to overcrowding, lack of food and an increase in predators. Humans do not suffer from predation to any real extent and can make as much food as they like with their advanced technologies and agricultural methods. Also, improvements in health, medicine and disease eradication mean that mortality rates have decreased enormously in recent times.

On 27 June 2000 at 11.00 a.m. GMT, the US Census Bureau estimated the world population to be over 6 billion or 6,079,411,189 exactly! Ten seconds later, it was estimated at 6,079,411,222 — an increase of 33. In other words, between births and deaths, three more people were being added to the population every second at that time. This is an increase of over 240,000 people per day or 88 million in a year! (This rate of increase is slightly less than in 1994 when the highest rate of increase was recorded.)

The current rate of increase is not sustainable and will have to be reduced. The appalling losses suffered by human populations during wars and famine make virtually no impact on the global population curve. National contraceptive policies such as taxes on 'extra' children in some Eastern countries have some effect, but clearly may interfere with basic human rights.

Mathematically, the requirements are simple; if adult humans throughout the world only reproduced once in every seven years, the population curve would start to come under control. However, the moral issues are complex and the efforts required to reduce the world population are immense.

SUMMARY

- The *Biosphere* is a true ecosystem — no part is completely isolated from the rest.
- *Environmental factors* (both abiotic and biotic) affect the *distribution* and *abundance* of living organisms.
- *Abiotic factors* are *non-living* factors such as temperature, water availability and soil type.
- *Biotic factors* are *living* factors, resulting from the presence and activities of other living organisms.

- Abiotic factors include *climatic*, *edaphic* (*soil*), *geographic* and *chemical* factors.
- Biotic factors are usually relationships such as *competition*, *predation*, *parasitism* and the *effects of humans*.
- A *food chain* is the path along which energy (in food) is transferred in an ecosystem.
- A *food web* is a set of interconnected food chains.
- A *pyramid of numbers* represents the numbers and types of organisms in a food chain.
- Organisms survive by *managing energy flows* and *recycling nutrients*.
- Human impacts affect the balance of an ecosystem.
- Beneficial human impacts have been made in the areas of agriculture, transport and communication, health and medicine, conservation and resource management.
- The most harmful human impact is pollution.

EXTENDED SUMMARY

- *Pyramids of numbers* are often distorted. The shape is restored if *biomass* is calculated.
- The common ecological relationships are *competition*, *predation*, *parasitism* and *symbiosis*.
- The *predator/prey* relationship is subject to many variables.
- Human control of the *human population curve* has become essential, but will be difficult to achieve.

KEY WORDS

The essential terms in ecology listed in sections [142]–[144] at the start of this chapter should be learned.

Ecology	The study of plants and animals in their natural environment.
Energy flow	The pathway of energy movement from one organism to the next due to feeding relationships.
Pyramid of numbers	A diagram representing the numbers and types of organisms in a food chain.

Niche	The position occupied by an organism in its ecosystem.
Conservation	The wise management of the environment.
Pollution	Any human addition to the environment that leaves it less able to sustain life.
Competition	When organisms of the same or different species 'fight' for necessary resources that are in short supply.
Predation	A relationship where one organism, the *predator*, kills and eats another organism, the prey.
Parasitism	A relationship where one organism, the parasite, benefits from another, the host, and does harm to it.
Population	A group of organisms of one species.

QUESTIONS

1. *What is ecology and why is it important?*
2. What is the primary source of energy for all organisms? What is the significance of *photosynthesis* in ecology?
3. What are environmental factors? Give three examples.
4. What is the difference between abiotic and biotic factors in ecology? Give three examples of each. Explain, with one example, why the difference is not always clear-cut.
5. With reference to a woodland, choose a term from the list below to best match the following:

   a. a list of all the plants and animals;
   b. the total mass of leaves;
   c. the beetles;
   d. the soil pH;
   e. the entire woodland;
   f. the plants;
   g. the light intensity.

   biomass, abiotic factor, community, ecosystem, producers, population.

6. Draw a simple food chain. Mark clearly on it the producers, consumers, carnivores, herbivores, plants and animals. What do the arrows in the chain represent?
7. State two consequences of the energy losses from a food chain.
8. Using the woodland food web diagram (Fig. 4.5):

   a. Write out five different food chains within the web.
   b. Draw a pyramid of numbers for any of these chains.
   c. Name four herbivores and four carnivores.
   d. List the organisms in the second trophic level.
   e. State three effects of trapping and killing the slugs and snails.

9. What is a *niche*?
10. Explain the difference between energy flow and nutrient flow in an ecosystem.
11. What is the main difference between the carbon cycle and the nitrogen cycle?
12. Outline three consequences of a breakdown of the nitrogen cycle.
13. Give examples of three beneficial human impacts on the environment. What, in your opinion, is the greatest impact?
14. What is pollution? Choose an example and describe its cause, its effects and suggestions for its control.
15. What is conservation and what are the advantages of practising it?
16. Discuss the reasons for a build-up of waste in urban areas. What is *landfill* and what are the difficulties associated with it? What other methods are available for dealing with urban waste?

EXTENDED QUESTIONS

17. Explain what is meant by *competition*. Give three examples of competition taking place. How does competition benefit the ecosystem?

18. What is *symbiosis*? Name three types of symbiosis and give an example of each.

19. What is *overgrazing*? Why is it important and what normally guards against it in an ecosystem?

20. What factors regulate a normal population curve? How do these factors apply to the human global population curve?

21. Briefly outline the effects of war, famine, disease eradication and contraception on the human population curve.

22. The diagrams represent pyramids of numbers for two different food chains.

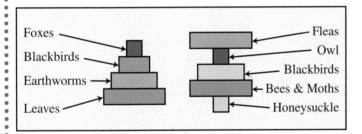

a. Redraw the diagrams and mark the trophic levels on each.
b. Explain why the pyramids have different shapes.
c. Redraw both pyramids as pyramids of biomass.

OPTIONAL ACTIVITIES

- List the various ways in which you yourself are affected by abiotic, biotic and climatic factors.
- Construct microenvironments to demonstrate the effects of acid rain. Use clear lunch-boxes or glass petri dishes, some germinating seedlings and buffer solutions.

Procedure:
Label four dishes or boxes for each seed type used.
Place ten seeds on damp tissue paper in each container and cover with another layer of tissue paper.
Label each dish pH 7, 6, 5 and 4.
Prepare four buffer solutions of pH 7, 6, 5 and 4. Check the pH of each with a pH meter or pH paper.
Water the seeds each day with the appropriate buffer solution.
Observe each day and record the number of seeds germinating.
Present all data in the form of a bar chart showing % germination in each of the conditions.
Repeat with different seed types.

- List all the food you have eaten in the last 24 hours and trace each one back to its plant origins.
- Present a report on any of the man-made problems currently facing our planet.

For information on websites dealing with subjects covered in this chapter, see www.my-etest.com.

Now test yourself at
www.my-etest.com

Chapter 5
Study of an Ecosystem

SELECTION OF AN ECOSYSTEM

The basic principles of ecology that apply to any ecosystem have been explained in Chapter 4. To study these principles in practice, choose a convenient and suitable ecosystem and carry out a scientific study of it. Emphasis in this study should be on the following:

- using the correct techniques of fieldwork;
- recording data within the ecosystem;
- analysing the collected data.

Suitable ecosystems can be found within the following lists:

Terrestrial ecosystems

- a hedgerow;
- a small woodland;
- an overgrown back garden;
- waste land;
- an old brick or stone wall;
- a meadow;
- peat land;
- soil.

Aquatic ecosystems

- a stream;
- a canal;
- a freshwater pond or lake.

Marine ecosystems

- the rocky seashore;
- rock pools.

Fig. 5.2. An old stone wall.

Fig. 5.1. Uncultivated land.

Fig. 5.3. A freshwater lake.

Practical ecology is safe and can be very enjoyable, but there are some rules to be kept:

1. Always obtain permission to be on private property.
2. Be aware of hidden dangers — deep water (water is always deeper than it looks), advancing tides, slippery rocks, electric fences, dangerous animals such as bulls or dogs!
3. Leave the habitats as undisturbed as possible. Do not collect more than necessary and replace upturned rocks and stones exactly as you found them.

4. Observe the *Country Code*: close gates behind you, do not litter, do not damage fences or hedges and do not start fires.
5. Protected wildlife cannot be collected. Protected organisms include frogs and frogspawn, badgers, hedgehogs, bats, otters and bog orchids.

Fig. 5.4. A gravel-bedded stream with beeches.

6. Wear clothing and footwear to suit the conditions and the time of year.
7. Wash your hands after all work and always before eating.

One final thought — would anyone know afterwards that you had visited the environment? You should leave no evidence of any sort.

Ecosystems and habitats are highly varied. Even habitats of the same kind vary in different parts of the country. Woodlands in Mayo are different to those in Kilkenny; the rocky seashore on the west coast of Ireland is different to the more sheltered east coast. This text cannot describe in detail all possible ecosystems that might be encountered in Ireland. The guidelines within this section should be applied to the ecosystem you have chosen. All of the knowledge, understanding and skills that are developed within your study can be applied to other ecosystems.

OVERVIEW OF THE SELECTED ECOSYSTEM [151]

Resources needed for this section

Guidebooks.
Biological keys.
Camera.
Drawing sheets and pencils.
Hand lens.
Measuring tape.
Ropes.
Compass.
Wall charts and posters.
Reference collections.
Internet access.

The selected ecosystem should be visited as many times as possible and at different times of the year. On your first visit, you need to form a general overview of the ecosystem. This will include:

1. *Drawing a simple map* (see fig. 5.5). Use a measuring tape, long ropes, a compass, a pencil and graph paper to draw a simple map. Mark on it a scale, the direction of north, any non-living features, such as walls, paths, etc., and any other prominent features. Indicate slope by including approximate contour lines.
2. *Making a list of important abiotic factors.* Depending on the habitat choice, this could include factors such as temperature, light, pH, water and air currents, soil content, slope and dissolved oxygen. Methods of measurement are described later in this chapter.
3. Identifying a number of habitats within the ecosystem, e.g. in a woodland — shrub layer, canopy, tree stump, etc; at the seashore — rock pool, lower shore, splash zone, etc.
4. *Finding and identifying organisms.* Methods of collection are described in later.

Choose *ten organisms* from the ecosystem (five plants and five animals) for identification and closer study. Make a drawing of each organism or photograph it. A digital camera will produce images that are instantly printable or can be used in a computer presentation. Compare each drawing or photograph to a textbook photo, a wall chart or a reference collection.

USING KEYS

A biological key can be used to classify each of the ten organisms. A key is a set of carefully structured questions.

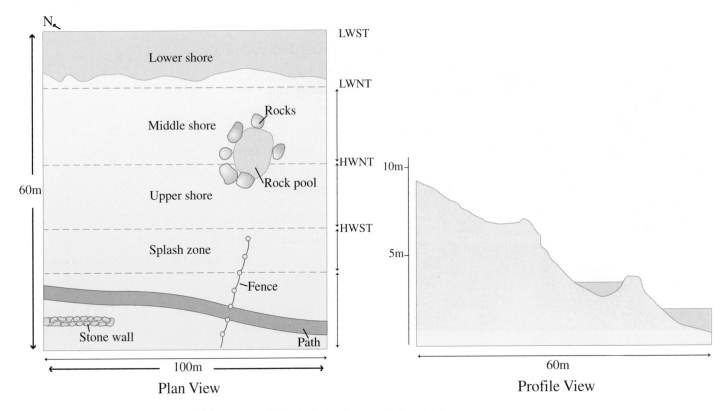

LWST - Low Water Spring Tide   HWNT - High Water Neap Tide
LWNT - Low Water Neap Tide   HWST - High Water Spring Tide

Fig. 5.5. Sample map of seashore habitat.

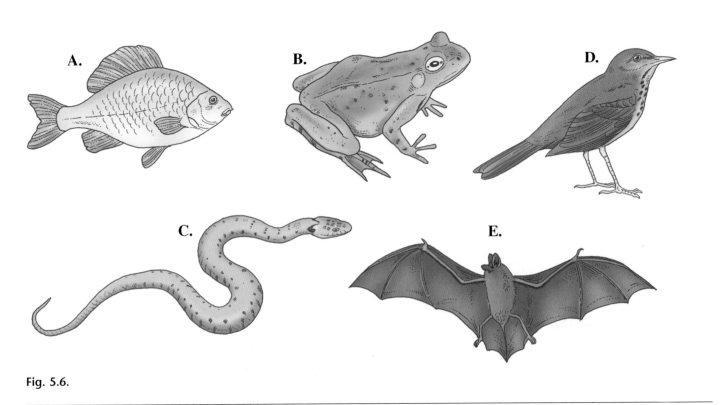

Fig. 5.6.

Each answer leads to a specific, new question until the identification is complete. Once a name has been found, it can be used to gather more information on the organism, through textbooks, encyclopaedias or the Internet. Keys are available for either detailed or general classification. Beware though — keys seem easy to use but give no warning if you happen to make a mistake and proceed in the wrong direction. Answer each question as carefully as possible and start again if any questions seem strange. The simplest keys have questions for which there are only two answers (usually *yes* or *no*) but some questions may have multiple answers. Keys may be written as lists of questions or drawn as diagrams. Each branch in the diagram is termed a *node* and represents a question.

The following is a simple key for identifying five animals:

Table 5.1. Key for identification of animals in 5.6.

Question	Answer	Then:
1. Does it have wings?	Yes	Go to Q4
	No	Go to Q2
2. Does it have legs?	Yes	It is a frog
	No	Go to Q3
3. Does it have fins?	Yes	It is a fish
	No	It is a snake
4. Does it have feathers?	Yes	It is a bird
	No	It is a bat

The same key can be represented as a diagram:

Mandatory activity #2: Using keys to identify plants and animals

Appendix A lists the characteristics of the main groups of living organisms.

Optional Activities:

1. Choose six people within your class and write a key designed to identify any one of the six.
2. Make a collection of objects on a table and write a key to identify them.

Besides keys, other methods of identifying organisms include using guidebooks, posters, reference collections kept in the laboratory, using libraries, the Internet or asking someone who is likely to know!

Reporting on organisms. For each of the ten organisms, a report should be presented. This normally includes:

- a photograph if possible;
- a simple, labelled drawing;
- a simple description of its appearance;
- its location within the habitat;
- any variation within the population — weight, size, height, colouring or other features;
- diet and mode of nutrition. If possible, observe it feeding or examine its feeding apparatus and maybe the contents of its stomach;

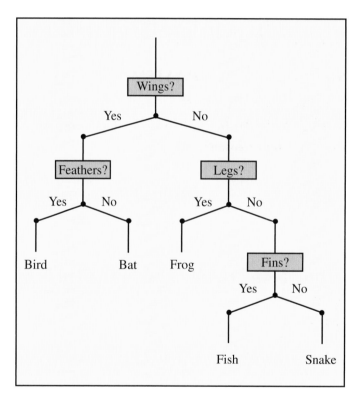

Fig. 5.7. Branching key.

- known predators;
- any observed behaviour;
- method of reproduction — for plants, include a drawing of flower parts and a note of its method of pollination (by wind or insects).

Use the same headings for each organism.

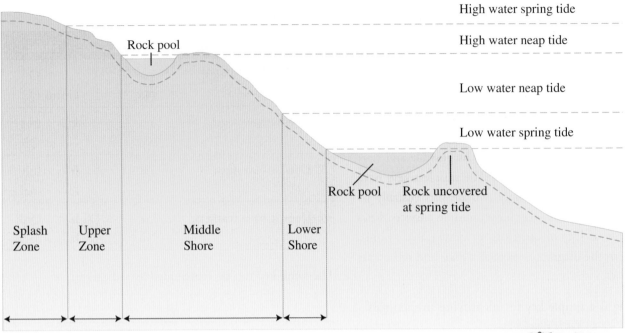

Fig. 5.8. Seashore zonation.

STUDY OF THE ECOSYSTEM
Collecting Organisms   [152]

Resources needed for this section (depending on the ecosystem chosen)

Small mammal traps.

Jam jars.

Stones.

Wooden covers.

Wooden boards.

Pooters.

Sweep nets.

Insect nets.

Plankton nets.

Fish nets.

Tullgren funnel.

Paper and pencil.

Identify a number of habitats within the ecosystem chosen. Mark the various habitats on the map and assign each organism to its correct place.

In a woodland ecosystem, individual habitats include the ground layer, the herb layer, the shrub layer, the canopy of mature trees, the soil and the bark of fallen trees (see fig. 5.9). Rocky seashore habitats include the upper, middle and lower shore, the splash zone and the rock pools (see fig. 5.8).

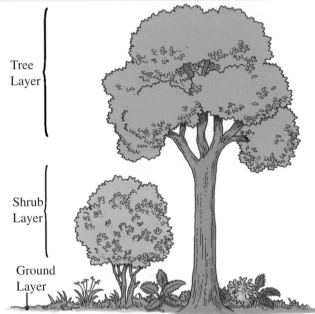

Tree layer e.g. oak, ash, beach. Includes a *canopy* of leaves.
Shrub layer e.g. bushes of hazel, hawthorn and young trees.
Herb layer e.g. non-woody plants, bracken, bramble, bluebells and seedlings.
Ground layer e.g. moss, grass, lichens and fungi.

Fig. 5.9. Woodland zonation.

Mandatory activity #1:
Using apparatus to collect organisms

Collecting equipment

PITFALL TRAP

The pitfall trap is used to collect small animals that move on the ground surface. It consists of a jam jar buried level with the ground surface. The opening is covered by a piece of wood or a flat rock supported by small stones. The cover keeps the rain out and helps protect the trapped animals from predators. Bedding or bait can be placed in the jar. The position of the traps should be recorded on the map and the traps inspected and emptied regularly.

SMALL MAMMAL TRAP

Mammal traps are suitable for collecting mice and voles. Each trap is made from light metal and is usually about the size of a shoebox. The door is held open by a spring and closes once the mammal is inside. Bait and bedding can be placed inside to allow the trapped animal to settle down. The traps should be inspected regularly and never forgotten or abandoned. Mark their positions on the map and open mammal traps carefully!

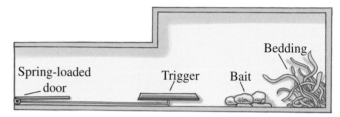

Fig. 5.12. Small mammal trap.

POOTERS

Pooters are used to collect spiders and small insects from leaf litter on the ground or directly from the bark and foliage of plants. The user sucks through the shorter tube and 'hoovers' the insects into the jar. A piece of muslin cloth prevents the insects travelling any further. The collected animals can be identified and then released. Never carry a pooter in your pocket: you may fall on it.

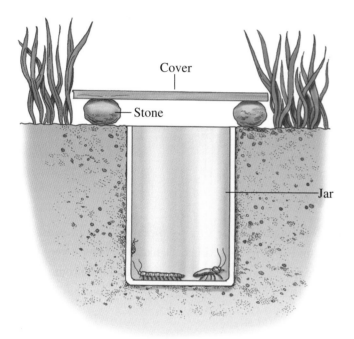

Fig. 5.10. Pitfall trap.

CRYPTOZOIC TRAP

Cryptozoa are 'secret animals' which hide by day and are normally only active at night. Woodland examples include slugs and woodlice. A cryptozoic trap is a sheet of wooden board or a flat rock left lying on the ground. Cryptozoa shelter underneath by day and can be inspected and collected by turning the board over. The position of the board should be marked on the map.

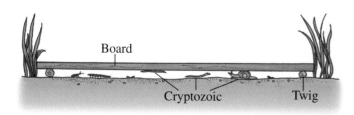

Fig. 5.11. Cryptozoic trap.

Fig. 5.13. A pooter.

TULLGREN FUNNEL

Tullgren funnels are used in the laboratory to extract small animals from soil samples. The sample is supported in the funnel by wire mesh, and an electric light is placed above the soil surface. The heat and light force small animals to move to the bottom of the funnel and fall into the water in the container.

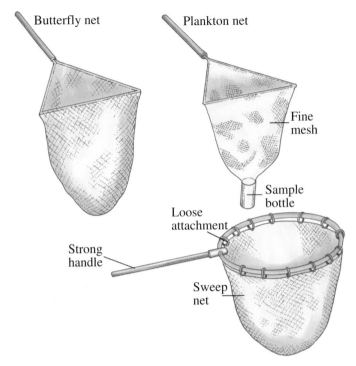

Fig. 5.15. Nets.

Fig. 5.14. Tullgren funnel.

NETS

Sweep nets have strong handles to sweep through long grass. Butterfly nets have shorter handles. Fish nets are very strong and have varying mesh size to suit different fish and shrimp collections. Plankton nets have very fine mesh with a sample bottle attached at the bottom.

DIRECT SEARCH

Walk through the habitat, turning over any rocks, boulders or fallen tree branches. At the seashore, turn over seaweed and rocks at the bottoms of pools. Identify and record any plants or animals discovered and then replace everything as it was found.

STUDY OF THE ECOSYSTEM
Measuring Organism Distribution   [153]

Resources needed for this section

Marked strings or ropes — at least 30 m long and marked every 50 cm.
Tent pegs.
Quadrat frames.
Point quadrat.
Cellulose paint or other suitable marker.
Metre sticks.
Recording sheets and pencils.

Surveys

QUALITATIVE SURVEYS

A *qualitative survey* of an ecosystem produces *a list of the organisms present*. It does not indicate which organisms are more common and contains no numbers.

Examples of qualitative surveys include:

1. *Line transects:* Lay a long rope or measuring tape (a *transect line*) in a straight line across the habitat. Identify and record all organisms touching the line. Line transects are suitable only for non-moving organisms.
2. *Quadrats:* Quadrats are usually made from wood, metal or plastic. They are square and vary in size — usually measuring 0.5 m or 1 m on each side. Tiny quadrats (10 cm square) are used for moss and lichen communities. Throw quadrats *at random* within the habitat and identify and record all organisms found within them.
3. *Use of pitfall traps, pooters and nets.*
4. *Use of Tullgren funnels for soil samples.*
5. *Direct search.*

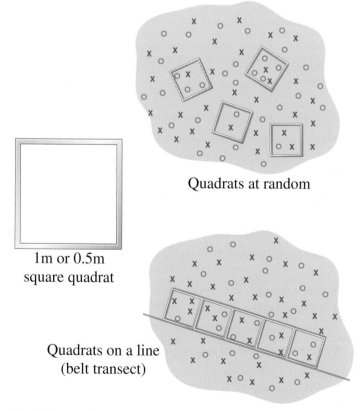

Quadrats at random

1m or 0.5m
square quadrat

Quadrats on a line
(belt transect)

Fig. 5.16. Quadrats thrown.

QUANTITATIVE SURVEYS

A *quantitative survey* of an ecosystem produces information on the *distribution* and *abundance* of an *individual species*. *Distribution* refers to where the organisms *are* (or are likely to be found) and *abundance* (or population size) refers to their *number*. It is important to remember that quantitative surveys are always done for a single species at a time. Studying an individual species is termed *autecology*.

> *Mandatory activity #3:*
> *Quantitative survey of part of the habitat*

Quantitative surveys for plants (or animals with little movement, e.g. limpets and barnacles)

1. ESTIMATING THE DISTRIBUTION OF A PLANT

   A line transect

   - Lay six transect lines parallel to each other and across the habitat.
   - Record their positions on the map.
   - Walk along the lines and mark on the map where the plant under survey touches each line.

   A belt transect

   - Lay out the transect lines as above, but space each line pair 1 m apart.
   - Record their positions on the map.
   - Use the marks on the lines to divide the area in between into 1 m square areas (similar to quadrats) — or else lay a quadrat at each metre mark on the line.
   - Mark on the map or on a table where the chosen plants are found.

2. ESTIMATING THE SIZE OF A PLANT POPULATION

   - Mark out, measure and calculate the area under survey.
   - Throw eight quadrats *at random* within the area.
   - Count the number of plants found within each throw.
   - Record the results in a chart.
   - Knowing the size of quadrat used, calculate the number of plants found per square metre.

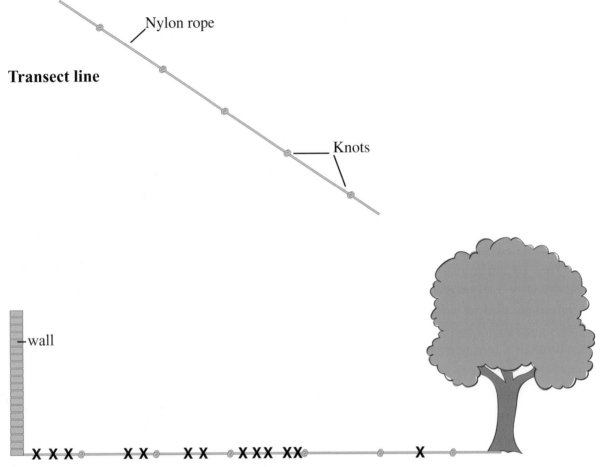

Fig. 5.17. Using line transects to investigate distribution of moss plants near a wall.

- Calculate the number of plants within the entire area.

Sample results:

Area under survey = 60 m × 10 m = 600 m².

Table 5.2. Estimating population size

Quadrat throw	1	2	3	4	5	6	7	8
Number of plants within each throw	0	2	0	2	2	3	1	0

Area of one quadrat = 0.5 × 0.5M = 0.25 m²
Area of 8 quadrats = 0.25 × 8 = 2 m²

2m² contained ten plants in total.
So 1m² contains five plants (the *plant density* — number of plants per square metre).
So 600m² (the total area) contains approximately 3,000 plants.

3. ESTIMATING THE PERCENTAGE FREQUENCY OF A PLANT

Frequency is estimated by the number of quadrats in which a particular organism occurs. Quadrats are thrown at random as above and a record kept of each time the particular plant is found. This is then written as a percentage of the total number of throws.

Percentage frequency is easy to calculate and gives a quick comparison between two species in the habitat.

- Mark out the area under survey.
- Throw ten quadrats (to simplify the maths!) *at random* within the area.
- Record whether or not the particular plant was found within each quadrat.
- Calculate the % frequency.
- Repeat for another species and compare.

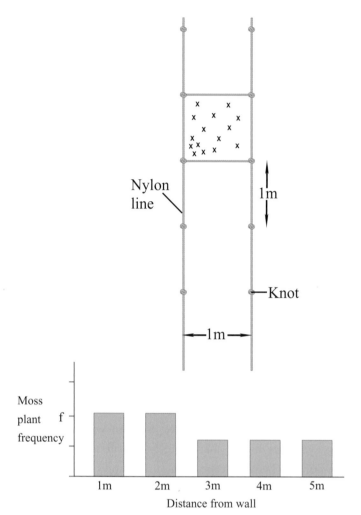

Fig. 5.18. Belt transect.

Table 5.3. Estimating population frequency

Quadrat throw	1	2	3	4	5	6	7	8	9	10
Was the plant found or not?	no	yes	no	yes	yes	yes	yes	no	yes	yes

In this example, the plant was found in seven out of ten random throws.

$$\% \text{ frequency} = 7/10 \times 100/1$$
$$= 70\%$$

4. ESTIMATING THE PERCENTAGE COVER OF A PLANT

Percentage cover refers to how much of the ground is covered by the plant being surveyed. Any part of the ground covered by leaves, stems or flowers is included. Percentage cover is a useful way of assessing the dominance of a plant and its contribution to the habitat. Cover

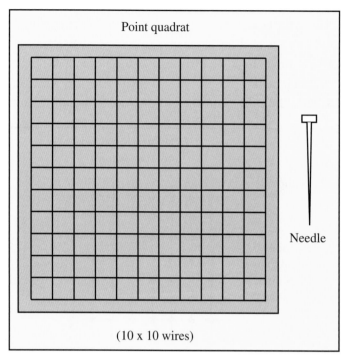

Fig. 5.19. Point quadrat and needle.

is estimated using a *point quadrat*. This is a quadrat of standard size but with a wire grid of 10 × 10 wires stretched across it.

The wires of the quadrat cross over 100 times to form 100 sample points. A needle is lowered to the ground at each sample point and a record kept of how many times it touches the plant under survey. Point quadrats are delicate and should not be thrown! An 'ordinary' quadrat is thrown at random in its place.

- Throw a quadrat at random.
- Replace the quadrat with a *point quadrat*.
- Use a needle to explore the 100 sample points.
- Record how many times the needle touches the plant being surveyed.
- Express this as a percentage of the total number of samples. If, say, 27 plant 'touches' are recorded out of 100 sample points, the % ground cover is 27%.
- Repeat and average the results.

Quantitative surveys for animals

1. ESTIMATING THE DISTRIBUTION OF AN ANIMAL

- Mark out and measure the area under survey.

- Divide the area into a grid to produce sample points.
- Mark the grid on the map.
- Set pitfall traps or carry out a direct search at each sample point.
- Record on the map where the animal is found.

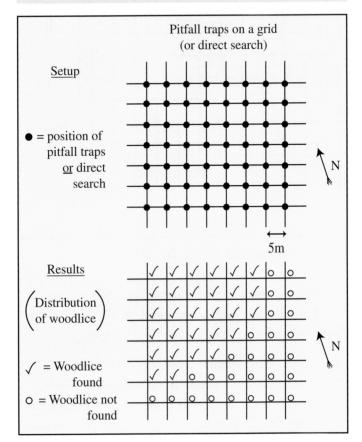

Fig. 5.20. Diagram of grids.

2. ESTIMATING THE SIZE OF AN ANIMAL POPULATION

This method uses the technique of *capture–recapture*. A sample of the population is captured and their number recorded. Then each animal is discreetly marked (using brown cellulose paint) and released at the place of capture. The marking must be permanent enough not to rub off or wash away too soon but at the same time must not interfere with the animal's gas exchange or camouflage. After 24 hours, another sample of animals is captured and counted. Within this sample will be some marked animals (the recaptures) and their number will indicate the population size.

- Capture as many animals as possible. Use pitfall traps or direct search.

- Record the number captured, e.g. 200.
- Mark each with cellulose paint on its ventral surface.
- Release the animals at the place of capture.
- On day two, again capture as many as possible.
- Record the number captured, e.g. 180.
- Also record the recaptures (any that are marked), e.g. 30.
- Release all at the place of capture.
- Apply the capture–recapture formula below.

Sample results:

Number caught on day 1 = 200

Number caught on day 2 = 180 of which 30 were marked (the recaptures).

$$\text{Population size} = \frac{\text{captures (day 1)} \times \text{captures (day 2)}}{\text{recaptures}}$$

$$= \frac{200 \times 180}{30}$$

$$= 1{,}200 \text{ animals}$$

The formula gives an accurate estimate with relatively large samples but is inaccurate for small samples. The relationship between captures and recaptures is also called the *Lincoln Index*.

Display of results after surveying

All survey results should be recorded on paper and then transferred to a suitable display. Results are best kept in tables, graphs, diagrams, histograms or pie charts. Tables are suitable for most data and are easy to construct. Proper display of results makes interpretation of the data much easier.

Possible sources of error in measuring and gathering data

Besides simple errors such as misusing measuring tapes or confusion over measuring units, it is worth bearing in mind that there are important sources of error in ecological surveying.

- Measurements are being applied to a natural world that is in a constant state of change. Accuracy can depend on the size and stability of the population. Populations are constantly changing due to the cyclical effects of both predators and parasites.

- Often, accidental discoveries are chanced upon which can distort data.
- The sample size affects accuracy. Large samples give more accuracy, but sometimes it is not possible to obtain a large sample. Conclusions have to be qualified if their underlying samples are small.

To reduce error:

1. All surveys should be repeated and the results averaged. More surveys may have to be done at different times during the year.
2. All samples should be as large as possible. Data from small samples is of little use.
3. Quadrats must be thrown *at random* rather than placed over interesting, colourful or easily identified organisms.
4. Be alert for false assumptions. If a crow is observed eating a dog whelk, this does not mean that it never eats anything else, or that it *always* eats dog whelks.
5. Avoid common measuring errors:

   - Record the measuring units used and do not change units during the survey.
   - Calibrate or zero all equipment before starting.
   - Record measurements immediately in a proper notebook, not on scraps of paper.
   - Repeat and average all measurements.
   - Record time, date and location of measurements.

PRESENTING DATA

Data collected from surveys can be presented in many ways. Use a combination of the following throughout your report:

1. Continuous prose

For example, 'limpets were recorded on all of the rocks in the middle shore and, to a lesser extent, in the lower shore. No limpets were found on the rocks of the upper shore or in the splash zone'.

2. Tables

For example, 'the results of our search are summarised as follows…'.

Table 5.4. Sample data.

Quadrat throw	1	2	3	4	5	6	7	8
Number of plants within each throw	0	2	0	2	2	3	1	0

3. Bar charts

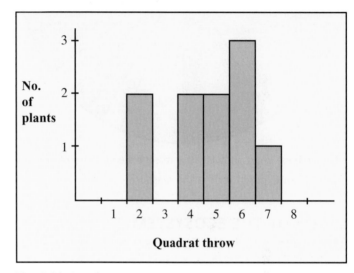

Fig. 5.21. Bar chart.

4. Graphs

For example, 'the frequency of daisies close to the hedge is shown on the graph'.

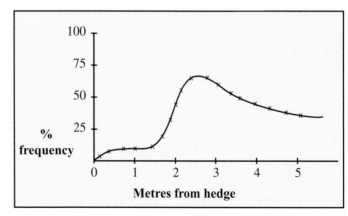

Fig. 5.22. Graph of frequency v distance.

5. Clock diagrams and pie charts

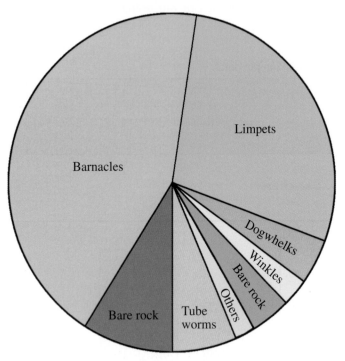

Fig. 5.23. Pie chart showing the relative frequencies of animals found on an exposed rock at the seashore.

STUDY OF THE ECOSYSTEM
Measuring Abiotic Factors [154]

> ### Mandatory activity #4:
> ### To investigate three abiotic factors

Resources needed for this section

pH solution (or soil testing kit).
Test tubes.
Barium sulphate powder.
Spatula.
pH chart.
Plastic bags.
Soil thermometer.
Maximum / minimum thermometer.
Incubator.
Large tin cans.
Large basin.
Trowel.
Large graduated cylinder.
Compass.

Sample bottles.
Spirit level.
Kitchen paper insert.
Oxygen meter.
Canes.
Sighting poles or metre sticks.

Abiotic factors are *non-living* factors that affect the *distribution* and *abundance* of organisms. The relationship between an organism and these factors will decide the suitability of the habitat. For example, ferns need *dampness* and *shade* to complete their life cycles and will not find a dry, bright habitat suitable.

1. Measuring edaphic factors

Edaphic factors are factors related to *soil*.
Soil should never be poured into laboratory sinks or drains.

Measuring soil pH

- Collect soil samples in plastic bags.
- Label each bag with date and location.
- Add 1 cm barium sulphate, 5 cm of soil sample and 1 cm of universal indicator to a clean test tube.
- Fill the tube to near the top with distilled water.
- Shake well and allow to stand.
- Compare the colour of the indicator to the colour chart.

Table 5.5. Soil pH

Soil sample	Indicator colour	Soil pH
1.		
2.		
3.		

Barium sulphate binds soil particles together, causing them to fall to the bottom quickly. Otherwise their colour will add to the colour of the indicator and give an inaccurate reading.

Why is distilled water used rather than tap water?

MEASURING PERCENTAGE AVAILABLE WATER IN SOIL

Available water is soil water loosely held between soil particles and available to plants.

- Weigh a suitable dish.
- Weigh the dish with a soil sample and subtract to find the sample weight.
- Warm the soil at 30 °C in an incubator to remove available water (this cannot be done correctly by heating the soil with a Bunsen flame). The soil can be dried at room temperature but this may take a few days.
- Reweigh the sample.
- Repeat warming and weighing until no further weight loss is obtained.
- $$\% \text{ available water} = \frac{\text{weight loss} \times 100}{\text{weight of original sample}}$$

Table 5.6. Available soil water

Weight of dish	
Weight of dish + soil	
Weight of fresh soil	
Final weight of dish + dry soil	
Weight of dry soil	
Loss in weight	
% available water	

MEASURING TOTAL SOIL WATER

Total soil water includes *available water* and *unavailable water* – the portion of water held tightly by soil particles and not available to plants.

- Weigh a suitable dish.
- Weigh the dish with a fresh soil sample and subtract to find the sample weight.
- Warm the soil at 100 °C in an incubator or oven to remove total water.
- Reweigh the sample.
- Repeat warming and weighing until no further weight loss is obtained.
- $$\% \text{ total water} = \frac{\text{weight loss} \times 100}{\text{weight of original sample}}$$

Table 5.7. Total soil water

Weight of dish	
Weight of dish + soil	
Weight of fresh soil	
Final weight of dish + dry soil	
Weight of dry soil	
Loss in weight	
% total water	

MEASURING HUMUS CONTENT

Humus is a black, sticky, fibrous jelly formed from dead and decaying organic matter. It improves soil quality — binding particles together and neutralising the soil pH.

- Collect soil samples in plastic bags.
- Label each bag with date and location.
- Use a previously dried soil sample. Soil should be heated to no more than 100 °C in an oven until no further weight loss is found (as above).
- Weigh a heat-proof dish and lid.
- Weigh the dish and lid with the dried soil sample.
- Heat the sample strongly to burn off the humus.
- Allow to cool and reweigh.
- Repeat until no further weight change is recorded.
- Express the weight loss as a percentage of the original soil sample.

Table 5.8. Humus content

Weight of dish	
Weight of dish + soil	
Weight of fresh soil	
Weight of fully dried soil	
Final weight of dish + burnt soil	
Weight of burnt soil	
Loss in weight due to burning	
% humus	

MEASURING MINERAL CONTENT

Many kits are available to test for soil minerals — the manufacturer's instructions should be followed. Almost all tests involve the addition of a test chemical with distilled water to the sample and then the use of a colour chart for estimating the mineral content.

For example, to test for nitrates:

- Add diphenylamine and distilled water to the soil sample.
- Allow to stand for five minutes.
- Compare the colour to the colour chart (a blue/brown colour indicates a high nitrate content, an orange/yellow colour indicates a low nitrate content).

MEASURING SOIL TEMPERATURE

- Use a soil thermometer and measure temperatures at different depths and in different locations.
- Record all data within a table.

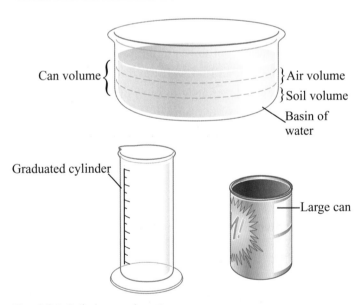

Fig. 5.24. Soil air experiment.

MEASURING SOIL AIR CONTENT

- Fill a large basin with water and mark the water level.
- Remove one full can of water from the basin.
- Empty the can into a large graduated cylinder to find the can volume.
- Punch holes in the base of the can.

- Turn the can upside down and press it gently into the soil.
- Carefully dig up the can, then level off the soil within it.
- Add this soil sample to the basin. The water level will rise — but not to the same mark. This 'missing volume' was occupied by the air in the soil.
- Add water from the graduated cylinder to restore the original level in the basin.
- The % air in the sample $= \dfrac{\text{missing volume} \times 100}{\text{can volume}}$

2. Measuring air temperature

- Use a maximum/minimum thermometer to record the highest and lowest temperatures during any period.
- Ideally the thermometer should be placed in a screened box (a Stevenson screen) at various stations within the habitat.
- Use the data to record the *daily temperature range* and the *mean (average) daily temperature* for each station. A graph is best to show monthly temperature changes.

Extreme temperatures are rarely found in Ireland. A temperature of 33.3 °C was recorded in Kilkenny in 1887 and a temperature of −19.1 °C in Sligo in 1881.

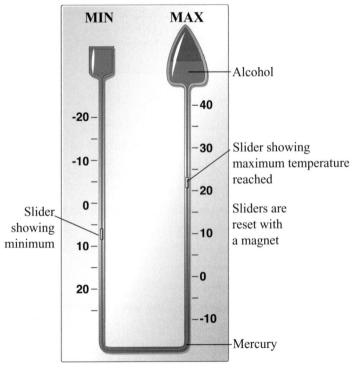

Fig. 5.25. Max/min thermometer.

3. Measuring light intensity

- Use a light meter at different stations within the habitat and at different times.
- Record all data to show *light duration* (length of day) and *maximum intensity*.
- Display the data using tables and graphs.
- Records should be kept over months or an entire year if possible.

4. Measuring water currents

Measuring water currents is potentially hazardous and great care should always be taken. This measuring should *always* be done in groups!

- Mark the waterway on the map.
- Mark two points ten metres apart along the water's edge.
- Time how long it takes for a floating object to move between the points.
- Record the speed (speed = distance / time).
- Note the direction of movement.
- Plot the current direction on the map and use a compass to indicate north.

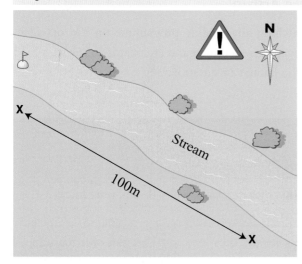

Fig. 5.26. Measuring water currents.

5. Measuring slope

- Position two survey poles (or metre sticks) 10 metres apart.
- Position a sighting tube (kitchen paper insert) horizontally with a spirit level as shown.

- Record the height of the sighting tube.
- View through the tube and ask your assistant to slide his/her finger up and down their metre stick until you can see it.
- Record the height of the finger.
- Calculate the rise or fall of the ground.
- The slope $= \dfrac{\text{rise or fall}}{10}$

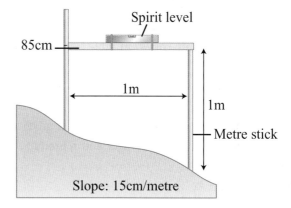

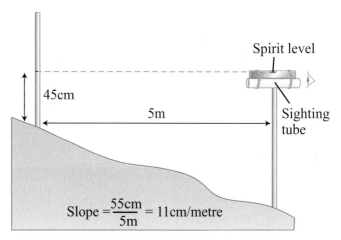

Fig. 5.27. Measuring slope.

6. Measuring dissolved oxygen

- Obtain water samples in clean sample bottles, filling the bottles gently and completely.
- Keep water agitation to a minimum.
- Label all bottles with date, time and location.
- Use an *oxygen meter* to measure oxygen concentration in parts per million (ppm).
- Record all data in a table.

ORGANISM ADAPTATIONS [155]

Adaptation is any characteristic of an organism that makes it more likely to survive and reproduce within the ecosystem. Adaptations have *survival value*. Plants and animal populations respond to both daily and seasonal changes in the environment by changing their *structures* or *behaviours*.

Using your observation, data collection and any other method, note the adaptations of any of the organisms found in your ecosystem and explain the purpose of them.

Table 5.9 gives examples of adaptations and their purposes in common organisms are shown in table 5.9.

(NB: Beware of *teleology*!

Don't say: 'Greenfly are green to avoid capture by predators.' when what you mean is: 'Green greenfly in a green environment are more likely to live longer and reproduce.')

ENERGY TRANSFER [156]

Food chains and food webs are diagrams showing feeding relationships within ecosystems. The arrows of the diagrams represent energy flow (see Chapter 4, section [146]).

The primary source of energy for all living organisms is the sun. Light energy from the sun is trapped by green plants, converted to chemical energy and stored in food (by the process of *photosynthesis*). Plants are producers of food for themselves and for all other organisms. Animals (herbivores) eat the plants and use the food energy to maintain their own lives. Other animals eat some of these herbivores and so obtain their energy. This feeding relationship establishes *a pathway of energy flow* from one organism to the next.

Suggested Activity

Constructing chains, webs and pyramids for the selected ecosystem:

- List all of the organisms identified within the ecosystem.
- Group the organisms into plants, herbivores and carnivores.
- Construct as many food chains as possible using your observations and all collected information. All food chains must start with a plant and must have arrows in the correct direction.
- Find which parts of the food chains interconnect with others and draw a food web.
- Using data collected from quantitative surveys, construct pyramids of numbers for each food chain.

Suggested Activity

While watching any wildlife programme on TV or video, list the organisms identified and afterwards construct a food web for the habitat in question.

Table 5.9. Adaptations

Organism	Structural adaptation	Advantage	Behavioural adaptation	Advantage
Limpet	Thick shell	Resists tidal forces	Grips rock tightly when touched	Resists tidal forces
Seaweed	Air bladders	Helps to float near the water surface	Releases sex cells into the sea	Uses tides for reproduction
Earthworm	Dark brown colour on upper surface	Camouflage	Retreat from light	Avoids predators during daytime
Honeysuckle	Scented flowers	Attracts insects for pollination	Grips onto any supports and climbs	Finds more light for photosynthesis
Spider	Chewing mouthparts	For eating prey	Spins a web of silk	Traps prey

CONCLUSION OF THE ECOLOGICAL STUDY   [157]

Each student should present the results of the ecological study in the form of a *portfolio* (a portable, written report).

The portfolio should be within a bound science notebook or a ring binder with plastic-covered pages. Alternatively, information can be used to design a web page or other computer presentation.

The portfolio should include:

- The choice of ecosystem.
- An overview of the ecosystem, including photographs, maps, diagrams, measurements, etc.
- A list of the habitats within the ecosystem.
- A list of the plants and animals present.
- Information gathered on individual organisms — shape, size, variation, feeding methods, drawings and photographs, etc.
- Methods used to collect and identify organisms.
- The details and results of all surveys. Results should be presented clearly within tables, bar charts, graphs and diagrams. Include dates, times and locations with all data.
- The details and results of all abiotic measurements.
- A table of adaptations found within the ecosystem.
- Diagrams of food chains, food webs and pyramids of numbers.
- Descriptions of any ecological issues related to the ecosystem. This might include data gathered on pollution or other human impacts. Surveys done before and after human impacts should be compared.
- Attractive and easy-to-read portfolios can be produced using word-processing and spreadsheet programmes on computers. Spreadsheets can easily convert data into professional-looking bar charts and graphs.

SUMMARY

- An ecological study requires:

  - choice of a suitable ecosystem;
  - using the correct techniques of fieldwork;
  - recording data within the ecosystem;
  - analysing the collected data.

- Practical ecology is safe — but there are rules to be kept.

- An overview of an ecosystem includes:

  - mapping;
  - listing important abiotic factors;
  - collecting and identifying organisms.

- Methods of identifying organisms include using keys, guidebooks, posters, reference collections, libraries, the Internet or asking someone who knows.
- A full report is made on all organisms.
- Organisms are collected using pooters, cryptozoic traps, pitfall traps, small mammal traps, Tullgren funnels, nets and direct search.
- Qualitative surveys produce a list of which organisms are present in the ecosystem.
- Quantitative surveys estimate the distribution and abundance of individual species.
- Results are best displayed within tables, graphs, diagrams, histograms or pie charts.
- Ecological surveys can contain many sources of error.
- The adaptations of organisms have survival value.
- Energy is transferred within ecosystems through food chains and food webs.
- Results of an ecological survey can be presented in a portfolio.

KEY WORDS

Key	A set of carefully structured questions used to identify organisms.
Pitfall trap	Used to collect small animals that move on the ground surface.
Cryptozoic trap	A wooden board or a flat rock left lying on the ground.
Cryptozoa	'Secret animals' — who always try to remain hidden.
Pooter	Used to collect small animals by 'hoovering' them into a jar.

Tullgren funnel	Used in the laboratory to extract small animals from soil samples.
Qualitative survey	Produces a list of the organisms present in the ecosystem.
Line transect	A length of rope laid across the habitat to mark a line of study.
Belt transect	Two ropes laid parallel to survey non-moving organisms in between.
Quadrat	A square frame made from wood, metal or plastic and used to survey non-moving organisms.
Quantitative survey	Provides information on the *distribution* and *abundance* of an *individual species*.
Frequency	The number of quadrats in which a particular organism occurs.
Distribution	Refers to where organisms are likely to be found.
Abundance	Refers to the number of organisms (or population size).
Autecology	Studying the ecology of an individual species.
Percentage cover	Refers to how much of the ground is covered by an organism.
Point quadrat	A quadrat of standard size but with a wire grid of 10 × 10 wires stretched across it. Used to estimate percentage cover.
Abiotic factors	Non-living factors that affect the distribution and abundance of organisms.
Edaphic factors	Related to soil.
Available water	Soil water loosely held between soil particles and available to plants.
Unavailable water	Soil water held tightly by soil particles and not available to plants.
Humus	A black, sticky, fibrous jelly formed from dead and decaying organic matter.
Adaptation	Any characteristic of an organism that makes it more likely to survive and reproduce within the ecosystem.
Portfolio	A portable, written report.

QUESTIONS

1. List five rules that must be observed during practical ecology.
2. Describe the steps you would take to draw a simple map of an ecosystem.
3. What is a biological key? Use the following key to identify the animals A, B, C and D in fig. 5.28.

1.	No shell	Go to 2.
	Hard shell	Limpet
2.	Legs in fives	Go to 4.
	Legs not in fives	Go to 3.
3.	Has antennae	Shrimp
	Has tentacles	Go to 5.
4.	No division between body and legs	Starfish
	Thin legs, divided from body	Brittle star
5.	Tentacles on upper side	Sea anemone
	Tentacles on lower side	Jellyfish

4. Use the following key to identify the drawings of five Irish amphibians in fig. 5.29.

1.	Aquatic larva, small size	Go to 2.
	Adult organisms, can leave the water	Go to 3.
2.	Very dark, almost black	Frog or toad tadpoles
	Light colour, long and thin	Newt tadpoles

A.

B.

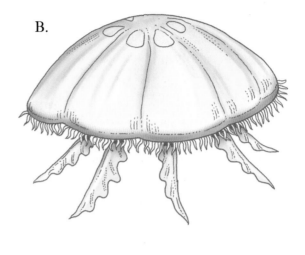

C.

D.

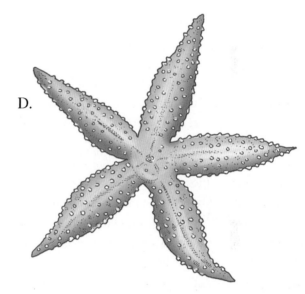

Fig. 5.28. Four seashore animals.

3.	Strong hind legs, smooth skin	Common frog, *Rana temporaria*
	Strong hind legs, warty skin, yellow stripe on back	Natterjack toad, *Bufo calamita*
	All limbs short and thin, smooth skin	Common newt, *Triturus vulgaris*
4.	Dark back, spots underneath	Male newt
	Uniform light brown, no spots underneath	Female newt

5. Draw a diagram of each of the following and say how they are used:

   a. pooter;
   b. pitfall trap;
   c. Tullgren funnel;
   d. cryptozoic trap.

6. Explain the difference between a *quantitative* and a *qualitative* survey. Name three methods for conducting a qualitative survey.

7. Name an animal you have studied during your investigation and explain how its numbers could be estimated using capture–recapture.

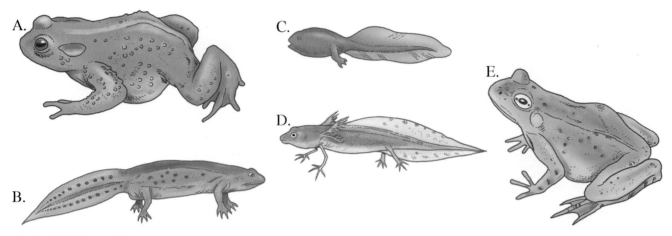

Fig. 5.29. Irish amphibians.

Include in your answer an outline of:

a. how you would capture the animals;
b. how you would mark the animals;
c. how you would release the animals; and
d. how you would calculate the approximate population size.

What are the weaknesses of this method?

8. In an investigation of a population of woodlice, animals were trapped on three occasions using pitfall traps. The trapped woodlice were counted, marked on their under surface and released in the same area. On two subsequent occasions, woodlice were trapped again, counted, and then released. The following data was collected:

Number of woodlice first trapped and marked	220
Number of woodlice trapped on 2nd occasion	183 of which 30 were marked
Number of woodlice trapped on 3rd occasion	210 of which 35 were marked

(i) Why were the woodlice marked on their undersurface?
(ii) Why are trapped animals always released in the same area?
(iii) Estimate the woodlice population size.

9. Construct a profile transect of a seashore from the following data: (all measurements in metres). Mark on the profile the distribution of limpets.

Distance from path	0	3	6	9	12	15	18	21	24	27
Vertical distance	6.6	6.5	6.3	5.2	3.1	1.9	0.8	0.5	0.2	0.0
Limpets found	no	no	no	no	yes	yes	yes	yes	no	no

10. A lawn, 50m², was surveyed using a 1m² quadrat to obtain an estimate of the number of earthworms it contained. The results of the survey were as follows:

Quadrat number	1	2	3	4	5
Number of earthworms	25	18	27	20	10

Calculate

(i) the average number of worms per quadrat;
(ii) the total number of worms in the lawn estimated by this method (*LCO 1991*).

What are the limitations of this survey method?

11. The following data was collected during an investigation of a soil sample:

Weight of original sample	210g
Weight after drying at 30 °C	151.2g
Weight after drying at 100 °C	130.2g
Weight after burning at 250 °C	117.6g

Calculate:

(i)   % available water in the original sample;

(ii) the % of total water;

(iii) the % of humus.

State two possible sources of error during the investigation.

12. In an experiment to measure the amount of air in a soil sample, a can was filled carefully with undisturbed soil. The soil was transferred to a large graduated cylinder and its volume recorded at 800 ml. Then 200 ml of water were added to the cylinder. The total volume in the cylinder settled to 880 ml.

   Using the data provided, calculate the percentage of air in the soil sample.
   Point out a serious flaw in the outlined procedure and one other source of error.

13. Name five organisms identified during your ecological study and explain how each is adapted to its environment.

14. Explain the value of each of the following adaptations:

   a. a carrot;

   b. a tree without leaves in the winter;

   c. a cat's fur;

   d. the scent of roses;

   e. birds migrating.

OPTIONAL ACTIVITIES

- Design a key to identify any playing card from a pack (the winning key will have the fewest questions).
- Design and complete a questionnaire to assist in your ecological study.
- Use capture–recapture to estimate the number of sweets, buttons or beads in a jar.
- Use the Internet or library resources to write a report on an extreme environment, e.g. a desert, the Antarctic, a rainforest, etc.
- Carry out soil pH testing on samples from the home of everyone in the class. Present the class data to relate pH to local area.

For information on websites dealing with subjects raised in this chapter, see www.my-etest.com.

Now test yourself at
www.my-etest.com

Chapter 6
Cell Biology

Learning objectives

After your study of this chapter, you should be able to:

- use the light microscope as a precision instrument;
- prepare plant and animal tissue for microscopic examination;
- appreciate the similarities and differences between plant and animal cells;
- describe in detail the structure and function of cell organelles;
- consider the nucleus as the control centre of the cell.

Extended learning objectives

- Define and compare prokaryotic and eukaryotic cells.

Mandatory activities

#5 Using the light microscope.
#6 Examining plant cells.
#7 Examining animal cells.

ORIGINS OF CELL THEORY

Robert Hooke (1635–1703) was a noted English scientist and a contemporary of Isaac Newton. In 1662, Hoote examined sections of cork with a convex lens and first used the word *cell* to describe repeating units within the tissue that looked like tiny prison cells. Using an improved microscope, he carried out further investigations and published his drawings in his main work *Micrographica* in 1665. Since that time, it has generally been accepted that all living organisms are composed of cells.

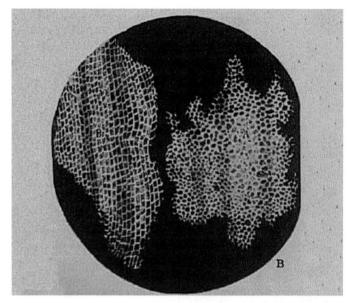

Fig. 6.2. Cork tissue.

'... I could exceedingly plainly perceive it to be all perforated and porous... these pores, or cells,... were indeed the first microscopical pores I ever saw, and perhaps, that were ever seen, for I had not met with any Writer or Person, that had made any mention of them before this.'

Robert Hooke

Magnifying (convex) lenses had been known since the earliest of times but were first used regularly in biology by Anton van Leeuwenhoek, a Dutch draper who worked in his father's drapery in the late 1600s. He manufactured his own lenses to examine the quality of fabric in the shop. Leeuwenhoek was probably the first human being to see bacteria. He made his own microscopes and described everything he could view: the cells of trees; the structure of bacteria; blood cells; protozoans in rainwater (*'little animalcules'*); algae in lake water; roundworms; and spermatozoa. In 1684, he produced the first description of red blood cells and estimated them to be 25,000 times smaller than a grain of sand.

A single convex lens (or *hand lens* or 'magnifying glass') is also known as a simple microscope. Around this time, two lenses were regularly combined together to form a compound microscope with much greater magnification. (The compound microscope was probably invented in about 1590 and the telescope in 1608, but neither were then used for scientific purposes and needed Galileo and then Leeuwenhoek to advance their importance.)

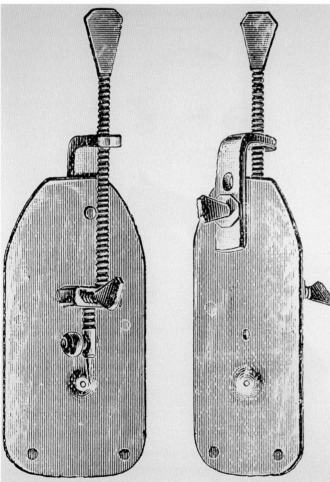

Fig. 6.1. Hooke (above) and Leeuwenhoek microscopes.

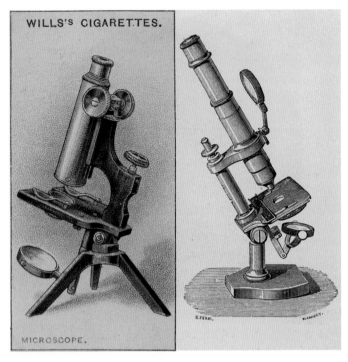

Fig. 6.3. Later microscopes.

Matthias Jakob Schleiden.
(Nach einer Lithographie von Hoffmann.)

In the 1800s, lenses improved enormously in quality and cell organelles began to reveal themselves. Robert Brown first described the nucleus of a cell in 1831. In 1839, Matthias Schleiden (examining plants) and Theodor Schwann (examining animals) proposed their *Cell Theory*. The theory contained two main parts:

- all living organisms are made from cells;
- activities of organisms are the outward expression of internal processes.

In other words, the cell was the structural and functional unit of all living organisms.

In 1858, Rudolf Virchow stated that cells could only arise from pre-existing cells — '*omnis cellula e cellula*' (all cells come from cells). By 1890, most cell organelles had been described including the *golgi apparatus* and *mitochondria*.

From 1930 on, the electron microscope revealed the details of the structure of the smallest cell organelles.

Theodor Schwann.
(Nach einer Lithographie von Hoffmann.)

Fig. 6.4. Schleiden and Schwann.

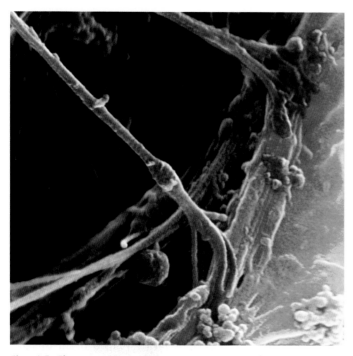

Fig. 6.5. Electron micrograph of human nerve cells.

MODERN CELL THEORY

1. Cells are the basic building blocks of all living organisms.
2. All cells arise from pre-existing cells.
3. Cells contain all the information required for cell activity.
4. Cells are the functional units of all biochemistry.

Nowadays, the importance of individual cells has given way to the importance of how cells work together.

MICROSCOPES   [211]

Two types of microscope are in common use today: the light microscope and the electron microscope.

The light microscope

FEATURES OF THE LIGHT MICROSCOPE

- It uses light rays and at least two convex glass lenses.
- It can magnify up to $1400\times$ at the very most.
- It can separate objects about 0.2 μm apart (1μm = one millionth of a metre or one thousandth of a millimeter).
- It is portable and relatively inexpensive — suitable for

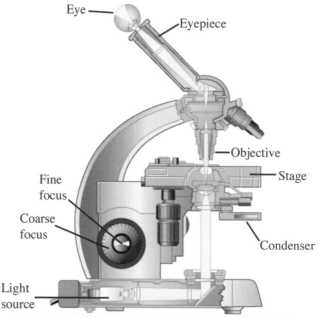

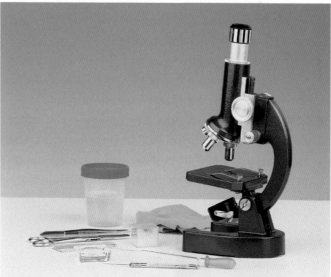

Fig. 6.6. Light microscope.

daily use in schools, colleges, hospitals and laboratories.
- It can examine living tissue — but usually the tissue sample must be thin enough to allow light to pass through.
- It reveals the nucleus, cell organelles, cell walls, vacuoles and chromatin.

Mandatory activity #5: Use of the light microscope

GENERAL USE OF THE LIGHT MICROSCOPE

N.B. The microscope is a precision instrument and needs to be treated gently at all times. Do not bump it off the desk or allow any part to become wet or stained. Focussing should be done gently and slowly and the microscope should not be moved unless its bulb is cold.

1. Adjusting the lenses:

- Place the microscope on the tabletop — not on books or pages.
- Check that the lenses are clean. Clean lenses with lens tissue only; do not rub them with ordinary tissue paper.
- Move the low power lens into position. A faint click is heard when the lens is correctly aligned.
- Use the coarse focus wheel to move the stage close to the objective lens.
- Place the slide to be examined on the stage.
- Look through the microscope and turn the coarse focus wheel. Always turn the wheel to move the lens *away* from the slide — never towards it.
- Keep both eyes open! If you find this difficult, persevere! The image from the other eye is ignored after a few minutes. One eye closed leads to eyestrain.
- Click the high power lens into position. The image should be almost in focus without any adjustment. Use the fine focus wheel to improve the image but always move *away* from the slide to prevent an expensive collision.

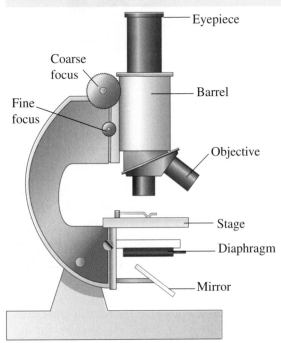

Fig. 6.7. Light microscope.

2. Adjusting the light:

- Adjust the mirror to give even light. If an electric bulb is fitted, try covering it with a piece of thin paper to even the light.
- If the condenser is being used, used the flat side of the mirror. Otherwise, use the concave side.
- Adjust the condenser to illuminate the object as best as possible.
- Adjust the iris diaphragm so that the object is not over-illuminated. Better results are usually obtained by *darkening* rather than brightening the object.

The electron microscope

FEATURES OF THE ELECTRON MICROSCOPE

- It uses a beam of electrons rather than a beam of light and focusses them with electromagnets.
- The image is a *photomicrograph* — a grainy, black and white picture.
- It has about 500 times the power of the light microscope.
- It magnifies up to about 500,000 times. At this extreme, a dressmaking pinhead appears to have a diameter of several kilometres and a typical cell seems the length of a classroom.
- It reveals the details of organelles and cell structures such as cilia, flagella and membranes.
- It is very expensive and not portable at all. Expensive training is required to use it.
- Objects viewed are usually within a vacuum and therefore dead. Are they still the same as when they were living?

The Transmitting Electron Microscope (TEM) sends electrons *through* objects and reveals the most detail.

The Scanning Electron Microscope (SEM) photographs reflected electrons *from surfaces* and reveals three-dimensional structures. It has less detail but can be used on slightly larger specimens.

CELL STRUCTURE AND FUNCTION   [212]

All plant and animal cells have:

1. a nucleus;

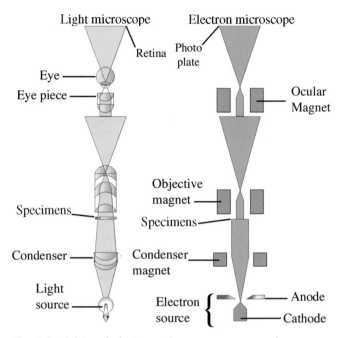

Fig. 6.8. Light and electron microscopes compared.

Fig. 6.8(a). The electron microscope.

2. cytoplasm;

3. a cell membrane (or plasma membrane).

The *nucleus* is the control centre of the cell. It contains genetic instructions within its DNA and directs all of the cell's activities.

The *cytoplasm* is mostly water but contains many cell *organelles* ('little organs').

The *cell membrane* encloses the cell contents. It is very thin and not easily seen with the light microscope.

In addition, plant cells have a thick cell wall outside the cell membrane. The wall is made from cellulose fibres.

Table 6.1. Differences between plant and animal cells

Plant cells	Animal cells
Have a cell wall outside the cell membrane.	No cell wall — just the membrane on the outside.
Contain plastids including chloroplasts.	No plastids.
Large, permanent vacuoles.	Small, temporary vacuoles.

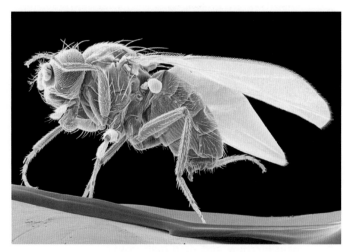

Fig. 6.9. SEM of a red-eyed fruit fly.

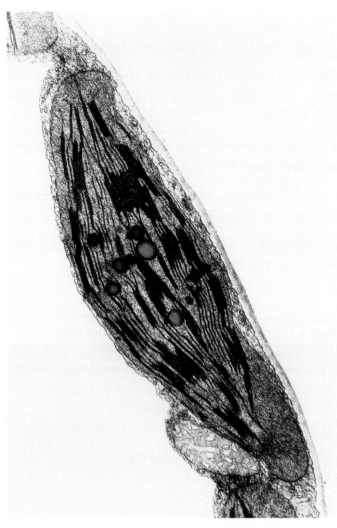

Fig. 6.10. TEM of a chloroplast from a tomato plant.

Practicals

Mandatory activity # 6: Examining plant cells

- Peel a thin layer of epidermis from inside one of the fleshy layers of an onion bulb.
- Lay the tissue in a drop of water on a microscope slide.
- Hold a cover slip at 45° and lower gently to exclude any air bubbles.
- Add a few drops of iodine solution to one side of the cover slip (treat all stains as hazardous and avoid direct contact).
- Draw the stain across the tissue by soaking up fluid on the other side with filter paper.
- Focus under low and then high power.
- Observe the nucleus, nucleoli, chromatin, cytoplasm and cell wall.

- Make a labelled drawing of what you see. Bear in mind that all cells are three-dimensional.
- Repeat the preparation using scrapings of raw potato or moss leaves (see fig. 6.13).

Mandatory activity #7: Examining animal cells

- Gently scrape the inside of your own cheek with a sterilised wooden spatula.
- Place the cheek scrapings on a microscope slide with a drop of water.
- Hold a cover slip at 45° and lower gently to exclude any air bubbles.
- Add a few drops of methylene blue stain to one side of the cover slip (treat all stains as hazardous and avoid direct contact).
- Draw the stain across the tissue by soaking up fluid on the other side with filter paper.
- Focus under low and then high power.
- Observe the nucleus, nucleolus, chromatin, cytoplasm and the position of the cell membrane.
- Make a labelled drawing of what you see (see fig. 6.14).

CELL ULTRA STRUCTURE   [213]

The prefix *ultra* means *beyond*. *Cell ultra structure* refers to the structures of the cell hidden beyond the range of the light microscope — but revealed by the electron microscope. The nucleus of the cell is easily seen with a light microscope but its details are clearer when viewed with an electron microscope.

The nucleus

Nearly all living cells have a single, prominent nucleus (mature red blood cells in mammals and phloem sieve tubes in plants do not). The nucleus contains the *chromosomes* of the cell. These are clearly visible only during cell division. When a cell is not dividing, chromosomes form a mass of threads referred to as *chromatin*. The chromosomes are made from DNA (*deoxyribonucleic acid*) and protein and they direct the growth and activity of the entire cell (and so direct the entire organism too). The nucleus is covered by a *nuclear membrane* with thousands of pores in it for communication

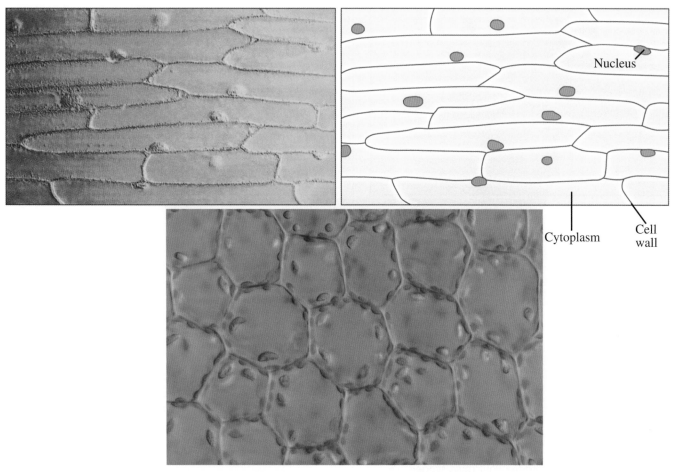

Fig. 6.11. Plant cells seen with the light microscope.

with the cytoplasm. These nuclear pores are only visible with the electron microscope but cover one third of the nuclear surface. A *nucleolus* ('little nucleus') is sometimes seen inside the nucleus; it is a temporary store of RNA that disappears during cell division.

FUNCTIONS OF THE NUCLEUS

- Directs the growth, development and activities of the cell.
- Makes faithful replicas of the DNA for new cells.
- Carries out cell division to form new cells.
- Instructs the formation of enzymes and hormones.

The cytoplasm

This is the transparent, slightly viscous liquid that fills the inside of the cell. It is mostly water and contains the nucleus and various other cell *organelles* ('little organs'). It is retained within the cell by the cell membrane.

The cell membrane (or plasma membrane)

This is a thin skin of protein and lipid forming a boundary between the cell contents and the outside. The membrane is not solid and is self-sealing if broken open, i.e. it is a fluid, moving barrier. It consists of two layers of phospholipid molecules forming a greasy, lipid bilayer around the perimeter of the cell. The 'heads' of the lipid molecules are *hydrophilic* — they are attracted to water. The tails of the molecules are *hydrophobic* — they repel water.

Large protein molecules float freely within the bilayer. Carbohydrate molecules are often fixed to proteins and lipids on the outer side of the membrane. These *glycoproteins* and *glycolipids* are involved in making contact with other cells and in cell protection. There are temporary pores throughout the membrane.

The functions of the membrane include:

- allowing diffusion of gases;

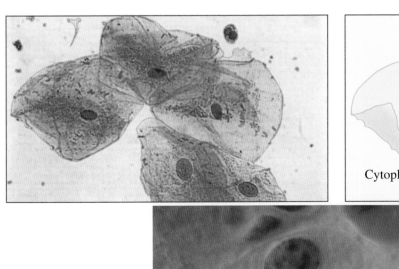
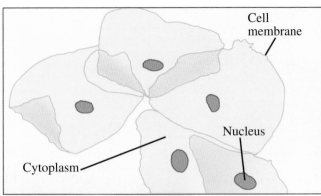
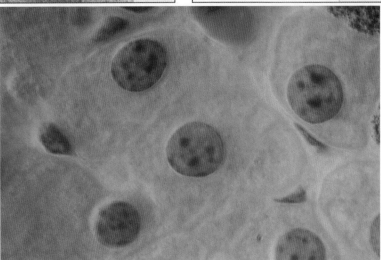

Cell membrane

Nucleus

Cytoplasm

Fig. 6.12. Animal cells seen with the light microscope.

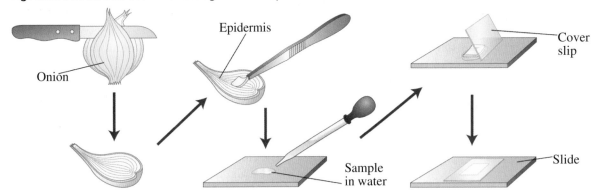

Onion

Epidermis

Sample in water

Cover slip

Slide

Fig. 6.13. Preparing epidermis for examination.

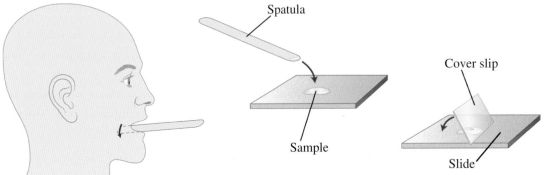

Spatula

Sample

Cover slip

Slide

Fig. 6.14. Preparing saliva for examination.

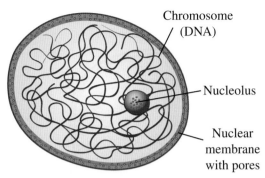

Fig. 6.15. Cell nucleus.

- allowing the passage of water by osmosis;
- allowing the transmission of light;
- actively moving specific chemicals from one side to the other;
- defending the cell against attack;
- generating nerve impulses (as in nerve cells).

The cell membrane is discussed further in Chapter 10.

The cell wall

The plant cell wall lies outside the membrane and so is not a cell organelle. It is composed of tiny microfibrils of cellulose and other polysaccharides. It is very strong and contributes strength, protection and shape to the cell. It is however fully permeable and has no control over the entry and exit of materials. Adjacent plant cells are glued together by an intercellular cement of calcium pectate — the *middle lamella*.

Plastids

Plastids are oval, double-membraned containers found in the plant cell cytoplasm. The most important plastids are chloroplasts, which contain green chlorophyll. These are the organs of photosynthesis and are found in the cells of the green parts of the plant (see section [224])

The inner membrane of the chloroplast forms parallel strands of membrane called *lamellae*. Circular piles of membrane (the *grana*) contain the chlorophyll; the rest of the chloroplast is filled with a matrix of water, starch, loose membranes, scraps of DNA and some ribosomes — a mixture termed the *stroma*.

Other plastids found in plant cells include *leucoplasts* (for storing starch, e.g. in potato cells) and *chromoplasts* (for storing coloured pigments, e.g. in flower petal cells).

Vacuoles

Plant cells have permanent vacuoles. These are fluid-filled spaces bounded by a membrane (the *tonoplast*). They contain cell sap — a mixture of food, minerals, pigments and water.

(Animal cells have smaller, temporary vacuoles sometimes called *vesicles*.)

Mitochondria

These are cylinder-shaped organelles found in most cells.

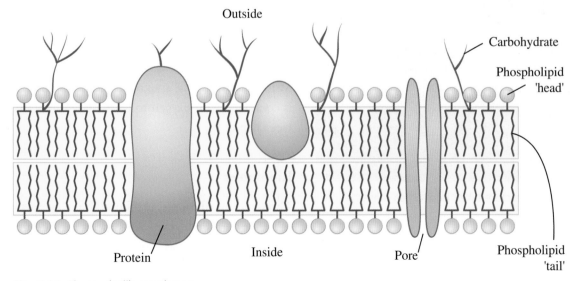

Fig. 6.16. Plasma (cell) membrane.

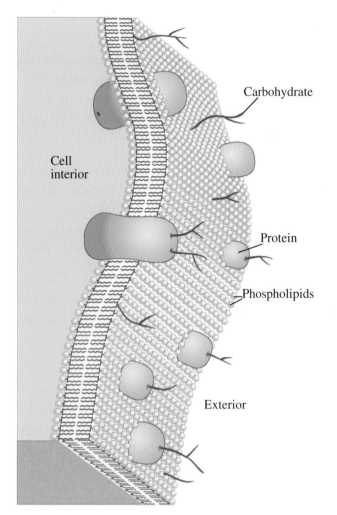

Fig. 6.17. Membrane structure.

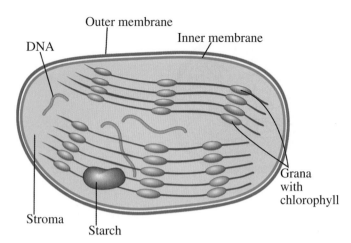

Fig. 6.19. Simplified diagram of chloroplast structure.

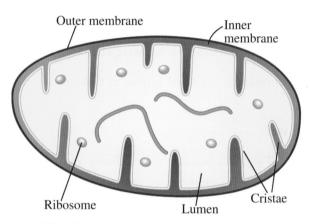

Fig. 6.20. Mitochondrion structure.

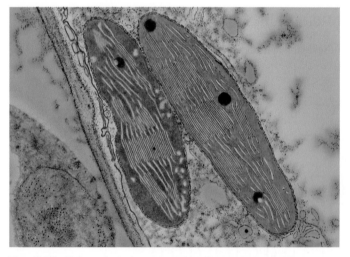

Fig. 6.18. Chloroplast structure taken from a pea plant.

Their number in the cytoplasm indicates the activity of the cell; two to three are found in skin cells and about 800 in muscle cells. They have an outer, smooth membrane and an inner, folded one. The foldings (*cristae*) give a large surface area to the interior. The cristae increase in number as cell activity increases. The lumen contains a matrix of water, food, enzymes, some ribosomes and small portions of DNA. Mitochondria are the sites of aerobic respiration; where food is combined with oxygen to release large amounts of energy (see chapter 9.

Ribosomes

Thousands of ribosomes are found in the cytoplasm of every cell. They are tiny, grain-like structures made from protein and RNA. They act as '*protein factories*': they are the places where enzymes and other proteins are made. DNA in the nucleus directs the ribosomes and they follow nuclear

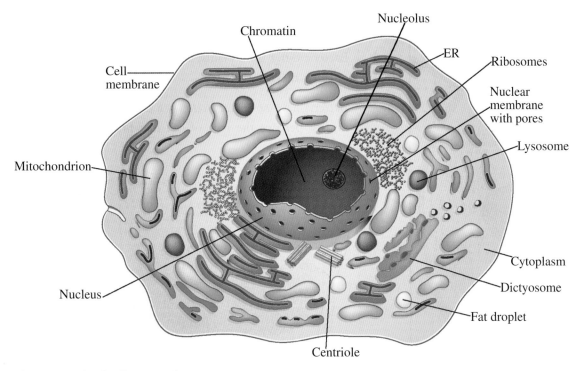

Fig. 6.21. Animal cell — complete.

instructions brought to them by messenger RNA (mRNA). Several ribosomes often lie along a single strand of mRNA to form a *polysome*.

Some ribosomes lie free in the cell and make enzymes and other proteins for internal use. Other ribosomes are attached to folded membranes (the *endoplasmic reticulum* or *ER* of the cell) and make enzymes and other proteins for secretion to the outside.

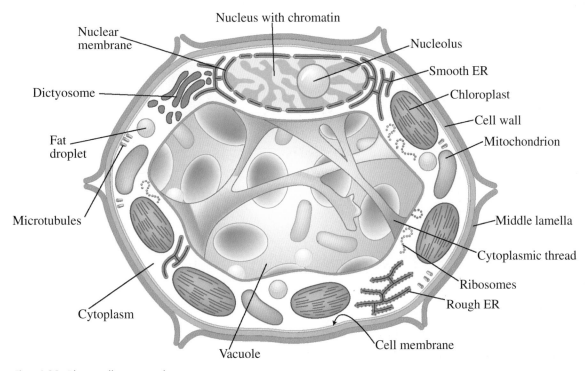

Fig. 6.22. Plant cell — complete.

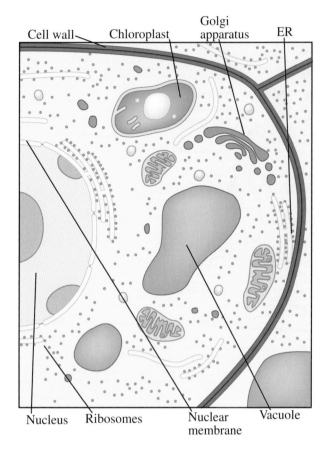

Fig. 6.23. Drawing from a root cell TEM.

Table 6.2. Structural differences between plant/animal cells

Structure	Plant cells	Animal cells
Cell wall	yes	no
Plasma membrane	yes	yes
Permanent vacuoles	yes	no
Tonoplast	yes	no
E.R.	yes	yes
Golgi apparatus	yes	yes
Lysosomes	yes	yes
Nucleus	yes	yes
Nuclear membrane	yes	yes
Chloroplasts	yes	no
Mitochondria	yes	yes
Ribosomes	yes	yes
Centrioles	no	yes

PROKARYOTIC CELLS   [H211]

Bacteria differ from plants, animals and fungi in the type of cell that they possess.

Bacteria have *prokaryotic cells* — a cell type with an ancient history, perhaps the type of cell that first appeared on the

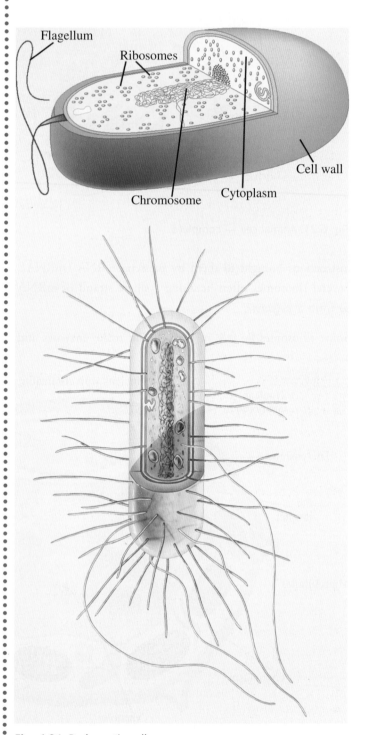

Fig. 6.24. Prokaryotic cells.

Earth millions of years ago. Prokaryotic cells do not have a definite nucleus and have few cell organelles.

Plants, animals and fungi possess *eukaryotic cells* — a more 'modern' and more advanced cell type. Eukaryotic cells have a definite nucleus, bounded by a nuclear membrane, and many cell organelles.

Prokaryotic cells	Eukaryotic cells
No distinct nucleus	Distinct nucleus
No nuclear membrane	Nucleus bounded by a
Single, circular	nuclear membrane
chromosome of DNA	Many chromosomes of
	DNA
Have ribosomes	Have ribosomes
No mitochondria	Have mitochondria
No plastids	Have plastids
Cell wall contains	Cell wall will contain
protein	cellulose or chitin
Very small cell size,	Larger cell size, 10–100 μm
1–10 μm	

Greek lesson: *pro* = before *karyon* = nucleus
                eu = good *karyon* = nucleus

SUMMARY

- Cells are the smallest units of living organisms that show the characteristics of life.
- Cells were discovered soon after the invention of the compound microscope.
- The light microscope reveals basic cell structure.
- The electron microscope reveals the details of cell structure.
- The nucleus is considered the control centre of every cell.
- The nucleus contains chromosomes of DNA and a nucleolus containing RNA.
- The nuclear membrane is porous.
- The cytoplasm contains numerous organelles carrying out various life processes.
- All cells are bounded by a cell membrane.
- Cell membranes are formed from a phospholipid bilayer and protein molecules.

- Cell membranes are semi-permeable.
- Plant cells have some differences to animal cells — in particular they possess a fully permeable cell wall of cellulose and also plastids.
- Vacuoles are permanent in plant cells and usually temporary in animal cells.
- Chloroplasts carry out photosynthesis.
- Mitochondria carry out respiration.
- Ribosomes manufacture protein.

EXTENDED SUMMARY

- Prokaryotic cells have no nuclear membrane and few organelles.
- Bacteria are prokaryotic.
- Eukaryotic cells have a nuclear membrane and many membrane-bounded organelles.
- Fungi, plants and animals are eukaryotic.

KEY WORDS

Microscope	An instrument that uses lenses to produce a magnified image.
Photomicrograph	An image produced by an electron microscope.
TEM	A transmitting electron microscope, which sends electrons *through* objects.
SEM	A scanning electron microscope, which photographs reflected electrons from surfaces.
Condenser	Focusses light rays to illuminate objects as well as possible.
Iris diaphragm	Adjusts the amount of light passing through the microscope.
Nucleus	The control centre of the cell.
Cytoplasm	The watery region of the cell containing many cell *organelles*.

Cell membrane	A thin, greasy skin of protein and phospholipid around the perimeter of the cell. It encloses the cell contents.
Hydrophobic	Repelling water (literally 'water-fearing').
Hydrophilic	Attracting water (literally: 'water-loving').
Nucleolus	A temporary store of RNA within the nucleus.
Cell wall	A wall of cellulose outside the cell membrane of plant cells.
Plastids	Oval, double-membraned containers found in the cytoplasm of plant cells.
Chloroplasts	Plastids containing green chlorophyll. The site of photosynthesis in plant cells.
Leucoplasts	Plastids that store starch.
Chromoplasts	Plastids that manufacture and store coloured pigment.
Vacuoles	Fluid-filled spaces bounded by a membrane. Permanent in plant cells, temporary in animal cells.
Mitochondria	Cylinder shaped organelles that carry out respiration.
Ribosomes	Tiny, grain-like structures made from protein and RNA. They act as *'protein factories'*.

EXTENDED KEY WORDS

Prokaryotic cells	Primitive cells that do not have a definite nucleus and have few cell organelles.
Eukaryotic cells	Cells that have a definite nucleus, bounded by a nuclear membrane, and many cell organelles.

QUESTIONS

1. Distinguish between the members of each pair by writing a brief note on each term:

   a. leucoplast and chloroplast;
   b. ribosome and polysome;
   c. cell wall and cell membrane;
   d. nucleus and nucleolus;
   e. light microscope and electron microscope;
   f. SEM and TEM;
   g. chloroplasts and mitochondria.

2. State the basic principles of modern cell theory.
3. What is the advantage of using stains when examining tissue under the microscope? Name two microscopic stains and the tissues they might be used on. Are there any disadvantages in the use of stains?
4. Draw up a chart to compare light and electron microscopes. Include at least five comparisons.
5. Briefly explain the functions of the following microscope parts:

   a. condenser;
   b. objective lens;
   c. coarse focus wheel;
   d. iris diaphragm;
   e. stage;
   f. eyepiece.

6. Which of the following can be seen with: (i) the light microscope? (ii) the electron microscope?

   a. cell wall;
   b. cell membrane,
   c. nucleolus;
   d. glycoproteins;
   e. chromatin;
   f. microfibrils;
   g. cytoplasm;
   h. vacuoles;
   i. nuclear pores.

7. Why are no chloroplasts observed in the microscopic examination of onion cells?

8. Match the list of structures to the list of functions:

Nucleus: Manufactures proteins
Chloroplast: Controls entry and exit of
                    materials
Cell wall: Makes food using sunlight
Nucleolus: Directs the cell's activities
Ribosome: Extracts energy from food
Cell membrane: Stores RNA
Mitochondrion: Maintains the cell shape

9. Draw and label a typical plant cell and a typical animal cell as seen with the electron microscope.

10. What are prokaryotic cells? Which living organisms possess them? State whether each structure on the following list is found in prokaryotes, eukaryotes or both:

a. cell membrane;

b. chromosome;

c. cell wall;

d. ribosomes;

e. nuclear membrane;

f. mitochondria;

g. chromoplasts;

h. DNA;

i. nuclear pores.

OPTIONAL ACTIVITIES

■ Use the microscope to examine human hair roots and split ends, torn paper, fluff samples, crystals of salt and sugar, threads of different fabrics, pollen grains, pencil and biro marks.

■ Write with the tiniest handwriting you can manage and examine the sample under low power. What do you notice about the letters?

■ Obtain line samples from five blue biros. Ask your assistant to choose one biro and write something. See if you can decide which biro was used — by forensic analysis!

■ Use a hand lens to examine flower parts or animals parts, e.g. flies, woodlice, earthworms or pond worms.

■ Experiment with looking through two convex lenses to see what distances give the best magnification. DO NOT look directly at the sun or other light sources! Van Leeuwenhoek almost blinded himself from watching gunpowder explode under a microscope. A home-made microscope can be constructed from cardboard tubes, adhesive tape and two convex lenses.

For information on websites dealing with subjects covered in this chapter, see www.my-etest.com.

Now test yourself at
www.my-etest.com

Chapter 7
Cell Metabolism and Enzymes

CELL METABOLISM   [221]

Metabolism is a term for all of the chemical processes occurring inside a living organism. It is sometimes used in connection with specific processes e.g. protein metabolism, glucose metabolism, etc.

All living organisms are made from cells, so metabolism really refers to *chemical reactions within cells*. Examples of metabolism include:

1. *respiration* in all cells — where nutrients are broken down to release much needed energy;
2. *tissue growth* from other nutrients in the diet;
3. *photosynthesis* in plant cells — where carbohydrates are made from simple chemicals.

There is an overall equation to represent the important process of photosynthesis:

Sunlight + carbon dioxide

$$+ \text{ water} \xrightarrow{\textit{chlorophyll}} \text{glucose} + \text{oxygen}$$

This equation suggests that by mixing sunlight, carbon dioxide and water in the presence of chlorophyll, glucose and oxygen will be formed. This does not tell the full story of what happens inside plants; the equation is only a *summary* of a complicated *metabolic pathway* by which glucose is formed. This pathway is typical of all metabolism — it is a long series of gentle chemical reactions involving intermediates, rather than one sudden, perhaps violent reaction creating the desired products. A metabolic pathway is safer and more efficient than a single step reaction — better to dismantle a house brick by brick and reuse the materials than to blow it up! Metabolic pathways are complicated but they are guided at every step by *metabolic enzymes*.

SOURCES OF ENERGY [222]

Energy is the ability to do work (or to do anything!). It is measured in *joules* and *kilojoules*.

Nothing can 'happen' anywhere in the world (or in the universe) without energy to make it happen. It is the motivator behind every single event that ever takes place anywhere. This rule applies in biology and so living organisms always require an input of energy to continue to live and carry out their life processes. Generally, living organisms obtain their energy either directly from the sun or from energy-rich chemicals — food.

The primary source of energy for all life on Earth is the sun. The sun produces a vast amount of heat and light energy (*solar energy*), which is absorbed by plants. The light energy is then converted to chemical energy by the process of *photosynthesis*. This resulting chemical energy is stored in *nutrients* in the plants and these are passed along *food chains* to

all other living organisms. The energy-rich nutrients end up inside the cells of the food-chain members and this energy is now referred to as *cellular energy*.

To demonstrate the release of energy from food:

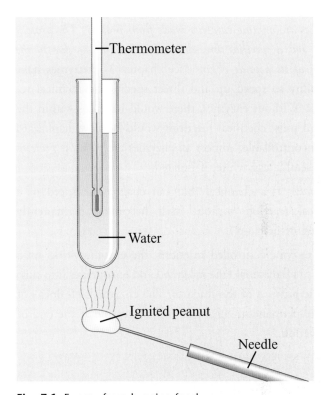

Fig. 7.1. Energy from burning food.

RESOURCES NEEDED:

Peanut.
Mounted needle.
Test tube.
Bunsen.

- Wear safety glasses.
- Record the temperature of the water.
- Position the peanut on the end of the needle and ignite the nut in a Bunsen flame.
- Heat the water until it boils or the nut burns out.
- Record the final temperature of the water.

The burning nut releases its food energy in the form of heat, which can raise the temperature of the water. This demonstration is similar to the controlled burning of food in cells through the metabolic pathway of respiration.

ENZYMES [223]

In any one cell, up to 1,000 different chemical reactions may be taking place at any one time — despite the very overcrowded conditions. The fact that these reactions are ordered and controlled is due to the presence of *metabolic enzymes* within the cell.

Enzymes are organic catalysts made from protein. The protein always has a specific, three-dimensional shape — due to the folding of its peptide chains (see chapter 3). Enzymes have the ability to speed up and direct specific biochemical reactions. Without enzymes, there would be chaos within the cell and most chemical reactions would be slow, haphazard and uncontrollable. Almost all enzymes are *globular proteins* and resemble egg white, if isolated.

(A *catalyst* is a chemical that can change the speed of a chemical reaction without itself becoming permanently changed or used up.)

In all enzyme-controlled reactions, the enzyme works on a specific raw material (the *substrate*) and encourages it to turn into the *products* of the reaction. The enzyme itself does not become permanently changed and is reusable at the end of the reaction.

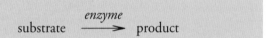

$$\text{substrate} \xrightarrow{\text{enzyme}} \text{product}$$

The word '*enzyme*' originally meant '*in yeast*'. The first successful extraction and identification of an enzyme was carried out by *Eduard Buchner* at the end of the 19th century. He demonstrated that fermentation could be done by an enzyme alone and did not require living yeast cells.

Enzyme structure

All enzymes are made from protein and all proteins are formed from long chains of amino acids (see section [**134**]). The primary structure of an enzyme is the order of amino acids in its chains. The secondary structure is the way in which the chains are folded in three dimensions. The folding produces shapes (*active sites*) on the surface of the enzyme that correspond to the shapes of specific substrate and product chemicals.

As a result of this folding, enzymes can have unlimited variation in structure — which is necessary if they are to catalyse thousands of *different* chemical reactions. Without this

variety of enzyme structure, life is unlikely to have evolved past a single cell stage if it reached that at all.

The properties of enzymes

- Enzymes are made from protein.
- *Enzymes originate in cells* — but do not have to be within cells to function.
- *Enzymes are reusable* — they are catalysts and are not permanently changed during the reaction although they become worn out and have to be replaced from time to time.
- *Enzymes work very quickly* — their reactions have a high *turnover number*. This is the number of substrate molecules that are changed per minute by one molecule of enzyme. Typical numbers are in the region of 6,000, although *carbonic anhydrase*, an enzyme involved in gas transport in the blood, has a turnover number of 36,000,000.
- *Enzymes are sensitive to temperature changes* — their activity decreases if they stray from their optimum (most suit-

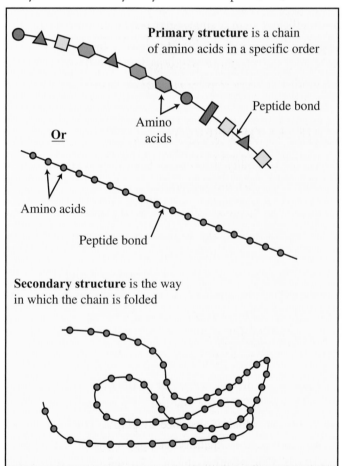

Fig. 7.2. Enzyme structure (primary and secondary).

able) temperature. Human enzymes work at their fastest rate at 37 °C — human body temperature.

- *Enzymes are deactivated by extremes of heat or cold.* Most proteins (and so enzymes too) are permanently *denatured* above a temperature of 45°C.

- *Enzymes are sensitive to pH changes.* Any deviation from the optimum (most suitable) pH will decrease enzyme activity, although different enzymes have different requirements for their optimum. For example, pepsin in the stomach works best at about pH 2, while blood enzymes usually work best at pH 7.4 and trypsin in the duodenum prefers pH 8.5.

- *Enzymes are specific.* Usually an enzyme will only catalyse one single reaction — this helps to keep order in the cell and prevents unwanted reactions at the wrong time.

- *Enzymes are reversible.* This is a complicated property, but an enzyme can make a reaction run in either direction depending on the build-up or disappearance of substrate or products.

NB: Organisms must try to spend all of their lives between the minimum and maximum conditions for their enzymes (i.e. they must always stay under the curves above).

Enzymes heated above their maximum temperatures are *denatured* — irreversibly destroyed by the heat. Egg white heated in a frying pan is denatured protein. It is impossible to turn it back into its original, fluid and transparent state.

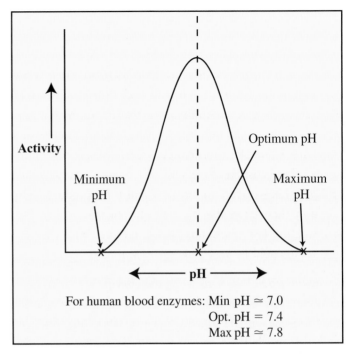

For human blood enzymes: Min pH ≃ 7.0
Opt. pH = 7.4
Max pH ≃ 7.8

Fig. 7.4. The effect of pH on enzyme activity.

[H221]

How enzymes work

Most chemical reactions are difficult to start — they need some energy (*activation energy*) to get them going. Enzymes

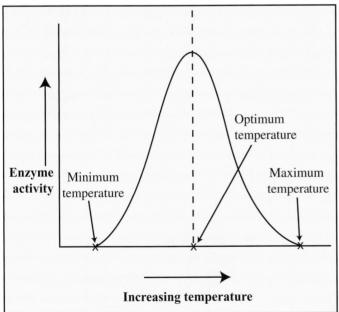

Fig. 7.3. The effect of temperature on enzyme activity.

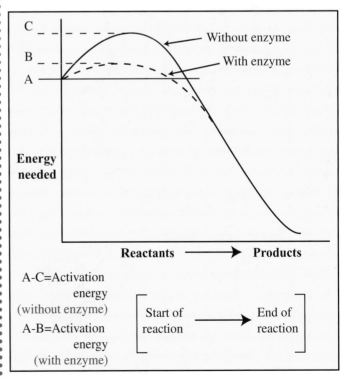

A-C=Activation energy (without enzyme)

A-B=Activation energy (with enzyme)

Start of reaction → End of reaction

Fig. 7.5. Activation energy.

are able to lower the amount of activation energy needed and so encourage the reaction to proceed (fig. 7.5).

Every enzyme has a specific shape on its surface (the *active site*) that attracts and fits substrate molecules exactly. Once substrate molecules are attached to the site (forming an *enzyme–substrate complex* or *E.S.C.*), they find themselves in a position favourable to chemical reaction (e.g. forced to touch other substrate molecules or having chemical bonds broken). They react without delay and form products. The products then leave the site and the enzyme is reusable. Without the favourable positioning on the active site, the substrates would be very slow to react at all.

Optimum activity refers to when the enzyme is turning substrate into product at the fastest possible rate. Slight changes in environmental pH and temperature affect the shape of the active site and the enzyme's ability to catalyse reactions. All enzymes have an optimum temperature and an optimum pH where their activity is at a maximum.

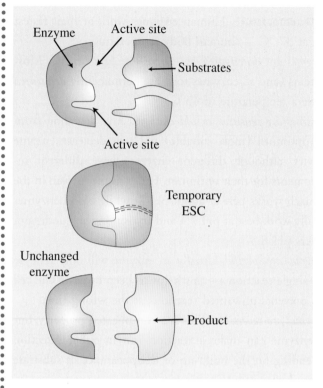

Fig. 7.7. Active-site mechanism of enzyme activity.

High temperatures *denature* enzymes as they disrupt the bonding between the amino acid chains and so alter the shape of the active site. Substrate molecules cannot now attach to the enzyme. This effect of heat is permanent and irreversible.

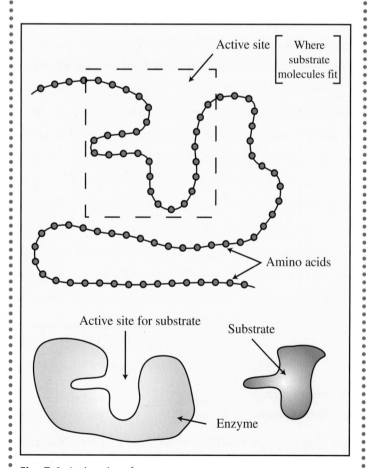

Fig. 7.6. Active site of an enzyme.

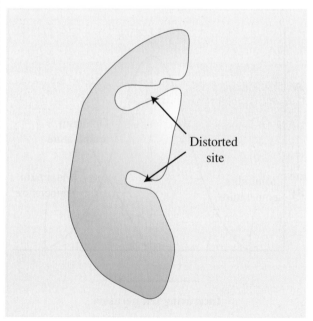

Fig. 7.8. Denatured enzyme with distorted active site.

Naming enzymes

When enzymes were first classified in Biology, they were given fairly arbitrary names (such as pepsin, ptyalin, trypsin) containing little information as to what they were or did.

A more modern approach is to add the letters *-ase* to either the substrate they work on (e.g. amy*lase* digests amylose, malt*ase* digests maltose) or to the type of reaction they catalyse (e.g. dehydrogen*ase*, oxidoreduct*ase*, etc.). Pepsin is now better described as a *protease*.

Bioprocessing with immobilised enzymes

It has long been established that enzymes will work outside living cells and it is also clear that they can be better catalysts of chemical reactions than anything else (due to their high turnover numbers). So the use of enzymes in industry and medicine has always seemed a good idea — except for the problem of removal of the enzyme when the reaction is over.

A solution to this problem has been found where enzymes are *immobilised* by attachment to some insoluble supporting material — usually beads of resin, fibres of collagen or sometimes a gel. The bonding of the enzyme to the support is usually *physical* (and usually reduces the enzyme activity a lot). Chemical bonding is more difficult to do but gives greater enzyme activity. A typical arrangement includes the enzyme attached to beads of resin in a tower. The beads are alternated with washed, fine sand. Substrate is added at the top and the products are drawn off at the bottom.

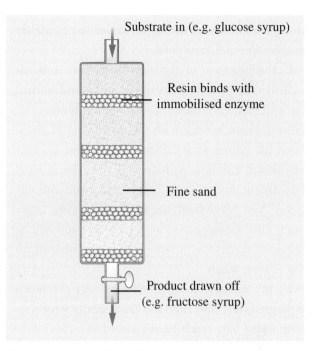

Fig. 7.9. Bioprocessing with immobilised enzymes.

Scissors.
Large beaker.
Sieve.
Freezer bags.

In this experiment, sucrose is converted to glucose and fructose by the enzyme *invertase*.

Sucrose (table sugar) is widely available but is not often used in the food industry, as it is not particularly sweet unless added to foods in large amounts. Immobilised enzymes in bioreactors can be used to convert sucrose into the much sweeter glucose and fructose. These are then added to foods and give a sweet taste in small amounts. There is no risk of contaminating the food with the enzyme, if the enzyme is immobilised.

This activity probably needs about two days to complete.

Day 1 — Immobilising the enzyme

1. Dissolve 3 g of sodium alginate (or calcium alginate) in 100 ml of water to make a 3%$^{w/v}$ solution. Sodium alginate is the salt of a natural polysaccharide extracted from marine brown algae. The solution is best prepared by adding the powder to agitated water, rather than vice versa, to avoid the formation of

> ### Mandatory activity # 16:
> ### To prepare a bioreactor using enzyme immobilisation

RESOURCES NEEDED

(*Recipes for all solutions are given in Appendix B.*)

10 ml of invertase concentrate.
200 ml 2%$^{w/v}$ sucrose solution.
50 ml 3%$^{w/v}$ sodium alginate solution.
200 ml 3%$^{w/v}$ calcium chloride solution.
25 ml plastic syringe.
Clinistix or *Clinitest* tablets for glucose testing.
Plastic soft-drink bottle.

clumps. Continuous stirring is needed to completely dissolve the sodium alginate.

2. Add the invertase to the sodium alginate and stir well. If time permits, leave the solution undisturbed for up to 20 minutes to eliminate air bubbles.

3. Fill the plastic syringe with the mixture.

4. Hold the syringe approximately 20 cm over a beaker of calcium chloride solution and drip the mixture into the beaker to form beads of alginate and enzyme. Aim for a bead size of about 2 mm; larger beads have a relatively small surface area and will be slower to react. The enzyme is now immobilised on the alginate beads.

5. Pour the calcium chloride solution and the beads through a sieve and rinse the beads gently with running water. The beads can be stored in a clean container until needed.

Day 2 — Manufacturing glucose and fructose from sucrose

Two alternative methods are given.

- Fill a freezer bag with immobilised enzyme bags and sucrose solution.

- Suspend the bag from a retort stand.
- Cut a tiny hole in the end of the bag.
- Collect the emerging drops.
- Test for glucose using *Clinistix*.
- Test the original sucrose solution in the same way and compare.

Or

- Cut the base off a suitable plastic bottle — use a scissors, not a knife! Plug the neck of the bottle with glass wool.
- Fill the bottle with immobilised enzyme beads.

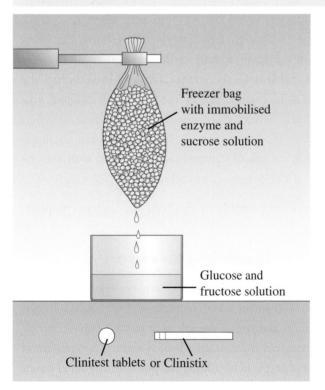

Fig. 7.10. To demonstrate the working of immobilised enzymes.

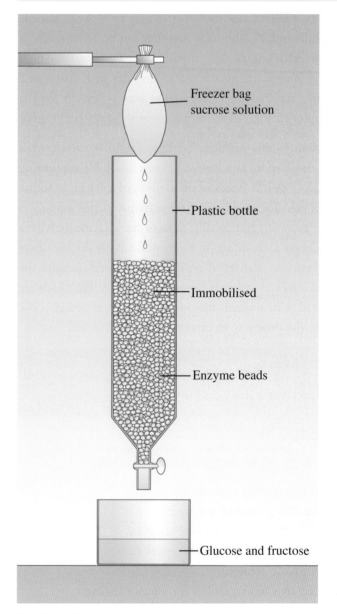

Fig. 7.11. Alternative set-up.

- Allow the sucrose solution to drip slowly through the bioreactor. Use a burette with the tap slightly open — or a freezer bag with a pinhole in the end.
- Collect the product at the other end.
- Test for glucose with *Clinistix*.
- Test the sucrose solution in the same way and compare.

The alginate beads can also be placed within the bottle with alternate layers of washed fine sand.

Advantages of enzyme immobilisation

- The enzyme is highly reusable, cutting costs for the manufacturer.
- The product is not contaminated with the enzyme, This reduces reaction reversal and also the possibility of allergic reactions to enzymes within the product.
- The enzyme is very stable and controllable when immobilised.
- The arrangement is perfect for multi-step processes — different enzymes can be added to different parts of the enzyme tower.

Applications of immobilised enzymes

- Gasohol (a biofuel for cars — used in Brazil!) is made from sugar cane.
- Antibiotic and steroid production.
- Waste treatment.
- Nitrogen-fixing to produce nitrate.
- Glucose syrup production for sweets.
- Vinegar production.

Enzyme experiments

RESOURCES NEEDED

(*Recipes for all solutions are given in Appendix B.*)

Starch agar plates.
Milk agar plates.
Mayonnaise agar plates.
Amylase solution.
Raw potato.
Cork borer.
Starch solution.
Iodine solution.

Dropping tile.
'20-volume' hydrogen peroxide solution.
Range of buffer solutions.
Electric water bath.
Thermometer.
Test tubes.

N.B. Treat all chemicals as potentially hazardous. Wear safety glasses and rinse all skin contact with lots of running water.

To demonstrate catalase activity

The enzyme known as catalase, occurs in many plant and animal tissues. It breaks down poisonous hydrogen peroxide into harmless oxygen and water. It has a very high turnover rate and can produce a foam of oxygen in a test tube.

$$\text{hydrogen peroxide} \xrightarrow{\text{catalase}} \text{oxygen} + \text{water}$$

METHOD

- Use a cork borer to cut discs of raw potato. The discs should be about 1 cm in diameter and 0.5 cm in height. Store the discs in water until needed.

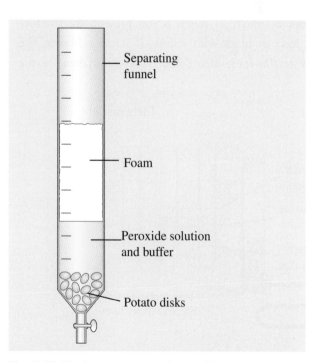

Fig. 7.12. To demonstrate catalase activity.

- Place five discs into each of the two test tubes.
- Add equal amounts of pH 7 buffer solution to each tube.
- Add hydrogen peroxide solution to one and an equal amount of water to the other.
- Observe the reaction and, after five minutes, measure the height of any foam produced.
- Repeat the experiment using similar size pieces of apple, liver, kidney and muscle (raw meat). For a fair comparison, add equal size discs and keep all materials at the same temperature, i.e. room temperature.
- Compare the difference between using whole discs and chopped up discs of tissue. Comment on your observations.

Mandatory activity #11: To demonstrate the effect of pH on the rate of enzyme activity

Amylase is an enzyme that converts starch to maltose. It is found in intestinal juice and in saliva. An amylase solution can be prepared by keeping a small amount of water in the mouth for as long as possible and then 'spitting' it into a 250 ml beaker. Collect about 50 ml of saliva and dilute it to 200 ml with water. Alternatively, amylase is available from commercial suppliers.

In this experiment, an amylase solution is added to a starch solution at various pHs. Every minute, a drop of the mixture is removed and tested with iodine for the presence of starch. If starch is still present, the mixture turns navy or black with iodine. If starch is absent, the iodine retains its golden colour. The time taken for the

starch to completely disappear is noted. The simplest way to do this is to fill the wells of a spotting tile with iodine before starting and then test drops from each test tube every minute.

$$starch \xrightarrow{amylase} maltose$$

METHOD

- Prepare a water bath at 37 °C.
- Warm all solutions to this temperature by standing them in the bath before beginning.
- Pour equal amounts of starch solution into four test tubes.
- Add equal amounts of different buffer solutions to each tube e.g. pH 7, 6, 5, 4.
- Check the pH with pH paper or a pH meter and record the readings.
- Label the test tubes.
- Add equal amounts of the same amylase solution to each tube and stir quickly while noting the time.
- Every minute, remove one drop from each tube and test with iodine for the presence of starch.
- Note the time taken for the starch to disappear from each tube.
- Do not continue longer than ten minutes with any tube.
- Repeat the entire experiment using water instead of amylase solution as a control.
- Display your results in the form of a table.
- Draw a graph of pH against time taken for starch to disappear. Put pH on the horizontal axis. Mark on the graph the optimum pH for this enzyme.

Mandatory activity #12a: To demonstrate the effect of temperature on the rate of enzyme activity

This experiment is similar to #11. Tubes containing amylase, starch and optimal buffer are placed at different temperatures and the time taken for starch to disappear is noted.

METHOD

- Prepare a water bath at 37 °C.

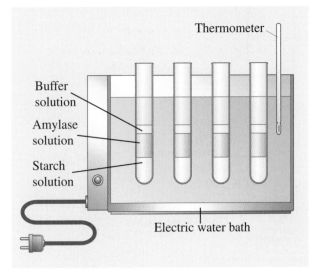

Fig. 7.13. To demonstrate the effect of pH on amylase activity.

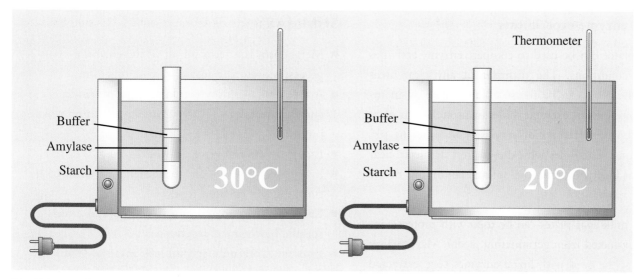

Fig. 7.14. To demonstrate the effect of temperature on amylase activity.

- Warm all solutions to this temperature by standing them in the bath before starting.
- Pour equal amounts of starch solution into two test tubes.
- Add equal amounts of pH 7 buffer solution to each tube.
- Add a measured amount of water to one tube — as a control.
- Label the test tubes.
- Add an equal amount of amylase solution to the other tube and stir quickly while noting the time.
- Every minute, remove one drop from each tube and test with iodine for the presence of starch.
- Note the time taken for the starch to disappear from each tube.
- Do not continue longer than ten minutes with any tube.
- Repeat the entire experiment with water baths of different temperatures e.g. 40°C, 30°C, 25°C, 20°C.
- Display your results in the form of a table.
- Draw a graph of temperature against the time taken for starch to disappear. Put the temperature on the horizontal axis. Mark on the graph the optimum temperature for this enzyme.

Mandatory activity #12b: Demonstration of enzyme denaturation due to high temperature

This experiment uses starch-agar substrate. Starch-agar is a mixture of starch solution and a setting agent, agar powder (a seaweed extract). The mixture is poured into petri dishes and then allowed to set as a gel. Holes are cut in the agar and amylase solution is poured into the wells formed. The dishes are incubated at constant temperature for 12–24 hours to allow the enzyme to diffuse through the agar. Then the dishes are flooded with iodine solution. Navy/black areas show the presence of starch, golden areas show that starch has been digested.

METHOD

- Use a cork borer to cut three holes in a starch–agar plate.
- Label each hole A, B, C on the underneath of the plate.
- Fill hole A with amylase solution at pH 7, hole B with boiled amylase solution and hole C with amylase at pH 6.
- Close the dish and incubate it at 35 °C for 12–24 hours.
- Flood the dish with iodine solution.
- Pour off any surplus iodine after three minutes.
- Record any clear areas around the holes.

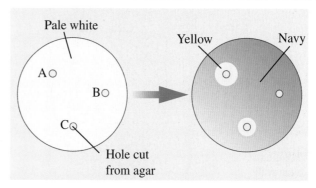

Fig. 7.15. To demonstrate amylase activity on starch–agar plates.

Alternative enzyme experiments

Starch-agar plates can be used to compare enzyme activities in different conditions. The diameter of any clear areas formed on the plate can be measured and taken as an indication of activity. For example, holes in a starch–agar plate can be filled with mixtures of amylase and different pH buffer solutions. The holes with the greatest diameter clear areas (i.e. not black) indicate the optimal conditions of the experiment.

In addition, milk-agar plates can be used with protease enzymes (e.g. extracted from germinating seeds). Mayonnaise-agar plates can be used with lipase enzymes (e.g. extracted from germinating sunflower seeds). Both of these types of plate have a milky-white appearance. Clear areas form around the holes if the enzymes are active.

(See mandatory activity #22 in Chapter 27 for more information on enzymes in germinating seeds.)

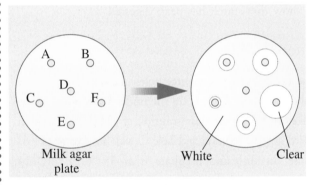

Fig. 7.16. To demonstrate the effect of pH on rate of enzyme activity.

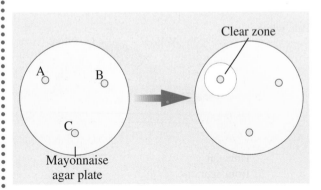

Fig. 7.17. To demonstrate enzyme denaturing

SUMMARY

- Metabolism is a term for all of the chemical processes occurring inside a living organism.
- A metabolic pathway is a long series of gentle chemical reactions involving intermediates by which a product is formed.
- Energy is the ability to do work.
- Living organisms obtain their energy either directly from the sun or from food.
- Enzymes have the ability to speed up and direct specific biochemical reactions.
- Enzymes work on a specific raw material (the *substrate*) and turn it into the *product* of the reaction.
- Enzymes are not permanently changed and are reusable. They are catalysts.
- The primary structure of an enzyme is the order of amino acids in its chains.
- The secondary structure is the way in which the chains are folded in three dimensions.
- Enzyme properties:

    – originate in cells;
    – made from protein;
    – reusable;
    – fast rate of reaction;
    – sensitive to temperature;
    – denatured by extreme temperatures;
    – sensitive to pH and other reaction conditions;
    – specific;
    – reversible.

- Enzymes can be *immobilised* by attachment to a supporting material.

EXTENDED SUMMARY

- Enzymes have highly specific active sites.
- Enzymes lower the activation energy of reactions.
- Enzyme activity is best in an optimal environment.
- Denatured enzymes have altered active sites.

KEY WORDS

Metabolism	Chemical reactions within cells.
Metabolic pathway	A series of enzyme-controlled steps leading to a final product.
Energy	The ability to do work.
Enzymes	Organic catalysts made from protein.
Catalyst	A chemical that can change the speed of a chemical reaction without itself being permanently changed.
Substrate	A specific raw material for an enzyme to work on.
Active site	A site on the surface of the enzyme that corresponds to the shape of a specific substrate.
Denatured enzyme	An enzyme irreversibly destroyed by heat.
Enzyme–substrate complex	A temporary joining of an enzyme to its specific substrate.
Immobilisation	Attachment of an enzyme to an insoluble supporting material.

EXTENDED KEY WORDS

Activation energy	Energy required to start a chemical reaction.
Optimum activity	When an enzyme is turning substrate into product at the fastest possible rate.

QUESTIONS

1. What is meant by the term metabolism?
2. What is a metabolic pathway? Give three examples.
3. Up to 1,000 different chemical reactions can take place in a single cell. How does the cell avoid confusion in its metabolism?
4. What is the original source of the energy found inside parasitic fleas?

5. What are enzymes and why are they important in biology?
6. Why are many enzymes necessary in a metabolic pathway?
7. Draw simple diagrams to explain the primary and secondary structures of enzymes.
8. List nine properties of enzymes.
9. What is meant, in relation to enzymes, by:

   a. minimum temperature;

   b. maximum temperature;

   c. optimum temperature?

10. What system is used to name enzymes? Describe briefly what each of the following enzymes probably does:

    a. lipase;

    b. protease;

    c. ATPase;

    d. oxidase;

    e. invertase;

    f. sucrase.

11. The equation for photosynthesis in plants is:

    $$\text{sunlight} + 6CO_2 + 6H_2O \xrightarrow{\textit{chlorophyll + enzymes}} C_6H_{12}O_6 + 6O_2$$

    The equation for aerobic respiration in all cells is:

    $$C_6H_{12}O_6 + 6O_2 \xrightarrow{\textit{resp. enzymes}} 6CO_2 + 6H_2O + \text{Energy}$$

    What do you notice about these two equations? Why might they both be considered a bit misleading?

12. State two factors that affect enzyme activity. Draw a graph to summarise the effects of one of the factors.

13. An experiment was carried out to investigate the effect of temperature on the rate of enzyme reaction. The following results were obtained:

Temperature (°C)	5	10	15	20	25	30	35	40	45	50
Reaction rate (mg of product/ sec.)	0	1.1	2.4	3.7	5.2	7.0	8.6	9.9	3.4	0

Plot the results on a labelled graph. Mark the minimum, maximum and optimum temperatures of the enzyme on the graph. What factors should be kept constant during this experiment?

14. What is bioprocessing? Give three examples of applications of bioprocessing.

15. Design an experiment to detect the presence of amylase, protease and lipase in biological washing powder.

OPTIONAL ACTIVITIES

- Compare peanuts, biscuits and bread for their energy content. Use equal amounts of each and see how much they heat equal amounts of water. Explain the results you obtain.
- Use milk-agar plates to compare the digestive powers of different biological washing powders.
- Experiment with immobilising other materials in sodium alginate beads. Try yeast cells or ground-up nettle leaves. Use immobilised yeast cells to construct a bioreactor designed to turn glucose into alcohol.

Now test yourself at
www.my-etest.com

Chapter 8
Photosynthesis

DEFINITION OF PHOTOSYNTHESIS

Nutrition is the process of obtaining *energy* and *matter* in order to drive the metabolism of the cells. Both energy and matter are found in *nutrients* (see chapter 3.

There are two principal types of nutrition:

1. *Heterotrophic nutrition* — where existing foods are eaten by organisms and broken down to provide ready-made nutrients. The word '*heterotrophic*' means '*other-feeding*'.

This method of nutrition is found in all animals (including humans), all fungi and most bacteria.

Fig. 8.1. Horses feeding.

2. *Autotrophic nutrition* — where nutrients are first made by organisms themselves from simple, inorganic chemicals and an input of energy. The word '*autotrophic*' means 'self-feeding'.

Plants (and some bacteria) use sunlight to make their own food — the process of *photosynthesis*.
[Besides photosynthesis, there are other forms of autotrophic nutrition. For example, *Nitrosomonas* and *Nitrobacter* are common nitrifying bacteria found in the soil. They have the ability to make their own food — but do not use sunlight energy. Their nutrition is by *chemosynthesis* — they use the energy released from the addition of oxygen to ammonia and nitrite found in the soil. This is an *exergonic reaction* — one that releases energy. The bacteria convert these chemicals to nitrate, which is taken up and used by plants. The bacteria represent an important step in the recycling of nitrogen in nature.]

Photosynthesis is a chemical process that takes place in the chloroplasts of green plants. Chloroplasts are organelles found in the cells of the green parts of the plant — the leaves and sometimes the stems. Photosynthesis takes place during the daytime when light is available to the plant. Sunlight energy is absorbed by green chlo-

rophyll and used to turn carbon dioxide and water into carbohydrate and oxygen gas.

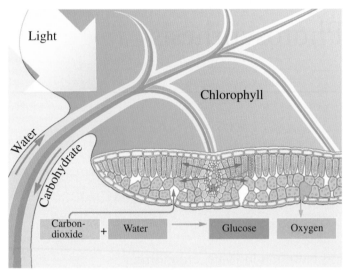

Fig. 8.2. Photosynthesis in the leaf.

Sunlight is provided by the sun. (Plants can use artificial light — fluorescent light sources are best.)

Carbon dioxide enters the leaves from the outside air or is already present in the cells left over from respiration.

Water enters the plant through the roots and travels upwards through the xylem cells to the leaves.

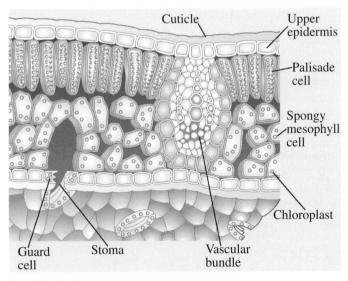

Fig. 8.3. Leaf structure.

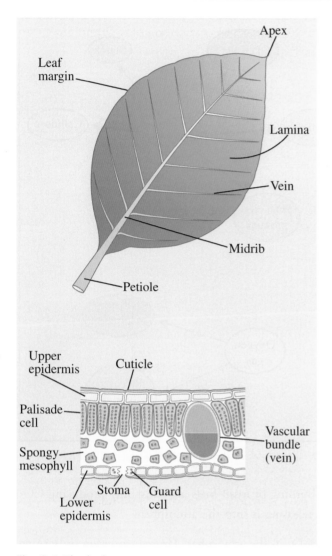

Fig. 8.4. The leaf.

The transverse section of the leaf reveals the detail of the leaf structure. The functions of the different parts are:

Cuticle	Waterproofs the leaf and prevents both flooding and water loss.
Upper epidermis	A sheet of transparent cells to let light pass through.
Palisade cells	The site of most photosynthesis. Cells stand vertically to increase the chances of light rays hitting their many chloroplasts.
Spongy mesophyll cells	Loosely packed to allow free movement of gases.

Vascular bundle	Supports the leaf and contains vascular (transporting) tissue to supply water and remove photosynthesis products.
Lower epidermis	A sheet of protective cells.
Stomata (singular *stoma*)	openings to allow the movement of oxygen, carbon dioxide and water vapour.
Guard cells	Adjust the openings of the stomata. Stomata are normally open in daytime and closed at night.

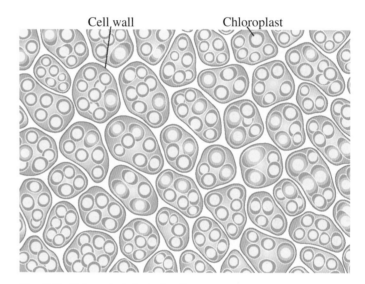

Fig. 8.5. Chloroplasts in leaf cells.

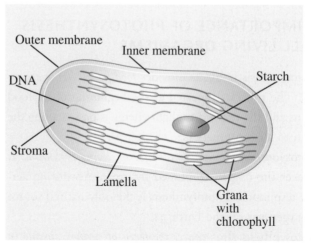

Fig. 8.6. Chloroplast structure.

105

The overall process of photosynthesis is represented by the following equation:

sunlight + carbon dioxide + water

$$\xrightarrow{\text{chlorophyll}} \text{glucose} + \text{oxygen}$$

Or

sunlight + $6CO_2$ + $6H_2O$

$$\xrightarrow{\text{chlorophyll}} C_6H_{12}O_6 + 6O_2$$

N.B. Chlorophyll acts as a *catalyst* for the process — it helps photosynthesis take place but is not itself permanently changed or used up in any way.

THE IMPORTANCE OF PHOTOSYNTHESIS TO THE PLANT

- The glucose formed by photosynthesis can be used for respiration to provide the plant with energy.
- Some glucose can be stored in the form of starch for later use.
- Some glucose can be converted to cellulose and used in the formation of cell walls for new cells.
- With the addition of minerals absorbed from the soil, glucose can be converted into pigments, vitamins, fats, oils and proteins — all used in the ongoing growth, development and reproduction of the plant.
- Some of the oxygen formed is used for plant respiration.

THE IMPORTANCE OF PHOTOSYNTHESIS TO ALL LIVING ORGANISMS

- Photosynthesis in plants provides *food for all living organisms*. The process is located at the beginning of all food chains and the trapped sunlight energy is passed along the chain to all consumers (see chapter 4).
- Photosynthesis provides *oxygen for all living organisms*. It replaces the oxygen consumed by organisms during aerobic respiration. Photosynthesis is the only natural source of oxygen gas on the Earth.
- Photosynthesis also *reduces the levels of carbon dioxide* in the atmosphere. This is important because respiration and

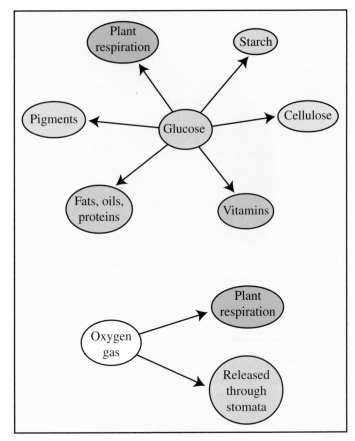

Fig. 8.7. Summaries of the utilisation of glucose and oxygen.

the burning of fossil fuels are constantly producing CO_2 and releasing it into the atmosphere.

Excess CO_2 in the atmosphere (from respiration or burning fossil fuels) can trap heat from the sun and raise the temperature of the surface of the Earth. This *'greenhouse effect'* produces a small rise in the Earth's overall temperature — *global warming*. The effects of global warming are also discussed in chapter 4.

Photosynthesis is a vital part of the control of CO_2 levels. Phytoplankton are microscopic, green plants floating near the surface of the sea. They carry out huge amounts of photosynthesis and they are the biggest single factor in the removal of CO_2 from the atmosphere. Most of the carbohydrates that they form from their photosynthesis fall to the bottom of the ocean and stay there — acting as a *carbon dump* for CO_2 from the atmosphere. The photosynthesis of the world's forests also reduces CO_2 levels, as carbon is absorbed and effectively stored in young trees. Accumulation of carbon dioxide is worsened by the vast scale of destruction of young trees in rain forests.

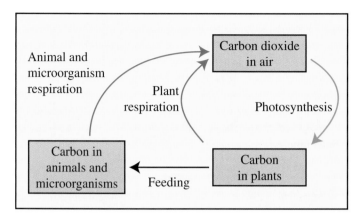

Fig. 8.8. The carbon cycle.

SIMPLE EXPERIMENTS ON PHOTOSYNTHESIS

RESOURCES NEEDED

Suitable plants.
Alcohol.
Water bath or other heat source.
Iodine solution.
Tin foil.
Plastic bags.
Soda lime.

When photosynthesis takes place, most of the glucose formed is stored in the leaf as starch. The following four experiments all involve allowing a plant to photosynthesise in different conditions and then looking for any starch that has been made.

The standard procedure in testing for starch involves boiling the leaf in water to disrupt the cell membranes, heating it in alcohol to extract the chlorophyll, dipping it in water to soften the tissue and flooding the leaf with iodine to locate any starch. Alcohol must not be permitted near any flames.

To show the need for chlorophyll

- Obtain a variegated plant (leaves have chlorophyll unevenly distributed) and store in the dark for 48 hours (this is *destarching*, removing old starch).
- Select a leaf and draw or photograph it — to keep a record of chlorophyll distribution).
- Expose the plant to strong light for 6–12 hours.
- Boil the leaf in water for five minutes.

- Turn off all flames and heat the leaf in a test tube of alcohol until all chlorophyll is removed.
- Dip the leaf in hot water to rehydrate it.
- Place the leaf in a dish and flood it with iodine solution.
- Draw or photograph it and compare it to the original.
- Black areas indicate that starch is present, golden areas indicate that no starch is present.

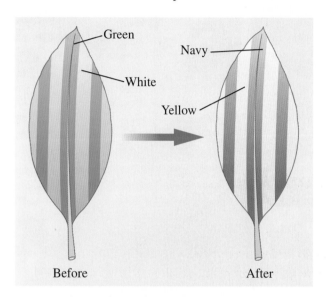

Fig. 8.9. The need for chlorophyll.

To show the need for sunlight

- Destarch a plant by storing it in darkness for 48 hours.
- Cover part of one leaf in loose tin foil.
- Expose the plant to strong light for 6–12 hours.
- Test for starch as above.

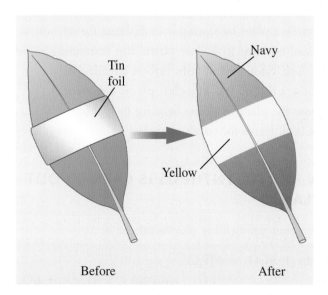

Fig. 8.10. The need for sunlight.

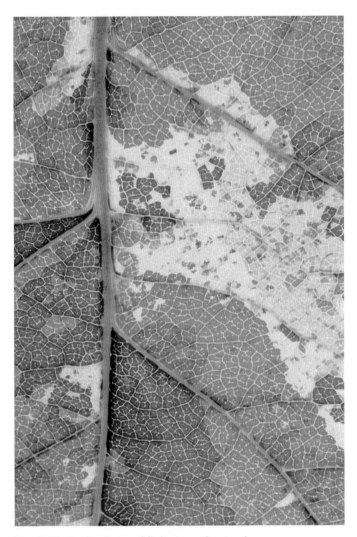

Fig. 8.11. Leaf cells need light to make starch.

To show the need for carbon dioxide

- Destarch a plant by storing it in darkness for 48 hours.
- Enclose one leaf in a clear plastic bag containing some *soda lime*. Soda lime absorbs carbon dioxide gas.
- Enclose a second leaf in a clear plastic bag alone.
- Expose the plant to strong light for 6–12 hours.
- Test both leaves for starch as above.

HOW PHOTOSYNTHESIS IS CARRIED OUT BY PLANTS

The equation representing photosynthesis is:

$$\text{Sunlight} + 6CO_2 + 6H_2O \xrightarrow[\text{chlorophyll}]{} C_6H_{12}O_6 + 6O_2$$

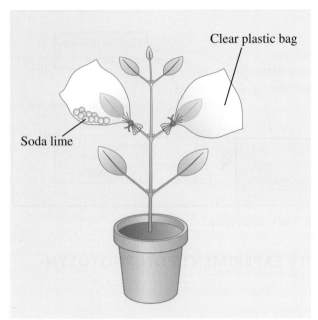

Fig. 8.12. To show the need for CO_2.

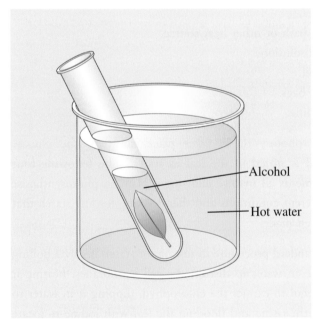

Fig. 8.13. Removal of chlorophyll.

This is only a summary of the formation of food and oxygen. It indicates the reactants necessary, the products formed and the catalyst required, without any hint as to *how* the products are constructed. Mixing the three ingredients above with chlorophyll in a test tube will not produce any food.

Photosynthesis is a long sequence of enzyme-controlled reactions. The products of any one step in the sequence form the raw material for the next step. The entire sequence is a typical *metabolic pathway*.

The main steps in the formation of glucose are as follows (all steps are directed by enzymes within the chloroplasts):

1. The first phase of reactions requires light — the *light stage* — and is located in the grana of the chloroplast.

   - Sunlight energy is absorbed by chlorophyll in the chloroplasts of the leaf cells.
   - Some of the trapped energy is used to split water molecules into electrons, hydrogen ions (or *protons*) and oxygen.
   - Protons are added to a *pool of protons* that will act as a source of hydrogen.
   - Oxygen is either used within the cell or released to the atmosphere.
   - Trapped energy generates a flow of electrons.
   - This energy in the electrons is temporarily stored within a chemical termed ATP. Enzymes are essential for this energy-transfer process.

   In summary: protons (hydrogen ions), oxygen and ATP are produced during the first stage of photosynthesis.

2. The second phase of reactions does not require light and is located in the stroma of the chloroplast. It is termed the *dark stage*.

   - Carbon dioxide and protons from the proton pool are joined together to form carbohydrate of the general formula $C_x(H_2O)_y$ — i.e. containing carbon and oxygen (from carbon dioxide) and hydrogen (from the pool of protons).
   - ATP provides the energy for this construction (this is the energy that will remain within the food as it passes along the food chains to other organisms).

N.B.

- *Chlorophyll* is located in the *grana* of the chloroplasts. It contains the enzymes necessary to direct the photosynthesis reactions.
- *Sunlight* is a mixture of different colours (the 'rainbow' colours). Most of these colours are absorbed strongly by chlorophyll and so are used by the plant, but some portions of sunlight are poorly absorbed (particularly green

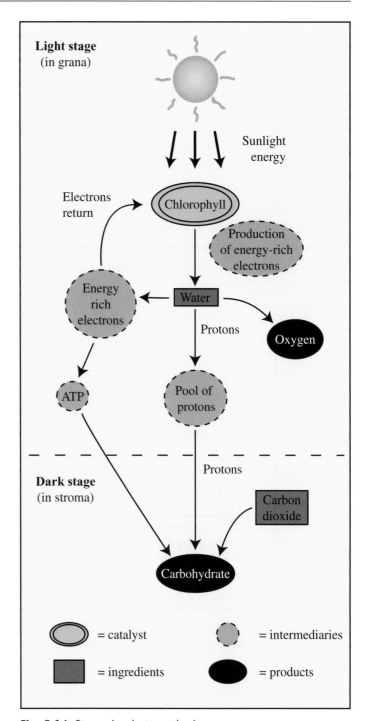

Fig. 8.14. Stages in photosynthesis.

light) and are reflected away from the plant. Plants appear green as a result of the large quantities of green light being reflected off their surfaces.

The absorption and use of energy by the plant is unavoidably inefficient. Of all the energy arriving at the leaf, no more than 6% of it will end up in manufactured glucose. The rest of it is either used to drive the photosynthesis reactions or is quickly lost from the leaf to the exterior. Extra light intensity increases the rate of photosynthesis up to a point; after that, the plant is light-saturated and extra light makes little difference.

■ *Artificial light* can be utilised by plants but may need extra violet and red added (no green component is necessary). Artificial light allows photosynthesis to take place at night as well as during the day and in theory should double the plant's output. Plants, however, require some periods of darkness to allow them to balance their various reactions. Overall, a plant photosynthesises better in alternate light /dark conditions than in continuous light.

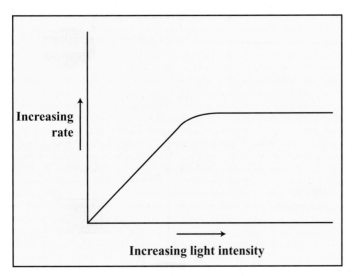

Fig. 8.15. Graph of light v rate of photosynthesis.

■ *Carbon dioxide* is supplied to the chloroplasts either directly from cell respiration in the leaf or by diffusion from the air through the stomata on the underside of the leaf.

The addition of extra CO_2 (the atmosphere only has 0.03% CO_2) by enrichment in a greenhouse does improve the rate of photosynthesis — but only up to a point. Plants can achieve high rates of photosynthesis if they are not limited by the supply of carbon dioxide, but they must have high levels of light intensity and an optimum temperature at the same time. This technique of CO_2 enrichment is used by horticulturalists to make plants grow faster.

■ *Water* is obtained either from cell respiration in the leaf or absorbed from the soil by root hairs and passed up to

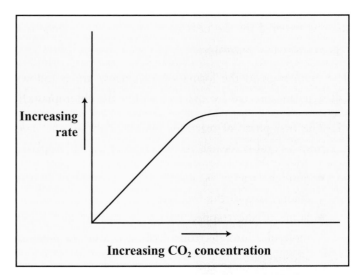

Fig. 8.16. Graph of CO_2 v rate of photosynthesis.

the leaf through tunnels of xylem cells in the root and stem. The mechanism for this is linked to transpiration. The path of water movement within the plant can be shown by the use of coloured dye or by radioactive labelling. Simply place a fresh, leafy cutting in a solution of water and some red or blue food dye. In a short space of time, the dye will have travelled to the leaves via the xylem cells. Section the stem at any point and examine the tissues under a microscope (see chapter 17 for more on xylem tissues).

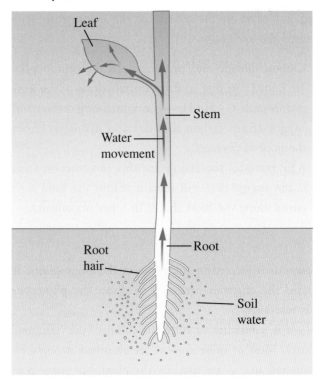

Fig. 8.17. The water path.

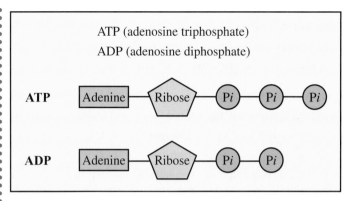

Fig. 8.19. ATP structure.

ATP is constructed by the addition of one inorganic phosphate (Pi) molecule to adenosine diphosphate (ADP). Energy is required to attach the extra Pi unit and so the formation of ATP is endergonic. However, if ATP is reconverted to ADP (by the removal of one Pi unit), the reaction is exergonic — energy is released. This reversible reaction is a convenient method of either storing or releasing energy in a cell and of transferring energy from one cellular process to another.

$$ADP + Pi + energy = ATP + H_2O$$
$$ATP + H_2O = ADP + Pi + energy$$

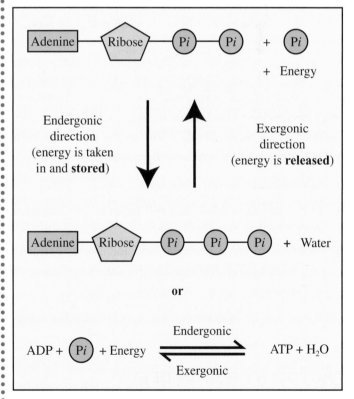

Fig. 8.20. ADP/ATP interchange.

Fig. 8.18. Blue dye moving through celery xylem.

ROLES OF ATP AND NAD/NADP   [H 22II]

Most chemical reactions in biology are *endergonic* — they require an *input* of energy in order to take place. Examples of endergonic reactions include muscle contractions, building new tissues for growth and repair, movement of materials across cells and membranes etc.

These reactions are rarely driven *directly* by the energy in food or sunlight; instead they are coupled with *exergonic* (energy-*releasing*) reactions as follows:

A reaction that produces energy is coupled or paired with a reaction that *requires* energy.

ATP invariably joins the two types of reaction together and assists in the transfer of energy between them.

ATP (**a**denosine **tri**phosphate) is made from adenine, ribose and three inorganic phosphate units (Pi) joined as follows:

For example, suppose a muscle cell is preparing to contract. This contraction requires energy and the energy is normally supplied from the respiration of some glucose.

Energy from respiration (which is exergonic) is used to construct ATP and then the breakdown of ATP drives the muscle contraction (which is endergonic). In effect, ATP couples the exergonic respiration to the endergonic muscle contraction. Note that the respiration does not have to occur *to order* (i.e. as the muscle cell demands), it just has to maintain a daily stockpile of ATP to match the cell's possible requirements.

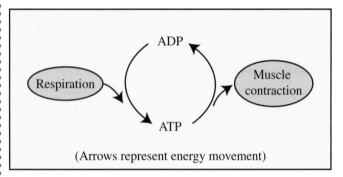

(Arrows represent energy movement)

Fig. 8.21. Energy coupling.

Photosynthesis produces ATP from sunlight energy.

Respiration produces ATP from chemical energy in food.

ATP is an intermediary for energy transfer.

NAD and NADP$^+$ (*nicotinamide adenine dinucleotide* and *nicotinamide adenine dinucleotide phosphate*) are coenzymes (enzyme activators) made from nicotinic acid (a B-complex vitamin). They have the ability to accept and carry both hydrogen ions and electrons during metabolic reactions.

The two chemicals are very similar:

- NAD is found in respiration and assists in the formation of ATP.
- NADP$^+$ is found in photosynthesis and used to transport both electrons and hydrogen to the site of formation of carbohydrate.

NAD and NADP$^+$ are intermediaries for electron and hydrogen transfer.

PHOTOSYNTHESIS IN DETAIL

The following is a summary of the process of photosynthesis:

$$\text{LIGHT} + 6CO_2 + 6H_2O \xrightarrow{\text{chlorophyll}} C_6H_{12}O_6 + 6O_2$$

The equation shows the necessary ingredients, the catalyst and the products of photosynthesis but gives little information as to how the glucose is made. Simply mixing the above chemicals and exposing them to light will not make food. The process is complicated and overseen by hundreds of plant enzymes. Photosynthesis is a two-stage process:

A *light stage* — which is light-dependent. The light stage is also termed a *photo stage* and uses light to provide a supply of electrons, protons and energy.

A *dark stage* — which is light-independent. The dark stage is a *synthetic stage* where the carbohydrate is synthesised from carbon dioxide and the products of the light stage.

Both stages take place during the daytime and both are located in the chloroplasts of the plant leaf cells. The light stage is located in the grana and the dark stage is located in the stroma.

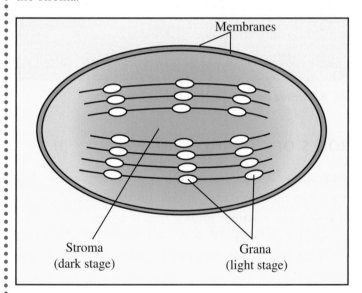

Fig. 8.22. Chloroplast — locating the stages.

The light stage

'Chlorophyll' is not one single chemical but a mixture of different pigments including *chlorophyll a*, *chlorophyll b* and many *carotenoids*.

These various pigments contained within chlorophyll are organised into *photosynthetic units*. Most of the pigments are light-gathering or *antenna pigments* — these absorb the sunlight. At the centre of each unit is a molecule of chlorophyll a. All of the energy gathered by the antenna pigments is funnelled towards chlorophyll a, which forms a *reaction centre*. This concentrates the light energy at one site. The reaction centre then emits a stream of highly energised electrons.

These *excited* electrons follow one of two pathways:

- Some transfer their energy to the formation of ATP and then return directly to the chlorophyll pigments.
- Others join with $NADP^+$ and protons from the proton pool to form $NADP^-$ and then NADPH.

This loss of electrons leaves chlorophyll *electron-deficient*.

The electron-deficient chlorophyll splits water into electrons, protons and oxygen. The protons contribute to the proton pool and the oxygen is mostly released. Electrons are returned to the chlorophyll to restore it to its original state.

IN SUMMARY

Light releases energised electrons from chlorophyll.

Some of these transfer their energy to ATP.

Others are used (with protons from split water molecules) to form NADPH, which acts as a temporary store of hydrogen.

Oxygen is released.

N.B. Chlorophyll regains all the electrons it releases — either directly or indirectly; it is unchanged overall — a true catalyst.

N.B. Herbicides, such as *paraquat*, often work by inhibiting NADPH formation.

The dark stage

The protons and electrons in NADPH combine with CO_2 to form carbohydrate. All carbohydrates have the general formula $C_x(H_2O)_y$, the carbon and oxygen atoms are supplied by carbon dioxide and the hydrogen atoms by NADPH.

ATP provides the energy required for this construction. Energy contained in carbohydrates (such as those in sweets and chocolate) can be traced back through ATP and the light stage and ultimately to the sun.

N.B. Both ADP and $NADP^+$ return to the light stage and are reused.

IN SUMMARY

CO_2 requires hydrogens (protons) and energy to form glucose.

NADPH from the light phase provides the hydrogens.

ATP from the light phase provides the energy.

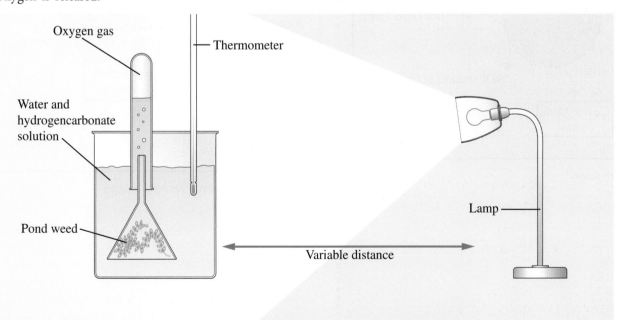

Fig. 8.23. To demonstrate the effect of light (or CO_2) on the rate of photosynthesis.

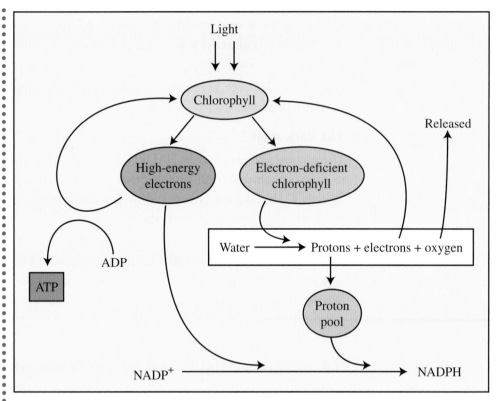

Fig. 8.24. Electron and proton pathways.

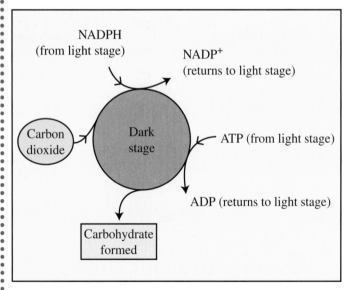

Fig. 8.25. Dark stage.

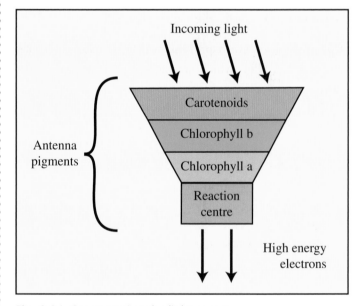

Fig. 8.26. Concentrating the light energy.

Table 8.1. Light stage and dark stage compared

Light stage	Dark stage
Located in the grana	Located in the stroma
Light-dependent	Light-independent
Produces ATP	Consumes ATP
Chlorophyll involved	Chlorophyll not involved
$NADP^+$ accepts protons	NADPH releases protons
O_2 released	CO_2 consumed

Mandatory activity #13: To show the effect of light intensity or carbon dioxide levels on the rate of photosynthesis

RESOURCES NEEDED:

Elodea or any suitable aquatic plant.
Test tube.
Large beaker.
Clear glass funnel.
Sodium hydrogencarbonate solutions ranging from $0.1\%^{w/v}$ to $2.0\%^{w/v}$ (see Appendix B).
Bench lamp.
Water bath.
Thermometer.

In these experiments, the rate of production of oxygen by a plant is measured against varying environmental conditions. An aquatic plant is used so that any oxygen released by the plant can be seen and collected. Light intensity is varied by adjusting the distance between the lamp and the plant. Carbon dioxide levels are varied by adjusting the concentration of sodium hydrogencarbonate in the water.

METHODS

■ Allow all solutions, apparatus and water to stand at room temperature before starting.
■ Obtain some fresh *Elodea* (Canadian pond weed) and cut the stem at a slant under water.
■ Position the *Elodea* under the funnel as shown in the fig. 8.27. Make sure that the cut end faces upwards.

Fig. 8.27. Production of oxygen gas from pond weed.

A. To show the effect of light intensity on the photosynthesis rate

■ Add excess sodium hydrogencarbonate powder to the water to ensure there is no shortage of carbon dioxide.
■ Position the lamp close to the plant and record its distance.
■ Allow the plant to adjust.
■ Count the oxygen bubbles per minute that emerge from the cut stem.
■ Repeat for different lamp distances.
■ Record all data on a chart.
■ Draw a graph to show the photosynthesis rate plotted against the lamp distance.

B. To show the effect of carbon dioxide levels on the photosynthesis rate

■ Set up the plant as shown, but replace the water with $0.1\%^{w/v}$ sodium hydrogencarbonate solution.
■ Position the lamp close to the plant and record its distance. Do not move the lamp during the experiment (why?).

- Allow the plant to adjust.
- Count the oxygen bubbles per minute that emerge from the cut stem.
- Repeat with different solutions of sodium hydrogencarbonate.
- Record all data on a chart.
- Draw a graph to show the photosynthesis rate plotted against the sodium hydrogencarbonate concentration.

N.B.: In both investigations the water bath maintains a constant temperature.

SUMMARY

- *Nutrition* is the process of obtaining *energy* and *matter* in order to drive the metabolism of the cells.
- *Heterotrophic nutrition* is where existing foods are eaten by organisms and broken down to provide ready-made nutrients.
- *Autotrophic nutrition* is where organisms make nutrients from inorganic chemicals and an input of energy.
- *Photosynthesis* is a chemical process that makes carbohydrate and oxygen from sunlight, water and carbon dioxide.
- *Photosynthesis* takes place in chloroplasts in the leaf cells.
- Photosynthesis is represented by:

$$\textbf{sunlight} + \textbf{6CO}_2 + \textbf{6H}_2\textbf{O} \xrightarrow{\text{chlorophyll}} \textbf{C}_6\textbf{H}_{12}\textbf{O}_6 + \textbf{6O}_2$$

- *Photosynthesis* in plants provides food and oxygen for all living organisms.
- *Photosynthesis* reduces the levels of carbon dioxide in the atmosphere.
- *Photosynthesis* is a two-stage process.
- *The first phase* of reactions requires light — the light stage.
- *The second phase* of reactions does not require light — the dark stage.
- *Addition of extra CO_2* improves the rate of photosynthesis — but only up to a point.
- *Extra light intensity* increases the rate of photosynthesis up to a point.

- *Water movement* within the plant can be shown by the use of coloured dye.

EXTENDED SUMMARY

- *Endergonic reactions* require an *input* of energy.
- *Exergonic reactions* release energy.
- *ATP* assists in the transfer of energy between exergonic and endergonic reactions.
- *Photosynthesis produces ATP* from sunlight energy.
- *Respiration produces ATP* from chemical energy in food.
- *NAD and NADP$^+$* are intermediaries for electron and hydrogen transfer.
- *The light stage* is also termed a photo stage and uses light to provide a supply of electrons, protons and energy for the dark stage.
- *The dark stage* is a synthetic stage, where carbohydrate is synthesised from carbon dioxide and the products of the light stage.
- *Chlorophyll* is not one single chemical but a mixture of different pigments.

KEY WORDS

Autotrophic	'Self-feeding'.
Heterotrophic	'Other-feeding'.
Photosynthesis	Using sunlight to make food.
Exergonic reaction	One that releases energy.
Endergonic reaction	One that requires an input of energy.
Catalyst	Changes the speed of a chemical reaction but is not itself permanently changed.
Greenhouse effect	When excess CO_2 in the atmosphere traps heat from the sun and raises the temperature of the surface of the Earth.
Global warming	A rise in the Earth's overall temperature due to excess CO_2 in the atmosphere.

Proton pool	A source of hydrogens for photosynthesis.
ATP	An intermediary for energy transfer.
Antenna pigments	Chlorophyll pigments that are light gathering.
Reaction centre	A concentration of light energy at one site.

QUESTIONS

1. How does animal nutrition differ from plant nutrition? Why is it that animals tend to be highly mobile compared to plants?

2. Write down the two forms of the equation summarising photosynthesis (word and chemical forms). What are the waste products of photosynthesis?

3. Draw a large, labelled diagram of a transverse section of a typical leaf. Describe a function for each labelled part. Mark on the diagram:

    a. Where water and carbon dioxide enter the leaf.
    b. Where oxygen and glucose might leave.

4. State four different fates for the glucose formed after photosynthesis.

5. What is the importance of photosynthesis to plants? To animals?

6. Summarise, in your own words, Diagram 8.14, showing the stages of photosynthesis.

7. Describe the effect of each of the following on the rate of photosynthesis:

    a. increasing the light intensity;
    b. increasing the CO_2 concentration;
    c. increasing the temperature.

8. Why do leaves look green? What colour are they during the night? What would be the most efficient colour for a plant? What would be the least efficient colour?

9. In an experiment to show the effect of light intensity on the rate of photosynthesis, what conditions must be held constant?

10. Design an experiment to show the effect of changing temperature on the rate of photosynthesis. What conditions must be held constant during the experiment?

11. What would be the consequences for all living organisms if only red light reached the Earth? If only green light reached the Earth?

EXTENDED QUESTIONS

12. Distinguish between exergonic and endergonic reactions. Give one biological example of each.

13. Describe, using diagrams, the difference between ADP and ATP.

14. Explain what *energy coupling* means. Explain the roles of ATP and ADP during energy-coupling processes.

15. Summarise the purposes of the light stage and the dark stage.

16. How is a supply of excited electrons maintained during the light stage?

17. Trace the path taken by energy from the time it crosses the cuticle of the leaf until it is stored inside a starch molecule. A bulleted list of points is a suitable answer style.

18. Why does the 'dark stage' only occur in light?

OPTIONAL ACTIVITIES

- Write down the names of all the foods that you have eaten so far today and try to trace their origin back to photosynthesis in plants. N.B. sugar beet and cocoa beans are parts of plants!

- Chloroplasts can be immobilised in beads of sodium alginate in the same way as enzymes were in Chapter 7. Grind up some freshly picked nettle leaves in sucrose solution (to stop the chloroplasts bursting) and mix with sodium alginate solution. Drip the mixture from a syringe, as outlined in Chapter 7, into a solution of calcium chloride to form immobilised chloroplast beads. Add the beads to warm water (25°C) and illuminate them with a bench lamp. Record the time taken for ten beads to rise from the bottom of the container (why do they rise?). Repeat with the bench lamp at different distances and draw a graph of your findings.

■ In 1618, the Belgian scientist, Jan Baptista van Helmont (1579–1644), carefully weighed a 2-kg young willow tree and about 90 kg of soil. He then allowed the tree to grow in the soil for five years with the addition of nothing except rainwater. The tree grew to about 80 kg, but the soil lost virtually no weight at all. Van Helmont concluded that the tree was made of water. How would you explain his results? Consider repeating van Helmont's experiment using a bean seedling and a small pot of soil growing over a period of six months.

■ Try to prepare and examine leaf transverse sections. Hold a piece of holly leaf in a slit in a bottle cork and cut thin slices with a *backed* blade. Keep the blade wet at all times and cut *away* from yourself! Prepare several sections and examine in water under the microscope. Vascular bundles may look unusual if they have been cut obliquely. Stain the preparation with iodine: lignified tissue will turn yellow and any starch will turn black.

■ Use the Internet, or other resources, to research the topic of *global warming*. Prepare a report to the class on the causes, effects and solutions.

For further information on websites dealing with subjects covered in this chapter see www.my-etest.com.

Now test yourself at
www.my-etest.com

Chapter 9
Respiration

ENERGY AND RESPIRATION

In chapter 7, energy was defined as the ability to do work. All living organisms need energy available to them in order to stay alive and to drive their metabolism. They obtain this energy either directly from the sun or from energy-rich nutrients in food. The cells of all organisms then store their energy in a chemical form (usually inside sugars and fats) until it is required. When a cell requires energy for some purpose, these chemical stores are broken down by *respiration* to release their energy.

Respiration is the controlled release of energy from energy-rich chemicals in cells.

It is a pathway of chemical reactions directed by enzymes (a *metabolic pathway*) and it takes place in all living cells at all times of the day and night.

(Respiration should not be confused with *breathing*, the process of taking in oxygen and removing carbon dioxide gas. Breathing and respiration are very closely connected (the oxygen taken in is needed for most respiration and the carbon dioxide being removed is a product of respiration) but the two processes are not the same. Respiration is a complex metabolic pathway and is located within all living cells — in the roots of plants, in the head of a spider, in human feet and toes, in the heart and stomach and so on. Breathing refers to an *exchange of gases*, and in humans is located in the lungs and airways.)

There are two types of respiration:

Anaerobic respiration — which does not use oxygen gas in releasing energy from food.
Aerobic respiration — which uses oxygen gas to release energy from food.

Anaerobic respiration can occur in the presence of oxygen but does not require oxygen. One might think that anaerobic respiration would be a less-restricted and better method to use within the human body, as no oxygen needs to be supplied, but it is a very inefficient process — producing only small amounts of useable energy from food. On its own, it could not keep up with the energy requirements of large plants or animals. Strict anaerobes are usually tiny, relatively inactive organisms, such as some bacteria.

Aerobic respiration is a much more efficient process, producing about 19 times as much energy as anaerobic respiration from the same amount of food. The only 'price to pay' is that the aerobic organism needs an uninterrupted supply of oxygen gas.

AEROBIC RESPIRATION

Aerobic respiration is a complex metabolic pathway controlled by enzymes, but it can be summarised by a single equation showing reactants and products:

$$\text{Glucose} + \text{oxygen gas} \rightarrow \text{carbon dioxide} + \text{water} + \text{energy}$$

or

$$C_6H_{12}O_6 + 6O_2 \rightarrow 6CO_2 + 6H_2O - 2875 \text{ kJ}$$

(the minus sign indicates a *release* of energy)

Glucose (the most commonly available energy-rich food in cells) is combined with oxygen gas to form carbon dioxide and water with a release of energy.

Within this equation summary, two main events take place:

Stage I

Glucose is converted by enzymes into to an intermediate chemical, *pyruvic acid* (or 'pyruvate'). This stage takes place within the cytoplasm of the cell, releases a small amount of energy and does not require any oxygen.

Stage II

Pyruvic acid enters the mitochondria of the cell and is broken down, in the presence of oxygen, into carbon dioxide and water, with a release of large amounts of energy.

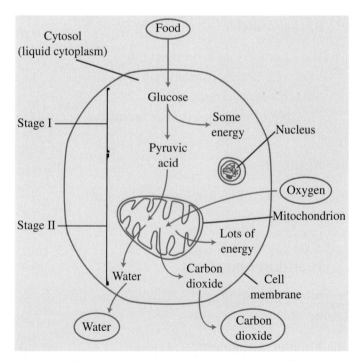

Fig. 9.1. Aerobic respiration in the cell.

Table 9.1. Summary of the two stages of aerobic respiration

Stage	Location	Purpose	Products	O_2 needed?
I	Within the *cytosol* — the liquid portion of the cytoplasm	Converts glucose to pyruvic acid	Pyruvic acid, some energy	No
II	Within the mitochondria	Converts pyruvic acid to CO_2 and H_2O	CO_2, H_2O, large amounts of energy	Yes

ANAEROBIC RESPIRATION

In *anaerobic* respiration, stage I takes place as above, but stage II does not — due to lack of either oxygen or mitochondria (anaerobic respiration does not use oxygen gas but can still take place in its presence). After stage I, pyruvic acid is either converted to alcohol and carbon dioxide or to *lactic acid* (or 'lactate'), i.e. two different metabolic pathways are found at this point in different living organisms. Both alcohol and lactic acid are energy-rich compounds — indicating that little energy has been released to the cell during anaerobic respiration.

The two possible outcomes of anaerobic respiration are:

> 1. **glucose → alcohol + carbon dioxide + energy**
>
> or
>
> $$C_6H_{12}O_6 \rightarrow 2C_2H_5OH + 2CO_2 - 210 \text{ kJ}$$

Glucose (without oxygen) is converted to ethanol (*alcohol*) and carbon dioxide, with the release of some energy.

This happens, for example, in yeast cells during the *fermentation* of sugars. This single equation is worth billions of euro to all the brewing companies around the world and is one of the oldest examples of *bioprocessing*. The production of beer dates back to at least 6000 BC in Babylon. The same metabolic pathway is used in the baking industry where the CO_2 expands with the heat of an oven to raise yeast bread. The alcohol evaporates from the bread — leaving a sweet taste. Bread found in Switzerland has been dated back to about 8000 BC.

> 2. **glucose → lactic acid + energy**
>
> or
>
> $$C_6H_{12}O_6 \rightarrow 2CH_3CHOHCOOH - 150 \text{ kJ}$$

Here, glucose (without oxygen) is converted to lactic acid, with the release of some energy.

This other type of anaerobic respiration is seen, for example, in bacteria in milk. *Lactic acid bacteria*, natural to all milk, convert milk sugar to lactic acid to obtain energy. The acid then makes the milk curdle and 'go sour'. Lactic acid bacteria are not destroyed by pasteurisation, so all pasteurised milk will eventually go sour — although the respiratory enzymes of the souring bacteria can be slowed by refrigeration. Human muscle tissue, if deprived of oxygen, is capable of anaerobic respiration for short periods of time but accumulating lactic acid will soon lead to a cramp in the muscles.

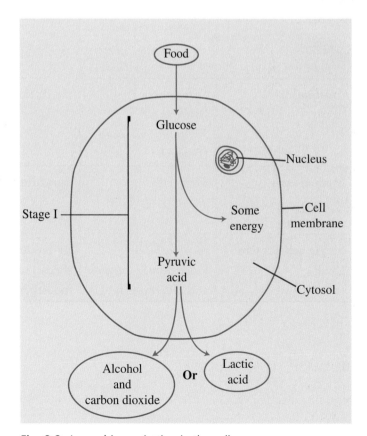

Fig. 9.2. Anaerobic respiration in the cell.

Table 9.2. Use of microbial fermentation in industry

Product	Microorganisms	Added to...	Effect	Notes
Cheese	Lactic acid bacteria	Warm milk	Produces an acid pH to sour the milk.	Rennet then added to complete the process.
Blue cheese	*Penicillium roqueforti* (blue mould)	Blocks of cheese	Alters fats to change cheese flavour. Blue spores produce colour.	Mould added with sterile needles.
Yoghurt	*Streptococcus thermophilus* and lactic-acid bacteria	Concentrated skimmed milk with added sugar or starch	Bacteria replicate, adding flavours. pH lowers due to lactic acid production.	Ethanol and other compounds produce characteristic flavour.
Beer	*Saccharomyces* (yeast)	Wort — a liquid extracted from malted barley and hops	Sugars converted to ethanol and carbon dioxide.	*S. cerevisiae* used for beer, *S. carlsbergenesis* used for lager.
Wine	Natural yeasts	Must — crushed grapes	Sugars converted to ethanol and carbon dioxide.	Red wines obtained if red grape skins present, white wines obtained if either red or white grape skins removed.
Antibiotics	*Streptomyces* (bacterium), *Penicillium notatum* (fungus)	Sterile nutrients	Organisms reproduce and secrete antibiotic.	Fermentation stopped when high levels of antibiotic are present.
Methane gas	*Methylophilus*	Agricultural waste	Methane gas released.	Cheaper than coal but more expensive than natural gas.
Single cell protein (SCP)	*Methylophilus* (bacterium), *Candida* and *Fusarium* (fungi)	By-products from cheese, sugar and oil industries	Blocks of microorganism formed.	Used as animal feed or meat substitutes for humans.

The cramp will ease when the circulation removes the lactate and the oxygen supply returns. The muscle needs massage or rest.

In both aerobic and anaerobic respiration, the release of energy is mediated by cellular enzymes.

MICROBIAL RESPIRATION IN INDUSTRY

Microorganisms can be added to a whole range of substrate materials and their respiration exploited to make useful and saleable products. *Fermentation* is the term used for the anaerobic breakdown of organic nutrients by microorganisms.

There are two types of fermentation:

- *Solid substrate fermentation* — This involves growing microorganisms on solid or semi-solid raw material. Examples include mushrooms (fungi) growing on compost, bread making (yeast within dough), cheese making and methane gas production from sewage.
- *Aqueous fermentation* — This is done either in closed fermenters (*batch fermentation*) or in open fermenters (*continuous fermentation*).

In a batch or closed fermenter, nothing moves in or out during the process except for the release of waste gases. This type of fermentation is easy to run and the fermenting vessels can be used for various types of reaction. Besides temperature, close monitoring of the process is not essential and contamination is not disastrous, as only one batch of ferment will be lost.

In continuous or open fermentation, nutrients are added continually as the product is drawn off. All variables of the reaction (temperature, pH, substrate concentration etc.) have to be monitored constantly throughout the process. The system can run indefinitely and the terms lag phase, log phase etc. do not apply to the microorganisms (see chapter 16). The method can use smaller fermenting vessels and is very efficient, but contamination or loss of control of the reaction will be disastrous. The system is also prone to blockage of the various valves and pipes.

Immobilised whole bacterial cells are sometimes used for complex fermentations. Cells of this sort are relatively cheap to produce, have a fast reaction rate and give a high degree

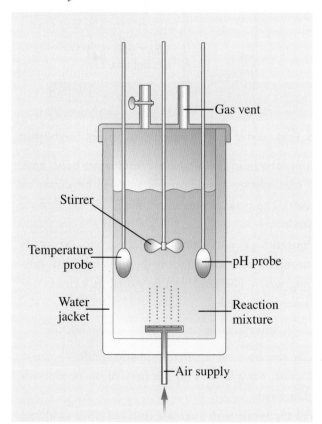

Fig. 9.3. A batch fermenter

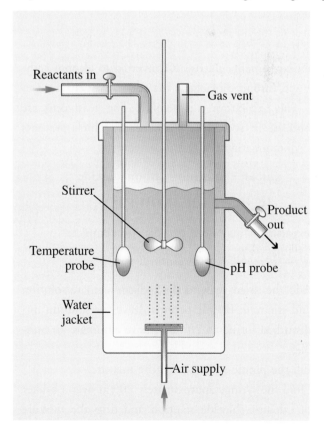

Fig. 9.4. A continuous fermenter.

of control over the reaction. Cells are fixed to gel, collagen fibres or resin beads and placed in the fermenter. Immobilised cells are used to manufacture steroids, antibiotics and alcohols. They are also used in waste treatment.

Mandatory activity # 15: The preparation of alcohol using immobilised yeast cells and continuous fermentation

RESOURCES NEEDED:

(*Recipes for all solutions are given in Appendix B.*)

20 g dried yeast powder.
100 ml 3%$^{w/v}$ sodium alginate solution.
100 ml 3%$^{w/v}$ calcium chloride solution.
250 ml 5%$^{w/v}$ glucose solution.
Large plastic lemonade bottle.
Glass wool or cotton wool.
25 ml plastic syringe.
Washed silver sand.
Wine hydrometer.
Large beaker.
Freezer bag.
Scissors.
Sieve.

In this experiment, glucose is converted to alcohol (ethanol) and carbon dioxide by the respiratory enzymes in yeast. The respiration is anaerobic. The yeast cells are immobilised in sodium alginate beads, which prevents them contaminating the end product.

glucose → ethanol + carbon dioxide

$$(C_6H_{12}O_6 \rightarrow 2C_2H_5OH + 2CO_2)$$

The experiment may need two days to complete.

Day 1 — Immobilising the yeast cells

1. Add the dried yeast to the sodium alginate solution and stir well. If time permits, leave the solution undisturbed for up to 20 minutes to eliminate air bubbles.
2. Fill the plastic syringe with the mixture.
3. Hold the syringe approximately 20 cm over a beaker of calcium chloride solution and drip the mixture into the beaker to form beads of alginate and yeast.

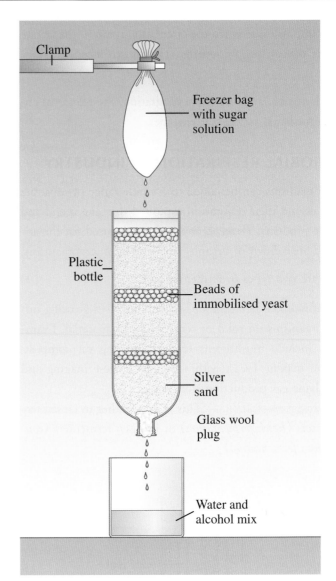

Fig. 9.5. Production of alcohol by continuous fermentation by yeast.

Aim for a bead size of about 2 mm; larger beads have a relatively small surface area and will be slower to react. The yeast is now immobilised on the alginate beads.

4. Pour the calcium chloride solution and the beads through a sieve and rinse the beads gently with running water. The beads can be stored in a clean container until needed.

Day 2 — Manufacturing alcohol from glucose solution

1. Cut the base off a suitable plastic bottle — use a scissors, not a knife! Plug the neck of the bottle with glass wool.
2. Fill the bottle with alternate layers of silver sand and immobilised yeast beads.

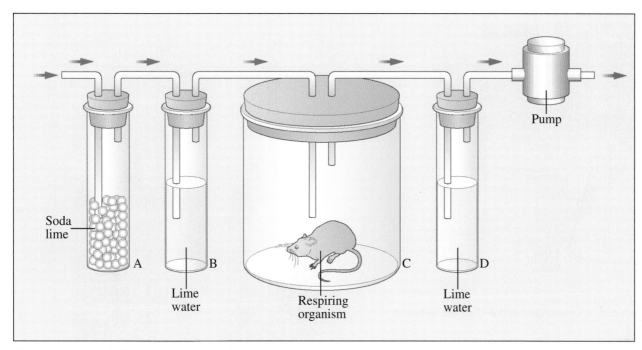

Fig. 9.6. Release of CO_2 from respiring cells.

3. Fill a freezer bag with the glucose solution.
4. Suspend the bag from a retort stand.
5. Cut a tiny hole in the end of the bag.
6. Allow the glucose solution to drip slowly through the bioreactor.
7. Collect the product at the other end.
8. Test for alcohol by measuring the relative density with a wine hydrometer.

Advantages of yeast immobilisation

- The yeast is highly reusable — cutting production costs.
- The product is not contaminated with yeast.
- The procedure is gentle and stable.

Uses

As a *bioreactor* for the production of alcohol by continuous fermentation.

To demonstrate the release of CO_2 from respiring cells.

- Set up the apparatus as shown in fig. 9.6.
- Enclose a small mammal or suitable small invertebrates (earthworms, snails, woodlice, etc.) or germinating peas in container C.
- Observe any changes.
- Repeat with no animals.

- Repeat with a green plant. (Cover container C with a black cloth to prevent photosynthesis. Why?)

If using a small mammal, a large container (a bell jar) is needed — but a result will be obtained within a class period. *Do not put a small mammal in too small a container.* Invertebrates may need a few days to produce a clear result.

- The pump draws air through the apparatus.
- Container A absorbs CO_2 from the air.
- Container B stays clear to show that CO_2 has been removed.

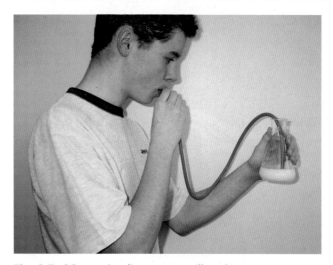

Fig. 9.7. CO_2 turning lime water milky white.

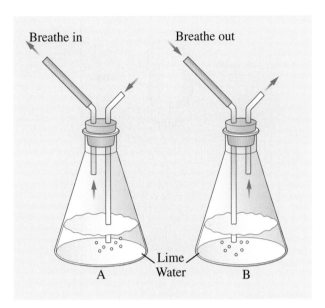

Fig. 9.8. Showing that inhaled and exhaled air are different.

- Respiration takes place in the tissues of organisms in C.
- Container D turns milky-white, showing the presence of CO_2.

Figure 9.8 compares inhaled and exhaled air. Flask A turns milky white slowly — showing that there is a small amount of CO_2 in the room air.

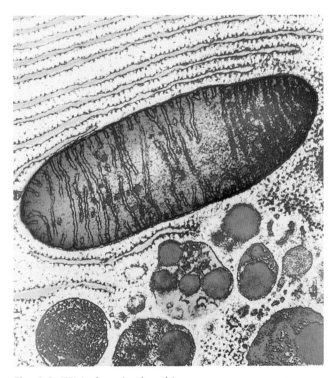

Fig. 9.9. TEM of a mitochondrion.

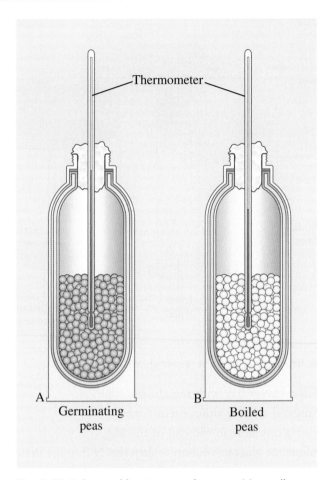

Fig. 9.10. Release of heat energy from respiring cells.

Flask B turns milky-white quickly — showing that there is a larger amount of CO_2 in respired air.

Figure 9.10 demonstrates the release of heat energy from respiring cells.

- Flask A reaches a higher temperature than flask B due to heat released during respiration.
- *Sterilise all equipment and peas in Milton solution before starting — to prevent microbial respiration.*

RESPIRATION IN DETAIL   [H 22IV]

Stage I

All respiration, whether aerobic or anaerobic, begins with the process of *glycolysis* within the cytoplasm of the cell.

Glycolysis (which means '*sugar-splitting*') is a series of enzyme-controlled reactions in which six-carbon sugar molecules (usually glucose) are broken down into three-carbon *pyruvate* molecules. Glycolysis generates two ATP molecules from every glucose molecule broken down.

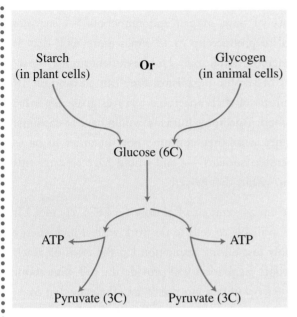

Fig. 9.11. Stage I of respiration — glycolysis.

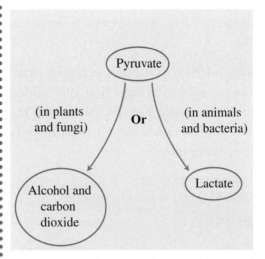

Fig. 9.12. Fate of pyruvate in anaerobic conditions.

If *no oxygen* is present in the cell (i.e. anaerobic conditions), the pyruvate molecules are converted to *ethanol and carbon dioxide* (typically in plant cells and fungal cells) or *lactate* (in animal cells and most bacterial cells) with no further production of ATP. Common examples of this type of respiration include the fermentation of sugars by yeast (in the brewing and baking industries), the souring of milk by lactic acid bacteria and the appearance of cramp in muscles starved of oxygen.

Anaerobic respiration is a very inefficient process as the waste products, ethanol or lactate, still have a high energy content. Animals can save and re-metabolise lactate for additional energy if oxygen returns (cramps disappear with restoration of the oxygen supply to the muscles), but ethanol is toxic to cells and is usually released by plants and fungi.

Stage II

If *oxygen* is present in the cell (i.e. aerobic conditions), further respiration of pyruvate from glycolysis is possible with a greater yield of energy.

Each pyruvate molecule enters the lumen of the mitochondrion and is converted, by respiratory enzymes, to CO_2 and an intermediate compound called acetyl coenzyme A (acetyl CoA). The CO_2 is toxic and is released from the cell.

Acetyl CoA now enters into a cycle of biochemical reactions — the Krebs cycle (named after Sir Hans Krebs who first described it). During this cycle, an electron transport system operates, which removes energy-rich electrons from acetyl CoA and other intermediaries. CO_2 and water are also produced. As the *excited* electrons move through the electron transport system, their energy is transferred to molecules of ATP. The transport system is located on the *cristae* of the mitochondria. The electrons are ultimately transferred to oxygen, which combines with hydrogen to form water.

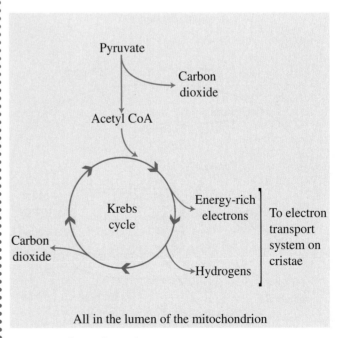

Fig. 9.13. The Krebs cycle.

This electron transport system only operates if oxygen is present in the cell.

(Sir *Hans Krebs* (1900–1981), a German biochemist, established the details of the pathway of stage II in 1937 during his work at Sheffield University. For this, he received the Nobel Prize in 1953. Krebs carried out his respiration experiments on pigeon breast muscle.)

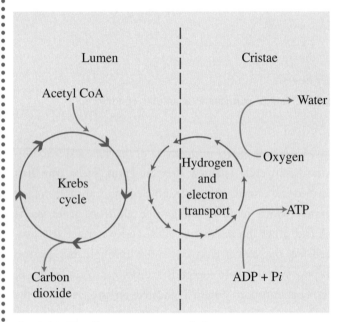

Fig. 9.14. The electron transport chain.

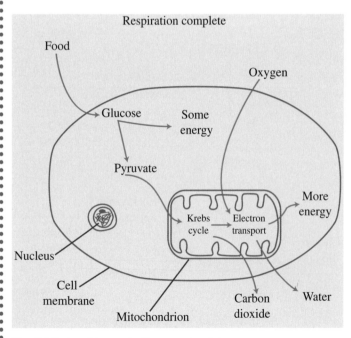

Fig. 9.15. Aerobic respiration — complete.

The presence of both oxygen and mitochondrial enzymes allows a cell to produce up to 19 times more ATP than it could in anaerobic conditions. This has an enormous impact on the lives of aerobic organisms; they can accomplish 19 times the efforts of their anaerobic relatives given the same amount of food. 'Anaerobic humans' would have to consume daily 19 times what they consume now in order to be as active as 'aerobic humans' — and would have to carry this extra weight within themselves!

Most of the energy content of glucose (-2875 kJ/mol.) is never made available to cells to do work with. Much energy is unavoidably lost during respiration (in the form of heat). At best, aerobic respiration will provide the cell with about 40% of the energy within glucose — an efficiency that compares well with the best petrol engines and their efficiency of about 25%. Anaerobic respiration has a low efficiency (about 2%), as the waste products (either alcohol or lactate), still have a high energy content.

SUMMARY

- *Respiration* is the controlled release of energy from energy-rich chemicals in cells.
- *Respiration* can be aerobic or anaerobic.
- *Anaerobic respiration* does not use oxygen gas in releasing energy from food.
- *Aerobic respiration* uses oxygen gas to release energy from food.
- *Aerobic respiration* is 19 times as efficient as anaerobic respiration.
- *Aerobic respiration* is summarised by:
  $$C_6H_{12}O_6 + 6O_2 \rightarrow 6CO_2 + 6H_2O - 2875kJ$$
- *Aerobic respiration* is a two-stage process.
- *Anaerobic respiration* is summarised by:
  $$C_6H_{12}O_6 \rightarrow 2C_2H_5OH + 2CO_2 - 210kJ$$
  or
  $$C_6H_{12}O_6 \rightarrow 2CH_3CHOHCOOH - 150kJ$$
- *In all respiration*, the release of energy is mediated by cellular enzymes.
- *Fermentation* is the term used for the anaerobic breakdown of organic nutrients by microorganisms.
- *Solid substrate fermentation* involves growing microorganisms on solid or semi-solid raw material.

■ *Aqueous fermentation* involves growing microorganisms on liquid material — either in closed fermenters (batch fermentation) or in open fermenters (continuous fermentation).

EXTENDED SUMMARY

■ *All respiration* begins with the process of glycolysis within the cytoplasm of the cell.

■ *Glycolysis* is a series of enzyme-controlled reactions in the cytosol where glucose is broken down into pyruvate molecules.

■ *Glycolysis* generates two ATP molecules from every glucose molecule broken down.

■ *In anaerobic conditions*, pyruvate is converted to ethanol and carbon dioxide or lactate, with no further production of ATP.

■ *In aerobic conditions*, pyruvate enters the lumen of the mitochondria and is converted to CO_2 and acetyl CoA.

■ *Acetyl CoA* takes part in the Krebs cycle.

■ *An electron transport system* removes energy-rich electrons from acetyl CoA.

■ *Excited electrons* transfer their energy to ATP.

■ *Electrons* are ultimately transferred to oxygen, which combines with hydrogen to form water.

■ *The electron transport system* only operates if oxygen is present in the cell.

KEY WORDS

Respiration	The controlled release of energy from energy-rich chemicals in cells.
Breathing	An active exchange of gases in an organism.
Anaerobic respiration	Does not require oxygen gas in releasing energy from food.
Aerobic respiration	Which does require oxygen gas in releasing energy from food.
Cytosol	The liquid portion of the cell cytoplasm.
Fermentation	The anaerobic breakdown of organic nutrients by microorganisms.
Bioprocessing	Using the enzymic activities of living organisms to obtain a useful product.
Batch (closed) fermentation	Where nothing moves in or out during the process.
Continuous (open) fermentation	Where nutrients are added continually as the product is drawn off.
Glycolysis	A series of enzyme-controlled reactions converting glucose to pyruvate molecules.
Acetyl coenzyme A	An intermediate compound within the Krebs cycle.
Krebs cycle	A cycle of biochemical reactions within stage II of aerobic respiration.

QUESTIONS

1. What is meant by respiration? In which of the following locations does respiration take place:

   a. petals;
   b. toes;
   c. the heart;
   d. hair;
   e. the lungs;
   f. bacteria;
   g. the ear;
   h. leaves during the daytime;
   i. hooves;
   j. kidneys;
   k. an onion bulb.

2. Distinguish between aerobic and anaerobic respiration. What would be the consequences for humans if they were anaerobic organisms?

3. Summarise, in your own words, the two stages of respiration.

4. Respiration is sometimes referred to as *tissue respiration* or *cellular respiration*. Why are these

terms unnecessary? What is '*artificial respiration*'? Why is this term confusing?

5. What is fermentation? Give five examples of the use of fermentation in industry.

6. Explain why an overused muscle becomes cramped. How will the cramp eventually go away? Why are fit runners less prone to cramps than unfit ones?

7. The equation:

$$C_6H_{12}O_6 + 6O_2 \rightarrow 6CO_2 + 6H_2O$$

can be used to describe both the *burning* of glucose and the *aerobic respiration* of glucose. What are the differences between the two processes?

EXTENDED QUESTIONS

8. Draw a labelled diagram of a mitochondrion within a cell. Mark on the diagram the locations of glycolysis and the Krebs cycle.

9. What is the role of acetyl CoA in aerobic respiration?

10. Ethanol is a high-energy chemical. How does this reflect on the efficiency of anaerobic respiration?

11. An adult male is fed 800 g of carbohydrate during a 24-hour period and is measured to have made 85 kg of ATP during the same period. How is this large amount of ATP explained? His body weight is only 72 kg.

OPTIONAL ACTIVITIES

The action of yeast on bread dough can be used to demonstrate alcoholic fermentation.

Mix together 200 g strong, white flour, 10 g sugar and 50 ml of yeast suspension. Stir well until a smooth, soft dough is formed. Pour the mixture into a 500 ml measuring cylinder and leave in a warm place. Observe and account for the change in volume. Mixture runniness can be adjusted by altering the quantity of water.

Equal amounts of mixture can be used to half-fill test tubes. Design and carry out experiments to show the effect of temperature or pH on the rate of yeast action.

Never, ever, taste or eat anything from the school laboratory!

Now test yourself at www.my-etest.com

Chapter 10
Movement Through Cell Membranes

INTRODUCTION

Every living cell carries out thousands of chemical reactions within itself — its *cell metabolism*. There is a high demand for various raw materials and there will be many products left over when metabolic reactions are completed — resulting in a lot of movement in and out of the cell. All of this entering and exiting has to take place across the cell membrane (or *plasma membrane*), which is a thin skin surrounding the cytoplasm of every cell and a barrier between the inside of the cell and the outside environment. The cell membrane is *semi-permeable* — it allows the passage of some materials but not others.

Cells need to set up a *dynamic balance* between themselves and their environment; the nature of the cell membrane plays a huge part in maintaining this balance. The balance is termed *dynamic*, as there is a constant movement across the membrane.

The cell membrane is responsible for:

- controlling the passage of materials in and out of the cell;
- recognising foreign particles;
- sensing the needs of the cell.

Plant cells have a second, thicker barrier — the *cell wall* — just outside the cell membrane, but this is fully permeable to everything and contributes only strength and support to the cell. It is not involved in controlling the entry or exit of any materials.

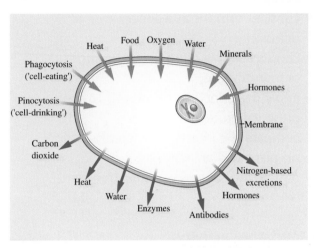

Fig. 10.1. Movements across the animal cell membrane.

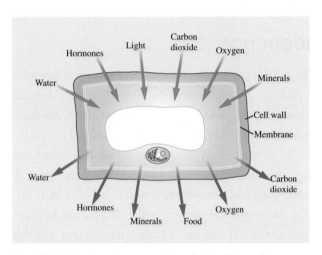

Fig. 10.2. Movements across the plant cell membrane.

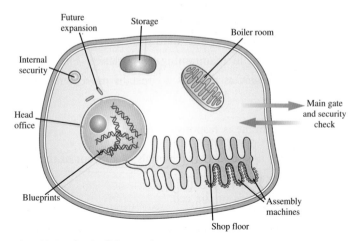

Fig. 10.3. The 'cell factory'.

THE NATURE OF THE CELL MEMBRANE (THE PLASMA MEMBRANE)

The cell membrane is too thin to show up clearly with a light microscope, but electron micrographs show that it has the appearance of a double layer of fat with lumps of protein floating like icebergs on its surfaces. It consists of two layers of phospholipids embedded with protein molecules. The membrane is fluid, not solid. You might imagine it as a sheet of *cling film* around the cell, but it is more like a skin of soft grease on top of a cup of water. If you push your finger through and then take it out, the grease layer reseals itself. Carbohydrate molecules are often fixed to proteins and lipids on the outer side of the membrane. These *glycoproteins* and *glycolipids* are involved in making contact with other cells and in cell protection. Temporary pores are found throughout the membrane.

Singer and Nicholson proposed this modern theory of membrane structure in 1972.

Membranes are not just found around the outsides of cells but inside them too. They encircle the nucleus of most cells and are found around all cell organelles — mitochondria, plastids, ribosomes, etc. — in effect making these into *mini-cells* themselves. Membranes are also folded to form the ER, the Golgi apparatus and other cell parts (see chapter 6).

Membranes determine the nature of both the cell and organelle contents and therefore determine what the cell can and cannot do.

CROSSING THE MEMBRANE

Some substances seem to cross the cell membrane easily, and others never seem to cross. For this reason, the membrane is always described as *semi-permeable,* that is, it allows some substances to cross and resists others.

(A *sieve* is also semi-permeable — the size of the pores determines what passes through the sieve and what does not.)

Materials may cross the cell membrane by many different methods. The three most important methods are:

- by *diffusion*;
- by *osmosis*;
- by *active transport*.

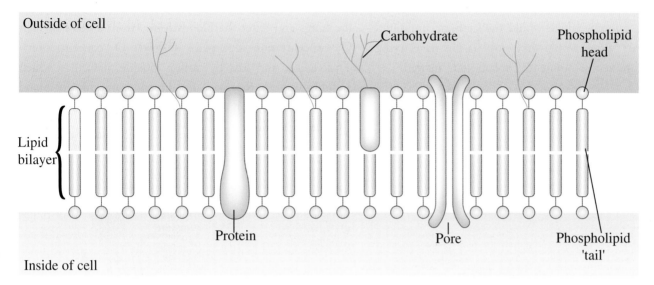

Outside of cell

Carbohydrate

Phospholipid head

Lipid bilayer

Protein

Pore

Phospholipid 'tail'

Inside of cell

Fig. 10.4. Cell membrane ultra structure.

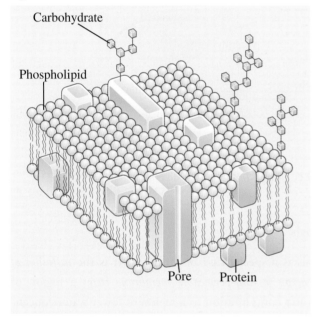

Carbohydrate

Phospholipid

Pore   Protein

Fig. 10.5. The cell membrane.

Diffusion

This is the *movement of materials from a place of high concentration to a place of lower concentration.*

This is an idea that is generally understood by everyone and could be renamed *spreading out.* Everyone knows instinctively that perfume (or air freshener) sprayed into one corner of a room will not stay there for long. They spread themselves across the room (moving from a region of higher to a region of lower concentration) until they are evenly concentrated everywhere. Similarly, food colouring added down the side of a glass of water will eventually spread itself evenly

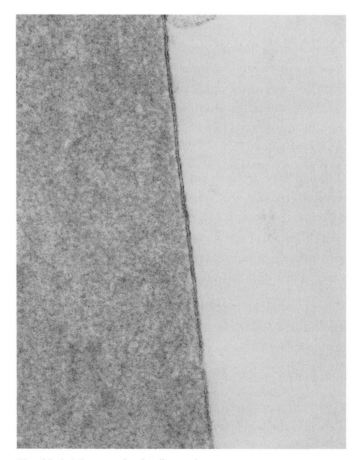

Fig. 10.6. Micrograph of cell membrane.

through the water. All materials in the universe try to obey the rule of diffusion — it is because their molecules are constantly vibrating and colliding with one another, so creating a natural tendency to spread out. Gases, liquids and dissolved solids are best at diffusion as their molecules are more free to move.

(After filling a room, where would the perfume molecules try to go next? When would they stop? Is this page trying to fill the room at this moment? Explain your answer.)

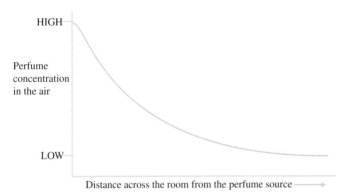

Fig. 10.7. The concentration gradient.

The perfume is moving down an imaginary, mathematical slope known as the *concentration gradient*. Notice that the slope is steeper at the start, which indicates that diffusion is faster over the earlier, short distances. Redraw the graph to show the distribution of perfume if the room was sealed and left for 24 hours.

Diffusion may be taken as '*free*', i.e. it is completely automatic, using only the kinetic (movement) energy of the molecules involved. Random collisions between molecules have the effect of spreading out the molecules evenly. In a cell, diffusion processes do not draw on the cell's energy stores in any way.

Moving *up* the concentration gradient is very difficult and requires an input of energy. This type of movement is equivalent to trying to put all of the perfume back into the bottle!

Biological examples of diffusion:

- the diffusion of oxygen from the alveoli of the lungs into the bloodstream;
- the diffusion of digested food from the intestine into the blood;
- the diffusion of urea from the bloodstream of a foetus into the bloodstream of the mother in the placenta;
- the diffusion of water from the soil into plant root-hair cells.

Different types of particle diffuse independently of each other. For example, oxygen molecules leave the air space of the lungs and enter the bloodstream (from a place of high O_2 concentration to a place of lower O_2 concentration). They ignore and pass by carbon dioxide molecules, which are diffusing in the opposite direction out of the blood (from a place of high CO_2 concentration to a place of lower CO_2 concentration).

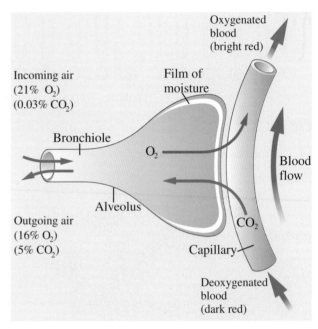

Fig. 10.8. Gas exchange in the alveolus.

Osmosis

Osmosis is a special case of diffusion. It is the *diffusion of water across a semi-permeable membrane* from a region of high water concentration to a region of lower water concentration.

Mandatory activity #14: Demonstrating osmosis
RESOURCES NEEDED

Visking tubing.
Water.
Starch solution.
Sucrose solution.
Iodine solution.
Plastic syringe.
Glass tube.
Large beakers.
Rubber bands or string.

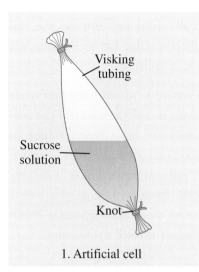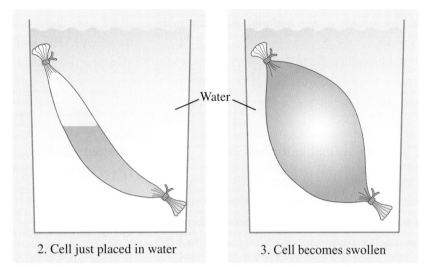

1. Artificial cell   2. Cell just placed in water   3. Cell becomes swollen

Fig. 10.9. Visking tubing experiment.

To demonstrate osmosis, a model cell can be constructed from *visking tubing* (an artificial semi-permeable membrane). The tubing is filled with strong sucrose solution, tied with rubber bands or string and placed in a container of water. The tubing now resembles a cell with its semi-permeable membrane.

- Soften a length of visking tubing by holding it under water.
- Tie a knot at one end.
- Use a syringe to fill the tubing with strong sucrose solution.
- Tie the other end of the tubing and rinse both knots well with tap water.
- Place the model cell in water and record its appearance.
- Record its appearance after 30 minutes and compare.

Water molecules move from the region of higher water concentration to the region of lower water concentration — in this case into the model cell. Sucrose molecules would 'like' to move from the more sugary to the less sugary region (i.e. out of the tubing), but the molecules are too large to fit through the semi-permeable membrane pores. Despite the inpouring of water, the visking tubing doesn't burst, as it is strong. The model cell swells and eventually osmosis has to stop as no more water molecules can fit in.

FURTHER DEMONSTRATIONS OF DIFFUSION AND OSMOSIS:

1.
   - Use a syringe to place starch solution at the base of a still container of water.
   - Immediately test a sample of water at the surface for the presence of starch. Starch solution turns black in the presence of iodine.
   - Retest the water surface after 30 minutes and compare the result.
2.
   - Tie a closed 'bag' of visking tubing to the end of a glass tube.
   - Use a syringe to fill the bag with starch solution.

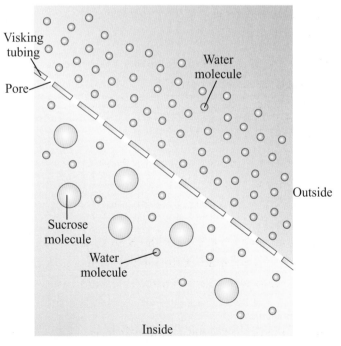

Fig. 10.10. Close-up of the cell 'boundary'.

■ Rinse the outside of the bag and glass tube with clean water.

■ Place the bag and tube in a container of water and record the height of liquid within the tube.

■ Record the change of height after 30 minutes.

Differences between animal and plant cells

Animal and human cells do not possess cell walls and, if they are placed in watery environments, are unable to resist the inflow of water for very long. For this reason, they have to be *osmoregulated* by some sort of active process to keep their water concentrations constant and prevent rupture of the cell membrane (see Chapter 22). Unicellular organisms, such as *Amoeba*, can suffer a constant inpouring of water from their environment. *Amoeba* collects surplus water in a contractile vacuole and periodically 'squirts' it to the outside. Otherwise, its membrane would rupture from internal water pressure.

On the other hand, if animal cells are placed in strong sugar or salt solutions, they will *lose* water by osmosis. The cells collapse and may develop characteristic wrinkling on the membrane surface — *crenation*.

Plant cells have a cell wall positioned outside the cell membrane. The wall is fully permeable but very strong and able to resist either bursting or collapse.

If plant cells are placed in watery solutions, they *gain* water by osmosis. This water collects in cell vacuoles and the cells begin to swell. The cells does not burst however (due to their cell walls); instead an internal pressure builds up which eventually stops any further entry of water. The cells are very swollen or *turgid*. Plant cells function best in this turgid condition. Notice that osmosis stops although there is still a concentration difference across the cell membranes.

If plant cells are placed in strong sugar or salt solutions, they *lose* water by osmosis. The cells do not, however, collapse (due to their cell walls); but their cytoplasm loses a lot of water and becomes stuck to the inside of the cell membrane. These cells are described as *plasmolysed* and cannot function. They can be restored to their normal condition by immersion in water.

All cells immersed in strong sugar or salt solutions lose water by osmosis (the water in the cell crosses the membrane to the less watery region). This happens in bacterial cells too, so sugar or salt solutions are commonly used for the pres-

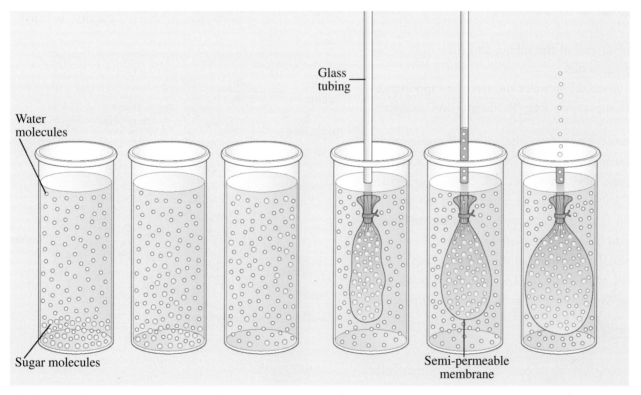

Fig. 10.11. Diffusion and osmosis.

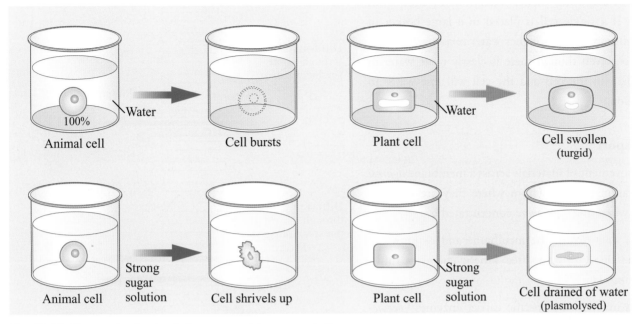

Fig. 10.12. Plant and animal cells in water and in sugar solution.

ervation of food. The solutions absorb water from the bacteria by osmosis and so prevent any bacterial growth. This preservation method is cheap, but the preserving solutions are consumed with the food and must have an acceptable taste. The use of salt to preserve meat and fish dates back hundreds of years. Sugar syrup is used to preserve tinned peaches and other fruits.

Use of the words 'concentrated' and 'dilute'

When using these words in Biology, always make it clear as to which chemical the words refer to. In the fig. 10.14, solution A is more concentrated with regard to *orange* but solution B is more concentrated with regard to *water*. To simply say that either solution is 'the concentrated one' may lead to confusion.

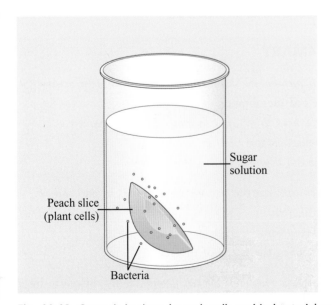

Fig. 10.13. Osmosis in tinned peach cells and in bacterial cells.

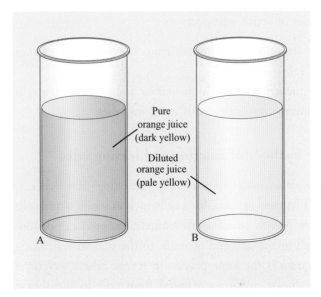

Fig. 10.14. 'Concentrated' and 'Dilute'.

Also, beware of confusing 'higher water concentration' with 'more water'. If a single cell is placed in a large beaker of strong salt solution, it has a higher water *concentration* than its environment even though there is clearly more water in the beaker than in the cell and the cell will lose water to the salt solution.

Active transport

This is the movement of materials across a membrane *against* the concentration gradient (from where they are *less* concentrated to where they are *more* concentrated).

It is done by enzymes in the membrane and requires cell energy (rather than using the 'free' kinetic energy of diffusion and osmosis).

The enzymes involved are specific carrier enzymes (*permeases*) and only certain specific chemicals are moved.

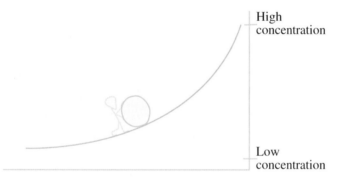

Fig. 10.15. Moving against the gradient.

Examples of active transport:

- The absorption of minerals from the soil by plant root hair cells.
- The movement of sodium ions in and out of nerve cells during the transmission of nerve impulses.

Other methods of entering and leaving cells:

- *Pinocytosis* and *phagocytosis* ('cell drinking' and 'cell eating') happen in specialised cells such as white blood cells where liquids or solids are entirely enclosed in portions of cell membrane and taken in to the cells in vesicles.
- *Exocytosis* is the same process in reverse where secretions (like breast milk) are released from cells in membrane vesicles.

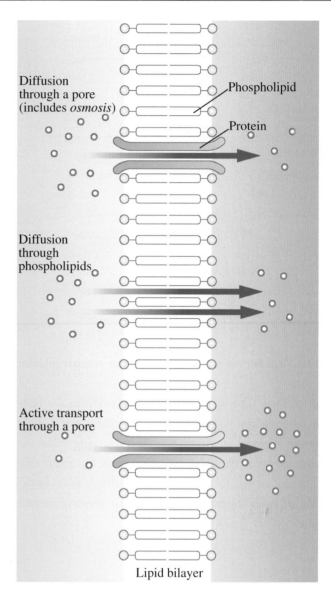

Fig. 10.16. Crossing the membrane.

SUMMARY

- *Cell metabolism* results in a lot of movement across the cell membrane.
- *Cells need to set up a dynamic balance* between themselves and their environment.
- *The cell membrane is responsible for:*

  - controlling the passage of materials in and out of the cell;
  - recognising foreign particles;
  - sensing the needs of the cell.

- *Materials may cross the cell membrane* by diffusion, by osmosis or by active transport.

- *Diffusion* is the movement of materials from a place of high concentration to a place of lower concentration.
- *Osmosis* is the diffusion of water across a semi-permeable membrane from a region of high water concentration to a region of lower water concentration.
- *Animal cells* do not possess cell walls and, if they are placed in watery environments, are unable to resist the inflow of water for very long.
- *Plant cells* have a cell wall, which is fully permeable but able to resist either bursting or collapse.
- *Plant cells become turgid* when placed in watery solutions.
- *Plant cells become plasmolysed* when placed in less watery solutions.
- *Sugar or salt solutions* are commonly used for the preservation of food. These solutions absorb water from the bacteria by osmosis and so prevent any bacterial growth.
- *Active transport* is the movement of materials across a cell membrane against the concentration gradient.

KEY WORDS

Semi-permeable	Allows the passage of some materials but not others.
Diffusion	The movement of materials from a place of high concentration to a place of lower concentration.
Concentration gradient	A mathematical slope representing the smooth transition from a more concentrated to a less concentrated region.
Osmosis	The diffusion of water across a semi-permeable membrane from a region of high water concentration to a region of lower water concentration.
Visking tubing	An artificial, semi-permeable membrane.

Osmoregulation	Water and salt balance.
Crenated	When animal cells have collapsed due to water loss.
Turgid	When plant cells are swollen with water.
Plasmolysed	When plant cells have lost water due to osmosis.
Active transport	Movement of materials across the cell membrane against the concentration gradient.
Pinocytosis	'Cell eating'.
Phagocytosis	'Cell drinking'.
Exocytosis	Release of secretions from cells in membrane vesicles.

QUESTIONS

1. What is the explanation for the large amounts of 'traffic' across cell membranes?
2. Why is the balance between a cell and its environment considered *dynamic*?
3. State three differences between the cell wall and the cell membrane.
4. What is meant by the term *semi-permeable*? What sort of chemicals are most likely to pass through a semi-permeable membrane?
5. Explain the process of diffusion. What is the connection between diffusion and kinetic energy? Using the word 'diffusion' in your answer, explain why pregnant women should not smoke.
6. Define *osmosis*. Why does osmosis occur so frequently in biology?
7. Compare the behaviour of an onion cell and a blood cell when:

   a. placed in distilled water;
   b. placed in strong sugar solution.

   Draw simple, labelled diagrams of the cells after this treatment.
8. Comment on the following statements:

   a. Carbon dioxide passes out of cells because it is poisonous.

b. If water neither enters nor leaves a cell, it must be equally concentrated on both sides of the cell membrane.

9. How does sugar solution preserve tinned fruit?

OPTIONAL ACTIVITIES

- Pour some food colouring gently down the side of a still glass of water. Observe the movement of the colour. When will the colouring stop moving through the water?
- Make a semi-permeable membrane model. Cut holes in a plastic drink bottle. Fill the bottle with a mixture of large buttons and small plastic beads. Cut the holes large enough so that only the beads can escape. The model works best when it is shaken. This gives the 'molecules' their 'kinetic energy' to collide with one another.
- Obtain a sheet of epidermal cells from between the layers of a red onion or from the outside of a stick of rhubarb. Tulip petals or thin slices of beetroot can also be used. All of these cells have a water-soluble pigment in their cytoplasm.
- Place the cells on a microscope slide in a drop of distilled water and cover with a cover slip. Leave for five minutes and examine. Note the distribution of the coloured pigment — the cells are turgid. Repeat with tissue in strong sucrose solution and compare the results. Draw labelled diagrams of the cells in each case.
- Cut two strips of fresh raw potato about 5 mm × 5 mm × 5 cm long. Weigh the strips as accurately as possible. Place one strip in a test tube of distilled water and the other in a test tube of strong sucrose solution. Leave for 30 minutes. Examine, measure and weigh both samples. Comment on your findings.
- Place a small handful of raisins in distilled water, cover and leave for a few days. Describe any changes.
- Place a wilted lettuce leaf in a bowl of water. Why does it recover its crispness?

Now test yourself at
www.my-etest.com

Chapter 11
Cell Continuity and Cell Diversity

Learning objectives

After your study of this chapter, you should be able to:

- explain the need for cell reproduction;
- distinguish between haploid and diploid cells;
- draw a circular diagram to illustrate the cell cycle;
- construct a chart to compare mitosis and meiosis;
- explain the complementary roles of fertilisation and meiosis in maintaining the diploid number;
- collect and present information on cancer and cancer prevention;
- outline the process of tissue culture.

Extended learning objectives

- Describe, in detail, the four phases of mitosis.

INTRODUCTION

No cells (nor living organisms) can live forever. The continuity of life depends on *cell reproduction* taking place at

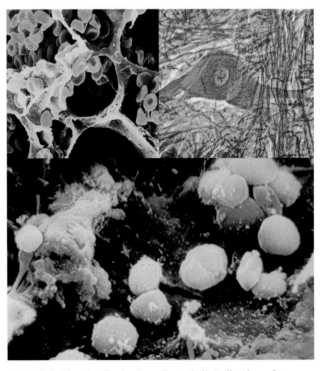

Fig. 11.1. Blood cells, brain cells and digitally cloned sperm cells.

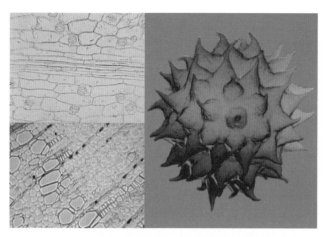

Fig. 11.2. Epidermal cells, xylem cells and pollen.

some time. This will produce new, younger cells that can continue the process of living. New cells must replace older ones for growth and repair to take place. New organisms will obviously require new cells to grow from.

Cell reproduction depends on copying the instructions written on the cell DNA and then passing on the copy to the new cells. This copying and passing on must be done *faithfully*. No mistakes in the DNA copies are allowed (*zero tolerance!*) as any such mistakes would multiply with each cell generation and quickly bring chaos to the organism.

Most new cells formed will be used for growth and repair of the existing organism. Some new cells, however, will form reproductive cells (sperms, eggs or spores) and will pass on instructions to a completely new organism. This new organism will continue the process of cell division and cell reproduction.

CHROMOSOMES [231]

Chromosomes are threads of DNA wrapped in protein (see Chapter 12). Chromosomes contain all of the instructions necessary for the growth and activity of the cell. These instructions will, in turn, determine all the characteristics of the living organism — its appearance, structure, abilities, etc.

In non-dividing cells, the chromosomes are long and thin and difficult to see. They lie in the nucleus and form a dark mass of threads called *chromatin*. During cell division, the chromosomes shorten and thicken and can be counted if their number is not too great.

The number of chromosomes in the cells of different living organisms varies, but in any one organism, the number is usually constant in every cell. For example, humans have 46 chromosomes in almost every cell, fruit flies have eight per cell, mice have 40 and dandelions have 24. The size of this number does not in any way indicate the advancement of the species; some wild grasses have 256 chromosomes per cell. (It's not the size of a book that matters; it's what's written in it).

In most cells, chromosomes are found to occur in pairs, i.e. each chromosome has a natural partner in the cell with identical length and similar information written on it in similar locations. These pairs of chromosomes are called *homologous pairs* and are due to the fact that each member of the pair has arisen from one of the two sex cells that formed the organism (i.e. each member of the pair was originally donated by either the male or the female parent). Having two of everything in the cell is a good design plan as, in general, there is a 'spare copy' of every piece of genetic information if anything goes wrong.

Humans have 46 chromosomes per cell, forming 23 homologous pairs. Homologous pairing is only visible at certain times during cell division.

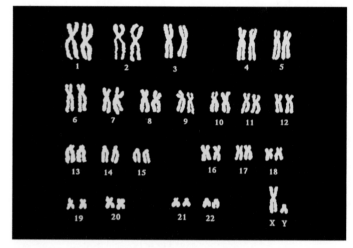

Fig. 11.3. Chromosomes of a human male.

[232]

A nucleus or cell in which homologous pairs of chromosomes are found is said to be in the *diploid* condition (written as *2n*). In humans, the diploid number is 46; that is to say, human diploid cells contain 46 chromosomes or

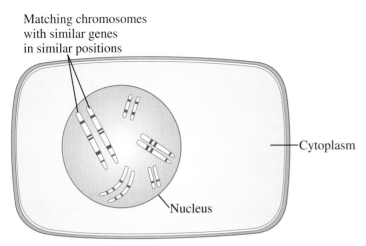

Fig. 11.4. Homologous pairs of chromosomes in a cell with ten chromosomes.

23 homologous pairs. The diploid condition occurs in almost every cell in the body. Human sex cells, however, are *haploid* (written as *n*) — they contain only one member of each pair of chromosomes and this reduces the chromosome number of the cell by half. Human sex cells contain only 23 chromosomes each — the human haploid number. When sex cells join in *fertilisation*, the diploid number is restored for the next generation.

Diploid (*2n*) — refers to nuclei or cells containing chromosomes in homologous pairs.

Haploid (*n*) — refers to nuclei or cells containing unpaired chromosomes.

Cells divide repeatedly by *mitosis* to produce new, identical cells. Mitosis does not change the cell chromosome number in the new cells. Mitosis generally takes place in diploid cells, but haploid mitosis is common.

Haploid cells are formed from diploid cells by a type of cell division called *meiosis*. Haploid cells never themselves divide by meiosis as this would lead to a further, useless division of the chromosome number.

The human life cycle is summarised in fig. 11.5.

THE CELL CYCLE   [233]

The complete life of a cell (the *cell cycle*) has five parts:

1. *Cell division* — By *mitosis* or *meiosis* depending on whether the chromosome number is to be unchanged or halved.

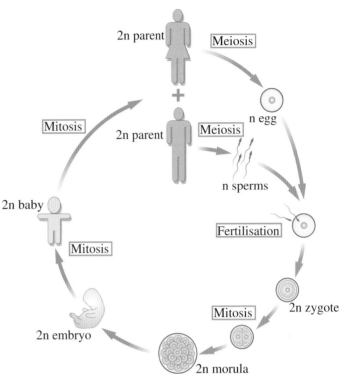

Fig. 11.5. Simple life cycle showing meiosis and fertilisation.

2. *Cytokinesis* (*or division of the cytoplasm*) — When the cell separates into daughter cells.
3. *Growth* — When new organelles are made and the cell carries out its various functions.
4. *Synthesis of new DNA** — When faithful copies of the cell DNA are made for further cell division.
5. *Further growth** — When the cell prepares for further cell division.

Stages 2–5 are often grouped together and termed *interphase* — the misnamed *resting phase* of cell life. Under the microscope, the cell appears inactive during this phase but it is, in fact, extremely busy.

Figure 11.6 summarises the cell cycle.

Cell division mechanisms — mitosis and meiosis

Two different types of cell division can be found within a cell cycle:

* Many cells never divide again after they have grown and do not enter into stages 4 and 5 above. Examples include skin and nerve cells, and guard cells from plant leaves. On the other hand, bone marrow cells never stop dividing and can complete their cell cycle every 8–10 hours.

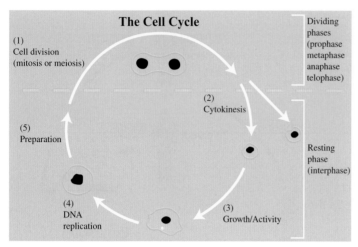

Fig. 11.6. Circular diagram of cell cycle.

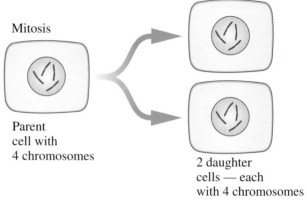

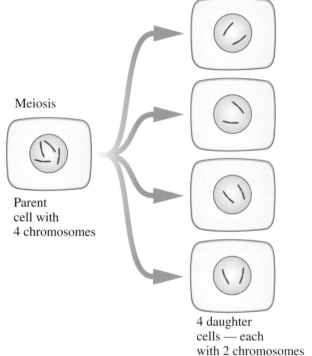

Fig. 11.7. Mitosis and meiosis.

MITOSIS

Mitosis produces *two daughter cells*, each with *the same number of chromosomes as the parent cell*. Mitosis is a *replication division* — it produces identical cells for growth and repair of the organism or for asexual reproduction. Single celled organisms, such as *Amoeba* or yeast, use mitosis exclusively for reproduction.

Mitosis is by far the more common method of cell division of all organisms and it conserves the chromosome number: diploid parent cells produce diploid daughter cells and haploid parent cells produce haploid daughter cells. *Mitosis always produces faithful copies of the parent cell DNA.*

In animals and humans, mitosis occurs throughout the body. In plants, mitosis is generally confined to specific growing regions (meristematic regions): stem buds, stem tips and root tips.

MEIOSIS

Meiosis produces *four daughter cells*, each with *half the number of chromosomes of the parent cell*. Meiosis is a *reduction division* — it halves the chromosome number, producing haploid cells from diploid cells. It is generally reserved for making sex cells and spores.

There is a convention in cell division that newly formed cells are referred to as *daughter cells* regardless of their origin or destiny. Even newly formed haploid cells in the testis are referred to as daughter cells.

Mitosis and cancer

WHAT IS CANCER?

Cancer occurs when cells lose their normal regulation over both their dividing rate and the number of divisions they undergo. Cancerous cells will continue to divide (by mitosis) to form more cells without control or order.

All organs of the body are made up of cells. Normally, cells divide to produce more cells only when the body needs them. If cells divide when new ones are not needed, they form a mass of excess tissue, called a *tumour*. Some tumour cells stay together and tend not to spread. These groups of

Air spaces

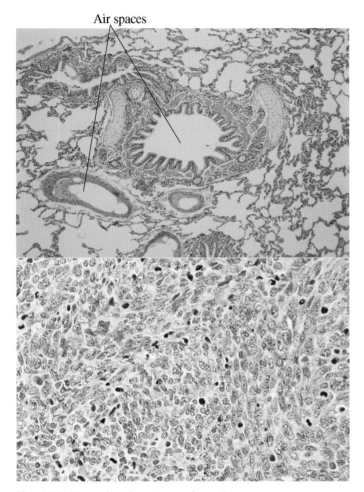

Fig. 11.8. Normal and cancerous lung tissue.

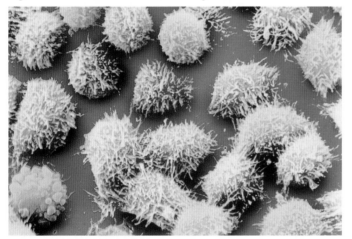

Fig. 11.9. Cancer cells.

cells are called *benign tumours*. Other tumour cells invade nearby organs or travel through the lymphatic system and bloodstream to new body sites. These groups of cells are called *malignant tumours* or *cancer*. Cancer cells can also break away from a malignant tumour and travel through the

body to form new tumours in other parts of the body. The spread of cancer is called *metastasis*.

WHAT ARE THE SIGNS AND SYMPTOMS OF CANCER?

Early diagnosis is extremely important in cancer treatment and cancer often produces symptoms that you can watch for. The word **CAUTION** can remind everyone of the most common warning signs of cancer:

- change in bowel or bladder habits;
- a sore that does not heal;
- unusual bleeding or discharge;
- thickening or a lump in the breast or any other part of the body;
- indigestion or difficulty in swallowing;
- obvious changes in a wart or mole;
- nagging cough or hoarseness.

These symptoms are not *always* warning signs of cancer. They are more likely to be caused by less serious conditions. However, it is important to see a doctor if you have any of these symptoms — only a doctor can make a diagnosis. Early cancer does not usually cause pain.

A biopsy is the only certain way to know whether a medical problem is cancer. In a biopsy, the doctor removes a tiny sample of tissue and examines it under a microscope to check for cancer cells.

HOW IS CANCER TREATED?

Cancer is treated with *surgery, radiation therapy, chemotherapy* (use of strong drugs), or *hormone therapy*. Doctors may use one method or a combination of methods. The choice of treatment depends on the type and location of the cancer, whether the disease has spread, the patient's age and general health, and other factors.

Many cancer patients take part in carefully planned clinical trials testing new treatment methods. These studies are designed to improve cancer treatment for everyone.

CAN CANCER BE PREVENTED?

The majority of cancers are prevented by not smoking, by avoiding the harmful rays of the sun, and choosing foods with less fat and more fibre. In addition, regular check-ups and self-examinations can reveal cancer at an early stage, when treatment is likely to be more effective.

WHAT IS THE MOST IMPORTANT ADVICE?

- Don't smoke cigarettes. If you do smoke, stop now. *This is the single most important thing you can do to protect yourself from cancer.* The Irish Cancer Society has information and programmes that can help you to give up smoking. Visit www.cancer.ie/education/schools.html for more information.

- Avoid too much sunlight; always wear protective clothing in strong sunlight and use sunscreen creams on your skin.

- Eat as much fruit and vegetables as you can every day. Fruit and vegetables will lower your risk for some kinds of cancer.

- All women should learn to examine their breasts for lumps. In addition, all women should have a *mammogram* (an X-ray examination of the breast tissue) every three years. Breast cancer is the most common form of cancer in women.

- All women should have a *cervical smear test* done every three years from the time they begin to have intercourse. A smear test (also called a Pap test after the doctor that originated it) is designed to check for cancer of the cervix. Cancer of the cervix is the second most common cancer in women.

- Prostate cancer is the most common cancer in men, especially older men. A doctor will discuss early detection tests and their benefits and drawbacks.

- All men should learn to examine their testes for lumps.

- Avoid unnecessary X-rays and harmful chemicals.

For more information about cancer, contact the Irish Cancer Society at www.irishcancer.ie/ or at The Irish Cancer Society, 5 Northumberland Road, Dublin 4. Telephone: 01 668 1855, Freephone 1800 200 700.

SUMMARY OF MITOSIS   [234]

1. The cell enters mitosis from interphase where it has been copying its DNA and preparing itself for division.
2. The chromosomes coil up on themselves to prevent breaking. This has the additional advantage to scientists that they can now be seen with a microscope and count-

ed. The nuclear membrane begins to dissolve to allow chromosome movements.

3. Each chromosome reveals an identical copy of itself.
4. Fibres form within the cell and the chromosomes, with their identical copies, attach to these. The fibres contract and pull the chromosomes and identical copies apart. This produces two groups of identical genetic material within the cell.
5. Nuclear membranes form around each group of chromosomes. The chromosomes start to uncoil and become less distinct.

(See [H231] below for more details.)

Cytokinesis will now divide the cytoplasm to form two new, identical daughter cells each with the same number of chromosomes as the parent cell. As the cytoplasm divides, organelles and biomolecules are partitioned into the two new cells.

[235]

N.B. The primary function of mitosis in multicelled organisms is to make new, identical cells for growth, development and repair. The new cells will contain a *faithful* copy of the genetic instructions contained in the pre-existing cells.

In single-celled organisms, mitosis is used as a method of asexual reproduction: the parent organism divides by mitosis to form two 'daughter' organisms.

[236]

Meiosis

Meiosis — produces *four daughter cells*, each with *half the number of chromosomes of the parent cell*. Meiosis is a *reduction division* — it halves the chromosome number, producing haploid cells from diploid cells. It is generally reserved for making sex cells and spores.

[237]

The significance of meiosis

- It maintains the original, parental chromosome number within the population, as haploid cells can unite in fertilisation to restore the original diploid number. Other-

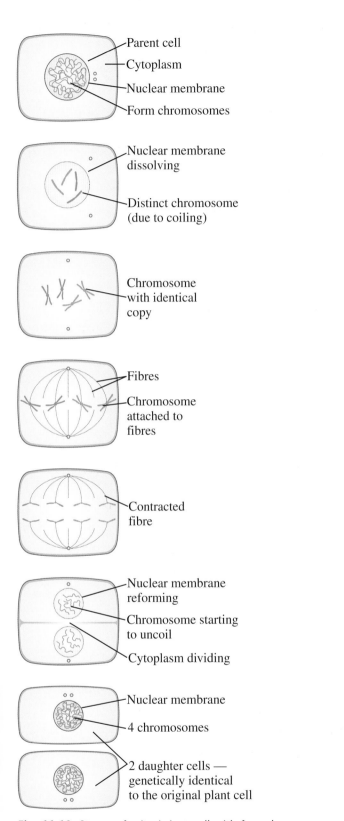

Parent cell
Cytoplasm
Nuclear membrane
Form chromosomes

Nuclear membrane dissolving

Distinct chromosome (due to coiling)

Chromosome with identical copy

Fibres
Chromosome attached to fibres

Contracted fibre

Nuclear membrane reforming
Chromosome starting to uncoil
Cytoplasm dividing

Nuclear membrane
4 chromosomes

2 daughter cells — genetically identical to the original plant cell

Fig. 11.10. Stages of mitosis in a cell with four chromosomes.

wise, a doubling of the chromosome number would take place with each generation. In this regard, meiosis and fertilisation are complementary processes.

■ It introduces genetic variation into any population as it rearranges the combinations of genes of the parents.

DETAILED STUDY OF THE STAGES OF MITOSIS [H231]

The process of mitosis is a continuous one but is divided into four stages or *phases* for convenience of study. Cells always enter mitosis from *interphase*.

Interphase is the longest phase in the cell cycle. It is a non-dividing stage and is not part of mitosis. During interphase, the cell appears inactive but it is busy using its genetic information to direct and carry out all its biochemical functions. It also makes accurate copies (replicas) of its DNA in preparation for cell division. The chromosomes are usually invisible and the nuclear membranes and nucleoli are intact.

The four phases of mitosis are:

1. *Prophase*: The chromosomes become visible due to coiling and condensing on themselves. Each chromosome has already replicated itself and the replicas (or *chromatids*) are joined to each other at a centromere. The nucleoli disappear, the nuclear membrane starts to dissolve and (in animal cells only) centrioles form from the centrosome and migrate to opposite poles of the cell.

2. *Metaphase*: In all cells, a series of microtubules of protein (the spindle) appears from the cell poles. The centromeres of the chromosomes attach to the flat plane of the spindle equator.

3. *Anaphase*: This is the shortest and most dramatic phase. The spindle microtubules contract and pull the sister chromatids apart. The chromatids are dragged to the opposite poles of the cell.

4. *Telophase*: The chromatids (now called chromosomes) are at opposite poles of the cell and start to uncoil and disappear. A nuclear membrane forms around each group and nucleoli reappear.

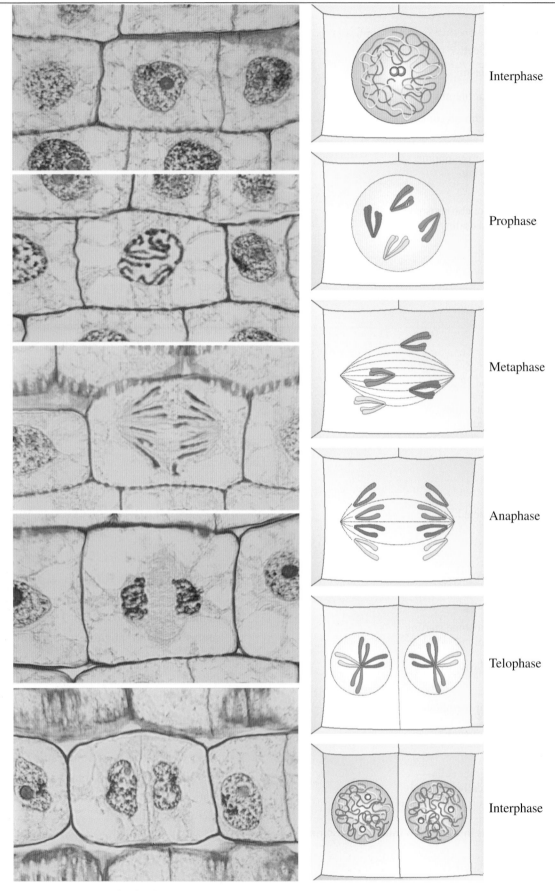

Fig. 11.11. Stages of mitosis.

Interphase

Prophase

Metaphase

Anaphase

Telophase

Interphase

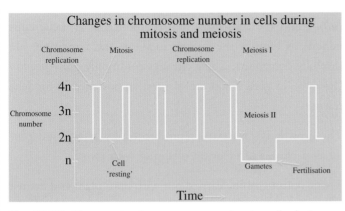

Fig. 11.12. Changes in chromosome number in cells during an animal life cycle.

After mitosis has finished, the process of *cytokinesis* will divide the cell cytoplasm to form two daughter cells. In plant cells, a line of vesicles or bubbles appears and forms cell membranes and a new cell wall (the cell plate). In animal cells, a ring of microfilaments constricts the equator of the cell forming the two new cells.

CELL DIVERSITY   [240]

Tissues, organs and systems

Most familiar living organisms are multicellular — they have thousands of cells working together to maintain the organism and to meet its needs in life. These cells are not all identical — they *diversify* their structure early on in their lives to suit the functions that lie ahead of them. Nerve cells are long and thin and electrically irritable, muscle cells can contract, skin cells are waterproof and so on.

Also, these thousands of cells are not scattered at random through the body of the organism, they are arranged into groups of cells that form *tissues* and *organs*. This increases the efficiency of the organism enormously.

(If blocks of *Lego* represented cells, a three-year-old child might attempt to make a lego animal by randomly joining all the blocks together. An older child knows that a better result is obtained by grouping the blocks according to an overall plan).

A tissue is a group of cells of similar structure that performs a specific function.

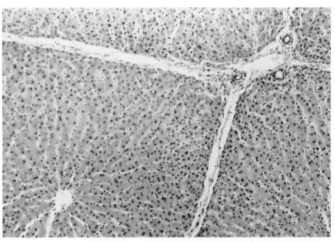

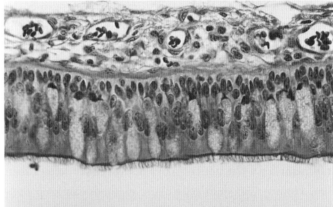

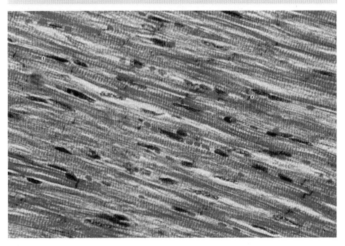

Fig. 11.13. Human and other tissues: liver, epithelium and cardiac muscle.

Examples of animal tissue are *skin tissue* found in layers for protection, *muscle tissue* for movement, a *drop of blood* for transport. Plant examples include *epidermis tissue* for protection, *xylem tissue* for transporting water upwards and *parenchyma* for storing starch in potatoes. In each of these examples, the cells within the tissue are similar and there is an *overall, intended function*.

An organ is a collection of tissues. It has a clear, overall structure and performs one or more functions.

For example, the *kidney* in mammals contains various tissues: blood, smooth muscle, connective tissue, etc. and performs the functions of excretion and osmoregulation. Clearly this allows great complexity and efficiency in the design of the animal. Other examples of organs are: the *liver*, the *skin*, the *eye*, the *ear* in animals, and, in plants, the *leaf* and the *flower*.

In most animals, organs work together in *organ systems*, e.g. the *digestive system* includes the stomach, the intestine, the liver, the pancreas, etc. The *circulatory system* includes the heart, the arteries, the veins, the blood, etc.

Organ systems are not well developed in plants.

Tissue culture

Organs removed from the human body can be kept alive for transplant for a few hours — but not for much longer than that. However, modern cell-culture methods can keep *individual cells* alive almost indefinitely. This is called *tissue*

culture and the cells grow and reproduce in artificial containers, as long as the culture medium and conditions are carefully controlled. These cultures commonly grow *in vitro* (literally 'in glass') and are of great importance in modern science.

The growth is an asexual reproduction by *mitosis* and produces a cluster of identical offspring — a *clone*.

Tissue culture can be carried out with both plant and animal cells.

In plants, cells cut from the parent plant become *meristematic* — they divide repeatedly on the culture medium and entire plants may grow from single cells. Often cells without cell walls are formed — called *protoplasts* — which are easier to work with when making genetic changes.

In animals and humans, the tissue culture technique is usually as follows:

- *Primary cells* are removed from a suitable source — the heart or liver.
- Enzymes are used to separate these into *individual cells*.
- The cells are placed in a *culture medium* that is precisely

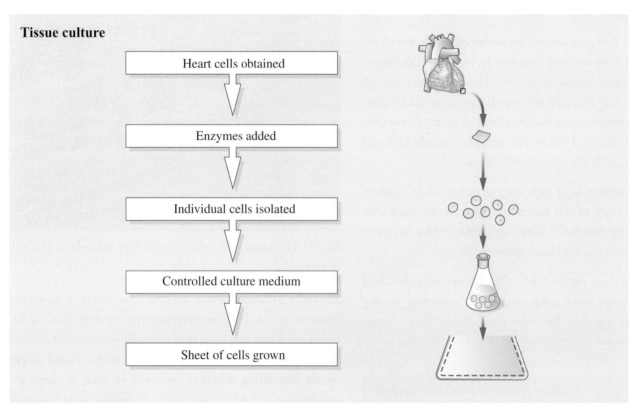

Tissue culture

Heart cells obtained

↓

Enzymes added

↓

Individual cells isolated

↓

Controlled culture medium

↓

Sheet of cells grown

Fig. 11.14. Steps in tissue culture.

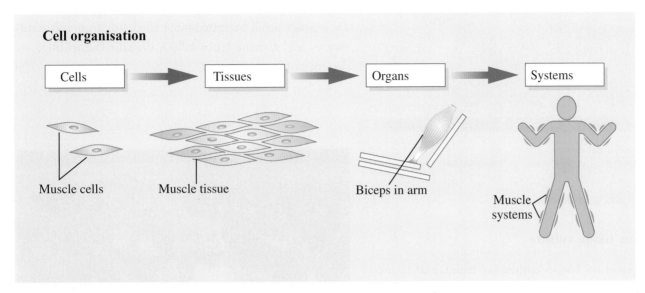

Fig. 11.15. Cell organisation.

controlled. All conditions including temperature, pH and nutrients must be exactly right. Conditions must be sterile.

- The cells become *undifferentiated* — they lose their characteristics and usually their ability to make enzymes and hormones.

- The cells *continue to grow* into clones but must have contact with the surface of the container. This means that only monolayers (sheets of cells) are first grown. However, the monolayers can be 'trained' to grow on synthetic frameworks and produce more complicated structures.

In general, embryonic animal and human cells produce the best results in tissue culturing as they have much greater powers of regeneration. Plant cells grow as lumpy *calluses* and are not restricted to growing in sheets.

Uses of animal/human tissue culture

Tissue and organ regeneration. Replacement human earflaps have been formed from 'seeding' a plastic framework with cartilage cells and growing them in conditions rich in oxygen and nutrients. A human foreskin, taken from a newborn baby, can grow enough skin cells to cover six football pitches. Sheets of skin cells are used to treat burn patients. Cultured neural stem cells can be used to repair tears and gaps within nerves.

Cancer research. Known carcinogens (cancer generators) are added to cultures for study.

Oncogenes (cancer-causing genes) can be added to the tissue DNA to study their effects.

Virus cultivation. Viruses can only live in living cells and cannot be kept anywhere else. *HeLa cells** are commonly used to incubate and 'grow' viruses.

Metabolism experiments are conducted on enzyme pathways within tissues

Drug testing is carried out more accurately and more safely on tissues rather than on an entire organism.

Monoclonal antibodies (MCAs) are extracted from cultured lymphocytes. These antibodies are used in pregnancy testing kits, in 'magic bullet' cancer treatments, in diagnosing infectious diseases and in making vaccines.

---

* **HeLa cells**: On 1 February 1951, a woman, Henrietta Lacks, entered a hospital in Baltimore with a kidney tumour. Henrietta Lacks died from her illness but a sample of her kidney tissue continued to grow in the hospital laboratory. The reasons for this are still not clear. Doctors found that her kidney cells had reverted to a more primitive form and would grow indefinitely on sheets of glass given the right conditions of nutrients, moisture, oxygen and temperature. Since then, her cells have been distributed to almost every hospital and virus laboratory in the world and are used to store viruses. Henrietta Lacks' cells (named *HeLa cells*) are still growing and are used for virus culturing throughout the medical community.

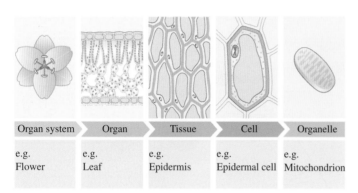

Organ system	Organ	Tissue	Cell	Organelle
e.g. Flower	e.g. Leaf	e.g. Epidermis	e.g. Epidermal cell	e.g. Mitochondrion

Fig. 11.16. Organs to organelles.

Uses of plant tissue culture

Micro-propagation — Tissue samples are maintained to preserve samples of rare plants.

Disease-free plants, e.g. King Edward potatoes, are grown from uncontaminated tissue cultures.

New hybrids, e.g. tomato/potato plants have been formed from mixing tissue samples and are under testing at the moment.

Drought-resistant and *herbicide-resistant* varieties are formed and tested.

Plant drugs are all harvested more efficiently from tissue culture — e.g. codeine (pain killer), digitalis (heart drug), or spearmint (for flavouring).

Fig. 11.18. Tobacco plants.

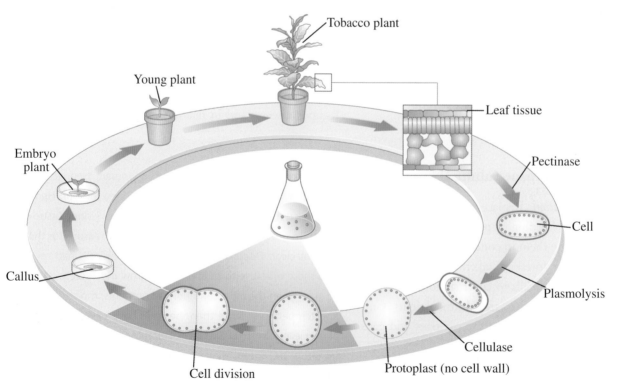

Fig. 11.17. Tissue culture flow chart.

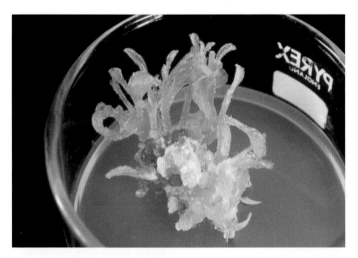

Fig. 11.19. Plant cells in cell culture.

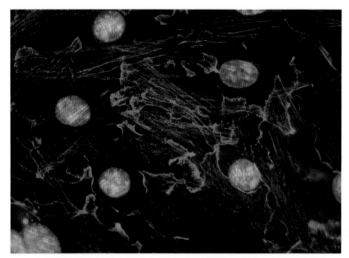

Fig. 11.21. Fibroblast cells in culture. Nuclei have nucleolar 'necklaces'.

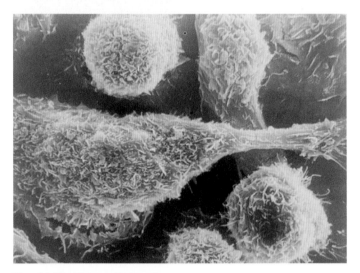

Fig. 11.20. HeLa cells in culture.

SUMMARY

- *The continuity of life* depends on cell reproduction.
- *Diploid* (*2n*) refers to nuclei or cells containing chromosomes in homologous pairs.
- *Haploid* (*n*) refers to nuclei or cells containing un-paired chromosomes.
- *The complete life of a cell* (the cell cycle) has five parts:

  - cell division — by mitosis or meiosis;
  - cytokinesis or division of the cytoplasm;
  - growth — when new organelles are made and the cell carries out its various functions;
  - synthesis of new DNA — when faithful copies of the cell DNA are made for further cell division;

  - further growth — when the cell prepares for further cell division.

- *Mitosis* — produces two daughter cells, each with the same number of chromosomes as the parent cell.
- *Meiosis* — produces four daughter cells, each with half the number of chromosomes of the parent cell.
- *Newly formed cells* are referred to as daughter cells.
- *Cancerous cells* will continue to divide by mitosis to form more cells without control or order.
- *Cells enter mitosis* from interphase.
- *Mitosis in a cell takes place as follows:*

  - the chromosomes coil up on themselves to prevent breaking;
  - the nuclear membrane begins to dissolve to allow chromosome movements;
  - each chromosome 'reveals' an identical copy of itself;
  - fibres form within the cell and the chromosomes, with their identical copies, attach to these;
  - the fibres contract and pull the chromosomes and identical copies apart;
  - nuclear membranes form around each group of chromosomes;
  - the chromosomes start to uncoil and become less distinct.

- *The significance of mitosis:*

  - it produces identical cells for growth, repair and development;
  - it is used by unicellular organisms for reproduction.

- *The significance of meiosis:*

  - it produces haploid cells, which can unite in fertilisation and restore the original diploid number;
  - it introduces genetic variation into any population.

- *A tissue* is a group of cells of similar structure that performs a specific function.
- *An organ* is a collection of tissues with a clear, overall structure and performs one or more functions.
- *In most animals*, organs work together in organ systems.
- *Tissue culture* is when cells are grown and reproduced in artificial conditions.
- *The stages of animal tissue culture are:*

  - primary cells are removed from a suitable source;
  - enzymes are used to separate these into individual cells;
  - the cells are placed in a sterile culture medium that is precisely controlled;
  - the cells become undifferentiated, losing their characteristics;
  - the cells generally grow as monolayers or sheets;
  - plant cells, however, form calluses and are not restricted to growing in sheets.

EXTENDED SUMMARY

- Mitosis is a continuous process but is arbitrarily divided into four phases: prophase; *metaphase; anaphase; and telophase.*

KEY WORDS

Chromosomes	Threads of DNA wrapped in protein.

Homologous pairs	Pairs of chromosomes with identical length and similar information in similar locations.
Diploid (2n)	Refers to nuclei or cells containing chromosomes in homologous pairs.
Haploid (n)	Refers to nuclei or cells containing unpaired chromosomes.
Cell cycle	The complete life of a cell.
Cytokinesis	Division of the cell cytoplasm.
Interphase	The resting phase of the cell cycle.
Mitosis	A cell division that produces two daughter cells, each with the same number of chromosomes as the parent cell.
Meiosis	A cell division that produces four daughter cells, each with half the number of chromosomes of the parent cell.
Benign	Not cancerous.
Malignant	Cancerous.
Metastasis	The spread of cancer from its primary location.
Tissue	A group of cells of similar structure that performs a specific function.
Organ	A collection of tissues with a clear, overall structure and function.

QUESTIONS

1. List the stages of the cell cycle. What is meant by *interphase*? Why is it misleading to describe interphase as a resting phase?
2. What is meant by *cytokinesis*? In what way is cytokinesis different in plant and animal cells?
3. Distinguish between the following pairs of words:

a. mitosis and meiosis;

b. haploid and diploid;

c. chromatin and chromosome;

d. replication and reduction.

4. If human sex cells contained 46 chromosomes each rather than 23, what would happen to the chromosome number of human cells after one generation? After two generations? After three? After one million years of reproduction?

5. Decide whether the following statements apply to mitosis, meiosis or both processes:

a. produces identical cells;

b. may occur in haploid or diploid cells;

c. chromosome number is reduced;

d. only occurs in diploid cells;

e. used for asexual reproduction;

f. increases variety in the population;

g. used for growth;

h. takes place after interphase.

6. Prepare a simple chart to compare mitosis and meiosis. Both similarities and differences are allowed in your comparison.

7. Decide whether the following statements are true or false:

a. diploid cells can divide by mitosis;

b. diploid cells can divide by meiosis;

c. haploid cells can divide by mitosis;

d. haploid cells can divide by meiosis;

e. diploid cells always have even numbers of chromosomes;

f. haploid cells always have odd numbers of chromosomes.

8. What is cancer and how can it affect the body? Give one similarity and one difference between cancer cells and normal body cells. What are the signs of cancer in the body? List five ways in which you can protect yourself against cancer.

9. Draw simple, labelled diagrams to show the behaviour of chromosomes during mitosis.

10. Reorder the following words: tissues, systems, cells, organs.
    Explain the reason for the new ordering.

11. What is tissue culture? What are the steps that are taken in culturing animal cells?

12. What uses can be made of animal tissue cultures?

13. What are HeLa cells and why are they of use in hospital laboratories?

EXTENDED QUESTIONS

14. Name the four phases of mitosis and draw simple, labelled diagrams to represent each one.

15. What is the major feature of each of the four phases of mitosis?

OPTIONAL ACTIVITIES

■ Write down a short message on a piece of paper and then whisper it quickly to the person beside you. Ask them to whisper it to the next person and so on around the classroom. Ask the last person to hear the message to write it down. Compare this to the original. Why is it necessary that mitosis copies the genetic information in a cell faithfully and without the slightest mistake?

■ Use pipe cleaners and string to make two-dimensional models of the stages of mitosis. Different class groups should take on different stages.

■ Make a *flick-book* to animate mitosis.

■ Plan and launch a cancer prevention/awareness week within your school.

■ Draw diagrams of the different stages of mitosis onto squares of cardboard. Shuffle the cards and ask a partner to reorder them.

■ Prepare unlabelled diagrams of the stages of mitosis, photocopy them and practice labelling them from memory.

■ Examine prepared microscope slides of mitosis.

■ Remove the organs from a plastic human model and practice identifying and replacing them.

- Photocopy a blank outline of the human body and practice drawing different organ systems in their correct location.
- Research a particular organ system and present a summary of your findings to the class.
- View the *Self Repair* episode of the BBC's *Superhuman* series presented by Professor Lord Winston.
- Use the internet to research the life, death and contribution of Henrietta Lacks to Biology.
- It is possible to clone cauliflower tissue using the following technique, if conditions are kept sterile at all times:

  - Cut a tiny portion (5mm) from the white part of a fresh cauliflower.
  - Divide the portion into three parts using a scalpel.
  - Soak the tissue pieces in dilute Domestos solution for about ten minutes.

  - Use a sterile tweezers to rinse each piece in sterile distilled water. Four or five rinses are necessary.
  - Soak the samples in three changes of sterile water at least.
  - Add the samples to test tubes of sterile plant tissue growth medium observing aseptic technique at all times.
  - Cover and incubate at room temperature for a few weeks.

For information on websites dealing with topics covered in this chapter see www.my-etest.com.

Now test yourself at
www.my-etest.com

Chapter 12
Genetics and DNA

Learning objectives

After your study of this chapter, you should be able to:

- define a species;
- distinguish between acquired and inherited variation;
- consider genes as specific portions of DNA;
- relate gene structure to enzyme production;
- outline the structure of DNA and compare it to RNA;
- outline the process of replication and its importance;
- describe the technique of genetic profiling and its applications;
- list the steps involved in protein synthesis;
- consider the cell as similar to a factory.

Extended learning objectives

- Explain the importance of base pairing in DNA.
- Describe, in detail, the processes of transcription and translation.
- Read, transcribe and translate the triplet code within DNA.

Mandatory activity

#17 Separating DNA from a plant tissue extract.

VARIATION OF SPECIES   [251]

A species describes any group of organisms that resemble one another and have the ability to reproduce with one another. Examples include cats, frogs, woodlice, geraniums, dandelions and humans.

The number of species that have been named and recorded in biology so far illustrates the *diversity of living organisms*. Estimates vary but there are probably between three million and 30 million different species identified at present — half of which are terrestrial insects! Given such huge numbers, an orderly system of classification is necessary for their study. This system is outlined in Chapter 16.

Species never reproduce outside their group. Cats, dogs, greenfly, oak trees and humans can only reproduce with their own kind. The range of species indicates a huge *genetic diversity* on the Earth, with the genetic differences between species being such that crossbreeding is impossible. Further diversity is found within species: although all species members are obviously very similar, there is plenty of room for uniqueness and individuality within the group. This is particularly obvious within the human species.

A *population* refers to a group of the same species within a geographical area, e.g. the humans living in Kilkenny or the ladybirds within a garden.

The term *variation* refers to the differences between the members of a population.

Any two members of a population will resemble each other, but no two members will ever be exactly the same. This is particularly obvious in a population of humans. Variations between two individuals of the same species may be *acquired* or *inherited*.

Acquired variations are 'picked up' during the life of the organism and are *not* passed on to the next generation.

Fig. 12.1. Mother cat and kittens.

Examples of acquired variations in humans include suntans, a broken arm, a shaved head or the ability to ride a bicycle. Information about these events is not 'written into' the sex cells and these features are not expected to appear automatically in any future children.

Inherited variations are a result of what is 'written' into the chromosomes of the organism. Chromosomes are the threads of DNA in the nucleus of every cell that direct all cell activity. Examples of human inherited variations include eye colour, tallness, dimples, skin type and hair type. These features develop as a result of instructions in the genetic code of the cells and they are passed to the next generation through the chromosomes of the sex cells.

(Some population variations are not easily classified as acquired or inherited. One example of this is the variation found in human intelligence. A controlled study of this '*nature versus nurture*' debate requires many sets of identical twins that have been separated at birth. These would have grown up with identical genetic influences but different environments. These studies are very difficult to carry out given the time involved and the difficulty in finding a large enough supply of such twins. Intelligence does, however, appear to have both genetic and environmental components.)

Fig. 12.2. Cloned sheep.

Variation is of great advantage to populations. Variety improves the members' chances of adapting to environmental change. If all the population members were too similar, they would not have the variety to respond to some sudden changes such as the appearance of diseases, parasites or new predators. Populations with a high degree of variation can adapt and evolve to cope with changing conditions. Populations where all members are genetically identical are termed *clones*. Such populations are not capable of much adaptation or evolution and tend to be short-lived.

GENETICS, HEREDITY AND EXPRESSION   [252]

Genetics is the study of the mechanism of inheritance.

All cells arise from pre-existing cells and they obtain their instructions from these 'parents'. On a larger scale, all living organisms obtain their instructions from their parent organisms — usually through the contents of the parents' sex cells. The parental DNA contains all the information that is necessary to form the new organism from food and oxygen.

Heredity refers to all materials and information passed from one generation to the next or to later generations. Almost all hereditary information is passed to new generations by way of DNA molecules in sex cells. The possession of genetic material or information is no guarantee that the information will be used in any way.

Expression refers to when hereditary information is *activated* or 'switched on'. Dark (or blond) hair, tongue-rolling and pale skin are all expressions of underlying genetic instructions.

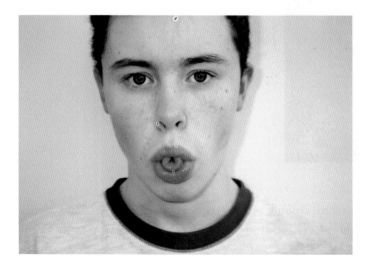

Fig. 12.3. Tongue-rolling.

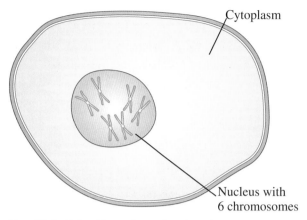

Fig. 12.4. Cell with nucleus, showing chromosomes.

Tongue-rolling in humans is an example of inherited variation within a group. Tongue-rollers express their inherited genetic information by controlling the muscles of their tongues to form a U-shape. Identify the tongue-rollers within your class group. Can non-rollers learn to roll their tongues?

DNA AND THE GENETIC CODE   [253]

The nucleus of a cell contains threadlike structures called *chromosomes*. When cells are not dividing, the chromosomes form an indistinct mass of threads called *chromatin*. If cells are preparing to divide, the individual chromosome threads shorten and thicken and are more easily seen.

Each chromosome is a length of DNA wrapped in protein. About two-thirds of any chromosome is protein and one-

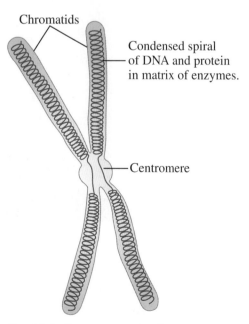

Fig. 12.5. Chromosome detail.

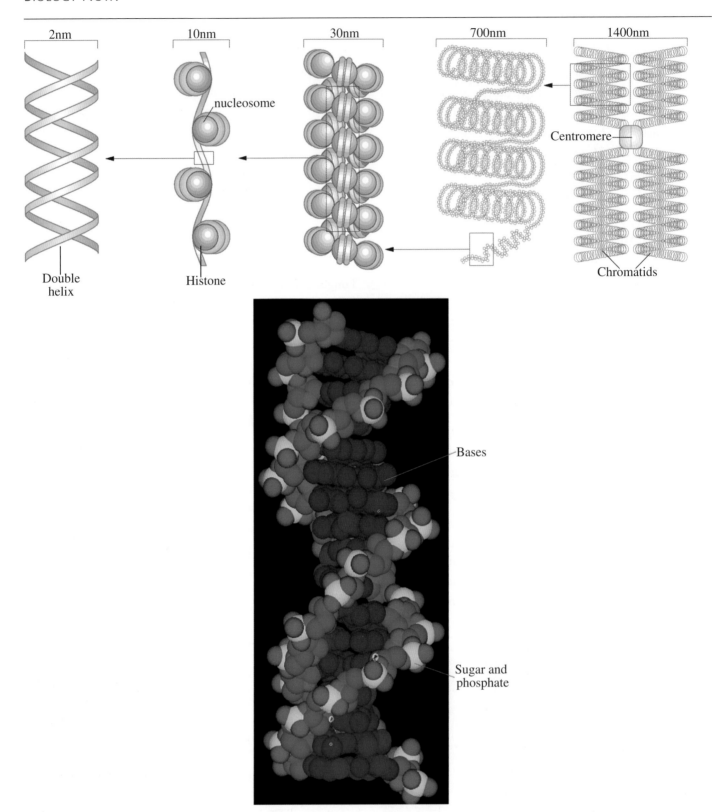

Fig. 12.6. Packing of the DNA molecule.

third is DNA. Some of this protein forms a support for the DNA, the rest is mainly enzymes. The DNA molecule is wrapped around beads of protein (called *histones*) to form units called *nucleosomes*. These nucleosomes are then tightly packed around a protein backbone forming a long, dense thread. The thread is further coiled to form the chromosome.

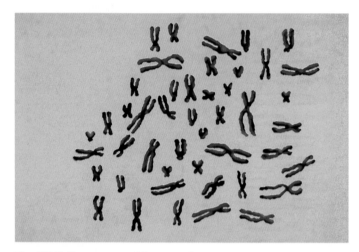

Fig. 12.7. Karyogram of human chromosomes.

Although chromosomes are microscopic, this repeated coiling ensures they contain enormous lengths of DNA. The average human chromosome contains 4 cm of DNA. There are almost 2 metres of DNA in total in any single human cell.

When cells are not dividing, every chromosome consists of two identical strands or *chromatids*, joined at a *centromere*.

All human cells (except sex cells) contain 46 chromosomes capable of forming 23 chromosome pairs. Other organisms have different chromosome numbers.

Table 12.1. Chromosome number in diploid cells of animals and plants

Humans	46	Alligators	32
Apes	48	Carp	104
Cows	60	Jellyfish	20
Horses	64	Earthworms	32
Pigs	38	Fruit flies	8
Sheep	54	Snails	54
Rabbits	44	Frogs	26
Hedgehogs	48	Wheat	42
Mice	40	Barley	14
Bats	44	Sunflowers	34
Chickens	78	Mushrooms	8
Blackbirds	80	Ferns	104

A *gene* is a hereditary unit on a chromosome. It is a portion of a chromosome that controls the development of a particular characteristic, e.g. humans have genes for colour vision, for nose shape, for hair pigment and for haemoglobin formation. A gene is a specific region of the DNA in a chromosome that contains the instructions for developing these characteristics. The position of a gene on its chromosome is called the *locus* of the gene.

Genes work by directing the production of specific enzymes in cells. These enzymes then have an effect on the cell's metabolism. Normal colour vision in humans is the result of an enzyme acting on the development of colour-sensitive pigments in the cells in the retina of the eye. This enzyme is made precisely by the retinal cells — following the instructions of the gene for colour vision. If this gene is damaged or faulty, the correct enzyme is not made and the colour vision cells fail to produce the correct amounts of pigment. This condition is termed *colour deficiency* or 'colour blindness'.

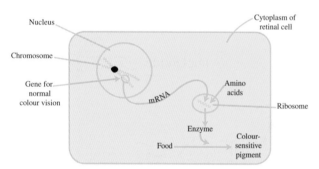

Fig. 12.8. Gene directing enzyme production.

DNA   [254]

During the twentieth century, as scientists worked to identify which part of the cell contained the genetic material, they knew in advance that any genetic chemical would have to have certain properties:

- it would have to be able to *store* vast amounts of information;
- it would have to be able to *replicate* itself — to make faithful copies of itself to pass on to new cells;
- it would have to be chemically *stable*. Random changes in the chemical could have enormous effects on the cell and the organism (yet *some* changes would have to be possible to produce variation within the population).

Many different chemicals are found in cells, some with very complicated structures, but the *nucleic acids* of cells are the only biomolecules that can store *information*. They have a structure that makes it possible for them to carry a *genetic code*. This code can represent all the information needed for the organism to develop and function correctly. Two types of nucleic acid are found within cells: DNA and RNA.

STRUCTURE OF DNA

DNA **d**eoxyribo**n**ucleic **a**cid) is a very long molecule made from very simple chemicals. It consists of two chains of repeating units, or *nucleotides*, wrapped around each other in a double spiral, similar to a very long, twisted ladder. This double spiral is termed a *double helix*. Each nucleotide consists of a five-carbon *sugar* known as *deoxyribose*, a *phosphate* unit and one of four *bases* — adenine, thymine, guanine and cytosine (or A, T, G and C).

Nucleotides link together to form long chains. Alternating sugars and phosphates form the backbone of the chain. Two

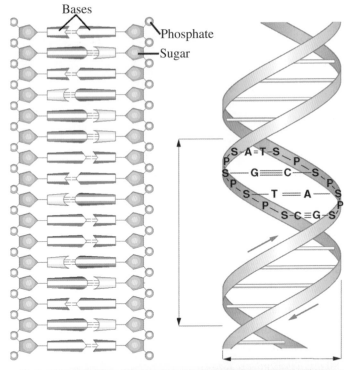

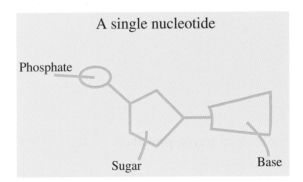

Fig. 12.9. Single nucleotide.

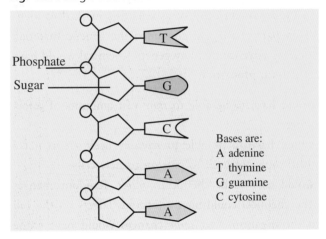

Bases are:
A adenine
T thymine
G guamine
C cytosine

Fig. 12.10. A chain of nucleotides.

Fig. 12.11. Molecule of DNA strands.

such chains are wrapped around each other to form the double helix. Sugars and phosphates form the two parallel sides of the ladder and the bases of the nucleotides join in pairs to form the rungs of the ladder.

The ladder takes a complete turn every ten rungs. The *base pairing* follows strict rules: *adenine always pairs with thymine* and *guanine always pairs with cytosine*. Any other pairing would mean that the rungs of the ladder would not all be of the same length. The two nucleotide chains run in opposite directions — they are *antiparallel*. Hydrogen bonds join the base pairs and hold the two chains or *strands* of DNA together.

Mandatory activity #17: To extract DNA from plant tissue

RESOURCES NEEDED

25 g sodium chloride.

80 ml washing-up liquid.

Kiwi fruit (or onion cells).

Coarse filter paper, e.g. coffee filter paper.

Protease enzyme (optional).

Ice cubes.

Water bath.

Thermometer.

Methylated spirits, ethanol or isopropanol.

In this experiment, DNA is isolated from the rest of the cell contents by taking advantage of its different physical and chemical properties.

Kiwi fruit cells are mashed to break up their cell walls. A salt/detergent mixture is used to break up the fatty cell membranes and the mixture is heated to inactivate enzymes and remove membrane portions. DNA is soluble in water and passes through a filter. Protease removes final traces of enzymes. DNA is insoluble in cold organic solvent and appears out of solution. All stages should be performed gently as the DNA strands break easily. The entire procedure may take up to one hour.

N.B. The organic solvents are highly flammable and no naked flames are allowed.

N.B. AT NO STAGE should anyone attempt to eat the kiwi fruit!

PROCEDURE

- Add 25 g sodium chloride to about 80 ml of washing-up liquid. Add water to make up the volume to 1 litre.
- Stir the solution gently to dissolve the salt, but do not allow the mixture to foam excessively.
- Peel, chop and mash a kiwi fruit (or onion) and place in a 250 ml beaker.
- Add 100 ml of the salt/detergent mixture and mix well but gently.
- Heat the mixture in a water bath at 60°C for 15 minutes.
- Cool the mixture and filter it through coffee filter paper.
- Collect about 5 ml of filtrate in a test tube and add a few drops of protease solution.
- Pour ice-cold methylated spirits gently down the side of the test tube to form a 1 cm layer on the surface.
- Use a wire loop to lift white strands of DNA from between the layers of water and organic solvent.

[H25V]

As all DNA molecules have the same backbones of sugar and phosphate, the genetic code must lie within the sequence of bases within the helix. The sugar/phosphate parts are *non-coding* structures, the *base sequence* is the *coding structure* of the molecule. Also, as adenine always pairs with thymine and guanine with cytosine, each strand of DNA is a 'mirror image' of the opposite strand.

Fig. 12.12. Watson and Crick at Cambridge in 1953.

This structure of DNA was first proposed by James Watson and Francis Crick, working in Cambridge in 1953. They based their model on information gathered by Rosalind Franklin and Maurice Wilkins, who calculated the spacings between the DNA parts by X-ray crystallography. (X-rays are fired at the DNA and their pattern of scattering after they hit the molecule is photographed and analysed.)

Watson and Crick saw immediately that their model contained a built-in method of perfect replication. Each strand could act as a mould or *template* for the opposing strand if the helix unwound itself. Their model satisfied all the requirements: it could contain infinite amounts of code, it was stable and it could replicate itself.

Adenine and guanine have double-ringed molecular structures and are called *purine bases*. Thymine and cytosine have single-ringed structures and are called *pyrimidine bases*. The number of purines always equals the number of pyrimidines in any DNA molecule — evidence that led to the discovery of the rule of *base pairing*. Adenine always joins to thymine with two hydrogen bonds. Guanine always joins to cytosine with three hydrogen bonds. Watson and Crick knew that the molecular length of an A–T pair was identical to that of a G–C pair and saw that this would produce rungs of equal length in the DNA ladder.

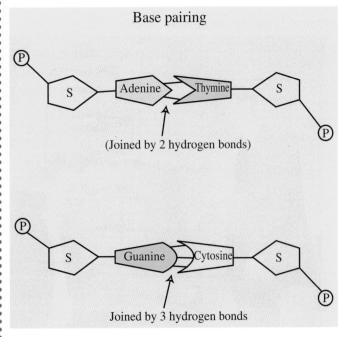

Base pairing

(Joined by 2 hydrogen bonds)

Joined by 3 hydrogen bonds

Fig. 12.13. AT and GC couples.

Watson, Crick and Wilkins received the Nobel Prize for their work in 1962; Rosalind Franklin had died in 1958 at the age of 37 and was not awarded for her contribution. The discovery of the structure of DNA was possibly the biggest scientific breakthrough of the twentieth century.

STRUCTURE OF RNA

RNA (**ri**bo**n**ucleic **a**cid) is found both in the nucleus and in the cytoplasm of cells. It has a similar structure to DNA but with the following differences:

- it is a *single strand* of nucleotides — forming a single helix, which resembles one half of a twisted ladder;
- it is a much *shorter* molecule, consisting of about 1,500 nucleotides;
- the sugar is *ribose*;
- thymine is replaced by *uracil*.

The functions of RNA within the cell are discussed later.

REPLICATION OF DNA

Replication means exact copying with no mistakes. When cells divide, copies of the 'parental' DNA must be made for the new 'daughter' cells. The genetic code is complicated and very precious to cells and an exact copying mechanism is required to rule out any mistakes. Any mistakes in copying would quickly multiply through the organism with each cell generation — with disastrous results.

Watson and Crick saw that their DNA model suggested a foolproof copying mechanism. As a result of the base pairing rule, (A–T and C–G), each strand of DNA can act as a template for the making of a complementary strand.

Steps in DNA replication:

1. The DNA strand is 'unzipped' by an enzyme, *DNA helicase*. This unzipping or opening takes place at hundreds of different positions on the DNA molecule at the same time. Starting at one end of the molecule and working to the other end would take too long and would make the DNA rotate very rapidly (like unwinding strands from a piece of string).
2. Free nucleotides are attached to the exposed bases by *DNA polymerase*. The rules of base pairing are observed

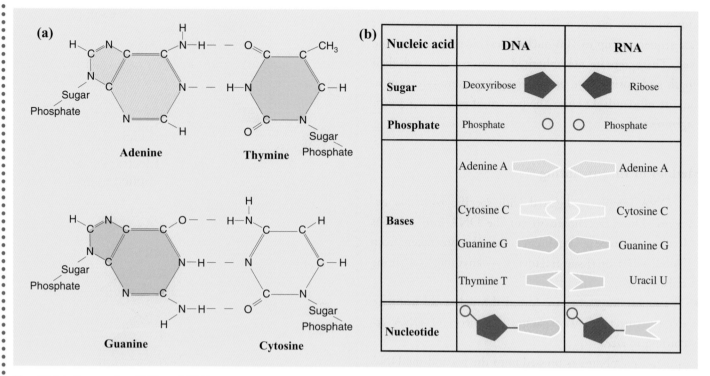

Fig. 12.14. Comparing RNA and DNA.

and each strand acts as a template for a new and complementary strand.

3. Adjacent nucleotides join together.

Replication produces two identical copies of the original DNA. Each new molecule keeps, or *conserves*, an original strand together with a completely new strand. This is termed *semi-conservative* replication. Replication takes place before the actual mechanics of cell division (see Chapter 11, section [230]). With mitosis, it ensures that the genetic code is *faithfully* transmitted to the next cell generation.

DNA PROFILING

DNA profiling — or *'DNA fingerprinting'* — was developed by Alec Jeffries at Leicester University in 1984.

Principle: All human chromosomes have sections of DNA

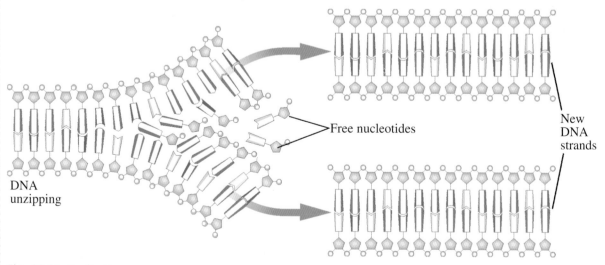

Free nucleotides

New DNA strands

DNA unzipping

Fig. 12.15. Replication.

with no known function. Typically these sections have short base sequences (up to 100 nucleotides) that repeat over and over. These repeats are inherited from parents and their length and position are *unique* to each person — except in the case of identical twins. The pattern of repeats is a *genetic fingerprint*.

Method of fingerprinting

- A DNA sample is digested with specific *restriction enzymes*. These are chosen to cut the DNA into portions leaving the repeat sites intact. Samples are taken from blood, saliva or tissue fragments — anything containing cells.

- The repeat fragments are forced through a gel using an electric current. This separates the pieces of DNA according to *size*.

- A nylon membrane is pressed onto the gel and the DNA fragments attach to it. The DNA is completely invisible at this stage.

- DNA probes are added to the nylon. A DNA probe is a strand of DNA that is complementary to the base sequence of a repeat fragment. It attaches to the fragment and labels it with radioactive phosphorus.

- An X-ray photograph is taken of the nylon membrane. The DNA fragments are revealed as dark bands. The pattern of banding is unique to each individual and similar to a computer bar code label.

Applications

- *Paternity disputes*: DNA fingerprinting is used to establish the natural parents of any child. Half of the banding of the child's DNA will be found in each natural parent.

- *Forensic science*: Forensic scientists use DNA fingerprinting. Criminals can be identified from traces of body fluids left at the scene of the crime. DNA fingerprinting can be done from tiny amounts of DNA, including the amount in single hair follicles and in the saliva on the back of a stamp.

- *Genetic screening*: The same technique can examine DNA samples and screen them for altered genes. Cystic fibrosis genes and other genetic defects can be identified at an early embryo stage. Parents can also be screened and in-

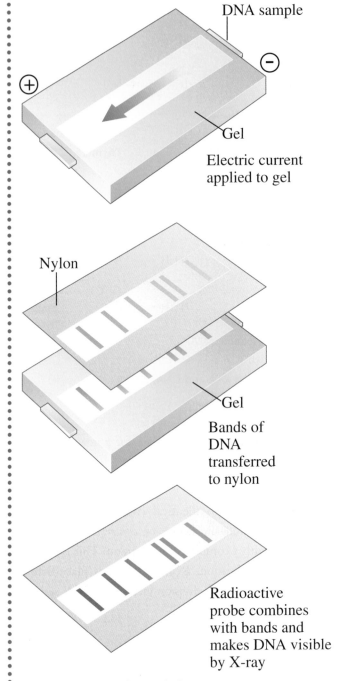

Fig. 12.16. Genetic fingerprinting.

formed on the possibilities of certain genetic combinations arising in any children they might have.

- *Genetic archaeology*: Modern-day populations can be linked with, say, Viking ancestors.

PROTEIN SYNTHESIS [255]

All cell activity is directed by enzymes. Every feature of the developing organism is due to the action of a specific enzyme. The development in humans of brown eyes or tallness

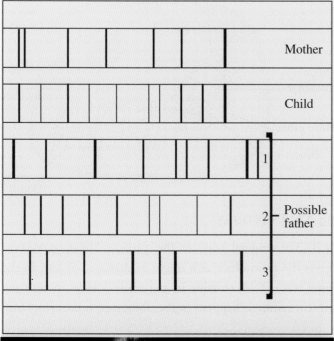

Fig. 12.17. Examining DNA banding.

can only take place if the cells involved have the appropriate *enzyme* to convert food into the required chemicals — brown pigment or growth hormone. A supply of the necessary food alone is not enough; enzymes must change the food into exactly what is needed.

Enzymes are proteins and so are constructed from long chains of amino acids (see Chapter 11, section [130]). The order of the amino acids in the chain determines the properties of the enzyme. The formation of these specific proteins requires:

- *A supply of amino acids.* There is a pool of amino acids from the organism's diet within the cytoplasm of every cell.
- *Instruction as to which amino acids should be joined together.* These instructions are contained in the sequence of bases in the DNA molecule — the *genetic code*. Every *gene* contains the instructions for the manufacture of one specific enzyme.
- *An assembly site.* Most proteins are constructed in the *ribosomes* in the cytoplasm of the cell.

A *messenger* is needed to carry copies of the genetic information from the DNA in the nucleus to the ribosomes in the cytoplasm.

STEPS IN PROTEIN SYNTHESIS

The example used here concerns the production of the brown eye colour in the iris cells in the human eye.

1. The DNA in the region of the eye-colour gene opens up and exposes its sequence of bases.
2. This code is faithfully copied (by *transcription*) onto a molecule of messenger RNA (mRNA).
3. mRNA leaves the nucleus and travels to the ribosomes in the cytoplasm.
4. The ribosomes *translate* the code and use it to assemble amino acids in the correct sequence to form a specific protein.
5. The new protein is folded to give the correct, functional shape — in this case the enzyme for 'brown eyes'.
6. The enzyme converts dietary nutrients into brown pigment.

N.B. Any mistake in the genetic code results in the formation of an incorrect enzyme (a nonsense enzyme) and no

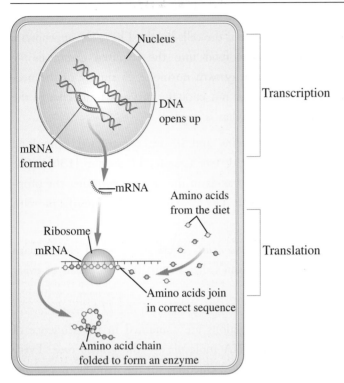

Fig. 12.18. Protein synthesis.

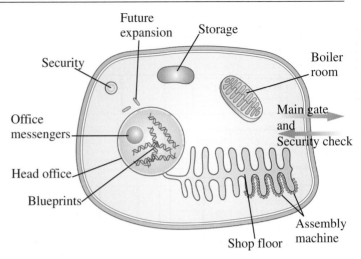

Fig. 12.19. Cell factory.

N.B. The original copy of the 'precious' blueprints never leaves the main office as it might be damaged or lost. In the same way, DNA remains in the nucleus even though the protein synthesis happens in the ribosomes in the cytoplasm.

brown pigment is formed. The eyes will be blue, grey or green instead (depending on the action of other genes). Such a mistake is *genetic* and can be inherited by children and grandchildren.

Note that there are two main processes at work:

- *transcription* — where the genetic code is faithfully copied by mRNA;
- *translation* — where the copied code is converted into the correct chain of amino acids.

THE CELL FACTORY

The cell can be considered as a *factory* in the following way:

- Raw materials enter the factory from outside — i.e. food passes across the cell membrane.
- The blueprint for the factory's output is kept in the office — the DNA kept in the nucleus.
- A messenger carries a copy of the plans down to the shop floor — mRNA travels from the nucleus to the ribosomes.
- The assembly workers join raw materials according to the copied plans — amino acids are joined in the ribosomes as instructed.
- The product is made correctly — a specific enzyme is formed.

THE PROCESS OF PROTEIN SYNTHESIS
[H25 VI]

Twenty kinds of naturally occurring amino acids are used to make proteins and DNA must be able to code for each one of them. Watson and Crick realised that a *triplet code* would be enough to specify 20 kinds of amino acid.

(Each base cannot simply represent an amino acid as there are only four kinds of base and 20 kinds of amino acid. Similarly, grouping the bases in twos does not generate enough code — there are only 16 ways (try it!) of writing the letters A, T, G and C in pairs; still not enough. Grouping the bases in triplets allows 64 different arrangements — enough to code for 20 amino acids. The code is described as *degenerate* — several groupings of bases have the same meaning. This code is also *universal*. The same group of bases represents the same amino acid in virtually every living organism — whether bacteria, jellyfish, dandelions or humans! The universality adds to the evidence supporting the Theory of Evolution and suggests common ancestry amongst all living organisms.)

Each group of three bases (termed a *codon*) represents a particular amino acid. CGG in DNA represents the amino acid alanine, GCT represents arginine, and so on. Certain codons act as punctuation marks — TAC means 'start here' and ACT means 'stop'.

1. Position	2. Position				3. Position
	U	C	A	G	
U	Phenyl-alanine	Serine	Tyrosine	Cysteine	U
	Phenyl-alanine	Serine	Tyrosine	Cysteine	C
	Leucine	Serine	Stop	Stop	A
	Leucine	Serine	Stop	Trypto-phan	G
C	Leucine	Proline	Histidine	Arginine	U
	Leucine	Proline	Histidine	Arginine	C
	Leucine	Proline	Glutamine	Arginine	A
	Leucine	Proline	Glutamine	Arginine	G
A	Isoleucine	Threonine	Asparagine	Serine	U
	Isoleucine	Threonine	Asparagine	Serine	C
	Isoleucine	Threonine	Lysine	Arginine	A
	Isoleucine (Start)	Threonine	Lysine	Arginine	G
G	Valine	Alanine	Aspartic acid	Glycine	U
	Valine	Alanine	Aspartic acid	Glycine	C
	Valine	Alanine	Aspartic acid	Glycine	A
	Valine	Alanine	Aspartic acid	Glycine	G

Fig. 12.20. The genetic code.

(The code is always translated from mRNA, which has copied a 'mirror image' of the DNA code. Also RNA contains the base, uracil, instead of thymine. So TAC on the DNA molecule is transcribed as AUG, ACT as UGA, etc.)

Protein synthesis in more detail:

Transcription in the nucleus

1. The hydrogen bonds in the appropriate gene region of the DNA break.
2. The DNA strands unwind and expose the base sequences.
3. Free nucleotides of RNA attach to one exposed strand of DNA and then join to one another. This produces a single strand of mRNA *with a mirror image (or complementary copy) of the base sequence.*
4. mRNA leaves the nucleus and travels to the ribosomes in the cytoplasm.
5. The gene closes over until required again.

Translation in the ribosomes

1. Amino acids combine with short lengths of RNA called *transfer RNA* or *tRNA*. Each tRNA molecule has a

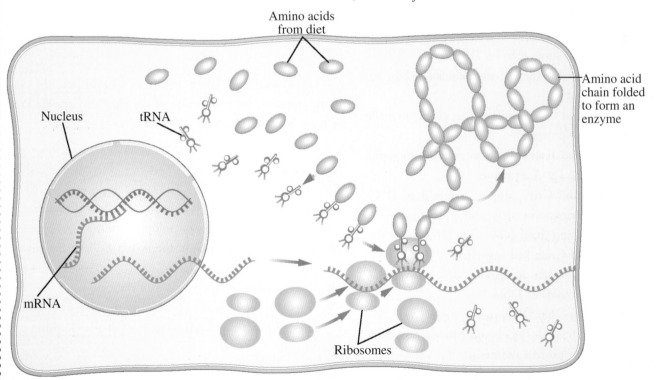

Fig. 12.21. Protein synthesis.

specific amino acid at one end and a sequence of three bases — an *anticodon* — at the other.

2. The ribosomes (made from *ribosomal RNA* (*rRNA*)) attach to the mRNA strand and move along it, reading the code. The mRNA bases are read in groups of three.

3. Complementary molecules of tRNA line up against the mRNA.

4. The adjacent amino acids are joined together by peptide bonds.

5. The ribosomes continue to the end of the mRNA strand and produce a chain of correctly sequenced amino acids.

6. The chain is folded to form a specific enzyme.

LANDMARKS IN THE STUDY OF DNA

- 1869 — Miescher isolates DNA from white blood cells but does not name it.

- 1923 — Feulgen develops a stain for DNA and shows that it is always present within chromosomes.

- 1928 — Griffith demonstrates a *transforming principle* within bacteria that can both copy itself and direct cell activities.

- 1941 — Beadle and Tatum propose the *one gene–one enzyme* hypothesis.

- 1944 — Avery, MacLeod and McCarty purify the *transforming principle* and show it to be DNA.

- 1950 — Chargaff shows the one-to-one relationships between bases in DNA.

- 1952 — Hershey and Chase confirm that genes are made from DNA and not protein.

- 1953 — Wilkins and Franklin use X-ray crystallography to show parts of the DNA structure.

- 1953 — Watson and Crick propose a model of DNA that allows for information storage and replication.

- 1958 — Meselson and Stahl prove that DNA replicates itself as Watson and Crick had suggested.

- 1958 — Kornberg isolates an enzyme, *DNA polymerase*, that will replicate strands of DNA.

- 1961 — Crick shows that DNA uses a 'triplet' code. Nirenberg deciphers the code. Jacob and Monod propose a model for regulating protein synthesis.

- 1966 — Weiss and Richardson discover DNA ligase for joining portions of DNA.

- 1971 — Arber and Smith discover restriction enzymes for chopping up DNA. Nathans uses restriction enzymes to construct a genetic map

- 1976 — The first genetic engineering company *Genentech* is formed.

- 1982 — Sanger devises a method for gene sequencing: determining the exact code of bases within a gene.

- 1984 — Jeffreys develops genetic fingerprinting.

- 1987 — Sinsheimer proposes the human genome project to map, describe and *sequence* (write down the order of bases) every single human gene.

- 1990 — The Human Genome project begins.

- 1994 — Venter and Smith plan the computerising of the project.

- 1999 — The first human chromosome (# 22) is completely sequenced.

- 2000 — The project is completed five years 'early' with the assistance of Venter and his private sector company *Celera Genomics*. Between 80,000–100,000 human genes are sequenced. The genetic blueprint of humans, *Adam II*, is finally written. It will probably form the basis of all medical discovery for the next hundred years.

Today, we are learning the language in which God created life. With this profound new knowledge, humankind is on the verge of gaining immense, new power to heal.

— US President William Jefferson Clinton on the announcement of the completion of the Human Genome Project, on Monday, 26 June 2000.

SUMMARY

- *Organisms are classified* to cope with their diversity.
- *Species never reproduce* outside the group.
- *Characteristics* result from the action of both heredity and environment.
- *DNA* is found in the nucleus of the cell.
- *The DNA molecule* is capable of both replicating itself and of instructing the formation of enzymes within the cell.
- *Variations between two individuals* of the same species may be acquired or inherited.

- *Genes work* by directing the production of specific enzymes in cells. These enzymes then have an effect on the cell's metabolism.
- *DNA* consists of two chains of repeating units, or nucleotides, wrapped around each other in a double helix.
- *Each nucleotide* consists of a five-carbon sugar known as deoxyribose, a phosphate unit and one of four bases — adenine, thymine, guanine and cytosine.
- *The genetic code* lies within the sequence of bases within the helix.
- *RNA* is found both in the nucleus and in the cytoplasm of cells.
- *RNA* has a similar structure to DNA but is single-stranded, shorter, contains the sugar ribose and replaces thymine with uracil.
- *DNA replication* involves the following steps:

  - the DNA strand is unzipped;
  - free nucleotides are attached to the exposed bases — each strand acts as a template for a new, complementary strand;
  - adjacent nucleotides join together following the base pairing rule.

- *DNA profiling* searches for short base sequences that repeat over and over. These patterns of repeats are unique to each person — except in the case of identical twins.
- *Every feature* of the developing organism is due to the action of a specific enzyme.
- *Protein synthesis* involves the following steps:

  - the DNA in the region of a gene opens up and exposes its sequence of bases;
  - this code is faithfully copied (by transcription) onto a molecule of mRNA;
  - mRNA travels to the ribosomes in the cytoplasm;
  - the ribosomes translate the code and use it to assemble amino acids in the correct sequence to form a specific protein;
  - the new protein is folded to give the correct, functional shape.

- *The cell operates* as a highly-organised factory.

EXTENDED SUMMARY

- *The structure of DNA* was first proposed by James Watson and Francis Crick working in Cambridge in 1953.
- *The sugar / phosphate backbones* are non-coding structures in DNA, the base sequence is the coding structure of the molecule.
- *The number of purines* always equals the number of pyrimidines in any DNA molecule — evidence that led to the discovery of the rule of base pairing.
- *Adenine* always pairs with thymine and guanine with cytosine.
- *Each group of three bases* (a codon) represents a particular amino acid.
- *Transcription* involves the following steps:
- the hydrogen bonds in the appropriate gene region of the DNA break;

  - the DNA strands unwind and expose the base sequences;
  - free nucleotides of RNA attach to one exposed strand of DNA to produce a single strand of mRNA with a mirror image or complementary copy of the base sequence;
  - mRNA leaves the nucleus and travels to the ribosomes in the cytoplasm.

- *Translation* involves the following steps:

  - amino acids combine with short lengths of tRNA;
  - each tRNA molecule has a specific amino acid at one end and a sequence of three bases — an anticodon — at the other;
  - the ribosomes attach to the mRNA strand and move along it, reading the code;
  - complementary molecules of tRNA line up against the mRNA;
  - the adjacent amino acids are joined together by peptide bonds;
  - the ribosomes continue to the end of the mRNA strand and produce a chain of correctly sequenced amino acids;
  - the chain is folded to form a specific enzyme.

KEY WORDS

Species	A group of organisms that resemble one another and have the ability to reproduce with one another.
Population	A group of the same species within a geographical area.
Variation	The differences between the members of a population.
Acquired variations	These are 'picked up' during the life of the organism and not inherited.
Inherited variations	These are a result of what is 'written' into the chromosomes of the organism.
Clone	A population where all members are genetically identical.
Genetics	The study of the mechanism of inheritance.
Heredity	Refers to all materials and information passed from one generation to the next or to later generations.
Expression	This refers to when hereditary information is *activated* within cells.
Histones	Beads of protein supporting DNA.
Nucleosomes	Packing units of DNA formed from groups of histones.
Gene	A hereditary unit on a chromosome, which contains the coding for a specific enzyme.
Double helix	A double spiral structure found in DNA.
Nucleotide	A structural unit in nucleic acids made from a five-carbon *sugar*, a *phosphate* unit and a base.

Replication	Exact copying.
Messenger RNA (*mRNA*)	A short length of RNA that carries a copy of genetic code from the nucleus to the ribosomes.
DNA helicase	An enzyme that 'unzips' complementary strands of DNA.
DNA polymerase	An enzyme that attaches free nucleotides to exposed DNA bases.
Restriction enzymes	They slice up DNA molecules into specific units.
DNA probe	A strand of DNA that is complementary to the base sequence of a DNA fragment.
Ribosomes	Organelles in the cytoplasm where proteins are made.
Transcription	The faithful copying of the genetic code onto mRNA.
Translation	The conversion of the copied code into the correct chain of amino acids.

EXTENDED KEY WORDS

Purine bases	Double-ringed molecular bases such as adenine and guanine.
Pyrimidine bases	Single-ringed molecular bases such as thymine, cytosine and uracil.
Base pairing	Adenine always joins to thymine (or uracil), guanine always joins to cytosine.
Codon	A group of three bases coding for a specific amino acid.
Ribosomal RNA (*rRNA*)	Used to construct ribosomes.
Transfer RNA (*tRNA*)	Lengths of RNA with an anticodon at one end and a specific amino acid at the other.

QUESTIONS

1. What is a species? List twenty Irish examples.
2. What is meant by variation? Explain the difference between acquired variation and genetic variation. Decide whether the following human variations might be acquired or genetic:

    a. dimples;
    b. long fingernails;
    c. good hearing;
    d. short-sightedness;
    e. ability to ride a bicycle;
    f. ability to play the violin.

3. What is a clone? Are all twins clones? Are any? What are the consequences of a lack of variation within a population?
4. What are chromosomes made from? What is the advantage of the repeated coiling within chromosomes?
5. Why are genes considered to be hereditary units? Summarise exactly what it is that genes do.
6. What do the letters DNA stand for? Draw a labelled diagram of a DNA nucleotide. How many kinds of nucleotide are found in DNA?
7. Explain the terms:

    a. *antiparallel*;
    b. *double helix*;
    c. *complementary strands*.

8. With reference to the experiment to extract DNA from kiwi fruit, explain the purpose of each of the following steps:

    a. mashing the kiwi fruit;
    b. adding salt and detergent;
    c. heating the mixture;
    d. filtering the mixture;
    e. adding protease;
    f. gently pouring ice cold organic solvent onto the mixture.

    If the experiment is carried out on animal tissue, no mashing is required. Why is this?

9. Construct a chart to compare DNA and RNA. Include reference to length, base content, helical form, sugars, location in the cell, function.
10. What is replication? When and where is DNA replicated?
    Explain the following statement: 'One strand of DNA can act as a template for a new, complementary strand'.
11. What is genetic fingerprinting? Outline the principle behind the process.
    What are the main stages in preparing a genetic fingerprint? State three applications of the technique.
12. Explain how a gene can direct the formation of brown eyes.
13. What is the base pairing rule within DNA? A length of DNA has the following base sequence: ATGACCTGACAATGCTGTTAC.
    What is the order of bases in its complementary strand? How would the sequence be transcribed by a mRNA molecule?
14. What are the differences between transcription and translation? Where do these processes occur?

EXTENDED QUESTIONS

15. Explain the roles of DNA helicase and DNA polymerase in DNA replication.
16. If adenine represents 20% of the base content in a length of DNA, what percentages will each of the other three bases represent?
17. What are purines and pyrimidines? What clue did the purine/pyrimidine ratio give to the structure of DNA?
18. Explain why the genetic code is considered degenerate. The processes of transcription and translation of the genetic code are identical in earthworms and in humans. What does this suggest?
19. Name three types of RNA found in cells. State a location and a function for each kind.

OPTIONAL ACTIVITIES

- Visit a zoo, a Natural History museum or botanic gardens to observe the diversity of life.
- Visit the Natural History Museum, London at http://www.nhm.ac.uk/.
- Collect the class fingerprints as an example of genetic variation. Dip fingers into talcum powder and then press them gently onto adhesive tape. Stick the tape onto black card, label the card and look for particular features — loops, scars, triangular sections, etc. Try to solve a class 'crime' by reference to the fingerprint collection!
- Collect information for a report on diversity within the class. Suitable features include: tallness, eye colour, tongue-rolling ability, shoe size, cucumber tasting ability, ear lobes, blood groups, freckles, nose profile (straight or convex when viewed from the side), hair type, hair colour, etc. Present the information using bar charts or pie charts.
- When discussing eye colour, it is best to consider brown, hazel, green and blue as the only colours.
- Research your family tree to try and establish characteristic links with past generations.
- Mark a long piece of rubber tubing or rope with as many pieces of coloured paper or tape as you can. Hold one end fixed and twist the other end as many times as possible to illustrate the coiling of DNA within chromosomes.
- Use a DNA modelling kit to construct a model of a half-turn of the DNA molecule.
- Compare DNA with videotape. Refer to length, information stored, need for translation, ease of copying, possibility of copying mistakes, possibility of editing.

Read:

Anne Sayre, *Rosalind Franklin and DNA* (Norton).

James D Watson, *The Double Helix* (Penguin).

Francis Crick, *What Mad Pursuit* (Penguin).

Matt Ridley, *Genome* (Fourth Estate).

Now test yourself at
www.my-etest.com

Chapter 13
Genetic Inheritance

Learning objectives

After your study of this chapter, you should be able to:

- distinguish between sexual and asexual reproduction;
- explain and use genetic terminology;
- predict the possible outcomes of simple genetic crosses;
- illustrate genetic inheritance;
- distinguish between probability and certainty;
- use a Punnett square;
- illustrate how sex is genetically determined.

Extended learning objectives

- Review the contribution of Gregor Mendel to genetics;
- state and illustrate Mendel's Laws;
- predict the possible outcomes of dihybrid crosses;
- discuss the restrictions imposed by gene linkage;
- outline and illustrate the inheritance of sex-linked conditions;
- outline the importance of plasmids.

INTRODUCTION

There are two kinds of reproduction in biology: *sexual* and *asexual*.

In asexual reproduction, only one parent is involved and the offspring are genetically identical to that parent. No sex cells are required. Examples include the division of *Amoeba* to form daughter *Amoebae*, spore formation in mosses and ferns, and cuttings taken from a geranium plant.

Asexual reproduction is found in all bacteria, fungi and plants and in a few, primitive animals such as flatworms.

In sexual reproduction, there are generally two parents. They make reproductive cells called sex cells or gametes, which join together by fertilisation to form a diploid zygote. The zygote develops into an embryo and eventually into another adult.

The new individual resembles its parents but is not identical to either of them, instead being a mixture of the genetic features of both.

Sexual reproduction is found in all animals and plants, most fungi and some bacteria.

Gametes (or sex cells) are reproductive cells containing single sets of chromosomes (they are *haploid*). Gametes are capable of *fusion* — they can join together in the process of fertilisation to form a zygote. The zygote has a double set of chromosomes (it is *diploid*) and can develop into a new organism. A zygote contains the genetic information of both gametes.

Gametes are formed either directly or indirectly by *meiosis* (see chapter 11). Meiosis is a type of cell division that produces four daughter cells, each with half of the original number of chromosomes in the parent cell. Meiosis is a *reduction division* — it halves the chromosome number, producing haploid cells from diploid cells. It is generally reserved for making sex cells and spores.

Male gametes (from male parents) are capable of their own movement and are relatively small. Female gametes (from female parents) are not capable of their own movement and are relatively larger with generous amounts of food.

(The word 'male' refers to the parent that makes the sex cell that moves, and the word 'female' refers to the parent that makes the sex cell that doesn't move!)

GENETIC TERMINOLOGY

Genetics	The study of the mechanism of inheritance.
Chromosome	A long thread of DNA embedded in protein. Species usually have a fixed number of chromosomes in their cells e.g. human cells contain 46 chromosomes (but only 23 in their sex cells). Chimpanzees have 48, a mosquito has six and a tomato plant has 24 chromosomes per cell.
Gene	A portion of a chromosome controlling the development of a particular characteristic, e.g. in humans, there are genes for eye colour, for tallness, for heart valve development, etc.
Locus	The position of a gene on a chromosome.
Dominant	When a gene is working normally and expressing itself in the organism. A dominant gene is denoted by a capital letter, e.g. T, C, X, etc.

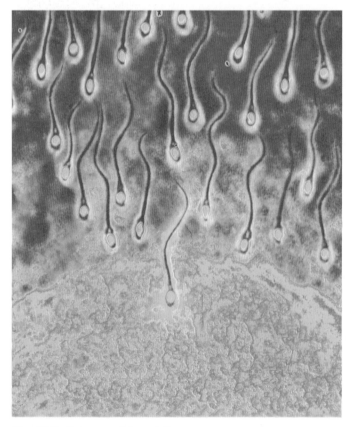

Fig. 13.1. Sperms arriving at the egg.

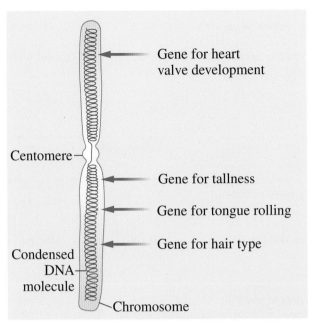

Fig. 13.2. Genes on a chromosome.

(N.B. Notice that both the chromosomes and the genes occur in *pairs*.)

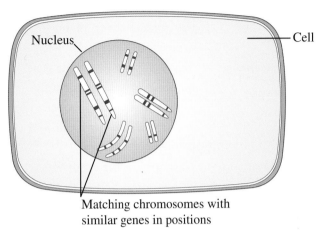

Fig. 13.3. Homologous pairs of chromosomes in a cell with 10 chromosomes.

Recessive	When a gene is *not* working and therefore not expressing itself. A recessive gene is denoted by a small letter e.g. t, c, x, etc.
Homologous chromosomes	Chromosomes that form matching pairs during meiosis. Homologous chromosomes have similar genes in similar positions.
Alleles	Alternative forms of genes. Most genes have *two* alternative forms — a dominant form or a recessive form.
Homozygous	When the members of a pair of genes have the same form, for example, TT, cc, AA, FF, hh, ww, etc. Organisms with this condition are referred to as '*pure breeding*'.
Heterozygous	When the members of a pair of genes have different forms, for example, Tt, Rr, Aa, Ff, etc. (Traditionally, the capital letter is written first.) Organisms with this condition are referred to as '*carriers*'.
Genotype	The genetic constitution of an individual, for example, Tt, aa, RR, Gg, etc. An organism's genotype is a description of the 'condition' of its genes, that is, which are dominant and which are recessive.
Phenotype	The expression of the genotype, for example, 'tall', 'blond hair', etc. An organism's phenotype describes its 'appearance' or how it 'turned out' as a result of its genes. Phenotype may be clearly visible, as in freckles or tallness or brown eyes, but can also be internal, as in having normal colour vision or liver function.

F1 generation	'First filial generation', i.e. the 'children' of any organisms.
F2 generation	'Second filial generation', i.e. the 'grandchildren' of any organisms.
Incomplete dominance	When a single dominant gene in a heterozygote is not fully expressed. This can happen with colours in particular and is explained later.
Diploid (2n)	Having a double set of chromosomes within the nucleus (or having chromosomes in pairs). In human cells, the diploid number, 2n, is 46.
Haploid (n)	Having a single set of chromosomes within the nucleus. In human sex cells, the haploid number, n, is 23.

Simple genetic crosses

Remember:

- Characteristics in organisms are generally controlled by *pairs of genes* located on pairs of homologous chromosomes.
- *Meiosis* ensures that only one member of any gene pair will be found in any gamete.
- *Fertilisation* restores the gene and chromosome pairs.

Seed colour in pea plants is controlled by a single pair of genes. These genes have two allelic forms: the yellow form and the green form. The yellow form of the gene is dominant and represented by the letter Y. The dominant gene works normally and produces a yellow colour within the seed coat. The green form of the gene is recessive and represented by the letter y. Green plants do not have the correct genetic instructions for producing yellow seed coats and instead are green.

Homozygous pea plants have genotypes of YY or yy. YY plants produce yellow seeds and yy plants produce green seeds.

Heterozygous pea plants have a genotype of Yy. These plants produce yellow seeds.

1. Suppose a homozygous yellow seed plant is crossed with a green seed plant:

Phenotypes of parents	Yellow seeds	Green seeds
Genotypes of parents	Y Y	y y
Gametes that can be formed	all Y	all y
Genotypes of possible offspring in F1 generation		all Y y
Phenotypes of F1 generation		all with yellow seeds

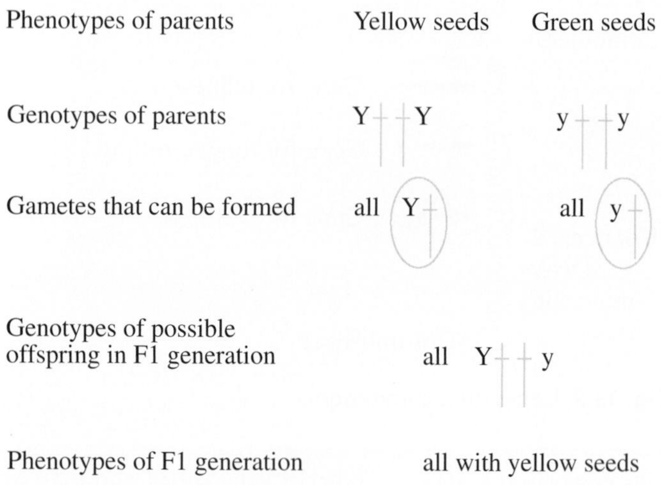

Fig. 13.4. YY crossed with yy.

N.B. The characteristic (seed colour) is controlled by a *pair* of genes, but only one member of the pair is found in the gametes (due to meiosis). Fertilisation restores the gene pair in the next generation.

All the F1 plants receive a dominant Y gene from one parent and so will all be yellow, regardless of what they receive from the other parent.

The seeds of Yy plants are no less yellow than YY plants. Having two copies of the dominant gene does not mean that a YY plant will make twice as much yellow pigment as a Yy plant — in the same way that having a spare copy of a recipe for chocolate cake does not mean that the cake has to be made twice!

Also, it is not possible to determine the genotype of a yellow plant by simply noting that it has yellow seeds. It could be homozygous, YY, or heterozygous Yy. However, the genotypes of green seed plants are always known: they are yy.

2. Suppose one of these heterozygous F1 plants is crossed with a green seed plant:

Parental phenotypes	Yellow seeds	Green seeds
Parental genotypes	Y ┃┃ y	y ┃┃ y
Possible gametes	(Y) or (y)	all (y)
Possible genotypes in F2 generation	Y ┃┃ y	y ┃┃ y
Possible phenotypes in F2 generation	Yellow seeds	Green seeds

Fig. 13.5. Yy crossed with yy.

N.B. Heterozygous plants make *equal amounts* of Y and y gametes. This means that yellow seed plants are as likely to occur in the F2 generation as green seed plants are. There is an expected ration of 1:1 between the two phenotypes.

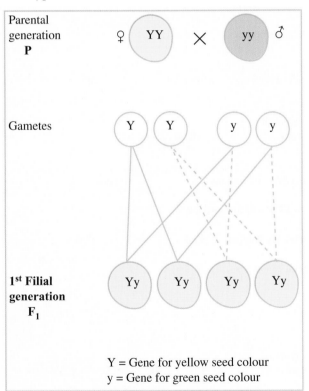

Y = Gene for yellow seed colour
y = Gene for green seed colour

Fig. 13.6.

Probability and certainty

An expected ration of 1:1 does not mean that equal amounts of the two plants *will* be obtained. If a coin is tossed 100 times, heads is just as likely as tails each time and a result close to 50 heads and 50 tails is the most likely outcome. It is possible to obtain a result of 60:40 or even 99:1, as the coin has no memory of the previous outcomes. These results are not *wrong*, but are just not expected. However, it is *certain* that the coin will either turn up heads or tails and will not turn up any other result.

Try tossing coins in class and average the results obtained. Compare the results for large numbers of trials and small numbers: see *Optional activities* below.

3. Supposing two heterozygous plants are crossed:

Parental phenotypes	Yellow seeds		Yellow seeds	
Parental genotypes	Y ┃ y		Y ┃ y	
Possible gametes	(Y) or (y)		(Y) or (y)	
Genotypes of F1 plants	Y┃Y	Y┃y	Y┃y	y┃y
Phenotypes of F1 plants	Yellow seeds	Yellow seeds	Yellow seeds	Green seeds

Fig. 13.7. Yy crossed with Yy.

A Punnett square (designed by Dr R.C. Punnett) is used to show the possible combinations of genotypes. See fig. 13.8.

	Y	y
Y	YY	Yy
y	Yy	yy

Fig. 13.8. A Punnett Square.

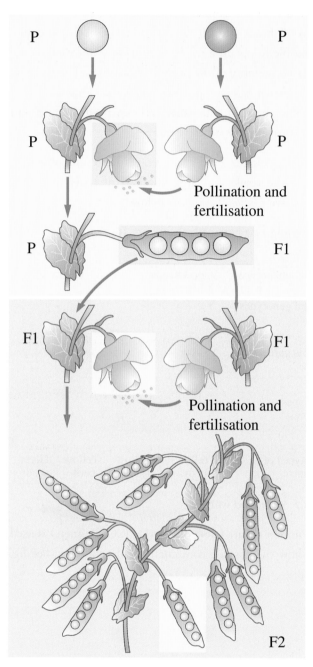

Fig. 13.9. Pea plants.

Phenotypes of F1: 3/4 of plants have yellow seeds 1/4 have green seeds

A ratio of 3:1 yellow:green plants is expected.

Of the yellow plants, 2/3 are likely to be heterozygous and 1/3 homozygous

N.B. It is important in genetic crosses to use a good layout such as above. Use circles to represent sex cells only and make sure to point out genotypes and phenotypes separately. Also be sure to make a clear difference between upper and lower case letters which otherwise look similar, e.g. S/s or M/m. Otherwise, your good work may be wasted!

Incomplete dominance is when a single dominant gene in a heterozygote is not fully expressed.

In primroses, petal colour is controlled by a single pair of genes. The red flower allele, R, is *incompletely dominant* over the white flower allele, r. Plants with the genotype RR are red, rr plants are white and Rr plants are pink. In the heterozygous plants (Rr), the single dominant gene does not make enough red pigment and the red colour is diluted.

4. If a red and a white flower are crossed:

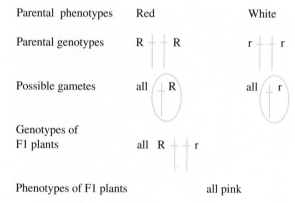

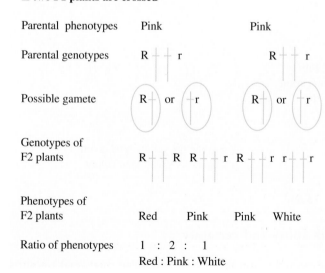

Fig. 13.10. Red and white primroses crossed.

N.B. Incomplete dominance does not affect the expected genotypes or change the genetic rules; it affects some of the phenotypes.

(When predicting the expected ratios of offspring in genetics, certain assumptions are made: that fertilisation is a random process, that all offspring are equally likely to survive and that large numbers of offspring or trials are being counted)

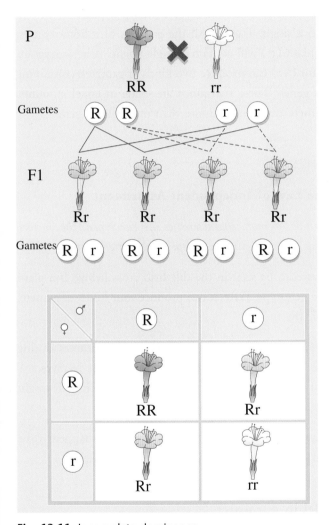

Fig. 13.11. Incomplete dominance.

DETERMINATION OF SEX

All human cells (except sex cells) contain 23 pairs of chromosomes. One pair is known as sex chromosomes and determine whether a person is male or female. The other 22 pairs are non-sex (autosomal) chromosomes.

Two kinds of sex chromosomes are found in humans:

1. a long chromosome (termed the X chromosome); and
2. a short chromosome with relatively few genes (the Y chromosome).

Females have two X chromosomes and males have an X and a Y chromosome.

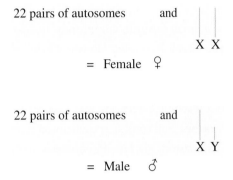

Fig. 13.12. Diagram of x and y chromosome arrangements for male and female.

Sex in humans is inherited in the same way as tallness in pea plants:

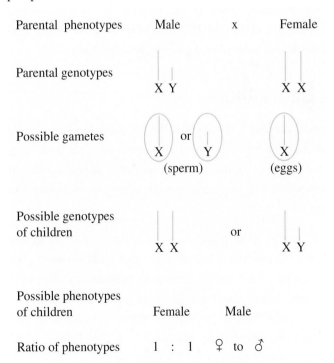

Fig. 13.13. Inheritance of sex.

Half of the male sperm cell contain an X chromosome, the other half contain a Y chromosome. All of the female eggs contain a Y chromosome.

Almost all higher animals use the same system of determining sex (although female birds are XY and male birds are XX!).

THE ORIGIN OF THE SCIENCE OF GENETICS   [H 25] [H25 I]

Johann Gregor Mendel (1822–1884)

Mendel was born into a small farming community in Moravia in what is now the Czech Republic. He was a brilliant student at school, but family resources were limited and so he entered an Augustinian monastery in Brno to continue his education and start a teaching career. He was a successful and popular biology teacher but took a special interest in the pea plants in the monastery garden. He crossed many different varieties of the pea plant, *Pisum sativum,* and made extensive notes of the mathematical ratios of the offspring.

Mendel worked for eight years with his experiments and then published his findings but had difficulty in obtaining any understanding or recognition. He eventually abandoned his studies and turned to the running of the monastery's finances. It was only in 1900, 16 years after his death, that his work was rediscovered and his genius appreciated.

Mendel's experiments

Mendel worked with many different plants and some animals but his main work concentrated on the edible pea, *Pisum sativum.* He studied the inheritance of seven different characteristics in the pea plant. His experiments usually had three parts:

- He would allow plants to self-pollinate for many generations to produce a line of plants that he knew were 'pure breeding'. This was important to prevent any later confusion. These plants would be his parental generation.
- He would then cross-pollinate different varieties of parentals by transferring pollen with a tiny brush. These plants would produce an F1 generation.
- He allowed the F1 plants to self-pollinate and produce an F2 generation. He then counted the offspring by phenotype.

MENDEL'S LAWS   [H25 II]

1. The Law of Segregation

Characteristics are controlled by pairs of 'factors', but only one of these factors can be carried in a gamete.

If we substitute the word *gene* for *factor*, this law states that the members of the gene pair are *segregated*, or taken away from one another. As a consequence of meiosis, only one member of each gene pair will enter any gametes.

All the gametes of a homozygous, tall pea plant (TT) will contain a single T gene. All the gametes of a homozygous, dwarf plant (tt) will contain a single t gene. A heterozygous, tall plant (Tt) can produce two kinds of gametes: containing T or t genes. These two kinds are made in equal amounts. No gamete can contain more than one tallness gene.

[H25 III]

2. The Law of Independent Assortment

Where two or more characteristics are concerned, the 'factors' for these enter the gametes independently of each other.

This law can be seen in the dihybrid cross below. If a plant has the genotype TtRr, it can produce four kinds of gamete: TR, Tr, tR, tr.

The members of each gene pair enter the gametes during meiosis *independently* of the others. If a gamete receives a T gene, it does not have to receive an R gene with it. It might receive an R gene or an r gene.

This law is not true if the genes in question happen to be located on the same chromosome (i.e. are linked).

Mendel in retrospect

Gregor Mendel is rightly considered to be the father of modern genetics. His genius, clear thinking and good mathematics, together with a degree of luck, paved the way for all later genetic advances.

- Mendel understood that the outcome of his work was based on probability. He was the first scientist to apply good statistical methods in his work. He counted very

Fig. 13.15. Original sample from Mendel's study of inheritance of seed colour.

Fig. 13.14. Mendel.

large numbers of plants (over 20,000), which meant that his results should be closer to the theoretical outcome and should rule out chance. Ironically, one of his attempts at publication was turned down with the advice to 'do more experiments'!

- Mendel never actually wrote down the two 'laws'; other scientists did this after his death.
- Mendel was lucky in the seven traits he chose to study. They were all single gene traits and they all existed on separate chromosomes.
- Pea plants are normally self-pollinating, which reduces the possibility of contamination by other pollen.
- Mendel may have discovered ratios and effects due to *gene linkage* (genes occurring on the same chromosome and therefore likely to be inherited together), but either ignored them or deleted them (which was bad scientific method!). He could not have understood evidence of linkage, as he did not know what a *chromosome* was.
- Some of Mendel's results were almost too good to be true. Perhaps he made 'adjustments' to his numbers, given that

he knew the theoretical outcome. His notebooks were burned and little evidence of his detailed work remains.
- Mendel made all of his discoveries without any knowledge of genes, chromosomes, alleles or meiosis. He referred to genes as 'factors'.

THE DIHYBRID CROSS [H25 IV]

The dihybrid cross shows the simultaneous inheritance of two characteristics at the same time.

For example, in the pea plant the allele for tallness (T) is dominant over that for dwarfness (t) and the allele for round seeds (R) is dominant over that for wrinkled seeds (r).

Suppose a homozygous tall plant with round seeds is crossed with a dwarf plant with wrinkled seeds:

Parental phenotypes:	Tall, round	×	dwarf, wrinkled
Parental genotypes:	TTRR	×	ttrr
Gametes:	all TR		all tr
Genotypes of F1 plants:			all TtRr
Phenotypes of F1 plants:			all tall with round seeds

If two of these F1 plants are crossed:

Parental phenotypes:	tall, round	×	tall, round
Parental genotypes:	TtRr		TtRr
Gametes:	TR, Tr, tR, tr		TR, Tr, tR, tr

Genotypes of F2 generation:

As there are four kinds of gamete from each parent, fertilisation can happen in 16 different ways (4×4). A Punnett square is used to show the possible combinations of genotypes.

	TR	Tr	tR	Tr
TR	TTRR	TTRr	TtRR	TtRr
Tr	TTRr	TTrr	TtRr	Ttrr
tR	TtRR	TtRr	ttRR	TtRr
tr	TtRr	Ttrr	ttRr	ttrr

Phenotypes of F2 generation:

Within this table, there are only four different phenotypes:

– all, round seed plants;
– tall, wrinkled seed plants;
– dwarf, round seed plants;
– dwarf, wrinkled seed plants.

They occur in a ratio of 9:3:3:1.

GENE LINKAGE

Living organisms have many more genes than chromosomes. Any chromosome can have thousands of genes located on it. Genes that are located on the same chromosome are said to be *linked*.

Linkage	Where genes happen to be located on the same chromosome.

As linked genes are 'tied' to one another, they tend to be inherited together.

Assume that a doubly heterozygous animal (AaBb) is crossed with a homozygous, recessive partner (aabb). If the genes in question happen to be located on separate chromosomes, the heterozygous *parent* can produce four kinds of gametes and the expected outcome is as follows:

Genotypes of Parents: AaBb $\times$ aabb
Possible Gametes: AB or ab   all ab
F1 generation: AaBb   aabb

These two kinds of offspring occur in the ratio of 1:1.

Genotypes of Parents: AaBb $\times$ aabb
Possible Gametes: AB, Ab, aB, ab   all ab
F1 Generation: AaBb   Aabb   aaBb   aabb

The expected ratio of the four kinds of offspring is 1:1:1:1 — given that the first parent can make equal amounts of its four kinds of gametes.

If, however, the genes in question are *linked*, A to B, the heterozygous parent can only make two kinds of gamete as A is inherited along with a and B with b.

Example of gene linkage

In the fruit fly, *Drosophila melanogaster*, grey body (+) is dominant over black body (b), and normal wings (+) are dominant over vestigial or undeveloped wings (vg). These genes are located on the same pair of chromosomes.

(Geneticists use the symbol + [or *wild type*] to represent the most common variation found within a species).

A grey fly with normal wings, homozygous for both characteristics, is crossed with a black fly with vestigial wings. All of the offspring are grey with normal wings. One of these F1 flies is crossed with a black, vestigial winged fly.

If the wing and colour genes happened to be located on separate chromosomes, the expected outcome would be as in fig. 13.16.

Parental phenotypes	Grey body, normal wings			Black body, vestigial wings
Parental genotypes	++ ++			bb vgvg
Possible gametes	all (+ / +)			all (b / vg)
F1 generation genotypes	all +b +vg (all grey with normal wings)			
Parental genotypes	bb vgvg		+b +vg	
Possible gametes	all (b / vg)	(+ / +) (+ / vg) (b / +) (b / vg)		
Genotypes of F2 generation	+b +vg	+b +vgvg	bb +vg	bb vgvg
Phenotypes of F2 generation	Grey, normal wings	Grey, vestigial wings	Black, normal wings	Black, vestigial wings
Ratio of phenotypes	1 :	1 :	1 :	1

Fig. 13.16. If genes are *not* linked.

However the genes are linked and the actual outcome is shown in fig. 13.17.

Parental phenotypes	Grey body, normal wings	Black body, vestigial wings
Parental genotypes	+ | + + | +	b | b vg | vg
Gametes	all (+ / +)	all (b / vg)
Genotypes of F1 generation	all + | b + | vg (all grey/normal wings)	
Parental genotypes	b | b vg | vg	+ | b + | vg
Gametes	all (b / vg)	(+ / +) or (b / vg)
Genotypes of F2 generation	+ | b + | vg	b | b vg | vg
Phenotypes of F2 generation	Grey/normal wings	Black/vestigial wings
Ratio of F2 phenotypes	1 : 1	

Fig. 13.17. If genes are linked.

Notice that, for the first parent of the F2 generation, any sex cell containing a dominant wing gene (+) also contains a dominant colour gene (+) as the genes are *linked* to each other. Only two kinds of sex cell are produced by the first parent, in contrast to four kinds when the genes were located on separate chromosomes.

Gene linkage reduces the variety of sex cells and contradicts Mendel's second law — the Law of Independent Assortment.

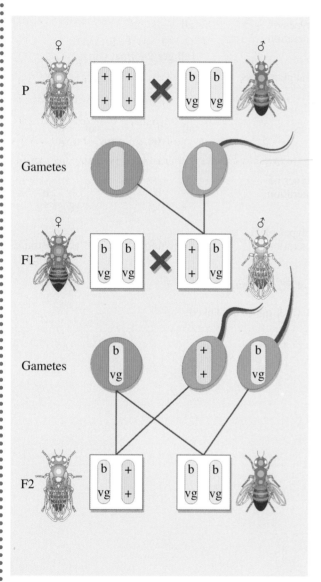

Fig. 13.18. Gene linkage.

Sex linkage

(See also determination of sex in section [256] above.)

Genes are sex-linked if they are located on sex chromosomes.

The human Y chromosome is physically very short and contains virtually no genes at all apart from the testis determining factor gene: TDF. The human X chromosome contains many genes, including ones not directly related to sex. As far as these genes are concerned, males have only one copy as they only have one X chromosome. Females have two copies of these sex-linked genes as they have two X chromosomes.

Haemophilia (inability to clot the blood due to a missing clotting factor) is caused by a recessive gene located on the X chromosome.

The following human genotypes are possible:

Genotype	Phenotype
H H XX	normal female
H h XX	carrier female
h h XX	haemophiliac female
H XY	normal male
h XY	haemophiliac male

Fig. 13.19. Sex linkage.

N.B. There are no carrier males for this condition.

Figure 13.20 shows the possible outcome if a carrier female marries a normal male.

N.B. In this example, haemophilia can only arise in the male children as this father gives an X chromosome with a normal gene to every daughter.

Haemophilia is said to be 'carried by females and suffered by males'.

In fact, females can be haemophiliacs if they have a carrier mother and a haemophiliac father. This is unlikely, however, as haemophiliac females are rare.

Other human sex-linked conditions are *colour blindness* (25 times as many males as females have red–green colour deficiency) and *Duchenne Muscular Dystrophy* (DMD), named after Dr Duchenne who first described the condition in Paris in the 19th century. Both conditions are due to recessive genes on the X chromosome. Inheritance of the condition follows the same rules as for haemophilia above.

DMD is a genetic condition where muscle fibres are gradually wasted away. At present there is no cure. About one in every 3,500 male births will have DMD. Female carriers often have a mild form of the disease. The male child will have a severe and progressive muscle weakness.

Non-nuclear inheritance

DNA is not always found in the cell nucleus. It is also found in mitochondria and in chloroplasts. This *extra-chromosomal* ('outside the chromosomes') DNA is generally circular and contains about 120 genes related to the function of the organelle. It has a slightly different genetic code and is not directly related to the nuclear DNA. Mitochondria and chloroplasts are self-replicating and their DNA has an independent existence from nuclear DNA.

Bacteria also contain loops or lengths of extra-chromosomal DNA called *plasmids*. These can be transferred from one bacterium to another — a process equivalent to sexual reproduction in bacteria. Plasmids are utilised in genetic engineering (see Chapter 15). They may yet be of serious consequence to humans as there are many examples of bacteria transferring their antibiotic resistance from one species to another via plasmids. Plasmid transfer is yet another reason for restricting the use of antibiotics.

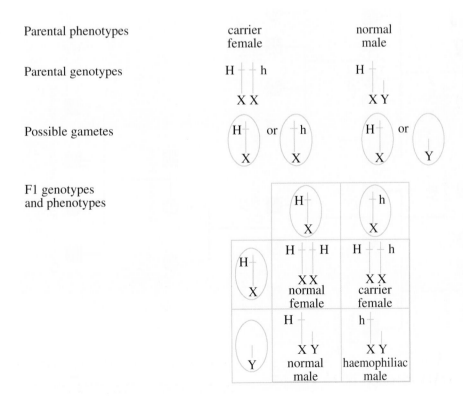

Fig. 13.20. Carrier female marries a normal male.

The Spread of Haemophilia through the Royal Houses of Europe

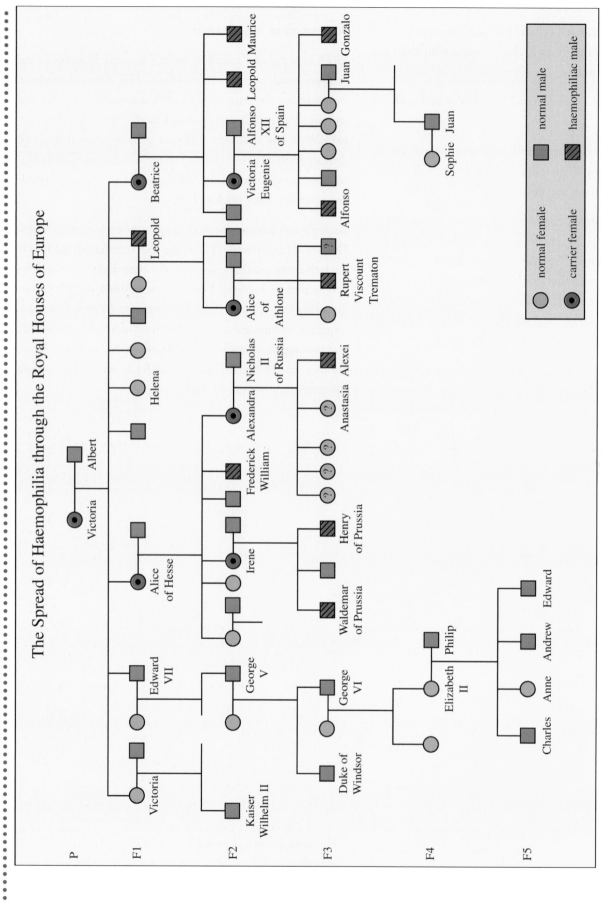

Fig. 13.21. Family tree of royal families of Europe, showing the inheritance of haemophilia.

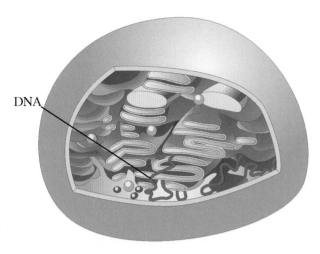

DNA

Fig. 13.22. Chloroplast with DNA.

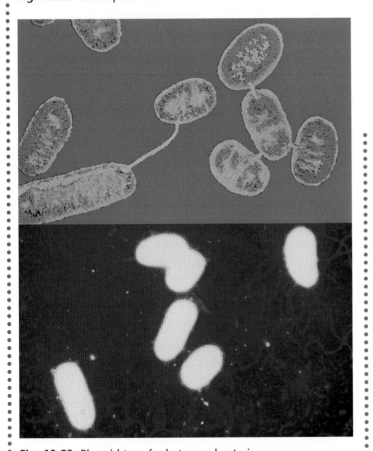

Fig. 13.23. Plasmid transfer between bacteria.

SUMMARY

- *There are two kinds* of reproduction in biology: sexual and asexual.
- *In asexual reproduction*, one parent is involved and the offspring are genetically identical to that parent.

- *In sexual reproduction*, there are two parents. They make haploid gametes, which join together by fertilisation to form a diploid zygote. The zygote develops into an embryo and eventually into another adult.
- *Gametes* are reproductive cells containing single sets of chromosomes (they are haploid).
- *Gametes are formed* either directly or indirectly by meiosis.
- *Characteristics in organisms* are controlled by pairs of genes located on pairs of homologous chromosomes.
- *Meiosis* ensures that only one member of any gene or chromosome pair will be found in any gamete.
- *Fertilisation* restores the gene and chromosome pairs.
- *Probability* is an estimate of how likely an event is.
- *Human females* have two X chromosomes in every cell, males have an X and a Y chromosome in every cell.

EXTENDED SUMMARY

- *Gregor Mendel* is rightly considered to be the father of modern genetics.
- *Mendel studied* the inheritance of seven different characteristics in the pea plant.
- *The Law of Segregation:* Characteristics are controlled by pairs of 'factors', but only one of these factors can be carried in a gamete.
- *The Law of Independent Assortment:* Where two or more characteristics are concerned, the 'factors', for these enter the gametes independently of each other.
- *The dihybrid cross* shows the simultaneous inheritance of two characteristics at the same time.
- *Linkage* is where genes happen to be located on the same chromosome.
- *Linked genes* are 'tied' to one another and tend to be inherited together.
- *Gene linkage* reduces the variety of sex cells and contradicts Mendel's second law.
- *Genes are sex-linked* if they are located on sex chromosomes.
- *Haemophilia,* colour blindness and Duchenne Muscular Dystrophy are sex-linked conditions.

- *DNA is not always found* in the cell nucleus, it is also found in mitochondria and in chloroplasts.
- *Mitochondria* and chloroplasts are self-replicating.
- *Bacteria* contain loops or lengths of extra-chromosomal DNA called plasmids.

KEY WORDS

All of the genetic terms listed at the beginning of the chapter should be learned.

Gametes	Haploid, reproductive cells containing single sets of chromosomes.
Punnett square	A mathematical grid used to show the possible combinations of genotypes arising from parents.
Incomplete dominance	When a single dominant gene in a heterozygote is not fully expressed.

EXTENDED KEY WORDS

Autosomes	Non-sex chromosomes.
Pisum sativum	The pea plant used by Mendel in his studies.
Linkage	Where genes happen to be located on the same chromosome.
Drosophila melanogaster	A fruit fly commonly used in genetic study.
Extra-chromosomal DNA	DNA that is not part of a chromosome, usually found in chloroplasts and mitochondria.
Plasmids	Loops or lengths of extra-chromosomal DNA found in bacteria.

QUESTIONS

1. Explain the difference between sexual and asexual reproduction. Which method leads to more variation in a population and why?

2. In mice, long ears are dominant over short ears. A homozygous, long-eared mouse is mated with a short-eared mouse. Decide whether each of the following outcomes is *certain*, *possible* or *impossible*:

   a. no offspring will arise;
   b. all offspring will be long-eared;
   c. half of the offspring will be short-eared;
   d. all female offspring will be like the mother.

3. True or false?

   a. If a phenotype is known, the genotype will always be known.
   b. Recessive heterozygote pea plants do not exist.
   c. If two heterozygous, tall pea plants are crossed, four kinds of fertilisation are possible.
   d. It is possible that a tossed coin turns up heads 100 times in a row.
   e. Meiosis only takes place in diploid cells.

4. In pea plants, tall (T) is dominant over dwarf (t). A homozygous, tall plant is crossed with a dwarf plant and two of the F1 plants are crossed. Show, by diagrams, the genotypes and phenotypes of the F2 generation.
   If two tall pea plants produce some dwarf plants, what are the genotypes of the parents?

5. In humans, brown eyes (B) are dominant over blue eyes (b). A brown-eyed parent and a blue-eyed parent produce four blue-eyed children over a number of years. What are the genotypes of the parents? What are the chances that the next child will be blue-eyed too?

6. In humans, normal skin (N) is dominant over freckled skin (n).
   State the genotype of each of the following:

   a. a homozygous, normal skin parent;
   b. a heterozygous, normal skin parent;
   c. a freckled skin parent.

   Show, by diagrams, how two freckled parents always produce freckled children.
   Show how two normal skin parents can produce a freckled skin child.

7. In pea plants, round seed (R) is dominant over wrinkled seed (r). Two wrinkled seed plants are crossed and one of the resulting F1 plants is crossed with a homozygous, round seed plant. State the genotypes of the parent plants and the F1 plants. Show, by diagrams, the results of the second cross.

8. Albinism is due to a recessive mutation of a single gene. Albinos are homozygous recessive (aa) for the gene and are unable to produce the pigment, melanin. This gives albinos pale skin, white hair and pink eyes.

   An albino woman marries a homozygous man and they have three children. Show how all the children are carriers for the disease.

   One of the children later marries another carrier. What are the chances that they will have an albino child?

9. In snails, plain shell (S) is dominant over speckled shell (s). Two heterozygous, plain snails are mated. State the genotypes and phenotypes of the parents. State the genotypes of any sex cells they might produce.

   Show, by diagrams, the possible genotypes and phenotypes of the F1 generation.

   Assess what percentage of the F1 generation is likely to:

   a. have a plain shell;
   b. have a speckled shell;
   c. be homozygous;
   d. be heterozygous.

10. Cystic fibrosis in humans is a genetic condition due to a recessive gene. A patient with the condition produces lots of mucus within their digestive system and lungs. Patients are homozygous, recessive. Heterozygous individuals are normal.

   The first child of two parents has cystic fibrosis. What are the genotypes of the parents? What are the chances that a second child will have the condition too?

11. In humans, the condition of *brachydactyly* (very short fingers) is due to the presence of a single, *dominant* gene.

   Can two parents, with normal fingers, produce a child with brachydactyly?

   Two parents with brachydactyly have a child with normal fingers What does this suggest about the parents' genotypes and the child's genotype?

12. In snapdragons, the gene for red flower (R) is incompletely dominant over the gene for white flower (r) and heterozygous plants have pink flowers.

   Draw a table to show all the possible genotypes and phenotypes of snapdragons.

   Show, by diagrams, the genotype and phenotype of the F1 plants if a plant with red flowers is crossed with a plant with white flowers.

   If two of these F1 plants are crossed, show that the chances of obtaining plants with white flowers is one in four.

13. Human ABO blood groups are determined by a single pair of allelic genes. The gene can have three forms: A, B or o. The A and B forms of the gene are equally dominant when present together. Both dominate the o form of the gene.

   The chart shows all possible genotypes and phenotypes:

Genotype	Phenotype
AA	**Group A**
AB	Group AB
Ao	Group A
BB	Group B
Bo	Group B
oo	Group O

   (i) State the possible genotypes of:

   a. a group A parent;
   b. a group B parent;
   c. a group AB parent;
   d. a group O parent.

(ii) Show how a group A parent and a group B parent can produce a group O child.

(iii) Will two group A parents always produce group A children?

(iv) Two group A parents produce five group A children over a number of years. What does this suggest about their genotypes?

(v) A group A mother has a group O child. Two men, one group A and the other group AB, both claim to be the father of the child. What does the blood group evidence suggest?

14. In shorthorn cattle, coat colour can be red (R), white (r) or, in heterozygous animals, roan. If two roan animals are crossed, what percentage of the offspring is likely to be roan?

What are the chances of obtaining a white animal from a roan and a white parent? From a roan and a red parent?

15. In fruit flies (*Drosophila*), normal wings (W) are dominant over stumpy (or *vestigial*) wings, (w). A biologist has three normal wing flies: A, B and C. When A and B were crossed, 124 normal wing flies were produced. When B and C were crossed, 78 normal and 28 stumpy wing flies were obtained.

State, with reasons, the genotypes of A, B and C.

16. What are sex chromosomes? What sex chromosomes occur in human males? In females? Draw diagrams to show how the sex of a child is inherited. A woman is pregnant for the seventh time. Her six children are all male. What are the chances that this next child is male too?

EXTENDED QUESTIONS

1. How many kinds of sex cell could be produced by organisms with the following genotypes?

a. AAbb
b. JjKk
c. Ccdd
d. RrSsTt
e. EEffggHHiiJJ

2. How many compartments would be needed in the Punnett squares used to work out the following crosses?

a. Aa × aa
b. Aa × Aa
c. AaBb × aabb
d. AaBb × AaBb
e. AaBbCc × AABbcc
f. AABBccDD × aabbCCdd

3. In pea plants, tall (T) is dominant over dwarf (t) and grey seed coat (G) is dominant over white seed coat (g). A homozygous, tall plant with grey seeds is crossed with a dwarf, white seed plant. All of the F1 generation are tall. One of the F1 plants is crossed with a dwarf, white seed plant. Give the genotype, phenotype and ration of the F2 generation.

4. In snapdragons, the gene for red flower (R) is incompletely dominant over the gene for white flower (r) and heterozygous plants have pink flowers. Tall (T) is dominant over dwarf (t). Use Punnett squares to show the genotypes and phenotypes that could arise from the following crosses:

a. a homozygous tall, red flowered plant with a dwarf, white flowered plant;
b. a dwarf, pink plant with a dwarf, white plant;
c. two heterozygous tall, pink plants.

5. Mendel crossed a tall pea plant with axial flowers (TtAa) with a dwarf plant with terminal flowers (ttaa). He obtained four types of offspring in a ratio of 1:1:1:1. Explain how this result complied with his two laws.

6. Mendel provided great insight into the mechanisms of inheritance.

a. State his two laws and then restate them using more modern terminology.
b. How well do his laws stand up in the light of modern knowledge?
c. In what ways was Mendel 'lucky' in his investigations?

7. What is meant by gene linkage? Draw labelled diagrams to show the genes and chromosomes of a heterozygous organism AaBb if:

   a. these genes occur on separate chromosomes;
   b. the genes are linked: A to B and a to b.

8. In *Drosophila*, grey body (G) is dominant over ebony body (g) and straight wing (S) is dominant over curled wing (s). The genes for these characteristics are linked. A grey, straight winged fly, homozygous for both conditions, is crossed with an ebony, curled wing fly. Two of the F1 flies are crossed. Show the genotypes and phenotypes of the F2 generation.

9. In sweet pea, purple flowers (P) are dominant over red flowers (p) and elongated pollen (L) is dominant over rounded pollen (l). A plant with the genotype PPLL is crossed with a double recessive plant (ppll). Two of the F1 plants are then crossed.

   a. State the phenotypes of the parent plants.
   b. Show the genotypes, phenotypes and ratio of the F2 generation:

      (i) if these genes occur on separate chromosomes;
      (ii) if the genes are linked.

10. What is meant by *sex linkage*?
   'Colour blindness in humans is a sex linked condition'. Explain exactly what this statement means.
   Draw chromosome diagrams to illustrate the genotypes of the following:

   a. a colour blind male;
   b. a normal male;
   c. a normal female;
   d. a carrier for the condition.

   Show how it is *possible* for a female to have colour blindness. Can a man's Y chromosome be inherited from his father's mother's father?

11. Why should humans be particularly interested in plasmid transfer between bacteria?

OPTIONAL ACTIVITIES

■ In humans, all eye colours are dominant over blue eyes, tongue-rolling is dominant over non-rolling, non-freckled skin is dominant over freckled skin, and free ear lobes are dominant over attached lobes.

Survey the class and prepare a chart to show the number of pupils showing dominant and recessive characteristics for each trait.

Characteristic	Number of pupils showing dominant condition	Number of pupils showing recessive condition
Eye colour		
Tongue-rolling ability		
Freckling		
Ear lobe type		

Calculate the percentage of the class showing the recessive condition of each characteristic.

■ Prepare a set of pairs of strips of paper marked with gene symbols. These will represent pairs of chromosomes of one parent. Prepare a second set in a different colour to represent a second parent, e.g.:

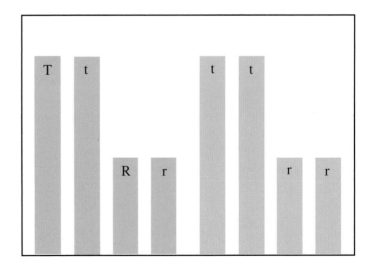

Choose one of *each* pair of chromosomes *at random* (eyes closed!) to form sex cells. Combine the sex cells of both parents and record the genotype and phenotype of the offspring.

Perform large numbers of 'crosses' to allow Mendel's ratios to emerge.

■ Gather information on the numbers of males and females in Ireland at different age levels. Make a written presentation of your findings.

■ Relevant information can be found within the Central Statistics Office web page at http://www.cso.ie/index.html or *LoCall*: 1890 313414.

Now test yourself at
www.my-etest.com

Chapter 14
Variation and Evolution

SOURCES OF INHERITED VARIATION [257]

As explained in Chapter 12, section [251], *Variation* refers to the differences between the members of a population.

Any two members of a population will resemble each other but no two members will ever be exactly the same. This is particularly obvious in a population of humans. Variations between two individuals may be *acquired* ('picked up' during the life of the organism) or *inherited*.

Inheritable (or genetic) variations in a population are very significant as they can be passed on to the next generation.

The main sources of inheritable variation are:

1. Sexual reproduction

- When parents make gametes, many genes enter the gametes independently of one another and so many different 'types' of gamete are made. Also, during the formation of the gametes by meiosis, random accidents produce new combinations of genes and further increase this variety.

- For example, one human sex cell may contain a dominant gene for a straight nose together with a recessive gene for fair hair. Another sex cell may have both dark hair and straight nose genes together and so on. This leads to variation amongst any children.

- The blending of the features of the male and female parents in fertilisation produces new combinations of features in the offspring.

- With the exception of identical twins, no two members of a family will ever be genetically the same — and there are millions of potential family members that could exist. Populations that use sexual reproduction will always have a high degree of variation.

2. Mutations

A mutation is a spontaneous change in a gene or chromosome.

Mutations are random events that affect individual genes or entire chromosomes.

Gene mutations are random changes to the gene structure. They may be changes as slight as the alteration of a single base in the DNA. They usually make the gene non-functional or recessive. The harm done depends on the importance of the gene involved. Both blond hair and sickle cell anaemia (where red cells take on a deformed shape and carry less oxygen) are due to single gene mutations. *Sickle cell anaemia* is due to a mutation of a gene (Hb^A) that is concerned with the structure of haemoglobin. The mutated gene (Hb^S) produces haemoglobin S rather than normal haemoglobin A. The mutation is common in black people in tropical climates.

The mutated haemoglobin is a poor oxygen carrier and distorts the shape of the red cells. Homozygotes for the disease ($Hb^S Hb^S$) suffer from severe anaemia with blocked blood capillaries and tend to have a short life expectancy. This means that sickle call anaemia is rare in any population. Much more common is *sickle cell trait*, which occurs in heterozygotes ($Hb^A Hb^S$). These heterozygotes have generally good health, with only some anaemia and tiredness. Heterozygotes also have the advantage of being resistant to severe forms of malaria. In this example, the same mutated gene, Hb^S, has an advantage in the heterozygous condition and a disadvantage in the homozygous condition.

Chromosome mutations are random changes to portions of chromosomes or to the chromosome number. They are potentially much more harmful given the large numbers of genes involved. Examples include: *deletions*, where entire chromosome portions are missing; *inversions*, where a portion of chromosome is turned the wrong way around; and *translocations*, where chromosome portions are attached to other chromosomes.

Changes in *chromosome number* tend to be harmful in animals and humans but beneficial in plants. Down's Syndrome is due to the presence of an extra 47th chromosome in the body cells.

Down's Syndrome patients possess three copies (a *trisomy*) of chromosome 21 in every body cell, rather than the normal two copies. The condition produces an alteration in some facial features, a reduced resistance to disease and a reduced IQ level. The condition occurs about once in every 700 births, but this frequency increases as a mother's age increases. The 21st chromosome in humans is tiny and contains few genes. Trisomies of other, larger human chromosomes are generally lethal.

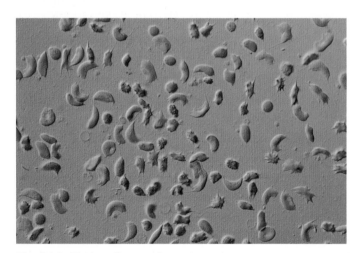

Fig. 14.1. Sickle cell anaemia.

Fig. 14.2. Three-year-old boy with Down's Syndrome.

Fig. 14.3. Red-eye *Drosophila* with white-eye mutants. Mutations in tree leaves.

Important points:

- All mutation events are *rare* in themselves, but if the condition they produce is not lethal, the mistakes tend to linger in the population and are passed on through many generations.
- Mutations at gamete formation (*germ cell mutations*) are important as they are passed on to the next generation.
- Mutations in body cells (*somatic mutations*) can be harmful but are *not* passed on to the next generation. Cancer is a somatic mutation — where cells revert to a primitive type and divide repeatedly. Cancers are potentially very harmful but are not inherited.
- As mutations are random changes, they are generally harmful and rarely to the benefit of the organism. (In a similar argument, it is possible to improve the picture quality of a TV by hitting it with a hammer, but not likely!). A tiny proportion of mutations are beneficial, however, and add variation to the population.

Mutations are either *spontaneous* (with no apparent cause) or caused by *mutagens*. A mutagen ('mutation generator') is any external agent likely to alter genes or chromosomes. Mutagens are, by their nature, very hazardous to biological tissue and should be avoided. Examples of mutagens include:

Chemicals: *mustard gas* — used in warfare in the past.
formaldehyde: once used as a biological preservative.
asbestos: used in the past for fireproofing and for reducing temperatures within car brake linings. Use is now illegal.
agent orange: a weed killer used by the American army in the Vietnam war to defoliate large stretches of jungle. Damages both somatic cells and reproductive cells.

Radiations: X-rays, cosmic rays, gamma rays and other ionising radiations harm DNA indirectly and their effects can accumulate in the body over years. They can also harm gametes. Ultraviolet radiation alters DNA structure directly and can cause somatic mutations in skin cells which produce skin cancer.

Viruses: The hepatitis B virus can cause liver cancer.

EVOLUTION   [258]

The word *evolution* means *unfolding* or *unrolling*.

Evolution is a gradual process resulting in the appearance of new species from previous forms over a long period of time. It explains how the enormous diversity of life appeared on the Earth.

EVOLUTION BY NATURAL SELECTION

Charles Darwin was an English naturalist who lived from 1809 to 1882. At the age of 22, he joined the crew of *HMS Beagle* on a five-year map-making journey through the southern hemisphere. The long voyage gave Darwin a chance to reflect on the variety of organisms he was observing. He was particularly influenced by the diversity of the

Fig. 14.4. Human evolution.

plants and animals inhabiting the Galapagos Islands off the west coast of South America and made extensive notes and observations. On his return, Darwin published many scientific papers, but he spent about 20 years working on his controversial theory that the members of a population could change over time. He then received a copy of an essay on evolution from Alfred Russel Wallace (who had also been travelling around the world) and realised it was a summary of his own beliefs. Darwin arranged for a joint paper on evolution to be presented to the Linnaean Society in 1858.

In 1859, Darwin published *On the Origin of Species by Natural Selection* to a mixture of acclaim and hostility. Many churchmen were particularly hostile to his work, as it suggested both that humans were related to apes and that all species had not been created separately as described in the Bible.

DARWIN'S OBSERVATIONS

1. In any natural population, the number of offspring is much greater than the number of parents.
2. Despite this, populations tend to remain at a constant level.

Conclusion: There is a '*struggle*' *for survival* and most offspring die without reproducing.

Fig. 14.5. Charles Darwin.

3. The members of any population have slight differences; no two organisms are exactly the same.

Conclusion: Some ('fitter') organisms are *more likely* to survive than others and will pass on their 'fitness' to the next generation.

Darwin called this process *Natural Selection* or '*Survival of the Fittest*' and stated that it would change the population over time. Natural Selection is the process where chance genetic variations in the population may give advantages to some organisms and make it more likely that they will survive. These favoured organisms then reproduce and pass on the advantageous variations to the next generation. Less favoured organisms tend to die young before passing their variations on by reproduction. Their disadvantages die with them and the population is overall slightly changed and now more suited to its environment.

Darwin's theory has been modernised with fossil dating and studies of geographical movements and is now referred to as *Neodarwinism*.

In summary, given the following:

- genetic variation in a population (due to mutation and sexual reproduction);
- pressure on the population to survive;
- a long period of time,

an *unfolding* of new and slightly different ('fitter') species will take place.

(Darwin's theory was in opposition to that of Jean Baptiste de Lamarck (1744–1829), who proposed the theory of *use and disuse*. Lamarck believed that, for example, giraffes obtained long necks by constantly stretching them to reach the leaves on tall trees. Darwin stated that giraffes born with long necks had a feeding advantage, were more likely to live longer and would pass their genetically long necks on to the next generation who, again, would have an advantage. Anyone believing that every human will soon lose his or her appendix due to disuse is guilty of Lamarckism! The appendix will only disappear from the population if being born without one confers an advantage of some sort.)

Fig. 14.6. Jean Baptiste de Lamarck.

Fig. 14.7. The evolution of long necks in giraffes.

Natural Selection is the driving force behind the Theory of Evolution. 'Fittest' means the most suitable to survive given the present conditions. It includes not just running ability but other adaptations such as suitable camouflage, appropriate digestive enzymes, extensive root systems and waterproofing on leaves. The expression *Survival of the Fittest* can be misleading. No organism, no matter how well designed, can survive through generations. It is better to think of copies of its *genes* surviving from generation to generation and giving advantages to their new owners.

NATURAL SELECTION IN ACTION

The peppered moth, *Biston betularia*, is common in Britain in the Midlands. It rests on the lichens on tree trunks and depends on its colouration for camouflage. Two forms of the moth are found: a light, speckled form and a dark form.

Prior to 1848, the dark form made up only 2% of the population, the rest being speckled. However, the frequency of the dark form then began to increase. By 1898, 96% of all moths in Manchester and other industrialised areas were dark and the speckled moths were rare.

The increase in population numbers of the dark moth was due to *Natural Selection*. The late 1800s was the time of the industrial revolution and soot from factories darkened the trees the moths landed on. Against a sooty background, birds could see the lighter coloured moths better and ate more of them. The speckled moths were likely to die before they could reproduce more of their kind. The dark moths were more likely to survive and leave dark offspring. The greater number of offspring left by dark moths increased their population frequency.

Fig. 14.8. Speckled and dark peppered moths.

Fig. 14.9. Katydid insect and pit viper.

N.B.

- *Genetic variation* existed within the population — due to mutation and sexual reproduction.
- Changing conditions placed new pressures on the population.
- No speckled moth turned itself into a dark moth.

EVIDENCE FOR EVOLUTION

All of the evidence for evolution is *circumstantial* — i.e. it appears to fit the facts of evolution *if evolution is true.* The Theory of Evolution can never be *'proved'* but, given the sheer size and weight of the supporting circumstantial evidence, it is the best theory available at present for the mechanism behind the unfolding of life over the age of the planet.

1. Comparative anatomy

Many of the anatomical structures of different organisms are strikingly similar. The forelimbs of a bat and a whale have similar bone structures. Humans, monkeys, mice and giraffes all have the same number of vertebrae in their necks, they suckle their young and they have diaphragms for breathing. Human, chicken, tortoise and fish embryos are strikingly similar if compared at an early stage. The similarities are not just external but found in their internal structure too.

The most likely explanation for these common relationships is that these animals all share a common ancestry and have inherited the same basic structures from these ancestors.

For example, the *pentadactyl limb* (fig. 14.11) is an arrangement of bones common to most higher vertebrates. It consists of a long bone followed by two parallel long bones, a group of small bones and then five sets of bones forming five digits (*'penta-dactyl'* means *'five digits'*).

This shared arrangement suggests a common ancestry. The details of the arrangement and the various bone shapes have been modified by the needs of the individual animals, but the basic plan of the limb is obvious and suggests a common ancestry.

2. Comparative biochemistry

Virtually all living organisms on the Earth share the same biochemistry. All use DNA and RNA as genetic molecules and share the same genetic code for protein synthesis. Respiration is performed in the same way in dandelions and humans, all plants use the same steps in photosynthesis. The same chemical, ATP, is used throughout biology for energy transfer. Again, this suggests a common ancestry.

3. The fossil record

Fossils are the dead and preserved remains of once-living organisms. Fossils are common on the earth and found in

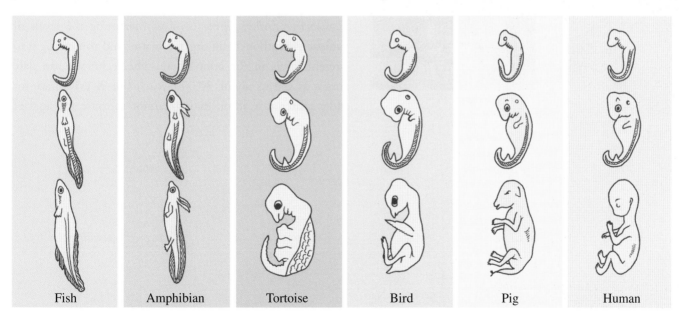

| Fish | Amphibian | Tortoise | Bird | Pig | Human |

Fig. 14.10. Compared embryos.

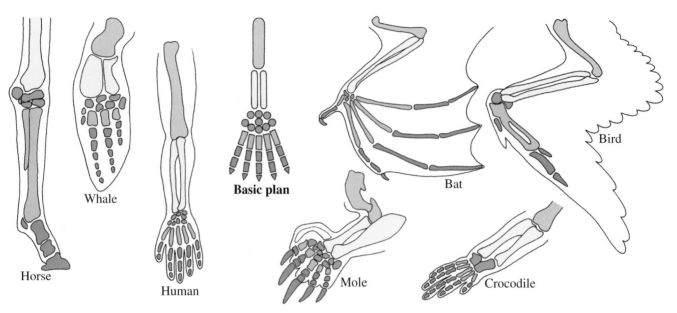

Fig. 14.11. Pentadactyl limbs.

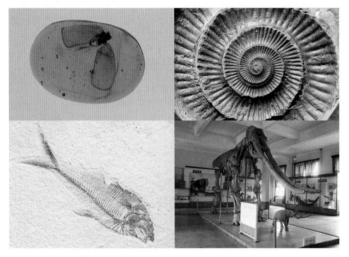

Fig. 14.12. Fossils.

sedimentary rock, ice and amber and in bogs (fig. 14.12). Generally the firmer parts of organisms form good fossils. The fossil records are very detailed for vertebrates (with bones), molluscs (with shells) and plants (with cell walls of cellulose). Fossils of flatworms and jellyfish are much less plentiful — their bodies having decomposed rapidly after death.

Some rocks and the fossils they contain can be accurately dated by radiometric dating.

Radioactive carbon dating involves measuring the levels of radioactive carbon-14 in organic matter and comparing it to present levels in the atmosphere. The technique can date fossils as old as about 30,000 years, but is inaccurate for older material. Carbon dating cannot measure the ages of fossils more than 60,000 years old and certainly not the ages of any that are millions of years old. *Potassium/argon dating* is used to date the rocks that contain older fossils and can be applied to rocks as old as 1,200 million years.

When the fossil record is studied, three observations can be made:

1. Many organisms were in abundance in the past but are not on the Earth now, e.g. the dinosaurs.
2. Many organisms are common on the Earth now, but have never been found as fossils, e.g. the modern horse.
3. If the fossils of related organisms are ordered according to their age, a pattern of simple to more complex anatomy is observed.

A study of the fossil record suggests ongoing changes in population members over long periods of time — with a direction of increasing complexity.

Example — the evolution of the modern horse

The study of horse fossils shows the existence of many intermediate forms between the ancestor of the horse, *Eohippus*, and the modern animal, *Equus*. A smooth transition from the 1/2 metre sized *Eohippus* to the present day 1.6m animal has been pieced together using fossilised teeth and limb bones.

The fossil record cannot provide a complete description of evolution as:

- generally fossils are only found for the harder structures of plants and animals;
- older fossils are difficult to date accurately;
- many fossils will never be discovered;
- many fossils are destroyed by erosion.

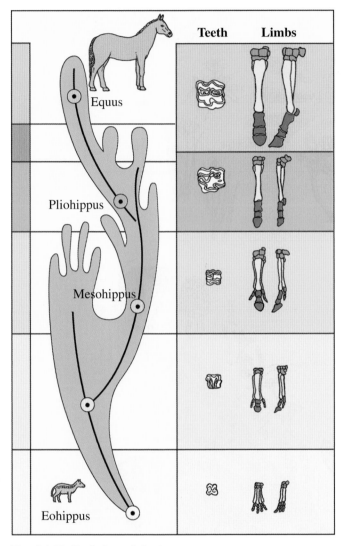

Fig. 14.13. Evolution of the horse.

Fig. 14.14. Evolution of plants.

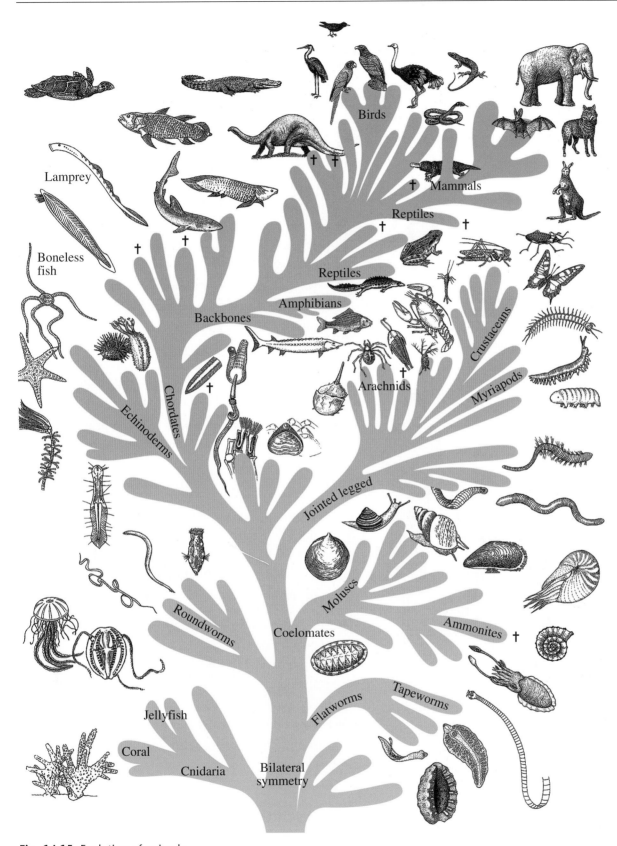

Fig. 14.15. Evolution of animals.

Fig. 14.16. Cultural evolution — technology.

Fig. 14.17. The evolutionary tree.

SUMMARY

- *Variations* between two individuals may be acquired or inherited.
- *The main sources* of inheritable variation are sexual reproduction and mutations.
- *Mutations* are random events that affect individual genes or entire chromosomes.
- *Gene mutations* are random changes to the gene structure.
- *Chromosome mutations* are random changes to portions of chromosomes or to the chromosome number.
- *Changes in chromosome number* tend to be very harmful in animals and humans but beneficial in plants.
- *Mutations* are either spontaneous or caused by mutagens.
- *Examples of mutagens* include chemicals, radiation and viruses.
- *Evolution* is a gradual process resulting in the appearance of new species from previous forms over a long period of time.
- *Darwin* drew two conclusions from his observations:

  - there is a 'struggle' for survival and most offspring die without reproducing;
  - some (the 'fitter') organisms are more likely to survive than others and will pass on their 'fitness' to the next generation.

- *Survival of the Fittest* leads to Natural Selection in populations.
- *Natural Selection* is the driving force behind evolution.
- *All of the evidence* for evolution is circumstantial.
- *Evidence for evolution* is drawn from comparative anatomy, comparative embryology and the fossil record.

KEY WORDS

Variation	Refers to the differences between the members of a population.

Acquired variation	'Picked up' during life.
Inherited variation	Passed on through sex cells.
Mutation	A spontaneous change in a gene or chromosome.
Gene mutations	Random changes to the gene structure.
Chromosome mutations	Random changes to portions of chromosomes or to the chromosome number.
Deletions	Where entire chromosome portions are missing.
Inversions	Where a portion of chromosome is turned the wrong way around.
Translocations	Where chromosome portions are attached to other chromosomes.
Trisomy	Three copies of the chromosome in a cell.
Germ cell mutations	Mutations at gamete formation.
Somatic mutations	Mutations in body cells.
Mutagen	Any external agent likely to alter genes or chromosomes.
Evolution	Unfolding or unrolling.
Natural Selection	Where organisms with favourable, genetic characteristics are more likely to survive, reproduce and pass their characteristics to the next generation. Also loosely termed 'Survival of the Fittest'.
'Fittest'	The organisms most suited to survive given the present conditions.
Neodarwinism	The modern form of Darwin's theory.
Lamarckism	The belief that favourable characteristics are acquired during life and then transmitted to the next generation.

Circumstantial	Evidence that appears to fit the given facts.
Pentadactyl	A limb with five digits.
Fossils	The dead and preserved remains of once-living organisms.

QUESTIONS

1. What is *variation*? Name two types of variation and give two examples of each type.
2. What are the main sources of variation within populations?
3. What are mutations? Explain the difference between a gene mutation and a chromosome mutation. State one example of each type of mutation in humans.

   Why are chromosome mutations generally much more harmful than gene mutations?

   Why are mutations in sex cells more significant than those in non-sex cells?
4. What is a *mutagen*? Name three types of mutagen and give one example of each.
5. What does the term '*evolution*' mean? Name the famous British scientist who published his Theory of Evolution in 1859. What was the title of his publication?
6. State the observations and conclusions on which the Theory of Evolution is based.
7. What is *Lamarckism*? Explain how giraffes may have obtained their long necks:

   a. According to Lamarck;
   b. According to Darwin.

8. The peppered moth population of Manchester demonstrated Natural Selection in action in the nineteenth century. Read the account of the moths in the text and answer the following questions:

   a. What caused the decline of the speckled form of moth?
   b. What advantage did the speckled form have before their numbers declined?

c. In what sort of environments might the speckled moths have continued to thrive?

d. Why did the dark moths become more frequent in certain areas?

e. Why are dark moths less frequent in industrial areas since 1965?

9. Explain what is meant by *circumstantial evidence*. Why is most of the evidence for evolution considered circumstantial?

10. List the types of evidence that support evolution and give one example of each.

11. Why will the fossil record always be incomplete?

12. Discuss the following:

a. Humans are descended from apes.

b. The human appendix gets shorter with every generation as it is not used. Soon it will have disappeared altogether.

c. Sharks and dolphins both have fins and so must be closely related.

d. Humans have used their technology to remove themselves from evolution.

e. Evolution on Earth is a thing of the past.

OPTIONAL ACTIVITIES

- Squash leaves between sheets of plasticine to simulate fossils formed in sedimentary rock.
- Use plasticine moulds and plaster of Paris to make casts of shells and chicken bones.
- Conduct a debate on *Evolution* versus *Creation*.
- Read *The Blind Watchmaker*, Richard Dawkins (Penquin).

For more information on websites dealing with subjects covered in this chapter see www.my-etest.com.

Now test yourself at
www.my-etest.com

Chapter 15
Genetic Engineering

INTRODUCTION

Genetic engineering is a technology designed to introduce new genes into cells. It dates from 1971 when Arber and Smith discovered *restriction enzymes* for chopping up specific portions of DNA. Organisms containing cells with transplanted DNA are termed *transgenic organisms* and have new and useful characteristics.

DNA made from genes of different organisms is called *recombinant DNA*. Genetic engineering is also known as *recombinant DNA technology*.

The tools of genetic engineering

1. *Restriction enzymes* are enzymes that can cut DNA molecules into pieces. They are highly specific and can produce exact DNA portions with 'sticky ends' for easy rejoining. If the same enzyme is used to cut both human and bacterial DNA, the 'sticky ends' will match and will join together. Complementary 'sticky ends' have complementary base pairing. A portion of DNA with the base sequence AGT exposed will join with another portion with a base sequence of TCA (see Chapter 12 for the base pairing rule).

   Restriction enzymes are extracted from bacteria and are named after their source. For example, *Eco*RI is named after the bacterium that produces it, *E. coli*.
2. *DNA ligase* is an enzyme used to join fragments of DNA. The process is called *annealing* and can only take place if the strands have complementary 'sticky ends'.
3. *DNA polymerase* is an enzyme used to replicate strands of DNA.
4. *Reverse transcriptase* is an enzyme used to make strands of DNA from RNA templates.

The main steps in genetic engineering

- A portion of DNA (or RNA) is identified as having useful characteristics and *isolated*.

- *Copies* of the DNA are made by gene cloning. This is often done inside bacteria.
- The multiple copies are inserted into a living organism that will *express* the gene.

Example: the manufacture of human insulin for diabetics

1. Insulin mRNA is extracted from healthy human pancreas cells.
2. Reverse transcriptase is used to make complementary DNA strands from the RNA.
3. The new DNA is copied many times by DNA polymerase.
4. DNA ligase inserts the copied DNA (cDNA) into tiny loops of bacterial DNA called *plasmids*.
5. Plasmids are inserted into *E. coli* bacteria and are incorporated in the bacterial chromosome.

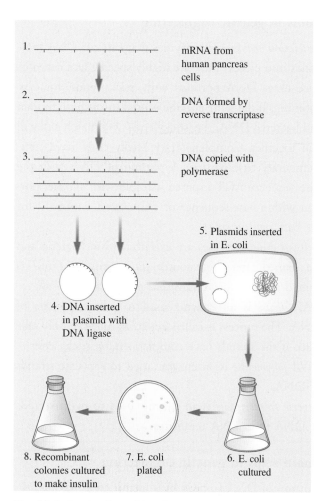

Fig. 15.1. Production of insulin.

6. The bacteria grow and reproduce — with multiple copies of the human insulin gene.
7. The bacteria are examined and any with the new, recombinant DNA are harvested.
8. These bacteria are cultured with lactose (which activates the insulin gene) to make human insulin.

APPLICATIONS OF RECOMBINANT DNA TECHNOLOGY

Humans

- Production of human insulin as above.
- Production of human blood clotting factor VIII for haemophiliacs. This will have the added advantage of being entirely free of contamination by HIV or hepatitis viruses.
- Production of human growth hormone.
- Replacement of faulty genes with normal ones will soon be possible, e.g. the repair of liver disorders and cystic fibrosis genes. This is referred to as *gene therapy*.
- Production of Interferon for cancer treatment.
- Production of antiviral vaccines.

Plants

- *Transgenic plants* such as tomatoes, apples and potatoes will have much improved characteristics — faster growth, better flavour and better disease and insect resistance. Tomato plants have been given genes that are fatal to caterpillars but not other animals (or humans!).

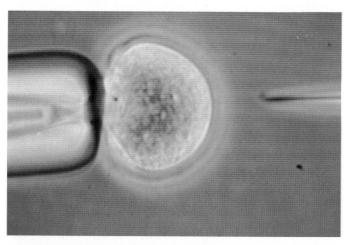

Fig. 15.2. Withdrawal of DNA and RNA from a cell by microinjection.

Animals

- Improved silk can be produced in silkworms.
- Strong adhesives can be made from barnacle genes.
- Improved milk and meat quality in farm animals.

Microorganisms

- Microorganisms are used as 'farms' for useful genes. Most gene cloning is done inside bacteria.
- Microorganisms are also used to transfer new genes to new sites. In a new treatment for cystic fibrosis (a genetic condition where mucus gathers inside the lungs), viruses containing normal genes will be introduced into the lungs. The viruses will enter the lung cells and incorporate the normal human genes into the lung DNA — so curing the condition.

DANGERS IN GENETIC ENGINEERING

Recombinant DNA technology is advancing at a very fast pace and many people are concerned that little attention has been given to possible dangers. Areas of concern include:

- 'Designer genes' may become available, where parents may wish to have embryos altered for trivial reasons such as eye colour, skin type, tallness, etc.
- Other gene functions within the organism may be affected by the appearance of new genes.
- New genes may 'leak' into the ecosystem and infect other species with unpredictable results. (At present, only 'disabled' species of microorganism are used — these have unusual nutrient requirements and cannot grow outside the laboratory.)
- The vast amounts of money that stand to be made can compromise the reliability of controls.
- The legal status of new, transgenic organisms is not clear.
- There is a general sense of an interference with the 'balance of nature'.

Clearly, genetic engineering offers enormous possibilities for the future. Its success will depend on our human ability to anticipate dangers and deal with them in advance. In this regard, genetic engineering is no different to any other scientific discovery in the past.

SUMMARY

- *Genetic engineering* is a technology designed to introduce new genes into cells.
- *Recombinant DNA* is DNA made from the genes of different organisms.
- *Genetic engineering* is also known as recombinant DNA technology.
- *Restriction enzymes* are enzymes that can cut DNA molecules into pieces.
- *Restriction enzymes are extracted* from bacteria and are named after their source.
- *DNA ligase* is an enzyme used to join fragments of DNA.
- *DNA polymerase* is an enzyme used to replicate strands of DNA.
- *Reverse transcriptase* is an enzyme used to make strands of DNA from RNA templates.
- *The main steps* in genetic engineering are:

  – a portion of DNA (or RNA) is identified as having useful characteristics and *isolated*;
  – *copies* of the DNA are made by gene cloning within bacteria;
  – the multiple copies are inserted into a living organism that will *express* the gene.

- *Recombinant DNA technology* is advancing at a very fast pace.

KEY WORDS

Restriction enzymes	Used for chopping up specific portions of DNA.
Transgenic	Organisms containing cells with transplanted DNA.
Recombinant DNA	DNA made from the genes of different organisms.
Recombinant DNA technology	An alternative name for genetic engineering.
Sticky ends	Matching ends of DNA molecules used to join both human and bacterial DNA portions together.

*Eco*RI	A restriction enzyme named after the bacterium that produces it, *E. coli*.
DNA ligase	An enzyme used to join fragments of DNA.
Annealing	The process of joining DNA fragments.
DNA polymerase	An enzyme used to replicate strands of DNA.
Reverse transcriptase	An enzyme used to make strands of DNA from RNA templates.
Plasmids	Tiny loops of DNA found in bacteria.
Gene therapy	Replacement of faulty genes with normal ones to correct health disorders.
Designer genes	Genes used to alter trivial conditions in organisms, e.g. eye colour, nose shape, etc.

QUESTIONS

1. What is genetic engineering? What is its alternative name? Explain what is meant by:

    a. transgenic organisms;
    b. recombinant DNA.

2. Name the enzymes that are commonly used in genetic engineering. What sort of enzyme is suitable for carrying out the following procedures?

    a. Making DNA from RNA.
    b. Joining DNA portions together.
    c. Chopping DNA into specific fragments.
    d. Copying DNA fragments.

3. What are plasmids? Why are they important in genetic engineering?

4. Outline the steps involved in the production of human insulin by genetic engineering.

5. What are restriction enzymes? Who first discovered them? If a portion of human DNA is to be attached to a bacterial plasmid, why is the same restriction enzyme used to prepare both DNA fragments?

6. Name the four different groups of organism within which recombinant DNA technology is used. Give two examples from each organism group.

7. What are 'designer genes' and why is there concern over their availability? State four other potential dangers in relation to the use of genetic engineering.

8. *Selective breeding* in agriculture is when animals or plants are reproduced together to form new individuals with, hopefully, good combinations of features. The technique is common in agriculture and produces, for example, cattle with good quality meat, potatoes that are disease-resistant, carrots with a good colour and taste, etc. *Genetic engineering* in agriculture attempts to do much the same. What is the difference between selective breeding and genetic engineering?

OPTIONAL ACTIVITIES

- Collect newspaper articles on genetic engineering and review them for good scientific technique.
- Present a report on good and bad aspects of genetic engineering. Visit *Genewatch UK* at http://www.genewatch.org/Home.htm for a discussion on the ethics of genetic engineering. Genewatch UK also maintain a database of genetically modified foods and have free briefings on many genetic engineering issues.
- Make a class list of the implications of having *designer genes* freely available to humans.

For more information on websites dealing with subjects covered in this chapter see www.my-etest.com.

Now test yourself at
www.my-etest.com

Chapter 16
Diversity of Organisms

Learning objectives

After your study of this chapter, you should be able to:

- explain the meaning of the term *species*;
- list the five kingdoms of living organisms;
- discuss the structure, growth and reproduction of bacteria;
- explain the origin and use of antibiotics;
- discuss the structure, growth and reproduction of fungi;
- illustrate the importance of both bacteria and fungi in medicine and industry;
- use safe microbial techniques to grow and study microorganisms;
- describe the structure and life of *Amoeba*;
- outline the classification of plants and animals.

Extended learning objectives

- Distinguish between prokaryotic and eukaryotic cell types.
- Draw and explain the typical bacterial growth curve.

Mandatory activities

#18 Investigation of the growth of leaf yeasts.
#15 The production of alcohol from yeast (see Chapter 9).

INTRODUCTION　　[311]

A *species* describes any group of organisms that resemble one another and have the ability to reproduce with one another.

At present, it is very difficult to say how many different species of living things are on the Earth. Current estimates range from six million up to maybe 120 million species. If you add to this all the discovered fossil species and any num-

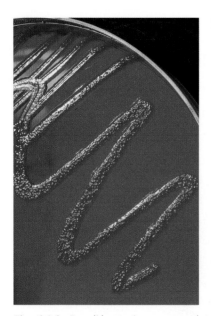

Fig. 16.1. *E. coli* bacteria on agar plate.

Fig. 16.3. Ferns.

Fig. 16.4. Buttercup.

Fig. 16.2. Bracket fungi.

Fig. 16.5. Carpenter ants.

Fig. 16.6. Trout.

Fig. 16.8. Red squirrel.

ber of existing, undiscovered species, the number would easily rise to over 500 million with many more to come through continuing evolution.

To study all of these organisms individually during a human lifetime of, say, 80 years, you would need to study about 12 creatures per minute, starting on the day you were born. You would still fall behind because of new evolutions during your own, very busy life!

Individual study of all organisms is very time-consuming. An alternative is to *classify* organisms, i.e. place them in groups. This is usually done according to similarities of

structure and now the groups may be studied rather than the individuals.

At present, organisms are first divided into five large groups or *kingdoms*. These kingdoms are then subdivided into smaller groups or *phyla*. These are, in turn, further subdivided and so on.

In addition to this, every organism is given a two-part Latin name to avoid international confusion over exactly which species is in question.

Fig. 16.7. Puffin.

Fig. 16.9. Charles Linnaeus (1707 – 1778).

The five kingdoms of living organisms are as follows:

1. *Monera.* These are single-celled organisms that lack a nuclear membrane (they are *prokaryotic* — see Chapter 6). They have very few cell organelles and are represented mostly by the bacteria.

2. *Protoctista* (or *protista*). These are also usually single-celled organisms, but with a more advanced cell type (they are *eukaryotic*). They may or may not make their own food. Many have become multicellular, though all their cells will be similar. This kingdom includes *amoeba* and the various *algae*.

3. *Fungi.* These are multicellular, eukaryotic organisms that have absorptive nutrition. They include mushrooms, bread mould and yeast (which is unicellular).

4. *Plants.* These are multicellular, eukaryotic organisms that make their own food using sunlight.

5. *Animals.* These are multicellular, eukaryotic organisms that ingest their food.

(Swedish botanist Carl Linnaeus (1707–1778) was the first to attempt to classify living organisms in a scientific manner. He decided on two major kingdoms — plants and animals. He was also responsible for the two-part Latin names given to all species.

The present five-kingdom system dates from only 1988 and comes from the work of Lynne Margulis and Karlene Schwartz, who first grouped single-celled eukaryotes together with multicellular algae.) Their system is based on the work of Robert H. Whittaker.

Table 16.1. A summary of the five kingdom system of classification

Kingdom	Cell type	Cell number	Nutrition	Diversity	Examples
Monera	Prokaryotic	Single-celled	Varied	Large number of phyla	Bacteria and cyanobacteria
Protoctista (protista)	Eukaryotic	Single- or multi-celled.	Varied	Algae, Protozoa	*Fucus* diatoms, *Amoeba*
Fungi	Eukaryotic	Multi-celled, except yeast	Absorptive	Four major phyla	Bread mould, mushrooms, yeast
Plants	Eukaryotic	Multi-celled	Photosynthetic	Six major phyla	Mosses, ferns, flowering plants
Animals	Eukaryotic	Multi-celled	Ingestive	Nine phyla	Sponges, jellyfish, flatworms, roundworms, segmented worms, arthropods, molluscs, echinoderms, chordates

Prokaryotic	describes a simple cell type with no nuclear membrane, no plastids and no mitochondria. Ribosomes are found loose in the cytoplasm.
Eukaryotic	describes an advanced cell type. Nuclear material is enclosed in a nuclear membrane and there are many cell organelles. See Chapter 6 for more information on this.

Some 'organisms' are difficult to classify:

Lichens

A lichen is a *commensalism* between an alga and a fungus (the two organisms live together for their mutual benefit).

Fig. 16.10. Lichens on white pine.

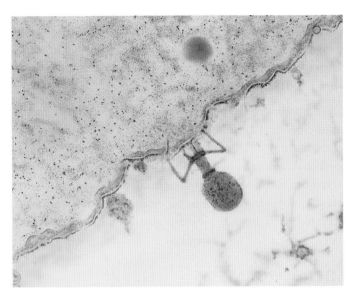

Fig. 16.11. A virus attached to a cell.

They are dual organisms — the two parts not being easily separated. They are therefore difficult to classify but are currently included with the fungi.

Viruses

It is debated whether viruses are living at all. They are extremely small and consist only of a protein coat, a nucleic acid core (DNA or RNA) and some enzymes. They do not demonstrate many (or perhaps any) of the characteristics of living organisms (see Chapter 26).

Prions

Certain types of cellular proteins have the peculiar property that when they are in an abnormal configuration, they will induce a corresponding normal protein to assume the same abnormal configuration. These proteins can set up a chain reaction leading to the progressive accumulation of abnormally configured proteins. Such proteins have been termed *prions* (from 'proteinaceous infectious particles').

Certain humans and animals seem to inherit genetically altered 'normal' protein. This protein has a tendency to form a small quantity of abnormally configured prion protein (PrP), which begins the chain reaction process. If other individuals become exposed to these proteins, e.g. by ingestion with food, disease can occur along with the potential of further transmission.

Prion diseases include *scrapie* in sheep and in goats, *bovine spongiform encephalopathy* (BSE or *mad cow disease*) in cattle, *feline spongiform encephalopathy* in cats and *Creutzfeldt–Jakob disease* (CJD) in humans.

Of major concern is the fact that prion disease can be spread across species. For example, the emergence of mad cow disease has been traced to the use of sheep-derived tissue as a food supplement to feed cows. The cow disease appears to have been further transmitted to humans. Human transmission has also occurred due to contaminated growth hormone prepared from human pituitary glands and from contaminated corneal transplants and surgical instruments.

MICROORGANISMS   [312]

The term *microorganism* is an informal way of grouping organisms of microscopic size. It includes bacteria, viruses, fungi and some protista. Microorganisms are immensely important in biology and occupy almost everywhere — including salt water, fresh water, terrestrial and elevated habitats.

MONERA — KINGDOM OF BACTERIA   [313]

Bacteria are single-celled, *prokaryotic* organisms found just about everywhere. Their cells are extremely small and they are usually found in vast numbers. They are fast-growing and very active cells and are of great significance to life on Earth.

Prokaryotic cells have no nuclear membrane and few cytoplasmic organelles. Bacteria have a cell wall, which is sometimes enclosed in a capsule or slime layer.

Bacteria are classified according to their shape. Four main shapes of bacteria are found:

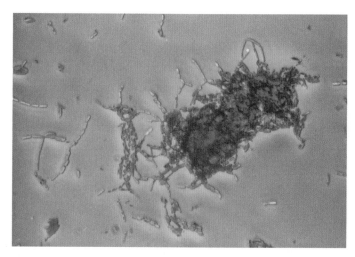

Fig. 16.12. Anthrax bacteria.

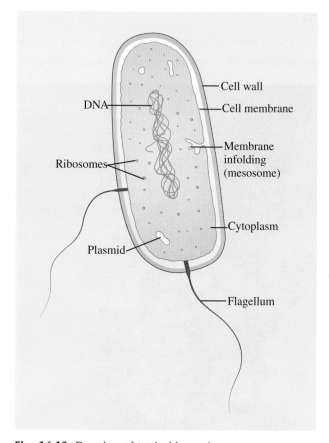

Fig. 16.13. Drawing of typical bacterium.

Spherical shape (*Cocci*), e.g.	*Streptococci* — cause sore throats; *Staphylococci* — cause food poisoning; *Diplococci* — cause pneumonia.
Rod shape (*Bacilli*), e.g.	*E. coli* — found in human intestines and therefore sewage; *Clostridium tetani* — causes tetanus in deep wounds;
Spiral shape (*Spirilli*), e.g.	*Spirillum minus* — causes Weil's disease (spread by rats);

Filament shape, e.g.	*Actinomyces* — cells remain attached after cell division and form threadlike (mycelial) colonies These bacteria are common in the soil and in the mouth.

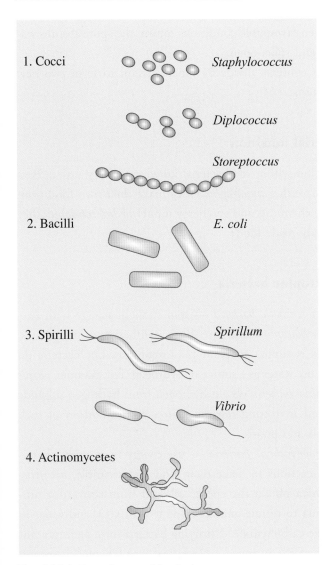

Fig. 16.14. Four shapes of bacteria.

1. Cocci — *Staphylococcus*, *Diplococcus*, *Storeptoccus*
2. Bacilli — *E. coli*
3. Spirilli — *Spirillum*, *Vibrio*
4. Actinomycetes

(N.B. Singulars/plurals are as follows: *bacterium/bacteria, coccus/cocci, bacillus/bacilli*).

REPRODUCTION OF BACTERIA

Reproduction is usually *asexual* (one parent) and is by binary fission. A single bacterium copies its DNA and then forms ingrowths of its cell wall. The cell then splits into two new bacteria. This may happen as rapidly as every 20 minutes, i.e. one bacterium in a wound with ideal conditions of temperature, nutrients and oxygen can become eight bacteria after one hour, 64 after two hours, 512 after three hours and so on — an enormous increase in numbers in a short period of time.

(Given this rate of reproduction, how many bacteria might be present after six hours? after 12 hours? after 24 hours? Why should wounds be cleaned as soon as possible?)

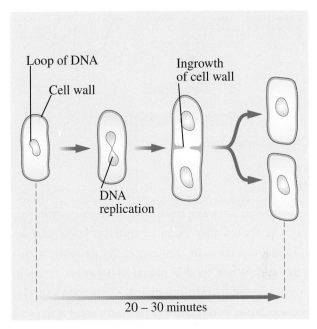

Fig. 16.15. Reproduction of a bacterium.

1. The bacterium prepares to reproduce by increasing its rate of respiration.
2. The DNA loop replicates itself.
3. The cell elongates and separates the new loops of DNA. The cell wall and membrane begin to infold.
4. Two identical bacterial cells are formed.

N.B. Most antibiotics work against bacteria by inhibiting cell wall synthesis. When exposed to the correct antibiotic, the bacteria become 'stuck' at stage three and then die.

The rapid rate of bacterial reproduction has important consequences:

- Wounds become heavily infected very quickly.
- Mutations within the bacterial population are very significant, e.g. antibiotic-resistant bacteria can suddenly appear in large numbers.
- Bacteria can transfer loops of DNA (plasmids) to other bacterial species and so transfer antibiotic immunities too.
- Bacteria can give very efficient returns of product when used in industry.

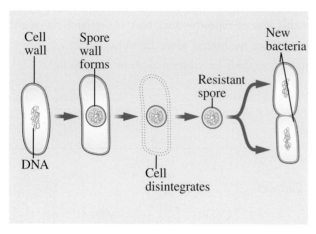

Fig. 16.16. Endospore formation.

Endospores

Many bacteria can form thick-walled endospores within parent cells. The spores often form in times of stress and are heat and chemical resistant. Endospore formation is a survival technique. When food is placed in a freezer, many of the bacteria respond by forming spores. These spores survive the low temperature and germinate when the food is thawed. Thawed food must be cooked and eaten without delay. Fast freezing in an expensive (and colder) freezer restricts spore formation. Trying to freeze too much food at the one time in a domestic freezer gives bacteria more time to form their spores.

Steps in endospore formation:

- The bacterium senses an unfavourable environment.
- The cell shrinks and becomes more rounded.
- A thick wall forms within the original cell wall.
- The rest of the cell disintegrates.
- The spore has minimal metabolism and can survive for long periods.

- When favourable conditions return, the spore absorbs water and splits open.
- The contents divide by binary fission to form two new bacteria.

Bacterial nutrition

Nutrition within the bacterial kingdom is very varied. Bacteria are either *autotrophic* (they make their own food from simple chemicals and an energy input) or *heterotrophic* (they eat ready-made food).

Autotrophic bacteria

- *Photosynthetic bacteria* — trap sunlight energy with *bacteriochlorophyll* and use it to synthesise carbohydrates. This is similar to plant photosynthesis, but bacteria do not use water as a source of hydrogen. For example, *purple sulphur bacteria* obtain hydrogen from hydrogen sulphide found in rotting organic matter at the bottom of rock pools and ponds.
- *Chemosynthetic bacteria* — use energy from other chemical reactions to make their food. For example, *nitrifying bacteria* obtain the energy released from converting ammonia to nitrate and combine it with CO_2 and water to make carbohydrate. Nitrifying bacteria form an important part of the nitrogen cycle in soil (see Chapter 4, section [148]).

Heterotrophic bacteria

- *Saprotrophic bacteria* — obtain their food in solution from dead and decaying organisms. The bacteria secrete extra-

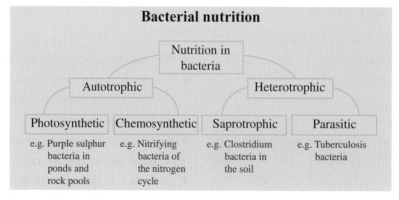

Fig. 16.17. Nutrition in bacteria.

cellular, digestive enzymes onto the food and then absorb the digested products. This contrasts with the feeding of animals and humans — where food is ingested whole and then digested internally. *Clostridium* bacteria in the soil are saprotrophic.

- *Parasitic bacteria* — obtain their food from a living source (or *host*). The parasitic relationship is beneficial to the bacteria but damaging to the host. *Mycobacterium tuberculosis* is a parasitic bacterium that grows within living lung tissue.

N.B. Parasitic bacteria attract a lot of attention but are relatively rare. Most bacteria are either autotrophic or saprotrophic.

The term '*saprotrophic*' replaces the older term '*saprophytic*' since bacteria and fungi are no longer grouped with plants.

Factors affecting the growth of bacteria

Bacterial growth is greatly affected by *temperature, humidity, pH, oxygen and suitable nutrients.*

Temperature	Most bacteria grow at 25–40 °C although some are active at near freezing temperatures and others produce spores that can survive boiling water for short periods of time.
Humidity	All bacteria, like all living things, need water to live but some can resist drying by forming resistant spores.
pH	pH 7.4 (the pH of blood) favours most bacteria but some (e.g. *acidophiles*) can tolerate extremes.
Oxygen	Most bacteria are *aerobic* — they need oxygen for respiration. Some bacteria are *facultative* — they can adapt if the oxygen disappears. Some bacteria are *strict anaerobes* — oxygen is lethal to them.

Nutrients	Some bacteria make their own food from sunlight or simple chemicals (*autotrophic bacteria*) but most of them (*heterotrophic bacteria*) have to find ready-made nutrients — either from living or dead tissue.

Other conditions that affect bacterial growth are external solute concentrations (including salt and sugar concentrations) and atmospheric pressure.

An understanding of the details of these factors is clearly important in the areas of food preservation and treatment of bacterial disease.

Table 16.2. Economic importance of bacteria

Beneficial bacteria	Harmful bacteria
Food/fuel industries	Cause disease (see below)
Role in nitrogen recycling (see chapter 4)	Cause food spoilage
Genetic research	Cause tooth decay — not strictly a disease
Antibiotics	
Silage-making	
Medicine	
Single-cell protein (a dietary protein substitute)	

Examples of useful bacteria:

Streptococcus is used in yoghurt and cheese making.
Methylophilus is used to make methane and methanol.
Leuconostoc is used in the sugar industry.
E. coli is used to make insulin, growth hormone and interferon (an antiviral drug).
Clostridium, *Nitrosomonas* and *Nitrobacter* recycle the dead remains of plants and animals in the soil.
Pseudomonas makes vitamin B_{12}.
Streptomyces produces antibiotics (see below).

Examples of harmful bacteria:

Salmonella causes food poisoning.
Mycobacterium causes TB.
Bordetella causes whooping cough.
Treponema causes syphilis.
Vibrio causes cholera.
Clostridium causes tetanus or botulism.

These harmful bacteria are examples of *pathogens* (or *pathogenic bacteria*). A pathogen is an organism that is capable of causing disease.

'*Pathogen*' = *pathos generator* or *disease generator*.
Pathology = *the study of the effects of disease.*

Many fungi and all viruses are also pathogens.

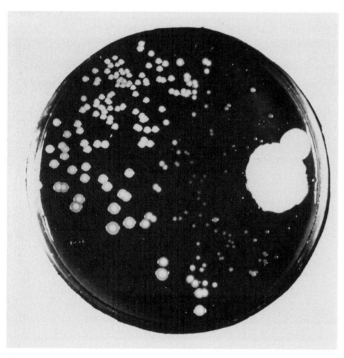

Fig. 16.18. Bacterial plate with fungus and antibiotic effect. Note the poor growth of the bacteria close to the fungus.

Antibiotics

Antibiotics are chemicals, secreted by some microorganisms, which prevent the growth of many bacteria (*antibiotic = against life*). Alexander Fleming discovered the first antibiotic, penicillin, in 1929 as a result of a chance accident in his laboratory. A bacterial plate was accidentally contaminated with *Penicillium* fungus and all bacteria near the fungus had died. The fungus was secreting a chemical to protect itself from bacterial attack. Fleming thought this chemical, *penicillin*, would make a good antiseptic but was unable to isolate the drug. In 1938, two scientists, Florey and Chain, collaborated to isolate and then test the drug. They succeeded by 1941 and the drug was in use in the second world war in Europe by 1944 — saving thousands of lives. Fleming, Florey and Chain shared the Nobel Prize in 1945, although Fleming had played no further part in the story since the original discovery.

Thousands of antibiotics have since been isolated — nearly all (but not penicillin) from bacteria. About 50 are in common use. Most of them work by *inhibiting cell wall synthesis* in the pathogens: the pathogen attempts to divide as normal but cannot complete the synthesis of new cell walls.

DANGERS IN THE OVERUSE OF ANTIBIOTICS

1. Overexposure increases the chances of resistant bacteria appearing. These will not be easily treated with existing antibiotics. New and stronger antibiotics then have to be developed to keep up. As a result of their rapid reproduction rate and high mutation rate, most bacterial colonies quickly develop a mixture of sensitive and resistant strains. If this mixed bacterial population is repeatedly exposed to antibiotics, the sensitive strains tend to die out and the resistant ones thrive in their absence. They will now require even stronger antibiotics — and the same process of 'natural' selection will repeat itself to select out even more resistant strains.
2. Antibiotics fed to animals generally improve their quality and growth but may accumulate in the food chain and cause problems to humans.
3. Many people are allergic to antibiotics.

KINGDOM OF FUNGI [314]

Fig. 16.19. Athlete's foot fungus.

Fig. 16.20. Mouldy bread.

Fig. 16.21. Fruit and vegetable mould.

Fig. 16.22. Toadstools.

Fungi are *eukaryotic* organisms with cell walls made mostly of chitin. They have *heterotrophic* nutrition and either feed on living tissue (*parasitic fungi*) or on dead organic matter (*saprotrophic fungi*). Fungi usually have a filamentous structure — the overall body of the fungus (*mycelium*) is made from branching, colourless threads or *hyphae*. Cell nuclei, cytoplasm and organelles tend to gather at the extremities of the hyphae, the rest of the fungus being almost empty. Fungi are usually multicellular with the famous exception of yeast, which is a unicellular fungus. All fungi are generally aerobic and they reproduce asexually by means of spores.

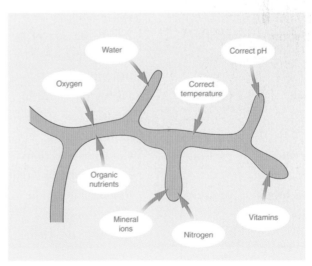

Fig. 16.23. Fungal needs.

N.B. Fungal nutrition is always heterotrophic — that is, they have to eat ready-made nutrients obtained from a living source (*parasitic* fungi) or a dead source (*saprotrophic* fungi).

Table 16.3. Examples of fungi

Fungus	Nutrition	Notes
Pin moulds	saprotrophic	Found in soil or on bread and rotten fruit, e.g. *Mucor* or *Rhizopus*.
Mushrooms	saprotrophic	The familiar parts are swollen reproductive organs — they may or *may not* be edible.
Yeast	saprotrophic	Single-celled — used in multimillion euro brewing and baking industries.
Penicillium	saprotrophic	Famous for producing penicillin for Alexander Fleming.
Ergot	saprotrophic	A woodland fungus that produces hallucinogenic chemicals.
Wet and dry rot	saprotrophic	Cause destruction of structural timbers in old buildings.
Ringworm	parasitic	Infects the skin of humans and other mammals.
Thrush	parasitic	Highly infectious in humans and difficult to treat.
Rusts and smuts	parasitic	Common infections of cereal plants.
Potato blight fungus	parasitic	Responsible for the Great Famine in Ireland in the 1840s.

In all cases, enzymes are released from the fungus onto the food. The food is digested *outside* the fungus and the digested products are then absorbed.

In the more advanced animals, food is digested *inside* the body of the animal.

Table 16.4. Economic importance of fungi

Examples of useful fungi	Examples of harmful fungi
Penicillium and *aspergillus* produce antibiotics.	*Amanita* (death cap fungus in woodland) is fatal if eaten.
Penicillium used for ripening cheese.	*Phytophthora* causes blight of potatoes and tomatoes.
Fusarium makes mycoprotein — a dietary protein substitute.	*Rhizopus* and *Penicillium* rot fruit.
Saccharomyces (yeast) used in brewing and baking.	*Merulius* causes dry rot.
Agaricus is the edible mushroom.	*Ceratocystis* causes Dutch elm disease.
Neurospora used in genetic research.	*Trichophyton* causes ringworm and athlete's foot.
Mucor helps to recycle organic matter in the soil.	*Candida* causes thrush and allergic reactions in humans.
Claviceps produces alkaloid drugs.	*Poria* stains paper in paper mills.

Rhizopus — the bread mould fungus

This is a grey, saprotrophic, pin mould found on bread and fruit. It produces a delicate, fluffy mycelium of hyphae with many sporangia (spore containers) that look like the heads of dressmaking pins. Rhizoids anchor the fungus to the substrate below (bread or fruit). The sporangia are held aloft by elongated sporangiophores. At the tip of each sporangiophore is a cup-shaped apophysis and a dome-shaped columella. Spores are formed by repeated mitosis and then covered in a protective coat. Spore release is by drying and fracture of the sporangium wall.

REPRODUCTION

Rhizopus has both a sexual and an asexual life cycle.

Asexual reproduction involves the formation of many spores by mitosis within a sporangium. These are released as above and will germinate in favourable conditions to form new but genetically identical fungi.

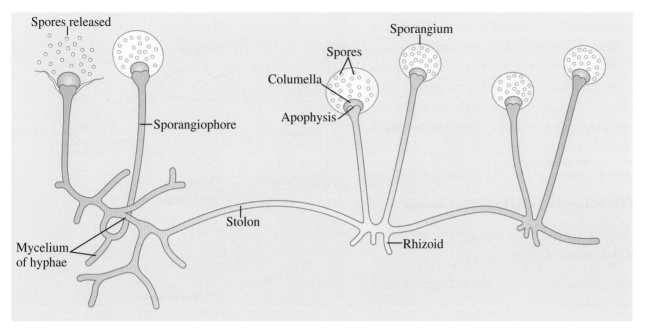

Fig. 16.24. Structure of *Rhizopus*.

Sexual reproduction involves two separate fungi and their sex cells or gametes. The fungi are physiologically different but termed + and − rather than male and female. The term 'male' refers to any parent that produces a sex cell that moves of its own accord. 'Female' refers to a parent that produces a sex cell that doesn't move of its own accord. As both sex cells of *Rhizopus* move equally, the terms 'male' and 'female' are not appropriate.

- Progametangia form on the adjacent hyphae of + and − fungi.
- Gametangia (gamete-producing cells) form on the ends of suspensors.
- The gametangia touch and join their nuclei ('gametes') together in fertilisation.
- A thick wall forms around the resulting zygote forming a zygospore.
- The zygospore germinates and produces a new fungal hypha.
- A sporangium forms immediately and releases spores.
- The spores form new *Rhizopus* fungi, which are a mixture of the genetic features of the two parents. All offspring will have the same physiological type: either + or −.

Yeast

This is a unicellular, saprotrophic fungus common on the surfaces of leaves and fruit and found in the soil. It is also

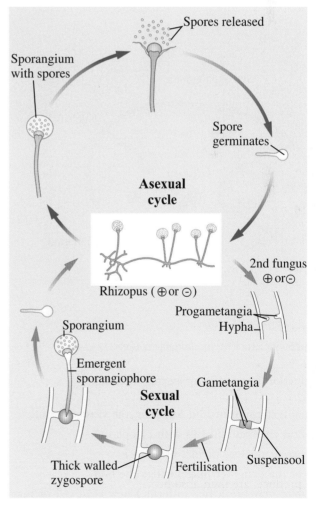

Fig. 16.25. Life cycle of *Rhizopus* — sexual and sexual reproduction.

a natural inhabitant of the intestines of most animals and humans. It is mostly anaerobic and has no need for oxygen. Its respiration lies at the heart of brewing and baking and is responsible for the billions of pounds generated by these enormous industries. The yeast family is known as the *Saccharomycetes* or literally 'sugar fungi'. (What do you think *Saccharomyces carlsbergenesis* is used for?)

Yeast respiration is summarised by the following equation:

$$C_6H_{12}O_6 + 6O_2 \Rightarrow 2C_2H_5OH + 2CO_2 + \textbf{Energy}$$

Glucose and oxygen are converted into alcohol and carbon dioxide — with a release of energy.

C_2H_5OH or *ethanol* is the alcohol that is found in beer, wine and other alcoholic drinks.

CO_2 or *carbon dioxide* is a gas that expands with heat and raises bread.

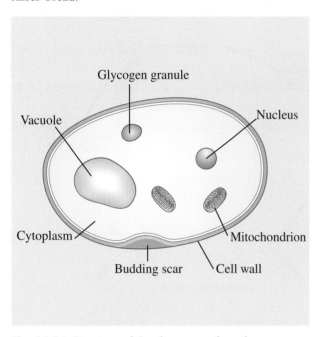

Fig. 16.26. Structure of *Saccharomyces* (yeast).

Reproduction in yeast is by asexual budding:

- a small extension or bud forms on the yeast cell wall;
- the bud enlarges and fills with cytoplasm;
- the parent nucleus divides by mitosis;
- one of the daughter nuclei enters the bud;
- this bud may break free to form a new yeast cell or may undergo its own budding while remaining attached to its own parent.

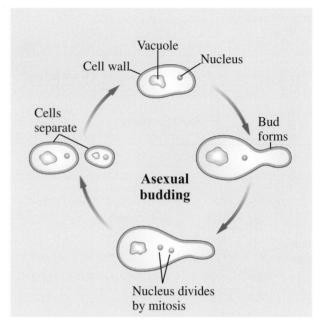

Fig. 16.27. Asexual reproduction in *Saccharomyces* (yeast).

LABORATORY PROCEDURES WHEN HANDLING AND GROWING MICROORGANISMS [315]

RESOURCES NEEDED

Petri dishes.
Nutrient agar powder.
Distilled or deionised water.
Autoclave or pressure cooker for sterilising all glassware and media.
Inoculating loop.
Cotton wool.
Bunsen burner.
Multodisks™.

- *Asepsis* means removing any possibility of infection by microorganisms.
- When working in a laboratory, in a hospital or near food, *aseptic technique* or *sterile technique* must be practiced at all times. This includes such activities as tying your hair back, wearing gloves, washing down surfaces, sterilising equipment, etc.
- *Antisepsis* refers to what you do to treat infection *after* it has occurred.
- *Sterile* means free from all living organisms including bacteria, fungi and their spores.

N.B. Sterile can also mean unable to produce sex cells — this is not relevant here.

1. Wash your hands before and after every procedure. Pupils (or teachers!) with cuts or plasters on their hands are not allowed work with microorganisms.
2. Wash all laboratory surfaces with disinfectant before and after all work.
3. Absolutely no eating or drinking is allowed in the lab. This includes chewing gum.
4. All cultures of microorganisms are presumed dangerous.
5. Sterilise all glassware, instruments and nutrients before and after your work.
6. Never open heavily infected dishes of microorganisms.
7. Incinerate all waste as far as possible. Nothing microbial should ever be thrown in waste paper bins for the cleaning staff!

INTRODUCTION TO MICROBIAL TECHNIQUE

Although microorganisms are found everywhere, they need to be grown in large numbers before they can be studied. Suitable growth media can be solid or liquid but must contain the correct nutrients and environmental conditions for the microorganisms. Hundreds of specialised media are available for specific microorganisms (see Appendix B) but a general-purpose medium such as *nutrient agar* is suitable for most schoolwork.

Agar is a gel extracted from seaweed. It is liquid when heated and then sets at room temperature. *Nutrient agar* consists of suitable nutrients mixed with agar gel and will support the growth of most common microorganisms.

All media must be sterilised before use — this is usually done in an autoclave or pressure cooker at a temperature of about 120 °C for 15 minutes.

1. Preparing sterile nutrient agar

1. Dissolve 28 g of nutrient agar powder in 1 litre of warm, distilled water (or see the manufacturer's instructions).
2. Pour about 125 ml of the mixture into several 250 ml conical flasks. Prepare as many flasks as are needed for your work.
3. Gently heat each flask over a Bunsen burner until the agar just starts to boil. Keep stirring throughout to dissolve all agar powder.
4. Remove each flask from the heat and plug the mouth with cotton wool.
5. Place the flasks of agar with some clean petri dishes and their lids in the autoclave or pressure cooker.
6. Sterilise the agar and dishes by heating to about 120 °C for 15 minutes.
7. Allow the flasks of agar to cool a little, but do not open them.

2. Pouring sterile agar plates

1. Light a Bunsen burner on the workbench.
2. Remove the cotton wool from the agar flask and pass the mouth of the flask through the flame (this is termed *flaming*).
3. Lift the lid of a sterile petri dish as little as necessary and pour about 0.5 cm of agar into the dish.
4. Replace the lid on the petri dish, pass the mouth of the flask through the Bunsen flame again and replace the cotton wool.

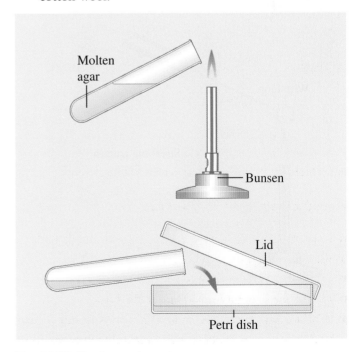

Fig. 16.28. Flaming and pouring.

5. Repeat for as many dishes as are needed.

6. Do not disturb or agitate the dishes until the agar has set (this should take about ten minutes).

N.B. Do not place the cotton wool plug on the bench surface during this procedure (why?). With a little practice, it is easy to hold the cotton wool in your 'other' hand while pouring.

3. Inoculating the sterile agar plates

1. Flame an inoculating loop and allow it to cool without touching anything. It will cool in a few seconds.

2. Use the loop to sample a possible source of microorganisms — fruit, water, milk, dust, hair, clothes, soil, etc.

3. Open a sterile dish as little as necessary and drag the loop gently across the agar surface as shown. This is termed *streaking* — the agar surface should remain unbroken.

N.B. Dishes can be left open to expose them to the air. To sample microorganisms on the skin surface, touch the agar directly with washed or unwashed fingers.

4. Close the lid and reflame the loop.

5. Seal each dish with adhesive tape or *parafilm*. Label the undersides.

6. Seal and label an unexposed dish as a control. This will check the sterility of the original plates.

4. Incubating the agar plates

- Incubate all plates upside-down in an incubator.
- For most common microorganisms, a temperature of 25 °C for at least 48 hours is suitable.
- Dishes are placed upside down to prevent a build-up of condensation.

5. Examining the plates

- All plates are examined without opening.
- Bacterial colonies are usually small, rounded and shiny but can have a range of colours according to type.
- Fungal colonies are usually large, textured and fluffy-looking.
- Control dishes should remain blank.
- A simple drawing should be made of each plate.

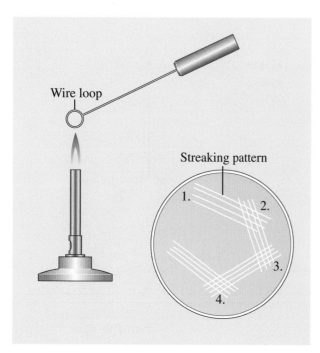

Fig. 16.29. Using the loop — flaming and streaking.

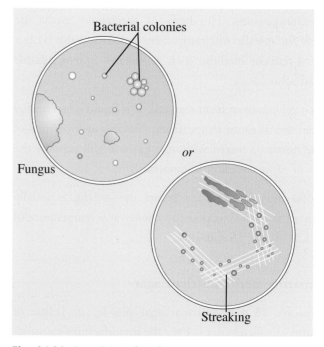

Fig. 16.30. Examining the plates.

Disposal

- All dishes and media should be resterilised without opening when work is finished. Use the autoclave again at 120 °C for 15 minutes. All glassware can then be washed safely in warm water and detergent.

6. Preparing a pure culture of microorganisms

The sterile nutrient agar plates exposed to possible sources of microorganisms as above produce mixed cultures containing a variety of species. To prepare a pure culture containing only one species of microorganism, use the following transfer technique:

1. Flame an inoculating loop in a Bunsen and allow it to cool in the air as before.
2. Barely lift the lid of a plate containing a mixed culture of microorganisms and use the loop to sample one single colony.
3. Streak the loop across the surface of an unexposed sterile plate.
4. Reflame the loop.
5. Incubate the new plate at about 120 °C for 15 minutes.

Many colonies of the same microorganism should be obtained — a pure culture. These cultures are suitable for comparing the strengths of disinfectants or antibiotics.

7. To demonstrate the effect of antibiotics on bacteria

Multodisks™ are star-shaped pieces of filter paper impregnated with various antibiotics. The discs are supplied in sterile wrapping.

1. Prepare a pure culture of bacteria as above.
2. Use a sterile tweezers to place a *Multodisk*™ on the agar surface *before* incubating the plate. Use minimal opening of the lid as before.
3. Incubate the dish upside-down at 25 °C for 48 hours.
4. Examine the dish without opening. Clear areas surrounding any specific antibiotic indicate bacterial sensitivity.

> ### Mandatory activity #18:
> ### To investigate leaf yeast using agar plates and controls
>
> RESOURCES NEEDED
>
> Petri dishes.
> Malt agar (or malt extract plus agar powder).
> Distilled or deionised water.
> Autoclave or pressure cooker for sterilising all glassware and media.
> Compass.
> Tweezers.

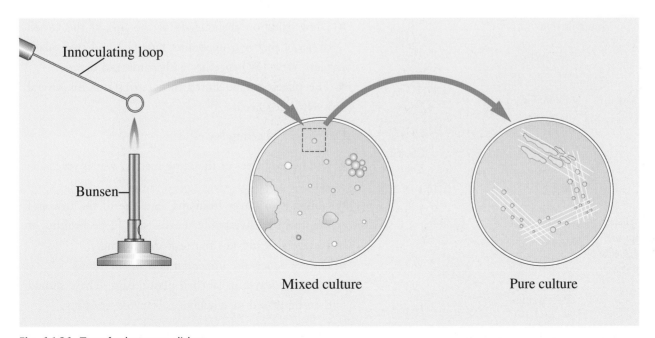

Innoculating loop

Bunsen—

Mixed culture

Pure culture

Fig. 16.31. Transfer between dishes.

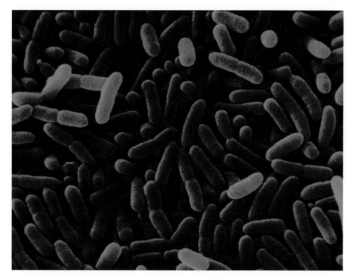

Fig. 16.32. *E. coli* pure culture.

Plastic bags with labels.
Kitchen paper.
2 cm cork borer or something similar.
Petroleum jelly.

Leaf yeasts are found on the surfaces of most leaves but particularly on ash and lilac. The yeasts can be cultured on malt agar plates, where they form pink colonies. Leaf yeasts are sensitive to pollution, so the number of colonies formed from any sample is a *pollution indicator* — large

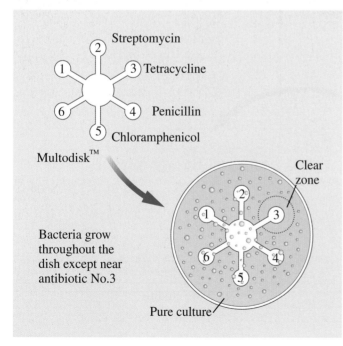

Bacteria grow throughout the dish except near antibiotic No.3

Fig. 16.33. Multodisks.

numbers of colonies indicating clean air and small numbers indicating polluted air.

In this experiment, malt agar plates are prepared and sterilised. Leaf samples are obtained and their yeasts are cultured on the plates. The yeast colonies are then counted to indicate air quality.

Leaves should not be sampled within four days after heavy rain or wind.

METHOD

Day 1 — preparing the malt agar plates. This work can be done at any time in advance.

- Three petri dishes are required for every tree — two for growing yeasts and one as a control.
- Prepare malt agar solution as described in Appendix B.
- Half-fill a 250 ml conical flask with agar and loosely plug the top with cotton wool.
- Sterilise the agar and the dishes in a dry oven or autoclave (or pressure cooker) at 121 °C for 15 minutes.
- Allow all materials to cool a little.
- Pour the malt agar into the petri dishes to a depth of about 0.5 cm and replace the lids. Use minimal opening and good aseptic technique as described in the previous experiments.
- Allow the agar to set at room temperature.
- Draw grids on the outside of the lids of the closed dishes. Label two quadrants East (E) and two quadrants West (W) together with name and date.
- The plates can be stored in a refrigerator for several weeks until needed.

Day 2 — Collecting leaves

- Use healthy trees of the same species. Ash is very suitable.
- Collect two leaves from the east side of the tree and two from the west side. Leaves should be healthy, of average size and not too near the ground.
- Do not touch the upper surfaces of the leaves.
- Store the leaves in labelled plastic bags. These should then be placed in lunchboxes to avoid crushing.

Day 3 — Preparing the leaf yeast cultures.

- Using a sterile tweezers, place the leaves topside up on clean kitchen paper.
- Use the cork borer to cut a 2 cm disc from each leaf.
- Turn over the lid of each malt agar dish and replace it to avoid contamination of the agar.
- Use petroleum jelly to attach the leaf discs to the inside of the lid — the East discs in the East quadrants and the West discs in the West quadrants. Attach the discs by their undersides.
- Turn the lid back over and replace it on the dish.
- Mark the bottom of the dish to correspond with the top.
- Label some unexposed dishes as controls.
- Leave all dishes to stand for 24 hours to allow yeast spores to fall onto the agar surface.
- Turn the dishes over and leave upside down for three to four days. Leaf yeasts will grow at room temperature and do not need an incubator.

Last day — Counting the yeast colonies.

- Record the number of colonies under each leaf disc. Yeast colonies have a salmon-pink colouring — ignore any other colonies.

- Make a drawing of the position of each colony on each dish.
- Total the number of colonies for each dish. Control dishes should be blank.
- Average all of the class results.

- 0–20 colonies per dish indicates poor air quality.
- 20–50 colonies per dish indicates moderate air quality.
- 50+ colonies per dish indicates good air quality.

KINGDOM OF PROTOCTISTA (OR PROTISTA)   [316]

This is a newly created kingdom (1988) for eukaryotic but simple organisms of varying types of nutrition. The kingdom includes both animal-like, heterotrophic creatures (*protozoa*) which are all single-celled and plant-like, autotrophic organisms (the *Algae*) which may be single-celled, filamentous or multi-celled. *Algae* include all of the common seaweeds.

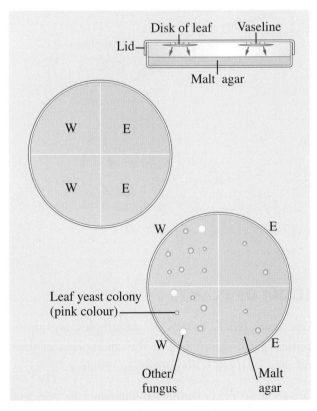

Fig. 16.34. Culturing leaf yeasts on malt agar.

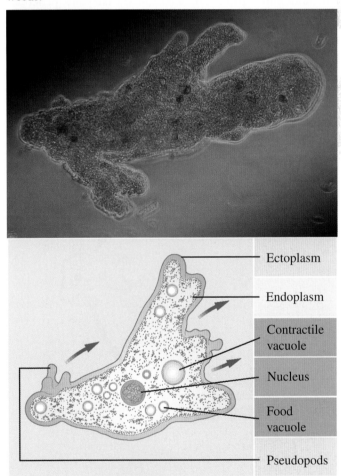

Fig. 16.35. *Amoeba* — structure.

One example of a protozoan is *Amoeba proteus*. *Amoeba* is a single-celled animal-like creature commonly found where fresh water and mud are together — in rain gutters and at the bottom of ponds.

Despite appearing simple in form, *Amoeba* is quite advanced in that it is capable of performing all the characteristics of living things inside just one cell.

Feeding in *Amoeba* is heterotrophic. It feeds by enclosing its food with a drop of water inside a temporary food vacuole (this is termed cell drinking or *pinocytosis*). *Amoeba* moves by forming false feet or *pseudopodia* and letting its cytoplasm flow into them. It reproduces asexually by *binary fission* — splitting in two to form two new *Amoebae*.

While *Amoeba proteus*, is harmless to humans, it does have tropical 'relations' that are important human parasites. Amoebic dysentery is caused by *Entamoeba histolytica*. Infection, which can last for years, brings vomiting, dysentery and abdominal pain. The *Entamoeba's* enzymes penetrate and digest human tissue. Infection is through faecal contamination of food or water through very poor standards of hygiene. Treatment of the disease is with anti-amoebic drugs.

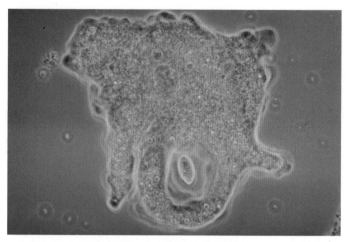

Fig. 16.37. *Amoeba* eating its prey.

Strangely, *Entamoeba* is usually confined to the tropics and the Arctic regions but not found in between. However, a huge outbreak occurred at the Chicago World Fair in 1933. Defective plumbing permitted sewage to contaminate the drinking water. There were over 1,000 cases of the disease with 58 deaths.

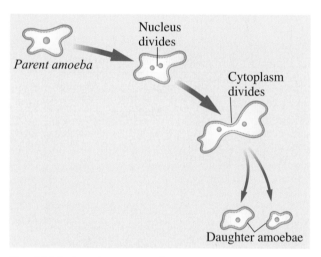

Fig. 16.38. *Amoeba* — reproduction.

KINGDOM OF PLANTS [317]

Plants are multi-celled, eukaryotic, autotrophic organisms. They possess green chlorophyll in the chloroplasts of their cells and they have cell walls containing cellulose.

There are six plant phyla within the kingdom; the principal phyla being as follows:

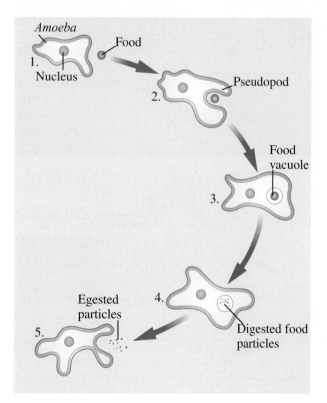

Fig. 16.36. *Amoeba* — feeding.

The Bryophytes	Small plants with no vascular tissue and no true roots — the mosses and liverworts.
The Pteridophytes or *ferns*	Plants with leaves tightly coiled when first formed. Spores are released from sporangia. No flowers, fruits or seeds are formed. A common example is *Dryopteris*.
The Conifers	These are large plants with needle shaped leaves. All plants bear male and female cones. They possess seeds but these are not enclosed in a fruit. Examples include Scots Pine and Larch.
The Angiosperms	This phylum includes all of the most common plants. Their seeds are enclosed in fruits and they produce flowers. Angiosperms (also called the 'flowering plants') are the dominant plant species on land. The phylum is subdivided into monocots and dicots.

Fig. 16.39. Moss.

Fig. 16.40. Liverwort.

- *Monocots* — have parallel leaf veins and one *cotyledon* or food store in their seed. Examples include grasses and cereals.
- *Dicots* — have reticulate (netted) leaf veins and two cotyledons in their seed. Examples include geranium, buttercup, rose, hawthorn, oak, sycamore, etc.

Fig. 16.41. Ferns.

All plants except the Bryophytes are *Tracheophytes*: that is, they have vascular tissue (xylem and phloem cells) for transport. This allows them to grow to a large size on land.

The Angiosperms are discussed in Chapter 17.

Fig. 16.42. Conifers.

Fig. 16.44. Deciduous trees.

gans. They never possess chlorophyll (unless they have eaten it) and their cells do not have cell walls.

As they need to find food, they generally have well-developed senses, nervous systems and locomotory organs.

The animal kingdom is divided into nine phyla, as shown in table 16.5.

(Note that the phyla are arranged roughly in the order in which they appeared on the Earth. Note also their increasing complexity.)

Fig. 16.43. A flower.

KINGDOM OF ANIMALS [318]

Animals are multi-celled, eukaryotic, heterotrophic organisms. Their cells are normally organised into tissues and or-

Fig. 16.45. Rye.

Table 16.5. Nine animal phyla within the kingdom

Phylum	Examples	Description	
Porifera (Sponges)	The breadcrumb sponge, *coral*	Multi-celled. Marine. No cell differentiation. Filter feeders. Lacking a nervous system.	
Cnidaria (Coelenterates)	*Hydra*, jellyfish, anemones	All aquatic. Most are marine. Diploblastic (two layers of cells separated by mesoglea). Radial symmetry. Stinging cells. Tentacles.	

All animals from here on in the table have *bilateral symmetry* (the left-hand side is a mirror image of the right-hand side, for better balance). They also have *triploblastic embryos*, i.e. their bodies are originally formed from three layers of cells (three germ layers).

Phylum	Examples	Description	
Platyhelminthes (Flatworms)	Liver fluke, tapeworms, pond worms	Flattened bodies. Most are hermaphrodite. Flame cells for excretion. One digestive opening.	

All animals from here on have two digestive openings — mouth and anus — for more efficient and continuous feeding.

Phylum	Examples	Description	
Aschelminthes (Roundworms)	*Ascaris*, potworms, threadworms, pinworms	Cylindrical shape. Smooth. Unsegmented.	

All animals from here on show varying degrees of metameric segmentation (a pattern of repeating body units). They also have triploblastic, coelomate embryos, a circulatory system with one or more pumps and a circulating fluid (blood). A *coelom* is a hollow, fluid-filled space within the body. It allows for independent movement of body organs (e.g. breathing, heartbeat, etc.) and for storage of food, urine, sex cells, etc.

Annelida (Segmented worms)	Earthworms, ragworms, leeches.	Segmented bodies with internal partitions (septa). Ventral nerve cord. Nephridia for excretion.	
Mollusca (Molluscs)	Slugs, snails, cockles, mussels, octopus, squid, cuttlefish.	Soft-bodied. Little segmentation. Most organs in a visceral hump protected by a shell. Sharp tongue (radula).	
Arthropoda (Arthropods)	Insects. Arachnids — spiders and scorpions. Crustaceans — crabs, lobsters, shrimps, barnacles, woodlice. Myriapods — centipedes and millipedes.	Jointed legs. Exoskeleton of chitin which is moulted.	
Echinodermata (Echinoderms)	Starfish, brittle stars, sea urchins, sea cucumbers.	Spiny skin. Marine. Pentaradial symmetry (anatomy in fives). Tube feet.	

Chordata	Includes fish, amphibians, reptiles, birds and mammals.	Dorsal nerve cord. Notochord of cartilage at embryo stage. Post-anal tail. Gill slits in embryos.	

These are the classes within the phylum Chordata.

Fish	Salmon, dogfish, shark, cod, mackerel. pike, eel.	Cold-blooded. Two-chambered hearts. Scales. Gills. External fertilisation.	
Amphibians	Frogs, toads, salamanders, newts.	Three-chambered hearts. Damp skin. Cold-blooded. Metamorphosis. Gills become lungs. External fertilisatiion.	
Reptiles	Lizards, snakes, crocodiles, alligators, tortoises, turtles.	Cold-blooded. Three-chambered hearts. Internal fertilisation. Lay eggs. Scales. Enamelled teeth.	
Birds	Crows, robins, hawks, seagulls, albatrosses, chickens, penguins.	Warm-blooded. Feathers. Wings. Four-chambered hearts. Lay eggs. Internal fertilisation. Most can fly.	

Mammals	Humans, monkeys, cats, dogs, sheep, cows, foxes, rhinos, giraffes, seals, dolphins, whales, bats, mice.	Warm-blooded. Hair/fur/blubber. Four-chambered hearts. Seven neck vertebrae. Sweat glands. Mammary glands.	

THE NATURE OF BACTERIA AND FUNGI   [H31I]

Bacterial cells are *prokaryotic* — they have a primitive cell structure with no definite nucleus and few cell organelles. Fungal cells are *eukaryotic* — they have a nucleus enclosed in a nuclear membrane and many cell organelles. Fungal cytoplasm and nuclei are similar in structure to plant and animal cells.

(See Chapter 6, section [211] for more details on this.)

GROWTH CURVES   [H31II]

Earlier, we stated that bacteria, given ideal growth conditions, can double their numbers every 20 minutes. This is true, but bacteria don't reproduce in this way at all times. When they first appear on a new substrate (in a wound, in soil, on meat, etc.), they take some time to 'settle in' and prepare themselves for reproduction. This is an *incubation period* and the bacteria use it to mobilise their food reserves and prepare themselves for reproduction. Binary fission then commences and the population numbers increase at an exponential rate — doubling as frequently as every 20 minutes as outlined. This huge increase quickly produces overcrowding within the population. Reproduction stops due to a lack of nutrients and a build-up of toxic excretions. Unless they are transferred to fresh substrate, the bacteria will die without further reproduction and the population numbers will start to decrease.

1. *Lag phase* — Bacteria settling in, the incubation period.
2. *Log phase* — Bacteria reproduce by binary fission and may double their numbers every 20 minutes — a logarithmic growth.
3. *Stationary phase* — Bacterial increase halts — due to lack of food and a build-up of toxic excretions.
4. *Decline phase* — Population decreases due to lack of food and a build-up of toxic excretions.

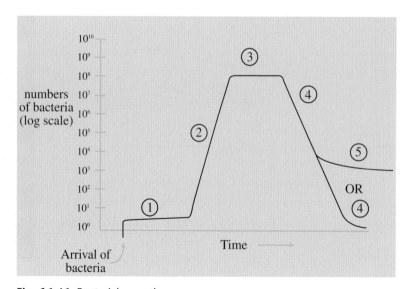

Fig. 16.46. Bacterial growth curve.

5. *Survival phase* — Population stabilises at a level that can be supported by the environment. Bacterial populations often decline abruptly to an unsustainable level.

On this curve:

■ when would a wound be best treated?
■ when would a wound be most infectious?

N.B. A *log scale* of numbers is useful for representing both very large and very small numbers on the same axis.

The shape of the growth curve is important in industries involving microorganisms. In Chapter 9, section [225] two methods of industrial fermentation — *batch fermentation* and *continuous fermentation* — are compared. In a batch flow process, all phases of the bacterial growth curve will occur — which means that the process is only efficient during one phase and not during all the others. In continuous flow, the microorganisms are maintained at optimum levels of population size and activity. Human population growth curves are discussed in Chapter 4, section [H14III].

SUMMARY

■ *Classification* of organisms involves placing them in groups according to similarities of structure. Done for ease of study and to observe trends in evolution.
■ *Kingdoms* are the major divisions of life on earth. At present, five kingdoms are recognised: monera; fungi; protoctista; plants; and animals.
■ *Carl Linnaeus* (1707–1778) was the first to attempt to classify living organisms in a scientific manner.
■ *Lynne Margulis* and *Karlene Schwartz* devised the present five-kingdom system, in 1988.
■ *Bacteria are single-celled*, prokaryotic organisms found just about everywhere.
■ *Bacilli often form endospores* in times of stress. These spores are heat- and chemical-resistant. Endospore formation is a survival technique.
■ *Nutrition within bacteria* is very varied. Bacteria are either autotrophic (they make their own food from simple chemicals and an energy input) or heterotrophic (they eat ready-made food).

■ *Bacterial growth* is greatly affected by temperature, humidity, pH, oxygen and suitable nutrients.
■ *Dangers* in the overuse of antibiotics include:

- overexposure increases the chances of resistant bacteria appearing;
- antibiotics fed to animals may accumulate in food chains and cause problems to humans;
- many humans are allergic to antibiotics.

■ *Fungi* are eukaryotic organisms with cell walls made mostly of chitin. They have heterotrophic nutrition and either feed on living tissue (parasitic fungi) or on dead organic matter (saprotrophic fungi).
■ *Fungi* usually have a filamentous structure — the overall mycelium is made from branching, colourless hyphae.
■ *Rhizopus* is a grey, saprotrophic pin mould found on bread and fruit.
■ *Yeast* is a unicellular, saprotrophic fungus common on the surfaces of leaves and fruit and found in the soil.
■ *Although microorganisms are found everywhere*, they need to be grown in large numbers before they can be studied. Suitable growth media can be solid or liquid but must contain the correct nutrients and environmental conditions for the microorganisms.
■ *Amoeba* is a single-celled, animal-like creature, commonly found where fresh water and mud are together.

EXTENDED SUMMARY

■ *Bacterial cells are prokaryotic* — they have a primitive cell structure with no definite nucleus and few cell organelles.
■ *Fungal cells are eukaryotic* — they have a nucleus enclosed in a nuclear membrane and many cell organelles.
■ *Growth in a bacterial population* is usually described by a growth curve.
■ *The shape of the growth curve* is important in industries involving microorganisms.

KEY WORDS

Species	Any group of organisms that resemble one another and have the ability to reproduce with one another.
Phylum	A major subdivision of a kingdom.
Monera	Single-celled organisms that lack a nuclear membrane — the bacteria.
Protoctista (Protista)	Single-celled organisms also, but with a eukaryotic cell type.
Fungi	Multicellular, eukaryotic organisms with absorptive nutrition.
Plants	Multicellular, eukaryotic organisms that make their own food using sunlight.
Animals	Multicellular, eukaryotic organisms that ingest their food.
Prokaryotic	Describes a simple cell type with no nuclear membrane, no plastids and no mitochondria.
Eukaryotic	Describes an advanced cell type with nuclear material enclosed in a nuclear membrane and many cell organelles.
Lichens	Commensalisms between an alga and a fungus — both living together for mutual benefit.
Microorganism	An informal name for organisms of microscopic size.
Cocci	Spherical-shaped bacteria.
Bacilli	Rectangular or rod shaped bacteria.
Spirilli	Spiral, motile bacteria.
Endospores	Thick-walled, reproductive bodies formed within some bacteria in times of stress.
Saprotrophic bacteria	Obtain their food in solution from dead and decaying organisms.
Parasitic bacteria	Obtain their food from a living source (or host).
Chemosynthetic bacteria	Use energy from other chemical reactions to make their food.
Photosynthetic bacteria	Trap sunlight energy with bacteriochlorophyll and use it to synthesise carbohydrates.
Pathogen	A 'disease generator' or a microorganism that causes disease.
Antibiotics	Chemicals, secreted by some microorganisms, which prevent the growth of many bacteria.
Mycelium	The overall body of a fungus.
Hyphae	Branching threads within a mycelium.
Gametangia	Gamete-producing cells.
Asepsis	The removal of any possibility of infection by microorganisms.
Antisepsis	The treatment of infection after it has occurred.
Sterile	Free of all living organisms including bacteria, fungi and their spores.
Nutrient agar	A growth medium consisting of suitable nutrients mixed with agar gel.
Flaming	Passing a wire loop or the mouth of a flask through a flame to kill any microorganisms.
Streaking	Using a wire loop to inoculate the surface of an agar plate with microorganisms.
Multodisks™	Star-shaped pieces of filter paper impregnated with various antibiotics.

Pseudopodia	Temporary cell projections or 'false feet' of *Amoeba*.
Binary fission	Splitting in two.
Bilateral symmetry	The left-hand side of an organism being roughly a mirror image of the right-hand side.
Triploblastic	Embryos consisting of three layers of cells (or three germ layers).
Metameric segmentation	A pattern of repeating body units. Found within most higher animals.
Coelom	A hollow, fluid-filled space within the body. Found in most higher animals at some stage of development.

EXTENDED KEY WORDS

Incubation period	The time taken by bacteria to prepare themselves for rapid reproduction.
Log phase	The phase of growth when bacteria reproduce by binary fission. The population may double its number as fast as every 20 minutes.

QUESTIONS

1. Name the five kingdoms of living organisms. For each kingdom, describe its main features and name three members.
2. What are the differences between prokaryotic and eukaryotic cells? Decide whether each of the following is prokaryotic or eukaryotic:

   a. mushroom;
   b. snail;
   c. *salmonella*;
   d. moss;
   e. human;
   f. *amoeba*;
   g. *streptococci*;
   h. yeast.

3. Latin words can be difficult to read, pronounce and spell. Why are they always used in the naming of living organisms?
4. In what ways are fungi different to plants? To animals?
5. What are *lichens* and what is unusual about them? Where are they commonly found?
6. Why is it difficult to classify viruses as living organisms?
7. Draw a large, labelled diagram showing the main structural features of a typical bacterial cell.
8. List the different shapes of bacteria and give one example of each.
9. Using simple diagrams, describe the asexual reproduction of bacteria. How do antibiotics interfere with this process? What are the consequences to humans of the rapid reproduction of bacteria?
10. What are endospores and why do bacteria form them? Why is it unsafe to refreeze thawed food?
11. Describe the four different methods of nutrition found in bacteria. Which of these methods is most similar to plants? To humans?
12. Bacteria can be either beneficial or harmful to humans. Give examples to support this statement. What are *pathogenic* bacteria?
13. List the factors that affect the growth of bacteria. Explain why each of the following food preservation techniques is successful:

    a. freezing;
    b. canning;
    c. smoking;
    d. pickling;
    e. drying.

14. What are antibiotics? Why is their concern about their overuse?
15. What are fungi? Explain how they are different to bacteria.

16. Fungi are either *saprotrophic* or *parasitic*. Explain the two underlined words and give five examples of each of these fungal types.

17. Draw a large, labelled diagram showing the structure of the common bread mould, *Rhizopus*. Is *Rhizopus* a saprotroph or a parasite?

18. Use diagrams to describe the asexual reproduction of *Rhizopus*.

19. For sexual reproduction to take place, two opposite forms of *Rhizopus* must come together. These forms are termed + and −. Why are they not described as male and female?

20. Write an equation to summarise the respiration of yeast. Why is this equation economically important?

21. Draw simple, labelled diagrams to show the reproduction of yeast. What is this method of reproduction called?

22. Explain the importance of each of the following when culturing microorganisms:

    a. no eating or drinking;

    b. using distilled water rather than tap water when making up nutrient agar;

    c. sterilising media before use;

    d. flaming the mouth of the agar flask;

    e. observing minimal opening of agar plates;

    f. flaming an inoculation loop before using it;

    g. flaming the loop after using it;

    h. sealing plates with tape;

    i. labelling the undersides of plates rather than the lids;

    j. incubating plates upside-down;

    k. incubating plates for at least 48 hours;

    l. using control plates.

23. To which *phyla* would organisms with the following descriptions belong?

    a. Spiny skin and an anatomy of five.

    b. Roots, stems and leaves but no transport system.

    c. Flattened bodies with one digestive opening.

    d. Have feathers.

    e. Red fruits.

    f. Have male and female cones.

    g. A soft body with a shell and a single foot.

    h. Dry, scaly skin.

    i. Wings and jointed legs.

    j. Segmented body with many setae.

OPTIONAL ACTIVITIES

■ Use slides, photos and acetates to practice the classification of organisms. Refer to the use of keys in Chapter 5.

■ Use the Internet to research the life cycle of *entamoeba histolytica*.

■ Design and carry out an experiment to test claims that one soap has greater disinfecting powers than another. Research the identification of edible and poisonous fungi.

For information on websites dealing with subjects covered in this chapter see www.my-etest.com.

Now test yourself at
my-etest.com

Chapter 17
Organisational Complexity in the Flowering Plant

- explain the key difference between a plant and an animal;
- list the functions of roots, stems and leaves;
- define and locate meristematic tissue within the plant;
- draw simple, labelled diagrams of the main types of plant cells;
- state the location and function of the important plant tissues;
- define and compare monocots and dicots.

Mandatory activity

#8 Preparing and examining a transverse section of a dicotyledonous stem.

NEEDS IN THE LIVES OF PLANTS

Fig. 17.1. Rape flowers.

The biggest single difference between a plant and an animal is food. A plant possesses chlorophyll and can make its own food by photosynthesis. An animal cannot make its own food and has to find and eat ready-made food. Because of this requirement, animals tend to be mobile and have good sensory and locomotory systems. Plants do not have the same need for mobility or awareness but they do have other needs if they are to photosynthesise successfully.

For photosynthesis (see Chapter 8), plants require:

- a supply of water and minerals;
- a supply of carbon dioxide and sunlight.
- the possession of chlorophyll

BASIC PLANT STRUCTURE

The typical plant is divided into two portions — a root system and a shoot system. The shoot system includes the stem and the leaves. The roots lie below the ground and the shoot above. Roots never bear leaves, flowers or fruit.

Types of roots

Tap roots — are developed from the radicle of the plant seed (see Chapter 27). A tap root is a large, main root with secondary roots branching out from it. Tap roots are found in most common dicot plants including rose, geranium, dandelion, sycamore, ash.

Adventitious roots — are roots that do not develop from the radical of the seed. They include fibrous roots, climbing roots in ivy, prop roots in maize and mangrove trees or balancing roots in water lilies and other floating plants.

Fibrous roots — consist of many equal-sized roots emerging from the stem base. There is no single, dominant root. Fibrous roots are found in most monocot plants, e.g. grasses, cereals and daffodils.

Functions of the plant's root system:

- Roots absorb water and minerals from the environment.
- Roots transport water, minerals, and food.
- Roots anchor terrestrial plants to the ground.
- Some roots store food, e.g. carrots and turnips.
- Some roots are involved in plant asexual reproduction, e.g. the swollen root tubers of the dahlia.

Plant shoots

Shoots consist of stems (branched or unbranched), leaves, flowers and fruit. Leaves emerge from stems at positions termed *nodes*. The smooth region between two nodes is termed an *internode*. Stems have a terminal (apical) bud at their apex (the very tip of the stem) and axillary buds in the angles (*axils*) between stem and leaf. Axillary buds form new branches and flowers.

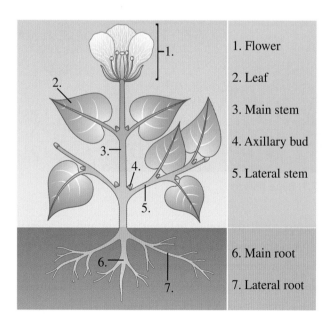

1. Flower

2. Leaf

3. Main stem

4. Axillary bud

5. Lateral stem

6. Main root

7. Lateral root

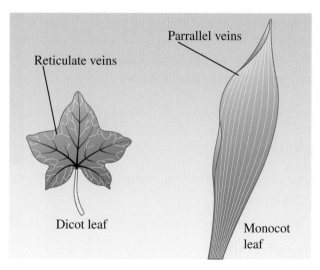

Reticulate veins

Parrallel veins

Dicot leaf

Monocot leaf

Fig. 17.2. Parts of a plant.

Functions of the plant stem:

- The stem transports water, minerals and food.
- The stem supports leaves and flowers.
- Many stems store food, e.g. celery, rhubarb and potatoes.
- Some stems are involved in asexual reproduction, e.g. the stem tubers of potatoes, the runners of strawberries.
- Stems may photosynthesise — if they are green.

Leaves

Leaves are broad, flattened structures attached to the stem at the stem nodes. The portion of a leaf attached to the stem is termed the *petiole*. Some leaves are directly attached without petioles and are termed *sessile* leaves, e.g. oak leaves. The flattened part of the leaf is termed the *lamina* and is supported by a midrib. Veins for transport and support branch from the midrib. Monocot leaves have parallel leaf veins, dicot leaves have netted or reticulate veins.

Functions of leaves:

- Leaves make food by photosynthesis.
- Leaves evaporate water by transpiration — to cool the plant and to move water and minerals up through the stem against gravity.
- Leaves exchange gases through their stomata to assist in respiration and photosynthesis.
- Some leaves store food, e.g. grass, cabbage, lettuce.
- Some leaves are involved in asexual reproduction, e.g. begonia or the bulbs of onions and tulips.

Plant tissues

As explained in Chapter 11, section [240], cells with similar structure and function are often grouped to form *tissues*, which, in turn, can be grouped to form *organs* and *systems* within living organisms.

To meet their needs efficiently, plants group their various cells into tissues and arrange the tissues about themselves. Besides certain reproductive structures (see Chapter 27), plants have little need for the development of *organs* — their needs are straightforward and are quite easily met by tissues. (Leaves are sometimes considered as photosynthesising organs and flowers as reproductive organs.)

Animals, on the other hand, have to move and respond rapidly to find and obtain their food. This leads to the development of highly specialised tissues — nerve tissue, muscle tissue, digestive tissue, etc. These tissues are then grouped into highly developed organs and organ systems.

Meristems

All flowering plants are formed from a multi-celled embryo in a seed. As the embryo develops, all of its cells are *meristematic*, i.e. they are capable of repeated cell division. These meristematic cells divide continually and group themselves to form tissues.

A tissue is a group of similar cells that performs a particular function (see Chapter 11, section [240]).

All tissues in plants develop in the same way:

- Cell division takes place within meristematic cells.
- The resulting cells are primitive (thin-walled, small and with a large nucleus) but develop into specific cell types.
- These cell types group themselves together to form plant tissues.

As the plant continues to develop, the tissues are arranged to form the various plant systems: roots, shoots, leaves, flowers, vascular systems and, finally, more seeds. This gives the flowering plant a fairly high degree of complexity but very few individual organs as found in animals.

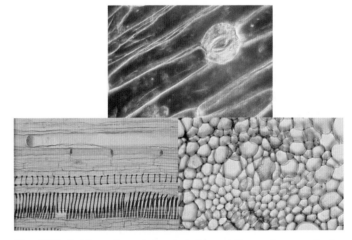

Fig. 17.3. Epidermal, vascular and storage tissues from a plant.

In developed plants, the meristematic tissue (meristems) is confined to certain regions of the plant.

Primary meristems are found at the plant extremities (apices) and used to increase plant length.

Secondary meristems (cambium) are found throughout the plant. They are generally for the development of the vascular system and for increasing the plant girth or diameter.

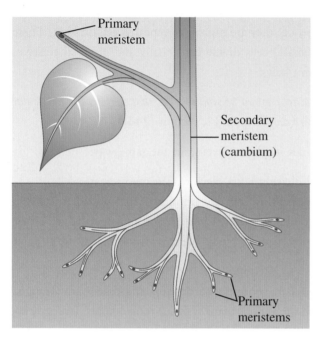

Fig. 17.4. Meristem locations.

Meristematic tissue divides to form:

- *Dermal tissue* — sheets of cells protecting the plant, e.g. epidermis tissue.
- *Vascular tissue* — tissue involved in transport, e.g. xylem and phloem tissue.

Xylem tissue is used for the transport of water and minerals upwards in plants. Xylem cell walls contain lignin, which is waterproof and very strong. Lignin makes cell walls impermeable and so kills the cells. Wood is formed from masses of xylem cells.

Phloem tissue is used for the transport (*translocation*) of food and other chemicals around the plant. Phloem tissue contains both sieve tubes and companion cells. Sieve tubes transport the food materials and sacrifice their

nuclei to allow better flow within their cell walls. Intermediate walls between phloem cells break down to form sieve plates to allow translocation. Companion cells maintain the sieve tubes.

Xylem and phloem cells are joined together to form tubes or pipelines within the plant. The tubes resemble drinking straws with thousands of tiny perforations allowing the contents to ooze out at any level. Many pipelines are bundled together in 'vascular bundles' — similar to bundles of drinking straws.

- *Ground tissue* — refers to all other tissues within the plant, e.g. *parenchyma*, *collenchyma* and *sclerenchyma*.

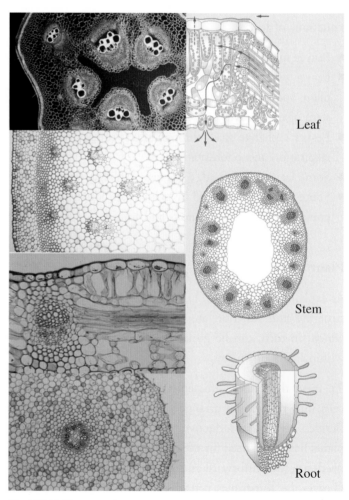

Fig. 17.5. Plant sections.

Tissue	Location	Function	Simplified drawing of cells
Epidermis	Outer surfaces	Protective	
Parenchyma	Leaf epidermis, leaf mesophyll, root cortex.	Food storage. Photosynthesis. Packing, protection.	
Collenchyma	In a ring near the outside of dicot stems, in midribs of leaves.	Strength and support.	
Sclerenchyma fibres	In and around vascular bundles, e.g. the 'threads' in celery stalks.	Strength and support.	
Sclerenchyma fibres	Scattered in pear fruit or together to form the protective covering of nuts.	Strength and protection.	
Xylem vessels	In vascular bundles or in wood.	Transport of water and minerals upwards in the plant. Strength and support.	

Xylem tracheids	In vascular bundles or in wood.	Transport of water and minerals upwards in the plant. Strength and support.	
Phloem sieve tubes and companion cells	In vascular bundles or in bark.	Movement of food and other complicated chemicals up and down the plant (*translocation*). Companion cells direct and maintain sieve tubes.	
			Phloem TS

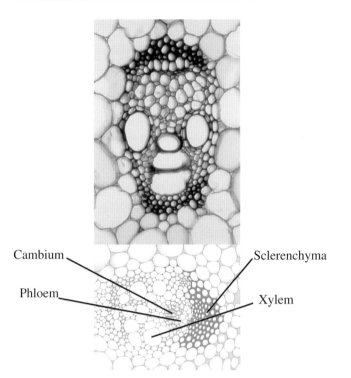

Cambium

Phloem

Sclerenchyma

Xylem

Fig. 17.6. Vascular bundles.

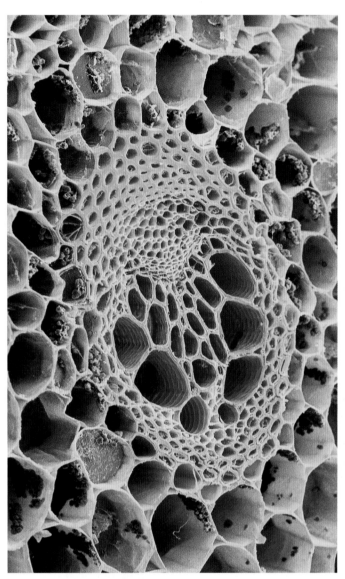

Fig. 17.8. Vascular bundle of a buttercup.

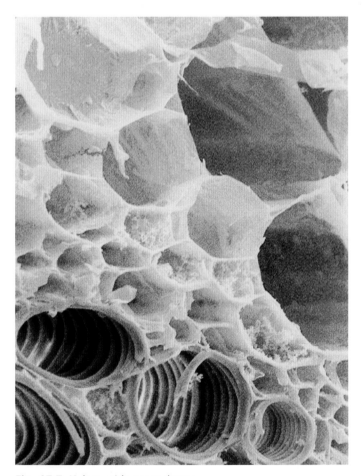

Fig. 17.7. Xylem with parenchyma.

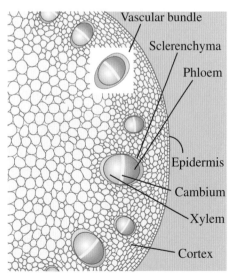

Vascular bundle

Sclerenchyma

Phloem

Epidermis

Cambium

Xylem

Cortex

Fig. 17.9. Dicot stem section.

Flowering plants are classified as either monocotyledonous plants (*monocots*) or dicotyledonous plants (*dicots*) depending on the structure of their embryos.

Table 17.2. Traits of monocots and dicots

Monocots	Dicots
Parallel leaf veins.	Reticulated (netted) leaf veins.
Embryos have a single cotyledon.	Embryos have two cotyledons.
Vascular bundles are scattered in the stem.	Vascular bundles are arranged in a circle in the stem.
Fibrous roots usually.	Single tap root usually.
Usually herbaceous, (non woody).	Often have woody growth.
Floral parts in threes.	Floral parts in fours or fives.
Examples: *Grasses, cereals, tulip, daffodil, asparagus.*	*Examples:* *Daisy, rose, geranium, cabbage, ash, elm, oak.*

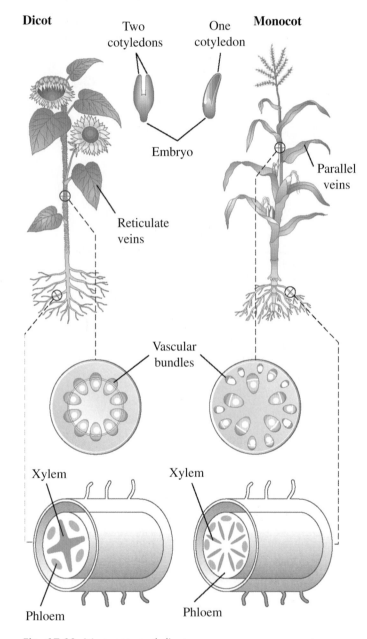

Fig. 17.10. Monocots and dicots.

The following table compares the two types of flowering plant:

Mandatory activity #8: Preparing a transverse section (TS) of a dicot stem

RESOURCES NEEDED

Suitable plant stems.
Microscope slides and cover slips.
Petri dish containing water.
Sharp, backed blades.
Scissors or scalpel.
Support material, e.g. foam, pith or carrot to hold stem tissue without crushing.
0.05% w/v toluidine blue stain.
Iodine solution.
Aniline sulphate stain.
30% glycerol.
Small paintbrush.
Tissue paper.

METHOD

■ Use *busy lizzie*, sunflower or buttercup stems.

- Practice sectioning the support material on its own (potato, carrot, pith, foam, etc.) before cutting the stems. Do not force the blade and keep both hands resting on the desk throughout (we are not studying the TS of a finger!). Use a single, slicing action rather than a sawing one.
- Use a scalpel to cut short, 2 cm lengths of stem.
- Cut the lengths from the internodes of the stem.
- Square off the ends.
- Place a stem piece in some support material, e.g. foam, pith or carrot. Ask your teacher to show you this.
- Use a backed blade to cut lots of thin transverse sections.
- Keep the backed blade wet at all times.
- Cut thin, transverse sections smoothly and quickly.
- Use the paintbrush to transfer the sections to a dish of water. Always cut lots of sections in order to get some suitable ones.
- Use the paintbrush to transfer the best sections to a dish of toluidine blue stain for about one minute.
- Transfer the stained sections to a dish of clean water to rinse away excess stain.
- Clean a microscope slide and cover slip so that it has no fingerprints.
- Place a drop of water (or 30% glycerol) in the centre of the slide. Glycerol lasts longer and makes the tissues more transparent.
- Use the brush to transfer the section to the drop of water.
- Hold the cover slip at an angle in the water and lower it gently to exclude any air bubbles.
- Dry around the edges of the cover slip with tissue.
- The preparation can be sealed on all for sides with clear nail varnish. These slides will keep for a month or two.
- Adjust the light of the microscope and examine the tissues under low power and then under higher power.
- Identify the various tissues. Lignified walls stain green, greenish-blue or bright blue. Non-lignified cell walls stain pink–purple. Nuclei should be visible and chloroplasts should be green.
- Draw and label the stem TS. A good 'map-diagram' does not have to show any individual cells, just the locations of the various tissues. If drawing individual cells, always use a double line for cell walls and include some indication of scale, e.g. the magnification.

To fully understand the 3-D arrangement of the tissues in the stem, sections should be made in other directions too. Use the same method for longitudinal sections (LS), making these about 1 cm long.

Experiment with other stains:

Iodine solution turns starch grains blue–black. Lignified cell walls stain golden and cellulose walls are unstained.
Aniline sulphate turns lignified cell walls bright yellow.
Sudan IV stains all fats orange or red.
Treat all stains as potentially harmful. Do not ingest them or allow them to touch your skin.

See Appendix B for more information.

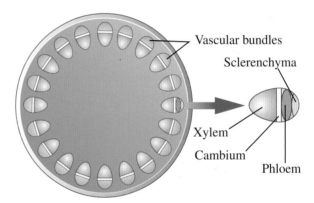

Fig. 17.11. Transverse section of a dicot stem.

SUMMARY

- The biggest single difference between a plant and an animal is to do with food.
- For photosynthesis, plants require a supply of water, minerals, carbon dioxide and sunlight.
- The typical plant is divided into two portions — a root system and a shoot system.
- Plants group their various cells into tissues and arrange the tissues about themselves.
- Besides certain reproductive structures and leaves, plants have little need for the development of organs.
- Meristematic cells divide continually and group themselves to form tissues.

- All tissues in plants develop in the same way:

  - cell division takes place within meristematic cells;
  - the resulting, primitive cells develop into specific cell types;
  - these cell types group themselves together to form plant tissues.

- Xylem tissue is used for the transport of water and minerals upwards in plants.
- Phloem tissue is used for the transport (translocation) of food and other chemicals around the plant.
- Flowering plants are classified as either monocotyledonous plants (monocots) or dicotyledonous plants (dicots) depending on the structure of their embryos.

KEY WORDS

Tap roots	Develop from the radicle of the plant seed.
Adventitious roots	Do not develop from the radical of the seed.
Fibrous roots	Equal-sized roots emerging from the stem base.
Nodes	Where leaves are attached to the stem.
Internodes	The smooth region between two nodes.
Apical bud	Found at the tip of the stem.
Axillary bud	Found where leaves are attached to the stem.
Petiole	Portion of a leaf attached to the stem.
Lamina	Flattened part of a leaf.
Meristem	Group of cells capable of repeated division.
Primary meristems	Found at the extremities of the plant. Used to increase plant length.
Secondary meristems	Found within the stem and root. Used to form vascular tissue and increase diameter.

Tissue	Group of similar cells that performs a particular function.
Dermal tissue	Sheets of cells protecting the plant.
Vascular tissue	Tissue involved in transport, e.g. xylem and phloem tissue.
Ground tissue	Refers to all other tissues within the plant.
Parenchyma	Thin-walled cells used for packing and storage.
Collenchyma	Thick-walled cells used for support.
Sclerenchyma	Lignified cells used for strength and protection.
Xylem	Lignified cells used for support and water transport.
Phloem	Used for translocation of food and hormones.
Lignin	Strong, and impermeable substance found in the cell walls of xylem and sclerenchyma cells. Kills the cells.
Monocots (monocotyledonous plants)	Embryos have one cotyledon or food store.
Dicots (dicotyledonous plants)	Embryos have two cotyledons.

QUESTIONS

1. Why are animals usually more mobile and much more aware than plants?
2. List four functions for each of the following:

   a. plant roots;
   b. plant stems;
   c. plant leaves.

3. What are *meristematic cells*? Where are they located in the plant? How are they involved in the formation of plant tissues?
4. Draw a labeled diagram of the arrangement of tissues in a non-woody, dicot stem.

5. Draw labelled diagrams of each of the following cell types:

   a. parenchyma;
   b. epidermis;
   c. xylem vessel;
   d. sieve tube;
   e. sclerenchyma fibre.

6. What are the functions of *collenchyma* and *parenchyma* in the plant?

7. Distinguish between:

   a. primary meristems and secondary meristems;
   b. xylem and phloem;
   c. xylem vessels and xylem tracheids;
   d. dermal tissue and ground tissue;
   e. monocots and dicots;
   f. terminal buds and axillary buds;
   g. lignified and non-lignified tissue;
   h. LS and TS.

8. When preparing a stem TS for examination under the microscope, explain why the following procedures are important:

   a. using a sharp blade to section the stem;
   b. supporting the stem in foam or carrot;
   c. avoiding stem nodes;
   d. keeping the blade wet;
   e. adding the sections to toluidine blue stain;
   f. cutting the sections as thin as possible;
   g. using a paintbrush to transfer the sections;
   h. using a cover slip.

9. State five differences between monocot and dicot plants.

OPTIONAL ACTIVITIES

- Make model xylem and phloem cells out of plastic lemonade bottles and stack them together as they would be in the plant. Use cardboard for sieve plates.
- Obtain a supply of plants and examine the root and shoot systems. Weeds from around the school grounds are very suitable.
- Examine pre-prepared slides showing plant tissues.
- Examine and identify monocot and dicot leaves and seeds. Make a reference collection.
- Make a chart to show similarities and differences of structure and function between xylem tissue and phloem tissue.

Now test yourself at
www.my-etest.com

Chapter 18

Organisational Complexity in Humans

INTRODUCTION   [322]

The primary need in the life of any animal is to find *food*. Unlike plants, animals cannot make their own food — instead they have to find it, capture it and eat it!

Everything else in the animal's life is secondary to this ever present need. The other important needs for shelter and suitable mates will not be met without food.

It is for this reason that animals — and humans — require a high degree of organisation within themselves. In most animals, organs and systems are highly developed. In its day-to-day search for food, an animal clearly has a great advantage in the possession of senses, a brain, muscles, bones and skin. Animal complexity develops in response to the animal's need for food.

The requirement to eat food leads to a need for a vascular system. Materials ingested will have to be moved around on the inside — the parts of the body that take in the food and gases are not the only parts in need. Food is not just needed in the stomach; it is needed in the ears, toes, kidneys, bones and all other living parts of the organism.

In very small animals, internal transport can be accomplished by *diffusion* and *active transport* (see Chapter 10). These processes can move substances from one location to another but are only fast over very short distances. Relying on only this method of transport leads to small, folded or flat animals such as *amoeba*, jellyfish and flatworms.

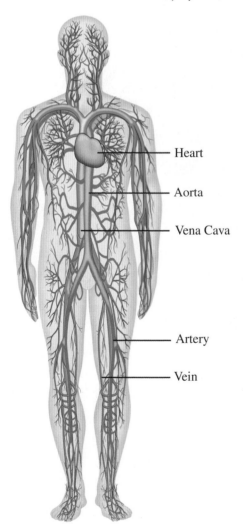

Fig. 18.1. The human vascular system.

Heart

Aorta

Vena Cava

Artery

Vein

Bigger and more active animals (such as humans) need a transport system or *vascular system*.

The typical vascular system will be composed of:

- *a circulating fluid* to transport everything — blood;
- at least one *pump* to move the fluid — a heart;
- *spaces* (in an open system) or *vessels* (in a closed system) for the fluid to move through;
- a *respiratory pigment* — to carry greater amounts of oxygen.

Closed systems — as in humans — are more efficient than open ones. They operate at higher fluid pressures and this results in faster transport and exchange.

The human vascular system

The human vascular system consists of a *closed double circulation* of blood pumped by a muscular heart inside closed blood vessels. The blood is generally under fairly high pressure, although the value of the pressure falls the farther the blood travels from the heart.

This circulating blood can transport anything soluble around the body, e.g. oxygen, carbon dioxide, proteins, vitamins, salt, water, hormones and many other substances.

Strangely enough, the blood does not touch most cells, tissues and organs directly; they are bathed in a fluid that is deliberately leaked from the system. This leaking fluid is almost colourless and termed *tissue fluid*.

The expression '*double circulation*' refers to the fact that the blood passes through the heart at least twice before reaching the same point again. One of these circuits passes through the lungs — the *pulmonary circulation*. The other and much longer circuit passes through the rest of the body systems — the *systemic circulation*.

To demonstrate the *double circulation*, try placing your finger on any part of fig. 18.2 and then move it in the direction of the blood flow to return to the same place.

What is the least number of times you pass through the heart? Is it possible to pass through the heart many times before returning to the same place?

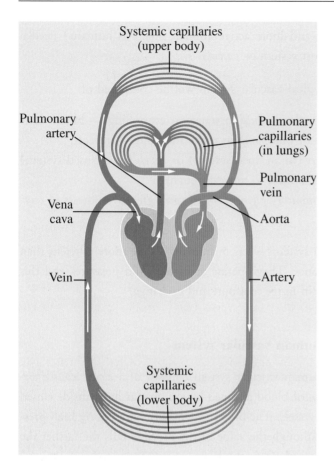

Fig. 18.2. The circulatory system.

A *portal system* is a blood supply that flows from one organ of the body directly to another organ — without passing through the heart. Portal systems begin and end with capillaries (see later).

Example: The hepatic portal vein brings blood (rich in digested food but lacking in oxygen) from the intestine directly to the liver.

THE HEART

The heart is a cone-shaped, hollow, muscular organ about the size of your closed fist. It is made from *cardiac muscle* — an unusual type of involuntary muscle that is very elastic and does not easily become tired. The heart lies to the front of the chest — underneath the breastbone and between the two lungs. It is surrounded by a membrane — the *pericardium* — which prevents friction with the nearby organs.

The heart has four pumping chambers — two lower chambers with very thick walls — the *ventricles*, and two upper, thinner chambers — the *atria*. (The *atrium* of an ancient

Roman dwelling was an entrance chamber.) The left-hand side of the heart is divided from the right-hand side by the *septum*.

Blood enters the right atrium from two 'great veins'. These are the *superior vena cava* (returning blood from the head, neck, arms and shoulders) and the *inferior vena cava* (returning blood from the abdomen and legs). (*Vena cava* is

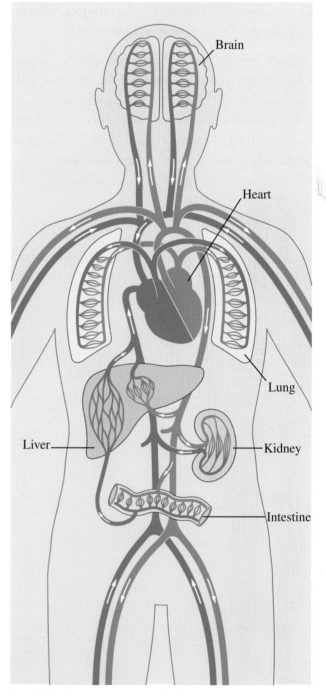

Fig. 18.3. Circulation in detail.

Latin for 'great vein'.) This blood leaves the right ventricle through the *pulmonary artery*, which branches left and right to the two lungs.

Blood enters the left atrium through four *pulmonary veins*, which return blood from the lungs. This blood leaves the left ventricle through the *aorta*, which curves like an umbrella handle and then lies behind the heart.

Within the heart, there are four *heart valves*. These are designed to ensure a one-way flow of blood at all times.

The cardiac muscle receives its own blood supply through cardiac or coronary blood vessels. It does not take oxygen or nutrients directly from the blood that it is pumping through its chambers.

Coronary arteries bring oxygenated blood from the base of the aorta to the heart muscle and coronary veins return deoxygenated blood directly to the right atrium.

Coronary heart disease

Atherosclerosis (literally *hardening of the blood vessels*) is a disease of human blood vessels. It kills more humans in the western world than any other single disease.

It is usually due to excess cholesterol from the diet forming fatty deposits under the inner lining of an artery. A raised lump of fatty deposits (an *atheroma*) in the artery will raise the patient's blood pressure and soon lead to the development of a blood clot (*embolus*). This clot will either block the artery completely or break away and block some other,

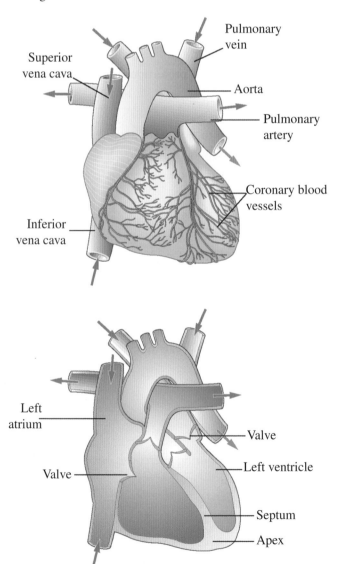

Fig. 18.4. The human heart.

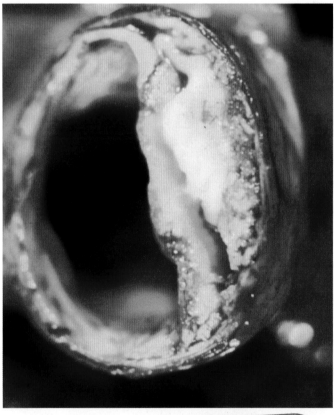

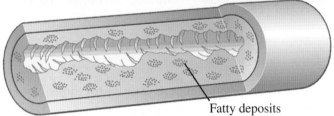

Fig. 18.5. Atheroma in an artery.

smaller blood vessel. This could lead to a stroke, if the blood supply to the brain is impaired.

If a blockage occurs in one of the coronary arteries, there will be a poor blood supply to some part of the heart. The pain from this — *angina* — is a warning that all is not well with the heart's blood supply. The condition may lead to failure of part or all of the heart — a heart attack.

Predisposing conditions for heart disease

1. SMOKING

- Burnt tobacco is highly toxic to the body. The nicotine in cigarettes stimulates the adrenal glands to secrete adrenaline and noradrenaline. These substances, in excess, cause the heart rate and blood pressure to increase and force the heart to work harder. This means that the heart muscle needs more oxygen. This excess stress on the heart can cause chest pain or angina.
- Platelets in the blood become sticky and clump onto the surface of lumps already present in the coronary arteries leading to a possible heart attack.
- Nicotine makes heart muscle more excitable and thus extra heartbeats can occur — a serious medical condition called *arrhythmia*.
- Sudden death from heart attack is very common in heavy smokers as nicotine and carbon monoxide can make heart muscle quiver (*fibrillate*) rather than contract. Heart fibrillation is immediately life-threatening.
- Carbon monoxide destroys the oxygen-carrying ability of the red blood cells (see later).
- Smoking increases the chest pain experienced by angina sufferers.
- Second-hand smoke from smouldering cigarettes contains high levels of carbon monoxide and other harmful chemicals. These can increase the heart rate and blood pressure of innocent bystanders — including friends, children, babies and pets.

2. LACK OF EXERCISE

Ideally, everyone should exercise three to five times a week for 20–60 minutes within their target heart rate (see below). If this is not possible, even moderate exercise is helpful —

walking, stair climbing, etc. Exercise not only helps to fight heart disease, it also lowers high blood pressure, protects bones against osteoporosis, reduces the chances of many cancers, reduces anxiety, improves sleep and lifts depression!

Aerobic exercise, such as walking, cycling, jogging and swimming, is recommended. If possible, resistance training, or weight lifting, should be included as it increases heart capacity and strength, decreases body fats and improves blood cholesterol levels.

The benefits of regular exercise include:

- stronger and better heart and lungs;
- a lowering of resting blood pressure;
- a decrease in body fat;
- a decrease in total cholesterol;
- an increase in overall energy with a more positive outlook;
- increased bone strength;
- increased suppleness and protection from injury.

When exercising:

- a frequency of three to five times a week is needed;
- exercise should last 20–60 minutes;
- stay roughly within your target heart rate (i.e. pulse not too slow and not too fast).

Calculating your target heart rate:

Maximum heart rate (MHR) = 220 − your age

The lower end of your target heart rate = MHR × 0.6

The upper end of your target heart rate = MHR × 0.8

For example: If you are 15 years old, your MHR is 220 − 15 = 205

205 × 0.6 = 123

205 × 0.8 = 164

Your target heart rate during exercise is between 123 and 164 beats per minute.

3. POOR DIET

Large amounts of saturated fat (animal fat) in the diet raises cholesterol levels and increase the risk of heart disease. Lowering dietary fat or replacing animal fats with fats of plant origin improves resistance to heart disease. Less fat in the diet is also a good way of losing weight and this reduces strain on the heart.

4. OTHER FACTORS

Age:	The risk of heart disease increases with age.
Sex:	At present, males are more susceptible than females. This may be changing.
Weight:	Excess body weight increases strain on the heart.
Heredity:	Family history is significant and can be a warning.
Stress:	Tends to raise adrenaline levels and increases the risk.

Treatments for heart disease include:

- change in lifestyle — no smoking and more exercise;
- protective diet — fewer animal fats;
- coronary bypass surgery — where blocked or diseased coronary blood vessels are bypassed with lengths of blood vessel removed from the patient's leg or chest. The bypass restores a full blood supply to the damaged portion of the heart.

The cardiac cycle (heart beat)

The cardiac cycle consists of alternate contraction (*systole*) and relaxation (*diastole*) of the muscle of the heart. (*Systole and diastole are pronounced 'systolee' and 'diastolee'.*)

The cycle is as follows:

- First, the two atria contract together and pump blood into the ventricles.
- Then, the two ventricles contract and pump the blood out of the heart through the two main arteries. The inner heart valves close at this time to stop the blood from re-entering the atria. This contraction of the ventricles is the main pumping action of the heart.
- After this, the outer valves close to stop blood from re-entering the ventricles and then the heart muscle takes a brief rest — the only rest it will get! The cycle now repeats itself — about 75 times per minute for a healthy adult at rest.

Heart phonetics

Heart sounds are due to the *closing* of the heart valves. First the outer heart valves close as the ventricles begin to contract, and then the inner valves close as blood tries to re-enter the heart from the two arteries.

The sounds are phonetically represented by: *lubb dup.*

Try saying this 75 times per minute!

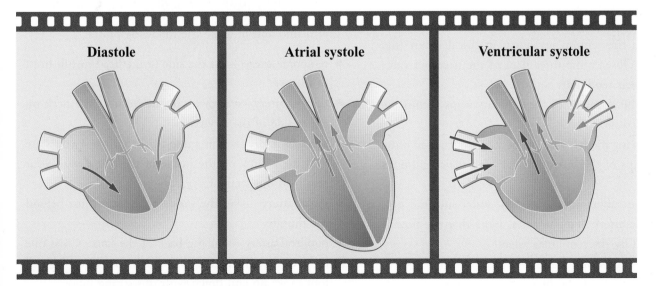

Fig. 18.6. Phases of heart beat.

Mandatory activity #9: Dissecting a bovine or sheep's heart

RESOURCES REQUIRED

Heart of a cow, ox, sheep, lamb or pig.
Dissecting instruments (scalpel, scissors, tweezers, needles).
Rubber gloves.
Rubber tubing and string or thread.

Try to obtain a heart with as much as possible of the atria and blood vessels intact. Consult your butcher over this or obtain preserved hearts from a laboratory supplier.

METHOD

1. Identify the front (ventral side) and the back (dorsal side) of the heart. The ventral side is more rounded and has coronary arteries lying in a clear diagonal. Also the left of the heart is thicker than the right.

2. Identify the following: the left and right atria; the left and right ventricles; the venae cavae; the pulmonary arteries; the aorta; the pulmonary veins; the coronary blood vessels.

3. Insert the rubber tube into the vena cava or directly into the right atrium. Clamp or tie the tube tightly and run water through the tube. Observe that the water emerges through the pulmonary artery.

4. Repeat with the tube inserted into a pulmonary vein or into the left atrium. Observe the water exiting through the aorta.

5. Cut from the right ventricle to the right atrium parallel to the septum as shown in the diagram (fig. 18.7). Observe the three flaps of the tricuspid valve with their tendinous cords.

6. Note the openings of the coronary veins within the right atrium.

7. Repeat for the left side of the heart and observe the two flaps of the bicuspid valve with their tendinous cords.

8. Use the rubber tubing to pour water into the pulmonary artery and the aorta. Note that the flow is resisted by the semilunar valves.

9. Cut upwards from each ventricle to its artery — in the direction of the blood flow. Examine the half-moon shaped flaps of the pulmonary and aortic valves.

10. Note the openings from the base of the aorta into the coronary arteries.

11. Note the relative thicknesses of the atrial walls, the left ventricle, the right ventricle and the septum.

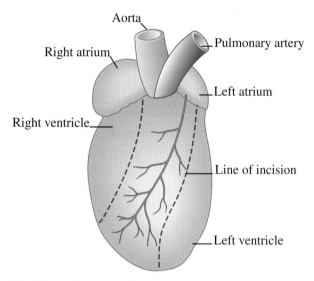

Fig. 18.7. Dissection of the heart-ventral view.

The pulse

The pulse is the change in pressure within arterial blood, as the ventricles alternately contract and relax.

This pressure change pulse can be felt at any location where an artery passes near to the surface of the body.

Try to find and measure the following pulses:

- temporal artery — at the side of the head just in front of the eye;
- carotid artery — high up in the front or the neck on either side of the larynx;
- brachial artery — this pulse is just visible if you stare into the hollow on the inside of the elbow with your arm held out straight;
- radial artery — on the inside of the wrist just behind the thumb;
- popliteal artery — at the back of the knee. Cross one leg over the other, relax, and watch your lower leg and foot move up and down with this strong pulse.

Mandatory activity #19: Investigating the effect of exercise on the pulse rate of a human

RESOURCES REQUIRED

Bench or stool, about 40 cm high.
Watch.

As the pulse is due to the contraction and relaxation of the heart, measuring the pulse rate indicates the rate of heart contraction. Students should work in pairs for this investigation. Students should be able to find a reliable pulse in their partner. Suitable pulses are at the wrist (radial artery) or at the temple just in front of the eye (temporal artery). The number of pulses or throbs per minute is counted. During times of quickly changing pulse rates (e.g. immediately after exercise), the number of pulses in 15 seconds should be counted and the answer multiplied by four.

METHOD

1. Work in pairs — one student exercising and the other measuring the pulses.
2. Ask the subject to relax but stand.
3. Obtain a resting pulse over one minute and record it.
4. Repeat twice more and find the average of the three resting pulses. This is the *normal, standing rate* for the subject.
5. Set definite exercise for the subject — e.g. stepping up and down on a 40 cm high bench every three seconds over two minutes (40 step-ups altogether!).
6. Record the pulse rate immediately on stopping over 15 seconds. Multiply this number by four. Repeat this measurement every 30 seconds until the pulse has returned to the normal standing rate.
7. If possible, repeat the experiment with more vigorous exercise, e.g. running a 100 m sprint.

N.B. A rapid return to the normal, standing rate after exercise is a sign of cardiovascular fitness.

8. Optional: Repeat the resting pulse part of the experiment to investigate the effect of posture on the heart rate. Ask the subject to lie down quietly for five minutes before recording their pulse. The subject might also like to try standing on their head!

TABLE OF RESULTS (ALL RATES ARE BEATS/MINUTE)

Pulse rate at rest I	
Pulse rate at rest II	
Pulse rate at rest III	
Average resting rate	
Pulse rate just after exercise	
Pulse rate after 30 seconds rest	
Pulse rate after 1 minutes rest	
Pulse rate after 1m 30s rest	
Pulse rate after 2 minutes rest	
Pulse rate after 2m 30s rest	
Pulse rate after 3 minutes rest	
Pulse rate after 3m 30s rest	

Blood pressure

Blood pressure within the circulation is due to:

- the contracting of the heart;
- the volume of blood within the system;
- the space available within the blood vessels.

Different values for blood pressure are obtained in different parts of the circulation. Generally the pressure goes down, as the blood moves further from the ventricles of the heart. The pressure is therefore highest in the arteries, less in the capillaries, lower still in the veins and negative (less than the air pressure in the room) in the vena cava.

Every time the ventricles contract (ventricular systole), the pressure rises in the nearby arteries. When the ventricles relax (ventricular diastole), the arterial pressure falls again. This alternate rising and falling of the arterial pressure is the familiar pulse and is easily felt anywhere an artery crosses a bone near the surface of the body.

When blood pressure is being measured, it is measured in the brachial artery of the upper arm. An inflatable cuff is used to measure the pressure required to stop the blood flow at this point. Two pressures are measured: the systolic pressure (as the ventricles contract) and the diastolic pressure (as the ventricles relax).

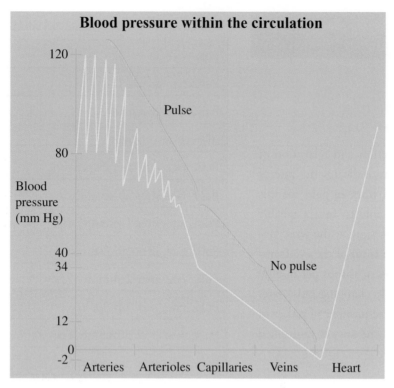

Fig. 18.8. Blood pressures within the circulation.

In the normal, healthy adult, these alternate pressures measured at the brachial artery of the arm would be:

120mmHg   When the ventricles are
           contracting   – *Systolic pressure*
80mmHg   When the ventricles are
           relaxed   – *Diastolic pressure*

This is usually written as: 120/80 mmHg or '120 over 80'.

If an artery is cut, the blood will come out quickly (due to the high pressure) and in spurts (due to the pulse or constant pressure change).

Blood pressures at other locations in the circulation:

Capillary pressure: about 32mmHg with no pulse.
Venous pressure: about 12mmHg with no pulse.
                       Blood flows out slowly if a vein is cut.
Vena cava pressure: – 2mmHg, i.e. *less* than the air pressure in the room — air would enter the blood vessel if it were cut.

THE HEART CYCLE AND HEART BEAT CONTROL   [H32 II]

The heart cycle is divided into three phases:

1. *Atrial systole* — lasting for 0.1 seconds.
   During this phase, the atria contract and top up the ventricles with blood. The ventricles are relaxed and about 70% full at the start of this phase, but 100% full by the end.

2. *Ventricular systole* — lasting for 0.3 seconds.
   The ventricles contract together, the cuspid valves close and blood is pumped out of the heart through the two main arteries. The semilunar valves are open at this time. This is the main pumping action of the heart.

3. *Diastole* — lasting for 0.4 seconds.
   All the chambers of the heart are relaxed. The semilunar valves close to prevent reflux of blood from the arteries. The heart muscle rests and blood flows passively into the heart from the veins.

The complete cycle lasts for 0.8 seconds, giving a resting pulse rate of 75 beats/minute.

Control of the heartbeat is *myogenic* (it comes from the heart muscle) and not *neurogenic* (coming from nerves). Living heart muscle excised from animals continues to beat on its own.

Cardiac muscle is highly specialised, it is not prone to fatigue and its fibres have cross branches for extra strength and elasticity.

The heartbeat is controlled as follows:

The heart contains two natural pacemakers — the *sinoatrial node* located in the top of the right atrium and the *atrioventricular node* in the septum at the top of the two ventricles.

- Every 0.8 seconds, the SA node produces an electrical spark.
- This sends a wave of electricity across the atria stimulating them to contract together — *atrial systole.*
- The wave of electricity hits the second pacemaker (the AV node).
- The AV node sends its own burst of electricity down wires buried in the septum (*Purkinje fibres* — collectively known as *bundles of His*).
- This wave now spreads up over the ventricles causing them to contract — *ventricular systole.*
- The heart relaxes.

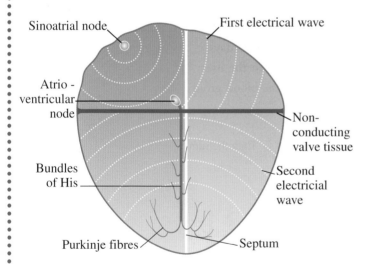

Fig. 18.9. Conduction of impulses within the heart muscle.

N.B. The valve tissue between the atria and ventricles is non-conducting and does not allow any waves to cross over. This prevents all four of the heart chambers from contracting together.

For patients with heartbeat irregularities, artificial battery-powered pacemakers are available to regulate the beat.

BLOOD VESSELS — ARTERIES, VEINS, CAPILLARIES

An *artery* is a blood vessel that transports blood *away from the heart* and under high pressure. Small arteries are called *arterioles*. Arteries have thick walls and a small internal diameter. They carry blood under high pressure and have a pulse.

A *vein* is a blood vessel that transports blood *towards the heart* and under low pressure. Small veins are called *venules*. Veins have thin walls and a large internal diameter. They carry blood under low pressure. Blood flow is sluggish in veins, particularly if against gravity, but is assisted by the presence of non-return valves and by the squeezing action of nearby arteries and muscles. Veins do not have a pulse.

A *capillary* is a microscopic, thin-walled blood vessel that is the site of exchange between the blood and the body tissues. Diffusion of dissolved substances can take place through capillary walls. Capillaries do not have a pulse.

N.B. The *only* place for substances (gases, nutrients, wastes, cells, hormones, etc.) to enter or leave the circulation is through the thin walls of the capillaries. No natural entry or exit can take place anywhere else in the circulation.

Table 18.1. Arteries, veins and capillaries

Arteries	Veins	Capillaries
thick elastic walls	thinner walls	very thin semi-permeable walls
no valves	have valves	no valves
high blood pressure	low blood pressure	medium blood pressure
blood has a pulse	no pulse	no pulse
mostly oxygenated blood	mostly deoxygenated	both kinds
carry blood from the heart	carry blood to the heart	carry from arteries to veins
small lumen	large lumen	Relatively large lumen. A diameter of 1/22nd of a human hair

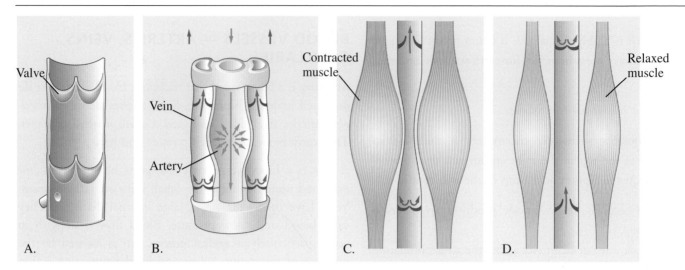

Fig. 18.10. Vein squeezing.

THE BLOOD

Blood is a fluid, connective tissue, which is pumped through the closed vessels of the circulatory system. It is the means by which materials are *transported* around the body and it also plays an important role in *defence* against disease.

55% of the blood volume is a liquid called plasma.

This encloses and transports:

- red blood cells (or *erythrocytes*);
- white blood cells (or *leucocytes*);
- platelets (or *thrombocytes*).

Red blood cells

- are biconcave discs;
- contain iron and haemoglobin to carry oxygen. *Haemoglobin* (a dark red pigment) has a high affinity for oxygen and combines with it to form *oxyhaemoglobin* (which is bright red). Oxyhaemoglobin can later release oxygen to body cells;
- have no nucleus or mitochondria;
- are made in the bone marrow of all bones in children and small bones only in adults;
- live for about 120 days;
- are destroyed in the liver;
- determine the blood group.

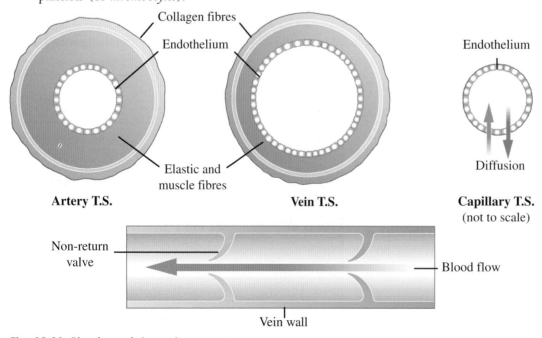

Fig. 18.11. Blood vessels in section.

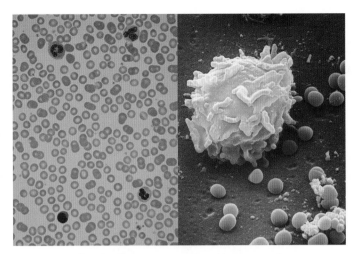

Fig. 18.12. Blood cells. Leucocyte attacking some throat bacteria (red).

White blood cells

- are larger, flattened discs;
- have a prominent nucleus;
- are made in the bone marrow or in lymphatic tissue;
- may make and carry *antibodies* to stick to foreign matter (see Chapter 26);
- may eat foreign matter within the circulation;
- only live for five to eight days.

Platelets

- are tiny fragments of bone marrow cells;
- are involved in blood clotting.
- have no nuclei or nuclear parts.

Plasma

- is a straw-coloured, watery liquid;

Erythrocytes   **Platelets**

Leucocytes

Lymphocyte   Granulocyte   Monocyte

Fig. 18.13. Blood components.

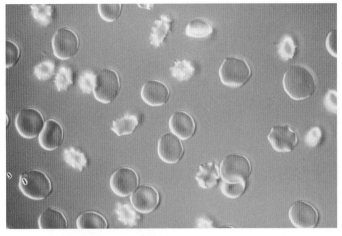

Fig. 18.14. Red cells trapped in a blood clot.

- makes up 55% of the blood volume;
- has a pH of about 7.4;
- transports everything — gases, nutrients, excretions, hormones, heat, blood cells and platelets.

Leukaemia

This disease is a cancer of the leucocyte-forming cells in the bone marrow. The cause is unknown but is often linked to exposure to radiation. The disease has different forms and is usually diagnosed by examination of the blood under a microscope. There are typically very high numbers of immature white cells, which may leave the patient prone to other disease.

Treatment is by *cytotoxic* (cell-killing) drugs, steroids and transfusions of blood or bone marrow from a suitable donor.

THE LYMPHATIC SYSTEM

Structure

- The lymphatic system is a set of branching tubes (the lymph vessels) that extends throughout the body.
- The tubes resemble veins (thin walls and valves) but do not contain blood.
- There are swellings in the tubes — lymph nodes.
- These swellings are concentrated mainly in the neck, armpits and groin.
- The largest vessel — *the thoracic duct* — opens into a vein in the left shoulder.
- Extensions of the lymphatic system — called *lacteals* — are found inside the villi of the small intestine.

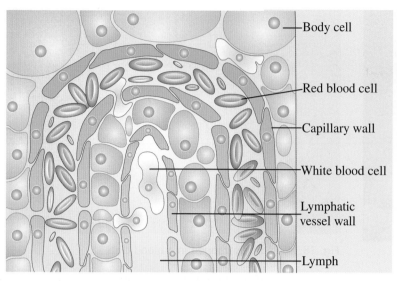
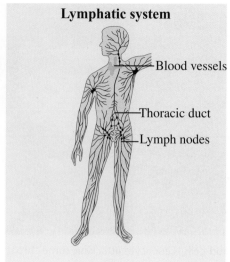

Fig. 18.15. Capillary and lymphatic vessel magnified.

- A watery fluid called lymph is found throughout the system.
- This fluid is at low pressure and does not have any pulse.
- Lymph moves in one direction only.

Functions

1. The lymphatic system returns lost water to the circulation. Capillaries are porous and they leak nourishing tissue fluid (*ECF or extra-cellular fluid*) onto the body's cells. Most of this fluid is later gathered up by the blood system, but some fluid remains behind. To avoid water-logging of the tissues at the extremities of the body, the lymphatic system sucks up this remaining fluid and returns it to the bloodstream in the left shoulder.

2. Lymph nodes trap and kill bacteria.

3. Lymph nodes can make lymphocytes and antibodies.

4. Lacteals transport fat from the intestine to the bloodstream.

5. The lymphatic system is used to transport some hormones.

N.B. Fluid within the lymphatic system is called lymph. The same fluid around the body cells is called tissue fluid or extra-cellular fluid (ECF).

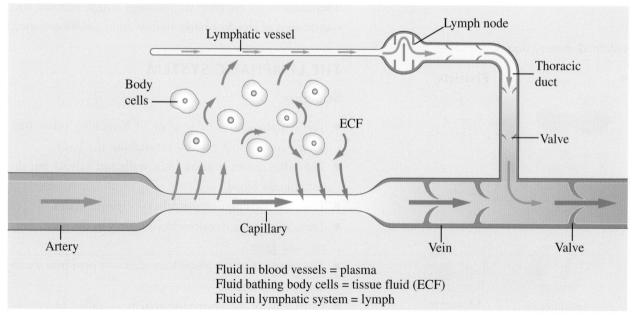

Fluid in blood vessels = plasma
Fluid bathing body cells = tissue fluid (ECF)
Fluid in lymphatic system = lymph

Fig. 18.16. Tissue fluid collection.

Oedema

Oedema is a swelling of the body (usually the lower legs and feet) due to too much fluid from the blood or lymph vessels lying in the tissue spaces. It may be due to a failing circulation or an unusual blood composition (too much water and salt or too little protein) due to a kidney complaint.

Elephantiasis

This is a dramatic example of how a parasite may alter the appearance of its host. This tropical disease is caused by a parasitic roundworm when eggs from it enter humans through mosquito bites. The young worms grow and live in the lymph vessels and eventually block them. The result of this is enormous swelling of the extremities (due to non-return of tissue fluid to the blood) leading to an elephant-like appearance of the limbs. Treatment is by removal of the worm, drainage of the gathered fluid and surgical repair of the damaged lymph vessels if necessary.

BLOOD CELLS   [H32 1]

Red blood cells

- Red cells have no nuclei and no mitochondria. They sacrifice these organelles to create more room for carrying oxygen.

- They are sometimes termed *corpuscles* — meaning *ghost cells*.
- They are made in the bone marrow from stem cells at a rate of five million per second.
- They outnumber white cells by about 400 to 1.

White blood cells

- White cells are made in the bone marrow and in lymphatic tissue.
- White cells are classified as *lymphocytes*, *monocytes* and *granulocytes*.
- *Granulocytes* are ingestive — they eat foreign material. They make up 60% of the white cell count and are very busy in the mouth, throat, intestine and at times of hay fever.
- *Monocytes* are non-granular and make up 6% of the white cell count. They are also ingestive and often leave the capillaries to engulf foreign matter.
- *Lymphocytes* make up 33% of the white cell count. They manufacture antibodies in response to any foreign material (antigens). They are small and non-granular cells (see Chapter 26 for more information on lymphocytes).

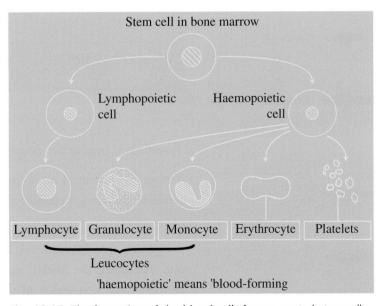

Fig. 18.17. The formation of the blood cells from a central *stem cell*.

BLOOD GROUPS

Almost all early attempts at blood transfusions were doomed to failure as the human *immune response* rejects any invading matter that the body considers *foreign*. If the blood of two individuals is incompatible, the donor's red cells stick together to form clumps (*agglutinate*) which block the smaller blood vessels of the recipient. In addition, haemoglobin leaks from the agglutinated cells and may eventually cause kidney failure.

Consequently, any blood transfer between two incompatible people will probably result in the death of the recipient. In modern transfusions, blood is screened or tested for compatibility before proceeding.

Many different systems are used to classify human blood, the most important being the *ABO system* and the *Rhesus system*.

In the ABO system, there are four blood groups covering the entire population of the world.

Group O — making up about 46% of the Irish population.
Group A — 42%.
Group B — 9%.
Group AB — 3%.

The grouping is determined by the presence or absence of proteins on the surface of the red blood cells. This is decided by the genetics (genotypes) of the natural parents.

These proteins can act as *antigens*. They may stimulate the production of *antibodies* within the recipient if they are classified as *foreign* by the recipient's immune system. Antibodies cause agglutination and then destruction of the 'foreign' blood cells.

The immune system will not produce antibodies against its own antigens but will produce antibodies against the other antigens of the ABO system as follows:

Table 18.2. Blood group antigens

Blood group	Occurrence (IRL)	Antigen on red cells	ABO antibody in plasma
Group A	42%	A	*anti-B*
Group B	9%	B	*anti-A*
Group AB	3%	A and B	neither *anti-A* nor *anti-B*
Group O	46%	neither A nor B	both *anti-A* and *anti-B*

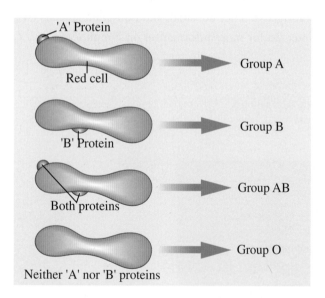

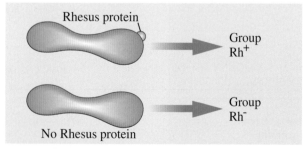

Fig. 18.18. Red cells with antigens.

Transfusions involve two people: the *donor* and the *recipient*.

The *recipient* is much more likely to be at any risk and the transfusion is always considered from *their* point of view.

For a safe transfusion, the recipient *must not* receive *anything foreign* into their bloodstream. If they do, their immune system will attack the foreign material with Antibodies. The clumping and destruction of the red cells that follows this will probably be fatal.

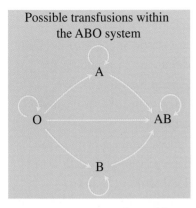

Possible transfusions within
the ABO system

Fig. 18.19. Diagram of possible transfusions.

The following diagram is a simple guide as to who might give blood to whom:

- Group O humans are known as *universal donors* — their blood can be *given* to anyone.
- Group AB humans are *universal recipients* — they can *receive* anyone's blood.

N.B. The above diagram only applies to transfusions of up to one litre of blood. In larger transfusions, the *donor's antibodies* may reach a high level within the recipient and the above diagram may not apply. As doctors can never say when a small transfusion might turn into a larger one, transfusions between *identical groups* are preferred.

The *rhesus system* contains only two blood groups:

- Rhesus positive (Rh^+)
- Rhesus negative (Rh^-)

Again, the grouping is determined by the presence or absence of a *rhesus protein* (first identified in rhesus monkeys and then in humans). In Ireland, about 85% of the population is Rh^+ and the other 15% are Rh^-.

Rh^- individuals consider Rh^+ to be *foreign*, but Rh^+ individuals can generally receive Rh^- blood safely.

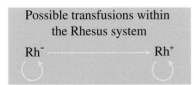

Possible transfusions within
the Rhesus system

Rh^- ⟶ Rh^+

Fig. 18.20. Possible rhesus transfusions.

SUMMARY

- *Animal complexity* develops in response to the animal's need for food.
- *Active animals* (*such as humans*) need a transport system or vascular system.
- *The human vascular system* consists of a closed double circulation of blood pumped by a muscular heart inside closed blood vessels.
- *The heart* is a cone-shaped, hollow, muscular organ.
- *The heart has four pumping chambers* — two atria and two ventricles.
- *Heart valves* are designed to ensure a one-way flow of blood at all times.
- *Predisposing conditions for heart disease* include smoking, poor diet and lack of exercise.
- *The cardiac cycle* consists of alternate contraction (systole) and relaxation (diastole) of the muscle of the heart.
- *Blood pressure* within the circulation is due to:

  - the contracting of the heart;
  - the volume of blood within the system;
  - the space available within the blood vessels.

- *Blood is a fluid, connective tissue*, which is pumped through the closed vessels of the circulatory system.
- *Blood is the means by which* materials are transported around the body and it also plays an important role in defence against disease.
- *Blood consists of* plasma, red blood cells, white blood cells and platelets.
- *The lymphatic system* returns lost water to the circulation.
- *Capillaries are porous* and they leak nourishing tissue fluid (ECF or extra-cellular fluid) onto the body's cells.
- *The lymphatic system* collects excess tissue fluid and returns it to the bloodstream.
- *Lymph nodes* trap and kill bacteria.
- *Lymph nodes* make lymphocytes and antibodies.
- *Lacteals transport fat* from the intestine to the bloodstream.
- *The lymphatic system* is used to transport some hormones.

EXTENDED SUMMARY

- *The heart cycle* is divided into three phases:

  - atrial systole — lasting for 0.1 seconds;
  - ventricular systole — lasting for 0.3 seconds;
  - diastole — lasting for 0.4 seconds.

- *Control of the heartbeat is myogenic.*
- *Cardiac muscle is highly specialised* — it is not prone to fatigue and its fibres have cross branches for extra strength and elasticity.
- *The heart contains two natural pacemakers* — the sinoatrial node and the atrioventricular node.
- *White cells* are classified as lymphocytes, monocytes and granulocytes.
- *The ABO system and the Rhesus system* are the two common blood-grouping systems.
- *For a safe transfusion*, recipients must not receive anything foreign into their bloodstream. If they do, their immune system will attack the foreign material with antibodies.

KEY WORDS

Diffusion	Movement of materials from high to lower concentration. Slow over large distances.
Vascular system	Transport system.
Respiratory pigment	Chemical, e.g. haemoglobin, designed to carry oxygen.
Double circulation	Blood must pass at least twice through the heart before returning to the same location.
Tissue fluid	Colourless fluid, rich in nutrients and gases, which leaks from the circulation and bathes all cells.
Pulmonary circulation	Circulation through the lungs.
Systemic circulation	Circulation throughout the body.
Portal system	A blood supply from one organ of the body directly to another organ without passing through the heart.

Cardiac muscle	Involuntary heart muscle — very elastic and not easily tired.
Pericardium	Membrane surrounding the heart, preventing friction.
Ventricles	Thick-walled, lower chambers of the heart.
Atria	Upper chambers of the heart.
Heart valves	Flaps preventing backflow of blood within the heart.
Atherosclerosis	Hardening of the blood vessels.
Atheroma	A raised lump of fatty deposits on the inner wall of a blood vessel.
Embolus	An internal blood clot.
Angina	Pain from the heart muscle due to lack of oxygen.
Arrhythmia	Irregular heart beat.
Fibrillation	A quivering of the heart muscle.
Pulse	A wave of pressure change within arteries due to the action of the ventricles.
Systolic pressure	Arterial blood pressure during ventricular contraction.
Diastolic pressure	Arterial blood pressure during ventricular relaxation.
Atrial systole	Contraction of the atria.
Ventricular systole	Contraction of the ventricles.
Diastole	Relaxation of the heart muscle.
Myogenic	Originating in the heart muscle.
Neurogenic	Originating in nerves.
Artery	A blood vessel that transports blood away from the heart and under high pressure.
Arteriole	A small artery.
Vein	A blood vessel that transports blood towards the heart and under low pressure.
Venule	A small vein.
Capillary	A microscopic, thin-walled blood vessel, the site of exchange between the blood and the body tissues.
Erythrocytes	Red blood cells.

Leucocytes	White blood cells.
Thrombocytes or platelets	Fragments of marrow cells needed for blood clotting.
Haemoglobin	A respiratory pigment within red cells. Used to carry oxygen.
Oxyhaemoglobin	Haemoglobin combined with oxygen.
Leukaemia	A cancer of the leucocyte-forming cells in the bone marrow.
Lymphatic system	A set of branching tubes that extends throughout the body. Used for returning tissue fluid to the circulation.
Lacteals	Extensions of the lymphatic system found within the villi of the intestine.
ECF	Extra-cellular fluid or tissue fluid.

EXTENDED KEY WORDS

Sinoatrial node	The main pacemaker of the heart.
Atrioventricular node	Secondary pacemaker of the heart.
Purkinje fibres	Conducting fibres within the septum.
Bundles of His	Bundles of Purkinje fibres.
Corpuscles	'Ghost' cells or cells with no nuclei.
Granulocytes	Ingestive white cells with granular cytoplasm.
Monocytes	Non-granular, ingestive white cells.
Lymphocytes	Non-granular white cells that make antibodies in response to antigens.

QUESTIONS

1. Explain why bulky animals have to have vascular systems.

2. Explain each of the following:

   a. double circulation;

   b. pulmonary circulation;

   c. systemic circulation.

3. What does a *closed circulation* mean? A closed circulation does not allow blood to bathe the cells and tissues of the body. How then are substances exchanged between the blood and the body cells?

4. Explain the function of each of the following:

   a. pericardium;

   b. aortic valve;

   c. tendinous cords;

   d. pacemaker;

   e. right ventricle;

   f. septum.

5. How does the heart muscle receive its own food and oxygen supply?

6. What is atherosclerosis? What are the main causes of this condition?

7. List seven different ways in which smoking can adversely affect the heart.

8. Explain the terms: *atrial systole, ventricular systole, diastole.* Briefly describe what happens during a complete heart cycle.

9. What is a pulse? Name four locations in the human body where a pulse can be easily detected. Why are pulses found at these locations?

10. List the four components of the blood and state the functions of each component.

11. Which blood component is being described in each of the following statements?

    a. *Are essential for clotting.*

    b. *Have nuclei.*

    c. *Are part of the immune system.*

    d. *Round biconcave discs.*

    e. *Contain haemoglobin.*

    f. *The liquid portion of the blood.*

    g. *Determine the blood group.*

    h. *Makes up 55% of the blood volume.*

12. Explain how arteries, veins and capillaries are adapted to their function.

13. List the following blood vessels in the order in which blood would pass through them:

    – *venules*;
    – *arteries*;
    – *capillaries*;
    – *veins*;
    – *arterioles*.

14. Which of the following could describe the flow of blood though an artery?

    a. Oxygenated blood moving slowly under low pressure.
    b. Oxygenated blood moving under high, steady pressure.
    c. Deoxygenated blood moving under high, surging pressure.
    d. Deoxygenated blood moving under medium pressure.
    e. Deoxygenated blood moving under low pressure but with a pulse.

15. Why is blood pressure necessary? What do people mean when they say they are 'suffering from blood pressure'? Why is normal blood pressure described as '120/80'?

16. How is tissue fluid formed? Which of its components are likely to be taken up by cells?

17. Describe the structure of the lymphatic system. In what way are plasma, lymph and tissue fluid similar? In what way are they different? Besides assisting in the return of leaked fluid to the circulation, in what other ways is the lymphatic system useful? Why does the thoracic duct open into a vein rather than an artery?

18. Explain the importance of each of the following adaptations in red cell structure:

    a. contain haemoglobin;
    b. have no nucleus;
    c. are thin and permeable;
    d. are flexible;
    e. have a biconcave shape.

EXTENDED QUESTIONS

1. Describe a complete heart cycle. Include reference to the time taken for the heart to complete each phase. What causes the heart sounds? At what precise moments are heart sounds heard?

2. Explain the terms myogenic and neurogenic. How has it been demonstrated that the heartbeat is myogenic?

3. Describe the electrical nature of the heartbeat. Include in your answer reference to two pacemakers and the Purkinje fibres. Why is it essential that the heart valve tissue does not conduct electricity?

4. Distinguish between lymphocytes, monocytes and granulocytes.

5. What is meant by the expressions: *universal donors*, *universal recipients*? Why are group O people considered universal donors? Combining the ABO and Rhesus blood group systems? Who are the most common and the least common people to meet in Ireland? What percentage of the Irish population is likely to be A^+, AB^-?

OPTIONAL ACTIVITIES

- If available, examine models and charts of the heart, blood and blood vessels.

- Examine prepared slides of artery and vein sections under the microscope.

- Rub oil on your finger between the nail and the first knuckle. Examine the skin under bright light and low power to observe capillaries.

- Use a Sphygmomanometer to measure blood pressure. Warning — this instrument must be used under supervision by a teacher.

- Examine a pre-prepared blood smear to identify some of these blood components. The blood cells are very small — high power and good microscope technique will be needed (see Chapter 6).

- Blood groups cannot be determined by microscopic observation. Determine your blood group using Eldon Cards — available from School Science Suppliers.

For further information on websites dealing with subjects in this chapter see www.my-etest.com.

Now test yourself at
www.my-etest.com

Chapter 19
Transport in the Flowering Plant

Learning objectives

After your study of this chapter, you should be able to:

- distinguish between diffusion and osmosis;
- list the materials within plants that are in need of transport;
- distinguish between the apoplast and symplast pathways of water movement;
- describe in detail the passage of water through a plant;
- define transpiration;
- relate stomatal opening to the rate of water movement;
- define translocation;
- give examples of plant food storage organs and explain their purpose.

Extended learning objectives

- Outline the elements of the cohesion-tension hypothesis.
- Summarise the evidence supporting the hypothesis.

Mandatory activities

#14. Demonstrating osmosis.

TRANSPORT FOR NUTRITION   [331]

Nutrition in the flowering plant is *autotrophic*: plants make their own food from simple nutrients and sunlight energy and they gather these ingredients from the surrounding environment.

Like animals, plants are multicellular and materials within them must be transported to and from individual cells. Many transport mechanisms are used within plants including *diffusion, osmosis, active transport, cytoplasmic streaming* and other methods (see Chapter 10, section [**226**]).

Revision of diffusion and osmosis:

- *Diffusion* is the movement of materials from a place of high concentration to a place of lower concentration.
- *Osmosis* is a special case of diffusion. It is the *diffusion of water across a semi-permeable membrane* from a region of high water concentration to a region of lower water concentration.

Mandatory activity #14: Demonstrating osmosis

(*See Chapter 10*).

RESOURCES NEEDED

Visking tubing.
Water.
Starch solution.
Sucrose solution.
Iodine solution.
Plastic syringe.
Glass tube.
Large beakers.
Rubber bands or string.

To demonstrate osmosis, a model cell can be constructed from *visking tubing* (an artificial semi-permeable membrane). The tubing is filled with strong sucrose solution, tied with rubber bands or string and placed in a container of water. The tubing now resembles a cell with its semi-permeable membrane.

- Soften a length of visking tubing by holding it under water.
- Tie a knot at one end.
- Use a syringe to fill the tubing with strong sucrose solution.
- Tie the other end of the tubing and rinse both knots well with tap water.
- Place the model cell in water and record its appearance.
- Record its appearance after 30 minutes and compare.

Water molecules move from the region of higher water concentration to the region of lower water concentration — in this case into the model cell. Sucrose molecules would 'like' to move from the more sugary to the less sugary region (i.e. out of the tubing) but the molecules are too large to fit through the semi-permeable membrane pores. Despite the inpouring of water, the visking tubing doesn't burst, as it is strong. The model cell swells and eventually osmosis has to stop as no more water molecules can fit in.

Further demonstration of diffusion and osmosis

EXAMPLE 1

- Use a syringe to place starch solution at the base of a still container of water.
- Immediately test a sample of water at the surface for the presence of starch. Starch solution turns black in the presence of iodine.

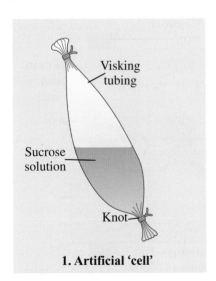
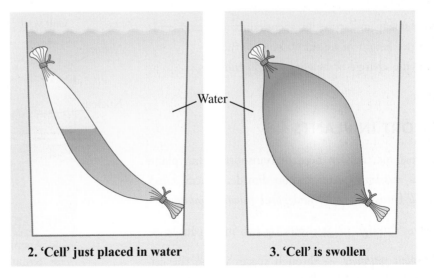

1. Artificial 'cell'   **2. 'Cell' just placed in water**   **3. 'Cell' is swollen**

Fig. 19.1. Visking tubing experiment.

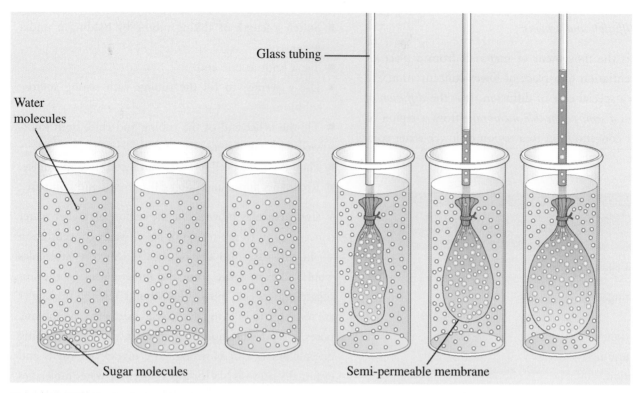

Fig. 19.2. Diffusion and osmosis.

■ Retest the water surface after 30 minutes and compare the result.

EXAMPLE 2

■ Tie a closed 'bag' of visking tubing to the end of a glass tube.
■ Use a syringe to fill the bag with starch solution.
■ Rinse the outside of the bag and glass tube with clean water.
■ Place the bag and tube in a container of water and record the height of liquid within the tube.
■ Record the change of height after 30 minutes.

TRANSPORT IN PLANTS

The principal materials in need of transport within plants are *inorganic nutrients* (water, carbon dioxide, mineral ions), *oxygen*, *foods* (mostly sugars) and *plant growth regulators*.

Water moves through plant tissues by two main pathways:

■ *The apoplast pathway* — through spaces within the cellulose cell walls and also through spaces within the non-living xylem cells. This route completely avoids living cytoplasm and meets little resistance. Ninety per cent of all water movement in a plant is by this pathway. Individual cells absorb most of their water directly from the apoplast pathway and fill up their vacuoles by osmosis.

■ *The symplast pathway* — through the contents of living cells. This route crosses the cell cytoplasm and passes through the cell walls via pits. The cell organelles provide considerable resistance and this pathway is slow.

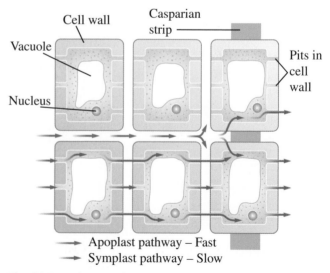

Fig. 19.3. Pathways of water movement in cells.

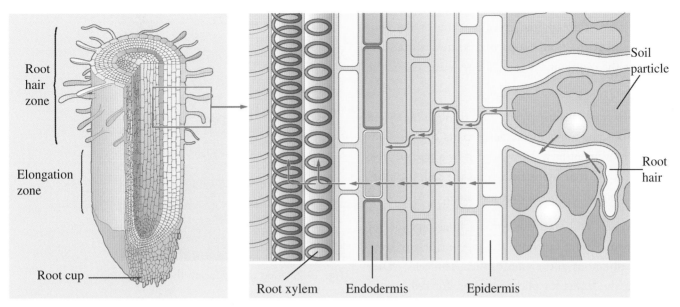

Root hair zone

Elongation zone

Root cup

Soil particle

Root hair

Root xylem Endodermis Epidermis

Fig. 19.4. Water crossing the root.

Table 19.1. Summarising transport of materials between plant cells

Material	Importance	Method of transport
Water	For photosynthesis and cell metabolism	Moves upwards within the xylem tissue
Mineral ions	For synthesising all plant components	Dissolved in water
Carbon dioxide	For photosynthesis	Diffuses through stomata and air spaces within the plant tissues
Oxygen	For tissue respiration	Diffuses through air spaces
Sugars and amino acids	For further growth, repair and reproduction	Move through phloem tissue
Growth regulators	For co-ordination of plant responses	Move by diffusion and active transport

Four important transports occurring within plants

1. UPTAKE AND TRANSPORT OF WATER

This begins at the root system of the plant. Most roots have a small root hair zone very close to the root apex and almost all water uptake is restricted to this region. Root hairs are extensions of the cells of the root epidermis and have a short life span. They grow between the soil particles and absorb soil water by *osmosis*.

Fig. 19.5. Root hairs.

Water now passes through the ground tissue of the root (along the apoplast and symplast pathways) towards the vascular tissue at the centre of the root. There, water enters the xylem cells.

Water can now flow (against gravity!) up through the xylem cells of the root and stem to the aerial parts of the plant. The upward movement of water is assisted by a *root pressure*. As water enters the root by osmosis from the soil, it pushes the water in front of it up the root and stem.

The xylem vessels and tracheids form a long pipeline for water movement. Water can leave the pipeline at any level, due to the perforations in the walls of the xylem cells. Water is required in the leaves for photosynthesis, for cell metabolism and growth and to maintain cell turgidity. However only a tiny proportion of the water in the plant (sometimes as little as 1%) is required by the leaves; the rest (up to 99%) is lost to the outside by evaporation through the stomata — the process of *transpiration*.

Transpiration is the evaporation of water from the surface of the leaf or stem.

This seemingly wasteful process has a purpose: as water is lost through the leaf stomata, more water is pulled up the xylem cells of the root and stem as replacement. As this water flows through apoplast and symplast pathways, leaf cells can use osmosis to absorb what water they need from the xylem. Transpiration maintains the flow of water and minerals from root to leaf despite the obstacle of gravity.

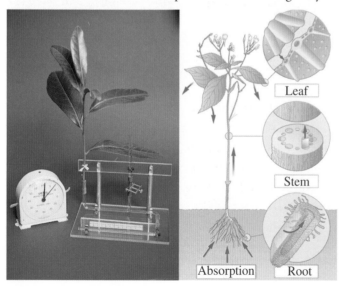

Fig. 19.6. Water movement.

Fig. 19.7. Using dye to locate the water pathway.

(Most animals are far less wasteful in their transport of liquids: they typically have enough energy and tissue organisation to form and operate a pump (a heart) working on a closed circulation with little fluid loss to the outside. However, a heart or series of hearts could never pump liquids to the height of a tall tree.

Transpiration is the best explanation for the plant's movement of water against gravity but water movement is assisted by *root pressure* where roots generate an upward force from soil water constantly entering their cell vacuoles. Root pressure does force water upward but never to the heights of tall trees. Water transport is also aided by *capillarity* — the tendency for water to creep through narrow tubes.)

The rate of transpiration usually follows a 24-hour repeating pattern: the rate is typically high by day and low or zero by night. This is partly due to the influence of many environmental factors (e.g. warmth increases the rate of evaporation) but mainly due to the behaviour of the stomata.

Stomata are found in the epidermis of most leaves and some stems. They tend to occur in the lower epidermis of leaves and are never found in root epidermis. Each stoma is a microscopic pore surrounded by two guard cells that are in turn surrounded by subsidiary cells. The guard cells are joined at either end but can flex in the mid-region and so change the diameter of the pore. By day, light seems to cause the stomata to open resulting in greater transpiration and a greater flow of water up through the plant. At night, the stomata of most plants close and prevent any transpiration or upward flow. The mechanism of stomatal opening is not clear and is not necessarily due to light — many stomata open before dawn. The waxy cuticle of leaves also restricts water loss.

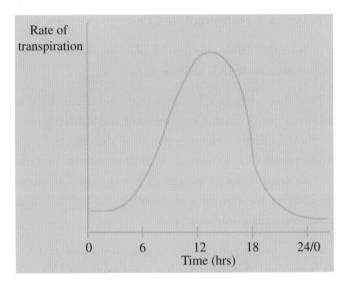

Fig. 19.8. Rate of transpiration over 24 hours.

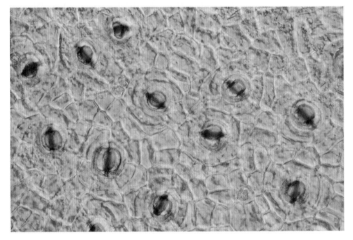

Fig. 19.9. Stomata.

2. UPTAKE AND TRANSPORT OF MINERALS

Mineral ions in plants combine with the sugars made by photosynthesis to form the building blocks of growth and to maintain the plant's metabolism. They are essential to the healthy life of the plant. The ions required include the *macronutrients*, which are calcium, potassium, sulphate, nitrate, phosphate, iron and magnesium, and also many *micronutrients* including manganese, copper, molybdenum, zinc and many others.

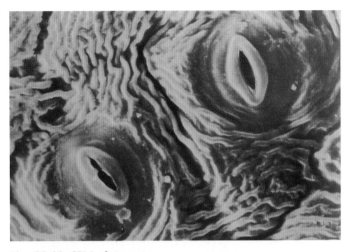

Fig. 19.10. SEM of stomata.

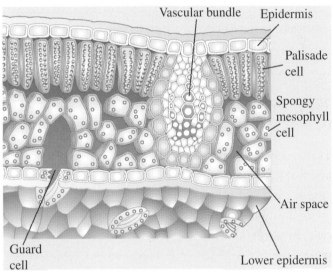

Fig. 19.11. Leaf structure.

There are various sources of mineral ions in the soil:

- Ions in solution in soil water — easily washed away (leached) from the soil.
- Ions adsorbed onto soil particles — held by electrostatic charges and not easily leached.
- Ions in humus, a black, fibrous material rich in ions and formed from the dead and decaying remains of plants and animals.
- Ions within the soil particles — not yet released by weathering.

Dissolved ions are adsorbed with water at the root tips but do not diffuse into the root through cells as water does; they

Table 19.2. Plant minerals

Macro-nutrient	Ionic form	Function	Ion-deficiency symptom
phosphorus	phosphate PO_4^{3-}	ATP, membranes, DNA, RNA	poor growth, dark green or spotted leaves
potassium	potassium ion K^+	enzyme function, cell membranes	poor growth, dark green or spotted leaves
nitrogen	nitrate NO_3^-	proteins and DNA/RNA	poor growth, chlorosis of older leaves
sulphur	sulphate SO_4^{2-}	amino acids, vitamins	poor growth, chlorosis of older leaves
calcium	calcium ion Ca^{2+}	cell walls, cell division	death of growing points
iron	iron(II) ion Fe^{2+}	chlorophyll, enzyme activation	chlorosis of young leaves
magnesium	magnesium ion Mg^{2+}	formation of chlorophyll	chlorosis of older leaves

are taken up by active transport across the root cell membranes. The ions now move quickly by the apoplast pathway or slowly by the symplast pathway. A cylinder of endodermis cells encloses the vascular tissue at the centre of the root. These cells have a strip of waterproof material — the *casparian strip* — on four of their six sides. The strip closes off the apoplast route and water with minerals can only continue moving through the endodermal cytoplasm. The active

transport required through the cell membranes and cytoplasm greatly slows the movement of the ions and regulates their flow. Otherwise, ions would quickly accumulate in the higher parts of the plant.

3. Uptake and transport of CO_2

Leaf cells require carbon dioxide for photosynthesis and they have two sources of CO_2 to draw from:

- All leaf cells produce CO_2 from respiration. This CO_2 is dissolved in cell water as carbonic acid and is directly used in photosynthesis without ever leaving the cells.
- Atmospheric CO_2 diffuses through open stomata into the leaf air space (spongy mesophyll layer). The CO_2 then dissolves in the film of water coating the leaf cells and enters the cells as carbonic acid.

In daytime, photosynthesis masks the production of CO_2 from respiration and the plant has a net intake of CO_2. At night, there is no photosynthesis and so the plant has a net output of CO_2. In certain dim conditions, it is possible to have a balance between the effects of photosynthesis and respiration and so have no net movement of CO_2 — this amount of light is the plant's *compensation point*.

4. Transport of photosynthesis products — carbohydrate and oxygen

Carbohydrate is made in the chloroplasts of the leaf by photosynthesis (see Chapter 8) and then transported to other parts of the plant that need it. Carbohydrates and other foods always travel in the phloem tissue and this movement is called *translocation*.

Translocation is the movement of organic materials within plants.

Phloem tissue consists of sieve tubes and companion cells (see Chapter 17, section [321]). Individual sieve tube cells (elements) are cylindrical and joined end to end to form a network of pipes running through the plant. Sieve elements have perforated end walls (sieve plates) but little cytoplasm and no nuclei. Companion cells are small and thin walled but have a large nucleus and are rich in cell organelles such as mitochondria and ribosomes. Companion cells attach to

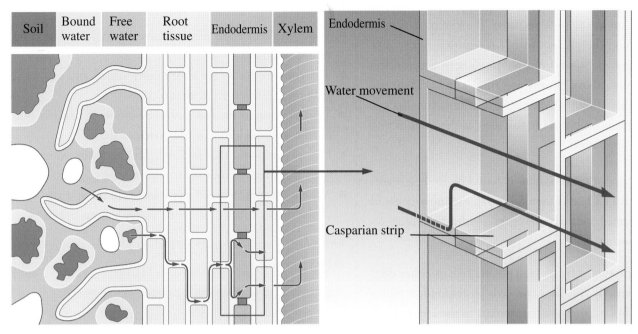

Soil	Bound water	Free water	Root tissue	Endodermis	Xylem

Fig. 19.12. The Casparian strip.

the sides of sieve tubes and communicate with them by continuous cytoplasm through tiny pores. It seems that companion cells regulate and maintain the metabolism of the enucleated sieve tubes.

Sugars from photosynthesis pass into the sieve tubes and are *translocated* through the plant to areas of growth, repair, development or storage. The speed of translocation is greater than that of diffusion alone and the process requires energy — supplied by aerobic respiration in the companion cells. The mechanism of translocation is not clear and its study is complicated by the fact that sugars may move at different speeds and in different directions within the phloem. One theory suggests that the sieve plates are crucial to translocation and act as electro-osmotic pumps controlled by the companion cells. Translocation is certainly an active process — killing the phloem cells with steam stops translocation instantly. In contrast, the flow of water in the xylem takes place through lignified, dead cells.

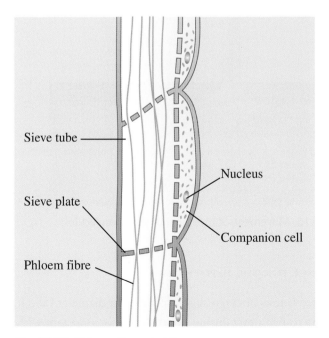

Fig. 19.13. Phloem tissue in LS.

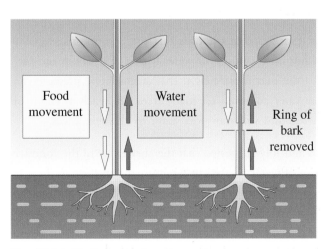

Fig. 19.14. Ringing experiment.

The destructive experiment of *bark ringing* provides evidence for translocation in the phloem tissue. If a complete ring of bark (containing the phloem tissue) is removed from a tree branch in summer, sugar from photosynthesis accumulates in a visible bulge above the missing ring. The leaves do not wilt — demonstrating that the xylem function is unaffected. If the main trunk is ringed, the tree dies, as the roots receive no sugar for respiration.

Further evidence of translocation is found by feeding plants with radioactive CO_2 and then following the movements of the newly formed radioactive sugars — the technique of *radioactive tracing*.

The oxygen produced by photosynthetic cells is either consumed immediately by the same cells in respiration or released, by diffusion, through the stomata to the atmosphere. In the balance of nature, this counteracts the general consumption of oxygen by combustion and respiration.

[H33 I]

The cohesion–tension model of water transport in the xylem

In 1895, the Irish plant physiologists H.H. Dixon and J. Joly proposed that water is *pulled* up a plant by a *tension* or negative pressure from above.

Water is continually being lost from leaves by transpiration. Dixon and Joly suggested that the loss of water in the leaves exerts a pull on the columns of water in the xylem below and draws more water up into the leaf.

It was understood at the time that the best pumps available could not lift a column of water higher than about ten metres — the maximum height that atmospheric pressure can *push* a water column. Yet many trees can reach a height of 80 metres and still transport water to all their leaves.

Dixon and Joly suggested that the answer lay in the cohesive strength of water — the strong, mutual attraction that water molecules have for one another. When water is confined to tubes of small diameter, the cohesive force imparts great strength to the water column. The 'pillars' of water in xylem cells are often stronger than steel wires of the same diameter.

THE ELEMENTS OF THE COHESION–TENSION HYPOTHESIS

- Water molecules are very cohesive — they tend to cling to one another.
- The cohesive forces are enormously strong and can resist pulling or tension from above.
- Transpiration in the leaf creates a tension or negative pull on the water columns in the xylem cells.
- Due to cohesion, this pull will lift the entire water column from leaf to root — regardless of its length.
- Adhesive forces between the water column and the walls of the xylem tubes protect the column from breaking.

The *cohesion–tension hypothesis* is also called the *transpiration-pull* hypothesis.

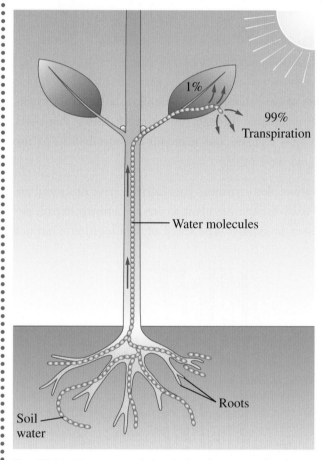

Fig. 19.15. Movement of the chain of water molecules.

EVIDENCE FOR THE HYPOTHESIS

1. Tree trunks undergo slight decreases in diameter (about one to two mm) during the day. This is consistent with a tension from above, but not with pushing from below.

2. In the morning, the upward movement of water begins in the higher, smaller branches before occurring in the trunk.

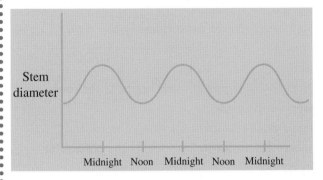

Fig. 19.16. Stem diameter over day/night.

3. If tall plants are forced to 'drink' from sealed containers of water, they do so without any decrease in upward flow rate — even though the resulting partial vacuum in the container is great enough to cause the remaining water to 'boil'.

MODIFIED PLANT FOOD STORAGE ORGANS [332]

In plants, the process of *perennation* refers to surviving the winter by means of a food store. *Perennials* are plants that survive from one year to the next. Perennation always involves laying down a large store of food usually in the form of starch. In winter, as growth is minimal, the store is barely used, but in the following spring it allows the plant to make a rapid growth burst and re-establish itself in the environment. In herbaceous (non-woody) perennials, the roots, stems or leaves are modified as food storage organs or *perennating organs*.

Roots as storage organs

In some dicots, the main tap root becomes fleshy and swollen with food, e.g. carrots and turnips.

Fig. 19.17. Carrots.

Fig. 19.18. Potatoes.

Stems as storage organs

Stem tubers are swollen, underground stems used to store food, e.g. potatoes.

Leaves as storage organs

An onion bulb is a collection of swollen, fleshy leaves used as a food store. Celery and rhubarb are leaf petioles also used to store food.

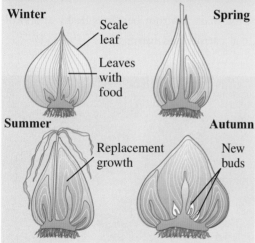

Winter — Scale leaf, Leaves with food

Spring

Summer — Replacement growth

Autumn — New buds

Fig. 19.19. Onion bulbs.

All of the perennating organs above are used to complete the plant's asexual life cycle (see Chapter 27).

SUMMARY

- *Plants are multicellular* and materials within them must be transported to and from individual cells.
- *Many transport mechanisms are used within plants,* including diffusion, osmosis, active transport, cytoplasmic streaming and other methods.
- *The principal materials in need of transport within plants* are inorganic nutrients (water, carbon dioxide, mineral ions), oxygen, foods (mostly sugars) and plant growth regulators.
- *Water moves through plant tissues by two main pathways* — the apoplast pathway and the symplast pathway.
- *Uptake and transport of water* begins at the root system of the plant.
- *Transpiration* maintains the flow of water and minerals from root to leaf, despite the obstacle of gravity.
- *Stomata* are found in the epidermis of most leaves and some stems.
- *The degree of opening of the stomata* is an important factor in determining the rate of transpiration.
- *Dissolved ions are absorbed with water* at the root tips and are taken up by active transport across the root cell membranes.
- *Ions are transported* quickly by the apoplast pathway or slowly by the symplast pathway.
- *Atmospheric CO_2* diffuses through open stomata into the leaf air space.
- *Carbohydrates and other foods always travel in the phloem tissue* — this movement is called translocation.
- *Bark ringing* provides evidence for translocation in the phloem tissue.
- *Further evidence of translocation* is found by feeding plants with radioactive carbon and then following its movements.
- *The oxygen produced by photosynthetic cells* is either consumed immediately by the same cells in respiration or released, by diffusion, through the stomata to the atmosphere.
- In *herbaceous (non-woody) perennials*, the roots, stems or leaves are modified as food storage organs or perennating organs.

EXTENDED SUMMARY

- In 1895, Dixon and Joly suggested that the loss of water in the leaves exerts a pull on the columns of water in the xylem below and draws more water up into the leaf.

■ Water molecules are very cohesive — they tend to cling to one another

■ Due to cohesion, an upward tension will lift an entire water column from leaf to root — regardless of its length.

KEY WORDS

Diffusion	The movement of materials from a place of high concentration to a place of lower concentration.
Osmosis	The diffusion of water across a semi-permeable membrane from a region of high water concentration to a region of lower water concentration.
Apoplast pathway	A pathway for water movement through spaces within the cellulose cell walls and within the non-living xylem cells.
Symplast pathway	A pathway for water movement through the contents of living cells.
Root hairs	Extensions of the cells of the root epidermis.
Root pressure	Pressure under which water passes from root cells into the xylem.
Transpiration	The evaporation of water from the surface of a leaf or stem.
Capillarity	The tendency of water to creep through narrow tubes.
Casparian strip	A strip of waterproof material on four of the six sides of root endodermis cells.
Translocation	The movement of organic materials within plants.
Bark ringing	The removal of a complete ring of bark from the trunk or branch of a tree.

Radioactive tracing	Feeding plants with radioactive CO_2 and then following the movements of the newly formed radioactive sugars.
Perennation	Surviving the winter by means of a food store.
Perennials	Plants that survive from one year to the next.
Perennating organs	Food storage organs used by plants to survive the winter.

EXTENDED KEY WORDS

Tension	A negative pressure that can move water within a plant.
Cohesion	Similar molecules clinging to one another.
Cohesion–tension hypothesis	Used to explain the upward movement of water in plants.
Transpiration-pull hypothesis	Alternative name for the cohesion–tension hypothesis.

QUESTIONS

1. Explain the difference between *diffusion* and *osmosis*.

2. List the materials that are in need of transport within plants. Briefly explain where each material comes from, where in the plant it is needed and how it is moved there.

3. Distinguish between the *apoplast* and *symplast* pathways within plants. Which pathway is faster and why?

4. Describe, in point form, the journey of a water molecule from the soil to the chloroplast of a leaf cell.

5. What is *transpiration* and why is it important to plants? How does sunlight affect transpiration? Why is transpiration considered a 'wasteful' process?

6. Name three ions needed by plants. Explain what these ions are needed for and how they are transported within the plant. How does the

absorption of ions from the soil differ from the absorption of water?

7. How do *root hairs* increase the rate of water absorption from the soil?

8. What is the *casparian strip*? How does it affect both the apoplast and symplast pathways?

9. What is *translocation*? In which part of the plant does it occur? What evidence is there to suggest that translocation takes place?

10. Explain how the loss of water vapour from a leaf causes a movement of water up from the roots.

11. Explain each of the following:

    a. perennation;
    b. perennating organs;
    c. perennials.

Give three examples of plant food storage organs. How are they of advantage to the plant?

EXTENDED QUESTIONS

1. Explain each of the following:

    a. cohesion;
    b. tension;
    c. capillarity;
    d. root pressure.

2. Summarise the *cohesion–tension hypothesis* of water movement in plants. What evidence exists to support the hypothesis?

OPTIONAL ACTIVITIES

- Obtain a prepared slide of a transverse section through a leaf. Examine under the microscope and draw and label the parts.
- Prepare your own leaf transverse section. Follow the instructions for *Mandatory activity #8* in Chapter 17. Use holly leaves and mount them in pith or some other support material before cutting. Also, try folding the leaf a few times before cutting.
- Make a *stomatal imprint* by coating the underside of a non-hairy leaf with clear nail varnish. Spread the varnish with a pin and allow to dry. Peel off the varnish with a tweezers and examine under the microscope. Alternatively, dip a leaf in acetone and press firmly onto some acetate to form a similar impression.

- String four fresh cherry leaves together with thread and weigh them on a sensitive balance. Hang them on a 'washing line' and allow to dry. Reweigh the leaves every 15 minutes and calculate the% weight loss over time.

  Try the following variations and compare the results to the original above:

  - Weigh a second bundle and hang the leaves exposed to wind or heat (from a hair drier).
  - Spread *Vaseline* on the upper surface of another bunch of leaves.
  - Spread *Vaseline* on the lower surface of another bunch of leaves.
  - repeat the experiment with leaves of different species and compare.

  Relate the results to the various habitats of the plants. Leaves from a *xerophyte* should show far less water loss than those of a *mesophyte*.

- Construct a simple *potometer* (literally 'drinking-meter') using graduated cylinders, water and oil (to stop evaporation). Use above as a guide. Use the potometer to demonstrate transpiration.
- Construct a model stoma. Take two long, cylindrical balloons and inflate them partially. Stick a length of sellotape down one side of each. Hold the balloons so that the sellotaped sides are touching each other. Fully inflate the balloons and observe the change in shape. What do the balloons represent?
- Examine a selection of modified roots, stems and leaves.
- Use the Internet to research the lives and work of H.H. Dixon and J. Joly. John Joly lectured in Trinity College, Dublin from 1883 to 1933.

Now test yourself at www.my-etest.com

Chapter 20
Nutrition in Humans

- list the stages of holozoic nutrition;
- explain the role of teeth and enzymes in digestion;
- describe the structure and function of all parts of the alimentary canal;
- describe the digestion and absorption of the main types of food;
- discuss the idea of a balanced diet;
- summarise the important facts concerning common diet-related conditions.

INTRODUCTION

Nutrition in living organisms refers to the process of obtaining energy and matter in order to stay alive. Nutrition is always either *autotrophic* or *heterotrophic* (see Chapter 3).

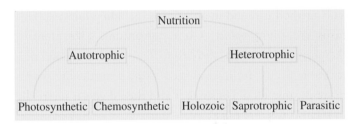

Fig. 20.1. Types of nutrition.

Autotrophic organisms manufacture their own food from simple, inorganic material and a source of energy. All plants and some bacteria are examples of autotrophs.

Heterotrophic organisms depend on an external source of organic food. All animals, fungi and some bacteria are heterotrophs. Fungi and most bacteria are either *saprotrophic* or *parasitic*. Animals are *holozoic*.

Saprotrophic nutrition

Saprotrophs obtain their food in solution. Digestive enzymes are released onto the food and digestion takes place externally. The digested products are then absorbed into the organism. This is found in many fungi and bacteria. This method is primitive and, because of the waiting involved, does not suit more advanced organisms under threat from predators.

Parasitic nutrition

A parasitic relationship is a very close relationship between two organisms. The parasite attaches itself onto or inside the host and takes food directly from it. Parasites cause great harm to their hosts but are often 'careful' not to kill them. Examples include some animals (e.g. tapeworms, liver fluke and fleas) and many fungi (e.g. those causing ringworm or potato blight). Parasites may sometimes behave in a saprotrophic way, i.e. they may feed on dissolved, organic food within the host, or in a holozoic way, i.e. they may feed directly off solid host tissue.

Holozoic nutrition

Animals ingest solid food and digest it internally. Ready-made food is located and identified by the organism using its senses. The food is taken inside a pouch or tube (an *alimentary canal*), is digested internally and then absorbed. This method is found in all animals including humans. Humans are *heterotrophic*, *holozoic* organisms. Like animals, they cannot construct their own food from inorganic materials as plants do; instead they locate and identify ready-made organic food, consume it and then digest it internally in their *alimentary canal*.

Stages of holozoic nutrition

1. *Ingestion*: Large pieces of food are taken inside the body.
2. *Digestion*: The food is broken down (by force and then by chemical action) into smaller particles. Solid food must be converted into a form suitable for absorption into the body cells.
3. *Absorption*: Small molecules of useful food pass through the body cells and usually into a distribution system, e.g. a blood circulation. These food molecules will eventually be *assimilated* by the body, i.e. incorporated within the body tissues and used.
4. *Egestion*: Unabsorbed or indigestible food (together with mucus, worn cells from the alimentary canal and a large amount of bacteria) is released from the body as *faeces*.

Heterotrophic organisms are often classified according to their appropriate diet.

Carnivores are animals that are equipped to eat other animals. They have the teeth and enzymes to feed exclusively on meat. Examples include cats and dogs.

Herbivores are equipped to eat plant food only. They do not have the correct teeth or enzymes for animal matter but often have chewing teeth and other adaptations of the alimentary canal suitable for plant cell walls. Examples include cows, sheep and rabbits.

Omnivores are animals that are equipped to feed on both plants and animals. They have varied teeth and enzymes, which are suitable for dealing with both types of food. Examples include pigs and humans.

N.B. Words such as *vegetarian* or *vegan* describe *human personal preferences* within the diet. A vegetarian is still equipped with the teeth and enzymes to deal with both plant and animal food. A cat with a preference for salad and potatoes is still a carnivore.

THE HUMAN DIGESTIVE SYSTEM [334]

The human alimentary canal is essentially a long, muscular tube open at either end. Food enters at one end and is digested by force and by chemical action. The digested food particles are absorbed through the tube wall, while undigested or unabsorbed food passes out at the other end.

Design features of the alimentary canal include:

- *Enormous vascular supply* — a large blood supply is needed to supply oxygen and to distribute the absorbed food particles.
- *Highly muscular* — food is moved along the alimentary canal by waves of involuntary, muscular contraction termed *peristalsis*.
- *Very long* (about nine metres in an adult) — this gives more time for the digestive and absorptive processes to take place efficiently. Food takes from 12 to 24 hours to travel from mouth to anus.
- *Highly folded* on the inside — this provides a greater surface area for absorption.
- *A marked degree of division of labour* — different parts of the canal perform different tasks. This leads to more efficiency and allows continuous functioning of some parts — even during sleep.

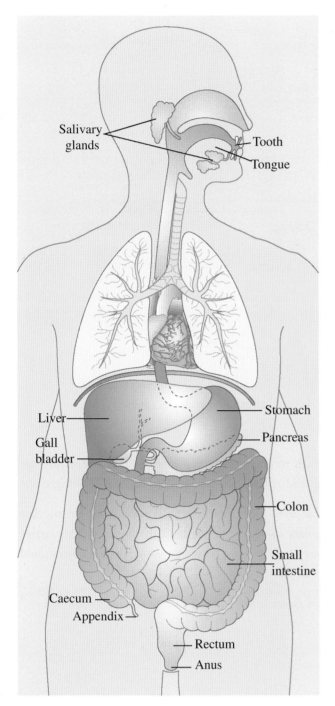

Fig. 20.2. Alimentary canal.

■ *Lined with secretory glands* on the inner surface — these pour digestive secretions and mucus into the *lumen* (hollow space) where the food is. Mucus lubricates the passage of the food and protects the canal from digesting itself.

The alimentary canal has *associated glands* that assist in the digestion, absorption and assimilation of food. These glands include the *salivary glands*, the *liver* with its *gall bladder* and the *pancreas*. A thin sheet of slippery membrane — the *peritoneum* — covers the canal, the associated glands, the main blood vessels and the inner lining of the abdominal cavity. This reduces friction between the different parts during movement. Inflammation of this membrane — due to bacterial infection or leaking of digestive juices — is called *peritonitis*. This is one of the symptoms of a ruptured appendix or *appendicitis*.

Macrostructure and basic function of the parts of the alimentary canal

THE MOUTH

The mouth (or buccal cavity) contains a muscular tongue and a set of teeth, which are firmly located in the upper and lower jawbones. The lips at the front of the mouth help to take in food and the tongue and teeth break the food into smaller pieces. The tongue manipulates the food but it is also a sense organ — it has rows of taste buds for tasting and recognising different types of food. The tongue is also important as an organ of speech.

Three pairs of *salivary glands* secrete saliva onto the food in the mouth. Saliva is mostly water but contains dissolved salts, mucus and the digestive enzyme, *amylase*. Secretion of saliva is controlled by the nervous system and is mostly a learned or conditioned response to the sight, smell or anticipation of food.

Saliva is necessary for speech, for lubricating and swallowing food and for diluting mouth acids. It has an antibacterial action and also protects the mouth from extremes of heat or cold. The enzyme, *amylase*, converts starch to maltose.

THE TEETH

Humans have two sets of natural teeth. A temporary set of 20 teeth (*milk teeth* or *deciduous teeth*) starts to emerge from the gums at about an age of six months; all of these teeth should be visible by the second birthday. A permanent set of 32 teeth begins to replace the temporary teeth after about the age of six and the temporary teeth are shed. Teeth are

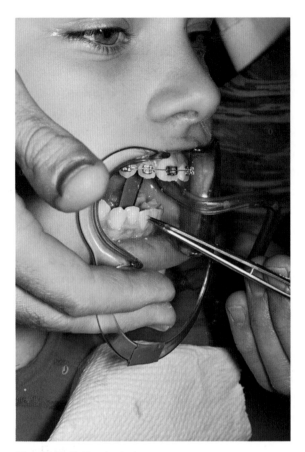

Fig. 20.3. Orthodonic braces.

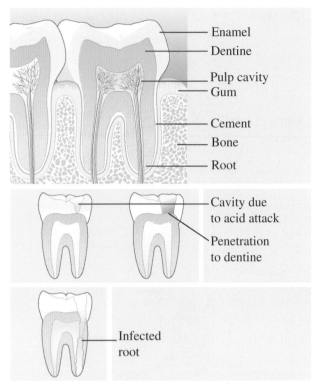

Fig. 20.4. Tooth structure and dental caries.

produced in this way in order to keep pace with the growth of the jawbones.

Each tooth has a crown, a root and a neck. The crown is visible outside the gum, the root is below the gum and the neck is at the gum level. The tooth is made from a tough material, *dentine*, surrounding a soft, pulp cavity of nerves, blood vessels and connective tissue. The dentine of the crown is covered in even tougher *enamel*. The shape of the crown varies with tooth function and diet — some are shaped for piercing and ripping, others for grinding and chewing.

N.B. *Eye teeth* are canine teeth. *Wisdom teeth* are the last four molars to appear at the back of the jaws. They arrive late due to lack of space on the growing jawbones but should be present by the age of 18–21.

A *dental formula* for humans can be written as follows:

$$\frac{2}{2}i \quad \frac{1}{1}c \quad \frac{2}{2}pm \quad \frac{3}{3}m$$

Table 20.1. Human teeth

Tooth type	Number in deciduous set	Number in permanent set	Shape of crown	Function
Incisors	8	8	Flat, square	Biting, cutting, nibbling
Canines	4	4	Conical	Gripping, tearing
Premolars	8	8	Cubic, cusped	Grinding, chewing
Molars	0	12	Cubic, cusped	Grinding, chewing, crushing.

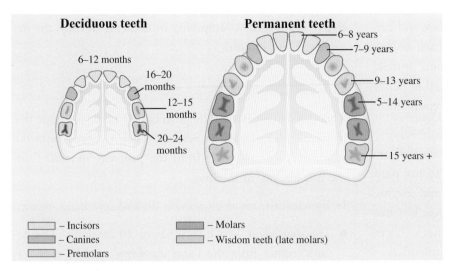

Fig. 20.5. Dental maps.

The formula indicates the numbers of each tooth type on one side of the mouth. The mouth is considered symmetrical. The formula is useless for describing the dentition of individual humans, as it cannot represent changes due to extractions.

THE OESOPHAGUS

The oesophagus is a muscular tube, about 25 cm long, running from the pharynx at the back of the mouth to the stomach. It is secretory on the inside, producing mucus to aid the passage of food, and has two layers of muscle for *peristalsis*. The muscle layers in the upper region are voluntary (i.e. under conscious control), while in the lower region they are involuntary. When empty, the oesophagus is flattened and closed.

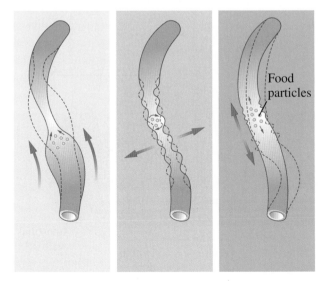

Fig. 20.6. Peristalsis.

Swallowing is initiated voluntarily and then completed involuntarily by reflex action.

- *Voluntary stage*: The food is mixed with saliva to form a moist bolus, and then the tongue moves the food to the back of the mouth.
- *Reflex stage*: The soft palate rises to close off the entrance to the nose and a small flap of tissue, the *epiglottis*, closes off the entrance to the trachea. The base of the tongue pushes the bolus into the pharynx. Waves of peristalsis in the oesophagus move the food towards the stomach — a journey of about three seconds.

THE STOMACH

The stomach is a J-shaped, muscular bag lying just under the diaphragm on the left-hand side of the abdominal cavity. Its exact shape varies with each individual and the amount of food in it. Entrance from the oesophagus is through a ring of muscle — the *cardiac sphincter*, and exit to the duodenum is through the *pyloric sphincter*. The stomach wall has three layers of muscle, which churn the food and perform peristalsis. The inner lining is folded and contains thousands of gastric glands, which secrete large volumes (one to two litres per day) of gastric juice, mostly at mealtimes. This juice is highly acidic and contains *hydrochloric acid* (HCl), *pepsinogen* (a precursor of the protein-digesting enzyme, *pepsin*) and *mucus*.

HCl kills most bacteria on the surface of the food and maintains a strong acid pH of about 2.0 — the optimum pH for the enzyme, pepsin. Pepsin is a strong protease and cannot be made in its active form within the stomach cells, as it would immediately digest their protein contents. Instead, inactive pepsinogen is formed and only converted to pepsin by contact with HCl in the stomach cavity. Pepsin breaks protein molecules into smaller polypeptides.

Large quantities of mucus coat the inner stomach wall and protect it from self-digestion. Lack of mucus at any point will lead to damage to the stomach wall by acid and enzymes — a *gastric ulcer*. The cause of ulcers is not clear but may be diet- or stress-related or due to bacterial attack. Ulcers are easily treated with many drugs including antibiotics.

The stomach also produces *lipase* to digest lipids and an '*intrinsic factor*' to aid in the absorption of vitamin B_{12} and protect against pernicious anaemia. The stomach absorbs alcohol and other drugs, water, glucose and some minerals.

The mixture of gastric juice and digested food (*chyme*) is released in small amounts into the duodenum through the pyloric sphincter and the stomach will be empty two to three hours after a meal.

Vomiting is the stomach's (and body's) method of protecting itself against unwanted or undesirable intake. Vomiting is a reflex action controlled by the *vomiting centre* of the brain stem. Various stimuli (fear, anxiety, motion impulses, drugs, poisons, disease, pregnancy hormones, distension of the stomach etc.) initiate the vomiting pathway: the oesophagus and cardiac sphincter relax, a quick breath is taken, the larynx rises, the diaphragm descends and the stomach is passively compressed — emptying its contents through the oesophagus and mouth.

THE SMALL INTESTINE

The small intestine is a long, muscular tube — about five to six metres in length in adults. It receives *chyme* from the stomach, *pancreatic juice* from the pancreas and *bile* from the gall bladder of the liver.

In humans, the small intestine is divided into three regions:

- The *duodenum* — which is about 30 cm long. 'Duodenum' comes from the Latin *duodecem* or '12', as it was first considered to be 12 finger widths in length.
- The *jejunum* — which is about 2.5 m long.
- The *ileum* — which is about 3 m long.

The duodenum is mainly secretory.

The jejunum and ileum are both secretory and absorptive in function.

The structure of the small intestine is highly related to function. The small intestine has two layers of muscle (longitudinal and circular) for the movement of food by peristalsis and has an extensive blood and lymph supply designed to transport digested and absorbed food to other parts of the body. The inner surface is thrown into folds lined with millions of leaf-shaped and finger-shaped *villi*. Each villus has its own individual blood and lymphatic circulation (see section [335] below).

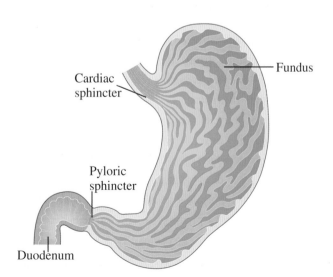

Fig. 20.7. Stomach.

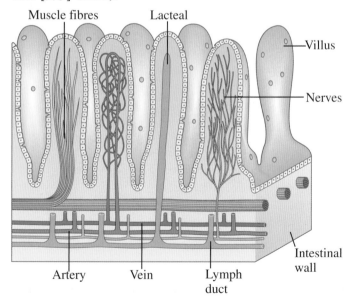

Fig. 20.8. Intestine and villi.

The entire intestine contains *intestinal glands* (the *Crypts of Lieberkühn*) and *Brunner's Glands* — in the duodenum only. Both types of glands secrete mucus and salts but no enzymes. Digestive enzymes are released from the *epithelial cells* lining the villi. These cells disintegrate (and are replaced) at a fast rate and release enzymes onto the food. The enzymes include *peptidases* (to complete protein digestion), *amylase, maltase, sucrase* and *lactase* for carbohydrate digestion, *lipase* for lipid digestion and *enterokinase* for the activation of pancreatic trypsin.

Peristalsis in the intestine is greatly aided by the presence of fibre in the diet. Fibre (plant cellulose and lignified cells) maintains the bulk of the intestinal contents and speeds up peristalsis. It also protects against bowel cancer, obesity and coronary heart disease. A daily intake of 30 g of fibre is recommended.

THE LARGE INTESTINE

The large intestine or *colon* is about one metre long. It includes the caecum and the appendix, which are small and have little function — a remnant of our pre-human, herbivore ancestors. The colon has no digestive role. Its function is to absorb water and some minerals, particularly iron. It does not contain any villi.

The small intestine and the large intestine always contain a large population of symbiotic bacteria. These include *E coli* — which use up any oxygen present, *Clostridium* and *Bacteroides*. The bacteria are beneficial in that that they manufacture *vitamin K* and *biotin* (a B vitamin) for their host. They also reduce the chances of fungal infection and may assist in the digestion of cellulose. The bacteria also produce gases such as carbon dioxide and methane.

Material remains in the colon for about 12 hours and then moves to the *rectum* where it will be egested as *faeces*. Faeces consist of mostly bacteria, unabsorbed food, cells from the intestinal lining and bile pigments. Egestion is through the anus.

THE PANCREAS

The pancreas is about the size of a large banana and lies under the stomach. It secretes *pancreatic juice* — an alkaline fluid containing many enzymes. Pancreatic juice contains *amylase* (to digest starch), *lipase* (digests fats), *trypsin* and other *proteases* (to digest protein and polypeptides). Pancreatic juice is secreted into the duodenum via the pancreatic duct. Production of the juice is stimulated by the presence of food in the duodenum.

Cells scattered within the pancreas — the *Islets of Langerhans* — secrete the hormone, *insulin*, directly into the bloodstream but not into the pancreatic juice (see Chapter 24).

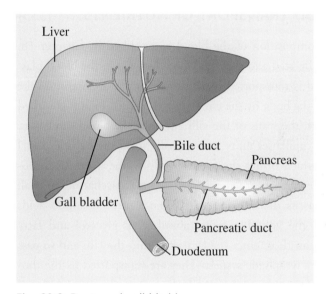

Fig. 20.9. Ducts and gall bladder.

THE LIVER AND BILE

The liver is the largest gland in the body. It lies in the upper abdomen under the diaphragm and mostly to the right-hand side. It is a *homeostatic organ* and can be described as a large chemical factory concerned with maintaining the body's metabolism at its optimum. It does this by modifying the nutrients absorbed from the alimentary canal to suit the body's needs.

The liver produces up to one litre of yellow/green bile continuously every day. The bile is stored in the gall bladder and the released through the bile duct directly onto food in the duodenum. This release is under both hormonal and nervous control.

Bile is 85% water with simple salts, bile salts, cholesterol, bile pigments and mucus. It is mainly an excretion from the liver but assists in the processes of digestion and absorption. Bile salts emulsify fats (convert them to tiny droplets) — increasing their surface area for digestion by enzymes. Bile also neutralises stomach acids. The bile pigments (*biliverdin* and *bilirubin*) are left over from the decomposition of haemoglobin in old red blood cells. They are the same pigments as seen in bruising under the skin where blood leaked from torn capillaries slowly decomposes.

The liver is discussed further in section [335] below.

BLOOD TRANSPORT OF NUTRIENTS [335]

The composition of the blood is described in Chapter 18. Most digested and absorbed food dissolves in the blood plasma and is transported first to the liver and then around the rest of the body by the circulation. Digested food is absorbed through the walls of the villi and into the blood capillaries. These capillaries unite to eventually form the hepatic portal vein, which brings the food directly to the liver. All carbohydrates are absorbed as digested monosaccharides and all proteins as di- or tripeptides. These turn to amino acids within the villi. Lipids are absorbed as glycerol and fatty acids, but these enter the lacteals within the villi and so pass into the lymphatic system. They are transported by the thoracic duct to the neck and left shoulder and enter the bloodstream there.

Transfer of digested nutrients to the liver

The liver has two blood supplies:

■ the *hepatic artery* arises directly from the aorta and brings oxygen for the very active liver cells;
■ the *hepatic portal vein* brings digested nutrients and deoxygenated blood directly from the stomach and intestines.

The liver also has a connection with the lymphatic system and a hepatic vein to return blood and metabolic products to the heart.

Summary of liver functions

1. METABOLIC CONVERSIONS

■ *Glycogen and glucose are interconverted* according to the body's needs.
■ Excess glucose in the bloodstream is converted to glycogen and stored for later use. Interconversion is done by *insulin* (for glucose to glycogen) and *adrenaline* (for glycogen back to glucose).
■ *Excess amino acids are deaminated* — their amino group is removed by liver enzymes and converted into urea, which is removed from the blood by the kidneys and excreted from the body in urine. The other parts of the

Table 20.2. Examples of chemical breakdown

Secretion	Role	Production site	Optimal pH	Optimal location of action	Products of action
Amylase	Converts starch to maltose	Salivary glands and pancreas	7	In mouth or intestine	Maltose
Pepsin	Converts protein to polypeptides	Wall of stomach	1.5	In stomach	Polypeptides
Lipase	Converts fats to fatty acids and glycerol	Pancreas	7.5	In intestine	Fatty acids and glycerol
Bile salts	Neutralise stomach acids and emulsify fats	Liver	7.5	In intestine	Fat droplets

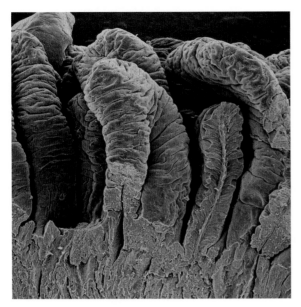

Fig. 20.10. SEM of intestinal villi.

amino acids are converted to carbohydrate. Urea moves from the liver to the kidneys via the bloodstream. (This journey includes passing through the hepatic vein, vena cava, heart, lungs, heart again, aorta and the renal artery (see Chapter 18).

- *Poisons are detoxified*. The liver destroys most of the drugs and poisons that enter the body (as best it can! Do not assume that the liver can absorb large amounts of alcohol without suffering in function in later life). The liver also produces its own toxins during metabolism, particularly hydrogen peroxide, and promptly detoxifies them with enzymes (the enzyme, *catalase*, instantly converts toxic hydrogen peroxide to oxygen and water). Heavy metals such as arsenic and lead will accumulate in the liver if ingested and eventually produce liver failure, as will excess paracetamol and alcohol taken over the long term.

2. STORAGE

- The liver stores glycogen to convert to glucose, if blood glucose levels fall.
- The liver also stores the fat-soluble vitamins A, D, E and K.
- Useful amounts of iron are found in the liver — retained from the destruction of old red blood cells.

3. PRODUCTION OF BILE

- Bile emulsifies fats and neutralises stomach acids — see section [**334**] above.

N.B. All cellular respiration produces excess heat and this includes the respiration of the very active liver cells. However, most of the liver cells' other reactions absorb heat (they are *endothermic* reactions). Overall, the temperature of the blood entering and leaving the liver is the same and the liver does *not* normally export large quantities of heat to the rest of the body as often stated.

A BALANCED HUMAN DIET   [336]

The food that we decide to eat makes up our *diet*. A balanced diet should consist of the correct proportions of the nutrients we need. What we need includes the following:

- *Fuel to provide energy*. This will be in the form of carbohydrates or lipids.
- *A source of nitrogen* for growth and repair. This will be in the form of proteins or amino acids.
- *Vitamins* to activate specific enzymes and protect against metabolic disease.
- *Minerals* for growth, repair and enzyme activation.
- *Water* as a general solvent and background medium.
- *Dietary fibre* to assist the alimentary canal.

Fig. 20.11. Variety in the diet.

Humans require *variety* within their diet to maintain interest and to ensure that all nutrients are obtained over any period of time. An individual's requirements depend on their age, sex, state of health, occupation and even climate and living conditions. Variety is obtained by sampling from different food groups such as:

- milk and milk products;
- meat, fish and poultry;
- breads and cereals;
- fruits and vegetables;
- other foods such as fats, oils and alcohol.

SOME MEDICAL DISORDERS OF THE DIGESTIVE SYSTEM

1. Dental decay and gum disease

CAUSE

- Bacteria combine with food particles to form plaque.
- Plaque clings to teeth — particularly in the hard-to-reach places.
- Some bacteria feed on gum tissue causing inflammation and bleeding of the gums — *periodontal disease*. Death of gum tissue leads to loss of the tooth.
- Bacterial metabolism produces acids, which digest tooth enamel and dentine.

PREVENTION

- Regular tooth brushing with a small amount of fluoride toothpaste.
- Reduce sugars in the diet.
- Not eating between meals.
- Eating high-fibre foods. Chewing strengthens gums and teeth.
- Regular dental checkups.

2. Stomach ulcers

CAUSE

A stomach ulcer (gastric ulcer) is an area of localised damage to the stomach lining. The cause may be stress- or diet-related or may just be due to bacteria. Ulcers are made worse by the failure of mucin to protect the stomach from its own digestive enzymes. Symptoms include pain, vomiting and bleeding. Ulcers of the duodenum are called *peptic ulcers* and are much more common.

TREATMENT

This is by antibiotics, a modified diet and/or lifestyle and by not smoking.

3. Appendicitis

This is a bacterial inflammation of the appendix.

SYMPTOMS

Pain is felt at the navel, and then travels to the right, lower abdomen. Nausea, vomiting and thirst are also common. All symptoms intensify if the appendix ruptures or bursts. This will lead to peritonitis from contamination of the body cavity with intestinal contents.

TREATMENT

This is almost always by surgical removal of the appendix. Alternatively, rest, antibiotics and a liquid diet are given.

4. Vitamin C deficiency — scurvy

CAUSE

Lack of vitamin C in the diet leads to a breakdown of collagen within the body's connective tissue (see Chapter 3).

SYMPTOMS

Bleeding from the gums, into the skin and into the body organs. Tenderness of the limbs. In extreme cases, haemorrhage and death.

TREATMENT

Eat lots of fresh food and vegetables. Do not overcook food as this destroys the vitamins.

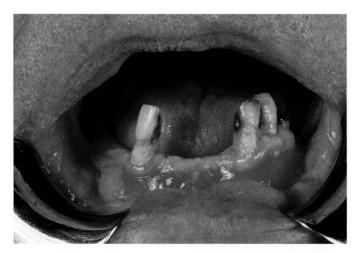

Fig. 20.12. Gum degeneration due to scurvy.

5. Iron deficiency — anaemia

CAUSE

Lack of iron in the diet leads to a shortage of haemoglobin for red blood cells. This leads to a low red cell count.

SYMPTOMS

These can vary but include:

- general tiredness and lack of 'energy';
- poor growth;
- unusual food cravings (e.g. chewing ice cubes!);
- pale skin is not necessarily a sign.

TREATMENT

- Eat good sources of iron. Wholegrain cereals, liver, kidney and red meat are the best sources. Milk contains very little iron. Iron is poorly absorbed and so about ten times the amount of iron needed must be swallowed.
- Take vitamin C (improves absorption).
- Avoid too much tea.
- Don't breastfeed after four to six months.

6. Slimming disorders
(a) Anorexia nervosa:

This is an extreme weight loss brought on by starvation.

The condition is most common in girls aged 12–18 years and coming from middle-class backgrounds. Anorexia can be fatal.

CAUSES

These are not clear but often include:

- family conflict;
- fears of 'growing up';
- sexual abuse.

SYMPTOMS

- Dramatic weight loss.
- Amenorrhoea (no periods).
- Low blood pressure.
- Osteoporosis.
- Injury from loss of body fat.
- Damage to heart muscle.

TREATMENT

- A controlled, healthy eating pattern.
- Weight gain.
- Counselling or therapy.
- Small, high-energy meals.

(b) Bulimia nervosa

This a condition involving 'binge' eating followed by self-induced vomiting. It is most common in girls aged 18–25 years old.

CAUSES

These are not known but may include those associated with anorexia above.

SYMPTOMS

- Acute stomach distension.
- Irregular periods.
- Erosion of teeth by gastric juice.

- Constant weight fluctuations.
- Depression.
- Low self-esteem.

TREATMENT

- Restore normal, healthy eating.
- Stop vomiting or other abusive behaviour.
- Counselling or therapy.
- Regular appointments with a doctor or dietician.

SUMMARY

- *Nutrition is always either autotrophic or heterotrophic.*
- *Humans are heterotrophic, holozoic organisms* — they locate and identify ready-made organic food, consume it and then digest it internally in their alimentary canal.
- *The stages of holozoic nutrition* are: ingestion; digestion; absorption; and egestion.
- *The human alimentary canal* is essentially a long, muscular tube open at either end.
- *The alimentary canal* has associated glands that assist in the digestion, absorption and assimilation of food. These glands include the salivary glands, the liver with its gall bladder and the pancreas.
- *Saliva* is mostly water but contains dissolved salts, mucus and the digestive enzyme, amylase.
- *Teeth* are made from enamel, dentine and a pulp cavity.
- *Humans have two sets* of natural teeth: a temporary set of 20 teeth and a permanent set of 32 teeth.
- *The stomach* is a J-shaped, muscular bag lying just under the diaphragm on the left-hand side of the abdominal cavity.
- *Vomiting* is the stomach's (and body's) method of protecting itself against unwanted or undesirable intake.
- *The small intestine* is a long, muscular tube — about five to six metres in length in adults.
- *It receives chyme* from the stomach, pancreatic juice from the pancreas and bile from the gall bladder of the liver.

- *The inner surface* is thrown into folds lined with millions of leaf-shaped and finger-shaped villi.
- *Intestinal enzymes* include peptidases, amylase, maltase, sucrase, lactase, lipase and enterokinase.
- *The function of the large intestine* is to absorb water and some minerals.
- *The small intestine and the large intestine* contain symbiotic bacteria.
- *Pancreatic juice* contains amylase, lipase, trypsin and other proteases.
- *The Islets of Langerhans* secrete the hormone, insulin, directly into the bloodstream
- *The liver* is the largest gland in the body. It is a homeostatic organ.
- *The liver produces* up to one litre of bile continuously every day.
- *Bile is* mainly an excretion from the liver but assists in digestion and absorption.
- *Bile salts* emulsify fats and neutralise stomach acids.
- *All carbohydrates* are absorbed as digested monosaccharides.
- *All proteins* are absorbed as di- or tripeptides.
- *Lipids* are absorbed as glycerol and fatty acids but enter the lymphatic system.
- *The functions of the liver* include:

  - interconversion of glycogen and glucose;
  - deamination of excess amino acids to form urea;
  - detoxification of poisons;
  - storage of glycogen;
  - storage of fat-soluble vitamins;
  - production of bile.

- *A balanced diet* should consist of the correct proportions of the nutrients we need.

KEY WORDS

Nutrition	The process of obtaining energy and matter in order to stay alive.
Autotrophic organisms	Manufacture their own food from simple, inorganic material and a source of energy.

Heterotrophic organisms	Depend on an external source of organic food.
Saprotrophs	Obtain their food in solution, e.g. many fungi and bacteria.
Parasites	Attach themselves onto or inside the host and take food directly from it.
Holozoic nutrition	Ingesting solid food and digesting it internally.
Ingestion	Taking large pieces of food within the body.
Digestion	Breaking down food by force or chemicals.
Absorption	When small molecules of useful food pass through the body cells and into a distribution system.
Assimilation	Incorporating and using food within the body tissues.
Egestion	Removal of unabsorbed or indigestible food from the body as faeces.
Carnivores	Animals that are equipped to eat other animals.
Herbivores	Animals that are equipped to eat plant food only.
Omnivores	Animals that are equipped to feed on both plants and animals.
Peristalsis	Involuntary waves of muscular contraction that move food along the alimentary canal.
Peritoneum	A thin sheet of slippery membrane covering the alimentary canal, the associated glands, the main blood vessels and the inner lining of the abdominal cavity.
Sphincter	An involuntary, circular muscle used to open or close portions of the alimentary canal.
Gastric ulcer	Damage to the stomach wall by acid and enzymes.

Peptic ulcer	Ulcer of the duodenal wall.
Chyme	A mixture of gastric juice and digested food.
Duodenum, jejunum and ileum	Regions of the small intestine.
Intestinal glands and Brunner's Glands	Secrete mucus and salts but no enzymes.
Colon	Large intestine.
Homeostatic organ	Maintains the body's metabolism at its optimum.
Bile	An excretion from the liver.
Biliverdin and bilirubin	bile pigments.
Hepatic portal vein	Brings digested nutrients and deoxygenated blood to the liver directly from the stomach and intestines.
Deamination	Removal of the amino group from amino acids.
Endothermic reactions	Require heat from their surroundings.

QUESTIONS

1. Explain each of the following words:

   a. *autotrophic;*

   b. *heterotrophic;*

   c. *holozoic;*

   d. *saprotrophic;*

   e. *parasitic.*

   What do holozoic, saprotrophic and parasitic organisms all have in common?

2. Explain the stages in holozoic nutrition. How many of these stages take place in the mouth?

3. The alimentary canal is essentially a long tube, open at both ends. Explain how its structure is related to its various functions.

4. Name the associated glands of the alimentary canal. What are the advantages of producing saliva?

5. Draw a labelled diagram of a human tooth. Name the different kinds of tooth and explain how each is adapted in shape for its function.

6. What are the functions of the stomach? How is it adapted for each function?

7. Why is the duodenum considered 'mainly secretory in function'?

8. What are villi? Draw a simple, labelled diagram to show the structure of a villus. How are they adapted for their function? How does the absorption of lipids differ from the absorption of other foods?

9. Why is the liver considered a homeostatic organ? List the various functions of the liver.

10. Draw a labelled diagram to show the blood circulation through the liver. Use the diagram to explain what is meant by a *portal system*.

11. What is a *balanced diet*? Why is the balanced diet of one individual likely to differ from that of another?

12. How might each of the following affect the dietary requirements of the individual concerned?

    a. Working in a hot, dry environment.
    b. Recovering from a broken leg.
    c. Suffering from anaemia.
    d. Suffering from rickets.
    e. Preparing to run a marathon.
    f. Trying to lose weight.

13. Why can eating sweets lead to tooth decay? How can saliva help to reduce tooth decay? Should 'an apple a day keep the dentist away'?

14. Explain each of the following:

    a. It is not possible to breathe and swallow at the same time.
    b. Indigestion medicines are usually alkaline
    c. The stomach cannot digest itself.
    d. Food moves automatically through the alimentary canal.
    e. Absorption of food from the small intestine is very fast and efficient.
    f. *E coli* in drinking water indicates sewage contamination.

15. Name the part of the alimentary canal where:

    a. saliva is produced;
    b. most water is reabsorbed;
    c. villi are found;
    d. bile is made;
    e. bile is stored;
    f. faeces are stored;
    g. acid is found;
    h. the cardiac sphincter is located;
    i. pepsinogen is made;
    j. peptic ulcers occur.

16. Answer the following questions in relation to the liver.

    a. Why does the hepatic portal vein only contain sugar at certain times of the day?
    b. What happens to excess amino acids?
    c. Why does the liver need two blood supplies?
    d. How does blood leave the liver? What happens the urea formed after deamination?
    e. Why is cod liver oil a good source of vitamins A and D?
    f. What is the function of the gall bladder?

17. Name the final digested products of each of the following: bread, meat, butter, sugar.

OPTIONAL ACTIVITIES

- Examine the skulls of various animals and try to deduce their natural diet.
- Place a marble in a rubber tube and try to move it from one end to the other. Stretching the tube is equivalent to relaxing longitudinal muscles, squeezing it is equivalent to contracting circular muscles.
- Examine an anatomical model of the alimentary canal. Note particularly the size and position of the liver.
- Examine prepared microscopic slides of sections of the various regions of the alimentary canal.

- Research any diet-related disorder of your choice and prepare a report for the class. Possibilities include osteoporosis, obesity, coeliac disease, diabetes, rickets and coronary heart disease (see Chapter 18).

For further information on websites dealing with subjects covered in this chapter see www.my-etest.com.

Now test yourself at
www.my-etest.com

Chapter 21

Homeostasis and Gas Exchange

Learning objectives

After your study of this chapter, you should be able to:

- define homeostasis;
- appreciate the need for both sensitivity and energy in homeostasis;
- distinguish between breathing, gas exchange and respiration;
- describe how the structure of the lungs suits its function;
- explain the breathing mechanism in humans;
- summarise the causes, prevention and treatment of asthma, bronchitis and emphysema;
- list the biological effects of smoking.

Extended learning objectives

Describe the role of CO_2 in controlling the rate of gas exchange.

Mandatory activities

#19. Investigating the effect of exercise on the breathing rate of a human.

HOMEOSTASIS [341]

The term '*homeostasis*' refers to maintaining a 'steady state' of conditions within the organism. (Homeostasis literally means 'standing the same'.)

NECESSITY FOR HOMEOSTASIS [342]

Conditions inside a living organism are completely different to the conditions in the outside environment. Some organisms live in deserts, some live at the seashore, some in snow, etc. Organisms cannot close themselves off completely from their surroundings and are always exchanging materials with

Fig. 21.1. Wolves in snow.

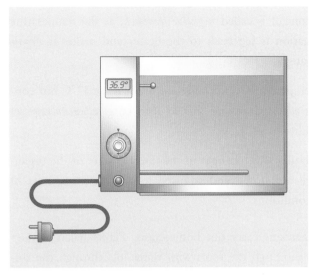

Fig. 21.2. Electric water bath.

the outside world. They must, however, maintain a constant internal environment for their metabolism to function properly no matter what is going on outside. They do this by *homeostasis*.

Humans, wolves and other mammals require a constant body temperature and relatively constant amounts of oxygen, carbon dioxide, water, food and urea in their blood. Organs that specialise in maintaining a constant internal environment include the liver, kidneys, lungs and skin. To maintain constant levels, any increase in any factor has to be balanced by a suitable decrease. A gain in body heat is balanced by a heat loss, a gain in CO_2 by a loss of CO_2, a loss in water by a gain in water and so on. Nerves and hormones regulate the various controlling mechanisms.

The process of homeostasis requires:

■ a *method of detecting change* — usually done in animals by nerves and/or hormones;

■ *a method of restoring normal conditions* — usually done by negative feedback;

■ an *energy input* — maintaining the difference between the inside and the outside requires a lot of energy.

An example of *homeostasis by negative feedback* can be seen in the working of a thermostatic water bath in a laboratory. These water baths can be set to maintain a constant water temperature regardless of the room temperature.

The important features of the water bath system are:

1. A temperature sensor
2. A normal or desired setting

3. A water heater
4. An energy input (electricity).

The system works as follows:

■ The bath is filled with water and the desired temperature is set (say 37°C).

■ The heater heats to the water to 37°C and beyond.

■ The sensor notices a temperature greater than 37°C and turns the electricity off.

■ The temperature falls below 37°C.

■ The sensor notices a temperature less then 37°C and turns the electricity back on.

■ This on/off cycle is repeated.

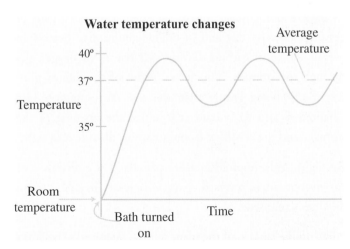

Fig. 21.3. Homeostasis.

This control is called *negative feedback*, as the temperature information is fed back to the heater and makes it *negate* the change.

The temperature is not maintained *exactly* at 37°C but constantly adjusted around this set level to give an *average* set of conditions of 37°C.

In a similar way, changes in the internal state of the organism are monitored and adjusted to give an average set of ideal conditions.

All organisms carry out homeostasis. Plants balance water intake thorough the roots with water loss through the stomata. They can also adjust stomatal opening to balance water loss with CO_2 requirements and heat loss due to evaporation. Leaves and stomata can be considered as excretory organs, but the amount of excretion done by plants is slight as they have little metabolic waste.

In humans and other mammals, the following conditions are constantly checked and maintained:

- water and salt balance (osmoregulation);
- glucose levels;
- calcium levels;
- carbon dioxide levels;
- urea levels;
- body temperature;
- blood pressure and blood pH.

GAS EXCHANGE IN PLANTS [343]

As part of homeostasis, plants use their leaves as organs of gas exchange. By day and in bright conditions, there is an overall intake of carbon dioxide and release of oxygen gas through the stomata. This is as a result of the rate of photosynthesis being *greater* than the rate of respiration (see Chapters 8 and 9). Guard cells adjust the opening of the stomata and are sensitive to both carbon dioxide and light.

By night, only respiration takes place and the direction of gas movement is reversed: oxygen is taken in and carbon dioxide is released.

Pores on the surface of the plant stem — *lenticels* — perform similar gas exchanges with much smaller volumes of gas.

Plant roots do not have any particular structures for gas exchange but do absorb some oxygen from the soil air and use it for small amounts of root respiration. It is tempting to see plant leaves as equivalent to the lungs in higher animals but lungs have ventilating mechanisms to deal with much larger volumes of gas and never reverse the direction of gas exchange.

BREATHING AND GAS EXCHANGE IN HUMANS [344]

Gas exchange in humans takes place through the *lungs*. *Breathing* refers to the mechanism of moving air in and out of the lungs. It is also termed *ventilation*. The purpose of breathing is to increase the rate of gas exchange across the internal lung surfaces. (Breathing and gas exchange should not be confused with *respiration* — the process of extracting energy from food in cells.)

The lungs are two spongy, pink organs situated in the thorax on either side of the heart. They lie in the airtight thoracic cavity and are wrapped in two *pleural membranes*. A lubricating fluid between the membranes allows them to slide over each other during breathing and reduces friction. The thoracic cavity is surrounded by the *ribs* and *intercostal muscles* and is separated from the abdominal cavity by a bell-shaped sheet of muscle and tendon tissue — the *diaphragm*.

Air enters the breathing system through the nostrils and mouth. It flows through the *pharynx* and then passes

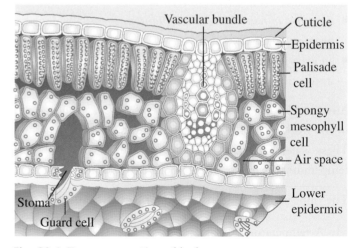

Fig. 21.4. Transverse section of leaf.

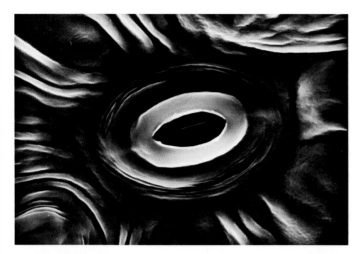

Fig. 21.5. Stoma.

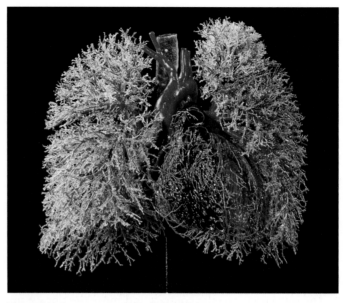

Fig. 21.7. Latex cast of the bronchial tree.

through the *larynx* (voice box) to the *trachea*. The entrance to the larynx (the *glottis*) is guarded by a flap of tissue supported by cartilage — the *epiglottis*. This closes during swallowing to keep food particles out of the lungs. It is not possible to breathe and swallow at the same time.

The trachea — or windpipe — is surrounded by C-shaped rings of cartilage to keep it permanently open, otherwise air pressure changes or neck movements could close it and cause temporary suffocation.

The trachea divides to form the left and right *bronchi* (singular — *bronchus*), which enter the lungs. Each bronchus divides repeatedly into smaller and smaller bronchioles —

forming a *bronchial tree*. The bronchi and larger bronchioles are also supported by rings of cartilage. The bronchial tree contains smooth muscle, which can adjust the diameters of the bronchioles. Too much constriction of the tubes causes the breathing difficulties of asthma.

The bronchioles eventually terminate in microscopic, thin walled sacs — the *alveoli* (singular — *alveolus*). Each lung contains about 350 million alveoli and has a surface area of about half of a tennis court — or about 90 times the area of the skin. The alveoli are surrounded by millions of blood

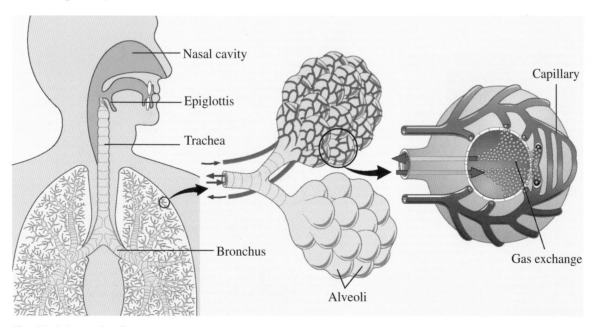

Fig. 21.6. Lung detail.

Nasal cavity

Epiglottis

Trachea

Bronchus

Alveoli

Capillary

Gas exchange

capillaries. They receive blood directly from the pulmonary arteries and return it to the heart by the pulmonary veins.

The breathing mechanism

Breathing is accomplished by altering the air pressure within the lungs in respect to the outside air pressure. If the air pressure in the lungs is *less* than outside, air will *enter* the lungs. This is called inspiration (or *breathing in*). If the air pressure in the lungs is *greater* than the outside air pressure, air will *leave* the lungs. This is called expiration (or *breathing out*).

INSPIRATION

- The diaphragm contracts and moves downwards.
- The intercostal muscles contract and move the ribcage up and out.
- This increase in chest volume lowers the air pressure within the lungs.
- Air is pushed into the lungs from outside.

EXPIRATION

- The diaphragm relaxes and moves upwards.
- The intercostal muscles relax and the ribcage moves in and down.
- This decrease in chest volume raises the air pressure within the lungs.
- Air is pushed from the lungs to the outside.

N.B. Although it *feels* as if air is *sucked* into the lungs when breathing in, it isn't! It is *pushed* from the outside into a space of lower pressure. The same thing happens when drinking through a straw. The drink is not 'sucked' up the straw: air pressure has been lowered at the 'mouth' end of the straw (by breathing in) and the air pressure in the room *pushes* the drink up the straw.

- *Inspiration is active,* as it requires muscle contraction; *expiration is passive* as the breathing muscles relax.
- Breathing is generally an involuntary activity and does not require conscious thought.
- Inspiratory and expiratory centres in the medulla oblongata of the brain control the rate of breathing. The rate is related to levels of carbon dioxide in the bloodstream: high CO_2 levels increase the rate, low levels decrease the rate. Exercise produces high levels of CO_2 from respiration and so increases the breathing rate. This removes the excess CO_2 faster and also supplies extra oxygen faster.

Carbon dioxide is also a controlling factor in gas exchange in plants. A decrease in CO_2 concentration (as would happen during daytime) opens the stomata. Stomata also open in response to light.

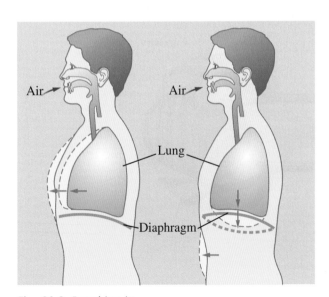

Fig. 21.8. Breathing in.

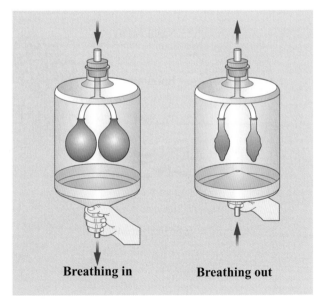

Fig. 21.9. Artificial lung.

Gas exchange in the alveoli

Gas exchange takes place through the walls of the alveoli and the walls of the blood capillaries.

- Oxygen leaves the alveolar air space, passes into the capillary and is taken up by *haemoglobin* in the red blood cells.
- Carbon dioxide leaves the blood plasma and passes into the alveolus air space.
- Water vapour also leaves the plasma and passes into the alveolar space.

The gases move by *diffusion* — each gas automatically moving from where it is more concentrated to where it is less concentrated.

Capillaries

- Capillaries are tightly packed (covering almost 90% of alveolar surface) — for a faster rate of gas exchange.
- They have thin walls — to reduce the distance for gas diffusion.
- They have a tiny internal diameter — to slow the movement of blood for more efficient gas exchange.

Table 21.1. Changes made to inspired air

Gases	Inspired air	Expired air
Oxygen	21%	16%
Carbon dioxide	0.03%	5%
Nitrogen	78%	78%
Water vapour	Variable	Saturated

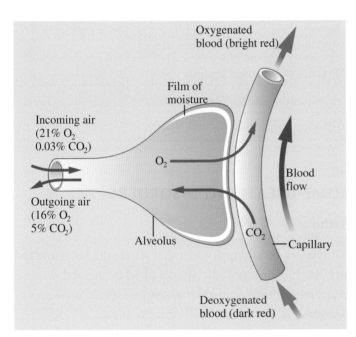

Fig. 21.10. Alveolus/capillary interface.

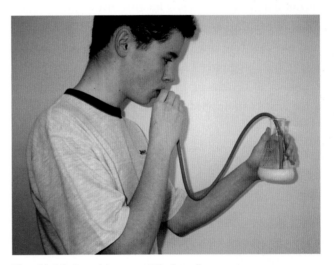

Fig. 21.11. Breathing out CO_2 into lime water.

Features of the alveoli and capillaries that suit gas exchange

Alveoli

- Alveoli have a large surface area — for a faster rate of gas exchange.
- They have thin walls — to reduce the distance for gas diffusion.
- They are moist — dissolved gases diffuse faster.

Protection of the airways

- Hair and mucus inside the nose trap larger dust particles and some bacteria.
- The trachea is lined with mucus to trap smaller foreign particles.
- Tiny hairs (cilia) lining the trachea move mucus with trapped particles upwards and out of the airway — in the manner of an escalator! The mucus is then swallowed.
- *Macrophages* leave the bloodstream to roam around the alveoli and digest any foreign matter.

Mandatory activity #19. Investigating the effect of exercise on the breathing rate of a human.

RESOURCES REQUIRED

Bench or stool, about 40 cm high.
Watch.

Students should work in pairs for this investigation. The number of breaths per minute will be counted. Breathing in and out counts as one breath. During times of quickly changing breathing rates (e.g. immediately after exercise), the number of breaths in 15 seconds should be counted and the answer multiplied by four.

METHOD

1. Work in pairs — one student exercising and the other measuring the breathing rate.
2. Ask the subject to relax but stand.
3. Obtain a resting breathing rate over one minute and record it.
4. Repeat twice more and find the average of the three resting rates.
5. Set definite exercise for the subject — e.g. stepping up and down on a 40 cm high bench every three seconds over two minutes (40 step-ups altogether!).
6. Record the breathing rate immediately on stopping over 15 seconds. Multiply this number by four. Repeat this measurement every 30 seconds until the breathing has returned to the normal rate.
7. If possible, repeat the experiment with more vigorous exercise, e.g. running a 100 m sprint.

N.B. A rapid return to the normal rate after exercise is a sign of cardiovascular fitness.

Table 21.2. Exercise experiment

Table of results (all rates are breaths/minute)

Breathing rate at rest I	
Breathing rate at rest II	
Breathing rate at rest III	
Average resting rate	
Breathing rate just after exercise	
Breathing rate after 30-second rest	
Breathing rate after 1-minute rest	
Breathing rate after 1m 30s rest	
Breathing rate after 2-minute rest	
Breathing rate after 2m 30s rest	
Breathing rate after 3-minute rest	
Breathing rate after 3m 30s rest	

SOME BREATHING DISORDERS

Asthma

Asthma is a breathing disorder that affects the lungs and the airways. It causes periodic attacks of wheezing and difficult breathing. *Asthma is a serious disease and should never ever be thought of as otherwise.*

During an asthma attack, the following changes take place within the lungs:

- Cells lining the airways make more mucus than normal. The mucus is thick and sticky and can clog the tubes.
- The bronchioles become swollen and stretched and the lungs may become inflamed.
- Muscle lining the bronchioles contracts and reduces the diameters of the tubes.

These changes decrease the lung volume and breathing becomes more difficult. Asthma attacks may start suddenly or may take a long time to develop. Attacks can be severe, moderate or mild. There may or may not be warning signs that an attack is about to start. Symptoms vary from person to person.

Typical symptoms of an asthma attack include:

- throat becomes itchy;
- coughing and wheezing;
- tightness of the chest as if the ribs are being pulled in;
- lips and fingernails may turn blue;
- difficulty in walking or talking;
- nostrils flare (widen) with each breath.

Asthma triggers

The following are commonly reported as bringing on asthma attacks:

1. ALLERGENS

Allergens ('allergy generators') are by far the most common triggers of asthma attacks — being responsible for about 90% of cases in children and 60% of adult cases. Common allergens include pollen, fruit mould, feathers, animal hair or fur, household dust and dust mites. Allergic reactions to medicines and foods also cause asthma attacks — particularly foods containing certain preservatives. Other allergens include cold air, perfumes, household chemicals, paint, and air pollutants such as coal dust, chalk dust and cigarette smoke. Cigarette smoke harms the lungs and airways of everyone but is particularly dangerous to asthmatics.

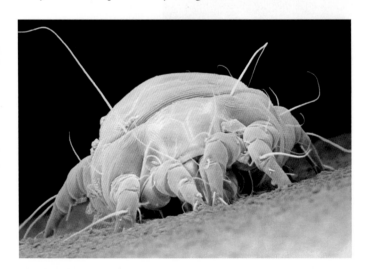

Fig. 21.12. House dust mite.

2. INFECTIONS

Bacterial and viral infections can irritate the airways and bring about an asthma attack. Mucus from sinusitis (a nasal infection) can clog the airways and bring on asthma symptoms.

3. EXERCISE

Although exercise is good for people with asthma, it can trigger an asthma attack. Patients need to consult their doctors over types and amounts of exercise.

4. STRESS

High levels of stress and anxiety can trigger asthmatic attacks.

Prevention of asthma attacks

- Identify your asthma triggers and avoid them.
- Recognise the signs of an asthma attack beginning.
- Take preventative medicine before attacks are likely — particularly if the air quality is poor or if you are planning exercise.
- Use a peak flow meter to indicate any change in the internal volume of your lungs.
- If you smoke, you must stop. Avoid cigarette smoke at all times.

Treatment of asthma

Two types of medication are available: *bronchodilators* and *anti-inflammatories*.

Bronchodilators relax the smooth muscle lining of the bronchioles and cause them to dilate. They are used during an asthma attack and give relief by increasing the lung volume.

Anti-inflammatories are used *before* any attacks. They coat the linings of the bronchioles and prevent any irritation or mucus build-up. They should be used regularly *regardless* of how the patient feels.

Both medications can be taken by *inhalers*.

Asthma is a serious disease and should never ever be thought of as otherwise. In the case of a severe asthma attack, take your asth-

ma medicine and get medical help immediately. People who have died from asthma attacks may have waited too long.

Chronic bronchitis

Chronic bronchitis, (*chronic* means *long-term*), is a common disease of the middle-aged and elderly. It is an inflammation and eventual scarring of the bronchial tubes within the lungs. It is one of the most common chronic medical conditions in Ireland.

SYMPTOMS

These include:

- a shortness of breath — even at rest;
- coughing during the night;
- difficulty with breathing, similar to asthma;
- increased mucus with frequent clearing of the throat.

CAUSES

Common causes are exposure to cold, damp, dust and particularly cigarette smoke. Smoking causes 90% of bronchitis cases and a smoker is ten times more likely to die from bronchitis than a non-smoker. Repeated chest infections produce slow destruction of the lung tissue and overproduction of mucus.

TREATMENT

- Stop smoking!
- Use bronchodilators to help breathing efforts.
- Take antibiotics to treat lung infections.
- Exercise to strengthen muscles, clear mucus and improve breathing.

PREVENTION

Avoid cigarette smoke and poor quality air.

In severe cases, bronchitis can turn to *emphysema* — a condition of irreversible lung damage and heart failure. The alveolar walls lose their ability to stretch and recoil and eventually break down. The lungs lose their elasticity and air becomes trapped within the lung tissue. The bronchioles lose their support and collapse. The disease can last about 20 years but is fatal. No real treatment is available for the lung damage short of a lung transplant.

Chronic bronchitis and emphysema are often found together and are now termed *chronic obstructive pulmonary disease* or *COPD.*

Medical conditions that are due to smoking

1. Cigarette smoke thickens the lining of the bronchioles and forms hard masses of cells. These cells may become cancerous and can grow within the lungs or spread to other parts of the body.
2. Nicotine is an addictive drug. It causes a brief rise in blood pressure and heart rate.
3. Cigarette smoke causes lung inflammation, overproduction of mucus and scarring which lead to bronchitis.
4. Lung inflammation leads to overproduction of white blood cells with leakage of digestive enzymes. Breakdown of the alveolar walls produces emphysema and heart failure.
5. Cigarette smoke is an *allergen* and can trigger asthmatic attacks.
6. Carbon monoxide in cigarette smoke combines with haemoglobin in the red cells and destroys it. This reduces the circulation's ability to carry oxygen.

Fig. 21.13. Dissection of smoker's lung.

7. Tar particles can coat the alveolar lining and reduce the surface area available for gas exchange. More rapid breathing will be necessary to make up this loss.

SUMMARY

- *Living organisms* need to maintain a constant internal environment for their metabolism to function properly. They do this by homeostasis.
- To maintain a constant environment, any increase in any factor has to be balanced by a suitable decrease.
- *The process of homeostasis requires*:

  - a method of detecting change;
  - a method of restoring conditions;
  - an energy input.

- *Plants use their leaves* as organs of gas exchange.
- *Lenticels on plant stems* perform similar gas exchanges with much smaller volumes of gas.
- *Gas exchange in humans* takes place through the lungs.
- *Breathing* is accomplished by altering the air pressure within the lungs in respect to the outside air pressure.
- *If the air pressure in the lungs is less* than outside, air will enter the lungs — inspiration.
- *If the air pressure in the lungs is greater* than the outside air pressure, air will leave the lungs — expiration.
- *Gas exchange takes place* through the walls of the alveoli and the walls of the blood capillaries.
- *Oxygen leaves the alveolar air space*, passes into the capillaries and is taken up by haemoglobin in the red blood cells.
- *Carbon dioxide and water vapour* leave the blood plasma and pass into the alveolus air space.
- *The gases move* by diffusion.
- *Alveoli have*:

  - a large surface area;
  - thin walls;
  - moisture to dissolve gases.

- *Capillaries have*:

  - thin walls;
  - a tiny internal diameter;
  - a high packing density (covering almost 90% of the alveolar surface);
  - a tiny internal diameter.

- *Asthma* is a serious disease and should never, *ever*, be thought of as otherwise.
- *During an asthma attack,* the following changes take place within the lungs:

  - Cells lining the airways make more mucus than normal.
  - The bronchioles become swollen and stretched.
  - Muscle lining the bronchioles contracts and reduces the diameters of the tubes.

- *Typical symptoms of an asthma attack include*:

  - itchy throat;
  - coughing and wheezing;
  - tightness of the chest;
  - lips and fingernails may turn blue;
  - difficulty in walking or talking;
  - nostrils flaring.

- *Common asthma triggers include*:

  - allergens such as pollen, fruit mould, feathers, animal hair or fur, household dust and dust mites;
  - bacterial and viral infections;
  - exercise;
  - stress.

- *Chronic bronchitis* is an inflammation and eventual scarring of the bronchial tubes within the lungs.
- *Causes of bronchitis* include exposure to cold, damp, dust, and particularly cigarette smoke.

EXTENDED SUMMARY

- *Inspiratory and expiratory centres* in the medulla oblongata of the brain control the rate of breathing.
- *High CO_2 levels* increase the breathing rate; low levels decrease the breathing rate.
- *Carbon dioxide* is also a controlling factor in gas exchange in plants.

KEY WORDS

Homeostasis	Maintaining a 'steady state' of conditions within the organism.
Negative feedback	When information is fed back into a controlling system to *negate* any change.
Osmoregulation	Water and salt balance.
Lenticels	Pores on the surface of the plant stem — used for gas exchange.
Pleural membranes	Two membranes covering the lungs and containing lubricating fluid to reduce friction.
Intercostal muscles	Muscle between the ribs, used to move the ribcage during breathing.
Diaphragm	A bell-shaped sheet of muscle and tendon used to ventilate the lungs.
Larynx	Voice box made from cartilage and containing the vocal cords.
Trachea	Windpipe.
Bronchi	The two main divisions of the trachea.
Bronchioles	Subdivisions of the bronchi.
Alveoli	Thin-walled air sacs at the ends of bronchioles. Sites of gas exchange.
Inspiration	Breathing in.
Expiration	Breathing out.
Diffusion	Movement of materials (especially gases) from where they are more concentrated to where they are less concentrated.
Macrophages	Types of white blood cell capable of wandering through body tissue, devouring foreign matter.
Asthma	A breathing disorder that affects the lungs and the airways.
Asthma triggers	Substances or situations that bring on asthma attacks.
Allergens	Allergy generators.
Bronchodilators	Drugs that relax the smooth muscle lining the bronchioles and cause them to dilate.
Anti-inflammatories	Drugs that coat the linings of the bronchioles and prevent any irritation or mucus build-up.
Chronic	Long-term.
Bronchitis	An inflammation and eventual scarring of the bronchial tubes within the lungs.
Emphysema	A condition of irreversible lung damage and heart failure.
Chronic obstructive pulmonary disease or COPD	Chronic bronchitis and emphysema found together.

EXTENDED KEY WORDS

Inspiratory and expiratory centres	Regions in the medulla oblongata of the brain controlling the rate of breathing.
CO_2	The principal controlling factor in gas exchange rates in both plants and animals.

QUESTIONS

1. What is *homeostasis*? Give an example of homeostasis in an animal and in a plant.
2. Explain why homeostasis requires both sensitivity and awareness.
3. What is negative feedback? Why is it impossible to maintain any internal biological factor precisely so that there are no changes?
4. Explain the differences between *breathing, gas exchange* and *respiration*. Why do we breathe?
5. How does the breathing system protect itself against damage?

6. How are alveoli and their capillaries adapted for gas exchange?

7. Describe the steps involved in breathing in and breathing out. Why is breathing out considered *passive*?

8. Explain each of the following:

   a. The lungs are wrapped in pleural membranes.

   b. Alveoli must maintain a film of moisture on their inner surfaces.

   c. The banning of smoky fuels from Dublin City resulted in a decrease in hospital admissions of patients with breathing disorders.

   d. The larger breathing tubes are supported by c-shaped rings of cartilage.

   e. When breathing in, air is *not* sucked into the lungs.

9. State whether each of the following is true or false. If false, state why.

   a. Pure CO_2 is breathed out of the lungs during expiration.

   b. Some bronchioles have rings of cartilage for support.

   c. Breathing is a voluntary activity.

   d. The epiglottis allows you to breathe and swallow at the same time.

   e. Respiration occurs in the lungs

10. In the photograph of the model lung, state which parts of the body are represented by the following:

    a. glass tubes;

    b. glass container;

    c. rubber balloons;

    d. opening to the outside;

    e. rubber sheet.

    Why do the balloons inflate when the rubber sheet is pulled down?

11. What is *asthma* and how is it caused? What treatments are available? Bronchodilators and anti-inflammatories are available for asthma patients. Explain how each medicine works.

EXTENDED QUESTIONS

12. Explain why it is that running makes you breathe faster.

13. Why is it dangerous to breathe in high levels of carbon dioxide?

14. State two factors that determine the degree of openness of stomata.

OPTIONAL ACTIVITIES

■ Refer to the end of Chapter 19 for information on how to make stomatal imprints and leaf transverse sections. Redraw the diagram of the leaf TS in Chapter 19 and mark arrows on it to show the movements of oxygen, carbon dioxide and water vapour.

■ Set up a demonstration of a smoking machine. See above.

■ Compare the breathing methods of each of the following:

   a. *Amoeba*;

   b. fish;

   c. earthworms;

   d. plants;

   e. insects;

   f. mammals.

■ Measure your *tidal volume* (the amount of air breathed in or out while resting) by breathing into a measuring cylinder filled with water and turned upside down in a basin of water. Any tube used as mouthpieces must be disinfected before and after use.

■ Make a long, plastic tube by cutting open and rolling up a supermarket bag. Try blowing and sucking through the tube to demonstrate the need for rings of cartilage around the trachea. Air pressure falls with air speed. The faster moving air in the tube has lower pressure than the still air outside and the tube will collapse each time. The harder you blow or suck, the more sudden the collapse.

N.B. **Caution!** Do not allow the plastic to cover your nose or mouth.

Now test yourself at
www.my-etest.com

Chapter 22

Excretion

EXCRETION   [345]–[346]

All living organisms create waste products from their metabolism. This waste is generally toxic to the organism and has to be removed. The removal of metabolic waste is termed *excretion*.

Excretion is an important part of homeostasis. Without excretion, wastes will quickly build up and interfere with the internal chemical and fluid balances of the organism.

PLANT EXCRETION   [345]

The metabolism of green plants is based on the photosynthesis of carbohydrates (containing carbon, hydrogen and oxygen) and they do not produce any nitrogen-containing waste.

Plants have a much 'cleaner' metabolism than animals: they convert their own carbohydrates to protein and fat, as they need them. Plants excrete large amounts of carbon dioxide by night through the stomata of their leaves. The leaves are acting as excretory organs in this case.

EXCRETION IN HUMANS   [346]

Animal metabolism is based around proteins and, as animals are eating food made elsewhere in the food chain, a lot of chemical 'processing' has to take place to produce the required tissues and enzymes. In humans, metabolism is complicated and large amounts of nitrogen-containing waste are manufactured, together with carbon dioxide from respiration. In the interests of homeostasis, excretory organs actively remove this metabolic waste before it accumulates to toxic levels.

(*Egestion* [removal of faeces through the rectum and anus] is not considered an excretion, as the faecal material is mostly unabsorbed food and not the waste products of any metabolism. Egested material has never been inside cells.

Secretion refers to the production of *useful* materials, e.g. saliva from salivary glands, oestrogen from ovaries or oil from the skin.)

Human excretory organs

- *The lungs* excrete carbon dioxide and water vapour (both made during respiration).
- *The kidneys* excrete water, salt and urea together as urine.
- *The skin* excretes small amounts of urea and salt in sweat.
- *The liver* excretes bile.

Is water ever an excretion? If water molecules have been newly created (as they are in respiration and anabolism) and if the body does not require them, these molecules are an excretion. However as water turns up in every living cell, it is impossible to say which molecules are created from metabolism and which are part of the diet. Some water molecules are unavoidably lost during excretion.

THE HUMAN URINARY SYSTEM

There are two kidneys, each the size of slightly less than a clenched fist. They lie at the back of the abdominal cavity on either side of the spine and are protected by the back muscles and by fat. The left kidney is slightly higher than the right kidney.

The kidneys receive blood from the aorta by the *renal artery* and return blood to the vena cava by the *renal vein*. Each

Table 22.1. Excretory organs

Organs	Location	Functions	Excretory products	Where Released
Lungs	Within the thorax	Excretion, gas exchange	CO_2 and water	To exterior
Skin	Covering the body	Excretion, protection, sensitivity, temperature control	Water, salt, some urea	To exterior
Kidneys	Mid-abdomen — either side of the spine and below the diaphragm	Excretion, osmoregulation	Urine (water, salt, urea)	To exterior
Liver	Upper abdomen — below the diaphragm and mostly on the right hand side	Metabolism, storage, bile production	Bile	Into the duodenum and then to exterior with the faeces

kidney is enclosed by a capsule of fibrous tissue and has a distinct outer part, the *cortex*, and a central part, the *medulla*. The medulla is divided into a number of cone-shaped areas called *pyramids*. The urine produced by the kidneys is carried away to the *bladder* by long, narrow, muscular tubes — the *ureters*. The upper end of each ureter is expanded within the kidney and called the *pelvis*. The bladder stores urine and then releases it to the exterior through a single tube — the *urethra*. In males, the urethra is shared by the reproductive system; it also conveys sperms to the exterior.

The human kidney has two main functions — both homeostatic:

1. *excretion* — it extracts water, salt and urea from the bloodstream and removes them to the exterior as urine;
2. *osmoregulation* — it adjusts water and salt concentrations within the body by adjusting the volume and concentration of the urine.

Urine is made in three stages:

■ *Filtration* — the blood is filtered to separate small chemicals from larger ones. Filtration takes place in the cortex of the kidney.

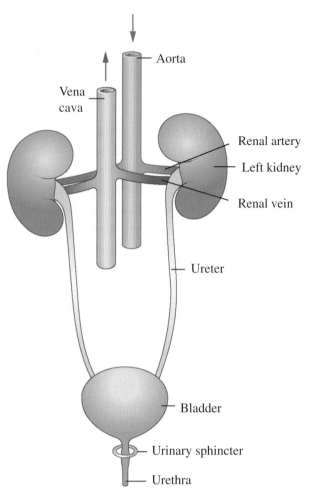

Fig. 22.2. The urinary system.

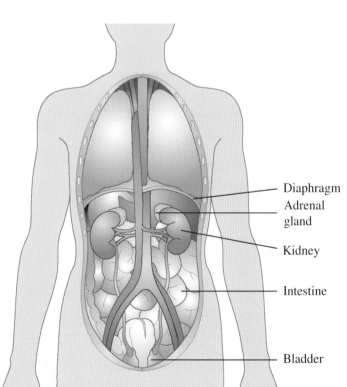

Fig. 22.1. Location of the urinary system.

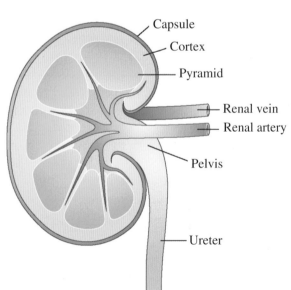

Fig. 22.3. Kidney LS.

- *Secretion and reabsorption* — the filtered chemical are sorted and useful ones are taken back into the bloodstream. Some wastes are secreted directly into the nephron from the blood. Secretion and reabsorption happen both in the cortex and the medulla regions.
- *Concentration* — the levels of water and salt are adjusted in the urine. Concentration is done mainly in the medulla of the kidney.

After the urine is formed, it collects in the pelvis of the kidney. From there, the ureters bring the urine to the bladder. The ureters do not transport urine by gravity, it is moved by *peristalsis* (a wave of muscular squeezing that occurs in ureters every ten seconds or so). When the bladder is full (with about 300 ml of urine in an adult), the ring muscles (*sphincters*) below it relax and the urine is emptied to the outside through the urethra — again by peristalsis.

Normal urine

The average human produces between one and 1.5 litres of urine per day. Urine contains water, salt, urea and some uric acid. It has a weak acid pH of about 6.0 and is coloured yellow due to urochrome — a pigment produced during protein metabolism. Urine should not normally contain glucose, proteins or blood cells. Glucose in the urine is often a sign of *diabetes*.

Kidney failure

Although everyone has two kidneys (a third, tiny kidney is sometimes found in girls!), it is possible to survive with only one.

If a patient has complete kidney failure from disease or damage, *haemodialysis* machines can act as artificial kidneys. *Dialysis* is a type of filtering. The patient's blood is diverted from the body and pumped through a bath of *dialysing fluid*. This contains all the nutrients that are normally in the blood but no toxins. Urea and salt will then diffuse out of the blood. Dialysis takes place across a *dialysing membrane* made from cellophane.

Kidney machines are expensive and the patient will need his or her blood 'cleaned' about three times per week. The procedure takes about six hours.

In younger patients, a *kidney transplant* is a better option, if a suitable donor can be found. Transplants are hampered by a shortage of kidneys and everyone is encouraged to carry a kidney donor card to allow use of their organs after death. The surgery is straightforward; any problems will be to do with *immunological rejection* of the new organ.

(A new and clearly controversial solution to the problem of suitable donors is the cultivation and genetic screening of human embryos. In October 2000, an American couple were the first in the world to announce that they had done just that to obtain suitable bone marrow cells for their sick daughter. They conceived multiple embryos and then screened them both for transplant suitability and for the illness of the daughter. Unsuitable embryos were discarded and a suitable one was replaced in the mother's womb. The baby was born healthy in October 2000 and had already donated bone marrow cells to his sister before the public announcement of what had taken place.)

Urinary tract infections (UTIs)

UTIs are due to the presence of bacteria within in the urinary tract. UTIs are common and pose serious health problems for thousands of people in Ireland every year. Women are especially prone to UTIs. Most infections arise from one type of bacterium, *E. coli*, which is not sexually transmitted. Infections from *Chlamydia*, *Mycoplasma* and *Neisseria* (gonorrhoea) are sexually transmitted and both partners have to be treated.

Symptoms of UTIs include:

- a frequent urge to urinate;
- a painful, burning feeling in the area of the bladder or urethra during urination;
- feeling tired or shaky;
- women feel an uncomfortable pressure above the pubic bone;
- a small amount of urine is passed;
- the urine itself may be cloudy.

A fever may mean that the infection has reached the kidneys. Other symptoms of a kidney infection include pain in the back or side below the ribs, nausea, or vomiting.

Treatment is by a full course of antibiotics together with lots of fluids. Acidic drinks such as cranberry juice can be of help.

Kidney stones

A kidney stone is a solid piece of material that forms in the kidney out of substances in the urine.

A stone may stay in the kidney or break loose and travel down the urinary tract. A very small stone may pass all of the way out of the body without causing too much pain. A larger stone may lodge in a ureter, in the bladder or the urethra. These stones can block the flow of urine and cause great pain. The most common type of stone is formed from excess calcium combining with excretory products. Stones are usually yellow/brown and can vary in size from that of a grain of sand to 2 cm in diameter!

Treatment is by *surgery* or by *shockwave lithotripsy* — stone-crushing using ultrasound. Patients prone to kidney stones are advised to drink lots of water and eat less meat.

The skin and temperature regulation

Temperature affects the rate of all chemical reaction and this includes the rate of metabolism within living organisms. Maintaining a suitable body temperature is one of the most important aspects of homeostasis.

Most organisms are active within the temperature range 10–42 °C; outside this range, enzymes either do not work or they are denatured and destroyed. (Some bacterial spores can survive brief exposure to boiling water (100°), although DNA is usually damaged above 85°. Some arctic plants can continue their metabolism at temperatures close to freezing (0°C).)

Animals are sometimes described as *cold-blooded* or *warm-blooded*. Cold-blooded animals are those whose temperatures vary with changes in the environment. Examples include fish, amphibians, reptiles and almost all invertebrates. Warm-blooded animals are those that maintain a constant temperature regardless of the temperature of the environment. This is a feature of all birds and mammals (including humans).

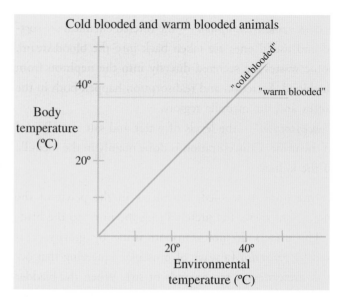

Fig. 22.4. Environmental temperature v. body temperature in cold-blooded and warm-blooded animals.

The terms '*warm-blooded*' and '*cold-blooded*' have fallen into disuse, as they can be misleading: a rattlesnake in the desert in daytime has a higher body temperature than a human but is still a 'cold-blooded' animal.

A better distinction is to look at how organisms *regulate* their body temperatures. *Ectotherms* gain heat directly from the environment, e.g. iguanas often bask in the sunshine in early morning to raise their temperature to a suitable level. *Endotherms* gain heat from metabolism within their bodies (from respiration) and then regulate the heat level by various physiological processes. *Endotherms* spend a lot of energy and effort on maintaining their constant temperature, but the advantages are great — enzymes are always working at their optimum temperatures and endotherms can remain active in temperature extremes.

Humans are endotherms — they gain body heat from their respiration and they regulate their heat loss through their skin.

The structure of the skin

The skin is divided into two layers: an outer *epidermis* and an inner *dermis*.

At the base of the epidermis is a layer of dividing cells — the *Malpighian layer*. These cells form new cells by mitosis and push them to the outside. These new cells contain *keratin* and become flattened and dense. Eventually they form the dead, *cornified layer*, which forms the outer part of skin and is constantly being rubbed off by contact with the surroundings. It takes about four weeks for new cells from the Malpighian layer to reach the outside.

The dermis is a much thicker and more complicated layer. It contains *collagen* and *elastin* fibres for strength and elasticity. There is an extensive supply of blood capillaries used for temperature regulation. The dermis also contains sensory cells and nerve endings for sensitivity. Hairs are formed in *hair follicles* set deep in the dermis. Each follicle has a tiny muscle to adjust the hair angle and a *sebaceous gland* producing oily *sebum*, which waterproofs the skin. *Sweat glands* are coiled, tubular glands opening to the outside through sweat ducts and tiny sweat pores. Sweat contains water, salt and some urea (it is similar to very dilute urine!), but sweating is more important as a temperature regulator than as an excretion.

Below the dermis is a layer of *adipose tissue*. The adipose cells are filled with fat droplets and act as an insulation, a protection and an energy store.

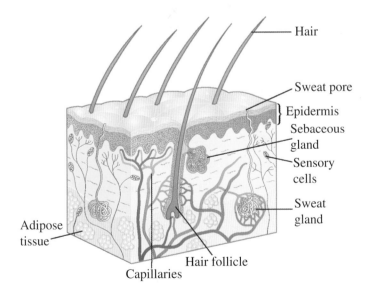

Fig. 22.5. Structure of the skin.

The functions of the skin

- *Protection* — the cornified layer is resistant to infection, water loss, physical injury and most ultraviolet radiation.

- *Sensory* — the skin can sense heat, cold, touch, pressure and pain using its receptors and nerve endings.
- *Excretion* — removal of some urea by the sweat glands.
- *Production of vitamin D* in the epidermis when exposed to ultraviolet radiation.
- *Temperature regulation* — see below.

Table 22.2. Responses of the skin to temperature changes

Conditions	Response	Advantage
Cold environment	Hairs stand on end	Trapped air is a good insulator
	Blood capillaries near surface constrict	Blood stays deep within the skin and pale skin loses little heat by radiation
	Brain stimulates muscle fibres to contract repeatedly (shivering)	Tissue respiration produces heat
Hot environment	Increased sweating	Evaporation cools the skin
	Blood capillaries near surface widen	Blood close to the surface radiates more heat from pink skin

Metabolism always produces excess heat and this must leak to the outside to prevent overheating of the body. A perfectly insulated human body would increase its temperature by 1° every hour — resulting in death in six to seven hours.

Exercise increases sweating and so water and salt loss. It is important then to drink lots of water before, during and after strenuous exercise. In extreme cases of dehydration, salt tables are also taken to replace lost salt and prevent muscle cramps.

THE NEPHRON   [H34 II]

Each kidney contains about one million microscopic, blind-ending tubes called *nephrons*. Each nephron is about 3 cm long (and a diameter of about one-tenth of a human hair), and has its own individual blood supply. The nephrons are the *functional units of the kidney* — they extract the urine from the blood.

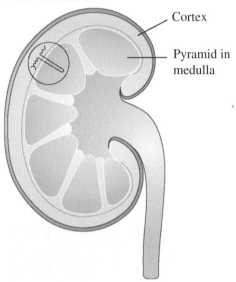

Cortex

Pyramid in medulla

Fig. 22.6. Nephron location.

The closed end of the nephron is shaped like a wine glass and called the *Bowman's capsule* (or *renal capsule*). Leading from this is the *proximal convoluted tubule* (*proximal* means 'at the near end', *convoluted* means twisted, *tubule* means 'little tube'). The tubule then forms a *loop of Henle* that lies deep in the medulla region. The nephron ends with a *distal convoluted tubule* (*distal* means 'at the far end'). Many distal tubules unite to form *collecting ducts*, which open into the pelvis of the kidney.

Blood arrives at each nephron via a branch of the renal artery — the *afferent arteriole*. This divides to form a knot of capillaries called the *glomerulus*, which is completely surrounded by and enclosed in the Bowman's capsule. The glomerular capillaries then unite to form the *efferent arteriole*, which divides again to form a network of capillaries surrounding the rest of the nephron. The capillaries finally unite again to form a branch of the renal vein.

Note that the glomerulus is supplied by the *afferent* arteriole and drained by the *efferent* arteriole (*afferent* means *carrying towards*, *efferent* means *carrying away from*).

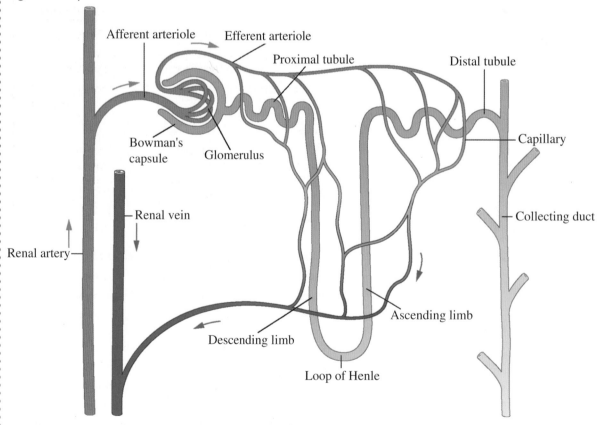

Afferent arteriole   Efferent arteriole

Proximal tubule

Distal tubule

Bowman's capsule   Glomerulus

Capillary

Renal vein

Collecting duct

Renal artery

Descending limb

Ascending limb

Loop of Henle

Fig. 22.7. The nephron and its blood supply.

How urine is formed

1. FILTRATION

The blood pressure within the glomerulus is high because:

- the diameter of the afferent arteriole is greater than the efferent arteriole;
- the incoming blood is arterial.

This high pressure forces any materials in the blood *of small molecular size* through pores in the walls of the capillaries and into the space within the Bowman's capsule.

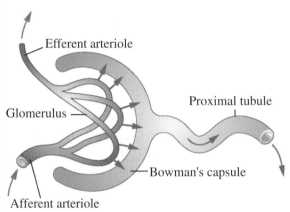

Fig. 22.8. Capsule detail.

Materials small enough to pass through the pores include:

- water;
- salt;
- urea;   } This is the glomerular filtrate
- glucose;
- amino acids.

Note that the filtrate is a mixture of wanted and unwanted substances but is not yet the same as urine. A filter can only separate substances according to size, not importance.

Materials too large to be filtered and so retained within the blood capillaries include:

- plasma proteins;
- most hormones;
- blood cells and platelets.

Some water is retained in the blood — necessary to allow it to continue to flow.

2. SECRETION AND REABSORPTION

As the filtrate passes along the proximal tubule, glucose, amino acids and some salt are reabsorbed into the blood capillaries by *active transport* (an energy-requiring process that moves materials from regions of low concentration to regions of high concentration — see Chapter 10). Some urea is reabsorbed by diffusion and large amounts of water are reabsorbed by osmosis.

Certain chemicals, such as uric acid and penicillin (if in the blood) are actively secreted from the blood into the proximal tubule.

The inner wall of the proximal tubule is covered in microvilli to increase its surface area and improve reabsorption. Large numbers of mitochondria provide the energy needed for active transport.

Table 22.3. Secretion and reabsorption in the proximal tubule

Substance	Direction moved	Process involved
Glucose	From tubule to bloodstream	Reabsorption by active transport
Amino acids	From tubule to bloodstream	Reabsorption by active transport
Salt	From tubule to bloodstream	Reabsorption by active transport
Water	From tubule to bloodstream	Reabsorption by osmosis
Urea	From tubule to bloodstream	Reabsorption by diffusion
Uric acid	From bloodstream to tubule	Secretion
K^+ and H^+ ions	From bloodstream to tubule	Secretion

3. CONCENTRATION

After leaving the proximal tubule, the filtrate within the nephron resembles very dilute urine. The loop of Henle is

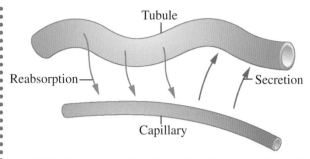

Fig. 22.9. Secretion and reabsorption in the proximal tubule.

now able to concentrate the urine to prevent unnecessary water loss. The ascending limb of the loop is waterproof and contains a set of enzymes (the *salt pump*), which extracts salt from the nephron by active transport and pumps it into the surrounding tissues. This creates a salty patch of tissue in the medulla of the kidney. Water then moves by osmosis from the descending limb of the loop in an attempt to dilute this salt. Water also leaves the nephron through the walls of the distal tubule and the collecting duct. Any water reabsorbed in this way cannot re-enter the loop and instead passes back to the blood capillaries. This results in the production of a small volume of concentrated urine which passes into the pelvis of the kidney and then to the bladder.

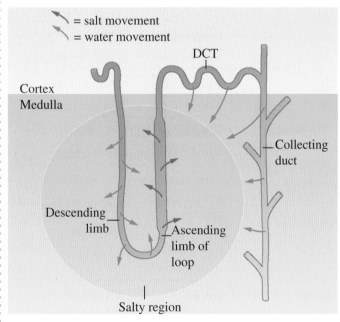

Fig. 22.10. Water movement in the medulla.

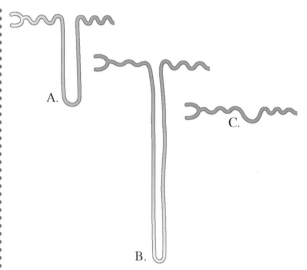

Fig. 22.11. Loops of Henle in camel, beaver and human compared. Which is which?

Control of water reabsorption

A pituitary hormone ADH controls water reabsorption. The pituitary gland monitors the concentration of water in the blood and secretes the hormone as necessary. ADH increases the permeability of the distal tubule and the collecting ducts.

(ADH is the **antidiuretic hormone**. *Diuresis* means *'water loss'*.)

SUMMARY

- *All living organisms* create waste products from their metabolism.
- *The removal of metabolic waste* is termed excretion.
- *The metabolism of green plants* is based on carbohydrates and they do not produce any nitrogen-containing waste.
- *Plants excrete large amounts of carbon dioxide* by night through the stomata of their leaves.
- *In humans, large amounts of nitrogen-containing waste* are manufactured together with carbon dioxide from respiration.
- *Human excretory organs* include the lungs, the liver, the skin and the kidneys.
- *The lungs* excrete carbon dioxide and water vapour.
- *The kidneys* excrete water, salt and urea together as urine.
- *The skin* excretes sweat.

- *The liver* excretes bile.
- *The human kidney has two main functions*: excretion and osmoregulation.
- *The kidneys extract water, salt and urea from the bloodstream* and remove them as urine.
- *Urine is made in three stages*:

  - *filtration* — separates small chemicals from larger ones;
  - *reabsorption* — the filtered chemicals are sorted and useful ones are taken back into the bloodstream;
  - *concentration* — reabsorption of water.

- *The average human* produces 1–1.5 litres of urine per day.
- *Haemodialysis machines* can act as artificial kidneys.
- *A kidney transplant* is an option for kidney failure, if a suitable donor can be found.
- *UTIs* are due to the presence of bacteria within in the urinary tract.
- *A kidney stone* is a solid piece of material that forms in the kidney out of substances in the urine.
- *Maintaining a suitable body temperature* is one of the most important aspects of homeostasis.
- *Cold-blooded animals* are those whose temperatures vary with changes in the environment.
- *Warm-blooded animals* are those that maintain a constant temperature regardless of the temperature of the environment.
- *Ectotherms* gain heat directly from the environment.
- *Endotherms* gain heat from metabolism within their bodies and then regulate it.
- *Humans are endotherms* — they gain body heat from their respiration and they regulate their heat loss through their skin.
- *The skin is divided into two layers*: an outer epidermis and an inner dermis. Below the dermis is a layer of adipose tissue.
- *Functions of the skin*:

  - *protection* — against infection, water loss, physical injury and most ultraviolet radiation;
  - *sensory* — the skin can sense heat, cold, touch, pressure and pain;
  - *excretion* — removal of some urea by the sweat glands;
  - *production of vitamin D*;
  - *temperature regulation*.

EXTENDED SUMMARY

- *Each kidney* contains about one million microscopic, blind-ending tubes called nephrons.
- *The nephrons* are the functional units of the kidney — they extract the urine from the blood.
- *Filtration* occurs when high pressure forces small materials in the blood through pores in the walls of the capillaries and into the space within the Bowman's capsule.
- *The glomerular filtrate* includes water, salt, urea, glucose and amino acids.
- *As the filtrate passes along the proximal tubule*, glucose, amino acids and some salt are reabsorbed into the blood. Some wastes are secreted directly into the nephron.
- *The loop of Henle* concentrates the urine to prevent unnecessary water loss.
- *A pituitary hormone* ADH controls water reabsorption.
- *ADH* increases the permeability of the distal tubule and the collecting ducts.
- *ADH* is the **antidiuretic hormone.**

KEY WORDS

Excretion	The removal of metabolic waste.
Egestion	The removal of unabsorbed and unwanted material.
Secretion	The production of useful materials from cells.
Cortex	The outer part of an organ.
Medulla	The central part of an organ.
Pyramids	Cone-shaped areas within the kidney medulla.
Ureter	A long, narrow and muscular tube carrying urine from the kidney to the bladder.

Pelvis	An expansion of the ureter within the kidney.
Urethra	A muscular tube carrying urine from the bladder to the exterior.
Osmoregulation	The control of water and salt concentrations within the body.
Peristalsis	An involuntary wave of muscular squeezing within a tube.
Sphincter	A ring muscle for opening and closing tubes.
Dialysis	Filtering by passing liquids through a membrane.
Haemodialysis	Filtering the blood.
Haemodialysis machines	Artificial kidney machines.
UTIs	Urinary tract infections, usually due to bacteria.
Kidney stone	A solid piece of material that forms in the kidney from substances in the urine.
Shockwave lithotripsy	Stone-crushing using ultrasound.
Cold-blooded animals	Those whose temperatures vary with changes in the environment.
Warm-blooded animals	Those that maintain a constant body temperature regardless of the temperature of the environment.
Ectotherms	Gain heat directly from the environment.
Endotherms	Gain heat from metabolism within their bodies and then regulate the heat level by various physiological processes.
Malpighian layer	A layer of dividing cells at the base of the skin epidermis.
Cornified layer	Dead cells that are filled with keratin.

Sebaceous gland	Glands within the skin that produce oily sebum.
Adipose tissue	Tissue made from cells filled with fat droplets.

EXTENDED KEY WORDS

Nephron	A microscopic, blind ending tube that is the functional unit of the kidney.
Bowman's capsule	Closed end of the nephron, shaped like a wine glass.
Proximal convoluted tubule	Twisted portion of the 'near' end of the nephron.
The loop of Henle	'Hairpin' region of the nephron.
Distal convoluted tubule	Twisted portion of the 'far' end of the nephron.
Afferent arteriole	Arteriole carrying blood towards the Bowman's capsule.
Glomerulus	A knot of capillaries within the Bowman's capsule.
Efferent arteriole	Arteriole carrying blood away from the Bowman's capsule.
Glomerular filtrate	A collection of small, soluble molecules that passes from the blood into the nephron.
Active transport	An energy-requirin process that moves materials from regions of low concentration to regions of high concentration
Salt pump	A set of enzymes that extracts salt from the nephron by active transport and pumps it into the surrounding tissues.
Diuresis	Water loss.
ADH	The ***antidiuretic hormone***.

QUESTIONS

1. Distinguish between excretion and egestion. Why is excretion of less importance to plants than it is to animals?

2. List the human excretory organs and state their main excretions.

3. Draw a large, labelled diagram of the human urinary system. Mark the following on the diagram:

   a. left kidney;
   b. cortex;
   c. medulla;
   d. pyramid;
   e. right ureter;
   f. bladder;
   g. urethra;
   h. renal artery;
   i. renal vein.

4. Explain the stages involved in the production of urine. Name three substances normally found in urine.

5. What treatments are available to a patient with complete kidney failure? How do these treatments compare?

6. What are UTIs? Are UTIs always sexually transmitted? List the symptoms of a UTI and explain how it might be treated.

7. Explain what kidney stones are and why they may cause a serious medical problem. What treatments are available?

8. List the functions of the skin. Explain how the skin can respond if the body is too hot, and if the body is too cold.

9. State whether each of the following is *true* or *false*. If *false*, give a reason for your answer.

   a. Urea is made in the kidneys.
   b. Plants do not excrete.
   c. The skin is an excretory organ.
   d. Urine leaves the bladder via the ureters.
   e. The outer layer of the skin is dead tissue.

10. Explain what *endotherms* and *ectotherms* are. Which category does each of the following belong to?

    a. human;
    b. rattlesnake;
    c. polar bear;
    d. frog;
    e. cat.

11. Distinguish between the members of the following word pairs by writing a short explanation of each:

    a. warm-blooded and cold-blooded;
    b. excretion and osmoregulation;
    c. urea and urine;
    d. renal artery and renal vein;
    e. cortex and medulla.

EXTENDED QUESTIONS

12. Draw a large, labelled diagram of a nephron and its blood supply. Mark letters on the diagram to show where the following take place:

    A. active secretion of salt;
    B. filtration;
    C. the action of ADH;
    D. collection of urine;
    E. reabsorption of glucose.

13. Explain the effect of each of the following on the composition of the urine:

    a. a salty meal;
    b. drinking two pints of water;
    c. a high protein diet;
    d. uncontrolled diabetes;
    e. high blood pressure;
    f. removal of the pancreas;
    g. destruction of the pituitary gland.

14. What is the glomerular filtrate? List the materials found within it. What do all these materials have in common? If a kidney is chilled during an operation, the glomerular filtrate resembles the urine in its composition. Why does this happen?

15. Explain the difference between secretion and reabsorption.

16. Fig. 22.11 shows the loops of Henle found within the kidneys of a *beaver*, a *camel* and a *human*. State which nephron belongs to which animal and explain the differences in length. Explain the differences in length.

17. Make a list of the parts of the urinary system that a molecule of urea would pass through on its way from the renal artery to the outside. Try and name at least ten locations in order.

OPTIONAL ACTIVITIES

- Examine a chart or plastic model of the human urinary system.
- Dissect a kidney. Obtain a pig's kidney from a pork butcher. Carefully remove any fat from the outside. Examine the outside of the kidney and identify the renal artery, renal vein and ureter. Slice the kidney longitudinally down the middle. Look for the cortex, medulla and pyramids. These parts are not particularly easy to see but should eventually be seen. Use as a guide.
- Write a report on *Unhealthy Urinary Systems* and present it to the class.
- Collect information on dialysis machines and kidney donor cards. Contact the Irish Kidney Association at Donor House, 156 Pembroke Road, Ballsbridge, Dublin 4 for information on kidneys, dialysis and transplants.
- Debate the idea of carrying kidney donor cards.
- *Extension material* — examine prepared microscope slides to show nephron structure.

For more information on websites dealing with subjects covered in this chapter see www.my-etest.com.

Now test yourself at
www.my-etest.com

Chapter 23
Responses in the Flowering Plant

Learning objectives

After your study of this chapter, you should be able to:

- distinguish between animal and plant responses;
- list the internal and external factors that regulate plant growth;
- define meristems;
- explain the naming of tropisms;
- outline the responses of phototropism and geotropism;
- name and give the functions of common growth regulators;
- discuss the growth regulator IAA.

Extended learning objectives

- Summarise the activity of IAA within the plant.
- Compare plant growth regulators with animal hormones.
- Explain phototropism in plant stems.

Mandatory activities

#20. Investigating the effect of IAA growth regulator on dicot plant tissue.

RESPONSES TO STIMULI   [350]

All organisms are in contact with their environment and it is in the nature of any natural environment to be full of constant change. Some of these changes are of advantage to organisms (e.g. the presence of food, water, shelter) and some are a disadvantage (e.g. approaching predators). Living organisms need to *detect* these changes and *respond* to them in order to either exploit the advantages or protect themselves from the disadvantages. The environmental changes are *stimuli* to the organisms and the ability to detect and respond is called *sensitivity*.

All living organisms display sensitivity to the external environment although this is much more obvious in animals than in plants.

Living organisms are also sensitive to their inner, biochemically-changing environment.

Fig. 23.1. Chicks responding to food.

STRUCTURES FOR RESPONSE [351]

Sensitivity in organisms is a complicated business and usually involves the development of specialised organs and systems. All plants and animals use a chemical messenger or *hormonal system* to respond to change. The hormonal system is highly developed in animals and humans. In addition, higher animals possess sense organs, nervous systems, muscles, bones and an immune system to respond to their environment.

In general, plants respond to change by modifying their *growth* and animals respond to change by modifying their *behaviour*.

RESPONSES IN THE FLOWERING PLANT [352]

Plants, like animals, must be sensitive to their environment and must be able to respond to change if they are to survive. We cannot expect plant sensitivity and response to match that of most animals however; plants lack electrical nervous systems and so cannot operate finely tuned sense organs or quick responding muscles. Also plants are, for the most part, anchored permanently in the ground and must stay there even if the environment is not entirely favourable.

All plant responses are quite slow and involve chemical modifications of their growth. If plants sense light, gravity or water, part of the plant will grow either towards or away from these stimuli as survival demands.

Growth regulation in plants

Plant growth is regulated by both external and internal factors. *External factors* include light, length of the day, gravity and temperature. *Internal factors* include the production of chemicals termed *growth regulators*. Growth regulators affect the *meristems* of the plant.

Fig. 23.2. Spiral tendril of a grape vine.

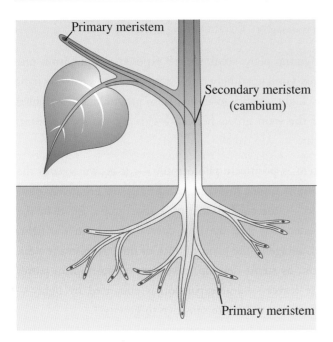

Fig. 23.3. Meristem locations.

A *meristem* is a group of plant cells that divides repeatedly by mitosis. Plants use their meristems for growth.

- *Apical meristems* are found at the extremities (*apices*) of the stem and root and are responsible mainly for primary growth, i.e. increases in *plant length*.
- *Lateral meristems* are found in the vascular bundles and are responsible for secondary growth, i.e. increases in *plant diameter*. Lateral meristems are also named *cambium tissue* and produce parallel rows of cells.

Growth in plants is a matter of increasing the size and length of new meristematic cells. The cells enlarge by taking in water, forming large vacuoles and then stretching and reforming their cellulose walls. This process is under hormonal control.

Plant growth is *localised* at meristems, whereas animal growth generally occurs throughout the body. Young stems and roots marked with bands of ink reveal growth near their primary meristems.

Plant movements

Plant movements are classified as follows:

1. *Tropisms* — part of a plant grows in a direction determined by a stimulus.

2. *Nasties* — growth responses of a plant where the direction of the movement is *not* determined by the direction of the stimulus, e.g. flowers opening at dawn.

3. *Taxes* — Movement of a *complete organism* or *gamete* in response to an external stimulus. The direction of the movement is determined by the direction of the stimulus, e.g. movements of male gametes in mosses and ferns.

The plant movements we are most concerned with here are tropisms.

Tropisms

A tropism is a growth movement of part of a plant in response to an external stimulus. The direction of the movement is determined by the direction of the stimulus.

Examples of tropisms

Phototropism	Plant shoots grow towards light and plant roots grow away from light.

Fig. 23.4. Phototropism.

Geotropism (or *Gravitropism*)	Shoots grow away from gravity, roots grow towards gravity.
Thigmotropism (or *Haptotropism*)	Shoots and tendrils of climbing plants grow around solid objects.
Hydrotropism	Roots grow towards water.
Chemotropism	Roots grow towards or away from dissolved chemicals.
Aerotropism	Pollen tubes grow away from free air.

All of the above tropisms clearly have survival value to the plant. (Explain how in each case.)

Tropisms are described as *positive* if the direction of movement is *towards* the stimulus and *negative* if the direction is *away from* the stimulus, e.g. plant stems are positively phototropic and also negatively geotropic.

Fig. 23.5. *Mimosa* responding to touch.

PHOTOTROPISM

When young plant seedlings are exposed to light from one side only (unilateral light), the stems grow towards the light source. Light appears to *inhibit* stem growth and the shaded side of the stem grows better — curving the stem *towards* the light.

The stem is positively phototropic — it grows *towards* the light. Roots under the same conditions are negatively phototropic — the shaded side of a root grows *less* than the illuminated side and the root curves away from the light. The advantage to the plant of both of these tropisms is clear. Later on, as stems develop leaves, the phototropism passes to these leaves — leaf expansion is enhanced by light — and stems are now more sensitive to gravity.

GEOTROPISM (GRAVITROPISM)

A plant placed horizontally will demonstrate geotropism — a growth response to 'unilateral' gravity. The stem will curve upwards and the root downwards — for obvious survival value. As in phototropism, the growth responses occur in the zones of elongation.

A young seedling attached to a slowly revolving clinostat no longer senses unilateral gravity and shows no geotropism.

PLAGIOGEOTROPISM

Plagiogeotropism ('plagio' means a new direction) is when lateral roots and branches grow at an angle to gravity.

THE REGULATORY SYSTEM FOR GROWTH

A *growth regulator* is a chemical substance (similar to a hormone but see later), which exerts a degree of control over plant growth.

There are five main types of growth regulator in plants. They interact with each other rather than work independently. Plant growth regulators operate in extremely low concentrations — making their extraction or study very difficult. (20,000 tonnes of stem tip are required to extract 1 g of IAA [indoleacetic acid] — the best-studied growth regulator). Consequently, there is little agreement on many aspects of their function.

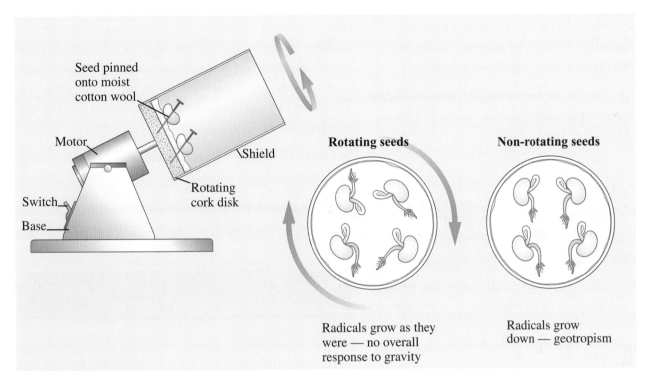

Fig. 23.6. Use of a clinostat.

IAA (Indoleacetic acid)

The most important growth regulator in plants is *auxin* or *IAA* (indoleacetic acid) — a chemical that also occurs in fungi and bacteria. It allows cellulose fibrils in cell walls to loosen and stretch. Cells then increase their water intake and form larger vacuoles inside larger cell walls — resulting in cell elongation and growth.

IAA is made at the stem tip (apex) by meristematic cells, and moves downwards through the plant tissues. This results in a decrease in IAA concentration as one moves away from

Table 23.1. Growth regulators

Regulator name	Function or effect	Industrial application
IAA (Indoleacetic acid)	Cell elongation Apical dominance Rooting Fruit ripening	Improved growth Deadheading to improve branching 'Rooting hormone' for cuttings. Production of 'virgin fruits' out of season.
2.4-D (synthetic IAA)	Excessive respiration	Selective weed-killer
Gibberellin	Stem elongation Synthesis of amylase	Better growth and germination Improves malting of barley in brewing.
Cytokinin	Increases cell division rate	Improved growth, delayed ageing.
Abscisic acid	Promotes leaf-fall	–
Ethene	Fruit ripening	Ripening after bulk transport.

the apex, and roots have far lower concentrations of IAA than stems. Plants, incidentally, are adapted for this uneven distribution, otherwise uneven growth would result.

The movement of IAA is by *active transport* from cell to cell and requires energy from cell respiration (although IAA can *diffuse* through agar and similar media).

OTHER EFFECTS OF IAA

- IAA inhibits the development of side branches from lateral buds — so maintaining the dominance of the main stem over lesser stems.

  (Apical dominance — the apex of the main stem inhibits the development of side branches below it. If the apex is removed however, side branches quickly appear — the theory behind pruning hedges and rose bushes to produce more branches.)

- IAA stimulates development of adventitious roots — lateral roots that originate directly from a stem. Plant cuttings dipped into 'rooting hormone' (a powder containing IAA) respond by growing roots quickly.

- IAA stimulates fruit formation in the absence of fertilisation. The resulting fruits (parthenocarps or 'virgin fruits') are seedless but can be sold out of season. Examples of virgin fruits are bananas, cucumbers, pineapples and some grapes. In normal fertilised fruits, the developing embryo produces IAA in order to stimulate the ripening process.

2,4-D (Synthetic IAA)

2,4-D is a synthetic auxin that stimulates unusual growth and high rates of respiration in plants. It is more effective on broad-leaved plants and is used as a selective weed killer. The broad-leaved weeds grow rapidly and then die of exhaustion. The narrow-leaved grass is only moderately stimulated. 2,4-D also delays fruit fall in plants and is used in low concentrations to delay pre-harvest fruit drop.

All plant growth regulators work in combination with one another. For example, cytokinin will only promote cell division in the presence of IAA. Neither IAA nor cytokinin will stimulate cell division on their own.

The interaction of different regulators is extremely difficult to study — differences in concentration of one microgram of one regulator may bring about complete reversal of function of other regulators! Changes in the proportion of cytokinin to IAA can promote either root or stem development in plant tissues.

Some growth regulators are *synergistic* to each other — e.g. gibberellin and IAA improve each other's effect.

Other regulators are *antagonistic* to each other — e.g. cytokinin and abscisic acid have opposing effects on plant ageing.

Mandatory activity #20. Investigating the effect of IAA growth regulator on dicot plant tissue

RESOURCES NEEDED

Six clean petri dishes and lids.
IAA powder or liquid (liquid is preferable).
Distilled water.
Graduated pipette or micropipette.
Ethanol.
60 mustard seeds.
Filter paper.
Dropper.
Ruler.

INTRODUCTION

In this investigation, mustard seeds are grown in different strength IAA solutions. The seeds grow in the dark in petri dishes and the development of their roots is assessed after 48 hours. The solutions involved contain tiny amounts of IAA and must be made up accurately. Any dilutions of IAA can be used, not necessarily the ones given below. All work should be done in near dark or in photographer's red light if possible, as IAA deteriorates in light. The absence of light also prevents the seedlings making their own supply of IAA.

Use distilled water throughout the experiment. The class should divide into five groups — each group will set up an entire experiment. The class results can be averaged afterwards.

PREPARATION

Solutions of IAA must be prepared in advance. This may appear a bit complicated but can be done quite easily. Each solution will be poured into a petri dish, so large quantities are not needed and amounts can be scaled down as suits.

THE IAA SOLUTIONS

Make a litre of stock IAA solution as follows:

Dissolve 100 mg of crystalline IAA (or the equivalent of liquid IAA) in about 2 ml of ethanol. Add 800 ml of distilled water and heat the mixture to about 80 °C for five minutes to evaporate the alcohol. Make up the solution to 1 litre with distilled water and allow to cool. This stock solution has a strength of 100 mg/L of IAA (*or 100ppm* [*parts per million*]) and will keep for over a month in a dark fridge.

Six solutions are needed in total:

- *Solution A contains 100 mg/l of IAA*
  Use the stock IAA solution prepared as above.
- *Solution B contains 1 mg/l of IAA*
  Add 1 ml of stock solution to 100 ml of water.
- *Solution C contains 0.01 mg/l of IAA*
  Add 1 ml of solution B to 100 ml water.
- *Solution D contains 0.0001 mg/l of IAA*
  Add 1 ml of solution C to 100 ml water.
- *Solution E contains 0.000001 mg/l of IAA*
  Add 1 ml of solution D to 100 ml water.

- *Solution F contains distilled water alone (as a control — for comparison).*
  Use 100 ml of distilled water.

PROCEDURE

- Place a sheet of filter paper in each petri dish.
- Label each dish with the name of the solution being used: A, B, C, etc.
- Pour 5 ml of solution A into dish A, solution B into dish B, etc.
- Place ten mustard seeds on the moist paper in each dish.
- Incubate the dishes in a warm, dark place, preferably an incubator, at 25 °C for 48 hours.

EXAMINATION

- Measure the length of the root of each of the ten seeds and record on the chart (see table 23.2). Calculate the average length.
- Repeat for each IAA solution and for the control solution.
- Compare the average root length of each dish with the average control length. Use the formula:

% change = ([average length of roots in IAA — average length of control roots in distilled water) × 100] / (average length of control roots).

Concentration of IAA	1	2	3	4	5	6	7	8	9	10	Total root length	Average length
100 mg/l												
1 mg/l												
0.01 mg/l												
0.0001 mg/l												
0.000001 mg/l												
Distilled water												

Concentration of IAA	Average root length (mm)	% change compared to control	Roots stimulated or inhibited?
100 mg/l			
1 mg/l			
0.01 mg/l			
0.0001 mg/l			
0.000001 mg/l			

If the formula produces a *positive* value, IAA has stimulated the roots. If the formula produces a *negative* value, IAA has inhibited the roots.

Transfer these results to a graph similar to the one below:

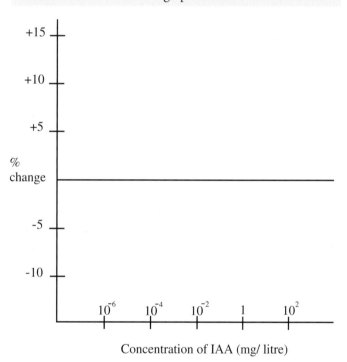

Responses of plants to adverse external environments

Many plants develop complicated responses to deal with recurring hardships. These responses are stimulated by the stress of the environment and contribute to the plant's survival.

- Arctic plants contain modified proteins that tend not to freeze during the winter. Heat-shock proteins attach to normal proteins within desert plants and prevent heat damage (denaturing) during the hottest periods of the day.

- Exposed, thin plants, such as cereals, develop hinge joints to allow some movement with the wind and to reduce the risk of fracture.

- The cactus has developed water storage tissue within its stem to retain precious water.

- The *Venus flytrap* typically grows in bogland deficient in nitrogen. It has responded by becoming carnivorous to supplement its mineral diet. Flies are lured into the traps by a scent and their bodies digested by enzymes. Nitrogen is then absorbed and circulated within the plant.

- Many tropical plants find transpiration difficult in humid conditions. They respond by developing guttation — the forced exuding of liquid water from special pores in the leaves. This maintains the upward flow of water and minerals from the soil.

Fig. 23.7. Snowdrops in spring.

Fig. 23.8. Hinge joints in cereals.

ADVANCED SUMMARY OF IAA IN PLANTS [H35 I]

The main features of the activity of IAA in plants are summarised as follows:

PRODUCTION

By primary meristems cells in plant stem tip.

INITIATION

Genetic plus synergistic/antagonistic effects of other growth regulators (i.e. other regulators either work with it or against it).

Fig. 23.9. Water storage in cactus.

TRANSPORT

IAA is moved through the plant by *active transport* from cell to cell (some diffusion takes place also, but this is slow). Oxygen is required to help provide energy for transport. Movement is mostly in the parenchyma cells around the

Fig. 23.10. A carnivorous plant — the venus flytrap.

Fig. 23.11. Guttation from Lady's mantle.

vascular bundles and is slower than translocation in the phloem.

SITE OF ACTION

IAA works within the *zones of cell elongation* in roots and stems.

FUNCTION

IAA allows cellulose fibrils in cell walls to loosen and stretch. Increased water intake forms large vacuoles inside the cells. Osmotic forces stretch the walls resulting in cell elongation and growth.

Effects of IAA within the plant

- Cell elongation and growth.
- Apical dominance (see below).
- Parthenocarpy — development of fruits without fertilisation. This occurs in bananas and pineapples and leaves these fruit seedless.
- Development of adventitious roots.
- Uneven distribution of IAA causes stem and root bending — necessary for plant tropisms.

Apical dominance describes the influence of a terminal bud on the lateral buds below it. IAA formed at the terminal bud of the stem (the stem apex) passes down the stem and inhibits the development of the lower, lateral buds. This prevents excessive branching of the stem. If the terminal bud is removed, the lateral buds are no longer inhibited and vigorous branching takes place. Gardeners regularly remove terminal buds to produce a thicker, more branched plant.

Comparing growth regulators with animal hormones

Plant growth regulators are often referred to as *plant hormones* but do not compare well to animal hormones. The term *plant hormones* may best be avoided.

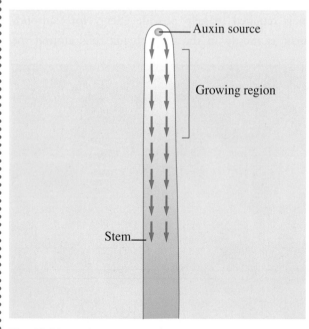

Fig. 23.12. Auxin movement.

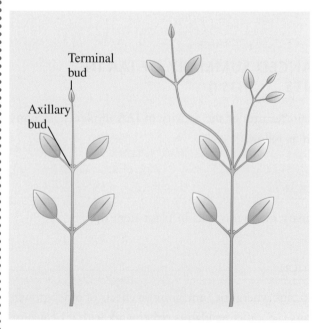

Fig. 23.13. Apical dominance removed.

Table 23.2. Plant growth regulators and animal hormones compared

Plant growth regulators	Animal hormones
Produced from unspecialised cells in certain plant regions	Produced by specific organs (endocrine glands)
Not always transported well — some manufactured 'on site' instead	Transported in blood and lymphatic systems and have specific 'target organs'
Effects are non-specific and determined by concentration and the presence of other substances	Effects are highly specific

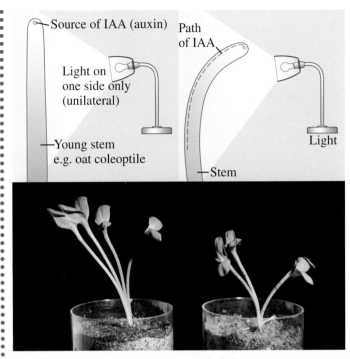

Fig. 23.14. Coleoptile bending towards light.

PHOTOTROPISM EXPLAINED   [H35 II]

Phototropism in the plant stem

The bending of a plant stem towards light is an example of phototropism. This tropism clearly has survival value and ensures maximum available light for the plant leaves. The mechanism for this tropism is traditionally believed to be as follows:

- Light inhibits the manufacture of IAA on the bright side of the stem tip and also causes exporting of IAA to the shaded side.
- More IAA travels down the shaded side of the stem than the bright side.
- The shaded side grows better and curves the stem towards the light.

The above mechanism is presently being critically examined.

- The experiments to support the mechanism were carried out on very young oat coleoptiles (sheaths covering very young stems). These are not necessarily representative of all stems.
- It has been discovered that contaminating fungi and bacteria on the stem can synthesise IAA and so make interpretation of results difficult.
- Experimental results are usually highly variable.

SUMMARY

- Living organisms need to detect changes and respond to them.
- All plants and animals use a chemical messenger or hormonal system to respond to change.
- In addition, higher animals possess sense organs, nervous systems, muscles, bones and an immune system to respond to their environment.
- Plants respond to change by modifying their growth.
- Animals respond to change by modifying their behaviour.
- All plant responses are slow and involve chemical modifications of their growth.
- Plant growth is regulated by both external and internal factors.
- External factors include light, length of the day, gravity and temperature.
- Internal factors include the production of chemicals termed growth regulators.
- When plants are exposed to light from one side only, the stems grow towards the light source. This is phototropism.
- The most important growth regulator in plants is auxin or IAA (indoleacetic acid).

- The movement of IAA is by active transport from cell to cell.
- The effects of IAA include the following:

  - IAA inhibits the development of side branches from lateral buds.
  - IAA stimulates development of adventitious roots.
  - plant cuttings dipped into IAA respond by growing roots quickly.
  - IAA stimulates fruit formation in the absence of fertilisation.

- All plant growth regulators work in combination with one another.
- Some growth regulators are synergistic to each other.
- Other regulators are antagonistic to each other.
- Many plants develop complicated responses to deal with recurring hardships.

EXTENDED SUMMARY

- Uneven distribution of IAA causes stem and root bending — necessary for plant tropisms.
- Plant growth regulators are often referred to as plant hormones but do not compare well to animal hormones.
- Phototropism explained:

  - light inhibits the manufacture of IAA on the bright side of the stem tip and also causes exporting of IAA to the shaded side;
  - more IAA travels down the shaded side of the stem than the bright side;
  - the shaded side grows better and curves the stem towards the light.

KEY WORDS

Sensitivity	The ability to detect change in the environment.
Meristem	A group of plant cells that divides repeatedly by mitosis.
Apical meristems	Found at the extremities (apices) of the stem and root.
Lateral meristems	Found within the vascular bundles.
Tropism	A growth movement of part of a plant in response to an external stimulus.
Phototropism	A tropism in response to light.
Geotropism (gravitropism)	Response to gravity.
Thigmotropism	Response to touch.
Hydrotropism	Response to water.
Chemotropism	Response to certain chemicals.
Aerotropism	Response to free air.
Plagiogeotropism	When lateral roots and branches grow at an angle to gravity.
Nasties	Growth responses of a plant where the direction of the movement is not determined by the direction of the stimulus.
Taxes	Movement of a complete organism or gamete in response to an external stimulus.
Growth regulator	A chemical substance that exerts a degree of control over plant growth.
IAA (indoleacetic acid or auxin)	An important growth regulator in plants.
Apical dominance	When the apex of the main stem inhibits the development of side branches below it.
Adventitious roots	Lateral roots that originate directly from a stem.
Parthenocarps	'Virgin fruits' formed without fertilisation.
2,4-D	A synthetic auxin that stimulates unusual growth.
Synergistic	Working together help each other.
Antagonistic	Having opposing effects.
Guttation	The forced exuding of liquid water from special pores in the leaves.

QUESTIONS

1. Explain what is meant by sensitivity in living organisms. How does sensitivity increase the chances of survival? In what way are plant responses different to animal responses?

2. Explain what meristems are. Name two kinds of meristem and state where they are found. How does plant growth differ from animal growth?

3. Define *tropism*. Give five examples of tropisms and explain the origin of the name of each. State how each tropism benefits the plant. Distinguish between positive and negative tropisms and give one example of each.

4. List the factors that regulate plant growth. What is a growth regulator? Name five growth regulators and state the function of each. Give three reasons why growth regulators are important in industry.

5. The most important growth regulator in plants is *IAA*.

   a. Where is IAA made?
   b. How does it promote plant growth?
   c. How does it move through the plant?
   d. Besides growth, what other effects does it have on the plant?
   e. What is the difference between IAA and 2,4-D?

6. With reference to mandatory activity #20, answer each of the following:

   a. What is the aim of the experiment?
   b. Which solution acts as a control solution?
   c. What is the purpose of the control?
   d. Give two reasons why the experiment is best done in the dark.
   e. Why are ten seeds used in each solution rather than one or two?
   f. What variables should be kept constant during the experiment?
   g. How is the effect of IAA measured?
   h. What result would suggest an inhibitory effect?

7. State four examples of plants responding to adverse external environments

EXTENDED QUESTIONS

8. Explain the term *apical dominance*. Outline how the stem maintains apical dominance during normal growth. What advantage is apical dominance to the plant?

9. Outline how the response of phototropism is most likely to occur in the plant stem. What criticisms are made of this mechanism?

10. Give three reasons why plant growth regulators do not compare well with animal hormones.

OPTIONAL ACTIVITIES

- Use the Internet or other resources to research the famous experiments of Dutch scientist Fritz Went on plant growth regulators. Other famous contributors to this area include Charles Darwin and his son, Francis, and also Peter Boyson-Jensen.

- Grow and maintain a Venus flytrap. Venus flytraps (*Dionaea muscipula*) can be bought at garden centres. Do not over-exercise the trap mechanisms, as the plants may die. Mimosa (originally a tropical weed) may also be bought and will also demonstrate a response to touch.

- Design an experiment to demonstrate phototropism. Use a cardboard shoebox and two petri dishes of germinating mustard seeds. Make sure to include a suitable control.

- Design a poster to show the commercial uses of plant hormones.

- Set up a clinostat to demonstrate geotropism. Ensure that the seeds used have an adequate water supply.

Now test yourself at
www.my-etest.com

Chapter 24
Responses in Humans

Learning objectives

After your study of this chapter, you should be able to:

- describe the anatomy of the human nervous system;
- explain the stimulus–response pathway;
- distinguish between different types of neuron;
- describe neuron structure;
- outline the features of the nerve impulse;
- describe the structure and function of the synapse;
- list the main senses of the body;
- describe the structure and function of the eye or ear;
- explain the major defects of vision or hearing;
- state the parts of the brain and their functions;
- describe a reflex arc;
- define a hormone;
- name the most important hormones and their function;
- illustrate hormone action by reference to thyroxine.

Extended learning objectives

- Summarise the control of thyroxine levels.

INTRODUCTION   [353]

The human nervous system consists of the following parts:

1. a central nervous system or *CNS* (the brain and the spinal cord); and
2. a peripheral nervous system or *PNS* (the *nerves* attached to the brain and spinal cord).

All of this nerve tissue is made from highly specialised cells called *neurons*.

The CNS is linked by the PNS to the tissues and organs of the body. These tissues and organs include *receptors* and *effectors*. Receptors are sensory cells that detect change in the environment. Receptors may be scattered through the body (e.g. pain receptors) or grouped together to form sense organs like the eye or ear. Effectors are capable of producing a response to stimulation and are either muscles (producing movement) or glands (producing secretions).

Changes in the outside environment are detected by the receptors and an *electrical impulse* is sent along the nerves of the PNS to the brain and spinal cord of the CNS. This impulse 'informs' the CNS of an outside change. The CNS may then send an impulse via the PNS to the effectors (muscles and glands) to bring about an appropriate response. This response may be simple (e.g. withdrawing a hand from a hot surface) or very complicated (e.g. talking to someone!).

Generally, the pathway of response to an external stimulus is as follows:

Stimulus → receptors → impulse → PNS
→ CNS → PNS → effectors → response

e.g. in figure 24.1, the pathway of response is:

visual stimulus → visual receptors in the eye → impulse → optic nerve → brain → spinal cord → leg muscles → legs, feet and lower body move

NEURONS

The entire nervous system is made from cells called *neurons* (singular = neuron). Neurons have two important properties:

- *irritability* (they can receive and respond to electrical messages); and
- *conduction* (they can transmit information from one place to another).

Neurons have many shapes and functions but all have three basic parts:

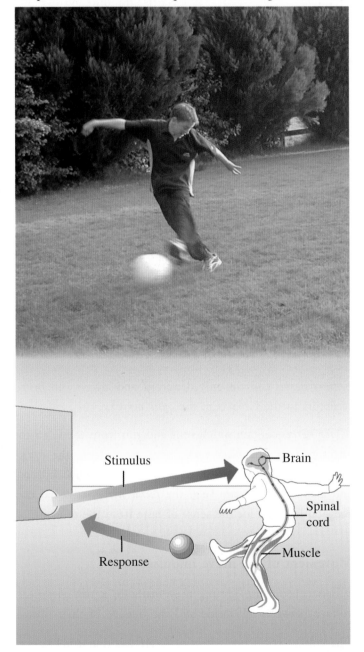

Fig. 24.1. Stimulus–response.

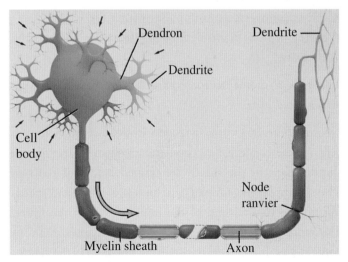

Fig. 24.2. Isolated motor neuron.

- a cell body containing the nucleus;
- a single fibre (dendron) or many fibres (dendrites) carrying impulses *towards* the cell body;
- a single fibre (axon) carrying impulses *away* from the cell body.

Neurons are classified by the number of their fibres:

- multipolar neurons have many fibres extending from their cell bodies;
- bipolar neurons have two fibres; and
- unipolar neurons have one fibre.

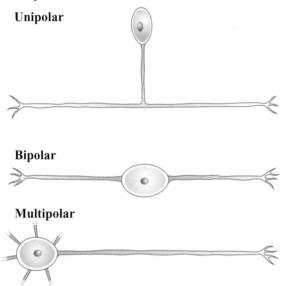

Fig. 24.3. Three shapes of neurons.

Neurons are also classified by their function:

- sensory neurons transmit impulses from receptors towards the CNS;
- relay neurons transmit impulses within the CNS;
- motor neurons transmit impulses from the CNS to the effectors.

The ends of motor neurons can attach to muscle fibres by a *motor end plate.*

Neuron fibres are often wrapped in cells called Schwann cells. These create a fatty insulation known as the myelin sheath. Gaps in the sheath are termed Nodes of Ranvier. The sheath has the advantage of both protecting and speeding up the transmission of the impulses within the fibres. The junctions between neurons are called synapses. Neurons contain tiny bubbles of transmitting chemicals (the neurotransmitter vesicles) to pass impulses across the synapses.

Table 24.1. Structure and function within the neuron

Structural unit of neuron	Function
Dendrites	Form synapses with other cells
Dendron	Carry impulses towards the cell body
Cell body	Contains the nucleus which directs the cell
Axon	Carries impulses away from the cell body
Myelin sheath	Insulates the axon
Schwann cells	Form the myelin sheath
Nodes of Ranvier	Gaps in the insulation which increase impulse speed
Vesicles	Contain neurotransmitter chemicals
Motor end plate	A special synapse with a muscle cell

Nerves

The fibres of neurons (dendrons or axons) are often bundled together and may even share myelin sheaths. These bundles are found in the PNS and are called nerves.

Sensory nerves contain only dendrons and always run from receptors to the CNS (e.g. the *optic nerve*).

Motor nerves contain only axons and run from the CNS to effectors (e.g. the *oculomotor nerve* for moving the eye). Many nerves are *mixed nerves* and contain both dendrons and axons side by side (e.g. the *facial nerve* for facial expression but also for the sense of taste from the tongue).

Movement of the nerve impulse

When neurons are resting, they maintain a tiny electrical voltage between the inside and the outside of their fibres.

The voltage (or *action potential — AP*) is due to a balance of sodium and potassium ions across the neuron membrane.

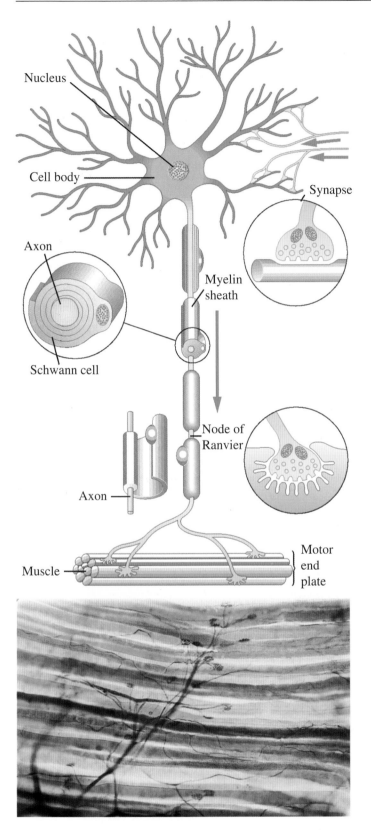

Fig. 24.4. The motor end plate.

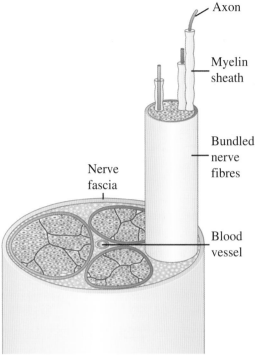

Fig. 24.5. A nerve.

If a neuron is irritated (by an impulse from another neuron or from a receptor cell), this AP is temporarily reversed. The reversal takes place at the site of the irritation and then runs along the entire length of the neuron. The neuron then restores its original balance and rests again.

The resting state of the neuron can be thought of as similar to a long line of dominoes standing on end. If the first domino is knocked over, all of the other dominoes will fall in turn, creating the effect of a movement from one end of the line to the other.

Nerve impulses have some interesting features that can be seen in the falling dominoes:

- The *all-or-nothing effect*. The impulse will travel the entire length of the neuron fibre or it will not travel at all. Once started, it cannot be stopped.
- The *threshold of stimulation*. The initial stimulation must be above a certain value before the impulse begins to travel. Touching the first domino very lightly has no effect.
- The *refractory period*. The neuron fibre needs a short time to recover (about 5 mSec) before it can transmit another impulse. The dominoes must be stood up again before the falling can be repeated.

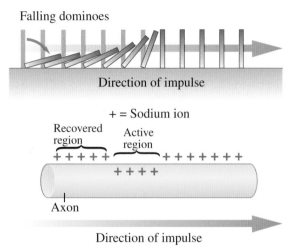

Falling dominoes

Direction of impulse

+ = Sodium ion

Recovered region   Active region

+ + + + +   + + + + + +

+ + + +

Axon

Direction of impulse

Fig. 24.6. Falling dominoes and the + / − impulse across axon membrane.

The speed of the impulse can be very fast (up to 250 mph!) and is quickest when the fibres have a large diameter and are myelinated.

Synapses

Synapses are the joints of the nervous system, the places where nerve cells meet. Synapses occur between the swollen tips (synaptic knobs) of the axon of one neuron and the dendrites of the next neuron. Special synapses called *motor end plates* are found between motor neurons and muscle tissue. The electron microscope shows that neurons do not actually touch one another at the synapse; there is a tiny gap — the *synaptic cleft*.

Transmission of an impulse across the cleft is done by the diffusion of a *neurotransmitter* substance. The most common neurotransmitter found is *acetylcholine*. When an impulse (or action potential) arrives at the synapse (in the presynaptic cell) it stimulates bubbles (vesicles) of acetylcholine to burst and release their contents into the cleft. Acetylcholine diffuses across the cleft and irritates the postsynaptic cell, generating a new action potential. This will start a new impulse. Enzymes in the postsynaptic cell then digest the acetylcholine to prevent its accumulation.

Synapses have many advantages:

- They ensure one-way transmission in the nervous system and prevent chaos.
- They protect against over-stimulation, as they will slow down if overloaded.

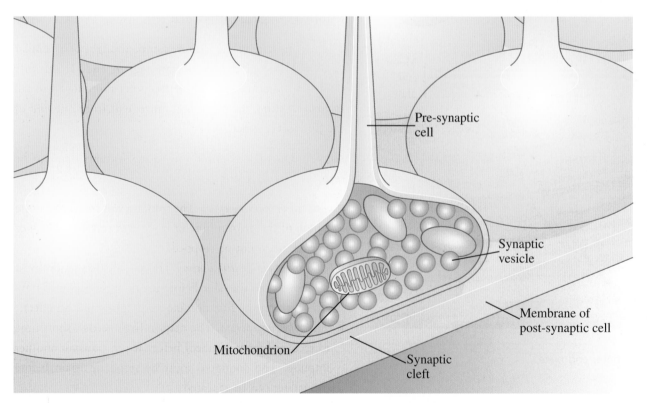

Pre-synaptic cell

Synaptic vesicle

Membrane of post-synaptic cell

Mitochondrion

Synaptic cleft

Fig. 24.7. The synapse.

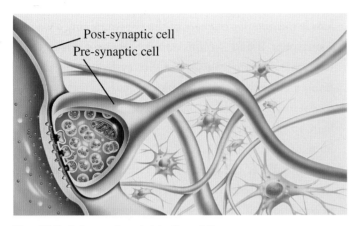

Fig. 24.8. Release of acetylcholine at the synapse.

- Their complicated interconnections allow for learning and memory.
- They ignore low-level stimulations — effectively removing 'background noise' (unwanted but unavoidable stimuli) from the nervous system.

On the other hand:

- Synapses are relatively slow and their number is often minimised by developing long axons and dendrons.
- They are prone to chemical alteration. Hallucinatory drugs, painkillers, anaesthetics and certain poisons can penetrate synapses and alter their function.

THE SENSES

The senses are receptor organs — or *collections of receptor cells.*

All cells are sensitive to change, but receptor cells specialise in detecting certain stimuli and converting them to electrical impulses. Receptor cells are translators (or transducers), converting various forms of energy (heat, light, chemical, kinetic, etc.) into the 'language' of the nervous system — electricity.

Most receptors are grouped together to form sense organs, e.g. the rod and cone cells are found only in the eye. The principal sense organs are: the eye, the ear, the nose, the skin and the tongue (the 'five senses').

All translated data from the senses must be *interpreted* by the brain before it is of any use to the body. How this interpretation is done is one of many enormous mysteries in the study of the nervous system.

N.B.: Students are required to study *either* the *eye* or the *ear*, but not both.

Table 24.2. The receptors

Receptor cell	Location	Energy sensed	Energy converted to
Rod and cone cells	Eye	Light	Electricity
Taste buds	Tongue	Chemical	Electricity
Olfactory buds	Nose	Chemical	Electricity
Hair cells	Cochlea of ear	Sound	Electricity
Hair cells	Vestibular apparatus of ear	Gravitational and kinetic	Electricity
Cells of carotid body	Carotid artery in neck	Chemical (O_2) and kinetic	Electricity
Skin receptors	Skin	Heat	Electricity
		Kinetic (touch, pressure)	Electricity
Stretch receptors	Skeletal muscle	Kinetic	Electricity

THE EYE

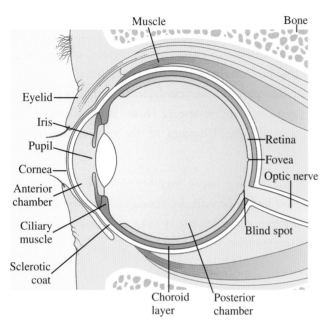

Fig. 24.9. The eye.

The human eyes contribute up to 70% of all sensory data that arrives in the brain. They are precious but well protected by the bony sockets of the skull. The front of each eye is protected by the eyelids and lashes and by an automatic blinking reflex. Tear glands produce tears that lubricate the surface of the eye and digest microorganisms.

The eyeball has three layers:

- *An outer tough sclera* (the 'white' of the eye). This maintains the round shape of the eyeball and has six muscles attached to it to rotate the eye. The front of the sclera is transparent and is called the cornea. The cornea lets light pass into the eye and helps to focus light rays.
- *A black, choroid layer* of nerves and blood vessels. This nourishes the eye and prevents internal reflection by absorbing stray rays of light. The ciliary body and iris are made from the choroid layer. The ciliary body is muscular and attached to the lens by suspensory ligaments. The lens is transparent and elastic and has a biconvex shape. Movements of the ciliary muscle alter the curvature of the lens to suit near or distant viewing. In front of the

lens is the *anterior chamber* of the eye containing a watery, transparent liquid — the *aqueous humour*. Behind the lens, the *posterior chamber* of the eyeball is filled with transparent jelly — the *vitreous humour*.

- *The retina* is a layer of photoreceptor cells and converts light to electricity. Two types of receptors are found in humans: rod cells and cone cells. Cone cells are mostly concentrated at the *fovea* of the retina, the region where vision is most sensitive and accurate. Cone cells are active in conditions of brightness and are used for colour vision. Rod cells are found (with some cone cells) on the rest of the retinal surface. Rods are active in dim light conditions and are used for black/white vision only. Most mammals (including cats, dogs and bulls!) have only black/white (monochrome) vision. Humans are unusual amongst mammals in having full colour vision.

The nerve fibres that carry impulses from the rods and cones to the brain lie on the inner surface of the retina, i.e. between the retina and the outside world. This means that we view the outside world through a fine mesh of neurons! These fibres leave the eye at the blind spot and unite to form the optic nerve. The blind spot has no rods or cones and is not sensitive to light.

Hold the book at arm's length, close your left eye and stare at the spot. Bring the book slowly towards you and note when the cross disappears and reappears. Repeat with both eyes open.

Fig. 24.10. Blind spot investigation.

Table 24.3. Summary of the functions of the parts of the eye

Structural unit of the eye	Function
Cornea	Focuses light and protects the eye
Anterior chamber	Focuses light
Iris	Adjusts pupil diameter
Pupil	Controls amount of light entering the eye
Lens	Focuses light
Suspensory ligaments	Adjust lens curvature
Ciliary muscle	Adjusts lens curvature
Posterior chamber	Focuses light and maintains eye shape
Sclerotic coat	Protects and covers the eye
Choroid layer	Contains blood vessels and absorbs stray light rays
Retina	Converts light to electrical impulses
Fovea	Most sensitive part of the retina
Blind spot	Light insensitive region
Optic nerve	Conducts electrical impulses to the brain

Colour vision and colour deficiency

Three types of cone cell are found in the human retina — each sensitive to one of the three primary colours: red, blue and green. The mechanism of colour vision is not fully understood but the cone cells probably measure the proportions of red, blue and green light in any observed colour and send appropriate messages to the brain. White light stimulates all three types of cone cell equally. Colour defi-

ciency ('colour blindness') in humans occurs in 8% of all men (but only in 0.4% of all women). Complete absence of colour vision is extremely rare. Much more common is the condition where all three pigments are present but are found with an incorrect intensity. This commonly produces red–green colour deficiency. Most colour-deficient people are completely ignorant of their condition until tested. Colour deficiency is a genetic, sex-linked disease. Like haemophilia, it tends to be carried by females and suffered by males.

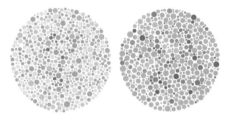

Fig. 24.11. Ishihara test for colour blindness. Which is the control?

Accommodation

This is the changing of the curvature of the lens to focus on either near or distant objects.

Incoming rays of light are bent (refracted) by the curved surfaces of the cornea and lens and brought to a sharp focus

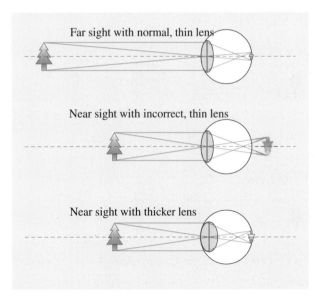

Fig. 24.12. Accommodation.

on the retina. Rays of light from near objects are strongly diverging and a strong, fat lens is needed to bring them to a focus. This is achieved by contracting the ciliary muscle and relaxing the suspensory ligaments. Rays of light from more distant objects are either weakly diverging or almost parallel and need less bending. The ciliary muscle relaxes, the ligaments tighten and the lens takes on a slimmer shape.

Corrective measures for vision defects

Near-sightedness and far-sightedness are two common *refractive errors* of the eye.

NEAR-SIGHTEDNESS OR MYOPIA

This is a very common condition, which affects about 30% of the population.

Symptoms: Near objects are seen clearly, but distant objects (e.g. blackboards, films, TV, etc.) are blurred.

Causes: Either the eyeball is too long or the lens (or cornea) is too curved for the distant, parallel light rays. The condition may be hereditary but is probably not caused by too much reading, poor diet or using dim light.

Correction: Glasses (or contact lenses) with *concave* lenses will alter the path of the incoming light rays to stop them focussing too soon. Laser surgery is available to change the curvature of the cornea but many eye specialists are worried about side effects concerning glare and night vision. In Britain, at the time of writing, no one who has had laser surgery for myopia is permitted to join the police or the fire services, or to train to be a pilot.

FAR-SIGHTEDNESS OR HYPEROPIA

Symptoms: Distant objects are seen clearly but near objects (newspapers etc.) are blurred.

Causes: Either the eyeball is too short or the lens (or cornea) has too little curvature for the diverging rays from a near object.

Correction: Glasses (or contact lenses) with *convex* lenses will decrease the divergence of the incoming light rays.

OTHER EYE CONDITIONS

Astigmatism is when the cornea has different curvatures in different directions — for example it can become barrel-shaped. Vision can be blurred at all distances and the patient can have eyestrain and poor concentration. The condition is treated with suitable glasses or contact lenses. A slight degree of astigmatism is found in almost everyone.

Lazy Eye is due to poor central vision in one eye only. It is unrelated to health problems and not corrected with lenses. It usually develops before the age of six. Treatment is by

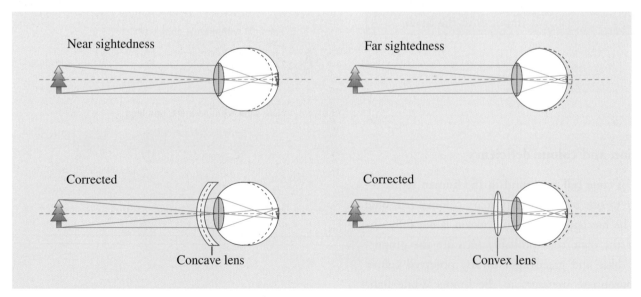

Fig. 24.13. Near-sightedness and far-sightedness corrected.

eye exercises (vision therapy) and eye patches. Early diagnosis will lead to a full recovery, otherwise treatment is difficult. The condition never corrects itself.

20/20 vision is a term used to describe perfect visual sharpness. It means that someone can see at 20 feet what should be seen at that distance. 20/50 vision would mean that you would have to be at 20 feet to see what you should see at 50 feet. 20/20 is not necessarily perfect eyesight; it takes no account of colour vision, eye coordination, peripheral vision or sense of depth.

Iris responses

In dim conditions, radial muscle fibres in the iris contract (and circular muscle fibres relax). This increases the diam-

eter of the pupil and admits more light to the eye to aid vision. In bright conditions, circular muscle fibres contract (and radial muscle fibres relax) and decrease the diameter of the pupil, lessening the amount of light entering the eye. Iris responses are an example of *reflex action* — an automatic response by the nervous system to a stimulus.

Many drugs, including alcohol and atropine, block the contraction of the circular muscle fibres and leave the eyes temporarily dilated.

Two eyes are better than one

Humans have stereoscopic vision — the visual fields of their two eyes overlap and each eye has a slightly different viewpoint of any object. The brain can combine these two slightly different images to give a 3-D impression of the object and a sense of depth and distance. A person with sight in one eye only will create a flat, 2-D image in their brain (like a photograph) and has difficulty judging distances.

THE EAR

The ear is the organ of hearing and also the organ of balance. It is divided into three parts: the outer ear, the middle ear and the inner ear.

Iris in bright light

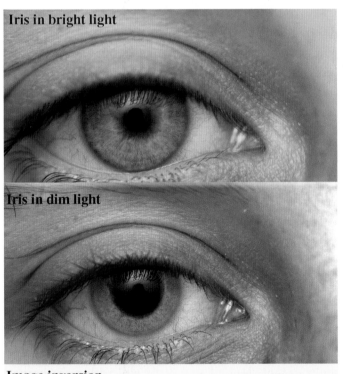

Iris in dim light

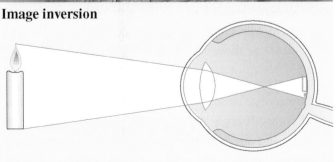

Image inversion

Fig. 24.14. Iris responding to light.

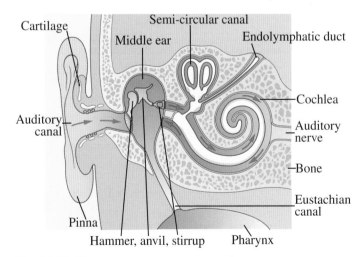

Fig. 24.15. The ear.

The **outer ear** includes the visible parts of the ear. The pinna is supported by cartilage and designed to collect sound waves, directing them through the auditory canal to the eardrum. The eardrum is a thin but strong sheet of connective tissue stretched across the base of the auditory canal.

The **middle ear** is an air-filled chamber containing the three *ear ossicles* or bones: the hammer, the anvil and the stirrup. The hammer is attached to the inner surface of the eardrum and the stirrup presses on the oval window of the cochlea. The Eustachian canal communicates between the middle ear and the pharynx. The canal is normally closed but opens with swallowing or yawning and allows movement of air between the middle ear chamber and the outside. This

ensures a balance of air pressures on both sides of the eardrum.

The **inner ear** is completely encased in the bones of the skull. It consists of the cochlea, the semicircular canals, the saccule and the utricle. The *cochlea* is a snail-shaped, coiled tube containing fluid, membranes and sensory cells that respond to vibrations. The semicircular canals, saccule and utricle are also fluid-filled and contain many sensory receptors that respond to changes in position or motion. There are three semicircular canals, each placed at right angles to the other two to respond to sudden changes in motion in any of three dimensions. The saccule and utricle detect the direction of gravity and give a sense of 'which way is up' at all times.

The mechanism of hearing

All sound originates from a vibrating source, e.g. hand clapping, movement of strings on a guitar, movement of vocal cords, etc. The speed of the vibration is termed its frequency and is measured in units of Hertz (Hz) (one Hertz means one vibration per second). The human cochlea has a hearing range of about 20 to 20,000 Hz, that is, it can respond to vibrations within this range. Vibrations outside this range are not detected.

(Dogs can detect vibrations up to 50 kHz and so hear many sounds that humans cannot. Bats transmit high-energy sounds of 100 kHz frequencies for echolocation — also undetected by humans. Ultrasound scanning in maternity hospitals uses 200 kHz frequencies that are unheard by mother, doctor or baby.

The upper end of the human hearing range tends to degenerate with age. Children can hear high frequency sounds that adults cannot. Musical sounds lie well within the hearing range — middle C has a frequency of 256 Hz and sounds below 40 Hz or above 10,000 Hz are not considered musical at all.)

Vibrations of a sound source produce ripples of vibration or sound waves through the air. These waves are gathered by the pinna and directed to the eardrum. The eardrum vibrates in response to the waves and moves the three ear ossicles. These tiny bones act as an amplifier: a small movement of

Table 24.4. Summary of the functions of the parts of the ear

Structural unit of the ear	Function
Pinna	Collects sound
Auditory canal	Directs sound to the eardrum
Cartilage	Supports the pinna
Hairs and wax glands	Trap and kill bacteria
Eardrum	Passes vibrations to the ear ossicles
Hammer, anvil and stirrup	Amplify and pass on vibrations to the cochlea
Eustachian canal	Equalises air pressures on either side of eardrum
Oval window	Passes vibrations into the cochlea
Cochlea	Converts vibrations into electrical impulses
Vestibular apparatus	Gathers information on motion and gravity — for balance
Auditory nerve	Conducts electrical impulses to the brain

the hammer bone generates a large movement of the stirrup bone which can make the sound up to 20 times louder that it originally was. The stirrup passes this amplified vibration through the oval window and into the fluid of the cochlea. Vibrations of this fluid stimulate the cochlear membranes and receptors to send electrical impulses along the auditory nerve to the hearing centres of the brain.

Corrective measures for hearing defects

There are two types of hearing loss:

- *conductive* — due to disorders in the outer or middle ear;
- *sensorineural* — due to disorders in the inner ear.

A *conductive hearing loss* may be due to a simple obstruction of the ear canal with wax or a foreign body, or a problem with the mobility of the eardrum or the three ossicles. Infections (arriving in the middle ear via the Eustachian canal) can cause stretching or rupture of the eardrum, or may prevent the free movement of the ear ossicles. All ear infections have to be taken very seriously; infection spreading to the cochlea can cause permanent damage to the eardrum or to the cochlea.

A *sensorineural hearing loss* may be due to disease of the membranes and receptors within the cochlea or due to damage to the auditory nerve. One of the most common causes of sensorineural loss is *exposure to excessive noise levels* — in the work environment or from audio equipment at concerts. This damage tends to be slow to accumulate but eventually serious and permanent.

An audiogram or hearing test can readily differentiate between the two types of hearing loss, and determine the degree of the loss.

Hearing aids can correct many hearing difficulties. They are miniaturised amplifiers designed to fit discretely, together with their power supply, within the auditory canal. They do not amplify all sounds, only those ones that the ear is less sensitive to. An audiologist will conduct an audiogram to assess which frequencies of sound may need amplification, then design the hearing aid accordingly.

A *cochlear implant* is a small electronic device that provides a sense of sound to children and adults who have severe hearing loss and who cannot hear or understand speech with hearing aids. While hearing aids make certain sounds louder and clearer, cochlear implants provide useful sound by directly stimulating undamaged nerve fibres in the cochlea.

A cochlear implant consists of three parts: a *receiver*, a *headpiece*, and a *speech processor*.

The *receiver* is the part that is implanted in the cochlea. It looks like a tiny disc about 1 cm in diameter. During delicate surgery, it is placed under the skin behind one ear, and a wire leading from the receiver to an electrode is placed in the fluid of the cochlea in the inner ear.

The *headpiece* is worn just behind the ear. It contains a microphone to pick up sound in the environment and also a transmitter to send the sound to the implanted receiver. The microphone and the transmitter are placed on the head behind the ear and held in place over the implanted receiver by tiny magnets. The *speech processor*, which amplifies the sounds picked up by the microphone, is worn on the body, either behind the ear or on a belt.

The system then works as follows:

- The microphone detects sounds in the patient's environment.
- The sound is sent to the speech processor.
- The speech processor transmits a special signal to the implanted receiver.
- The receiver passes the signal on to the fluid in the cochlea.
- The cochlea passes the information on to the brain.

Ten ways to recognise hearing loss

The following questions are used by the US National Institute on Deafness to help you determine if you need to have your hearing evaluated by a medical professional:

- Do you have a problem hearing over the phone?
- Do you have trouble following the conversation when two or more people are talking at the same time?
- Do people complain that you turn the TV volume up too high?
- Do you have to strain to understand conversation?
- Do you have trouble hearing in a noisy background?
- Do you find yourself asking people to repeat themselves?
- Do many people you talk to seem to mumble (or not speak clearly)?

- Do you misunderstand what others are saying and respond inappropriately?
- Do you have trouble understanding the speech of women and children?
- Do people get annoyed because you misunderstand what they say?

If you answered 'yes' to three or more of these questions, you may want to see an *otorhinolaryngologist* (an ear, nose and throat specialist) or an audiologist for a hearing evaluation.

THE SKIN

The skin is the largest (and most obvious) organ of the human body. Its structure is described in Chapter 22 where it is dealt with because of its role as an excretory organ.

The functions of the skin include:

- protection;
- sensation;
- excretion;
- production of vitamin D;
- temperature regulation.

The skin is sensitive to heat, cold, touch, pressure and pain. It contains receptors and bare nerve endings located just under the epidermis. These are sensitive to various stimuli of temperature and pressure. The receptors are not scattered evenly throughout the skin but concentrated at the fingertips and lips.

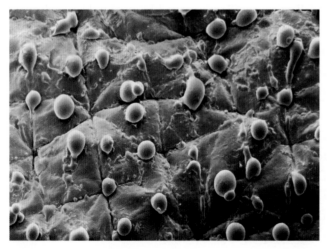

Fig. 24.16. Sweat droplets on the skin.

THE CENTRAL NERVOUS SYSTEM — BRAIN AND SPINAL CORD

We have already mentioned that the central nervous system (CNS) receives information from the senses of the body and can send appropriate responses to the muscles and glands. It can also store information for use at a later time and so modify the body's behaviour in the light of past events.

Almost all of this complicated neurological activity is performed by the brain; the spinal cord being relegated to performing simple reflexes and conveying impulses to and from the brain.

The brain and spinal cord are protected by:

- the bones of the skull and spine;
- three membranes — *the meninges* — lying on the surface of the CNS and enclosing watery cerebrospinal fluid;
- a blood/brain barrier — preventing many chemicals from leaving the capillaries and soaking directly into the delicate brain tissue.

Infection of the membranes is termed *meningitis*. Spinal meningitis is an infection of the membranes in the region of the spinal cord.

The Brain

The brain develops from the neural tube of the very young human embryo and initially is divided into three regions: forebrain, midbrain and hindbrain. As the embryo grows, the forebrain and hindbrain dominate the midbrain and conceal it.

In the adult human, the forebrain develops into the pituitary gland, the thalamus and hypothalamus, the pineal body and the huge cerebral hemispheres (or cerebrum). The midbrain becomes a small region concerned mostly with eye movements and the hindbrain forms the cerebellum and medulla oblongata.

The Spinal Cord

The spinal cord develops from the neural tube of the embryo and is enclosed within the vertebrae of the spine. It is enclosed and protected by the same membranes as the brain — the *meninges*.

Table 24.5. Regions of the brain

Brain region in embryo	Structures in adult brain	Function
Forebrain	Cerebrum	Higher mental activities such as voluntary movement, thought, abstraction, problem solving, language, musical skills, numeracy, processing sensory data.
	Olfactory lobes	Concerned with the sense of smell
	Pineal body	Controls sleep/wake cycle
	Thalamus	Gateway to the cerebrum for data and also the centre of emotions
	Hypothalamus	Monitors the body's internal environment. Controls hunger, thirst, body temperature, assists hormonal function of the pituitary
	Pituitary gland	Secretes hormones and regulates hormonal function through the body
Midbrain	Optic lobes	Control eye movements
Hindbrain	Cerebellum	Controls balance and coordination
	Pons	A 'bridge' of nerve fibres connecting the upper brain with the medulla
	Medulla oblongata	The 'brain stem' — regulates involuntary activity such as heartbeat, peristalsis, breathing, blood pressure, sneezing, coughing, vomiting, salivating, etc.

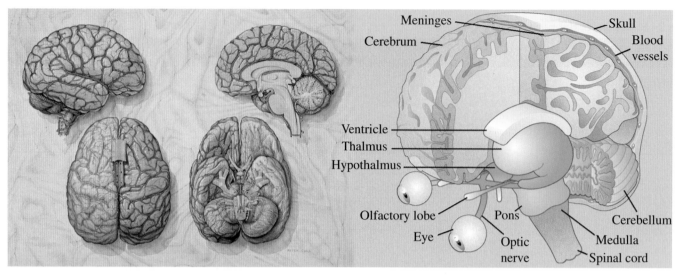

Fig. 24.17. The human brain.

The spinal cord has 31 pairs of spinal nerves attached to it, emerging from between the vertebrae. Each nerve is attached to the cord by two roots: a dorsal root and a ventral root. Within the cord is the tiny *central canal* containing cerebro-spinal fluid (CSF). CSF flows continuously through and around both the brain and spinal cord. The hollowness of the central nervous system is a remnant of the hollow neural tube of the embryo.

The inside of the spinal cord is grey and contains cell bodies and synapses. The outside of the cord is white and made from myelinated nerve tissue. (The brain is grey on the out-side and white on the inside!).

THE PERIPHERAL NERVOUS SYSTEM

The PNS contains nerve fibres — long threads containing axons and dendrons of the neurons. There are no cell bodies within the PNS; all cell bodies lie within the CNS tissue or within nerve ganglia (nerve swellings).

Spinal reflexes

A *reflex* is an automatic response to an external stimulus. Coughing, pupil movements, blinking, salivating and the knee-jerk are *simple reflexes* that do not have to be learned. Other reflexes have to be learned and are termed *conditioned reflexes*. They include such reflexes as increased salivation on hearing the clatter of dinner plates. Simple reflexes involve an arrangement of neurons called a reflex arc. The connec-

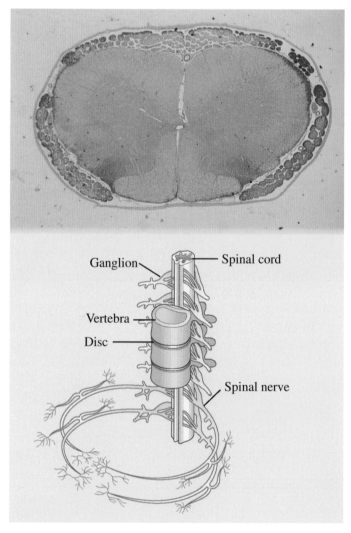

Fig. 24.18. The spinal cord in section.

tions of the arc usually lie within the spinal cord and the arc may not involve the brain, thus ensuring a quicker response.

Most simple arcs involve a minimum of three neurons:

1. a sensory neuron entering the spinal cord through the dorsal root;
2. a relay neuron within the grey matter of the cord; and
3. a motor neuron leaving the cord by the ventral root.

A few reflexes involve only two neurons; sensory and connecting.

One example of a reflex is the knee-jerk reflex:

- the patellar tendon is stretched by a sharp tap;
- stretch receptors in the muscle are stimulated;
- an electrical impulse travels along the sensory neuron to the spinal cord in the waist;
- the impulse enters the cord through the dorsal root and crosses the synapse in the grey matter;
- the impulse continues along the motor neuron leaving the cord by the ventral root;
- the impulse arrives at the motor end plate and stimulates the muscle to contract.

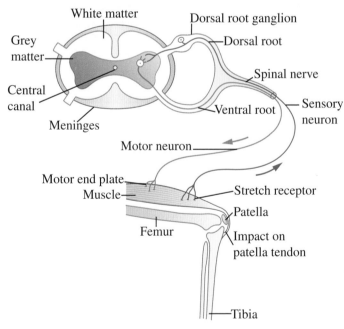

Fig. 24.19. Reflex arc within the spinal cord.

N.B.

- All synapses lie within the grey matter of the cord.

- The dorsal root ganglion contains the cell bodies of the unipolar sensory neurons.
- The brain is generally not involved — the 'reply' is automatic.
- The knee-jerk reflex is important for maintaining balance and posture. Any sagging or sudden movement results in an automatic muscle tightening.

Almost all reflexes involve additional sensory and motor neurons and are sometimes overridden by the brain, e.g. very hot food is not always instantly released by the hand. The brain is always informed of the reflex activity, e.g. the touch of the knee tap is 'felt' during the experiment.

Reflexes have great *survival value* — they obviously increase protection against harmful circumstances and the automatic reply has very little delay.

PARKINSON'S DISEASE

History

The disease is referred to in the Bible but was only first described clinically in 1817 by the London doctor, James Parkinson in his essay on 'the Shaking Palsy' or *paralysis agitans*. The disease was renamed Parkinson's Disease in 1869.

The disease

Parkinson's disease is a progressive neurological disorder that affects the control of voluntary movement. It affects 1.6% of people over the age of 65.

The cause

The cause of the disease is unknown but stems from a deficiency of the chemical dopamine in the brain. Dopamine is necessary to initiate and control voluntary movements. The disease is not considered genetic but minor abnormalities of chromosome #4 occur in many patients.

The symptoms

The three main symptoms are: *tremor* of the arms and hands and rest; *muscle rigidity*; and *slowness of movement*. Consequences of slowness are stooped posture, drooling of saliva and a shuffling walk. No two patients may have the same combination of symptoms and the difficulties of any patient can change by the hour. Patients describe themselves as being in an 'on' or 'off' condition, depending on the severity of their muscle rigidity.

Social implications

Communication skills are greatly impaired. Speech becomes laboured and monotonous and facial expression may reduce to give a 'mask-like face'. Handwriting is altered and less legible. People in contact with the patient may falsely assume poor intelligence and lack of cooperation on their part whereas in fact almost all patients retain their intellectual abilities throughout their physical disability. Patients suffer from lack of social contact, boredom and depression.

Treatment

The disease is considered progressive and incurable. Treatment is mostly by administering a mixture of drugs designed to cross the blood/brain barrier and replace missing dopamine. Long-term use of these drugs can give many unwanted side effects (including vomiting, nausea, hallucinations and uncommanded movements). Surgical treatment, originally abandoned, is now being reviewed. The highly controversial use of foetal brain tissue implants as a source of natural dopamine has also been explored.

THE ENDOCRINE SYSTEM

Hormones are *chemical messengers* that travel in the *bloodstream*. They are secreted by ductless or *endocrine* glands and travel throughout the body. They have a *slow but sustained* effect on specific *target organs*. Most hormones are made from proteins.

Endocrine means *inward secreting*. This refers to the fact that these glands do not have tubes or ducts to deliver their secretions. Instead they pass their secretions directly into blood

vessels within themselves. *Exocrine* (*eccrine*) glands, such as sweat glands and salivary glands, deliver their secretions through ducts.

Both the nervous system and the endocrine system are involved in communication but while nerves are more suited to sudden, short-lived activity, hormones suit slow, long-term responses.

Table 24.6. Nervous system and endocrine system compared

Nervous system	Endocrine system
Rapid transmission	Slow transmission
Good for short-term effects	Good for long-term effects
Impulses travel along specific nerve pathways	Hormones travel indiscriminately in the blood
Communication is electrical and chemical	Communication is chemical only
Increased frequency gives extra signal strength	Increased concentration gives extra signal strength
Stimulates muscle contraction or gland secretion only	Stimulates changes in metabolism

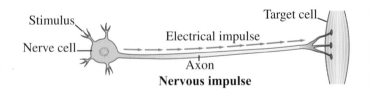

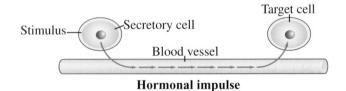

Fig. 24.20. Nervous and hormonal impulses.

Table 24.7. Location and function of hormonal glands

Gland	Location	Hormone secreted	Function
Thyroid	In the neck near the larynx	Thyroxine	Stimulates the basal metabolic rate (BMR)[1]
Parathyroids	Behind the thyroid	Parathyroid hormone	Regulates calcium metabolism
Adrenals	On top of the kidneys	Adrenaline (from medulla)	Stimulates 'fight or flight' response[2]
		Cortisol (from cortex)	Regulates glucose metabolism
Islets of Langerhans	In the pancreas	Insulin	Converts glucose to glycogen and so lowers blood glucose levels[3]
Ovaries	Lower abdomen	Oestrogen	Repairs inner lining of womb, stimulates secondary sexual development.
		Progesterone	Stimulates ovulation, maintains lining of the womb
Testes	In the scrotum	Testosterone	Stimulates secondary sexual development
Anterior pituitary	Below the hypothalamus of the brain	Thyroid stimulating hormone (TSH)	Stimulates thyroid production
		Follicle stimulating hormone (FSH)	Stimulates follicle development and oestrogen production in the ovaries. Stimulates sperm production in males
		Luteinising hormone (LH)	Stimulates ovulation and growth of the corpus luteum. Stimulates testosterone production in males
		Prolactin	Stimulates milk production by breast tissue
		Growth hormone	Stimulates growth

| Posterior pituitary | Below the hypothalamus of the brain | Antidiuretic hormone (ADH) | Stimulates water retention in the kidneys |
| | | Oxytocin | Stimulates contractions of the uterus |

THYROXINE AND THE THYROID GLAND

The thyroid gland lies in the front of the neck, just below the larynx and in front of the trachea. It uses iodine and the amino acid, tyrosine, to manufacture two iodine-containing hormones, one of which is thyroxine. The thyroid gland absorbs iodine from the bloodstream.

Thyroxine causes an increase in all tissue metabolism in all parts of the body and so controls the basal metabolic rate (BMR). It particularly stimulates respiration, protein synthesis, growth in children and glucose metabolism.

An overactive thyroid gland (*hyperthyroidism*) results in all metabolic reactions proceeding at too fast a rate. Symptoms include a raised heart rate, raised body temperature, sweating, weight loss, anxiety, and restlessness. Treatment is by surgical removal of a measured portion of the gland.

An underactive thyroid gland (*hypothyroidism*) results in the slowing of the metabolic reactions. The consequences of this very much depend on the age of the patient. In adults, symptoms include a slow heart rate, a fall in body temperature, weight gain, listlessness, lethargy, leathery skin and hair loss. The condition is known as *myxoedema*. Thyroid hormone tablets can be taken by mouth (unlike insulin) and the patient can expect to make a full recovery. Iodine deficiency in the diet will mimic an underactive gland.

In young children, lack of thyroxine will result in complete physical and mental retardation — a condition termed *cretinism*. Treatment is as for adults, but the condition is difficult to reverse if there is any delay. In particular, brain development can be severely impaired. Very young babies do not suffer at first, as they have received thyroxine from their mothers during pregnancy.

Hypothyroidism is much more common than hyperthyroidism.

A swelling of the thyroid is termed *goitre*. This can be due to an underactive gland, an overactive gland, a tumour or a lack of iodine in the diet.

Examples of the uses of hormone supplements in medicine

1. GROWTH HORMONE THERAPY

Human growth hormone (HGH) is a protein-based hormone made by the pituitary gland. It is necessary for normal growth in children. It is sometimes given as a supplement for the long-term therapy of children who have a growth failure. The hormone is given by injection three times a week over a period of many years until full growth is reached. The dosage is according to body weight and is monitored by regular blood tests and bone age measurements.

---

[1] BMR describes the rate at which the body carries out its metabolic activities while at rest.

[2] Adrenaline prepares the body to deal with emergencies (whether physical or mental). Its effects include converting glycogen to glucose and raising blood glucose levels, dilating the bronchioles of the lungs for deeper breathing, increasing heartbeat and blood pressure, dilating the pupil of the eyes, making hair stand on end, reducing blood flow to the alimentary canal. It gives an 'edge' to the body's performance but will leave you very tired afterwards.

[3] Failure to make insulin results in the condition of diabetes. Treatment is by injecting insulin as needed and controlling carbohydrates in the diet. Insulin must be injected directly into the blood as it is quickly digested and destroyed if swallowed.

2. HYPOTHYROIDISM (SEE ABOVE)

Patients with mild to severe hypothyroidism are treated with thyroid supplement. Diagnosis is by measuring the levels of thyroxine in the blood and comparing them to the levels of TSH, the pituitary hormone that normally controls thyroxine levels. A low level of thyroxine with a high level of TSH confirms thyroid failure. Treatment is by thyroid supplement. Animal thyroxine (T3) has been given to patients up to recently but is a little unpredictable in its effects. It is now replaced by synthetic thyroxine (T4) (see Chapter 15). Very little thyroxine is needed for treatment, but thyroid failure is an ongoing process and yearly blood tests are needed to avoid the dose becoming too low.

FEEDBACK MECHANISM OF HORMONAL CONTROL   [H35 II]

Thyroxine and the thyroid gland

CONTROL OF THYROID ACTIVITY

The secretion of thyroxine is stimulated by a pituitary hormone called TSH (the thyroid-stimulating hormone). The secretion of TSH is, in turn, inhibited by high levels of thyroxine — an example of *negative feedback control.*

Suppose the level of thyroxine in the bloodstream is low:

- the pituitary secretes TSH into the blood;
- TSH travels to the thyroid and stimulates thyroxine production;
- the level of thyroxine in the blood rises;
- this inhibits the production of TSH by the pituitary;
- less TSH means thyroid production decreases;
- secretion of TSH is no longer inhibited, etc.

This negative-feedback control mechanism means that the level of thyroxine in the blood does not change very much overall. Fairly equal levels of both TSH and thyroxine in the blood at any time is considered a sign of normal thyroid function, a large difference indicates an abnormality.

Most other hormone levels are controlled by the same mechanism.

The principle of negative feedback control is illustrated in the control of the temperature of a tropical fish tank or electric water bath. This method is illustrated in Chapter 21, section [341].

SUMMARY

- The human nervous system consists of:

  - a central nervous system or CNS (the brain and the spinal cord);
  - a peripheral nervous system or PNS (the nerves attached to the brain and spinal cord).

- *The entire nervous system* is made from highly specialised cells called neurons.
- *The pathway of response* to an external stimulus is as follows:

  Stimulus → receptors → impulse → PNS → CNS → PNS → effectors → response

- *Neurons all have three basic parts:*

  - a cell body containing the nucleus;
  - a single fibre (dendron) or many fibres (dendrites) carrying impulses towards the cell body;
  - a single fibre (axon) carrying impulses away from the cell body.

- *Sensory neurons* transmit impulses from receptors towards the CNS.
- *Relay neurons* transmit impulses within the CNS.
- *Motor neurons* transmit impulses from the CNS to the effectors.
- *Resting neurons maintain a tiny electrical voltage* between the inside and the outside of their fibres.
- *This voltage* (or *action potential — AP*) is due to a balance of sodium and potassium ions across the neuron membrane.
- *Irritation temporarily reverses the AP*. The reversal runs along the entire length of the neuron.
- *Transmission of an impulse across a cleft* is done by the diffusion of a neurotransmitter substance.
- *Receptor cells specialise in detecting certain stimuli* and converting them to electrical impulses.
- *The human eyes contribute up to 70%* of all sensory data that arrives in the brain.
- *Near-sightedness* is corrected by a suitable concave lens.

- *Far-sightedness* is corrected by a suitable convex lens.
- *In dim conditions,* the pupils dilate and admit more light to the eye to aid vision.
- *In bright conditions,* the pupils constrict, lessening the amount of light entering the eye.
- *Humans have stereoscopic vision.*
- *The ear is the organ of hearing* and also the organ of balance.
- *The ear is divided into three parts*: the outer ear; the middle ear; and the inner ear.
- *All sound* originates from a vibrating source.
- *There are two types of hearing loss*:

  – conductive — due to disorders in the outer or middle ear;
  – sensorineural — due to disorders in the inner ear.

- *Sound produces vibrations of fluid within the cochlea.* These stimulate the cochlear membranes and receptors to send electrical impulses along the auditory nerve to the hearing centres of the brain.
- *Hearing aids* can correct many hearing difficulties.
- *A cochlear implant* provides a sense of sound to children and adults who have severe hearing loss.
- *The skin is sensitive* to heat, cold, touch, pressure and pain.
- *The brain and spinal cord are protected by*:

  – the bones of the skull and spine;
  – the meninges;
  – a blood/brain barrier.

- *The PNS contains nerve fibres.*
- *Most simple reflex arcs* involve a minimum of three neurons: a sensory neuron entering the spinal cord through the dorsal root; a relay neuron within the grey matter of the cord; and a motor neuron leaving the cord by the ventral root.
- *While nerves are more suited* to sudden, short-lived activity, hormones suit slow, long-term responses.
- *Thyroxine* controls the basal metabolic rate (BMR).
- *An overactive thyroid gland* (hyperthyroidism) results in all metabolic reactions proceeding at too fast a rate.
- *An underactive thyroid gland* (hypothyroidism) results in the slowing of the metabolic reactions.

EXTENDED SUMMARY

- *The secretion of thyroxine* is stimulated by a pituitary hormone — TSH.
- *High levels of thyroxine* in turn, inhibit the secretion of TSH.
- *This negative feedback control mechanism* means that the level of thyroxine in the blood does not change much overall.

KEY WORDS

CNS	Central nervous system (the brain and the spinal cord).
PNS	Peripheral nervous system (the nerves attached to the brain and spinal cord).
Receptors	Sensory cells that detect change in the environment.
Effectors	Are capable of producing a response to stimulation.
Irritability	The ability to receive and respond to electrical messages.
Conduction	The ability to transmit information from one place to another.
Neurons	Nerve cells.
Schwann cells	Form a fatty insulation around neurons.
Myelin sheath	Completes the fatty insulation around neurons.
Nodes of Ranvier	Gaps in the myelin sheath.
Nerves	Bundles of nerve fibres.
Action potential (*AP*)	A tiny electrical voltage between the inside and the outside of nerve fibres.
Synapses	Where nerve cells meet.
Synaptic cleft	Microscopic gap within a synapse.
Acetylcholine	The most common neurotransmitter.
Senses	Collections of receptor cells.
Sclera	The 'white' of the eye.

Choroid layer	A layer of nerves and blood vessels within the eye.
Retina	A layer of photoreceptor cells at the back of the eye.
Accommodation	The changing of the curvature of the lens to focus on either near or distant objects.
Myopia	Near-sightedness.
Hyperopia	Far-sightedness.
Astigmatism	When the cornea has different curvatures in different directions.
Ear ossicles	Tiny bones within the ear — the hammer, the anvil and the stirrup.
Eustachian canal	Communicates between the middle ear and the pharynx.
Cochlea	A snail-shaped, coiled tube containing fluid, membranes and sensory cells that respond to vibrations.
Cochlear implant	A small electronic device that provides a sense of sound.
Meninges	Three membranes lying on the surface of the CNS.
Cerebrospinal fluid	A watery fluid surrounding and within the brain and spinal cord.
Reflex	An automatic response to an external stimulus.
Hormones	Chemical messengers that travel in the bloodstream.
Endocrine	Inward secreting.
Exocrine (eccrine) glands	Deliver their secretions through ducts.
Hyperthyroidism	Condition due to an overactive thyroid gland.
Hypothyroidism	Condition due to an underactive thyroid gland.
Myxoedema	Condition due to low levels of thyroxine in adults.
Cretinism	Condition due to low levels of thyroxine in children.

Goitre	A swelling of the thyroid gland.

EXTENDED KEY WORDS

TSH	The thyroid-stimulating hormone.

QUESTIONS

1. What do the letters CNS and PNS stand for? Name the parts of the CNS and the PNS.

2. What is a stimulus–response pathway? List the parts of the pathway in the case of accidentally touching something hot with your fingers.

3. What is a neuron? What are the basic parts of all neurons? What are the three types of neuron with regard to their function? Name the three shapes of neuron.
   Explain the difference between a neuron and a 'nerve'.

4. Draw a large, labelled diagram of a typical neuron. State a function for each labelled part.

5. What is an action potential?
   Explain what is meant by all-or-nothing in relation to the transmission of nerve impulses.

6. Fifty dominoes are stood on their ends and the first domino knocked over onto the second. All the dominoes fall in turn. In how many ways does this model illustrate the nature of the nerve impulse?

7. Why are axons unable to conduct impulses for a brief period after the last impulse has passed through?

8. Draw and label a diagram of a synapse. Mark the following locations on the diagram:

   a. where acetylcholine is manufactured;
   b. where acetylcholine is released;
   c. Where LSD might mimic the action of acetylcholine;
   d. where acetylcholine is broken down.

9. What is the connection between a sense organ and a receptor cell? Why are sense organs considered

energy converters? Give three examples of energy conversion within sense organs.

10. Draw and label a cross-section of the eye. State the functions of all labelled parts.

11. State the differences between rods and cones. What is red–green colour deficiency? Who are more likely to suffer from the condition? Is it easily treated?

12. Explain the following terms by writing a brief note on each:

    a. accommodation;
    b. astigmatism;
    c. lazy eye;
    d. myopia;
    e. hyperopia;
    f. convex;
    g. concave.

13. Why do elderly people often hold newspapers at arm's length to read them?

14. What are the functions of the ear? Name the three main parts of the ear.
    List, in order, the structures of the ear through which sound normally passes.

15. Why do ears pop when climbing a mountain or travelling in an aeroplane?

16. Name the two types of hearing loss and suggest how they can be corrected.

17. State a location and a function for each of the following parts of the CNS:

    a. cerebellum;
    b. medulla;
    c. meninges;
    d. pituitary;
    e. cerebrum;
    f. hypothalamus;
    g. H-shaped grey matter.

18. Define the terms 'reflex' and 'reflex arc'. State two examples of reflexes. In what ways do reflexes have great survival value?

19. As a doctor, you have just seen a patient that you have diagnosed as having Parkinson's disease. Write an account of your interview with the patient. Include reference to your initial impressions of them; the conversation you had with them; the questions you answered and the treatment you offered.

20. What is a hormone? Construct a chart to contain five examples of human hormones, their sources, their method of transport, target organs and effects.

21. Why is the hormone system suitable for communicating instructions regarding growth but not suitable for instructions regarding running?

22. In April 1986, nuclear power plant #4 in Chernobyl in Ukraine blew up and spread radioactive isotopes of iodine and other elements over a huge area of Eastern Europe. Doctors in the area immediately gave the population tablets of normal iodine to reduce the risk of certain tumours. What were the doctors concerned about?

23. Explain each of the following:

    a. Endocrine glands have a large blood supply.
    b. Virus infection of the pancreas can lead to diabetes.
    c. Hyperthyroidism is treated by surgery.
    d. A student is very tired after an exam.
    e. The ovaries are included in any list of endocrine glands.
    f. Hormones must be destroyed within the body.

24. Suggest a treatment for each of the following hormonal conditions:

    a. very retarded growth in a child;
    b. Cretinism;
    c. Grave's disease;
    d. diabetes;
    e. a very slow delivery of a baby;
    f. exam nerves.

EXTENDED QUESTIONS

25. What is negative feedback control?
26. Explain how the level of thyroxine is maintained at a fairly constant level in the blood.

27. The graph shows levels of glucose in the bloodstream during a normal day. Explain why the graph fluctuates up and down.

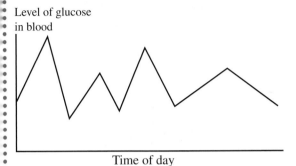

Level of glucose in blood

Time of day

OPTIONAL ACTIVITIES

- Examine microscope slides of a neuron. Draw and label all the parts that are clear to you.
- Use a model of the brain to locate and identify its major parts.
- Obtain prepared microscope slides of a spinal cord TS. Draw and label the main parts.
- Study the structure of the ear using a model or wall chart if these are available.
- Investigate the stimulus-response pathway as follows. Hold a ruler pointing downwards just above someone's hand. Drop the ruler without warning and measure how far it drops before they catch it. Calculate reaction time by the formula: t = √ distance 10).
- Repeat with the subject's eyes closed, relying on touch only for stimulus.
- Simple reflexes:

  - Gently blow air into a partner's eye; the eyelid will close.
  - Click your fingers near their eye and observe.
  - Sit with one leg crossed over the other. Tap below your kneecap and watch the lower leg move.
  - Shine a torch into your partner's eye. Observe the iris movement.
  - Drop lemon juice onto your partner's tongue and observe their facial muscles.

- Investigate the distribution of some receptors on the back of the hand as follows. Work in pairs — the subject should not look!

  - Pressure receptors — drag a pin gently across the back of the hand and record where the pressure is clearly felt.
  - Temperature receptors — heat a knitting needle with hot water and then dry. Drag it across the back of the hand and record where heat is clearly felt. Repeat with a needle chilled by standing in ice.

- Try placing the top on a biro at arm's length with only one eye open. Repeat with both eyes and compare. This will demonstrate the advantage of stereoscopic vision.
- Experiment with lenses. Use a concave and convex lens, a lighted candle and a cardboard screen.
- Research and write reports on any of the following:

  - paralysis;
  - Parkinson's Disease;
  - Motor Neuron Disease;
  - diabetes;
  - Gigantism;
  - Dwarfism;
  - Cretinism;
  - Cushing's Syndrome;
  - Addison's Disease.

For further information on subjects raised in this chapter see www.my-etest.com.

Now test yourself at
www.my-etest.com

Chapter 25

The Human Musculoskeletal System

INTRODUCTION [353 2]

SUPPORT AND MOVEMENT

One of the most obvious features of living organisms is *movement*. In animals, movement is directly related to the need to find food and to escape danger. Almost all animals use a system of muscles that contracts against a rigid framework or *skeleton*. Many types of skeleton are found in the animal world: insects, for example, have an *exoskeleton* of chitin for their muscles to work against; jellyfish twitch their muscles against an *endoskeleton* of jelly; and earthworms use a *hydrostatic* skeleton of pressurised fluid. In higher animals and in humans, muscles are attached to an endoskeleton of bone and cartilage.

The human skeleton consists of 206 bones. It is divided into two parts for study:

- the *axial skeleton* — which consists of the skull, the spine and the ribcage;

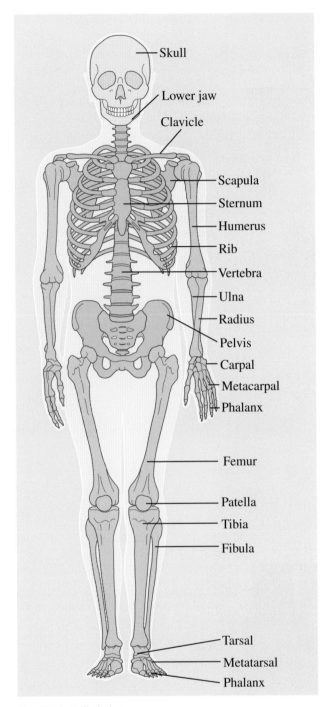

- Skull
- Lower jaw
- Clavicle
- Scapula
- Sternum
- Humerus
- Rib
- Vertebra
- Ulna
- Radius
- Pelvis
- Carpal
- Metacarpal
- Phalanx
- Femur
- Patella
- Tibia
- Fibula
- Tarsal
- Metatarsal
- Phalanx

Fig. 25.1. Full skeleton.

- the *appendicular skeleton* — which consists of the limb girdles and the limbs.

The skull protects the brain and the main sense organs: eyes, ears, nose and tongue. Nearly all its bones are fused together at immovable joints or *sutures*. The jaws hold the teeth (which are not bones), and the lower jaw is movable. The spine is made from 33 vertebrae forming a vertebral column.

The vertebrae enclose the spinal cord and have many surfaces for muscle attachment. The last nine vertebrae are fused together and to the pelvis. Discs of cartilage separate the first 24 vertebrae from each other. These discs are very tough on the outside but fluid on the inside; they act as shock absorbers and allow movement between the vertebrae.

N.B. Incorrect lifting can cause a disc to *prolapse* and compress the spinal cord. Keep your back straight and your legs bent!

The ribcage is formed from 12 pairs of ribs joined to the vertebrae at the back and to the breastbone or *sternum* at the front. The ribcage protects the heart and lungs and also functions in breathing.

The pectoral girdle consists of two collar bones (*clavicles*) and two shoulder blades (*scapulas*). The girdle attaches the arms to the ribcage and allows a wide range of movement.

The pelvic girdle is made from six fused bones and is joined to the lower vertebrae of the spine. The girdle attaches the legs to the spine and also protects the abdominal organs. No movement is possible between the pelvic bones and the lower spine.

The arms and legs show the pentadactyl (five-digit) limb arrangement found in most of the higher vertebrates — clearly evidence of a common ancestry.

Each arm and hand consists of a *humerus*, a *radius* and *ulna*, eight *carpals* (wrist bones), five *metacarpals* and 14 finger bones or *phalanges* (singular is *phalanx*). Each leg and foot consists of a *femur*, a *patella* (kneecap), a *tibia* and *fibula*, seven *tarsals* (ankle bones), five *metatarsals* and again 14 *phalanges*.

The largest single bone is the femur and the smallest is the *stirrup* within the ear. The *hyoid* bone, at the front of the larynx, is the only bone not connected to another bone.

FUNCTIONS OF THE HUMAN SKELETON

The human skeleton:

- allows muscles to transmit their force;
- maintains body shape;
- protects body organs;

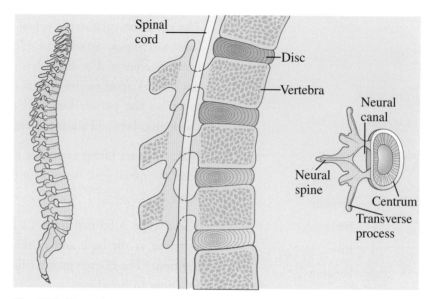

Fig. 25.2. The spine.

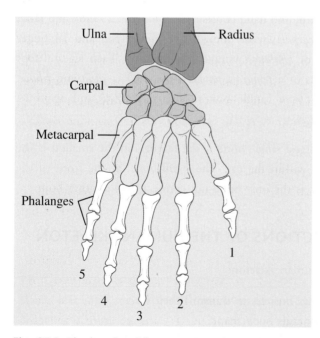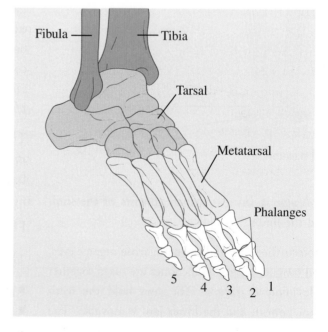

Fig. 25.3. The hand and foot.

- transmits sound;
- acts as a reserve of calcium;
- manufactures blood cells;
- anchors the teeth in place.

ANATOMY OF A LONG BONE

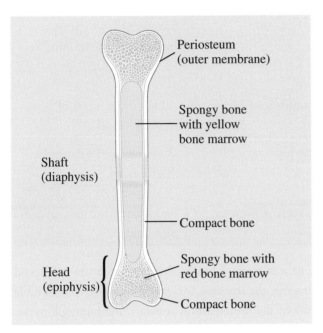

Fig. 25.4. Long bone.

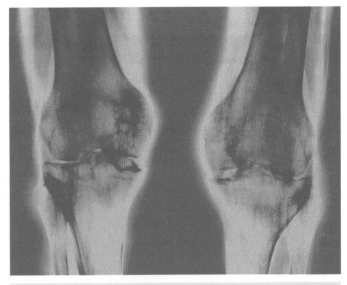

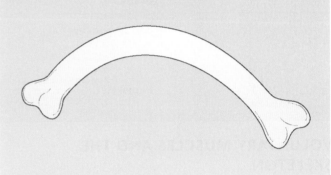

Fig. 25.5. Normal and arthritic knee joints. Also flexible, demineralised bone.

The typical long bone has a shaft and two heads. A tough membrane, the *periosteum*, covers the outside and forms an attachment with tendons. Bone tissue consists of a matrix of *collagen fibres* containing bone cells (*osteocytes*) that secrete calcium phosphate and other salts. Tiny canals run through the compact tissue bringing oxygen and nutrients to the bone cells. Collagen is resistant to tension and the calcium salts are resistant to compression, so the composite nature of bone combines these two properties.

Compact bone is found mostly at the bone shaft and is very dense. The bone tissue here is arranged in microscopic rings.

Spongy bone is found at the ends of the bone and within the shaft. It is less dense than compact bone and always contains soft marrow tissue. Red marrow (the site of red cell formation) is found within the bone ends and yellow marrow (mostly fat) within the shaft.

Cartilage (sometimes called young bone) consists of a protein matrix containing cartilage cells but no calcium salts. Blood vessels do not enter cartilage; oxygen and nutrients reach the cells by diffusion. Cartilage forms the entire skeleton of the embryo but is then replaced by bone. Cartilage is found in movable joints (see below), in rings around the trachea, supporting the nose and ears and forming the intervertebral discs.

Joints are places in the skeleton where two bones meet. Some joints, called sutures, do not allow any movement, but most joints allow some movement and cartilage is found in the joint to reduce friction.

Freely movable joints are usually *synovial* in design. A fibrous capsule surrounds the bones and secretes *synovial fluid* from its inner, *synovial membrane*. The fluid acts both as a shock absorber and as a lubricating oil. Cartilage protects the joint surfaces and ligaments prevent the bones from drifting apart.

Table 25.1. Classification of joints

Joint movement	Joint type	Example	Comment
Immovable	Sutures	Bones of skull, sacrum and pelvis	No movement, but jigsaw interlocking allows growth when young.
Slightly movable	Gliding joints	Wrist, ankle	Very little movement between any two bones, but overall movement increased by large number of bones present.
	Pivot joints	Between atlas and axis vertebrae	Allows movements of head in three planes.
Freely movable	Ball and socket	Shoulder, hip	Wide range of movements in all planes.
	Hinge	Fingers, toes, wrist, knee	Free movement, but in one plane only.

VOLUNTARY MUSCLES AND THE SKELETON

Muscles use tendons to transmit their forces to bones. A tendon is a strong cord of connective tissue made from collagen fibres. It is non-elastic and attached very firmly to both muscle and bone. In limb muscles, the tendon nearer to the centre of the body is termed the *origin* and attaches the muscle to a stationary bone. The tendon at the other end of the muscle, the *insertion*, attaches the muscle to a movable bone. When the muscle fibres contract, the joint will move. As muscles can only contract and relax, a second, opposite muscle is required to move the joint in the opposite direction. (Muscles can *pull* but not *push*!). The two muscles form an antagonistic muscle pair. As one contracts and shortens, the other relaxes and is stretched.

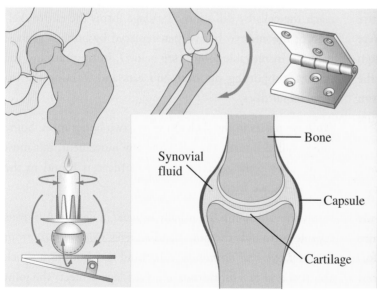
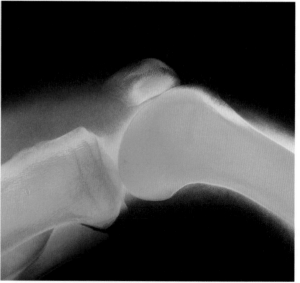

Synovial fluid — Bone — Capsule — Cartilage

Fig. 25.6. Synovial joints and X-ray of synovial knee joint.

An example of an antagonistic muscle pair is the biceps and triceps of the upper arm. To flex the arm, the biceps shortens and stretches the relaxed triceps. To extend the arm, the triceps shortens and stretches the relaxed biceps.

N.B.: As the biceps usually works against gravity, it tends to be thicker and stronger than the triceps, which is normally gravity-assisted. Russian astronauts who spent long periods in the space station *Mir* developed equal-sized biceps and triceps muscles, as they used both equally in the gravity-free conditions.

Tendons allow muscles to work at a distance, e.g. the muscles for moving the fingers are located further back in the hand and lower arm. This both lightens the fingers (for rapid movements) and allows them to be less bulky and more suited for precision work.

SKELETAL DISORDERS — OSTEOPOROSIS AND ARTHRITIS

Bone is an ever-changing tissue. Throughout the lifetime of an adult, old bone is removed (by reabsorption of the calcium salts) and new bone is added to the skeleton (by secretion of new calcium salts). During childhood and teenage years, new bone is added faster than old bone is removed. As a result, bones become larger, heavier, and denser. Bone

formation continues at a pace faster than reabsorption until peak bone mass (maximum bone density and strength) is reached during the mid-twenties. Even in adult years, two-thirds of the calcium phosphate in the skeleton is replaced every three weeks. After age 30, bone reabsorption slowly begins to exceed bone formation and there is a possibility of osteoporosis or brittle bone disease.

Osteoporosis

Osteoporosis is also called *brittle bone disease*. It develops when bone reabsorption occurs too quickly or if replacement occurs too slowly. This leads to bone fragility and an increased susceptibility to fractures of the hip, spine, and wrist.

PREVALENCE

- Of those affected by osteoporosis, 80% are women.
- One out of two women and one in eight men over age 50 will have an osteoporosis-related fracture in their lifetime.
- While osteoporosis is often thought of as an older person's disease, it can strike at any age.
- Most common fractures are of the spine (vertebral degeneration), followed by the hip, the wrist and then other fractures.

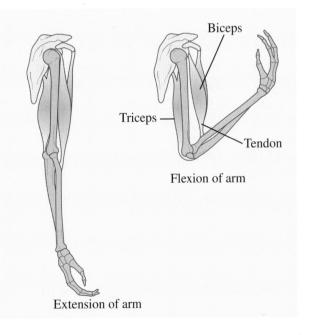

Fig. 25.7. Skeletal muscles.

SYMPTOMS

Osteoporosis is a silent disease. Patients will not know they have it until a fall or sudden movement results in a fracture or a collapsed vertebra. Bone density measurements can show the existence of the disease.

CAUSES

Some people are more likely to develop the disease than others. Risk factors (in order of importance) include the following:

- being female;
- being thin and/or of small frame;
- advanced age;
- a family history of osteoporosis;
- being postmenopausal (periods have ceased), including early or surgically induced menopause
- abnormal absence of menstrual periods (amenorrhoea);
- anorexia or bulimia;
- use of certain medications, such as corticosteroids and anticonvulsants;
- low testosterone levels in men;
- an inactive lifestyle;
- cigarette smoking;
- excessive use of alcohol.

PREVENTION

Osteoporosis is highly preventable, but not very treatable once it has taken hold. Building strong bones with high bone density during childhood and adolescence is the most important prevention. The following are essential aspects of protection:

- a balanced diet rich in calcium and vitamin D;
- weight-bearing exercise;
- a healthy lifestyle with no smoking and limited alcohol intake.

MEDICATIONS

Oestrogen and calcitonin are approved for osteoporosis treatment. Sodium fluoride, parathyroid hormone and vitamin D-related chemicals are currently under investigation.

Arthritis

Arthritis is an inflammation of the joints. It is a condition that can take hundreds of different forms but generally produces pain, swelling and limited movement. The inflammation often occurs at a site of joint damage, so fractures, stress, infection or other joint problems can bring on arthritis. It is a long-term or chronic condition. Diagnosis is by x-rays and blood tests.

The three most common forms of arthritis are:

- *Osteoarthritis* — which usually affects the weight-bearing joints: spine, ankles, knees, elbows and wrists. It is characterised by unwanted bone growth, poor movement and destruction of cartilage.
- *Rheumatoid arthritis* — an inflammation of the synovial membrane of the joints. It occurs in the hands and feet and tends to be equal on both sides of the body.
- *Fibromyalgia* — a long-term pain in the muscles and tissues surrounding the joints.

Less common forms of arthritis include *gout* (crystals of uric acid within the joints), *lupus* (inflammation of connective tissue) and *ankylosing spondylitis* (the bones of the spine beginning to knit together).

TYPICAL PATIENTS

- Osteoarthritis usually (but not always) occurs in older people.
- Anyone can get rheumatoid arthritis, including children and the elderly. However, the disease usually begins in the young to middle adult years. Women tend to outnumber men by three to one.

SYMPTOMS

- Pain and stiffness in the joints.
- Reduced mobility.
- Warmth in the joint due to an increased blood flow.
- Swelling.

CAUSES

Not known and may not be preventable. Stress on the joints, injury and infection can trigger arthritis.

TREATMENT

It is very important to begin treatment early before irreversible joint damage has occurred.

- *Drug therapy* is the most important treatment. Anti-inflammatory drugs can give very good relief. The newest are termed *COX-2 inhibitors*. Injections of *gold salts* have been given for the last 60 years. This treatment is beneficial for some patients only but can slow down the degeneration of cartilage and bone.

- *Cellular therapy* involves removing the type of white blood cell that mistakenly attacks joints in some forms of arthritis. The new, replacement cells do not appear to make the same mistake. This technique may replace drug therapy in the near future.

- *Physiotherapy* — maintaining joint movement is very important but often ignored by older patients.

- *Complementary medicine* — acupuncture, reflexology and relaxation therapy can be helpful in some cases. All 'alternative' treatments should be taken in conjunction with traditional medical therapy.

- *Fraudulent treatments* — arthritis suffers more than most diseases from claims for 'cures'. The use of magnets and antibiotics are a complete waste of precious time and money. At best, they can produce no more than a 'white coat' or placebo effect.

GROWTH AND DEVELOPMENT IN BONES [H35 IV]

Bone is the major skeletal tissue in vertebrates. It is originally formed in the embryo from another skeletal tissue — *cartilage*. *Hyaline* ('glassy') *cartilage* consists of a clear matrix of jelly-like *chondrin* embedded with cartilage cells called *chondrocytes*. Hyaline cartilage is found in the trachea and bronchi and forms the embryonic skeleton. *White fibro-cartilage* is similar but contains collagen fibres. Fibro-cartilage is found in the discs between the vertebrae. Cartilage never has an internal blood supply and tends not to repair itself well if damaged.

During embryonic growth, bone-forming cells (*osteoblasts*) replace the cartilage cells and secrete bone. Bone tissue spreads from the shaft of long bones to the heads. Cartilage remains only at the joint surfaces. Bones continue to grow

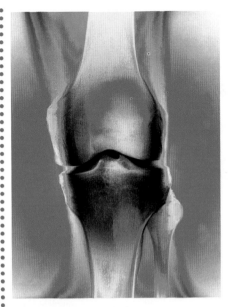

Fig. 25.8. Rheumatic bone.

for years but eventually stop increasing in size when adult proportions are reached. This limits the height of an individual. Further weight gain in adulthood does not result in a gain in height.

Bone is a *dynamic tissue* that is constantly changing. As explained above, two-thirds of the calcium phosphate in the skeleton is replaced every three weeks. Bone contains both *osteoblasts* (which secrete new bone) and *osteoclasts* (which break down the tissue and secrete calcium back intro the blood). It is important that the rate of bone production balances bone degeneration; otherwise conditions such as osteoporosis will occur.

The dynamic balance within bones is dependent on *diet* (calcium, phosphorus and vitamin D being essential), *physical exercise* and *hormone levels*. Stressing the bones with exercise increases the rate of osteoblast activity and makes bones healthier and stronger. Withdrawal of certain hormones such as oestrogen in the menopause can decrease osteoblast activity.

SUMMARY

- In animals, movement is directly related to the need to find food and to escape danger.
- Almost all animals use a system of muscles that contracts against a rigid skeleton.

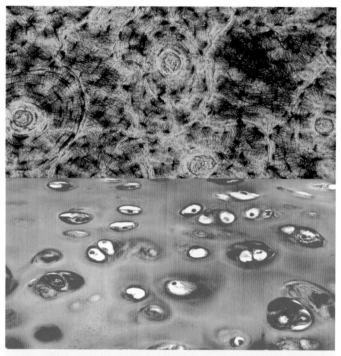

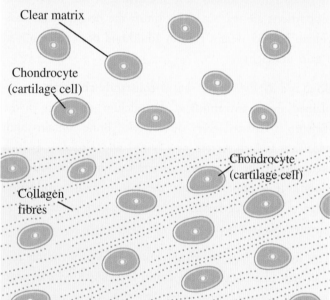

Fig. 25.9. Photo of compact bone (above) and cartilage (below).

- The human skeleton consists of 206 bones. It is divided into two parts for study.
- The axial skeleton — consists of the skull, the spine and the ribcage.
- The appendicular skeleton — consists of the limb girdles and the limbs.
- The skull protects the brain and the main sense organs.

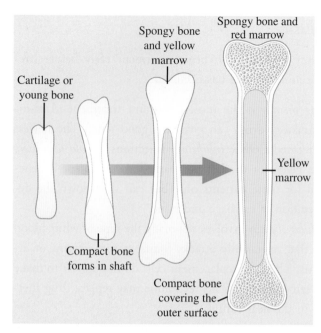

Fig. 25.10. Formation of a long bone.

- The spine is made from 33 vertebrae forming a vertebral column. Discs of cartilage separate the vertebrae from each other.
- The ribcage is formed from 12 pairs of ribs joined to the vertebrae at the back and to the breastbone or sternum at the front.
- The pectoral girdle consists of two collar bones (clavicles) and two shoulder blades (scapulas).
- The pelvic girdle is made from six fused bones and is joined to the lower vertebrae of the spine.
- The functions of the human skeleton are:

  - to allow muscles to transmit their force;
  - to maintain body shape;
  - to protect body organs;
  - to transmit sound;
  - to act as a reserve of calcium;
  - to manufacture blood cells;
  - to anchor the teeth in place.

- Bone tissue consists of a matrix of collagen fibres containing bone cells (osteocytes) that secrete calcium phosphate and other salts.
- Freely movable joints are usually synovial in design.
- Muscles use tendons to transmit their forces to bones.
- An example of an antagonistic muscle pair is the biceps and triceps of the upper arm.

EXTENDED SUMMARY

- Bone is the major skeletal tissue in vertebrates.
- Bone is originally formed in the embryo from another skeletal tissue — cartilage.
- Hyaline cartilage is found in the trachea and bronchi and forms the early, embryonic skeleton.
- Fibro-cartilage is found in the discs between the vertebrae.
- During embryonic growth, bone-forming cells (osteoblasts) replace the cartilage cells and secrete bone.
- Bones continue to grow for years but eventually stop increasing in size when adult proportions are reached.
- Bone contains both osteoblasts and osteoclasts.
- The dynamic balance within bones is dependant on diet, physical exercise and hormone levels.

KEY WORDS

Exoskeleton	A skeleton covering the outside of the body.
Endoskeleton	A skeleton lying within the body.
Hydrostatic skeleton	An endoskeleton of pressurised fluid.
Axial skeleton	Consists of the skull, the spine and the ribcage.
Appendicular skeleton	Consists of the limb girdles and the limbs.
Joints	Places in the skeleton where two bones meet.
Sutures	Immovable joints.
Osteocytes	Bone cells.
Collagen	A white, fibrous tissue, very strong and resistant to tension.
Compact bone	Dense bone found mostly at the bone shaft.
Spongy bone	Less dense than compact bone and containing soft marrow tissue. Found at the ends of the bone and within the shaft.
Cartilage	A protein matrix containing cartilage cells but no calcium salts.

Synovial fluid	A lubricating fluid within synovial joints.
Synovial membrane	Lines the inside of synovial joints and secretes synovial fluid.
Tendons	Strong cords of connective tissue made from collagen fibres. Used to attach muscles to bones.
Origin	The muscle tendon nearer to the centre of the body.
Insertion	The tendon at the far end of the muscle.
Antagonistic muscle pair	As one muscle contracts and shortens, the other relaxes and is stretched.
Osteoporosis	Brittle bone disease.
Arthritis	Inflammation of the joints.
Osteoarthritis	Characterised by unwanted bone growth, poor movement and destruction of cartilage.
Rheumatoid arthritis	An inflammation of the synovial membrane of the joints.
Fibromyalgia	A long-term pain in the muscles and tissues surrounding the joints.

EXTENDED KEY WORDS

Hyaline ('glassy') cartilage	Consists of a clear matrix of jelly-like chondrin embedded with cartilage cells.
Chondrocytes	Cartilage cells.
White fibro-cartilage	Cartilage containing collagen fibres.
Osteoblasts	Bone-forming cells.
Osteoclasts	Break down bone tissue and secrete calcium back intro the blood.

QUESTIONS

1. Give at least four reasons why animals (and humans) need to move.

2. Name three types of skeleton found in the animal world. Give one example in each case.

3. Name the main parts of the axial and the appendicular skeleton.

4. What are vertebrae? Name the important structure running through the vertebrae. What separates one vertebra from the next and what is its function? What would be the problem with designing a spine out of one single bone rather than many small ones?

5. What are *sutures*? The sutures in an unborn baby's skull are not completely fused and remain relatively free for about 18 months after birth. State two advantages of this.

6. Distinguish between:

   a. pectoral girdle and pelvic girdle;

   b. carpal and tarsal;

   c. femur and fibula;

   d. vertebrae and vertebrate;

   e. scapula and sternum.

7. The text lists seven functions of the skeleton. Give an example of each.
   Why is it important that an organism retains its shape?

8. Explain the difference between compact bone and spongy bone. Draw a simple diagram of a long bone and mark the two kinds of bone tissue on it. What is the *periosteum*?

9. State five examples of freely movable joints. The ball and socket joint in the shoulder gives a very wide range of movement to the arm. Explain why it would not be a good idea to have this joint at every location in the arm.

10. Draw a large, labelled diagram of a synovial joint. Use the diagram to explain the consequences of:

    a. extra fluid within the joint;

    b. torn cartilage;

    c. torn ligaments;

    d. arthritis.

11. How are muscles joined to bones? Distinguish between the *origin* and the *insertion* of a muscle. Draw a simple diagram showing the attachment of the biceps and triceps to the bones of the arm. Mark the origin and the insertion of the biceps on the diagram. Use the diagram to explain the working of an *antagonistic muscle pair*.

12. Explain the consequences of the statement: 'Muscles can *pull* but not *push*'.

13. Explain the following two observations:

    a. When a bone is left to stand in dilute acid, it retains its shape but becomes flexible.

    b. When a bone is burnt, it retains its shape temporarily but is fragile and crumbles if touched.

14. As a doctor, you have just seen a patient that you have diagnosed as having osteoporosis (or arthritis). Write an account of your interview with the patient. Include reference to your initial impressions of the patient, the symptoms you noticed, the conversation you had with him or her, the questions you answered and the treatment you offered.

EXTENDED QUESTIONS

15. Outline the development of bone from cartilage. At what age does this change take place?

16. Why is bone considered a *dynamic tissue*? Describe the behaviour of osteoblasts and osteoclasts. Would either cell type increase or decrease in activity at the site of a bone fracture? Explain your answer.

17. What factors affect the dynamic balance within bones? Give simple instructions for maintaining peak bone mass.

OPTIONAL ACTIVITIES

- Obtain a complete chicken or turkey leg and foot. Dissect away the loose tissue and demonstrate the action of the tendons. Also examine the joints for cartilage and ligaments.

- Observe the tendons in your wrist. Relax one hand with fingers nearly straight. Squeeze your wrist hard with the other hand to pull on the tendons. Observe the movement of your fingers.
- Use two lengths of cardboard, two rubber bands and a paper fastener to make a model of the biceps and triceps across the elbow joint.
- To demineralise a bone: place a chicken bone in dilute hydrochloric acid overnight. Rinse well and observe.
- To remove collagen from a bone, burn it at high temperature in a covered, heatproof dish.

- The Arthritis Foundation of Ireland is at 1 Clanwilliam Square, Grand Canal Quay, Dublin 2, Telephone: 01 6618188. They maintain a website at http://www.arthritis-foundation.com/ which contains comprehensive information.
- Contact the Irish Osteoporosis Society at 'Emoclew', Batterstown, Co. Meath, Telephone/Fax 01 8258159, for information on osteoporosis.

For more information on websites dealing with subjects covered in this chapter see www.my-etest.com.

Now test yourself at
www.my-etest.com

Chapter 26
Immunity and Viruses

Learning objectives

After your study of this chapter, you should be able to:

- define immunity;
- distinguish between non-specific and specific immunities;
- list the lines of defence protecting humans against microbial disease;
- explain the relationship between antigens and antibodies;
- compare active and passive immunities;
- outline the reasoning behind vaccination;
- describe the structure and reproduction of viruses;
- summarise the important facts concerning HIV.

Extended learning objectives

- Distinguish between cell-mediated and humoral-mediated immunity.
- Explain in detail the roles of T cells and B cells.

IMMUNITY   [353 3]

The human body is under constant attack from *pathogens* — microorganisms that cause disease. If they gain entry to the body, they will multiply and cause disease symptoms through tissue damage or the release of toxins. *Viruses* cause diseases such as colds, 'flu, mumps, measles, polio, chicken pox and AIDS. *Bacterial diseases* include typhoid fever, diphtheria, botulism, streptococcal throat and tuberculosis (TB). *Fungal diseases* in humans include ringworm, thrush and athlete's foot.

Immunity is the body's ability to resist disease. Humans have evolved a wide variety of ways of resisting microbial attack. These may be grouped as follows:

- *non-specific* or *innate immunities* (or *general immunities*) — these do not require previous exposure to the pathogen and work against microorganisms in general;
- *specific* or *acquired immunities* — these develop after contact with specific pathogens and protect only against those pathogens.

Approaching pathogens (or 'germs') will have to negotiate several lines of defence before producing disease symptoms in the host.

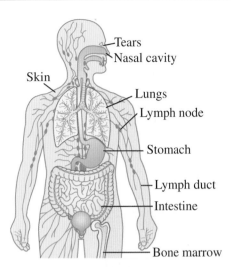

Fig. 26.2. Parts of the human immune system.

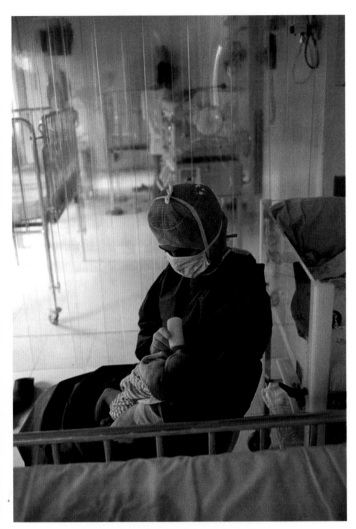

Fig. 26.1. Immune-deficient child within a plastic tent.

1. The first line of defence is an outer barrier of *non-specific immunities*, the most important being the skin. The epidermis of the skin contains keratin, which is germ-proof and waterproof. Sweat and sebum (oil) on the skin surface have an antiseptic effect. In addition the outer skin cells are continually flaking away and carrying pathogens with them. The importance of the skin should not be underestimated; as soon as it is cut or damaged, the risk of infection is extremely high. Also areas of the body *without* skin are at constant high risk. Ear, nose, throat and eye infections are common — all places where there is no natural skin barrier.

Other first line non-specific defences include:

- the acid barrier in the stomach, which kills germs on the surface of food;

- mucus, cilia and the coughing reflex in the trachea, which protect the lungs;

- the respiratory system, which contains scavenging *macrophages* that leave the bloodstream and attack any foreign matter within the airways;

- earwax, nose mucus, saliva and tear fluid, which all contain the digestive enzyme, *lysozyme*, which kills pathogens;

- commensal flora, which are natural populations of microorganisms living on and in the body. These compete with pathogens and restrict their activity. Overuse of antibiotics or mouthwashes can reduce their number and increase the chances of certain infections.

2. **The second line of defence** is also non-specific.

- The inflammatory response is triggered by the release of *histamine* from the damaged or attacked cells. Histamine causes the blood vessels in the infected area to dilate and bring more blood to the site. The site becomes red, swollen and tender, but there will be a high concentration of white blood cells and tissue fluid that has an antibacterial effect. Any discharge of pus is a mixture of white cells and dead bacteria.

- Blood clotting not only prevents the loss of blood but also the entry of pathogens.

- Certain types of white blood cell are *phagocytic* — they will identify and eat anything foreign inside the body. They will attack bacteria, fungi, dust or even soot particles (eaten by phagocytes in the lungs). Phagocytes are non-specific in their action. A few bacteria are resistant to them, e.g. tuberculosis bacteria.

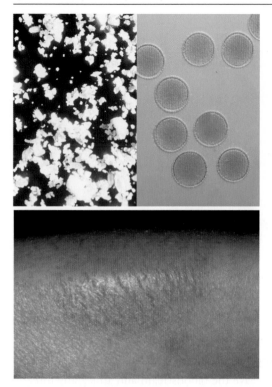

Fig. 26.3. Pollen grains and the immune response.

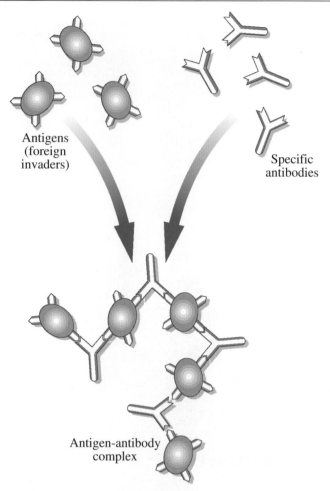

Fig. 26.4. Antigen–antibody reaction.

3. The third line of defence is specific and termed the *Immune Response*.

It is based on the body's ability to recognise *antigens* and make specific protein *antibodies* to destroy them.

An *antigen* is any chemical recognised by the immune system as being foreign. Antigens are large proteins that are found on the surfaces of bacteria, fungi and viruses, or in the secretions of these pathogens. They are, in fact, found on or in all biological tissue. They are 'learned' by the immune system and used to distinguish 'self' from 'non-self' or foreign material.

An *antibody* is a protein (an *immunoglobulin*) made by the immune system in response to an antigen. Each antibody is specific to only one type of antigen e.g. the anti-tetanus antibody is specific to tetanus bacteria and no other kind.

Antigens and antibodies bind together (to form the *antigen–antibody complex*) and this leads to the destruction of the antigen. The destruction happens in different ways: the antibody may digest the outer walls of the pathogen, the an-

tigen–antibody complex may be devoured by phagocytes or it may stick (agglutinate) to other complexes forming a harmless lump of tissue, which is later destroyed.

Antibodies are made by *lymphocytes* (a type of white blood cell) in the lymph nodes of the body.

ACTIVE AND PASSIVE IMMUNITIES, AND VACCINATION

Active immunity arises when the body manufactures its own antibodies in response to the arrival of a specific antigen. This happens in the normal course of exposure to infection and generally the immune system retains a memory of the pathogen to prevent repeated infection. For this reason, many diseases are 'once-only' events, e.g. mumps and measles.

Active immunity can be artificially induced by injecting a heat-treated or preserved form of the antigen into the blood (a *vaccine*). The body responds by making appropriate antibodies and relatively permanent protection is achieved.

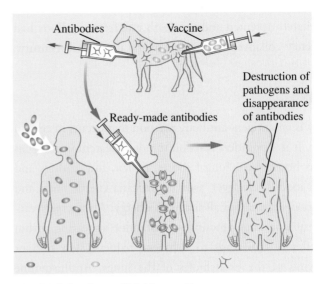

Fig. 26.6. Passive artificial immunity.

Active immunities are *delayed* but *long-lasting*, as the host retains a memory of how to make the antibodies.

The term *immunisation* applies to any artificial process that gives immunity to a patient. It includes both injection of ready-made antibodies and injection of vaccines.

Vaccination is a method of immunisation where a harmless (*attenuated*) form of the pathogen trains the immune system into making appropriate antibodies for long-term protection. Edward Jenner first described the technique in 1796.

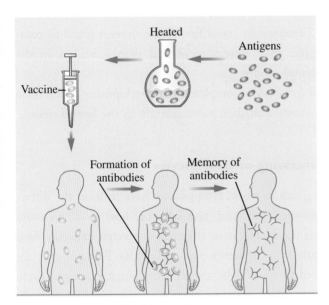

Fig. 26.5. Active artificial immunity.

Passive immunity arises when 'ready-made' antibodies turn up in the bloodstream. This often happens naturally; for example, a mother's antibodies cross into the baby's bloodstream via the placenta or in breast milk. This gives the baby a temporary protection against all the diseases the mother has had. Passive immunity can be brought about artificially too. Ready-made antibodies (usually from horse serum — refined horse blood plasma) can be injected to give a quick protection against a disease. Emergency antitetanus injections contain ready-made anti-tetanus antibodies.

N.B. Passive immunities are *immediate* but *short-lived*, as the host does not know how to make any more antibodies when the supply runs out.

Edward Jenner

Edward Jenner (1749–1823) was born in Gloucestershire in England, the son of a vicar. He trained in London as a surgeon and then returned to the country as a doctor and naturalist. At the time, deaths from smallpox were at a very high rate and 10% of all deaths in London were due to the virus. Jenner noticed that milkmaids in the dairies never contracted smallpox but instead suffered from the much milder cowpox disease. He correctly deduced that infection with cowpox protected against smallpox. On 14 May 1796, Jenner infected an eight-year-old boy with cowpox and allowed the mild disease to run its course. Then, in July, he injected smallpox-infected tissue into the boy's arm, and repeated the injections months later. The boy did not contract smallpox. Jenner repeated the process on others and then published his findings. The technique of vaccination was immediately accepted and the death rate from smallpox had completely collapsed by the end of the nineteenth century.

Allergy

Allergy is an antigen–antibody reaction that occurs in certain people. It is a pointless reaction to non-threatening allergens such as house dust, fungal spores, pollen, fur, feathers and certain foods. Hay fever, asthma, urticaria (nettle rash) and childhood eczema are all forms of allergy. An allergic reaction results in large amounts of histamine appearing within the sufferer. This leads to itchiness, redness, skin rash or narrowing of the bronchioles of the lungs. Antihistamine drugs relieve the condition. Some white blood cells release antihistamine chemicals that speed up recovery.

WHITE BLOOD CELLS AND THE HUMAN IMMUNE SYSTEM   [H35 III]

The human immune system consists of white blood cells (leucocytes) and lymphatic tissue. Bone marrow and the thymus gland (under the breastbone) are *primary lymphatic tissues*; the tonsils, spleen and the lymph nodes are *secondary lymphatic tissues*. All white blood cells are made from stem cells in the bone marrow. The white cells grow and mature in the primary lymphoid tissues and then migrate to the secondary lymphoid tissues.

White blood cells are very different to red blood cells in that they do their work outside the circulation and only use the blood for transport.

Types of white blood cell

1. *Granulocytes* — are large cells with irregular nuclei and granules in their cytoplasm. They are phagocytic cells; they engulf and devour any foreign matter by surrounding it and releasing digestive enzymes. Granulocytes can become *mast cells*, which release histamine to activate the immune response. *Neutrophils* (cells that stain with neutral dyes) are the most common sort of granulocyte.

2. *Monocytes* — are large cells with kidney-shaped nuclei. When formed, they are non-phagocytic but then develop into *macrophages*, which are the body's rubbish-collectors.

Macrophages leave the circulation and lie in wait for any foreign matter to arrive. They then surround it and digest it.

Granulocytes and monocytes are both *non-specific* in their action; they will defend the body against *anything* that is foreign to it.

3. *Lymphocytes* — are small, rounded cells with large nuclei. They are responsible for all of the *specific* responses of the immune system. Like other blood cells, they are formed in the bone marrow from stem cells. They then migrate to the lymph nodes by one of two routes:

   a. *T-lymphocytes* travel first to the thymus gland to complete their development and then move on to the lymph nodes.
   b. *B-lymphocytes* complete their development in the bone marrow and then move directly to the lymph nodes.

Pre-processing of lymphocytes

Before going to work, lymphocytes have to learn the difference between 'self' and 'non-self', i.e. how to differentiate between the body's natural cells and foreign material. At a very early stage, it seems that millions of T and B cells are produced to specifically match every possible antigen there could be. These cells are then naturally exposed to body tissues during their maturing in the thymus and bone marrow. Any that combine with the 'self' cells (cells naturally occurring in the body) are then destroyed, as they are not needed. The remaining cells will combine with 'non-self' antigens and are retained. These then travel to the lymph nodes and await 'activation' by foreign antigens.

Activation of lymphocytes

When lymphocytes and matching antigens come into contact, the lymphocytes respond by first forming identical copies, or clones, of themselves.

B-lymphocytes form two types of clone: *plasma cells and memory-B cells*. The plasma cells secrete antibodies, which combine with the antigen and destroy it. The memory-B cells retain a long term 'memory' of the antigen and can divide to form more memory cells and plasma cells if the

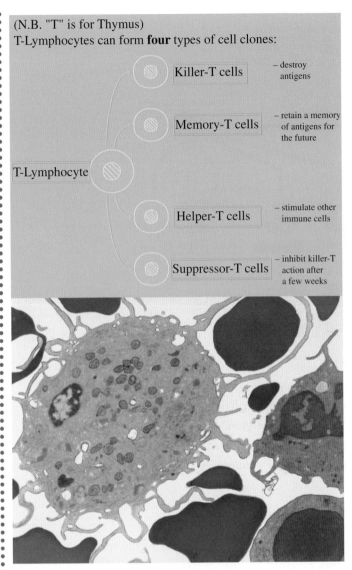

(N.B. "T" is for Thymus)

T-Lymphocytes can form **four** types of cell clones:

Killer-T cells — destroy antigens

Memory-T cells — retain a memory of antigens for the future

T-Lymphocyte

Helper-T cells — stimulate other immune cells

Suppressor-T cells — inhibit killer-T action after a few weeks

Fig. 26.7. Cells formed from T-lymphocytes. Also a macrophage eating foreign red blood cells.

- *Killer-T cells* cut tiny holes in the antigens and destroy them. They are particularly effective against fungi, parasites, cancer cells, transplanted tissue and some viruses.

- *Memory-T cells,* like memory-B cells, retain a 'memory' of the antigen and bring about a much faster response if the antigen ever returns.

- *Helper-T cells* secrete chemicals that stimulate the action of all other immune cells and greatly enhance their effect. Helper-T cells often secrete *interferon*, which stimulates the production of more B-cells. Helper-T cells are generally the host cells for the AIDS virus, HIV. A decline in the numbers of helper-T cells over a few months leads to a situation where the host is immune-deficient. The patient eventually dies, not from the HIV virus itself but from 'opportunistic' diseases that the body would normally resist.

- *Suppressor-T cells* inhibit the action of killer-T cells a few weeks after activation.

The response of T-lymphocytes is termed *cell-mediated immunity.*

T cells are only activated when antigens are brought to them by macrophages. If a macrophage encounters an antigen, it engulfs it and then transports it, partially consumed, to the lymph nodes and lymphocytes.

Vaccines work by stimulating the production of specific memory-B and memory-T cells without the risk of any disease. If the specific pathogen later turns up, the quick response of the memory cells destroys it before any symptoms are noticed.

same antigen should ever return. This response of B-lymphocytes is termed *humoral-mediated* (or *antibody-mediated*) *immunity* and is effective against bacteria and some viruses.

T-lymphocytes form four types of clone: *killer-T cells, memory-T cells, helper-T cells* and *suppressor-T cells.*

VIRUSES   [354]

Viruses are extremely small infectious agents and consist only of a protein coat, a nucleic acid core (DNA or RNA) and some enzymes.

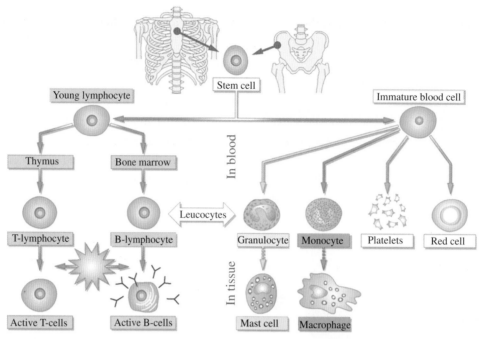

Fig. 26.8. Formation of blood cells.

Living or non-living?

In Chapter 2, we stated that all living organisms are deemed living if they possess cells and practice 'the seven characteristics of living organisms' — movement, growth, nutrition, awareness, excretion, respiration and reproduction. All familiar living organisms easily pass these tests, e.g. there is little doubt as to the biological difference between a cat and a hairbrush! Viruses, however, pose a problem when tested in the same way. They do not really possess *any* of the seven characteristics and it is the subject of much debate as to whether they should be considered as living organisms at all.

Also, viruses contradict traditional *cell theory*, first proposed by Schleiden and Schwann in 1839. This states that the cell is the structural and functional unit of all living organisms. The important points in their theory are:

- Cells are the basic building blocks of all organisms.
- All cells come from pre-existing cells.
- Cells contain all the information required for cell activity.
- Cells are the functional units of all biochemistry.

Viruses do not comply with any of the above points. They are *akaryotic*, that is, they do not have a cellular structure. They must use the existing cell machinery of a host cell to reproduce. They are described as *obligate parasites*, i.e. they are *obliged* to use living cells to complete their life cycle. Viruses will not grow on dishes of nutrients as bacteria do; they have to be cultured inside living cells — by the technique of *tissue culture* (see Chapter 11).

Basic structure

Viruses are extremely small. One of the smallest, the *poliovirus*, measures as little as ten nanometers (nm) in diameter (1 nm = 1 millionth of a millimetre). Most can only be seen with an electron microscope, although one of the biggest, the smallpox virus, can just be seen with the light microscope.

All viruses consist of a protein coat, a nucleic acid core and some enzymes. The nucleic acid is either DNA or RNA, but never both together. The protein coat (or *capsid*) is made from sub-units called capsomeres.

Virus shapes

There are three basic shapes of protein coat:

- *polyhedral* — the capsomeres form a multi-faceted (many faced) shape — very like a cut diamond (examples include the polio and herpes viruses);

- *helical* — the capsomeres are wrapped around the core in a spiral or helix (examples include mumps and 'flu viruses);
- *complex* — many viruses have complex shapes. *Bacteriophages* (viruses that attack bacteria) have a polyhedral head with a helical tail. The rabies virus is bullet-shaped and the smallpox virus has an outer double membrane. HIV is spherical with protein knobs extending from the outer surface.

Viral replication

Viral replication must take place inside a host cell. The virus needs to 'hijack' the host's cell machinery to complete its task. Replication (or 'Reproduction') proceeds as follows:

- The bacteriophage attaches itself to the wall of the host cell.

- Enzymes and a hollow spike cut an opening in the cell wall.
- The tail contracts and injects the nucleic acid core into the cell.
- Virus DNA is incorporated in the host's DNA
- Virus DNA takes over the host's existing cell machinery and directs it to form copies of virus coats and cores.
- Coats and cores are manufactured separately.
- The cores enter the coats to assemble the new viruses.
- The host cell bursts (*lyses*) from a build-up of lysozyme enzyme.
- Bacteriophages can now infect other host cells.
- This lytic cycle takes about 30 minutes.

1. Polyhedral

Protein coat containing RNA core

Polio virus

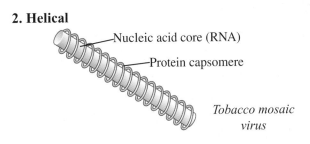

2. Helical

Nucleic acid core (RNA)

Protein capsomere

Tobacco mosaic virus

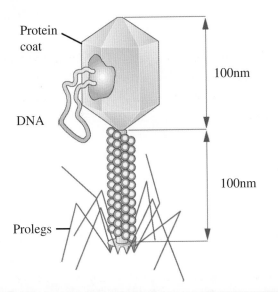

Protein coat

DNA

100nm

100nm

Prolegs

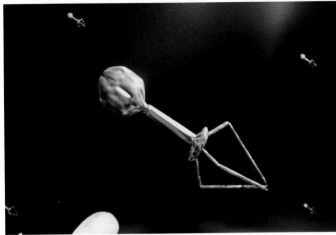

Fig. 26.9. A bacteriophage.

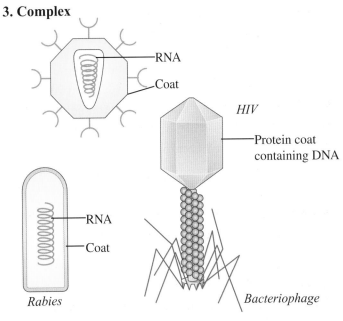

3. Complex

RNA

Coat

HIV

Protein coat containing DNA

RNA

Coat

Rabies

Bacteriophage

Fig. 26.10. Virus shapes.

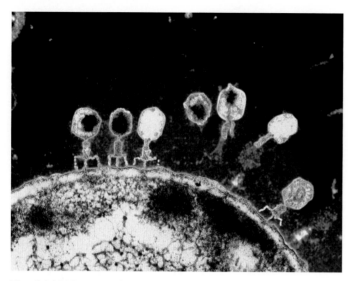

Fig. 26.11. Bacteriophage attack.

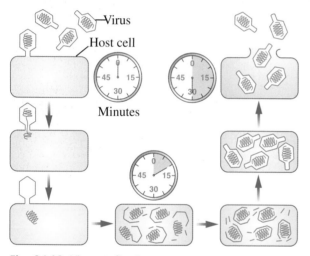

Fig. 26.12. Virus replication.

Fig. 26.13. Tobacco mosaic virus.

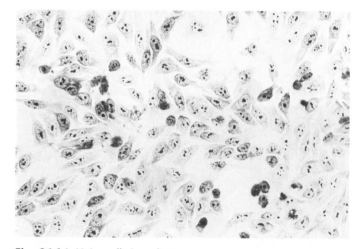

Fig. 26.14. HeLa cells in culture.

Defence against viruses

The immune system will defend the body against viruses in the usual way — by phagocytes and specific lymphocytes. Vaccines are available for most viruses. Antibiotics, such as penicillin, have no effect on viruses. *Interferon* — from white blood cells or cultured from bacteria — is used to control viruses.

Importance of viruses

Viruses are both economically and medically important.

(a) Harmful virus

Virus diseases include: colds, 'flu, mumps, measles, chicken pox, smallpox, genital herpes, cold sores, warts, viral hepatitis, German measles (rubella), rabies and AIDS (caused by HIV — see below). Most of these are considered 'once-only' diseases due to the memory of the body's immune system.

Tobacco mosaic virus (the first virus discovered — by the Russian, Dmitri Ivanovski, in 1892) attacks both tobacco and tomato plants, causing huge crop losses. Beet yellow virus attacks sugar beet, cabbages and spinach.

(b) Beneficial viruses

Viruses, cultured in HeLa cells (see Chapter 11) and other living tissue media, are used for research into genetic engineering and nucleic acid metabolism. Attenuated viruses are used to make vaccines.

The word *virus* was in use long before the discovery of microorganisms. The word comes from Latin and means *venom* or *poisonous* fluid. Until the nineteenth century, it was used to describe any infectious agent.

HIV

HIV stands for the **Human Immunodeficiency Virus**. It is an unusual virus disease in that it attacks the immune system of the body. It is responsible for causing AIDS or *Acquired Immune Deficiency Syndrome*.

VIRUS NATURE

HIV is a *retrovirus* — it contains RNA and uses it to make DNA within the host cells.

TRANSMISSION

HIV is transmitted from one person to another in sexual fluids and blood plasma. It may also be transmitted to babies through the placenta and in breast milk.

HIGH-RISK GROUPS

Those receiving blood transfusions, intravenous drug users (via contaminated needles), haemophiliacs receiving blood products and those with multiple sexual partners are high risk groups.

EFFECTS

HIV attacks and destroys *helper-T lymphocytes* in the immune system. These white blood cells normally stimulate other immune system cells. The virus remains dormant for a long time and may be activated by the body's response to a particular infection. After a long incubation period, the immune system deteriorates and the patient suffers from opportunistic diseases that they would normally be able to resist. This is an *immunodeficiency*. The patient eventually dies from diseases such as pneumonia and cancers, rather than from HIV itself. HIV can also attack brain cells directly.

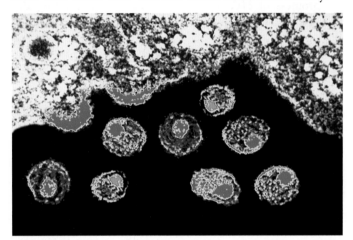

Fig. 26.15. HIV.

DIAGNOSIS

Blood tests will reveal the presence of HIV antibodies. The patient is then said to be 'HIV positive'. This only means that the virus has been present inside the person at some time in the past. It may be still there and active, it may be dormant or it may be gone.

TREATMENT

Two different vaccines are currently under test with mixed results. However, HIV constantly mutates and this makes the production of an effective vaccine difficult.

At present, there is no particular cure for the disease.

PROTECTION

- Avoid unknown or multiple sexual partners.
- Avoid contact with blood or bodily fluids from others.

- Use condoms during sex if your partner's status is unknown.
- Only use screened blood products.
- Never use contaminated needles.
- Avoid blood products in underdeveloped countries. Use extra holiday insurance to fly home immediately in emergencies.

STATISTICS

The Department of Health provides statistics in relation to the progress of HIV in Ireland. In a survey covering the period from 1986 to June 2000, the following data were gathered:

- 2,364 cases have tested positive — an increase of 169 in the last six months of this period.
- Of this total, 41% were drug users, 22.4% were homosexuals, 19.5% heterosexuals or risk unspecified, 17% were children, haemophiliacs and others. About half of all cases have died.
- A more detailed breakdown of these figures is available at: http://www.doh.ie/pdfdocs/stats_hivaids.pdf.

SUMMARY

- Non-specific immunities do not require previous exposure to the pathogen and work against microorganisms in general.
- Specific or acquired immunities develop after contact with specific pathogens and only protect against those pathogens alone.
- The first line of defence is an outer barrier of non-specific immunities:
  - the skin;
  - the acid barrier in the stomach;
  - mucus, cilia and the coughing reflex in the trachea;
  - macrophages in the respiratory system;
  - earwax, nose mucus, saliva and tear fluid;
  - commensal flora.
- The second line of defence is also non-specific:
  - the inflammatory response triggered by the release of histamine;
  - blood clotting;
  - phagocytic white blood cells.
- The third line of defence is specific and termed the Immune Response:
  - the body recognises antigens and makes specific protein antibodies to destroy them;
  - antigens and antibodies bind together — the antigen–antibody complex;
  - the antigen is destroyed.
- Active immunity arises when the body manufactures its own antibodies in response to the arrival of a specific antigen.
- Passive immunity arises when 'ready-made' antibodies turn up in the bloodstream.
- Active immunities are delayed but long lasting as the host retains a memory of how to make the antibodies.
- Passive immunities are immediate but short-lived.
- Vaccination is a method of immunisation where a harmless (attenuated) form of the pathogen trains the immune system into making appropriate antibodies for long-term protection.
- Viruses are akaryotic — they do not have a cellular structure.
- Viruses have to be cultured inside living cells.
- Viruses are extremely small.
- All viruses consist of a protein coat, a nucleic acid core and some enzymes.
- There are three basic virus shapes:
  - polyhedral — like a cut diamond;
  - helical — a spiral or helix;
  - complex.
- The stages in viral reproduction are:
  - enzymes cut an opening in the host cell wall;
  - nucleic acid is injected in;
  - virus DNA is incorporated in the host's DNA;
  - virus DNA directs the host cell to form copies of virus coats and cores;
  - the host cell bursts (lyses) and releases new viruses.

- The immune system will defend the body against viruses by phagocytes and specific lymphocytes.
- Vaccines are available for most viruses.
- Antibiotics, such as penicillin, have no effect on viruses.

EXTENDED SUMMARY

- The human immune system consists of white blood cells (leucocytes) and lymphatic tissue.
- Bone marrow and the thymus gland are primary lymphatic tissues.
- The tonsils, spleen and the lymph nodes are secondary lymphatic tissues.
- The types of white blood cell are:

  - granulocytes — phagocytic cells that can become mast cells;
  - monocytes — non-phagocytic cells that develop into macrophages — the body's rubbish-collectors;
  - lymphocytes — small, rounded cells with large nuclei — responsible for all of the specific responses of the immune system.

- When lymphocytes and matching antigens come into contact, the lymphocytes respond by first forming identical copies or clones of themselves.
- B-lymphocytes form two types of clone: plasma cells and memory-B cells.
- Plasma cells secrete antibodies, which combine with the antigen and destroy it.
- Memory-B cells retain a long term 'memory' of the antigen and can divide to form more memory cells and plasma cells if the same antigen should ever return.
- T-lymphocytes form four types of clone: *killer-T cells, memory-T cells, helper-T cells and suppressor-T cells.*
- Killer-T cells cut tiny holes in the antigens and destroy them.
- Memory-T cells retain a 'memory' of the antigen.
- Helper-T cells secrete chemicals that stimulate the action of all other immune cells and greatly enhance their effect.
- Helper-T cells often secrete interferon, which stimulates the production of more B-cells.

- Suppressor-T cells inhibit the action of killer-T cells a few weeks after activation.
- The response of T-lymphocytes is termed cell-mediated immunity.
- The response of B-lymphocytes is termed humoral-mediated (or antibody-mediated) immunity.

KEY WORDS

Pathogens	Microorganisms that cause disease.
Immunity	The body's ability to resist disease.
Non-specific or innate immunities	Do not require previous exposure to the pathogen and work against microorganisms in general.
Specific immunities	Develop after contact with specific pathogens and only protect against those pathogens alone.
Commensal flora	Natural populations of microorganisms living on and in the body.
Macrophages	Scavenging white blood cells that leave the bloodstream and attack any foreign matter.
Histamine	A chemical that causes the blood vessels in the infected area to dilate and bring more blood to the site.
Phagocytic cells	Identify and eat anything foreign inside the body.
Immune Response	The body's ability to recognise foreign invaders and to make specific protein antibodies to destroy them.
Antigen	Any chemical recognised by the immune system as being foreign.
Antibody	A protein made by the immune system in response to an antigen.

Antigen–antibody complex	Formed when antigens and antibodies bind together.
Agglutinate	Stick together.
Active immunity	When the body manufactures its own antibodies in response to the arrival of a specific antigen.
Vaccine	A heat-treated or preserved form of an antigen injected into the blood.
Passive immunity	When 'ready-made' antibodies turn up in the bloodstream.
Horse serum	Horse blood plasma with the clotting proteins removed.
Immunisation	Any artificial process that gives immunity to a patient.
Vaccination	A method of immunisation where a harmless form of the pathogen trains the immune system into making appropriate antibodies for long-term protection.
Viruses	Extremely small infectious agents. Made from nucleic acid and protein.
Cell theory	First proposed by Schleiden and Schwann in 1839 — states that the cell is the structural and functional unit of all living organisms.
Akaryotic	Having no cellular structure.
Obligate parasites	Required to use living cells to complete their life cycle.
Capsid	The protein coat of a virus.
Polyhedral	Many-faced or many-sided.
Capsomeres	Units of the capsid.
Helical	Wrapped in a spiral or helix.
Bacteriophages	Viruses that attack bacteria.
HIV	Human Immunodeficiency Virus.
AIDS	Acquired Immune Deficiency Syndrome.
Syndrome	A collection of symptoms.

Retrovirus	Contains RNA and uses it to make DNA within the host cells.

EXTENDED KEY WORDS

Granulocytes	Are large white blood cells with irregular nuclei and granules in their cytoplasm.
Mast cells	Modified granulocytes that release histamine.
Monocytes	Large cells with kidney-shaped nuclei.
Macrophages	The body's rubbish-collectors.
Lymphocytes	Small, rounded cells with large nuclei.
T-lymphocytes	Travel first to the thymus gland to complete their development and then move on to the lymph nodes.
B-lymphocytes	Complete their development in the bone marrow and then move directly to the lymph nodes.
'Self cells	Cells naturally occurring in the body.
Plasma cells	Secrete antibodies.
Memory-B cells	Retain a long term 'memory' of antigens.
Humoral-mediated immunity	An immune response through antibodies made by B-lymphocytes.
Killer-T cells	Cut tiny holes in the antigens and destroy them.
Memory-T cells	Retain a 'memory' of an antigen and bring about a much faster response if the antigen ever returns.
Helper-T cells	Secrete chemicals (e.g. interferon) that stimulate the action of all other immune cells.

| Suppressor-T cells | Inhibit the action of killer-T cells a few weeks after activation. |
| Cell-mediated immunity | An immune response through the action of T-lymphocytes. |

QUESTIONS

1. What are pathogens? Name three groups of pathogens and give three examples of each.

2. Define immunity. Explain the difference between non-specific immunity and specific immunity. Summarise the three lines of defence that pathogens have to negotiate within the human body.

3. Explain how each of the following helps to protect the body against microorganisms:

   a. macrophages;
   b. histamine;
   c. lysozyme;
   d. phagocytes;
   e. antibodies.

4. Name four regions of the head not protected by skin. Explain how each region defends itself against attack from microorganisms.

5. Explain the difference between active immunity and passive immunity. Why are passive immunities described as 'immediate but short-lived'? Why are active immunities described as 'delayed but long-lasting'?

6. What are the two types of immunisation used in medicine? If a deep cut is suspected of contamination with bacteria, doctors advise an immediate anti-tetanus injection. What do you think is contained in the injection? Doctors also prescribe a follow-up injection months later. What is contained in this second injection and why do the doctors think the follow-up is important?

7. What is a *vaccine*? Name three diseases which people are routinely vaccinated against. What criticisms could you make of Edward Jenner's experiments in discovering the technique of vaccination?

8. What is a virus? Why are viruses described as *obligate parasites*?
   Discuss whether or not viruses are living organisms.

9. State the three basic shapes of viruses and give two examples of each. Draw a simple, labelled diagram of a named virus.

10. Describe the reproduction of viruses within cells. What treatments are successful against viral infection?

11. Explain the difference between HIV and AIDS. A person is diagnosed as HIV$^+$ but does not suffer from AIDS. How can this happen? What steps can be taken to prevent infection with HIV?

12. True or false?

    a. You never catch the same cold twice.
    b. Kissing can spread AIDS.
    c. HIV attacks all blood cells.
    d. Antibiotics protect against colds and 'flu.
    e. Viruses can cause decay.

EXTENDED QUESTIONS

13. What causes organ rejection after certain transplants? What is an immunosuppressant drug? Why is it risky to treat rejection with immunosuppressants?

14. Distinguish between:

    a. primary lymphatic tissue and secondary lymphatic tissue;
    b. lymphocytes and monocytes;
    c. T-lymphocytes and B-lymphocytes;
    d. granulocytes and mast cells;
    e. killer-T cell and helper-T cells.

15. What is pre-processing of lymphocytes?

16. Construct a chart to compare T-lymphocytes and B-lymphocytes. Use the headings: site of formation, site of maturing, types of clone, type of action.

17. Distinguish between humoral-mediated and cell-mediated immunity.

OPTIONAL ACTIVITIES

- The following vaccines are often used in immunisation programmes. Use the Internet or other resources to research any of the diseases they protect against:

– Pertussis (whooping cough)
– Diphtheria
– Tetanus
– Polio
– Typhoid
– Rubella (German measles)
– Cholera
– Diphtheria-tetanus-pertussis (DTP)

– Tuberculosis (Bacillus Calmette Guérin or BCG vaccine)
– Mumps-measles-Rubella (MMR)
– Varicella (chicken pox, shingles)
– Meningitis C
– Influenza
– Measles
– Mumps
– Rabies
– Hepatitis A

Present a report to the class or design a poster to launch a public awareness campaign.
- Survey the class to gather information about their childhood diseases.

For information on websites dealing with subjects covered in this chapter see www.my-etest.com.

Now test yourself at
www.my-etest.com

Chapter 27

Reproduction in the Flowering Plant

Learning objectives

After your study of this chapter, you should be able to:

- distinguish between reproduction and growth;
- compare sexual and asexual reproduction;
- list the events in flowering plant sexual reproduction;
- describe the different methods of pollination;
- outline the process of fertilisation;
- describe the development of fruits and seeds;
- explain the need for seed dispersal and dormancy;
- list the factors necessary for germination and outline its main stages;
- state examples of plant asexual reproduction;
- compare seed reproduction with vegetative reproduction.

Extended learning objectives

- Outline the development of pollen grains and embryo sacs.

Mandatory activities

#21. Investigating the effect of water, oxygen and temperature on germination.
#22. Investigating the digestive activity in germinating seeds.

REPRODUCTION AND GROWTH   [360]

Fig. 27.1. Cherry blossoms.

Fig. 27.2. Swans with cygnets.

INTRODUCTION

Reproduction is the ability to produce more organisms of the same species. These organisms will be physically independent of their parents.

Growth is an increase in the *size* of an organism until parent size is reached. It usually includes an increase in complexity.

Organisms grow by increasing their *cell size* (through the addition of nutrients) and increasing their *cell number* (through mitosis). Growth is considered irreversible in biology.

Reproduction is a characteristic of all living organisms and is necessary for the continuity of life. All biological structures have a limited life span and no organism can live forever. Consequently, for life to continue on Earth, new, replacement organisms must be formed to carry on in place of the older, doomed parents.

There are two methods of reproduction in biology: *sexual and asexual.*

SEXUAL REPRODUCTION

Sexual reproduction involves two sources of special, haploid reproductive cells, or sex cells (*gametes*), made by meiosis. These gametes join together (by *fertilisation*) and form a diploid *zygote*. Given appropriate food and environmental conditions, this zygote develops into an embryo, which develops into a juvenile stage and eventually into another adult — and a potential parent capable of further reproduction.

In sexual reproduction, the new individual resembles its two parents but is not identical to either of them, instead being

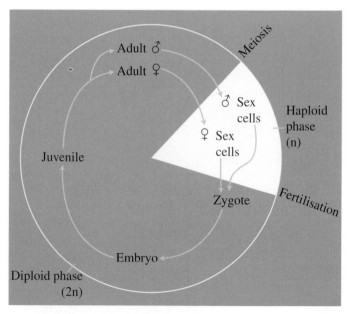

Fig. 27.3. The sexual life cycle.

a random mixture of the features of both. Normally, the two parents are termed male (♂) and female (♀). *Male parents make motile sex cells* (sex cells that can move themselves) and *female parents make non-motile sex cells* (sex cells that cannot move themselves).

(The male symbol, ♂, represents the spear of Hermes, the ancient Greek god. The female symbol, ♀, represents the mirror of Aphrodite, the beautiful ancient Greek goddess. The word '*hermaphrodite*', meaning containing both male and female reproductive organs, is a blend of the two names. Some invertebrates and almost all plants are hermaphrodite.)

N.B.

Haploid (n)	describes cells containing a single set of chromosomes.
Diploid (2n) (See Chapter 11.)	describes cells containing a double set of chromosomes.

Sexual reproduction is found in all animals and plants, most fungi and some bacteria. It is perhaps Nature's preferred method of reproduction, as it increases variety amongst the members of any population.

ASEXUAL (NON-SEXUAL) REPRODUCTION

This is where a part of a living organism breaks away and develops into a completely independent individual. No sex cells are involved and the new individual is genetically identical to its single parent.

Examples include a bacterial cell splitting in two (*binary fission*), spore formation in mosses and ferns and cuttings taken from a geranium plant.

Asexual reproduction is found in all bacteria, fungi and plants and in a few, primitive animals.

Table 27.1. Chart comparing sexual and asexual life cycles

Asexual life cycles	Sexual life cycles
Only one parent required	Two sources of sex cells required
No sex cells formed	Sex cells formed
No meiosis occurs	Meiosis occurs at some stage
No cell fusion occurs	Cell fusion (fertilisation) occurs
Offspring genetically identical to parents	Offspring combine the parental features
Little variety within the population	Lots of variety within the population
Found in bacteria, fungi, plants and some animals	Found in some bacteria, most fungi, all plants and animals
A relatively fast process	A relatively slow process

SEXUAL REPRODUCTION IN THE FLOWERING PLANT   [361]

Of all the plant forms on the Earth, flowering plants are the most successful. They inhabit just about everywhere and occur in enormous variety. They are found mostly on land and in their reproduction they tend to make great use of the terrestrial conditions there — in particular the wind and the presence of animals.

The sexual reproduction of flowering plants is highly evolved and features the following stages:

1. Flowers form, usually in the spring. The flowers produce male pollen and female ovules.

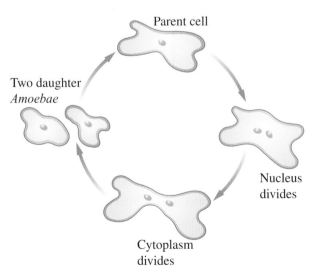

Fig. 27.4. Asexual life cycle of *Amoeba*.

Parent cell

Two daughter *Amoebae*

Nucleus divides

Cytoplasm divides

Petal   Carpel
          (♀)

(♂)
Stamen   Sepal

Fig. 27.5. Passion flowers, poppy and dog rose.

2. Male and female sex cells are formed by *meiosis*; male sex cells inside the pollen grains and female sex cells inside the ovules.
3. Pollination takes place; by wind or insects.
4. Fertilisation takes place inside the female ovule.
5. Embryos form inside seeds that are inside fruits. Unwanted flower parts now wither.

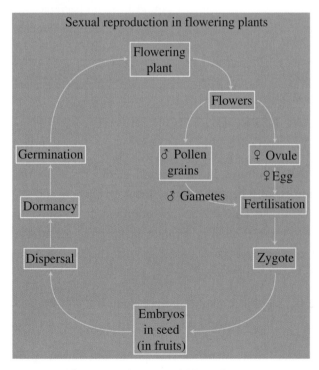

Fig. 27.6. Flowering plant sexual life cycle.

6. Fruits and seeds are dispersed from the parent plant.
7. Seeds lie dormant awaiting favourable conditions.
8. Seeds germinate.
9. An adult flowering plant develops.

FLOWERS

Flowers are reproductive organs. They contain the structures required for sexual reproduction to take place. Flowers consist of a central support or receptacle, on which are attached four groups of structures — all developed from modified leaves. Outermost are the *sepals*, then the *petals*. Within the petals are ♂ *stamens* and in the centre, one or more ♀ *carpels*.

Cherry blossoms

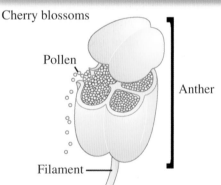

Fig. 27.7. The anther of the ♂ stamen.

- *Sepals* protect the young flower when it is a bud.
- *Petals* may be brightly coloured, scented and contain nectaries — pockets of nectar — for insect attraction. Alternatively the petals may be green, inconspicuous and reduced to suit wind pollination (see later).
- *Stamens* are the male parts of the flower. The *anther* forms pollen grains by *meiosis*. The grains are later released when

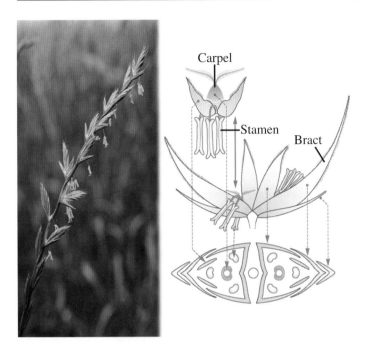

Fig. 27.8. Rye flowers (wind pollinated).

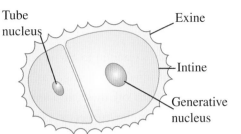

Fig. 27.10. Pollen grain.

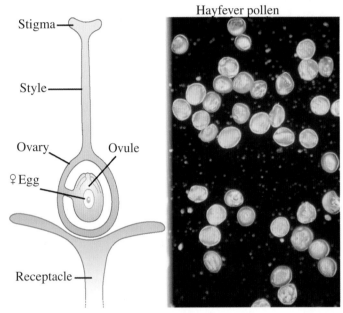

Fig. 27.11. Carpel with ovule and embryo sac.

the anther dries up, cracks and splits open. (This is called *dehiscence* and is an example of a plant making use of terrestrial conditions.) The *filament* supports the anther and transports water and nutrients to it.

- *Carpels* are the female parts of the flower. The *stigma* is a raised platform to receive pollen grains. The *style* supports the stigma and leads back to the ovary. The *ovary* contains many ovules, which develop an *embryo sac* by meiosis. The embryo sac contains a single female gamete — the egg. A single carpel or a group of fused carpels is also called a *pistil*.

N.B.

- Most plants have *monoecious* flowers, i.e. with both male and female structures present in the same flower. Some plants are *dioecious*, with separate male and female plants, e.g. willow, *Begonia*, Shepherd's purse and holly.
- Stamens and carpels are known as *essential flower parts* as they are the parts directly concerned in the process of reproduction. Sepals and petals are known as *accessory flower parts* — not directly concerned in reproduction.

At this point, it is a good idea to gather a collection of flowers for general examination. Draw exactly what you see in each case and try to identify the flower by use of keys, guidebooks or a reference collection. Name all of the parts observed.

Hay fever

Hay fever or *seasonal allergic rhinitis* is a *pollen allergy*. It is a very common condition in Ireland. It is often accompanied by asthma, another allergic condition.

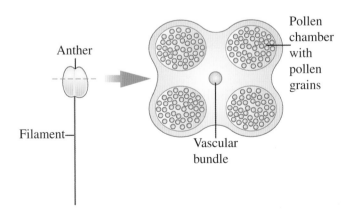

Fig. 27.9. Transverse section of anther.

CAUSE

The condition is due to the body's reaction to allergens (see Chapter 26) on the surfaces of inhaled pollen grains. Specific antibodies are formed to fight off these invaders and the resulting antigen–antibody complex triggers a release of histamine, which causes the symptoms of the condition. The allergens are completely non-threatening, but this does not stop the body from over-reacting.

SYMPTOMS

Repeated sneezing, itchiness in the eyes, nose, ears and throat, and difficulty in sleeping. A 'runny nose' is common too. Some people have a greater allergic tendency than others and suffer very badly from the condition. Extreme cases can lead to sinusitis — inflammation of the sinus cavities in the skull. Many sufferers develop growths within the nose — nasal polyps — and many develop asthma.

POLLEN TYPES

Wind-borne pollen grains are more likely to be the source of hay fever than insect-borne, heavier grains. The main culprits are grasses and cereals. The 'hay-fever season' is generally in late spring and early summer, when grasses produce their pollen. Many people suffer from allergy to fungal spores, which are found in damp places all year round.

TREATMENT

- Avoid the allergens if possible. Wear a mask if working in high-risk conditions. In extreme cases, some sufferers move house.
- Take antihistamines which will control the release of histamine in the body. There is a huge range of products available — an indication that no one product is particularly successful. Patients have to discover the best product for their individual case.
- Inhaled or injected steroids can give great relief but cannot be used in the long term.
- Complementary treatments such as acupuncture or restrictive diet can offer relief to some patients.

POLLINATION

This is *transfer of pollen from the anther of the stamen to the stigma of the carpel.*

- *Self-pollination* is when pollen lands on the stigma of the same flower (or on another flower on the same plant). This will lead to genetic self-fertilisation and little variety will result from this method of reproduction.
- *Cross-pollination* is when pollen reaches the stigma of another plant of the same species. This produces healthier variety in the offspring (a mixture of the features of the two parent plants is obtained). Cross-pollination needs the help of *wind* or *insects* to move the pollen grains to the stigma.

Table 27.2. Wind- and insect-pollinated flowers

Wind-pollinated (*anemophilous*) flowers	Insect-pollinated (*entomophilous*) flowers
No scent	Scented
Green colour	Bright non-green colours
No nectaries	Nectaries present
Small, light, smooth pollen grains	Large, sticky pollen grains
Very large numbers of pollen grains	Smaller numbers of pollen grains
Inconspicuous flowers	Conspicuous flowers
Inner flower parts exposed by reduced petals	Inner flower parts protected by petals
Examples: grasses and cereals	Examples: wallflower, buttercup, rose etc.

Some plants avoid self-pollination by the following methods:

- concealed inner parts, e.g. snapdragon;
- separate male and female flowers, e.g. willow and holly;
- chemical incompatibility — pollen fails to develop on its own stigma;
- male and female parts mature at different times, e.g. bluebells.

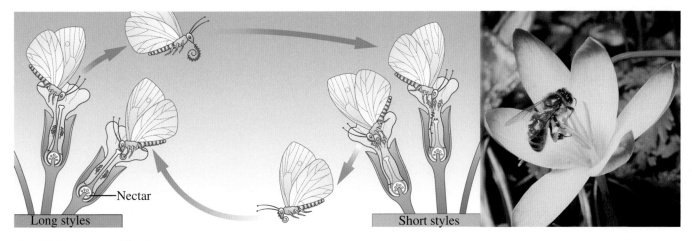

Nectar

Long styles

Short styles

Fig. 27.12. Insect pollination.

Controlled Cross-Pollination

Controlled cross-pollination is used in agriculture and horticulture as a method of producing new varieties of plant. Pollen is removed from the anthers of the donor plant (or ♂ parent) and rubbed onto the stigmas of the recipient (or ♀ parent). In this way the offspring *may* combine the advantageous features of the parents. Some precautions have to be taken during artificial cross-pollination:

- the stamens of the recipient are removed before they develop — to prevent self-pollination;
- the petals of the ♂ donor are removed — to give better access to the pollen;
- mature anthers are used as pollen sources — they contain mature pollen grains;
- the ♀ parents are always kept inside large plastic bags inflated with air — to prevent the entry of unwanted pollen.

(Compare this method of plant breeding to asexual *micropropagation* described later.)

FERTILISATION

Fertilisation is *the fusing of male and female haploid gametes to form a diploid zygote.*

In flowering plants, this takes place, unseen, in the ovules inside the female carpels of the flower. When pollen grains land on the stigma, they form tunnels (pollen tubes) that lead directly to the embryo sac of an ovule. A chemical released by the female ovule guides the pollen tubes. This is termed chemical attraction or *chemotaxis*.

Two male gametes are formed from a cell division within the pollen grain and these gametes pass down the pollen tube to the female embryo sac.

A double fertilisation now takes place:

1. One male gamete fuses with the female egg cell to form a zygote:

$$\text{♂ gamete (n)} + \text{♀ gamete (n)} \rightarrow \text{zygote (2n)}$$

   This zygote will quickly develop into an embryo plant.

2. The second male gamete fuses with two polar nuclei in the embryo sac to form a giant endosperm nucleus. This divides rapidly to form a mass of oily endosperm tissue — a food for the developing embryo:

$$\text{♂ gamete (n)} + \text{2 polar nuclei (n, n)}$$
$$\rightarrow \text{endosperm nucleus (3n)}$$

The triploid endosperm nucleus forms masses of triploid endosperm tissue; all of its cells contain three sets of chromosomes, which, in plants, often lead to rapid cell division.

N.B. After fertilisation, the *ovule* is referred to as a *seed* and the *ovary* is now a *fruit*.

SEED STRUCTURE

After fertilisation, the diploid zygote grows into a plant embryo, while the triploid endosperm tissue divides repeat-

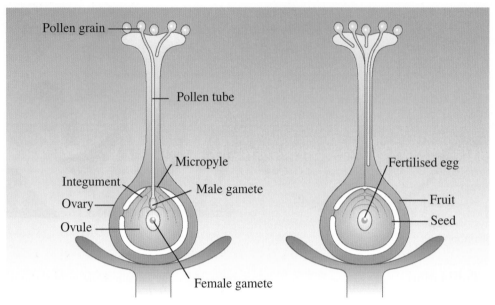

Fig. 27.13. Before and after fertilisation.

edly to form a food supply. This food supply on site is essential, as the embryo has no other way of feeding itself; there is no blood supply as in humans, and photosynthesis is not possible inside the completely dark seed.

The wall of the seed now hardens to form the seed coat or *testa* and all other flower parts wither away. Within the testa lie the plant embryo and its food supply. The embryo consists of:

1. a *radicle* — which will form the plant root;
2. a *plumule* — which will form the plant shoot; and
3. one or two *cotyledons* — which store food.

The embryo may be surrounded by an additional food supply — an oily *endosperm*.

- In some seeds (e.g. castor oil or sunflower) large amounts of endosperm are produced and the plant embryo remains quite small. These are described as *endospermic seeds*. Most monocots are endospermic.
- In other seeds (e.g. peas and beans) most of the oily endosperm is converted to sugar and then taken inside the cotyledons of the plant embryo. This results in a large embryo and little sign of any endosperm. These are *non-endospermic seeds*. Most dicots are non-endospermic.

Flowering plants are classified as either *monocots* (monocotyledonous plants) or *dicots* (dicotyledonous plants)

depending on whether their embryos have one or two cotyledons. Peas and beans are dicot plants, corn is a monocot.

Fig. 27.14. A germinating bean seed showing two cotyledons and an emerging plumule with leaves.

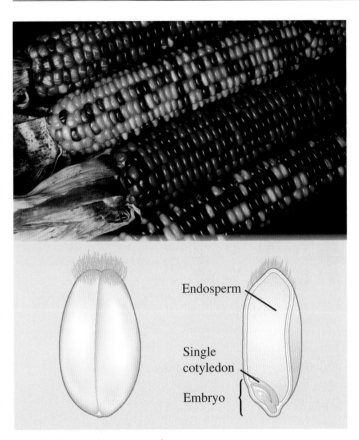

Fig. 27.15. Seed structure of corn.

Table 27.3. Monocots and dicots

Monocots	Dicots
One cotyledon in embryo	Two cotyledons in embryo
Parallel leaf veins	Leaf veins reticulated (netted)
Vascular bundles scattered through stem	Vascular bundles in a cylinder in stem
Cambium tissue in vascular bundles	No cambium in vascular bundles
Have tap roots usually	Have fibrous roots usually
Seeds generally endo-spermic	Seeds generally non-endo-spermic
Examples: geranium, rose, oak, wallflower.	Examples: grasses, cereals, bamboo, tulips

FRUIT FORMATION AND DISPERSAL

As the seeds develop, the ovary of the flower becomes the fruit and a fruit wall or pericarp now develops from the ovary wall. Fruit development is due to the action of growth regulators within the plant (see Chapter 23). Seeds lie within the fruit.

Fruit examples

Any seed container is usually a fruit, i.e. developed from the ovary of the flower. Besides the obvious oranges, lemons, plums, raspberries and cherries, fruits include brazil nuts, hazelnuts, peanuts, pea pods, tomatoes, cucumbers, peppers, sycamore 'helicopters', poppy capsules, apple cores and the 'pips' on the outside of strawberries.

Fig. 27.16. Cucumber and tomato fruits.

Fig. 27.17. Dandelion fruits and flowers.

In the fruit industry, it is possible to improve the size, appearance and even taste of fruits and vegetables by scientific technique. *Parthenocarpy* is the development of seedless fruits (*virgin fruits*). This can happen quite naturally or is sometimes brought about by genetic manipulation or the application of plant growth regulators. Examples of parthenocarps are: bananas, pineapples, figs, seedless grapes, some cucumbers and sometimes dandelions. Ethene (ethylene) is a plant growth regulator that is artificially applied in the fruit industry to ripen bananas, melons and tomatoes, and to 'degreen' oranges, lemons and grapefruit in time for arrival in the shops.

Fig. 27.18. Fruit formation and various fruits.

Dispersal

Dispersal is the scattering of seeds from the parent plant and fruits are developed with seed dispersal in mind. Unlike most animals, plants tend to be fixed in one place after they start to grow. To avoid competition between parents and offspring for precious resources, plants use their fruits to disperse their seeds before germination. It is to no one's advantage if the new plants attempt to grow on top of the parent — the survival rate of all involved will be lowered. Dispersal increases the chances of survival.

An examination of the fruit will usually reveal the method of dispersal employed by the plant.

Table 27.4. Fruits and dispersal

Description of the fruit	Probable agent of dispersal	Examples
Dry, shaped as wings or parachutes	Carried by the wind	Sycamore, dandelion
Soft, juicy, tasty, nutritious and often brightly coloured	Animals eat the fruits and egest the undigested seeds at a later time and place.	Berries, tomatoes, oranges
Tiny hooks on the fruit coat	Attach to animal fur then fall off later	Burdock, goose grass
Fruits are buoyant due to spongy pericarp and trapped air	Float away from aquatic parents	Lily, coconut
Fruit parts dry out unevenly and open with a sudden twisting motion	Seeds are catapulted away from the parent (*self-dispersal or active dispersal*)	Pea pods, wallflower, *busy lizzie*

Dormancy

Seeds regularly enter a state of dormancy before they germinate. Dormancy is a resting period where growth and development cease and metabolism is at the minimum necessary for survival.

There are two major advantages in having a period of dormancy:

1. The plant can avoid germination during unfavourable conditions (such as winter).
2. Dormancy allows more time for dispersal to be completed.

Dormancy is sometimes imposed on seeds by very harsh conditions. More usually though, the dormancy is 'planned' by the seed. This type of dormancy (*innate dormancy*) can be due to the impermeability of the seed coat or to genetic programming in the embryo.

Horticulturists are well aware of dormancy and overcome its delay by freezing seeds at -5 °C for a few weeks. Scoring or removal of the seed coat can also hasten germination.

Germination

Germination describes the emergence of the plant embryo from its seed. The essential conditions for germination are adequate water, a supply of oxygen and a suitable temperature. The effect of light on germination is quite variable; different seeds have different requirements and many require no light at all. For germination to occur:

- water is required for digesting food reserves and mobilising enzymes;
- oxygen is required for aerobic respiration, which will provide energy from the stored food;
- warmth is required for optimum enzyme function.

Mandatory activity #21. Investigating the effect of water, oxygen and temperature on germination

RESOURCES NEEDED

Germinating seeds (use beans, radish, lentil, lettuce, peas, mustard or cress, or any suitable seeds).
Test tubes.
Corks.
Cotton wool.
Oil.
Cold boiled water.
Refrigerator.
Tin foil.

In this investigation, a number of plant seeds are placed in different conditions to determine the necessary conditions for germination. The factors under investigation are light, temperature, oxygen and water. Ten seeds are used in each test tube rather than one or two, as some seeds may fail to germinate regardless of their conditions.

METHOD

1. Use suitable seeds as above and prepare test tubes as follows:

   - Tubes A and D contain moist cotton wool and ten seeds each.
   - Tube B contains dry cotton wool and ten seeds.
   - Tube C contains cotton wool, ten seeds, some cold, boiled water (gently poured) and a layer of oil. This tube contains no oxygen (see fig. 27.19).

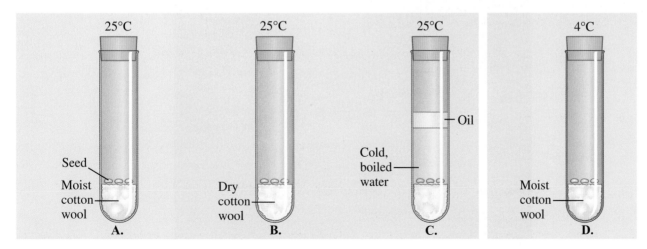

Fig. 27.19. To investigate the conditions necessary for germination.

2. Wrap all four tubes in tin foil to exclude light.

3. Place tubes A, B and C in a warm location. Place tube D in a fridge.

4. Prepare a second set of tubes as above but *do not* wrap these in tin foil.

5. Place tubes A, B and C in a warm location as before, but with light. Place tube D in a fridge with a light source.

6. Examine the eight tubes after about five to seven days and count the number of seeds that has germinated in each.

7. Calculate the % germination for each tube.

8. Record results on a suitable chart and report on your findings.

STAGES IN GERMINATION

1. *Water absorption.* Water enters the seed through a tiny opening — the micropyle (also used for the entry of the pollen tube into the ovule before fertilisation). This results in a dramatic increase in weight (up to 150%) and a swelling of the embryo tissue. Most water enters the seed by osmosis.

2. *Testa fracture.* The swelling embryo tissue fractures the seed coat, or testa. This allows the escape of inhibiting CO_2 gas and the entry of oxygen and water. The fractured testa will also allow the embryo to emerge.

3. *Mobilisation of food reserves.* The absorbed water activates the enzymes of the embryo and all stored food is quickly digested (*hydrolysed*) and moved to the parts of the embryo that need it. Respiration occurs at a very high rate in germinating seeds.

4. *The radicle emerges* and grows downwards to form the root.

5. (a) In some seeds, the *plumule* now emerges and grows upwards to form the plant shoot. The cotyledons of the embryo stay inside the seed, are drained of all food and shrivel up. This is termed *hypogeal germination* and is found in large, dry seeds such as peas, beans, wheat and maize. (*Hypogeal* means *below ground* and refers to the position of the cotyledons.) In wheat and maize, the plumule is protected by a sheath or *coleoptile*.

(b) In other seeds, *the cotyledons* are dragged out of the seed by the hypocotyl and pushed above the soil. They turn green and start photosynthesis as temporary *seed leaves*. True, foliage leaves soon replace them. This type of germination is termed *epigeal germination* and is found in small seeds such as sunflower, castor oil and cress. (*Epigeal* means *outside the ground* and again refers to the position of the cotyledons.)

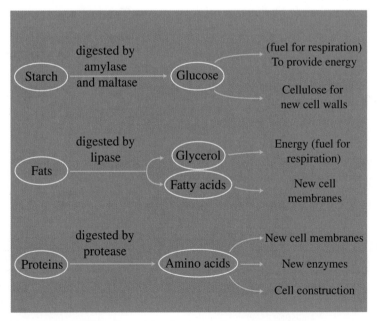

Fig. 27.20. Mobilisation of food reserves in germinating seeds.

Fig. 27.21. Hypogeal (above) and epigeal germination.

Mandatory activity #22. Investigating the digestive activity in germinating seeds

RESOURCES NEEDED:

Petri dishes containing starch agar (see Appendix B for preparation).

Pre-soaked peas, beans or maize 'seeds' (really maize fruits).

Backed razor blade.

Iodine solution.

In this investigation, seeds are cut open and their tissues left in contact with starch agar. Any active amylase will convert the starch to maltose. After a few days, the agar plates are flooded with iodine solution to see if any starch has been digested. A navy colour indicates that starch is still present, clear or yellow indicates that starch has been digested.

METHOD

1. Pre-soak the seeds in water for about two days. Drain the water and leave the seeds in a damp container for another day. Eight seeds are needed per group.
2. Boil half of the seeds in water for ten minutes.
3. Split all the seeds in half with a sharp, backed blade.
4. Place four boiled halves face down on one agar plate and four unboiled halves on another plate.
5. Cover the plates and leave in a dark, warm place for two to three days.
6. Flood each dish with iodine solution for about two minutes.
7. Pour off the iodine, place each dish on white paper and look for clear / yellow areas within the navy.

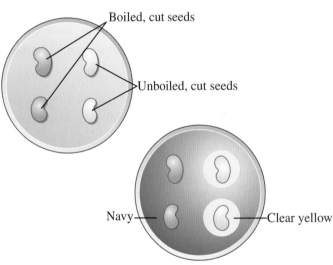

Fig. 27.22. To demonstrate the action of amylase in germinating seeds.

VEGETATIVE PROPAGATION (OR VEGETATIVE REPRODUCTION)

The term 'vegetative' refers to the non-sexual parts of the plant, i.e. the roots, stems and leaves. Propagation refers to a natural spreading-out by reproduction.

Vegetative propagation is when the roots, stems or leaves of a plant become modified to bring about an asexual reproduction. Typically, part of the plant becomes swollen with food and develops into a new, independent plant. This is an asexual process and the new plant will be genetically identical to its parent. Most plants are capable of this and the

Fig. 27.23. Carrots.

part of the plant involved is often quite a substantial organ. These organs are usually food stores such as rhizomes, bulbs, swollen roots and stems (root and stem tubers). They are called *perennating organs* and are a means of surviving the winter. Alternatively, vegetative propagation can be brought about artificially.

In each of the following examples of natural propagation, part of the plant is changed or modified to bring about asexual reproduction.

Modified roots

■ *Swollen tap roots* are main roots swollen with food. These survive the winter and carry on growth in the spring, e.g. carrots.

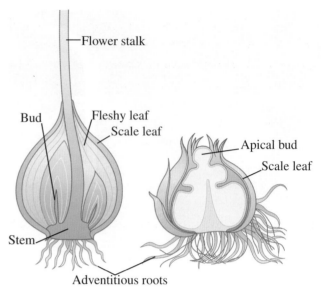

Fig. 27.25. Bulb and corm.

Modified stems

■ *Stem tubers* are swollen, underground stems. They survive the winter in the soil and new shoots grow in the spring, e.g. potatoes.

Fig. 27.24. Potatoes.

Fig. 27.26. Wild daisy.

- *Corms* are swollen stem bases. They have a stem tip and some buds, which will form new branches, e.g. crocus.
- *Rhizomes* are horizontal stems below the ground. New plants arise at the stem nodes and eventually detach themselves from the parent plant, e.g. iris.
- *Runners* are horizontal stems above the ground. New plants arise again at the stem nodes.

Modified leaves

- *Begonia* leaves fall from the plant and develop into new, identical offspring.
- *Bryophyllum* leaves form tiny 'plantlets'.

Modified buds

- *Bulbs* are buds swollen with food. They have fleshy leaves and a reduced stem, e.g. daffodils, onions.
- Buds sometimes grow into new plants, e.g. cactus.

Artificial propagation

Methods of vegetative propagation that *do not* occur in nature include the following. All require human intervention as used in agriculture and horticulture.

1. BUDDING

This method is used to propagate roses. A bud is removed from the plant to be propagated (the scion) and inserted into a T-shaped cut in the stem of a host plant (the stock). Wild roses are used as stock plants and the process is usually carried out in autumn.

Fig. 27.27. Begonia.

Fig. 27.28. Bryophyllum.

Fig. 27.29. Cactus.

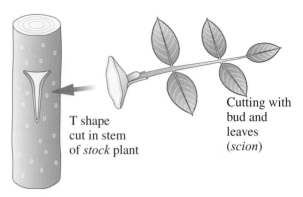

T shape
cut in stem
of *stock* plant

Cutting with
bud and
leaves
(*scion*)

Fig. 27.30. Budding.

Fig. 27.31. Geranium.

2. CUTTINGS

A healthy stem is cut from a parent and placed in damp soil to form a new plant. The stem is usually cut at an angle between two nodes. The cutting is often covered in plastic to give humid conditions. Dipping cuttings in rooting hormone can increase the chances of success. Geraniums, fuchsias and many other plants are propagated in this way.

3. GRAFTING

Grafting is similar to budding, but an entire twig is used as a scion, rather than a bud. The scion is inserted into a V-shaped notch in the stock and the joint is bound with tape. Wax can provide additional sealing. Success is more likely if the cambium cells (growing regions) of both stock and scion are aligned. Apples and pears are propagated by grafting.

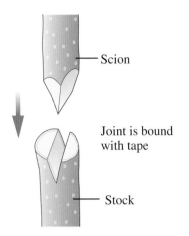

Fig. 27.32. Grafting.

4. LAYERING

A cut is made between two nodes on the stem of a suitable plant. The stem is pegged into damp soil to encourage the development of new roots at the cut. When established, the new plant can be separated from its parent. Alternatively, damp soil can be wrapped in plastic around the cut stem. Carnations are propagated by this method.

5. TISSUE CULTURE (MICROPROPAGATION)

Cells are extracted from the parent plant and separated with enzymes. When placed in sterile culture solution, they become *meristematic*, i.e. they divide repeatedly. Entire plants can grow from single cells. Often cells without cell

Fig. 27.33. Layering.

walls — termed *protoplasts* — are formed. Tobacco plants are regularly grown by tissue culture. See Chapter 11 for more information.

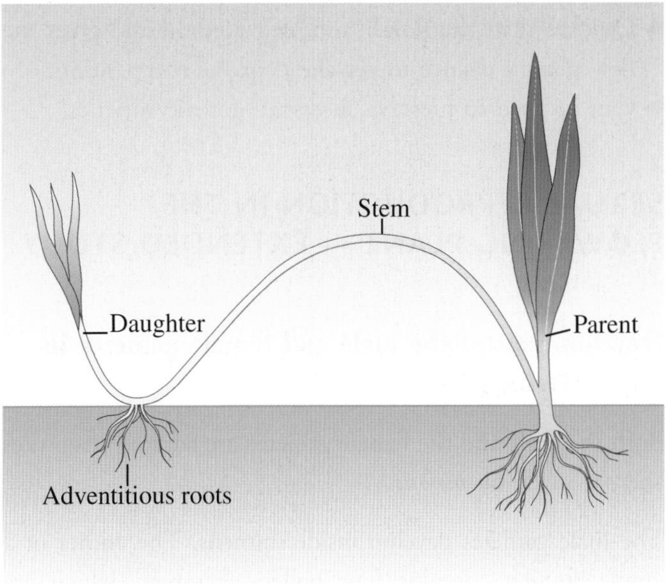

A simpler micropropagation is outlined in the optional activities at the end of the chapter.

Advantages of vegetative propagation

- Vulnerable seedlings can be avoided.
- Lots of food is immediately available to the new plant.

Table 27.5. Flowering plants classified by their life cycles

Life cycle	Description	Over-wintering?	Example
Ephemerals	Grow and flower quickly, often several times a year	Survive as seeds	Shepherd's purse
Annuals	Life cycle takes one year exactly	Survive as seeds	Saxifrage
Biennials	Life cycle takes two years	First winter — with perennating organs, second winter — as seeds	Carrot
Woody perennials	Many years of survival	Arial parts persist either with leaves (evergreens) or without (deciduous)	Pine — evergreen Oak — deciduous
Herbaceous perennials	Many years of survival	Survive as underground stems or buds	Iris, onions

- Quicker than the flower and seed method and gives the new plant a chance to get ahead of the competition.
- Can be used to preserve successful genetic varieties.

SEXUAL REPRODUCTION IN THE FLOWERING PLANT — EXTENDED STUDY
[H36 I]

Development of the male and female gametes in the flowering plant

Both the male and the female gametes are haploid structures and are made by *meiosis*.

The male gametes develop inside stamens. The anther of a young stamen contains four pollen chambers, which are filled with masses of diploid *microspore mother cells*. The chambers are lined with a layer of cells — the *tapetum* — that secretes sticky nutritive material. These microspore mother cells feed on the nourishing tapetum and then divide by *meiosis* to form haploid cells temporarily grouped in fours — *pollen tetrads*. Each of these daughter cells divides once by mitosis to form two, attached cells — a *generative cell* and a *vegetative or tube cell*. These two cells form the young pollen grain.

As the pollen grains mature, they develop a thin, inner wall — the *intine* — and a thick, outer wall — the *exine*. The exine has a characteristic appearance for each plant species and can often be used for plant identification, particularly important in the study of microfossils of pollen found in lake sediments and in peat. The exine has thin areas that will allow the later emergence of a pollen tube.

Pollen grains are released from the anther by *dehiscence*. The water supply to the anther is cut off by constriction of the filament. The walls of the pollen chambers then dry out and split longitudinally to release the grains to wind or insects.

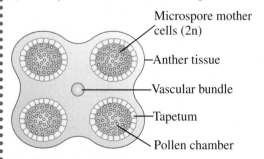

Fig. 27.34. Anther TS.

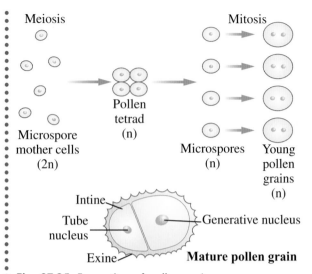

Fig. 27.35. Formation of pollen grains.

The female carpel consists of a stigma, a style and an ovary containing one or more ovules. Each ovule is made from a mass of tissue — the *nucellus*. This is covered by at least two sheets of cells — the *integuments*. The integuments quickly grow over the entire nucellus but leave a tiny opening — the *micropyle* — through which a pollen tube can later enter prior to fertilisation. The ovule is attached to the inner wall of the ovary by a short stalk and *placenta*.

A single *megaspore mother cell* develops within each ovule. This is a giant, diploid cell also called an *embryo sac mother cell*. This cell divides by *meiosis* to form four haploid daughter cells. Three of these disintegrate and the fourth divides three times by *mitosis* to form eight haploid nuclei. Three nuclei migrate to the top of the embryo sac and form *three antipodal cells*. Three more nuclei migrate to the bottom of the sac and form an egg cell with two *synergid* (minder) cells. The remaining two nuclei fuse to form a diploid *endosperm nucleus*.

N.B. *A double fertilisation results with the arrival of two male gametes from the pollen grain.*

One haploid male gamete fuses with the haploid egg cell to form a diploid zygote. This will develop into a diploid plant embryo.

The other haploid male gamete fuses with the diploid endosperm nucleus to form a giant, triploid endosperm nucleus, which will lead to the formation of endosperm food for the developing embryo.

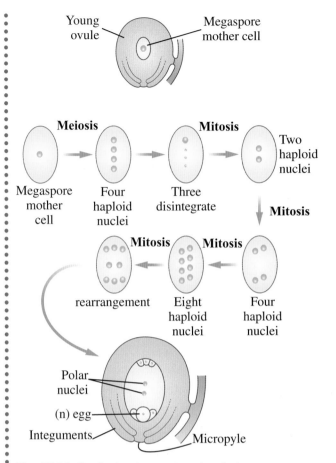

Fig. 27.36. Ovule development and meiosis.

After fertilisation, the *ovule* is referred to as a *seed*, and the *ovary* as a *fruit*.

SUMMARY

- *Reproduction* is a characteristic of all living organisms and is necessary for the continuity of life.
- *There are two methods of reproduction*: sexual and asexual.
- *Sexual reproduction involves two sources* of special, haploid reproductive cells, or sex cells (gametes), made by meiosis. The gametes fuse (fertilisation) to form a diploid zygote. The new individual is a blend of the features of the two parents.
- *Asexual (non-sexual) reproduction involves part of a living organism* breaking away and develops into a completely independent individual. No sex cells are involved and the new individual is genetically identical to its single parent.

- *Sexual reproduction features* the following stages:

  1. Flowers form — producing male pollen and female ovules.
  2. Male and female sex cells are formed by meiosis.
  3. Pollination takes place — by wind or insects.
  4. Fertilisation takes place inside the female ovule.
  5. Embryos form inside seeds that are inside fruits.
  6. Fruits and seeds are dispersed from the parent plant.
  7. Seeds lie dormant awaiting favourable conditions.
  8. Seeds germinate.
  9. An adult flowering plant develops.

- *Flowers consist of a central support* or receptacle, on which are attached four groups of structures.
- *Within the petals* are ♂ stamens and in the centre, one or more ♀ carpels.
- *Sepals protect the young flower* when it is a bud.
- *Petals may be* brightly coloured and scented — or may be green, inconspicuous and reduced.
- *Stamens* are the male parts of the flower.
- *Carpels* are the female parts of the flower.
- *Self-pollination* is when pollen lands on the stigma of the same flower (or on another flower on the same plant).
- *Cross-pollination* is when pollen reaches the stigma of another plant of the same species.
- *Cross-pollination needs the help* of wind or insects to moving the pollen grains to the stigma.
- *Fertilisation is the fusing of male and female haploid* gametes to form a diploid zygote.
- *Fertilisation takes place in the ovules* inside the female carpels of the flower.
- *A double fertilisation is usual*:

  ♂ **gamete (n) + ♀ gamete (n) → zygote (2n)**
  ♂ **gamete (n) + 2 polar nuclei (n, n)**
  → endosperm nucleus (3n)

- *After fertilisation*, the ovule is now referred to as a seed and the ovary is now a fruit.
- *The diploid zygote* grows into a plant embryo.
- *The triploid endosperm tissue* divides repeatedly to form a food supply.

- *Flowering plants are classified* as either monocots (monocotyledonous plants) or dicots (dicotyledonous plants) — depending on whether their embryos have one or two cotyledons.
- *Fruit development* is due to the action of growth regulators within the plant.
- *Seeds* lie within the fruit.
- *Plants use their fruits* to disperse their seeds before germination.
- *Dispersal reduces competition* and ensures a better chance of survival.
- *Advantages in dormancy*:

  - the plant can avoid germination during unfavourable conditions;
  - dormancy allows more time for dispersal to be completed.

- *The essential conditions for germination are* water, oxygen and a suitable temperature:

  - water is required for digesting food reserves and mobilising enzymes;
  - oxygen is required for aerobic respiration;
  - warmth is required for optimum enzyme function.

- *Stages in germination*:

  - water absorption;
  - testa fracture;
  - mobilisation of food reserves;
  - respiration;
  - the radicle emerges and grows downwards to form the root;
  - the plumule now emerges and grows upwards to form the plant shoot
    or
    the cotyledons are dragged out of the seed by the hypocotyl and pushed above the soil.

- *Artificial vegetative propagation* requires human intervention and is used in agriculture and horticulture. Methods include:

  - budding;
  - cuttings;
  - grafting;
  - layering;
  - tissue culture (micropropagation).

- *Advantages of vegetative propagation*:

  - vulnerable seedlings avoided;
  - food immediately available to the new plant;
  - quicker than the flower and seed method;
  - preserves successful genetic varieties.

EXTENDED SUMMARY

- *Male gametes* develop inside stamens.
- *The anther of a young stamen* contains four pollen chambers, which are filled with masses of diploid microspore mother cells.
- *Microspore mother cells* feed and then divide by meiosis to form haploid cells.
- *Each of these daughter cells* divides once by mitosis to form two cells — a generative cell and a vegetative, or tube, cell.
- *These two cells* form the young pollen grain.
- *Pollen grains* develop an intine and an exine.
- *The female carpel consists of* a stigma, a style and an ovary containing one or more ovules.
- *Each ovule* is made from a nucellus covered by integuments.
- *The integuments* leave a tiny opening — the micropyle — through which a pollen tube can later enter.
- *A single megaspore* mother cell develops within each ovule.
- *The mature embryo sac* contains an egg cell, an endosperm nucleus and other cells.
- *A double fertilisation* results with the arrival of two male gametes from the pollen grain.
- *One haploid male gamete* fuses with the haploid egg cell to form a diploid zygote.
- *The other haploid male gamete* fuses with the diploid endosperm nucleus to form a giant, triploid endosperm nucleus — which will lead to the formation of endosperm food for the developing embryo.
- *After fertilisation*, the ovule is referred to as a seed, and the ovary as a fruit.

KEY WORDS

Reproduction	The ability to produce more organisms of the same species.
Growth	An increase in the size of an organism until parent size is reached.
Gametes	Haploid cells, capable of fusion. Also called germ cells or sex cells.
Fertilisation	Fusion of two gametes to form a diploid zygote.
Male parents	Produce motile gametes.
Female parents	Produce non-motile gametes.
Hermaphrodite	Containing both male and female reproductive organs.
Haploid (n)	Describes cells containing a single set of chromosomes.
Diploid (2n)	Describes cells containing a double set of chromosomes.
Binary fission	Splitting in two.
Flowers	Sexual organs within most common plants.
Sepals	Protective leaves around young flowers.
Petals	Modified leaves surrounding the male and female flower parts.
Stamens	Male parts of the flower.
Anther	Part of the stamen, forms pollen grains by meiosis.
Filament	Supports the anther and transports water and nutrients to it.
Carpels	Female parts of the flower.
Stigma	A raised platform on the carpel. Receives pollen grains.
Style	Supports the stigma.
Ovary	Contains one or more ovules, which develop an embryo sac by meiosis.
Embryo sac	Contains a single female gamete — the egg.
Pistil	A single carpel or a group of fused carpels.
Monoecious	Plants with both male and female structures present in the same flower.
Dioecious	Plant species with separate sexes.
Pollination	Transfer of pollen from the anther of the stamen to the stigma of the carpel.
Chemotaxis	Chemical attraction.
Testa	Seed coat.
Radicle	Embryonic root.
Plumule	Embryonic shoot.
Cotyledons (seed leaves)	Embryonic leaves used as a food store.
Endosperm	An oily food store surrounding the embryo within seeds.
Endospermic seeds	Contain large amounts of endosperm.
Non-endospermic seeds	Contain little endosperm.
Parthenocarpy	The development of seedless fruits (virgin fruits).
Monocots (monocotyledonous plants)	Plants whose embryos have one cotyledon only.
Dicots (dicotyledonous plants)	Plants whose embryos have two cotyledons.
Dispersal	The scattering of seeds from the parent plant.
Dormancy	A resting period where growth and development cease.
Germination	The emergence of the plant embryo from its seed.
Hypogeal germination	Cotyledons remain under the ground.
Epigeal germination	Cotyledons emerge, turn green and begin photosynthesis.
Vegetative propagation	When the roots, stems or leaves of a plant become modified to bring about an asexual reproduction.
Perennation	Surviving the winter by means of a food store.

| Perennating organs | Food stores such as rhizomes, bulbs, swollen roots and stems (root and stem tubers). |
| Micropropagation | Growth of new plants by tissue culture. |

EXTENDED KEY WORDS

Tapetum	A layer of cells that lines the pollen chambers of the anther and feeds pollen mother cells with nutrients.
Pollen tetrads	Newly formed pollen grains in groups of four.
Intine	Thin, inner wall of pollen grains.
Exine	Thick, outer wall of pollen grains.
Dehiscence	The process of drying and splitting open.
Nucellus	A mass of tissue within the ovule.
Integuments	Two sheets of cells covering the ovule.
Micropyle	Tiny opening formed by the integuments.
Megaspore mother cell	A giant, diploid cell that develops within each ovule.

QUESTIONS

1. Explain the difference between reproduction and growth. What would be the consequences of a population failing to reproduce?

2. What rule is used throughout the whole of biology to tell the difference between male and female?

3. Reproduction can be *sexual* or *asexual*. To which method does each of the following statements refer?

   a. Only one parent necessary.
   b. Sex cells are produced.
   c. Offspring are a blend of parental features.
   d. Little variety arises within the population.
   e. A zygote is formed.
   f. Fertilisation takes place
   g. Meiosis is essential.
   h. Found in all plants and animals.

4. List the nine stages in flowering plant sexual reproduction.

5. Draw a large, labelled diagram of a named flower. Include the following labels: *sepal; petal; anther; filament; stamen; carpel; stigma; style; ovary; receptacle.* State one function for each of the labelled parts.

6. For each of the following, name the part of the flower involved:

   a. makes pollen;
   b. receives pollen grains;
   c. contains the C egg;
   d. secretes nectar;
   e. protects the young flower;
   f. contains ovules;
   g. supports the stigma;
   h. supports the filament.

7. What is pollination? Explain the difference between self-pollination and cross-pollination. Which method produces more variety within the population?

8. Name a wind-pollinated and an insect-pollinated plant. State five differences between a wind-pollinated and an insect-pollinated flower. Why might plants want to avoid self-pollination? What steps can they take to prevent it happening?

9. What is fertilisation? Briefly describe the events leading up to fertilisation from the time that pollen is carried into a flower. Draw a diagram of the route taken by a pollen tube on its way to the ovule.

10. Why is fertilisation in flowering plants described as a *double fertilisation*? Summarise what takes place. What are the functions of the two fertilisation events? What name changes are applied after fertilisation?

11. Draw a diagram to show the structure of a named seed. Include the following labels: testa, embryo,

cotyledon, radicle, plumule, endosperm. Give one function for each labelled part.

12. Zygote is to embryo as ovule is to .... and ovary is to ....

13. Explain the difference between endospermic and non-endospermic seeds. State one example of each.

14. What is a fruit? From which part of the flower do they develop? What are parthenocarps? Give three examples.

15. Why do flowering plants disperse their seeds? Name four agents of dispersal and name one plant using each agent. Which part of the plant is adapted for dispersal?

    Which dispersal agent is probably employed in each of the following cases?

    a. where fruits have an aerodynamic shape;
    b. where fruits have hooks on the outside;
    c. where fruits are nutritious;
    d. where fruits are spongy with many air pockets;
    e. where fruits dry out and split open.

16. What is a dormant state? What are the advantages to seeds of a period of dormancy?

17. Explain what is meant by germination. State the three essential conditions for successful germination and give the main reason that each condition is required.

18. Explain the main stages in the process of germination. Draw simple diagrams to show the difference between epigeal and hypogeal germination. Which of these germination methods gives the plant a quick start? Which suits smaller seeds?

19. Explain the difference between:

    a. monoecious and dioecious;
    b. essential flower parts and accessory flower parts;
    c. stamens and carpels;
    d. pollination and fertilisation;
    e. fruits and seeds;
    f. epigeal and hypogeal.

20. What is meant by *vegetative propagation*? What are *perennating organs* and what part do they play in reproduction? Name four perennating organs.

21. Choose any two methods of artificial propagation and describe, with a simple diagram, how each is brought about.

22. Explain the difference between:

    a. stock and scion;
    b. annuals and biennials;
    c. ephemerals and annuals;
    d. plant cells and plant protoplasts;
    e. budding and grafting;
    f. runners and rhizomes.

EXTENDED QUESTIONS

1. Draw a simple, labelled diagram of a transverse section across an anther. Mark on the diagram:

   a. the location where meiosis takes place;
   b. where nutrients are secreted;
   c. where water enters the anther;
   d. where the anther will eventually dry and split.

2. Explain the difference between:

   a. exine and intine;
   b. anther and filament;
   c. tube nucleus and generative nucleus;
   d. pollen mother cell and pollen grain;
   e. pollen grain and pollen tetrad.

3. Draw a simple diagram of an ovule. Mark the following on it:

   a. micropyle;
   b. integuments;
   c. nucellus;
   d. stalk;
   e. embryo sac.

4. State whether each of the following is haploid, diploid or triploid:

   a. megaspore mother cell;
   b. endosperm tissue;

c. generative nucleus;

d. embryo;

e. radicle;

f. nucellus;

g. tapetum;

h. synergid.

OPTIONAL ACTIVITIES

- Make a collection of a variety of flowers. Include at least one wind-pollinated flower in the collection. Use keys or reference books to identify each. Draw the flower parts that you can see, name the parts and state their function. Work through the flower from the outside in.

- Obtain microscope slides of microscopic sections of anthers and carpels. Draw what you see and compare your view with the drawings and photos in the text.

- View the BBC video series *The Secret Life of Plants*, presented by David Attenborough.

- Collect seeds of various types for examination. Include sunflowers seeds and beans in your collection. Draw the outsides of the seeds and then use a dissecting kit to split the seeds open along the long axis. Examine and draw the internal parts.

- Most pollen grains will germinate in sucrose solutions. Investigate this using a range of pollens mixed together so that *some* germination is seen. Lily pollen is available all year round. Pollen tube germination may take from one to three hours so plan accordingly.

  A suitable germination medium is 100 g/L sucrose in distilled water with 100 mg/L boric acid, and 300 mg/L calcium nitrate added. Add 20 g/L agar to form a solid medium (see Appendix B). These media do not have to be sterilised unless they will be stored. Pollen can be examined either in liquid or on solid medium. Use a microscope to follow development.

  Design an experiment to investigate the effect of calcium and boron on pollen tube growth.

- Practice taking cuttings from plants such as geranium, privet, laurel or *Begonia*. Place the cuttings in water to begin root development and then transfer to potting compost.

- Discuss the difference between 'weeds' and other plants.

- Extend mandatory activity #21 by using soda lime to investigate whether CO_2 is needed for germination.

- Research the class group on hay fever and other allergic conditions they might suffer. Present your class data using bar charts or other graphical methods.

- Seeds can be germinated in Ziploc plastic bags as follows:

  - Fold a paper towel to fit a bag.
  - Remove the towel and place a row of 6 staples in a line near the top.
  - Replace the towel in the bag and soak with water.
  - Position one seed gently above each staple.
  - Seal the bag and hang it in a suitable place.
  - Use this technique to investigate the effects of nutrients, vinegar, salt, sugar, etc. on germination.

- Make a collection of perennating organs.

- Dandelion and thistle fruits have rings of feathery hairs attached which seem to serve as parachutes during wind dispersal. The ring of hairs is termed a pappus (see above). Design and carry out an experiment to test if the pappus makes any difference to the movement of the fruits in the air.

- Suggestion: Collect at least 50 fruits and try dropping them from a fixed height (1 m) onto a large sheet of paper. Mark where each fruit falls. Repeat with a simulated draught (use a hair drier). Repeat with the pappus severed from each fruit. What factors would need to be held constant during the experiment?

- *Micropropagation* is a technique for growing large numbers of plants from a single parent. Investigate the use of dandelion root sections in sub-culturing new plants. Cut fresh dandelion root into circular segments about 3 mm thick. Sterilise them in Benlate or Milton solution for 20 minutes and then use a clean forceps to transfer them to the surface of soma sterile agar gel (1 g agar / 100 ml water). Make sure the segments are topside uppermost. Cover with cling film and leave under a lamp for a few weeks. The new plants can be sub-cultured further by cutting them again into smaller pieces. Observe aseptic technique throughout.

For information on websites dealing with subjects covered in this chapter see www.my-etest.com.

Now test yourself at
www.my-etest.com

Chapter 28
Reproduction in Humans

SEXUAL REPRODUCTION IN HUMANS   [362]

INTRODUCTION

Human reproduction is sexual. We use the process of sexual reproduction to pass copies of our genes on to the next generation. Compared to asexual reproduction (see Chapter 27), the complete process is slow, complicated and energy consuming — but it has the advantage that it produces *variation* within the population. Our parental genes are

Fig. 28.1. Newborn.

'reshuffled' during the complementary processes of *meiosis* (used to make our sex cells) and *fertilisation*. Variation makes the population more stable and healthy and allows the possibility of change with changing environmental conditions.

The principal features of human sexual reproduction are as follows:

- Two sources of gametes (sex cells) are required — the male (♂) and female (♀) parents. All mammals, including humans are unisexual — they possess either ♂ or ♀ sex organs but not both.
- Gametes are made by meiosis.
- The gametes are *haploid* — i.e. they contain a single set of chromosomes. Human gametes contain 23 chromosomes. All other human cells are *diploid* — they have a double set of 46 chromosomes.
- The gametes meet within the female reproductive system and fuse together — the process of fertilisation.
- A diploid *zygote* is formed.
- The zygote develops into a ball of cells or blastocyst.
- The blastocyst implants itself in the wall of the mother's womb and develops into an embryo.
- The embryo is nourished through a placenta and umbilical cord.
- A baby is born after about nine months. She will grow and develop through childhood and eventually become sexually mature itself.
- The new human individual is similar to both parents and a blend of the genetic features of each.

In the ♂ and ♀ reproductive systems, the gametes are produced within paired *gonads* or *primary sex organs*: sperms are produced within the testes and eggs within the ovaries. Associated with the gonads are the *secondary sex organs*, which are basically transport tubes and glandular structures designed to transport, receive and protect both the gametes

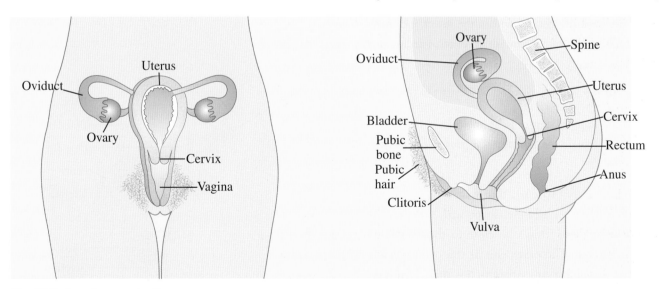

Fig. 28.2. Female reproductive organs.

and the developing embryo. The gonads are also endocrine glands and secrete important sex hormones.

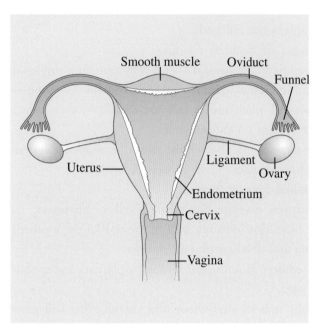

Fig. 28.3. Close-up of female reproductive organs.

THE FEMALE REPRODUCTIVE SYSTEM

The female reproductive system consists of:

- two paired *ovaries*;
- two *oviducts* or egg-tubes (also called *fallopian* tubes);
- the *uterus* or womb;
- the *vagina*.

The ovaries are quite small (about 3 cm × 1.5 cm), are oval in shape and are held in position within the lower abdomen by ligaments. These ligaments contain an ovarian artery and vein and a nerve supply.

The functions of the ovaries are:

- to produce the haploid egg cells by meiosis;
- to produce the female sex hormones *oestrogen* and *progesterone*.

Each oviduct is a short (10 cm), thin-walled tube. At one end, the oviduct opens in a funnel shape with a margin of fringes (*fimbriae*). These fringes lie close to the ovary but are not attached to it. The other end of the oviduct leads into the uterus through a tiny opening less than 1 mm in diameter.

The functions of the oviducts are:

- to provide a site for fertilisation;
- to carry the fertilised egg to the uterus.

The uterus or womb is a thick walled, muscular organ, measuring about 8 cm × 5 cm and shaped like an inverted pear. It has a smooth outer, muscular coat — the *myometrium* — and an inner mucous lining — the *endometrium*. The base of the uterus is narrow and known as the *cervix*. The cervix (or neck of the womb) opens into the vagina.

The functions of the uterus are:

- to protect and nourish the developing embryo;
- to assist in the delivery of the baby to the outside.

The vagina is a short (about 10 cm), thin walled, muscular tube leading from the cervix to the exterior at the *vulva*.

The functions of the vagina are:

- to receive the penis during sexual intercourse;
- to allow the delivery of the baby to the outside (the vagina is also called the birth canal).

THE MALE REPRODUCTIVE SYSTEM

The male reproductive system consists of:

- two paired *testes*;

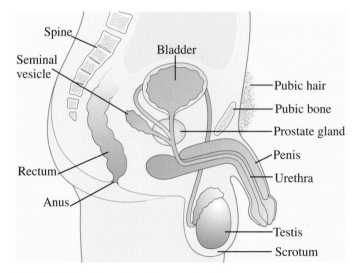

Fig. 28.4. Location of male reproductive organs.

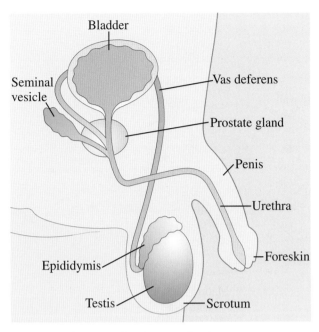

Fig. 28.5. Close-up of male reproductive organs.

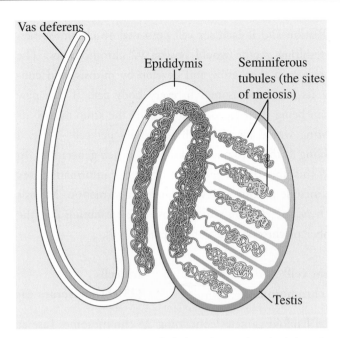

Fig. 28.6. Testis showing tubule location and meiosis location.

- two sperm tubes or *vas deferens* tubes (plural is *vasa deferentia* !);
- the *prostate gland*, *seminal vesicles* and *Cowper's glands*;
- the *urethra* within the *penis*.

The testes are small (3 cm), oval organs containing literally miles of microscopic, sperm-forming tubes — the *seminiferous tubules*. Between the many tubules lies connective tissue with patches of cells (*interstitial cells*) that produce the male sex hormone, *testosterone*. Each testis receives a blood and nerve supply via the testicular artery, vein and nerve. The testes are enclosed in an external pouch or *scrotum*, which maintains their temperature a little under normal body temperature — essential for healthy sperm production.

The seminiferous tubules leave the testis and immediately form the *epididymis* — a larger, coiled tube attached to the side of the testis. The epididymis (plural is *epididymedes*!) stores sperms and allows them to mature. Sperms leave the epididymis by the *vas deferens*, which carries the sperms past various glands and towards the urethra and penis.

The functions of the testes are:

- to produce the haploid, male sperms by meiosis;
- to produce the male sex hormone, testosterone, and secrete it into the bloodstream.

The two vas deferens tubes unite and merge with the *urethra* — a tube shared with the urinary system. At this point, the tubes pass a number of glands: the *prostate gland*, two *seminal vesicles* and two *Cowper's glands*. All of these glands contribute lubrication and nourishment to the sperms. This fluid together with the sperm cells constitutes semen.

The urethra carries either urine or semen to the outside and runs through the centre of the penis. The penis is the organ designed to bring about transfer of semen into the female reproductive system. During sexual excitement, the tissues of the penis fill with blood and it becomes erect.

MEIOSIS AND THE PRODUCTION OF SEX CELLS

Human gametes are formed in the testes and ovaries first by an *ordinary* cell division, called **mitosis**, and then by a *reduction* division, called **meiosis** (see Chapter 11).

All human body cells (somatic cells) contain 46 chromosomes arranged in 23 matching pairs. When new cells are required for growth and repair, existing cells divide by mitosis. This conserves the chromosome number so that the new body cells will also have 46 chromosomes each. Sex cells, however, will be required to *fuse* with each other at fertilisation and if each sex cell possessed 46 chromosomes, the resulting zygote would possess 92 chromosomes. The zygote would then grow and develop by mitosis, and conserve its 92 chromosomes in every body cell. If this new human being then reproduced itself by the same means, its offspring would have 184 chromosomes per cell — i.e. a doubling of the chromosome number at each generation. To avoid this unnecessary piling-up of genetic information, sex cells include *meiosis* somewhere in their formation. Meiosis is a *reduction division* which forms cells sustaining *half* the number of chromosomes of the parent cells.

parent cell $\xrightarrow{\text{*meiosis*}}$ **sex cells**
(46 chromosomes) **(23 chromosomes each)**

When haploid gametes containing 23 chromosomes fuse at fertilisation, the original, diploid number of 46 chromosomes is restored in the zygote.

Formation of the gametes

In the testes, cells lining the seminiferous tubules divide by *meiosis* to form millions of haploid spermatozoa. Sperms are formed continually throughout the life of the male from puberty to death. Sperm cells are small, motile and made in very large numbers.

In the ovaries, the production of haploid eggs follows a recurring cycle, the *ovarian cycle*, which is described in detail later. Within each ovary, tiny balls of cells — or *follicles* — develop at an early age. Each follicle contains a distinctive cell, the *primary oocyte*, which divides unevenly by meiosis to form a haploid egg and three polar bodies. The egg is later released from the mature ovarian follicle at the surface of the ovary — an event known as *ovulation*. The ovarian follicle then closes, fills with blood and forms the *corpus luteum*, or *yellow body*, within the ovary. Each ovulation leaves a tiny scar on the ovary surface. Egg cells are relatively large (about the size of the head of a dress-making pin), rounded and rich in nutrients.

SEX HORMONES AND SEXUAL DEVELOPMENT

From the onset of puberty until the age of about 45–50, every female secretes *follicle-stimulating hormone* (FSH) and

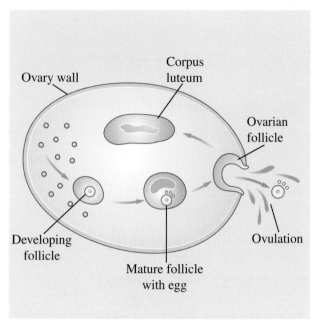

Fig. 28.7. Inside of ovary.

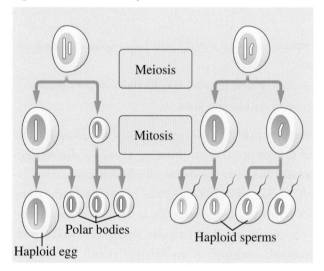

Fig. 28.8. Gametes made by meiosis.

luteinising hormone (LH) from her pituitary gland into the bloodstream.

FSH stimulates the ovaries to produce ovarian follicles — each containing a haploid egg cell — and also stimulates the ovaries to secrete the hormone *oestrogen*. Oestrogen is formed from cholesterol taken from the bloodstream and is first of all responsible for the development of the *female secondary sex characteristics* — development of the breasts, widening of the hips and growth of pubic hair. Oestrogen also stimulates the monthly repair of the inner lining of the womb after menstruation (discussed later).

The second pituitary hormone, LH, triggers ovulation. This is the release of the egg from the ovary and usually occurs on Day 14 of the average menstrual cycle. LH also stimulates the production of *progesterone* from the corpus luteum. FSH and LH also interact to regulate the menstrual cycle.

From the onset of puberty to the end of their natural lives, every male produces the same two hormones, FSH and LH, (retaining their female names) from his pituitary gland. These hormones bring about and maintain male sexual development. FSH stimulates the formation of sperms and LH stimulates the formation of *testosterone* in the interstitial cells of the testes. Testosterone, the male equivalent of oestrogen, is also made from cholesterol and is responsible for developing and maintaining the *male secondary sex characteristics* — development in size of the testes and penis, growth of body hair, deepening of the voice and greater muscle development.

THE MENSTRUAL CYCLE

In the human female, reproductive events occur in a cycle — the *sexual cycle* or *menstrual cycle*. Hormones secreted from the ovaries and from the pituitary gland regulate the events of the cycle. In the event of pregnancy, the cycle is altered and hormones from the placenta play their part.

In fact, the menstrual cycle involves two cycles of events: the *ovarian cycle* in the ovary and the *uterine cycle* in the uterus. These two cycles must be synchronised if humans are to reproduce successfully and the synchronisation is through the action of the ovarian and pituitary hor-

Table 28.1. Summary of reproductive hormones

Hormone	Source	Target	Function
FSH	Pituitary gland	Ovaries or testes.	Stimulates production of oestrogen in females. Stimulates sperm development in males.
LH	Pituitary gland	Ovarian follicle and corpus luteum in females. Seminiferous tubules in males.	Stimulates ovulation and progesterone production in females. Stimulates testosterone production in males.
Oestrogen	Ovary tissue	Entire body and specifically the endometrium of the womb.	Female sexual development and repair of the endometrium after menstruation.
Progesterone	Corpus luteum	Endometrium.	Maintains endometrium and maintains any pregnancy.
Testosterone	Interstitial cells of the testes	Entire body.	Male sexual development.
Oxytocin	Pituitary gland	Myometrium of uterus.	Stimulates contractions of the uterus, which dilate the cervix for birth.
Prolactin	Pituitary gland	Breasts.	Stimulates production of breast milk.

mones. The average menstrual cycle is about 28 days long but can be anywhere from 24–35 days. The most obvious feature of the cycle is the monthly loss of a small amount of blood, mucus and cell remains from the womb — *menstruation*. The onset of menstruation is always taken as Day 1 of the menstrual cycle and lasts four to five days.

1. The ovarian cycle

During the first 14 days after menstruation, a large ball of cells — the *ovarian follicle* — develops within one of the woman's ovaries (the two ovaries alternate in egg production). The development of the follicle is stimulated by the hormone FSH from the pituitary gland and the follicle contains a single, haploid *egg cell* — formed by meiosis. On Day 14 of the cycle (and under the influence of LH), the follicle bursts through the ovary wall and releases the egg into the abdominal cavity — this is the event of *ovulation*. The follicle now closes over, fills with blood and turns into

a yellowish mass of cells known as the *corpus luteum*, or yellow body. The corpus luteum becomes an endocrine gland and secretes progesterone into the bloodstream.

If the egg is ***not*** fertilised (almost always the case — otherwise up to 400 babies might be conceived per mother!), the egg dies after about 48 hours of life in the oviduct (by Day 16). The corpus luteum persists in the ovary for a while but eventually degenerates and no more progesterone is secreted. This withdrawal of progesterone triggers menstruation in the uterus and another ovarian cycle begins.

If, on the other hand, the egg ***is*** fertilised, the corpus luteum grows larger and continues to secrete progesterone. Progesterone inhibits menstruation and assists in the implantation of the embryo in the womb.

2. The uterine cycle

The inner lining of the uterus — the endometrium — un-

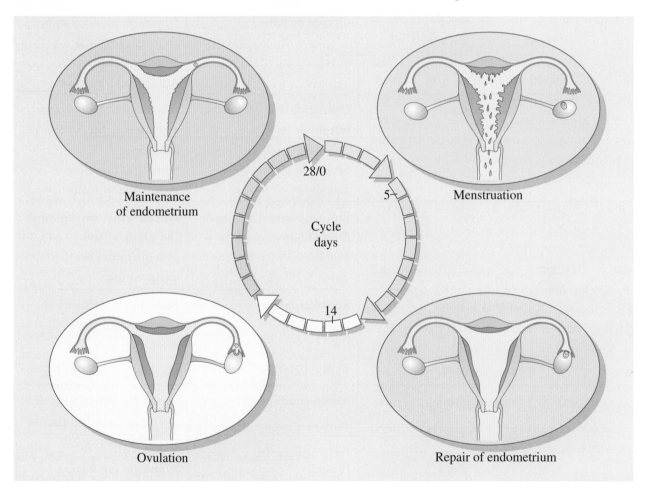

Fig. 28.9. Menstrual cycle.

dergoes a 28-day cycle of development, maintenance and degeneration. The onset of menstruation (the beginning of a *period*) is taken as Day 1 of the cycle and lasts about four to five days. From Day 5 to about Day 21, the endometrium repairs itself, developing tubular glands (producing glycogen and mucus) and also tiny, spiral arteries. The repair is mainly stimulated by the hormone oestrogen. If an egg has been fertilised, it will implant itself in the developed endometrium on about Day 21. Otherwise, the endometrium persists for another seven days, and then finally degenerates into the menstrual flow.

The females of almost all primates — humans, monkeys, apes and chimpanzees — have a menstrual flow, but most other mammals do not. Instead they have a period of time 'in heat' during which the female permits mating and is almost certain to be fertilised.

COPULATION

Copulation in humans is also termed *sexual intercourse*. It involves the insertion of the male's erect penis into the vagina of the female and the ejaculation of semen. Intercourse is preceded by a period of sexual arousal in both partners. This brings about a change in blood pressure within the penis and an erection in the male. The ejaculation takes place during a period of intense sexual excitement or orgasm. Ejaculation of sperm into the vagina is also called *insemination*.

The survival period for sperms within the female reproductive system is about one to five days at most. The egg can survive in the oviduct for up to 48 hours after ovulation. This would seem to suggest that fertilisation is only possible after having sex between Day 9 and Day 16 of the cycle. In the real world, the day of ovulation is not always predictable and certainly not guaranteed to occur on Day 14. Many factors such as age, health and mental stress can change the time that the egg is released. The fact that the previous cycle was 28 days long does not guarantee that the current one will be the same. This is particularly true for young women. Couples are urged not to rely on numbers alone as a method of avoiding pregnancy.

Intercourse in humans has important emotional and psychological dimensions and should never be considered as purely *biological* — but its biological significance is to facilitate *internal fertilisation*. Many simpler animals such as fish and amphibians employ external fertilisation where the sex cells meet outside the female body.

Internal fertilisation is employed by reptiles, birds and mammals (including humans). The *biological* consequences of internal fertilisation include the following:

- fertilisation is more likely;
- the developing embryo is within the mother and so protected;
- the embryo is guaranteed a food supply;
- a bond can develop between mother and baby.

BIRTH CONTROL

Couples can practice birth control (or more precisely control over conception) in order to either *plan* a pregnancy at a certain time or to *avoid* one.

Methods of birth control are very varied and no one method is considered perfect. Any method is likely to have physical, psychological or moral side effects and, when choosing a method, couples are strongly advised to discuss their choice with an expert adviser or doctor.

Table 28.2 is a review of the most common methods. It is not intended to be complete in its advice.

FERTILISATION

Fertilisation is the fusing together of two haploid gametes to form a diploid zygote.

In humans, fertilisation is internal and takes place within the upper third of the female oviduct.

There are three important biological aspects to fertilisation:

- the blending of a selection of genes from the two parents;
- the initiation of the development of an entirely new individual;
- the restoration of the diploid chromosome number.

Prior to fertilisation, about 3 cm^3 of semen is deposited in the female vagina after sexual intercourse. The semen is alkaline and contains from 80 to 150 million sperms. Semen

Table 28.2. Methods of birth control

CATEGORY	METHOD	DESCRIPTION	BIOLOGICAL PRINCIPLE	COMMENTS
Natural	Temperature method	Take body temperature every morning and keep a chart	Ovulation produces a temperature rise of 0.4 °C.	No chemical or medical intervention needed, therefore no side effects. Temperature can rise for other reasons.
	Billings method	Chart the texture of the secretions from the cervix and vagina	Texture changes just before ovulation.	High degree of discipline and organisation needed.
	Calendar method	Record dates of periods over six months	Ovulation occurs on Day 14 of the average cycle.	Many people have irregular periods.
Barrier	Condoms	Narrow tube of latex rubber covers the erect penis (or lines the vagina — the female condom).	Sperms cannot enter the uterus.	Good protection against diseases such as VD or AIDS.
	Diaphragm	A dome of soft rubber fitted over the cervix.	Sperms cannot enter the uterus.	Not a protection against disease.
	IUCD or 'coil'	Small copper and plastic coil fitted inside the womb.	Disrupts the implantation of the fertilised egg.	Egg dies *after* fertilisation. Coil must be fitted by a doctor.
Chemical	'Combined pill'	Contains both oestrogen and progesterone. Take one pill every day for 21 days, then a seven-day break.	Hormones prevent ovulation, alter the mucus of the cervix and alter the womb lining.	Promotes lighter, more regular periods. Side effects include sore breasts, nausea, some bleeding and, more rarely, blood clots.
	'Mini pill'	Progesterone only. Take one every day at the same time.	Alters the cervical mucus and the lining of the womb.	Suitable for older women (40+), smokers and diabetics.
	Injectable contraception	Progesterone by injection every 12 weeks.	Prevents ovulation, alters the mucus of the cervix and alters the womb lining.	Periods may stop or become heavier. Side effects will have to be endured for up to 12 weeks.

	Spermicide	Cream, foam, jelly or pessary forms available.	Kills sperm cells.	Ineffective on its own. Used in conjunction with other methods.
	Hormone implants (*Norplants*)	6 flexible matchsticks under the skin.	Prevents ovulation.	Lasts for 5 years.
'Emergency' chemical	Post-coital pill	Two pills (oestrogen and progesterone) within 60 hours of having sex, two more 12 hours later.	Disrupts the uterine cycle.	Nausea and vomiting are common. Theoretical risk of damage to a surviving foetus.
	Post-coital coil	Coil (as above) fitted up to five days after conception.	Disrupts the implantation of the fertilised egg.	Can be painful or spread vaginal infection. Egg killed *after* fertilisation.
Surgical	Vasectomy	Vas deferens tubes in male cut and ends tied off under anaesthetic.	Sperms' exit to penis is blocked and they are reabsorbed within the testis and epididymis.	A minor operation but considered irreversible. Semen (with no sperms) is still produced.
	Tubal ligation	Oviducts are cut and tied off.	Sperms and eggs cannot meet.	Involves major surgery under full anaesthetic and should be considered irreversible.

neutralises the natural acidity of the vagina and this then promotes the sperms' movement. They make their way quite rapidly to the oviducts — partly by swimming and partly aided by muscular contractions of the uterus and oviducts themselves. Only a small number of sperms will actually reach the upper regions of the oviducts, but if they encounter an egg there, fertilisation will take place.

Stages of fertilisation (during Days 14–16 of the average menstrual cycle)

1. Sperms are chemically attracted to the egg.
2. The *acrosome* (a bubble of digestive enzymes within the head of each sperm) releases its enzymes, which create an opening in the *zona pellucida* or egg covering.
3. The sperm head fuses with the egg cell membrane and the sperm nucleus enters the egg cytoplasm.
4. The sperm tail is lost.
5. The male and female nuclei fuse together and form the diploid zygote nucleus (by aligning these chromosomes) — this is the exact moment of the creation of the new life!
6. The zona pellucida alters both electrically and chemically. A spark of electrical charge repels other sperms. This is possibly the first thing 'done' by all humans! A membrane then forms to keep out any other 'invaders'.

Fig. 28.10. Egg with sperm.

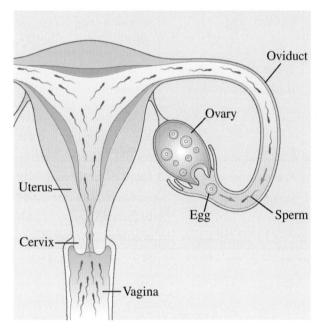

Fig. 28.11. Path of sperm.

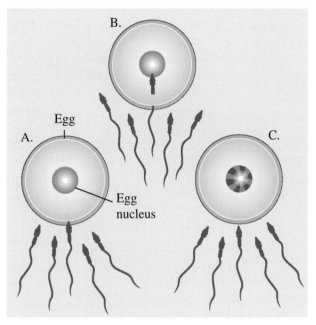

Fig. 28.12. Fertilisation.

- the ability of the blastocyst to implant itself in the endometrium;
- the correct hormonal environment for the developing embryo.

If any one of these conditions is not satisfied, infertility can result.

Typical causes of infertility are usually grouped as follows:

- 33% are due to male factors;
- 33% are due to female factors;
- 14% are due to a combination of male and female factors;
- 20% are unexplained.

Male infertility

The most common male infertility factors include *azoospermia* (no sperm cells made) and *oligospermia* (very few sperm cells made — or a *low sperm count*). Sometimes, sperm cells are poorly formed, or they die before they can reach the egg. In most cases, these problems have an endocrine or hormonal origin and are treatable with suitable drugs.

In rare cases, infertility in men is caused by a genetic disease such as cystic fibrosis, or by a chromosomal abnormality. Other male problems include impotence, premature ejaculation and inability to sustain an erection.

INFERTILITY

Infertility is any condition that makes conception and pregnancy difficult or impossible.

Although taken for granted by some, conception is complicated and success depends on many factors:

- the production of sufficient healthy sperm by the male;
- the production and release of healthy eggs by the female;
- the presence of unblocked oviducts to allow the gametes to meet;
- the ability of the sperm to fertilise the egg;

Female infertility

The most common female infertility factor is an ovulation disorder — often due to an endocrine gland failure. For example, high levels of the pituitary hormone, prolactin (*hyperprolactinaemia*), commonly inhibit ovulation. This condition is easily treated with appropriate drugs.

Other causes of female infertility include blocked or narrow oviducts (often due to pelvic inflammation) or *endometriosis* (described later). Congenital abnormalities (or birth defects) involving the structure of the uterus, oviducts and ovaries are also commonly found.

Most infertilities are successfully treated by drugs or surgery and these treatments are becoming more and more sophisticated every year. Many infertilities nowadays are stress-related, but these too are treatable.

In Vitro Fertilisation — IVF

In situations where women have blocked or absent oviducts, or where men have low sperm counts, IVF offers a chance of parenthood to couples who until recently would have had no hope of having a biologically related child. In IVF, eggs are surgically removed from the follicles of the ovary. The follicles are detected by *ultrasound* and the eggs removed by a hollow needle through the wall of the vagina. The eggs are then mixed with sperm in a glass petri dish (*in vitro*

means *in glass*) containing similar nutrients to the oviduct and at the correct temperature.

After about 40 hours, the eggs are examined to see if they have become fertilised by the sperm and have started cell division. These fertilised eggs or embryos are then placed in the women's uterus, thus bypassing the fallopian tubes. Generally one in three will survive and implant itself. Unused embryos can be stored in liquid nitrogen at −172 °C for use in the future — a situation with considerable moral and medical implications.

The success rate for IVF at present is about 18% and rising. This compares well with the chance of 20% in any given month that a reproductively healthy couple has of conception.

The first reported successful birth of an IVF, or *test-tube*, baby was that of Louise Brown in England in 1978.

Implantation

Twenty-four hours after fertilisation, the zygote commences cell division or *mitosis*. It thus passes through a two-cell stage, a four-cell stage, then an eight-cell stage and so on — an important process known as *cleavage*. After three to four days or so, a solid ball of cells (a *morula*) is formed, and this moves down the oviduct towards the uterus. The morula is transported by ciliary action (hairs lining the inside of the oviduct waft it along) and by a slow *peristalsis* or muscle contraction of the oviduct.

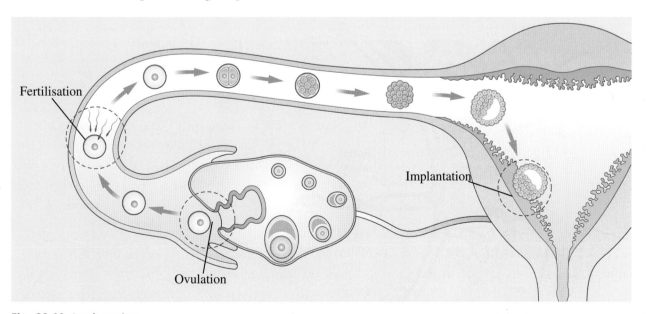

Fig. 28.13. Implantation

Further, complicated cell divisions of the morula produce a hollow ball of cells — the *blastocyst* — made from hundreds of cells or *blastomeres*. This arrives in the womb seven days after conception. The blastocyst buries itself in one of the pockets of the womb lining or endometrium — this is the process of *implantation*.

A disc of cells within the blastocyst develops into the embryo. The outer part of the blastocyst forms the *placenta* and the *amnion*. The amnion is a tough membrane that forms around the embryo and secretes amniotic fluid. The embryo floats in this fluid and is protected by it.

The placenta

The placenta is an organ of exchange between the mother and the foetus. It allows transport to take place between the two bloodstreams, although the two bloods do not mix. It is composed of both foetal and maternal tissue and measures about 20 cm across and 3 cm thick when fully formed.

The placenta attaches itself to the endometrium of the uterus and is connected to the foetus by the umbilical cord. The 'belly button' or '*umbilicus*' is the scar of this attachment. The cord contains two umbilical arteries and an umbilical vein — wrapped in a spiral to prevent kinking. There is no nerve tissue in the cord.

The main structural features of the placenta include:

- a huge surface area of villi — to allow faster diffusion;
- a very thin barrier between the maternal and foetal bloodstreams — making diffusion easier.

The placenta also manufactures hormones — especially progesterone and some oestrogen. These help to maintain the pregnancy.

Most soluble materials can pass across the placenta — generally in a direction from where they are highly concentrated to where they are less concentrated. For example, sugars, amino acids, vitamins, fatty acids, minerals, oxygen and water (and possibly alcohol, nicotine and other drugs too) are usually highly concentrated in the mother's blood and so cross into the foetal bloodstream. At the same time, carbon dioxide, urea and salt will be in high concentration in the foetal blood and so diffuse across the placenta to the mother's side. She will later excrete these from her own body.

Different methods of transport are used within the placenta:

- oxygen, carbon dioxide and urea cross by simple *diffusion* (i.e. soak across the placenta);
- glucose crosses by *facilitated diffusion* (i.e. is *helped* across by enzymes);
- amino acids cross by *active transport* (i.e. are *dragged* across by enzymes);
- maternal antibodies cross by *pinocytosis* (i.e. are *enclosed* within membranes in the placental villi).

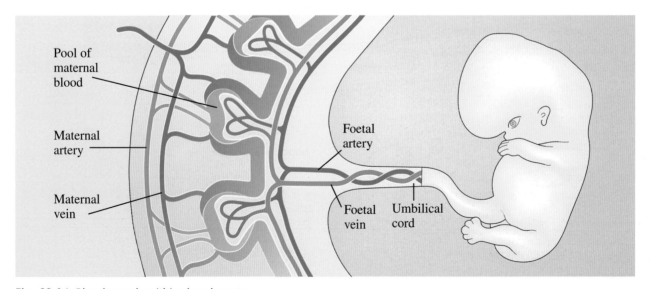

Fig. 28.14. Blood vessels within the placenta.

(See Chapter 10 for more information on substances crossing membranes.)

The maternal and foetal bloods will never actually mix — except briefly when the placenta is detached from the womb wall and expelled as the afterbirth. The bloods must not mix for various reasons:

- the blood groups may well be different;
- the blood pressures are different;
- many maternal hormones would pass, uncontrolled, into the foetus and cause undesirable changes.

Nausea in early pregnancy is due to high levels of progesterone from the corpus luteum in the ovary. Progesterone softens the connective tissue around the body (in preparation for birth) and this includes connective tissue in the stomach. This leads to heartburn and often nausea. After 12 weeks, placental progesterone replaces that from the corpus luteum and the nausea usually vanishes. Many mothers have no sickness at all; others console themselves with the thought that extra progesterone means a very stable pregnancy!

PREGNANCY TESTING

Human chorionic gonadotrophin, or HCG, appears in the mother's urine as soon as one week after conception. It can be tested for (with coloured HCG monoclonal antibodies) at home with a home testing kit after about two weeks or around the time of the 'missed' period. The urine sample will make the test stick appear blue if the user is pregnant.

SCANNING

In Ireland, pregnant mothers-to-be are routinely scanned by ultrasound at about four to five months. On the scan in figure 28.5:

- EDD is estimated date of delivery
- FEML is length of the femur (in millimeters)
- BPD is biparietal diameter — width of the head.

What is 20W5D?

BIRTH

Birth, or *parturition*, is the process whereby the baby leaves the womb and enters the outside world. There are three clear stages to the whole process:

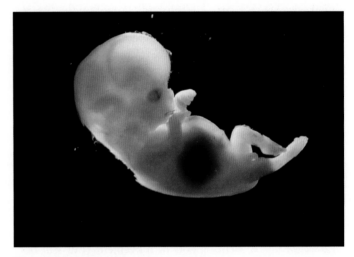

Fig. 28.15(a). Embryo at five weeks.

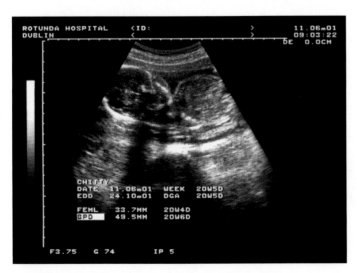

Fig. 28.15. Ultrasound scan of foetus at 20 weeks.

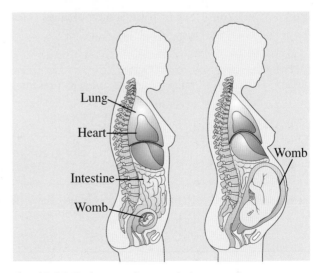

Fig. 28.16. Embryo at three and nine months.

Table 28.3. Pregnancy timetable (not for examination)

All times in this timetable are from the time of the last period and not from the day of conception: this is the normal convention used by doctors.

Time	Size	Development
14 days	–	Sperm and egg meet in oviduct.
17 days	–	Zygote divides by mitosis to form a solid morula.
18 days	0.1 mm	Morula becomes hollow — now termed a blastocyst.
21 days	0.2 mm	Blastocyst embeds in the endometrium — *implantation*.
4 weeks	1 mm	Blastocyst just visible to unaided eye. Three layers of cells are formed.
5 weeks	2 mm	Primitive organs and a beating heart are formed. Fish-like gill slits seen in neck region. Placenta forming. Spine and nervous system forming.
6 weeks	6 mm	Most internal organs formed and beginning to function.
7 weeks	1.3 cm	Limb buds grow rapidly. Heart beats and blood cells begin to move.
8 weeks	2.2 cm	All organs formed but very immature. Bones developing. Amnion and placenta formed. Embryo now called a *foetus*.
9 weeks	3 cm 2 g	Definite movements but not yet felt by the mother. Facial features developing.
10 weeks	4.5 cm 5 g	Recognisable face, fingers and toes.
11 weeks	5.5 cm 10 g	Foetus appears as a recognisable human baby. All organs well formed. Risk of congenital organ deformity or damage from drugs is now much lower.
12 weeks	6.5 cm 18 g	Lots of movement (but still not felt by mother). Some fat is laid down under the skin.
13 weeks	7.5 cm 30 g	Sex of baby is now obvious. Head is more rounded. Placenta is fully formed and will feed the baby from now on.
16 weeks	16 cm 135 g	Fingernails and toenails present. Baby covered in fine, soft hair (*lanugo*). Eyebrows and eyelashes grow.
20 weeks	25 cm 350 g	Very rapid growth, hair grows on head, muscles increase development.
24 weeks	33 cm 570 g	Rapid growth continues. Baby could survive only briefly if born now. Baby looks thin from lack of body fat.

28 weeks	37 cm 900 g	Foetus is viable — could survive independently outside the womb (but only has a 5% chance of doing so).
32 weeks	40 cm 1.6 kg	Greasy vernix (wax) covers entire body. 15% survival chance if born now.
36 weeks	46 cm 2.5 kg	Baby almost fully mature — 90% survival chance. Head is engaged in the mother's pelvic opening.
40 weeks	50 cm 3.4 kg	Average duration of pregnancy (280 days or 266 days after conception). Baby is born.

1. Contractions of the uterus

These are involuntary and due to the secretion of a hormone — *oxytocin* — from the pituitary gland. The contractions start slowly and then become more frequent as the hormone concentration builds up. The purpose of each contraction is not to push the baby out of the womb but to dilate the cervix to allow the baby's head to pass through. Often at this stage, the amnion ruptures or tears and the amniotic fluid is lost through the vagina — the *breaking of the waters*.

2. Delivery of the baby

Almost all babies are delivered vaginally, head first, with voluntary assistance from the mother. When the baby emerges, it inflates its lungs and breathes for itself for the first time. The umbilical cord is cut and tied, and an independent existence begins.

3. Delivery of the afterbirth

Ten or fifteen minutes after the baby is born, more (and gentler) contractions commence and these expel the placenta and the remains of the umbilical cord from the womb.

Multiple births

- *Non-identical twins* (dizygotic) are due to the simultaneous release of two eggs from the ovaries. They are fertilised by two different sperm cells. Each embryo will have its own placenta and amnion. The children will be similar and share a birthday but will be no more similar than any two children sharing the same parents.

- *Identical twins* (monozygotic) are formed if the morula divides in two *after* fertilisation. The embryos are genetically identical and will share a single amnion and one placenta with two umbilical cords.

- *Siamese twins* are formed when the morula starts to divide in two but does not complete the division. Depending on the extent to which they share internal organs, it may be difficult to separate the twins by surgery and keep both alive. The twins are monozygotic.

- *Triplets and quads* are rare but do occur. Higher multiple births are almost always as a result of some infertility treatment.

MILK PRODUCTION AND BREAST-FEEDING

Milk production in the breasts is termed *lactation*. Throughout pregnancy, the mother's breasts are prepared for milk production by the hormones oestrogen and progesterone. No milk is actually produced during this time however as progesterone inhibits the final secretory phase or lactation. With the loss of the placenta at birth, the levels of progesterone collapse and lactation begins. No milk is produced for the first few days: instead *colostrum* — a low fat liquid rich in maternal antibodies — is secreted. After three to four days, true milk containing fats, sugars and other nutrients appears.

Lactation is regulated by the pituitary hormone, *prolactin*, and will continue for as long as the mother allows the child to feed.

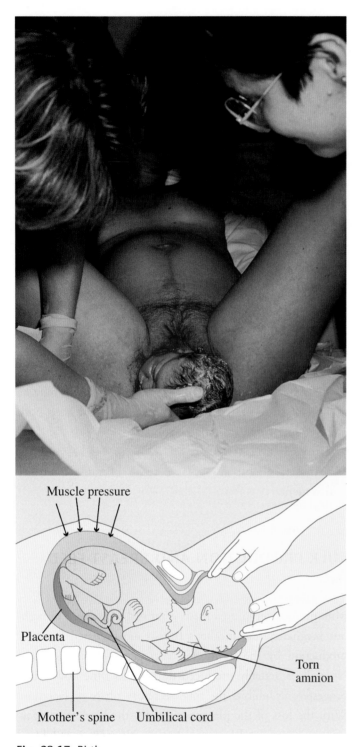

Fig. 28.17. Birth.

Fig. 28.18. Non-identical (dizygotic) twins (above). Identical (monozygotic) twins with father (middle).

Advantages of breast-feeding

1. Maternal antibodies in the colostrum and milk are extremely effective in providing immunity against disease throughout the feeding period.
2. The nutrients provided are correct for the child.
3. An important bond is established between mother and child.
4. Milk contamination is far less likely to occur.
5. Breast-feeding stimulates contractions of the womb, which helps restore it to its normal size.

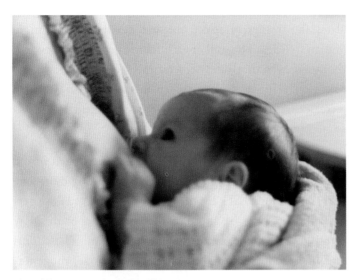

Fig. 28.19. Newborn feeding.

IMPLANTATION AND EMBRYO DEVELOPMENT [H36 II]

Twenty-four hours after fertilisation, the zygote commences cell division or mitosis. It thus passes through a two-cell stage, a four-cell stage, then an eight-cell stage and so on — an important process known as *cleavage*. After three to four days or so, it is a solid ball of cells (a *morula*) and is moving down the oviduct towards the uterus. The morula is transported by ciliary action (hairs lining the inside of the oviduct waft it along) and by a slow peristalsis, or muscle contraction, of the oviduct.

Further, complicated cell divisions of the morula produce a hollow ball of cells — the *blastocyst* — made from hundreds of cells or *blastomeres*. The outer blastomeres are flattened cells and appear like paving stones. These are *trophoblast cells* and will develop into the placenta and embryonic membranes. At one end of the blastocyst, a dense, flattened knot of smaller cells develops — the *embryo cells*. The blastocyst arrives in the womb seven days after conception and buries itself in one of the pockets of the womb lining or endometrium. This is the process of *implantation* and is not sensed by the mother.

The outer, trophoblast cells develop finger-like growths called *trophoblastic villi*. These form an attachment with the endometrium. Pools of maternal blood form in hollows, or *lacunae*, within the endometrium, and these pools surround the villi. The villi absorb oxygen and nutrients from the mother's blood and pass them to the embryo cells. The villi and lacunae grow and develop into the placenta.

Meanwhile the embryo cells continue to divide and undergo complicated foldings — *gastrulation* — to form a tiny (1 mm) human embryo. As the embryo grows into a larger

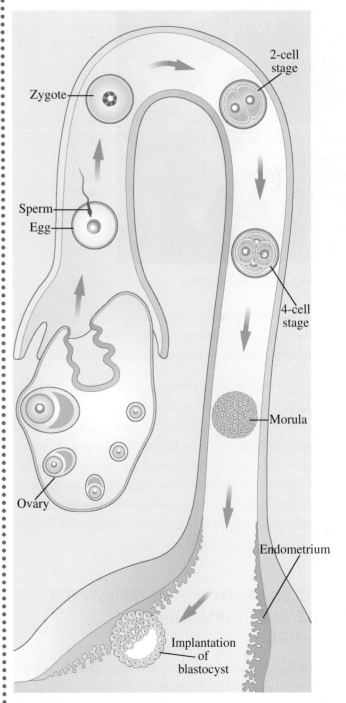

Fig. 28.20. Development of the blastocyst.

foetus, it is enclosed in a tough membrane, the *amnion*, which secretes a large quantity of watery amniotic fluid. The foetus floats weightlessly in this fluid and is protected by it.

Fig. 28.21. Foetus at 15 weeks.

Humans are *triploblastic* — their embryos are formed from three layers of cells: *ectoderm* on the outside, *endoderm* on the inside where food will pass and *mesoderm* in between.

Before eight weeks of development have passed, the ectoderm layer will have formed the skin, hair, nail, nervous system and parts of some hormonal glands. The endoderm will have formed all the inner linings of the digestive system and the mesoderm will have formed all the organs and tissues in between — the heart, blood and blood vessels, bone and cartilage, muscles, kidneys and reproductive organs. Development of all organs is complete by eight weeks, but the organs need much more time to mature.

DETAILED STUDY OF THE MENSTRUAL CYCLE AND HORMONAL CONTROL   [H36 III]

At the beginning of every menstrual cycle (Day 1), the pituitary gland releases follicle-stimulating hormone (FSH) into the bloodstream. FSH circulates in the blood and stim-

ulates the ovaries to select out and develop one or more ovarian follicles. The wall of each follicle becomes endocrinal (hormone-secreting) and secretes the female sex hormone, oestrogen. The level of oestrogen in the bloodstream now increases rapidly and this brings about the repair of the endometrium of the uterus.

On Day 11 of the cycle, the high level of oestrogen in the blood stimulates the production of luteinising hormone (LH) and more FSH by the pituitary gland. LH triggers ovulation on Day 14 and also the conversion of the now empty ovarian follicle into the corpus luteum. The corpus luteum is endocrinal and secretes the hormone, progesterone. Progesterone maintains the repair of the endometrium and inhibits the production of both FSH and LH. The endometrium now contains stored glycogen and spiral arteries, and is receptive to a fertilised egg.

If no fertilisation takes place:

■ The high levels of progesterone *inhibit* the production of both FSH and LH. The falling level of LH triggers the degeneration of the corpus luteum and no more progesterone is made. The endometrium is no longer maintained and menstruation commences. FSH reappears and a new cycle begins.

If the egg is fertilised:

■ The outer layer of the blastocyst becomes endocrinal and secretes the hormone, *human chorionic gonadotrophin* (HCG) into the mother's bloodstream. HCG maintains the levels of LH and thus the development of the corpus luteum. This, in turn, will continue to secrete progesterone for the first four months of the pregnancy. The endometrium is maintained and implantation can now take place.

Any drop in progesterone levels at any time will lead to a sudden degeneration of the endometrium — and a *miscarriage*. This is possible during the first four months and usually occurs at the times that a period would have been due.

After about 16 weeks, the placenta takes over the task of producing both oestrogen and progesterone for the rest of the pregnancy. Nausea in early pregnancy is generally due to the high level of progesterone made by the corpus luteum.

Placental progesterone is slightly different and nausea usually disappears with its arrival.

The placenta also secretes the hormone *relaxin*, which softens connective tissue throughout the body (in particular the connective ligaments of the bones of the pelvic girdle) to prepare the mother's body for the enlargement of the womb and the eventual birth of the baby.

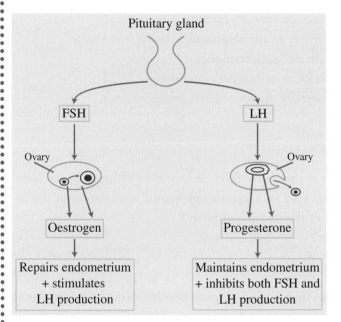

Fig. 28.22. The role of the pituitary in the regulation of the menstrual cycle.

MENSTRUAL DISORDER — ENDOMETRIOSIS AND FIBROIDS

Endometriosis

This is a condition in women where normal endometrial tissue (similar to that in the endometrium that lines the uterus) grows in the wrong place.

Common sites of unwanted growth are: the ovaries; the oviducts and ligaments; the space behind the uterus; the rectum; and the urinary bladder. Endometriosis is usually confined to the region of the pelvis.

This unwanted tissue responds to hormones just as normal endometrium does and so bleeds during a period. The bleeding has nowhere to go and results in scarring and tissue damage. Endometrium on the ovaries forms cysts of old blood — *chocolate cysts*.

The condition usually causes pain — especially during a period — and may lead to infertility. Endometriosis has many symptoms and can be difficult to diagnose.

CAUSES OF ENDOMETRIOSIS

The most widely accepted theories are:

- leakage of menstrual blood and tissue into the pelvis through open fallopian tubes;
- movement of endometrial cells throughout the pelvis via the circulation;
- abnormal, aggressive endometrial tissue;
- a defect in the immune system.

SYMPTOMS

The symptoms are:

- heavy or abnormal bleeding;
- severe abdominal pain;
- painful intercourse;
- severe cramps before and during a period;
- infertility.

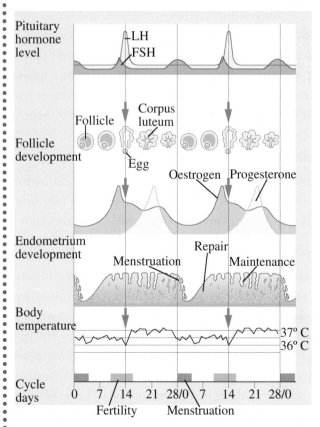

Fig. 28.23. Changes during the menstrual cycle.

Some women experience no physical symptoms at all but may have difficulty in conceiving.

Diagnosis

By examination through the navel with a laparoscope.

TREATMENTS FOR ENDOMETRIOSIS

1. Surgical

- Complete removal of unwanted endometrial tissue.
- Ablation (burning off of a surface) of the unwanted tissue by laser.
- Hysterectomy — chosen by some patients in extreme cases.

2. Hormonal

This is designed to suppress the response of endometrium to the woman's natural hormones. The menstrual cycle is suspended for about six months to allow healing and rest. Various side effects may arise (most treatable) and pregnancy is best avoided.

3. Emotional/social

The uncertainty of the condition, the pain and discomfort suffered and the effect of the condition on fertility and a normal sex life can all contribute to anxiety and stress in the patient. Communication with a sympathetic doctor, a fellow sufferer or a support group, such as the Endometriosis Society of Ireland (Telephone 01 8735702), can be of help.

4. Holistic

Diet, massage therapy, acupuncture, reflexology and herbal treatment can be of benefit to some patients and may help to develop a positive approach to controlling the condition.

Fibroids

Fibroids are benign (non-malignant) tumours in the muscle of the uterus. They can vary in size from 1 cm in diameter to the size of a tennis ball. They are rarely found in women less than 40 years old but occur in one in five by the age of 45. Often fibroids create no particular symptoms at all but they can cause pain or heavy periods and occasionally may block the oviducts by pressing on them. Large fibroids cause the wall of the uterus to feel lumpy during a medical examination.

CAUSES OF FIBROIDS

Not known.

SYMPTOMS

These are as follows:

- 25% of patients have no symptoms at all;
- heavy periods or abnormal bleeding;
- swelling of the abdomen;
- pain during intercourse;
- backache or bladder discomfort;
- infertility due to blocked oviducts (rare).

DIAGNOSIS

This is through a pelvic examination followed by an ultrasound scan or a laparoscopy (visual examination of the inside of the abdominal cavity).

TREATMENTS FOR FIBROIDS

- No intervention — most fibroids shrink and disappear as a woman gets older.
- Removal by *myomectomy* — small cuts are made on the surface of the uterus and each fibroid is removed. The operation is slow but safe.
- Anti-oestrogen hormone tablets can shrink fibroids but may lead to a risk of osteoporosis.
- *Hysterectomy* — complete removal of the uterus is carried out as a last resort

There is a higher risk of uterine cancer in women who suffer from fibroids; so all suspicions should be investigated thoroughly.

SUMMARY

- The principal features of human sexual reproduction are as follows:

  - Two sources of gametes (sex cells) are required.
  - Gametes are made by meiosis.

- The gametes are haploid.
- The gametes meet and fuse together — the process of fertilisation.
- A diploid zygote is formed.
- The zygote develops into an embryo.
- The embryo is nourished through a placenta and umbilical cord.
- A baby is born after about nine months.

■ The female reproductive system consists of:

- two paired ovaries;
- two oviducts;
- the uterus;
- the vagina.

■ The functions of the ovaries are:

- to produce the haploid egg cells by meiosis;
- to produce the female sex hormones — oestrogen and progesterone.

■ The male reproductive system consists of:

- two paired testes;
- two vas deferens tubes;
- the prostate gland, seminal vesicles and Cowper's glands;
- the urethra within the penis.

■ The functions of the testes are:

- to produce the haploid, male sperms by meiosis;
- to produce the male sex hormone, testosterone.

■ Human gametes are formed in the testes and ovaries by meiosis.
■ In the testes, cells lining the seminiferous tubules divide by meiosis to form millions of haploid spermatozoa.
■ In the ovaries, tiny balls of cells — or follicles — develop at an early age.
■ Each follicle contains a primary oocyte, which divides by meiosis to form a haploid egg.
■ The egg is later released from the mature ovarian follicle at the surface of the ovary — this is ovulation.
■ The ovarian follicle then closes and forms the corpus luteum.

■ FSH stimulates the ovaries to produce ovarian follicles and oestrogen.
■ Oestrogen is responsible for the development of the female secondary sex characteristics — development of the breasts, widening of the hips and growth of pubic hair.
■ Oestrogen also stimulates the monthly repair of the inner lining of the womb after menstruation.
■ LH triggers ovulation.
■ In males, FSH stimulates the formation of sperms and LH stimulates the formation of testosterone.
■ Testosterone is responsible for developing and maintaining the male secondary sex characteristics — development in size of the testes and penis, growth of body hair, deepening of the voice and greater muscle development.
■ The menstrual cycle involves two events: the ovarian cycle in the ovary and the uterine cycle in the uterus.
■ The stages of fertilisation are:

- sperms are chemically attracted to the egg;
- the sperm creates an opening in the zona pellucida or egg covering;
- the sperm nucleus enters the egg cytoplasm;
- the sperm tail is lost;
- the male and female nuclei fuse together to form the diploid zygote nucleus.

■ The zygote commences mitosis.
■ After three to four days or so, a morula is formed.
■ Further cell divisions produce a blastocyst.
■ The blastocyst implants itself in one of the pockets of the endometrium.
■ The embryo develops from a disc of cells within the blastocyst.
■ The placenta allows transport to take place between the maternal and foetal bloodstreams.
■ Most soluble materials can pass across the placenta.
■ The stages of childbirth are:

- contractions of the uterus;
- delivery of the baby;
- delivery of the afterbirth (the placenta).

■ Lactation is regulated by the pituitary hormone prolactin and will continue for as long as the mother allows the child to feed.

EXTENDED SUMMARY

■ The blastocyst is made from hundreds of cells or blastomeres.

■ The outer blastomeres are trophoblast cells and will develop into the placenta and embryonic membranes.

■ At one end of the blastocyst, a dense, flattened knot of smaller cells develops — the embryo cells.

■ The outer, trophoblast cells develop finger-like growths called trophoblastic villi.

■ The villi grow and develop into the placenta.

■ At the beginning of every menstrual cycle, the pituitary gland releases FSH into the bloodstream.

■ FSH stimulates the ovaries to develop one or more ovarian follicles.

■ The wall of each follicle secretes oestrogen.

■ Oestrogen brings about the repair of the endometrium of the uterus.

■ High levels of oestrogen in the blood stimulate the production of LH.

■ LH triggers ovulation and also the development of the corpus luteum.

■ The corpus luteum secretes progesterone.

■ Progesterone maintains the repair of the endometrium and inhibits the production of both FSH and LH.

■ If no fertilisation takes place:

  – progesterone inhibits the production of both FSH and LH;
  – the falling level of LH triggers the degeneration of the corpus luteum and no more progesterone is made;
  – the endometrium is no longer maintained and menstruation commences;
  – FSH reappears and a new cycle begins.

■ If the egg is fertilised:

  – the blastocyst secretes HCG into the mother's bloodstream;
  – HCG maintains the levels of LH and thus the development of the corpus luteum;
  – the corpus luteum continues to secrete progesterone;
  – the endometrium is maintained and implantation takes place;
  – after about 16 weeks, the placenta takes over the task of producing both oestrogen and progesterone for the rest of the pregnancy;
  – the placenta also secretes relaxin, which softens connective tissue throughout the body.

KEY WORDS

Haploid	A cell containing a single set of chromosomes.
Diploid	A cell containing a double set of chromosomes.
Gametes	Haploid cells capable of fusion — also termed sex cells.
Zygote	The immediate product of gametes fusing. Usually diploid.
Gonads	Organs capable of producing gametes. In humans these are testes and ovaries.
Fimbriae	A fringed margin on the edge of the oviduct.
Myometrium	The outer, muscular coat of the uterus.
Endometrium	The inner mucous lining of the endometrium — shed during menstruation.
Cervix	The narrow base of the uterus. Also termed the 'neck of the womb'.
Interstitial cells	Patches of cells within the testis that produce the male sex hormone, testosterone.
Scrotum	An external pouch holding the testes.
Epididymis	A coiled tube attached to the side of the testis.

Prostate gland, seminal vesicles and Cowper's glands	All contribute lubrication and nourishment to sperms.
Follicles	Balls of cells within each ovary.
Ovulation	Release of the egg from the ovarian follicle on the surface of the ovary, generally on Day 14 of the menstrual cycle.
Corpus luteum or yellow body	Forms from the ovarian follicle after ovulation and secretes progesterone.
Menstruation	The monthly loss of a small amount of blood, mucus and cell remains from the womb.
Copulation	Transfer of sperm. Also termed sexual intercourse in humans.
Acrosome	A bubble of digestive enzymes within the head of a sperm.
Zona pellucida	A membrane covering the egg.
Infertility	Any condition that makes conception and pregnancy difficult or impossible.
Azoospermia	When no sperm cells are made.
Oligospermia	When very few sperm cells are made.
Hyperprolactinaemia	Abnormally high levels of the pituitary hormone, prolactin.
In vitro	In glass.
Cleavage	Repeated division of the zygote.
Morula	A solid ball of cells formed before implantation.
Blastocyst	A hollow ball of cells that implants itself in the endometrium.
Blastomeres	The cells that form the blastocyst.
Implantation	When the blastocyst buries itself in one of the pockets of the endometrium.
Placenta	The organ of exchange between the mother and the foetus.

Umbilicus	The 'belly button' (or navel) — the scar of attachment of the umbilical cord.
Parturition (or birth)	The process whereby the baby leaves the womb and enters the outside world.
Colostrum	A low fat liquid rich in maternal antibodies, secreted from the breasts before milk is produced.
Lactation	Milk production in the breasts.

EXTENDED KEY WORDS

Trophoblast cells	Cells lining the blastocyst, form the placenta and embryonic membranes.
Trophoblastic villi	Finger-like growths that embed themselves in the endometrium during placenta formation.
Lacunae	Spaces within the placenta containing pools of maternal blood.
Gastrulation	Division and folding within the early embryo.
Amnion	A tough membrane, filled with amniotic fluid, in which the embryo lies.
Triploblastic	An embryo formed from three layers of cells — ectoderm on the outside, endoderm lining the gut cavity and mesoderm in between.
Endometriosis	A condition in women where normal, endometrial tissue grows in the wrong place.
Fibroids	Benign tumours in the muscle of the uterus.

QUESTIONS

1. Explain the difference between sexual and asexual reproduction. State one advantage of sexual

reproduction over asexual. State one advantage of asexual over sexual.

2. Summarise the essential stages of sexual reproduction.

3. Draw a simple, labelled diagram of the female reproductive system and mark the location of each of the following:

   a. ovulation;
   b. insemination;
   c. fertilisation;
   d. implantation;
   e. placenta development.

4. Match the sentence fragments to the correct parts of the female reproductive system:

   ovaries; uterus; cervix; oviduct; vagina.

   a. A muscular, pear-shaped organ.
   b. Makes eggs by meiosis.
   c. Secretes oestrogen.
   d. Inner lining is called the endometrium.
   e. Receives eggs from the ovary.
   f. Also called the birth canal.
   g. Base of the uterus.
   h. Held in place by ligaments.

5. Match the sentence fragments to the correct parts of the male reproductive system:

   prostate gland; urethra; testes; penis; epididymis; scrotum; vas deferens.

   a. Contains the testes.
   b. Provides nourishment for the sperms.
   c. Designed for sperm transfer.
   d. Makes testosterone.
   e. Tube shared with the urinary system.
   f. Stores sperms.
   g. Connects the epididymis and urethra.

6. Explain why meiosis is essential before the production of sex cells.

7. Vasectomy is a male sterilisation operation. It involves cutting and tying the vas deferens tubes under anaesthetic. After a vasectomy, explain why:

   a. the man will not father any children;
   b. his ability to have sex is unchanged;
   c. his semen cannot be DNA tested;
   d. his physical development is unchanged.

8. State the source and function of each of the following hormones:

   FSH; LH; oestrogen; testosterone; progesterone.

9. Summarise, in point form, the main events of:

   a. the ovarian cycle;
   b. the uterine cycle.

10. What is the corpus luteum? Explain what happens to the corpus luteum during a month when:

    a. an egg is fertilised;
    b. an egg is not fertilised.

11. Explain the significance of the following days during the average menstrual cycle:

    Day 1; Day 5; Day 14; Day 21; Day 28.

12. Fish use external fertilisation during their reproductive cycles. Typically, the female lays her eggs in the water and then a male covers them with sperm. List the biological hazards involved with this method and explain the advantages of internal fertilisation, used by mammals.

13. Name four methods of birth control. Briefly describe each method and point out any possible advantages and disadvantages as you see them.

14. What is fertilisation? Why is it considered such an important event in biology? Draw a simple diagram to show where, precisely, fertilisation takes place. Describe, in order, five events that occur during fertilisation.

15. What is infertility? List three causes each of male and female infertility.

16. Explain clearly the meaning of each of the following:

    implantation; blastocyst; cleavage; zygote; morula; blastomere.

17. Why must the embryo implant itself in the endometrium?

18. Explain how the placenta acts as a lung, digestive system and kidney for the foetus. Why is it that the maternal and foetal blood supplies are not allowed to mix?

19. The umbilical cord contains two arteries and one vein, wrapped in a spiral. Compare the blood within the arteries and the vein with regard to:

    a. oxygen content;
    b. carbon dioxide content;
    c. urea (urine) content;
    d. nutrient content.9

    Why are the blood vessels wrapped in a spiral?

20. What is the cause of nausea in early pregnancy? Why do some mothers feel it is a sign of a stable pregnancy? Why does it usually disappear after a few months?

21. What are the three stages of childbirth? Summarise what happens at each stage.

22. Outline the advantages of breast-feeding. For how long can a mother continue to breastfeed her child? What is the difference between colostrum and milk? Why are breast-fed babies not generally as prone to eye, ear and throat infections as bottle-fed babies are?

23. At the birth of twins, how can the nurses easily determine whether the twins are identical or not?

EXTENDED QUESTIONS

24. State a hormonal reason for the occurrence of each of the following:

    a. repair of the endometrium;
    b. ovulation;
    c. menstruation;
    d. production of oestrogen;
    e. degeneration of the corpus luteum;
    f. development of the corpus luteum after fertilisation;
    g. production of milk;
    h. contractions of the womb before childbirth.

25. Why is it that a breakdown of the corpus luteum early on in pregnancy can result in a miscarriage? Why does a breakdown later in the pregnancy have little effect?

26. For *either* of the conditions, *endometriosis* and *fibroids*, state:

    a. a description of the condition;
    b. a possible cause;
    c. three symptoms;
    d. two available treatments.

OPTIONAL ACTIVITIES

- Construct a table of the similarities and differences between sexual and asexual reproduction.
- If available, study plastic models and charts of the male and female reproductive systems.
- Place an egg in a coffee jar and fill the jar with water. Screw the lid on and try and break the egg by shaking. Repeat the experiment with no water in the jar! How is this relevant to reproduction?
- Design a pamphlet or poster for pregnant mothers explaining the dangers of smoking and drinking alcohol during pregnancy.
- Design and make a single acetate sheet to explain the formation and release of the egg in the ovary.
- Consider viewing any of the many rat dissections on the net to view the reproductive organs. Type *rat dissection* in any search engine. Preserved rats can be obtained and dissected at school.
- Visit the Irish Pregnancy Online Community at http://local.vhi.ie/communities/pregnancy/.
- Contact Cuidiú — the Irish Childbirth Trust — to gather information on childbirth. Cuidiú are at Carmichael House, Brunswick Street, Dublin 7, Telephone: 01 8724501.
- View the BBC video or interact with the CD-ROM entitled *The Human Body*.

For further information on subjects covered in this chapter, see www.my-etest.com.

Appendix A

List of Mandatory Activities

The numbering of the mandatory experiments follows the Department of Education and Science syllabus.

Fieldwork
1. Apparatus for collecting in ecology (page 56).
2. Using keys for plants and animals (page 55).
3. Quantitative survey of part of a habitat (page 59).
4. Investigating three abiotic factors (page 64).

Microscopy
5. Use of the light microscope (page 77).
6. Examining a plant cell (page 80).
7. Examining an animal cell (page 80).
8. Preparing a TS of a dicot stem (page 250).

Dissection
9. Dissecting a sheep's heart (page 260).

Laboratory activities
(each conducted during one double class period)
10. Test for starch, fat, reducing sugar and protein (page 20).
11. The effect of pH on the rate of enzyme activity (page 98).
12. The effect of temperature on the rate of enzyme activity (and denaturation of enzymes – higher level only) (pages 98, 99).
13. The effect of light intensity *or* carbon dioxide levels on the rate of photosynthesis (page 115).
14. Demonstrating osmosis (pages 134, 275).

Laboratory investigations
(each conducted over a series of class periods)
15. Producing alcohol from yeast (page 124).
16. Preparing cell or enzyme immobilisation (page 95).
17. Separating DNA from plant tissue (page 163).
18. Investigating the growth of leaf yeasts (page 229).
19. Investigating the effect of exercise on the breathing *or* pulse rate in humans (pages 261, 308).
20. Investigating the effect of IAA on plant dicot tissue (page 332).
21. Investigating the effect of water, oxygen and temperature on germination (page 401).
22. Investigating the digestive activity in germinating seeds (page 403).

Appendix B
Preparation of Solutions

Most solution strengths here are expressed as *percentage solutions*, i.e. the number refers to the number of grams of solute dissolved in 100g of solvent. For example, a 20 per cent glucose solution contains 20g of glucose dissolved in 100g of water (or 100ml of water). This solution strength is also written as 20 per cent$^{w/v}$. This system suits well for making up the solutions on this course and water is invariably the solvent used.

For more precision, each solution should be *made up to* 100ml in total rather than adding the solute to 100ml (or 100g) of solvent.

All solutions can, of course, be scaled up or down according to needs.

There is a trend towards the use of cm^3 rather than ml and dm^3 rather than litres. The author is aware of this but has avoided it here!

Chapter 3: Nutrition

Reducing sugar solution
Dissolve 20g of glucose or fructose in 100ml of water to make 20 per cent reducing sugar solution.

Starch solution
Mix 10g soluble starch powder with a little cold water. Pour, with constant stirring, into 1 litre of boiling water to make a 1 per cent solution.

Iodine solution
Dissolve 20g potassium iodide and 12.7g iodine crystals in 600ml water. Make up to 1 litre.

Bench sodium hydroxide solution
Dissolve 80g NaOH pellets in 800ml water and then make up to 1 litre. Stir constantly, wear eye and hand protection and preferably stand the glass vessel in ice as the heat released can crack the glass.

Copper sulphate solution
Add 1g $CuSO_4$ to 100ml water to make 1 per cent $CuSO_4$ solution.

DCPIP solution
Dissolve 1g DCPIP in 1 litre of distilled water to make 0.1 per cent solution.

Chapter 4: General Principles of Ecology

Buffer solutions
Best obtained commercially.

Chapter 6: Cell Structure

Iodine solution
Dissolve 20g potassium iodide and 12.7g iodine crystals in 600ml water. Make up to 1 litre.

Methylene Blue stain
Add 1g methylene blue and 0.5g NaCl to 100ml water. Also available commercially.

Chapter 7: Cell Metabolism and Enzymes

Invertase concentrate
Available commercially

Sucrose solution
Add 2g table sugar to 100ml water to make 2 per cent sucrose solution.

Sodium alginate (calcium alginate) solution
Add 3g sodium alginate (or calcium alginate) to 100ml water to make 3 per cent solutions.

Calcium chloride solution
Add 3g calcium chloride to 100ml water to make a 3 per cent solution.

Starch agar
Mix 2g of soluble starch with a little cold water. Add this to 100ml boiling water while stirring briskly. Mix 2g of agar powder with a little cold water. Add this to the boiling starch solution and continue stirring. Allow the mixture to cool a little and pour gently into clean petri dishes. Cover and allow to set.

Milk agar
Mix 2g of dried milk powder with 100ml cold water. Heat to boiling and stir constantly. Mix 2g of agar powder with a little cold water. Add this to the boiling solution and continue stirring. Allow the mixture to cool a little and pour gently into clean petri dishes. Cover and allow to set.

Mayonnaise agar
Mix one heaped teaspoon of mayonnaise with 100ml cold water. Heat to boiling and stir constantly. Mix 2g of agar powder with a little cold water. Add this to the boiling solution and continue stirring. Allow the mixture to cool a little and pour gently into clean petri dishes. Cover and allow to set.

Amylase solution
Add 0.5g amylase powder to 100ml distilled water to make a 0.5 per cent solution.
Alternatively – prepare a solution by rinsing the mouth with small amounts of distilled water and 'spitting' into a 100ml beaker. Collect about 20ml of saliva and dilute to 250ml with water. Prepare ahead of class time!

Starch solution
Mix 10g soluble starch powder with a little cold water. Pour, with constant stirring, into 1 litre of boiling water to make a 1 per cent solution.

Iodine solution
Dissolve 20g potassium iodide and 12.7g iodine crystals in 600ml water. Make up to 1 litre.

Hydrogen peroxide solution
Use '20 volume' H_2O_2 available commercially. Must be stored in the dark.

Buffer solutions
Best obtained commercially.

Chapter 8: Photosynthesis

Iodine solution
Dissolve 20g potassium iodide and 12.7g iodine crystals in 600ml water. Make up to 1 litre.

Sodium hydrogen carbonate solution

Add 0.1–2g NaHCO$_3$ to 100ml water to make the required range of solutions.

Chapter 9: Respiration

Sodium alginate (calcium alginate) solution

Add 3g sodium alginate (or calcium alginate) to 100ml water to make 3 per cent solutions.

Calcium chloride solution

Add 3g calcium chloride to 100ml water to make a 3 per cent solution.

Lime water

Available commercially.

Yeast suspension

Mix dried yeast powder in water as instructed on the packet.

Chapter 10: Movement Through Cell Membranes

Starch Solution

Mix 10g soluble starch powder with a little cold water. Pour, with constant stirring, into 1 litre of boiling water to make a 1 per cent solution.

Strong sucrose solution

Mix 34.2g sucrose to 1 litre of water to make a strong (1M) solution.

Iodine solution

Dissolve 20g potassium iodide and 12.7g iodine crystals in 600ml water. Make up to 1 litre.

Chapter 12: DNA

Protease solution

Available commercially.

Chapter 16: Diversity of Organisms

Nutrient agar

Dissolve 26g of nutrient agar powder in 1 litre of *distilled* water. Heat to boiling with constant stirring. Allow to cool slightly. Transfer to 250ml conical flasks. Plug loosely with cotton wool and tin foil. Incubate at 121°C for 15 mins.

NB: Use 'nutrient agar' powder, not 'agar' powder.

Malt agar

Measure out 20g of malt extract powder (or 20ml of liquid malt extract) with 20g agar powder. Add to 1 litre of distilled water and mix thoroughly. Heat to boiling with constant stirring. Allow to cool slightly. Transfer to 250ml conical flasks, plug loosely with cotton wool and tin foil. Incubate at 121°C for 15 mins.

Malt extract is available commercially.

Sodium alginate (calcium alginate) solution

Add 3g sodium alginate (or calcium alginate) to 100ml water to make 3 per cent solutions.

Calcium chloride solution

Add 3g calcium chloride to 100ml water to make a 3 per cent solution.

Chapter 17: Organisational Complexity in the Flowering Plant

Toluidine blue
Available commercially.

Iodine solution
Dissolve 20g potassium iodide and 12.7g iodine crystals in 600ml water. Make up to 1 litre.

Aniline sulphate stain
Make a saturated solution and add a few drops of concentrated H_2SO_4.
Also available commercially.

Glycerol
Make up a solution of 30g pure glycerine to 100ml with distilled water. This is 30 per cent glycerol. Also available commercially.

Sudan IV stain
Add 5g powder to 100ml of 70 per cent ethanol. Also available commercially.
Leave fresh sections in the stain for 20 minutes. Wash rapidly with 50 per cent alcohol to remove excess stain, and transfer to a drop of glycerol. Fats can be detected as droplets *within* cells and so distinguished from cutin (cuticle) or suberin.

Chapter 19: Nutrition in the Flowering Plant

Starch Solution
Mix 10g soluble starch powder with a little cold water. Pour, with constant stirring, into 1 litre of boiling water to make a 1 per cent solution.

Strong sucrose solution
Mix 34.2g sucrose with 1 litre of water to make a strong (1M) solution.

Iodine solution
Dissolve 20g potassium iodide and 12.7g iodine crystals in 600ml water. Make up to 1 litre.

Chapter 23: Responses in the Flowering Plant

IAA solutions
As explained in the text of the chapter.

Chapter 27: Reproduction in the Flowering Plant

Pollen grain germination medium
A suitable germination medium is 100g/L sucrose in distilled water with 100mg/L boric acid, and 300mg/L calcium nitrate added. Add 20g/L agar to form a solid medium. These media do not have to be sterilised unless they will be stored. Pollen can be examined either in liquid or on solid medium.

Appendix C

Guidelines on the Recording of Practical Work

Students (and all other scientists) must keep a record of their practical work. A hard-backed, practical notebook of A4 size is recommended. An *index* of the work done should be prepared and placed at the beginning of the notebook. The number and title of each mandatory activity should be filled in clearly. All diagrams should be large, clearly labelled and drawn with a 2B pencil.

The following headings are suggested:

1. Title and Date

2. An Introduction
This should be short but should describe clearly the purpose of the work.

3. Description of procedure
This should include:
• A clearly labelled diagram of all apparatus assembled, with reference to any adjustments necessary.
• The procedure outlined step by step.
• Details of all measurements taken.
• Description of all safety procedures.

4. Data presentation
All measurements, with the correct units, should be recorded and clearly presented as graphs or charts as appropriate.

5. Results, observations and conclusions
• All results and observations must be clearly presented.
• The correct units must be used and displayed.
• Relevant comments should be in the right place.
• A consideration of possible errors should be made.
• Pooling of results with other groups should be done if appropriate.

The most important aspects of each record are:
• The procedure
• The results
• The conclusions.

Glossary of Key Words

2,4-D: A synthetic auxin that stimulates unusual growth.

2n (diploid): Having a double set of chromosomes within the nucleus (or having chromosomes in pairs).

Abiotic factors: Non-living factors that affect the distribution and abundance of organisms.

Absorption: When small molecules of useful food pass through the body cells and into a distribution system.

Abundance: Refers to the number of organisms (or population size).

Accommodation: The changing of the curvature of the lens to focus on either near or distant objects.

Acetyl coenzyme A: An intermediate compound within the Krebs Cycle.

Acetylcholine: The most common neurotransmitter.

Acquired variations: Are 'picked up' during the life of the organism and not inherited.

Acrosome: A bubble of digestive enzymes within the head of a sperm.

Action potential (AP): A tiny electrical voltage between the inside and the outside of nerve fibres.

Activation energy: Energy required to start a chemical reaction.

Active immunity: When the body manufactures its own antibodies in response to the arrival of a specific antigen.

Active site: A site on the surface of the enzyme that corresponds to the shape of a specific substrate.

Active transport: An energy-requiring process that moves materials from regions of low concentration to regions of high concentration.

Adaptation: Any characteristic of an organism that makes it more likely to survive and reproduce within the ecosystem.

ADH: The antidiuretic hormone.

Adipose tissue: Tissue made from cells filled with fat droplets.

Adventitious roots: Lateral roots that originate directly from a stem and do not develop from the radical of the seed.

Aerobic respiration: Requires oxygen gas in releasing energy from food.

Aerotropism: Response to free air.

Afferent arteriole: Arteriole carrying blood towards the Bowman's capsule.

Agglutinate: Stick together.

AIDS: Acquired Immune Deficiency Syndrome.

Akaryotic: Having no cellular structure.

Alleles: Alternative forms of genes.

Allergens: Allergy generators.

Alveoli: Thin-walled air sacs at the ends of bronchioles. Sites of gas exchange.

Amnion: A tough membrane, filled with amniotic fluid, in which the embryo lies.

Anabolism: The joining of small chemicals to form larger chemicals.

Anaerobic respiration: Does not require oxygen gas in releasing energy from food.

Angina: Pain from the heart muscle due to lack of oxygen.

Animals: Multicellular, eukaryotic organisms that ingest their food.

Annealing: The process of joining DNA fragments.

Antagonistic: Having opposing effects.

Antagonistic muscle pair: As one muscle contracts and shortens, the other relaxes and is stretched.

Antenna pigments: Chlorophyll pigments that are light gathering.

Anther: Part of the stamen, forms pollen grains by meiosis.

Antibiotics: Chemicals, secreted by some microorganisms, which prevent the growth of many bacteria.

Antigen: Any chemical recognised by the immune system as being foreign.

Antigen-antibody complex: Formed when antigens and antibodies bind together.

Anti-inflammatories: Drugs that coat the linings of the bronchioles and prevent any irritation or mucus build-up.

Antisepsis: The treatment of infection after it has occurred.

Apical bud: Found at the tip of the stem.

Apical dominance: When the apex of the main stem inhibits the development of side branches below it.

Apical meristems: Found at the extremities (apices) of the stem and root.

Apoplast pathway: A pathway for water movement through spaces within the cellulose cell walls and within the non-living xylem cells.

Appendicular skeleton: Consists of the limb girdles and the limbs.

Arrhythmia: Irregular heart beat.

Arteriole: A small artery.

Artery: A blood vessel that transports blood away from the heart and under high pressure.

Arthritis: Inflammation of the joints.

Asepsis: The removal of any possibility of infection by microorganisms.

Assimilation: Incorporating and using food within the body tissues.

Asthma: A breathing disorder that affects the lungs and the airways.

Asthma triggers: Substances or situations that bring on asthma attacks.

Astigmatism: When the cornea has different curvatures in different directions.

Atheroma: A raised lump of fatty deposits on the inner wall of a blood vessel.

Atherosclerosis: Hardening of the blood vessels.

ATP: An intermediary for energy transfer.

Atria: Upper chambers of the heart.

Atrial systole: Contraction of the atria.

Atrioventricular node: Secondary pacemaker of the heart.

Autecology: Studying the ecology of an individual species.

Autosomes: Non-sex chromosomes.

Autotrophic: 'Self-feeding'.

Autotrophic nutrition: When foods are made from inorganic nutrients and usually sunlight energy.

Autotrophic organisms: Manufacture their own food from simple, inorganic material and a source of energy.

Available water: Soil water loosely held between soil particles and available to plants.

Axial skeleton: Consists of the skull, the spine and the ribcage.

Axillary bud: Found where leaves are attached to the stem.

Azoospermia: When no sperm cells are made.

Bacilli: Rectangular or rod shaped bacteria.

Bacteriophages: Viruses that attack bacteria.

Bark ringing: The removal of a complete ring of bark from the trunk or branch of a tree.

Base pairing: Adenine always joins to thymine (or uracil), guanine always joins to cytosine.

Batch (closed) fermentation: Where nothing moves in or out during the process.

Behaviour: The constant response of living organisms to their changing environment.

Belt transect: Two ropes laid parallel to survey organisms in between.

Benign: Not cancerous.

Bilateral symmetry: The left hand side of an organism being roughly a mirror image of the right hand side.

Bile: An excretion from the liver.

Biliverdin and bilirubin: Bile pigments.

Binary fission: Splitting in two.

Biology: The study of life and living organisms.

Biome: An ecological zone extending over a very large area.

Biomolecules: The basic chemical structures found within most organic chemicals.

Bioprocessing: Using the enzymic activities of living organisms to obtain a useful product.

Biosphere: The part of the Earth, including its atmosphere, which is inhabited by organisms.

Blastocyst: A hollow ball of cells that implants itself in the endometrium.

Blastomeres: The cells that form the blastocyst.

B-lymphocytes: Complete their development in the bone marrow and then move directly to the lymph nodes.

Bowman's capsule: Closed end of the nephron, shaped like a wine glass.

Breathing: An active exchange of gases in an organism.

Bronchi: The two main divisions of the trachea.

Bronchioles: Subdivisions of the bronchi.

Bronchitis: An inflammation and eventual scarring of the bronchial tubes within the lungs.

Bronchodilators: Drugs that relax the smooth muscle lining the bronchioles and cause them to dilate.

Brunner's Glands: Glands in the intestine that secrete mucus and salts but no enzymes.

Bundles of His: Bundles of Purkinje fibres.

Capillarity: The tendency for water to creep through narrow tubes.

Capillary: A microscopic, thin-walled blood vessel, the site of exchange between the blood and the body tissues.

Capsid: The protein coat of a virus.

Capsomeres: Units of the capsid.

Cardiac muscle: Involuntary, heart muscle: very elastic and not easily tired.

Carnivore: An animal that feeds exclusively on other animals.

Carpels: Female parts of the flower.

Cartilage: A protein matrix containing cartilage cells but no calcium salts.

Casparian strip: A strip of waterproof material on four of their six sides of root endodermis cells.

Catabolism: The breaking up of large chemicals to form smaller chemicals.

Catalyst: A chemical that can change the speed of a chemical reaction without itself being permanently changed.
Cell cycle: The complete life of a cell.
Cell membrane: A thin, greasy skin of protein and phospholipid around the perimeter of the cell. It encloses the cell contents.
Cell theory: First proposed by Schleiden and Schwann in 1839: states that the Cell is the structural and functional unit of all living organisms.
Cell wall: A wall of cellulose outside the cell membrane of plant cells.
Cell-mediated immunity: An immune response through the action of T-lymphocytes.
Cerebrospinal fluid: A watery fluid surrounding and within the brain and spinal cord.
Cervix: The narrow base of the uterus. Also termed the 'neck of the womb'.
Chemosynthetic bacteria: Use energy from other chemical reactions to make their food.
Chemotaxis: Chemical attraction.
Chemotropism: Response to certain chemicals.
Chloroplasts: Plastids containing green chlorophyll. The site of photosynthesis in plant cells.
Chondrocytes: Cartilage cells.
Choroid layer: A layer of nerves and blood vessels within the eye.
Chromoplasts: Plastids that manufacture and store coloured pigment.
Chromosome: A long thread of DNA embedded in protein.
Chromosome mutations: Random changes to portions of chromosomes or to the chromosome number.
Chronic: Long-term.
Chronic obstructive pulmonary disease or COPD: Chronic bronchitis and emphysema found together.
Chyme: A mixture of gastric juice and digested food.
Circumstantial: Evidence that appears to fit the given facts.
Cleavage: Repeated division of the zygote.
Clone: A population where all members are genetically identical.
CNS: Central nervous system (the brain and the spinal cord).
Cocci: Round shape bacteria.
Cochlea: A snail-shaped, coiled tube containing fluid, membranes and sensory cells that respond to vibrations.
Cochlear implant: A small electronic device that provides a sense of sound.
Codon: A group of three bases coding for a specific amino acid.
Coelom: A hollow, fluid-filled space within the body. Found in most higher animals at some stage of development.
Cohesion: Similar molecules clinging to one another.
Cohesion-tension hypothesis: Used to explain the upward movement of water in plants.
Cold-blooded animals: Those whose temperatures vary with changes in the environment.
Collagen: A white, fibrous tissue, very strong and resistant to tension.
Collenchyma: Thick-walled cells used for support.
Colon: Large intestine.
Colostrum: A low fat liquid rich in maternal antibodies, secreted from the breasts before milk is produced.
Commensal flora: Natural populations of microorganisms living on and in the body.
Community: The organisms that live in the habitat.
Compact bone: Dense bone found mostly at the bone shaft.
Competition: When organisms of the same or different species 'fight' for necessary resources that are in short supply.
Concentration gradient: A mathematical slope representing the smooth transition from a more concentrated to a less concentrated region.
Condensation: The joining of molecules together with the release of some water, e.g. during photosynthesis.
Condenser: Focusses light rays to illuminate objects as best as possible.
Conduction: The ability to transmit information from one place to another.
Conservation: The wise management of the environment.
Consumer: An organism that obtains its food from eating other organisms.
Continuity: All living organisms do their best to survive in their environment and then reproduce.
Continuous (open) fermentation: Where nutrients are added continually as the product is drawn off.
Control: A 'normal' situation used in experiments for comparison.
Copulation: Transfer of sperm. Also termed sexual intercourse in humans.
Cornified layer: Dead cells that are filled with keratin.
Corpus luteum or yellow body: Forms from the ovarian follicle after ovulation and secretes progesterone.
Corpuscles: Ghost cells or cells with no nuclei.
Cortex: The outer part of an organ.
Cotyledons (seed leaves): Embryonic leaves used as a food store.
Cowper's glands: Contribute lubrication and nourishment to sperms.
Crenated: When animal cells collapse due to water loss.
Cretinism: Condition due to low levels of thyroxine in children.
Cryptozoa: 'Secret animals': always try to remain hidden.
Cryptozoic trap: A sheet of wooden board or a flat rock left lying on the ground.
Cytokinesis: Division of the cell cytoplasm.

Cytoplasm: The watery region of the cell containing many cell organelles.
Cytosol: The liquid portion of the cell cytoplasm.

Deamination: Removal of the amino group from amino acids.
Decomposers: Microorganisms (fungi and bacteria) that bring about the decay of dead plants and animals.
Dehiscence: The process of drying and splitting open.
Deletions: Where entire chromosome portions are missing.
Denatured enzyme: An enzyme irreversibly destroyed by the heat.
Dermal tissue: Sheets of cells protecting the plant.
Designer genes: Genes used to alter trivial conditions in organisms, e.g. eye colour, nose shape etc.
Detrivore: An organism that feeds on dead plants and animals and on animal waste.
Dialysis: Filtering by passing liquids through a membrane.
Diaphragm: A bell-shaped sheet of muscle and tendon used to ventilate the lungs.
Diastole: Relaxation of the heart muscle.
Diastolic pressure: Arterial blood pressure during ventricular relaxation.
Dicots (dicotyledonous plants): Plants whose embryos have two cotyledons.
Diffusion: The movement of materials from a place of high concentration to a place of lower concentration.
Digestion: Breaking down food by force or chemicals.
Dioecious: Plant species with separate sexes.
Diploid (2n): Having a double set of chromosomes within the nucleus (or having chromosomes in pairs).
Disaccharides: Are made from pairs of single sugar biomolecules joined.
Dispersal: The scattering of seeds from the parent plant.
Distal convoluted tubule: Twisted portion of the 'far' end of the nephron.
Distribution: Refers to where organisms are likely to be found.
Diuresis: Water loss.
DNA helicase: An enzyme that 'unzips' complementary strands of DNA.
DNA ligase: An enzyme used to join fragments of DNA.
DNA polymerase: An enzyme that attaches free nucleotides to exposed DNA bases; used to replicate strands of DNA.
DNA probe: A strand of DNA that is complementary to the base sequence of a DNA fragment.
Dominant: When a gene is working normally and expressing itself in the organism.
Dormancy: A resting period where growth and development cease.
Double circulation: Blood must pass at least twice through the heart before returning to the same location.
Double helix: A double spiral structure found in DNA.
***Drosophila* melanogaster:** A fruit fly commonly used in genetic study.
Duodenum: Upper region of the small intestine.

Ear ossicles: Tiny bones within the ear: the hammer, the anvil and the stirrup.
ECF: Extra-cellular fluid or tissue fluid.
Ecology: The study of the interaction of living organisms with each other and with their natural environment.
EcoRI: A restriction enzyme named after the bacterium that produces it, E. coli.
Ecosystem: The habitat and community combined.
Ectotherms: Gain heat directly from the environment.
Edaphic factors: Related to soil.
Effectors: Are capable of producing a response to stimulation.
Efferent arteriole: Arteriole carrying blood away from the Bowman's capsule.
Egestion: Removal of unabsorbed or indigestible food from the body as faeces.
Embolus: An internal blood clot.
Embryo sac: Contains a single female gamete: the egg.
Emphysema: A condition of irreversible lung damage and heart failure.
Endergonic reaction: One that requires an input of energy.
Endocrine: Inward secreting.
Endometriosis: A condition in women where normal, endometrial tissue grows in the wrong place.
Endometrium: The inner mucous lining of the endometrium, shed during menstruation.
Endoskeleton: A skeleton lying within the body.
Endosperm: An oily food store surrounding the embryo within seeds.
Endospermic seeds: Contain large amounts of endosperm.
Endospores: Thick-walled, reproductive bodies formed within some bacteria in times of stress.
Endothermic reactions: Require heat from their surroundings.
Endotherms: Gain heat from metabolism within their bodies and then regulate the heat level by various physiological processes.
Energy: The ability to do work.
Energy flow: The pathway of energy movement from one organism to the next due to feeding relationships.

Enzymes: Organic catalysts made from protein.
Enzyme-substrate complex: A temporary joining of an enzyme to its specific substrate.
Epididymis: A coiled tube attached to the side of the testis.
Epigeal germination: Cotyledons emerge, turn green and begin photosynthesis.
Erythrocytes: Red blood cells.
Eukaryotic cells: Cells that have a definite nucleus, bounded by a nuclear membrane, and many cell organelles.
Eustachian canal: Communicates between the middle ear and the pharynx.
Evolution: Unfolding or unrolling
Excretion: The removal of metabolic waste.
Exergonic reaction: One that releases energy.
Exine: Thick, outer wall of pollen grains.
Exocrine (eccrine) glands: Deliver their secretions through ducts.
Exocytosis: Release of secretions from cells in membrane vesicles.
Exoskeleton: A skeleton covering the outside of the body.
Expiration: Breathing out.
Expression: Refers to when hereditary information is activated within cells.
Extra-chromosomal DNA: DNA that is not part of a chromosome, usually found in chloroplasts and mitochondria.

F1 Generation: 'First filial generation', i.e. the 'children' of any organisms.
F2 Generation: 'Second filial generation', i.e. the 'grandchildren' of any organisms.
Female parents: Produce non-motile gametes.
Fermentation: The anaerobic breakdown of organic nutrients by microorganisms.
Fertilisation: Fusion of two gametes to form a diploid zygote.
Fibrillation: A quivering of the heart muscle.
Fibroids: Benign tumours in the muscle of the uterus.
Fibromyalgia: A long-term pain in the muscles and tissues surrounding the joints.
Fibrous roots: Equal-sized roots emerging from the stem base.
Filament: Supports the anther and transports water and nutrients to it.
Fimbriae: A fringed margin on the edge of the oviduct.
Fittest: The organisms most suited to survive given the present conditions.
Flaming: Passing a wire loop or the mouth of a flask through a flame to kill any microorganisms.
Flowers: Sexual organs within most common plants.
Follicles: Tiny balls of cells within each ovary.
Fossils: The dead and preserved remains of once-living organisms.
Frequency: The number of quadrats in which a particular organism occurs.
Fungi: Multicellular, eukaryotic organisms with absorptive nutrition.

Gametangia: Gamete producing cells.
Gametes: Haploid cells, capable of fusion. Also called germ cells or sex cells.
Gastric ulcer: Damage to the stomach wall by acid and enzymes.
Gastrulation: Division and folding within the early embryo.
Gene: A portion of a chromosome controlling the development of a particular characteristic.
Gene mutations: Random changes to the gene structure.
Gene therapy: Replacement of faulty genes with normal ones to correct health disorders.
Genetics: The study of the mechanism of inheritance.
Genotype: The genetic constitution of an individual.
Geotropism (gravitropism): A plant's response to gravity.
Germ cell mutations: Mutations at gamete formation.
Germination: The emergence of the plant embryo from its seed.
Global warming: A rise in the Earth's overall temperature due to excess CO_2 in the atmosphere.
Glomerular filtrate: A collection of small, soluble molecules that passes from the blood into the nephron.
Glomerulus: A knot of capillaries within the Bowman's capsule.
Glycolysis: A series of enzyme-controlled reactions converting glucose to pyruvate molecules.
Goitre: A swelling of the thyroid gland.
Gonads: Organs capable of producing gametes. In humans: testes and ovaries.
Granulocytes: Large white blood cells with irregular nuclei and granules in their cytoplasm.
Gravitropism: A plant's response to gravity.
Greenhouse effect: When excess CO_2 in the atmosphere traps heat from the Sun and raises the temperature of the surface of the Earth.
Ground tissue: All plant tissue except the epidermis and the vascular tissue.
Growth: An increase in the size of an organism until parent size is reached.
Growth regulator: A chemical substance that exerts a degree of control over plant growth.

Guttation: The forced exuding of liquid water from special pores in the leaves.

Habitat: The place where an organism lives.
Haemodialysis: Filtering the blood.
Haemodialysis machines: Artificial, kidney machines.
Haemoglobin: A respiratory pigment within red cells. Used to carry oxygen.
Haploid (n): Describes cells containing a single set of chromosomes.
Heart valves: Prevent backflow of blood within the heart.
Helical: Wrapped in a spiral or helix.
Helper T cells: Secrete chemicals (e.g. interferon) that stimulate the action of all other immune cells.
Hepatic portal vein: Brings digested nutrients and deoxygenated blood to the liver directly from the stomach and intestines.
Herbivore: An animal that feeds exclusively on plant material.
Heredity: Refers to all materials and information passed from one generation to the next or to later generations.
Hermaphrodite: Containing both male and female reproductive organs.
Heterotrophic: 'Other-feeding'.
Heterotrophic nutrition: When existing foods are broken down to provide ready-made nutrients. Animals obtain food by eating.
Heterotrophic organisms: Depend on an external source of organic food.
Heterozygous: When the members of a pair of genes have different forms.
Histamine: A chemical that causes the blood vessels in the infected area to dilate and bring more blood to the site.
Histones: Beads of protein supporting DNA.
HIV: Human Immunodeficiency Virus.
Holozoic nutrition: Ingesting solid food and digesting it internally.
Homeostasis: Maintaining a 'steady state' of conditions within the organism.
Homeostatic organ: Maintains the body's metabolism at its optimum.
Homologous chromosomes: Chromosomes that form matching pairs during meiosis.
Homologous pairs: Pairs of chromosomes with identical length and similar information in similar locations.
Homozygous: When the members of a pair of genes have the same form.
Hormones: Chemical messengers that travel in the bloodstream.
Horse serum: Horse blood plasma with the clotting proteins removed.
Humoral-mediated immunity: An immune response through antibodies made by B-lymphocytes.
Humus: A black, sticky, fibrous jelly formed from dead and decaying organic matter.
Hyaline ('glassy') cartilage: Consists of a clear matrix of jelly-like chondrin embedded with cartilage cells.
Hydrolysis: Is the separation of molecules with the addition of water, e.g. during digestion.
Hydrophilic: Attracting water (literally 'water-loving').
Hydrophobic: Repelling water (literally 'afraid of water').
Hydrostatic skeleton: An endoskeleton of pressurised fluid.
Hydrotropism: Response to water.
Hyperopia: Far-sightedness.
Hyperprolactinaemia: Abnormally high levels of the pituitary hormone, prolactin.
Hyperthyroidism: Condition due to an overactive thyroid gland.
Hyphae: Branching threads within a mycelium.
Hypogeal germination: Cotyledons remain under the ground.
Hypothesis: A working assumption or 'educated guess'.
Hypothyroidism: Condition due to an underactive thyroid gland.

IAA (indoleacetic acid or auxin): An important growth regulator in plants.
Immobilisation: Attachment of an enzyme to an insoluble supporting material.
Immune response: The body's ability to recognise foreign invaders and to make specific protein antibodies to destroy them.
Immunisation: Any artificial process that gives immunity to a patient.
Immunity: The body's ability to resist disease.
Implantation: When the blastocyst buries itself in one of the pockets of the endometrium.
In vitro: In glass.
Incomplete Dominance: When a single dominant gene in a heterozygote is not fully expressed.
Incubation period: The time taken by bacteria to prepare themselves for rapid reproduction.
Infertility: Any condition that makes conception and pregnancy difficult or impossible.
Ingestion: Taking large pieces of food within the body.
Inherited variation: Variation passed on through sex cells.
Inorganic nutrients: Do not contain carbon.
Insertion: The tendon at the far end of the muscle.
Inspiration: Breathing in.
Inspiratory and expiratory centres: Regions in the medulla oblongata of the brain controlling the rate of breathing.

Integuments: Two sheets of cells covering the ovule.

Intercostal muscles: Muscle between the ribs, used to move the ribcage during breathing.

Internodes: The smooth region between two nodes.

Interphase: The resting phase of the cell cycle.

Interstitial cells: Patches of cells within the testis that produce the male sex hormone, testosterone.

Intestinal glands: Secrete mucus and salts but no enzymes.

Intine: Thin, inner wall of pollen grains.

Inversions: Where a portion of chromosome is turned the wrong way around.

Iris diaphragm: Adjusts the amount of light passing through the microscope.

Irritability: The ability to receive and respond to electrical messages.

Jejunum: Middle region of the small intestine.

Joints: Places in the skeleton where two bones meet.

Key: A set of carefully structured questions used to identify organisms.

Kidney stone: A solid piece of material that forms in the kidney from substances in the urine.

Killer T-cells: Cut tiny holes in antigens and destroy them.

Krebs cycle: A cycle of biochemical reactions within stage 2 of aerobic respiration.

Lactation: Milk production in the breasts.

Lacteals: Extensions of the lymphatic system found within the villi of the intestine.

Lacunae: Spaces within the placenta containing pools of maternal blood.

Lamarckism: The belief that favourable characteristics are acquired during life and then transmitted to the next generation.

Lamina: Flattened part of a leaf.

Larynx: Voice box made from cartilage and containing the vocal cords.

Lateral meristems: Found within the vascular bundles.

Lenticels: Pores on the surface of the plant stem – used for gas exchange.

Leucocytes: White blood cells.

Leucoplasts: Plastids that store starch (for storing starch).

Leukaemia: A cancer of the leucocyte forming cells in the bone marrow.

Lichens: Commensalisms between an alga and a fungus – both living together for mutual benefit.

Lignin: Strong and impermeable substance found in the cell walls of xylem and sclerenchyma cells. Kills the cells.

Line transect: A length of rope laid across the habitat to mark a line of study.

Linkage: Where genes happen to be located on the same chromosome.

Locus: The position of a gene on a chromosome.

Log phase: The phase of growth when bacteria reproduce by binary fission. The population may double its number as fast as every twenty minutes.

Loop of Henle: 'Hairpin' region of the nephron.

Lymphatic system: A set of branching tubes that extends throughout the body. Used for returning tissue fluid to the circulation.

Lymphocytes: Non-granular white blood cells that make antibodies in response to antigens.

Macrophages: Scavenging white blood cells that leave the bloodstream and attack any foreign matter.

Macrophages: Types of white blood cell capable of wandering through body tissue, devouring foreign mater.

Male parents: Produce motile gametes.

Malignant: Cancerous.

Malpighian layer: A layer of dividing cells at the base of the skin epidermis.

Mast cells: Modified granulocytes that release histamine.

Medulla: The central part of an organ.

Megaspore mother cell: A giant, diploid cell that develops within each ovule.

Meiosis: A cell division that produces four daughter cells, each with half the number of chromosomes of the parent cell.

Memory-B cells: Retain a long term 'memory' of antigens.

Memory-T cells: Retain a 'memory' of an antigen and bring about a much faster response if the antigen ever returns.

Meninges: Three membranes lying on the surface of the CNS.

Menstruation: The monthly loss of a small amount of blood, mucus and cell remains from the womb.

Meristem: A group of plant cells that divides repeatedly by mitosis.

Messenger RNA (mRNA): A short length of RNA that carries a copy of genetic code from the nucleus to the ribosomes.

Metabolic pathway: A series of enzyme-controlled steps leading to a final product.

Metabolism: The total of the chemical processes occurring within a living organism.

Metameric segmentation: A pattern of repeating body units. Found within most higher animals.

Metastasis: The spread of cancer from its primary location.

Microorganism: An informal name for organisms of microscopic size.

Micropropagation: Growth of new plants by tissue culture.

Micropyle: Tiny opening formed by the integuments.

Microscope: An instrument that uses lenses to produce a magnified image.

Mitochondria: Cylinder shaped organelles that carry out respiration.

Mitosis: A cell division that produces two daughter cells, each with the same number of chromosomes as the parent cell.

Monera: Single celled organisms that lacking a nuclear membrane – the bacteria.

Monocots (monocotyledonous plants): Plants whose embryos have one cotyledon only.

Monocytes: Non-granular, ingestive white blood cells.

Monoecious: Plants with both male and female structures present in the same flower.

Monosaccharides: Are the simplest sugar biomolecules.

Morula: A solid ball of cells formed before implantation.

Multodisks ™: Star-shaped pieces of filter paper impregnated with various antibiotics.

Mutagen: Any external agent likely to alter genes or chromosomes.

Mutation: A spontaneous change in a gene or chromosome.

Mycelium: The overall body of a fungus.

Myelin sheath: The fatty insulation completed.

Myogenic: Originating in the heart muscle.

Myometrium: The outer, muscular coat of the uterus.

Myopia: Near-sightedness.

Myxoedema: Condition due to low levels of thyroxine in adults.

n (haploid): Having a single set of chromosomes within the nucleus.

Nasties: Growth responses of a plant where the direction of the movement is not determined by the direction of the stimulus.

Natural selection: Where organisms with favourable, genetic characteristics are more likely to survive, reproduce and pass their characteristics to the next generation. Also loosely termed 'Survival of the Fittest'.

Negative feedback: When information is fed back into a controlling system to negate any change.

Neodarwinism: The modern form of Darwin's theory.

Nephron: A microscopic, blind ending tube that is the functional unit of the kidney.

Nerves: Bundles of nerve fibres.

Neurogenic: Originating in nerves.

Neurons: Nerve cells.

Niche: The position occupied by an organism in its ecosystem.

Nodes: Where leaves are attached to the stem.

Nodes of Ranvier: Gaps in the myelin sheath.

Non-endospermic seeds: Contain little endosperm.

Non-specific or innate immunities: Do not require previous exposure to the pathogen and work against microorganisms in general.

Nucellus: A mass of tissue within the ovule.

Nucleolus: A temporary store of RNA within the nucleus.

Nucleosomes: Packing units of DNA formed from groups of histones.

Nucleotide: A structural unit in nucleic acids made from a five-carbon sugar, a phosphate unit and a base.

Nucleus: The control centre of the cell.

Nutrient agar: A growth medium consisting of suitable nutrients mixed with agar gel.

Nutrients: Chemicals that supply energy and matter to organisms.

Nutrition: The process of obtaining energy and matter in order to survive.

Obligate parasites: Required to use living cells to complete their life cycle.

Oligospermia: When very few sperm cells are made.

Omnivore: An animal that feeds on both plants and animals.

Optimum activity: When an enzyme is turning substrate into product at the fastest possible rate.

Organ: A collection of tissues with a clear, overall structure and function.

Organic nutrients: Contain carbon.

Organisation: A structured plan designed to improve efficiency and increase the chances of survival.

Origin: The tendon nearest to the centre of the body.

Osmoregulation: Water and salt balance.

Osmosis: The diffusion of water across a semi-permeable membrane from a region of high water concentration to a region of lower water concentration.

Osteoarthritis: Characterised by unwanted bone growth, poor movement and destruction of cartilage.

Osteoblasts: Bone forming cells.

Osteoclasts: Break down bone tissue and secrete calcium back into the blood.

Osteocytes: Bone cells.

Osteoporosis: Brittle bone disease.

Ovary: Contains many ovules, which develop an embryo sac by meiosis.

Ovulation: Release of the egg from the ovarian follicle on the surface of the ovary.

Oxyhaemoglobin: Haemoglobin combined with oxygen.

Parasites: Attach themselves onto or inside the host and take food directly from it.
Parasitic bacteria: Obtain their food from a living source (or host).
Parasitism: A relationship where one organism, the parasite, benefits from another, the host, and does harm to it.
Parenchyma: Thin-walled cells used for packing and storage.
Parthenocarps: 'Virgin fruits' formed without fertilisation.
Parturition (or birth): The process whereby the baby leaves the womb and enters the outside world.
Passive immunity: When 'ready-made' antibodies turn up in the bloodstream.
Pathogen: A 'disease generator' or a microorganism that causes disease.
Pelvis: An expansion of the ureter within the kidney.
Pentadactyl: A limb with five digits.
Peptic ulcer: Ulcer of the duodenal wall.
Percentage cover: Refers to how much of the ground is covered by an organism.
Perennating organs: Food storage organs used by plants to survive the winter.
Perennation: Surviving the winter by means of a food store.
Perennials: Plants that survive from one year to the next.
Pericardium: Membrane surrounding the heart, preventing friction.
Peristalsis: An involuntary wave of muscular squeezing within a tube.
Peritoneum: A thin sheet of slippery membrane covering the alimentary canal, the associated glands, the main blood vessels and the inner lining of the abdominal cavity.
Petals: Modified leaves surrounding the male and female flower parts.
Petiole: Portion of a leaf attached to the stem.
Phagocytic cells: Identify and eat anything foreign inside the body.
Phagocytosis: 'Cell drinking'.
Phenotype: The expression of the genotype.
Phloem: Used for translocation of food and hormones.
Phospholipids: Fat-like substances with one fatty acid replaced by a phosphate molecule.
Photomicrograph: An image produced by an electron microscope.
Photosynthesis: Using sunlight to make food.
Photosynthetic bacteria: Trap sunlight energy with bacteriochlorophyll and use it to synthesise carbohydrates.
Phototropism: A tropism in response to light.
Phylum: A major subdivision of a kingdom.
Pinocytosis: 'Cell eating'.
Pistil: A single carpel or a group of fused carpels.
Pisum sativum: The pea plant used by Mendel in his studies.
Pitfall trap: Used to collect small animals that move on the ground surface.
Placenta: The organ of exchange between the mother and the foetus.
Plagiogeotropism: When lateral roots and branches grow at an angle to gravity.
Plants: Multicellular, eukaryotic organisms that make their own food using sunlight.
Plasma cells: Secrete antibodies.
Plasmids: Tiny loops of DNA found in bacteria.
Plasmolysis: When plant cells lose water due to osmosis.
Plastids: Oval, double-membraned containers found in the cytoplasm of plant cells.
Platelets: Fragments of marrow cells needed for blood clotting.
Pleural membranes: Two membranes covering the lungs and containing lubricating fluid to reduce friction.
Plumule: Embryonic shoot.
PNS: Peripheral nervous system (the nerves attached to the brain and spinal cord).
Point quadrat: A quadrat of standard size but with a wire grid of 10 x 10 wires stretched across it. Used to estimate percentage cover.
Pollen tetrads: Newly formed pollen grains in groups of four.
Pollination: Transfer of pollen from the anther of the stamen to the stigma of the carpel.
Pollution: Any human addition to the environment that leaves it less able to sustain life.
Polyhedral: Many faced or many sided.
Polysaccharides: Are made from long chains of many sugar biomolecules joined.
Pooter: Used to collect small animals by 'hoovering' them into a jar.
Population: A group of the same species within a geographical area.
Portal system: A blood supply from one organ of the body directly to another organ without passing through the heart.
Portfolio: A portable, written report.
Predation: A relationship where one organism, the predator, kills and eats another organism, the prey.
Primary meristems: Found at the extremities of the plant. Used to increase plant length.
Producer: An organism that makes its own food by photosynthesis or chemosynthesis.

Prokaryotic: Describes a simple cell type with no nuclear membrane, no plastids and no mitochondria.

Prostate gland: Contributes lubrication and nourishment to sperms.

Protoctista (Protista): Single celled organisms also but with a eukaryotic cell type.

Proton pool: A source of hydrogens for photosynthesis.

Proximal convoluted tubule: Twisted portion of the 'near' end of the nephron.

Pseudopodia: Temporary cell projections or 'false feet' of Amoeba.

Pulmonary circulation: Circulation through the lungs.

Pulse: A wave of pressure change within arteries due to the action of the ventricles.

Punnett Square: A mathematical grid used to show the possible combinations of genotypes arising from parents.

Purine bases: Double ringed molecular bases such as adenine and guanine.

Purkinje fibres: Conducting fibres within the septum.

Pyramid of numbers: A diagram representing the numbers and types of organisms in a food chain.

Pyramids: Cone-shaped areas within the kidney medulla.

Pyrimidine bases: Single ringed molecular bases such as thymine, cytosine and uracil.

Quadrat: A square frame made from wood, metal or plastic and used to survey non-moving organisms.

Qualitative survey: Produces a list of the organisms present in the ecosystem.

Quantitative survey: Provides information on the distribution and abundance of an individual species.

Radicle: Embryonic root.

Radioactive tracing: Feeding plants with radioactive CO_2 and then following the movements of the newly formed radioactive sugars.

Reaction centre: A concentration of light energy at one site.

Receptors: Sensory cells that detect change in the environment.

Recessive: When a gene is not working normally and therefore not expressing itself.

Recombinant DNA: DNA constructed from the genes of different organisms.

Recombinant DNA Technology: An alternative name for genetic engineering.

Reflex: An automatic response to an external stimulus.

Replication: Exact copying.

Reproduction: The ability to produce more organisms of the same species.

Respiration: The controlled release of energy from energy-rich chemicals in cells.

Respiratory pigment: Chemical, e.g. haemoglobin, designed to carry oxygen.

Restriction enzymes: Slice up DNA molecules into specific units.

Retina: A layer of photoreceptor cells at the back of the eye.

Retrovirus: Contains RNA and uses it to make DNA within the host cells.

Reverse transcriptase: An enzyme used to make strands of DNA from RNA templates.

Rheumatoid arthritis: An inflammation of the synovial membrane of the joints.

Ribosomal RNA (rRNA): Used to construct ribosomes.

Ribosomes: Organelles in the cytoplasm that manufacture proteins.

Root hairs: Extensions of the cells of the root epidermis.

Root pressure: Pressure under which water passes from root cells into the xylem.

Salt pump: A set of enzymes that extracts salt from the nephron by active transport and pumps it into the surrounding tissues.

Saprotrophic bacteria: Obtain their food in solution from dead and decaying organisms.

Saprotrophs: Obtain their food in solution, e.g. many fungi and bacteria.

Schwann cells: Form a fatty insulation around neurons.

Scientific method: A process of investigation based on observations and experiments.

Sclera: The 'white' of the eye.

Sclerenchyma: Lignified cells used for strength and protection.

Scrotum: An external pouch holding the testes.

Sebaceous gland: Glands within the skin that produce oily sebum.

Secondary meristems: Found within the stem and root. Used to form vascular tissue and increase diameter.

Secretion: The production of useful materials from cells.

Self cells: Cells naturally occurring in the body.

SEM: A scanning electron microscope, which photographs reflected electrons from surfaces.

Seminal vesicles: Contribute lubrication and nourishment to sperms.

Semi-permeable: Allows the passage of some materials but not others.

Senses: Collections of receptor cells.

Sensitivity: The ability to detect change in the environment.

Sepals: Protective leaves around young flowers.

Shockwave lithotripsy: Stone crushing using ultrasound.

Sinoatrial node: The main pacemaker of the heart.

Somatic mutations: Mutations in body cells.
Species: A group of organisms that resemble one another and have the ability to reproduce with one another.
Specific immunities: Develop after contact with specific pathogens and only protect against those pathogens alone.
Sphincter: A ring muscle for opening and closing tubes.
Spirilli: Spiral, motile bacteria.
Spongy bone: Less dense than compact bone and containing soft marrow tissue. Found at the ends of the bone and within the shaft.
Stamens: Male parts of the flower.
Sterile: Free of all living organisms including bacteria, fungi and their spores.
Sticky ends: Matching ends of DNA molecules used to join both human and bacterial DNA portions together.
Stigma: A raised platform on the carpel. Receives pollen grains.
Streaking: Using a wire loop to inoculate the surface of an agar plate with microorganisms.
Style: Supports the stigma.
Substrate: A specific raw material for an enzyme to work on.
Suppressor-T cells: Inhibit the action of killer-T cells a few weeks after activation.
Sutures: Immovable joints.
Symplast pathway: A pathway for water movement through the contents of living cells.
Synapses: Where nerve cells meet.
Synaptic cleft: Microscopic gap within a synapse.
Syndrome: A collection of symptoms.
Synergistic: Working together to help each other.
Synovial fluid: A lubricating fluid within synovial joints.
Synovial membrane: Lines the inside of synovial joints and secretes synovial fluid.
Systemic circulation: Circulation throughout the body.
Systolic pressure: Arterial blood pressure during ventricular contraction.

Tap roots: Develop from the radicle of the plant seed.
Tapetum: A layer of cells that lines the pollen chambers of the anther and feeds pollen mother cells with nutrients.
Taxes: Movement of a complete organism or gamete in response to an external stimulus.
TEM: A transmitting electron microscope, which sends electrons through objects.
Tendons: Strong cords of connective tissue made from collagen fibres. Used to attach muscles to bones.
Tension: A negative pressure that can move water within a plant.
Testa: Seed coat.
Theory: A hypothesis conformed by experiment.
Thigmotropism: Response to touch.
Thrombocytes (platelets): Fragments of marrow cells needed for blood clotting.
Tissue: A group of cells of similar structure that performs a specific function.
Tissue fluid: Colourless fluid, rich in nutrients and gases, which leaks from the circulation and bathes all cells.
T-lymphocytes: Travel first to the thymus gland to complete their development and then move on to the lymph nodes.
Trace elements: Elements essential in the diet but only required in tiny amounts.
Trachea: Windpipe.
Transcription: The faithful copying of the genetic code onto mRNA.
Transfer RNA (tRNA): Lengths of RNA with an anticodon at one end and a specific amino acid at the other.
Transgenic: Organisms containing cells with transplanted DNA.
Translation: The conversion of the copied code into the correct chain of amino acids.
Translocation: The movement of organic materials within plants.
Translocations: Where chromosome portions are attached to other chromosomes.
Transpiration: The evaporation of water from the surface of a leaf or stem.
Transpiration-pull hypothesis: Alternative name for the cohesion-tension hypothesis.
Triglyceride: The smallest lipid unit – made from three fatty acids attached to one glycerol molecule.
Triploblastic: Embryos consisting of three layers of cells (or three germ layers).
Trisomy: Three copies of the chromosome in a cell.
Trophoblast cells: Cells lining the blastocyst, form the placenta and embryonic membranes.
Trophoblastic villi: Finger-like growths that embed themselves in the endometrium during placenta formation.
Tropism: A growth movement of part of a plant in response to an external stimulus.
TSH: The thyroid-stimulating hormone.
Tullgren funnel: Used in the laboratory to extract small animals from soil samples.
Turgid: When plant cells are swollen with water.

Umbilicus: The 'belly button': the scar of attachment of the umbilical cord.
Unavailable water: Soil water held tightly by soil particles and not available to plants.
Ureter: A long, narrow and muscular tube carrying urine from the kidney to the bladder.

Urethra: A muscular tube carrying urine from the bladder to the exterior.
UTIs: Urinary tract infections, usually due to bacteria.

Vaccination: A method of immunisation where a harmless form of the pathogen trains the immune system into making appropriate antibodies for long-term protection.
Vaccine: A heat-treated or preserved form of an antigen injected into the blood.
Vacuoles: Fluid-filled spaces bounded by a membrane. Permanent in plant cells, temporary in animal cells.
Variable: Any condition that can change during an experiment.
Variation: Refers to the differences between the members of a population.
Vascular system: Transport system.
Vascular tissue: Tissue involved in transport, e.g. xylem and phloem tissue.
Vegetative propagation: When the roots, stems or leaves of a plant become modified to bring about an asexual reproduction.
Vein: A blood vessel that transports blood towards the heart and under low pressure.
Ventricles: Thick-walled, lower chambers of the heart.
Ventricular systole: Contraction of the ventricles.
Venule: A small vein.
Viruses: Extremely small infectious agents. Made from nucleic acid and protein.
Visking tubing: An artificial semi-permeable membrane.
Warm-blooded animals: Those that maintain a constant body temperature regardless of the temperature of the environment.

White fibro-cartilage: Cartilage containing collagen fibres.

Xylem: Lignified cells used for support and water transport.

Zona pellucida: A membrane covering the egg.
Zygote: The immediate product of gametes fusing. Usually diploid.

Index